Microsoft Official Academic Course
MICROSOFT EXCEL 2013

WILEY

Editor	Bryan Gambrel
Publisher	Don Fowley
Director of Sales	Mitchell Beaton
Technical Editor	Joyce Nielsen
Executive Marketing Manager	Chris Ruel
Assistant Marketing Manager	Debbie Martin
Microsoft Strategic Relationships Manager	Gene Longo of Microsoft Learning
Editorial Program Assistant	Allison Winkle
Content Manager	Kevin Holm
Production Editor	Jill Spikereit
Creative Director	Harry Nolan
Cover Designer	Tom Nery
Product Designer	Jennifer Welter
Content Editor	Wendy Ashenberg

This book was set in Garamond by BoxTwelve. and printed and bound by Courier/Kendallville. The covers were printed by Courier/Kendallville.

ISBN 978-0-470-13308-8

Printed in the United States of America

10 9 8 7 6 5 4 3 2 1

40311000071947

www.wiley.com/college/microsoft
or call the MOAC Toll-Free Number: 1+(888) 764-7001 (U.S. & Canada only)

Foreword from the Publisher

Wiley's publishing vision for the Microsoft Official Academic Course series is to provide students and instructors with the skills and knowledge they need to use Microsoft technology effectively in all aspects of their personal and professional lives. Quality instruction is required to help both educators and students get the most from Microsoft's software tools and to become more productive. Thus our mission is to make our instructional programs trusted educational companions for life.

To accomplish this mission, Wiley and Microsoft have partnered to develop the highest quality educational programs for Information Workers, IT Professionals, and Developers. Materials created by this partnership carry the brand name "Microsoft Official Academic Course," assuring instructors and students alike that the content of these textbooks is fully endorsed by Microsoft, and that they provide the highest quality information and instruction on Microsoft products. The Microsoft Official Academic Course textbooks are "Official" in still one more way—they are the officially sanctioned courseware for Microsoft IT Academy members.

The Microsoft Official Academic Course series focuses on workforce development. These programs are aimed at those students seeking to enter the workforce, change jobs, or embark on new careers as information workers, IT professionals, and developers. Microsoft Official Academic Course programs address their needs by emphasizing authentic workplace scenarios with an abundance of projects, exercises, cases, and assessments.

The Microsoft Official Academic Courses are mapped to Microsoft's extensive research and job-task analysis, the same research and analysis used to create the Microsoft Office Specialist (MOS) exams. The textbooks focus on real skills for real jobs. As students work through the projects and exercises in the textbooks they enhance their level of knowledge and their ability to apply the latest Microsoft technology to everyday tasks. These students also gain resume-building credentials that can assist them in finding a job, keeping their current job, or in furthering their education.

The concept of life-long learning is today an utmost necessity. Job roles, and even whole job categories, are changing so quickly that none of us can stay competitive and productive without continuously updating our skills and capabilities. The Microsoft Official Academic Course offerings, and their focus on Microsoft certification exam preparation, provide a means for people to acquire and effectively update their skills and knowledge. Wiley supports students in this endeavor through the development and distribution of these courses as Microsoft's official academic publisher.

Joe Heider
Senior Vice President, Wiley Global Education

Illustrated Book Tour

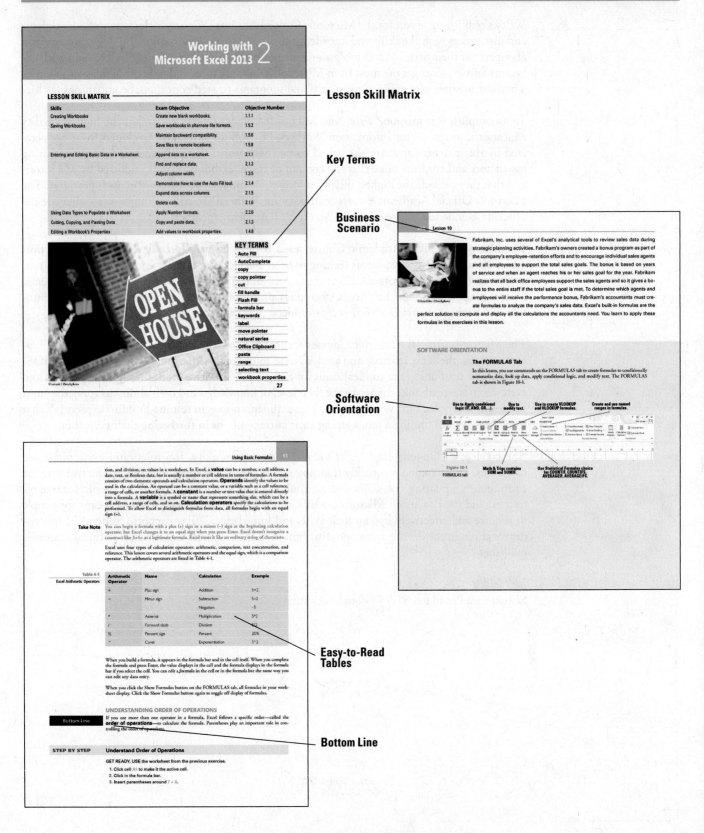

Lesson Skill Matrix

Key Terms

Business Scenario

Software Orientation

Easy-to-Read Tables

Bottom Line

Illustrated Book Tour

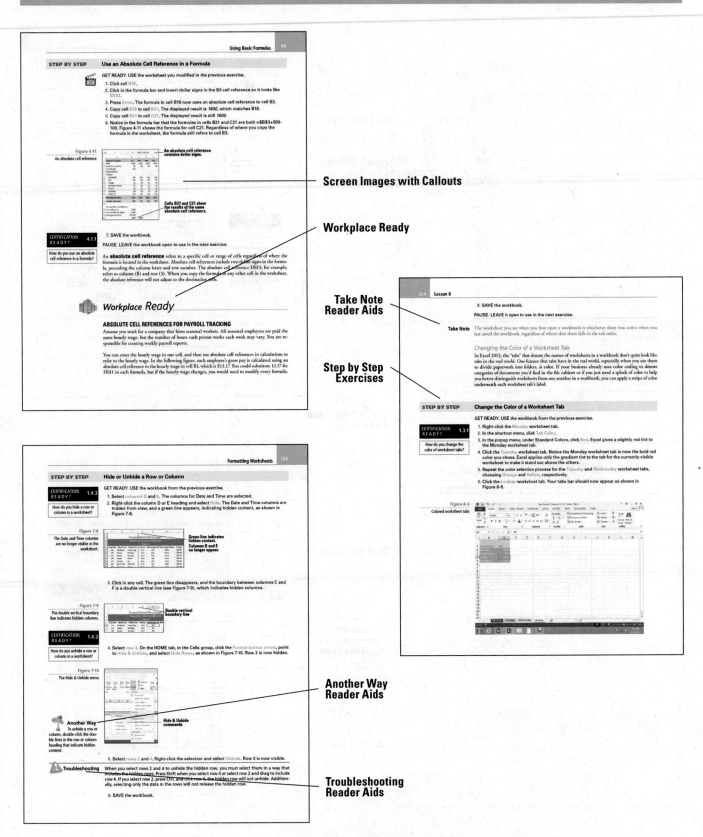

Screen Images with Callouts

Workplace Ready

Take Note
Reader Aids

Step by Step
Exercises

Another Way
Reader Aids

Troubleshooting
Reader Aids

Illustrated Book Tour

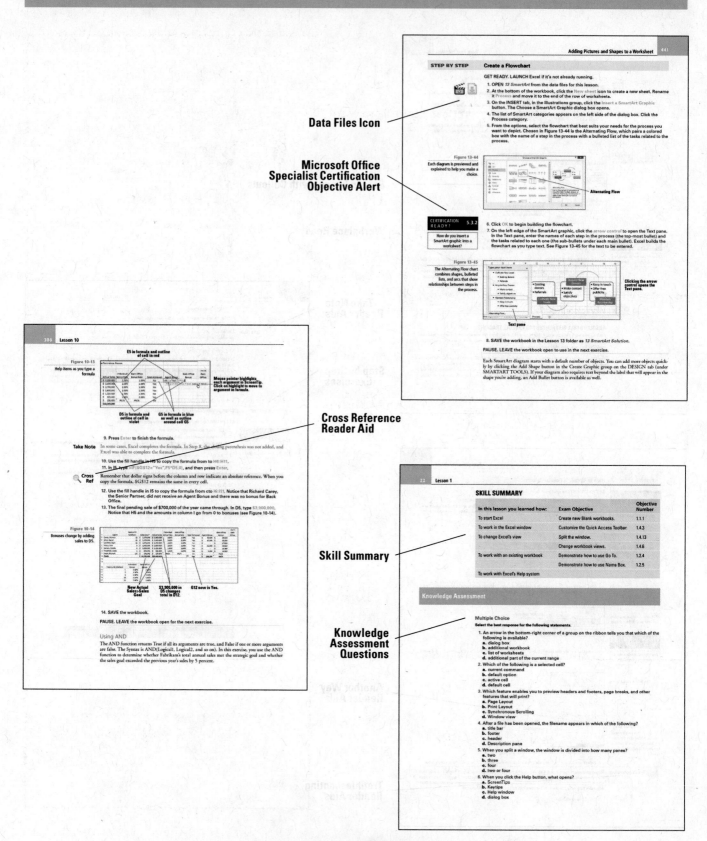

Data Files Icon

Microsoft Office
Specialist Certification
Objective Alert

Cross Reference
Reader Aid

Skill Summary

Knowledge
Assessment
Questions

Illustrated Book Tour

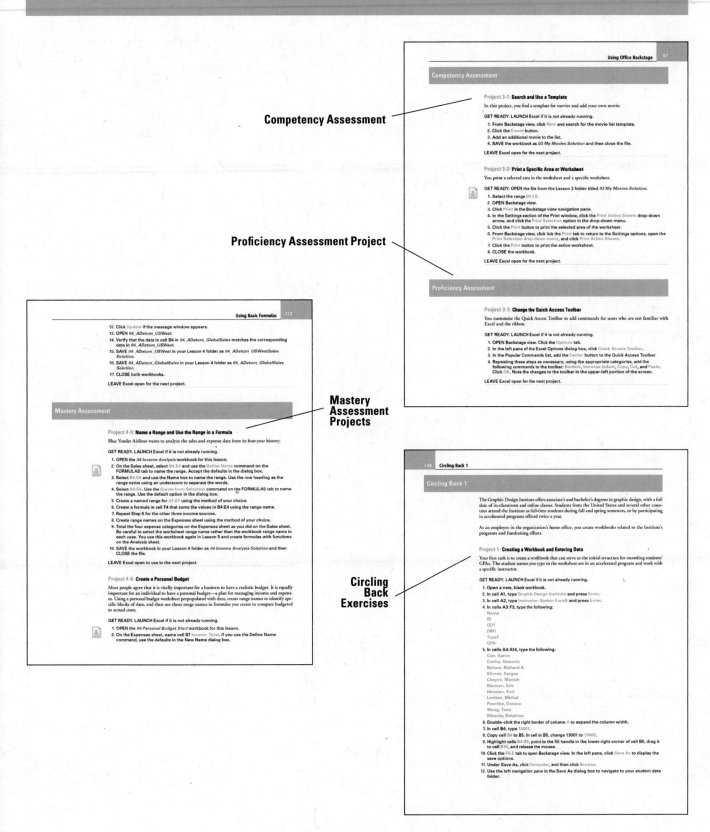

Competency Assessment

Proficiency Assessment Project

Mastery Assessment Projects

Circling Back Exercises

Using Office Backstage 87

Competency Assessment

Project 3-1: Search and Use a Template

In this project, you find a template for movies and add your own movie.

GET READY. LAUNCH Excel if it is not already running.

1. From Backstage view, click New and search for the movie list template.
2. Click the Create button.
3. Add an additional movie to the list.
4. SAVE the workbook as *03 My Movies Solution* and then close the file.

LEAVE Excel open for the next project.

Project 3-2: Print a Specific Area or Worksheet

You print a selected area in the worksheet and a specific worksheet.

GET READY. OPEN the file from the Lesson 3 folder titled *03 My Movies Solution*.

1. Select the range D5:L9.
2. OPEN Backstage view.
3. Click Print in the Backstage view navigation pane.
4. In the Settings section of the Print window, click the Print Active Sheets drop-down arrow, and click the Print Selection option in the drop-down menu.
5. Click the Print button to print the selected area of the worksheet.
6. From Backstage view, click lick the Print tab to return to the Settings options, open the Print Selection drop-down menu, and click Print Active Sheets.
7. Click the Print button to print the active worksheet.
8. CLOSE the workbook.

LEAVE Excel open for the next project.

Proficiency Assessment

Project 3-3: Change the Quick Access Toolbar

You customize the Quick Access Toolbar to add commands for users who are not familiar with Excel and the ribbon.

GET READY. LAUNCH Excel if it is not already running.

1. OPEN Backstage view. Click the Options tab.
2. In the left pane of the Excel Options dialog box, click Quick Access Toolbar.
3. In the Popular Commands list, add the Center button to the Quick Access Toolbar.
4. Repeating these steps as necessary, using the appropriate categories, add the following commands to the toolbar: Borders, Increase Indent, Copy, Cut, and Paste. Click OK. Note the changes to the toolbar in the upper-left portion of the screen.

LEAVE Excel open for the next project.

Using Basic Formulas 113

12. Click Update if the message window appears.
13. OPEN *04_ADatum_USWest*.
14. Verify that the data in cell B4 in *04_ADatum_GlobalSales* matches the corresponding data in *04_ADatum_USWest*.
15. SAVE *04_ADatum_USWest* in your Lesson 4 folder as *04_ADatum_USWestSales Solution*.
16. SAVE *04_ADatum_GlobalSales* in your Lesson 4 folder as *04_ADatum_GlobalSales Solution*.
17. CLOSE both workbooks.

LEAVE Excel open for the next project.

Mastery Assessment

Project 4-5: Name a Range and Use the Range in a Formula

Blue Yonder Airlines wants to analyze the sales and expense data from its four-year history.

GET READY. LAUNCH Excel if it is not already running.

1. OPEN the *04 Income Analysis* workbook for this lesson.
2. On the Sales sheet, select B4:E4 and use the Define Name command on the FORMULAS tab to name the range. Accept the defaults in the dialog box.
3. Select B5:E5 and use the Name box to name the range. Use the row heading as the range name using an underscore to separate the words.
4. Select A6:E6. Use the Create from Selection command on the FORMULAS tab to name the range. Use the default option in the dialog box.
5. Create a named range for A7:E7 using the method of your choice.
6. Create a formula in cell F4 that sums the values in B4:E4 using the range name.
7. Repeat Step 6 for the other three income sources.
8. Create range names on the Expenses sheet using the method of your choice.
9. Total the four expense categories on the Expenses sheet as you did on the Sales sheet. Be careful to select the worksheet range name rather than the workbook range name in each case. You use this workbook again in Lesson 5 and create formulas with functions on the Analysis sheet.
10. SAVE the workbook in your Lesson 4 folder as *04 Income Analysis Solution* and then CLOSE the file.

LEAVE Excel open to use in the next project.

Project 4-6: Create a Personal Budget

Most people agree that it is vitally important for a business to have a realistic budget. It is equally important for an individual to have a personal budget—a plan for managing income and expenses. Using a personal budget worksheet prepopulated with data, create range names to identify specific blocks of data, and then use those range names in formulas you create to compare budgeted to actual costs.

GET READY. LAUNCH Excel if it is not already running.

1. OPEN the *04 Personal Budget Start* workbook for this lesson.
2. On the Expenses sheet, name cell B7 Income_Total. If you use the Define Name command, use the defaults in the New Name dialog box.

---

140 Circling Back 1

Circling Back 1

The Graphic Design Institute offers associate's and bachelor's degrees in graphic design, with a full slate of in-classroom and online classes. Students from the United States and several other countries attend the Institute as full-time students during fall and spring semesters, or by participating in accelerated programs offered twice a year.

As an employee in the organization's home office, you create workbooks related to the Institute's programs and fundraising efforts.

Project 1: Creating a Workbook and Entering Data

Your first task is to create a workbook that can serve as the initial structure for recording students' GPAs. The student names you type in the worksheet are in an accelerated program and work with a specific instructor.

GET READY. LAUNCH Excel if it is not already running.

1. Open a new, blank workbook.
2. In cell A1, type Graphic Design Institute and press Enter.
3. In cell A2, type Instructor: Sachin Karnik and press Enter.
4. In cells A3:F3, type the following:
   Name
   ID
   GD1
   DM1
   Type1
   GPA
5. In cells A4:A14, type the following:
   Con, Aaron
   Cunha, Goncalo
   Byham, Richard A.
   Klimov, Sergey
   Chopra, Manish
   Davison, Eric
   Hensien, Keri
   Levitan, Michal
   Paschke, Dorena
   Wang, Tony
   Ribeute, Delphine
6. Double-click the right border of column A to expand the column width.
7. In cell B4, type 13001.
8. Copy cell B4 to B5. In cell in B5, change 13001 to 13002.
9. Highlight cells B4:B5, point to the fill handle in the lower-right corner of cell B5, drag it to cell B14, and release the mouse.
10. Click the FILE tab to open Backstage view. In the left pane, click Save As to display the save options.
11. Under Save As, click Computer, and then click Browse.
12. Use the left navigation pane in the Save As dialog box to navigate to your student data folder.

Preface

Welcome to the Microsoft Official Academic Course (MOAC) program for Microsoft Office 2013. MOAC represents the collaboration between Microsoft Learning and John Wiley & Sons, Inc. publishing company. Microsoft and Wiley teamed up to produce a series of textbooks that deliver compelling and innovative teaching solutions to instructors and superior learning experiences for students. Infused and informed by in-depth knowledge from the creators of Microsoft Office and Windows, and crafted by a publisher known worldwide for the pedagogical quality of its products, these textbooks maximize skills transfer in minimum time. Students are challenged to reach their potential by using their new technical skills as highly productive members of the workforce.

Because this knowledgebase comes directly from Microsoft, architect of the Office 2013 system and creator of the Microsoft Office Specialist (MOS) exams (www.microsoft.com/learning/mcp/mcts), you are sure to receive the topical coverage that is most relevant to students' personal and professional success. Microsoft's direct participation not only assures you that MOAC textbook content is accurate and current; it also means that students will receive the best instruction possible to enable their success on certification exams and in the workplace.

THE MICROSOFT OFFICIAL ACADEMIC COURSE PROGRAM

The Microsoft Official Academic Course series is a complete program for instructors and institutions to prepare and deliver great courses on Microsoft software technologies. With MOAC, we recognize that, because of the rapid pace of change in the technology and curriculum developed by Microsoft, there is an ongoing set of needs beyond classroom instruction tools for an instructor to be ready to teach the course. The MOAC program endeavors to provide solutions for all these needs in a systematic manner in order to ensure a successful and rewarding course experience for both instructor and student—technical and curriculum training for instructor readiness with new software releases; the software itself for student use at home for building hands-on skills, assessment, and validation of skill development; and a great set of tools for delivering instruction in the classroom and lab. All are important to the smooth delivery of an interesting course on Microsoft software, and all are provided with the MOAC program. We think about the model below as a gauge for ensuring that we completely support you in your goal of teaching a great course. As you evaluate your instructional materials options, you may wish to use the model for comparison purposes with available products.

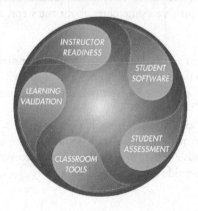

Illustrated Book Tour

PEDAGOGICAL FEATURES

The MOAC courseware for *Microsoft Office 2013 system* are designed to cover all the learning objectives for that MOS exam, which is referred to as its "objective domain." The Microsoft Office Specialist (MOS) exam objectives are highlighted throughout the textbooks. Many pedagogical features have been developed specifically for *Microsoft Official Academic Course* programs. Unique features of our task-based approach include a Lesson Skills Matrix that correlates skills taught in each lesson to the MOS objectives; Certification, and three levels of increasingly rigorous lesson-ending activities: Competency, Proficiency, and Mastery Assessment.

Presenting the extensive procedural information and technical concepts woven throughout the textbook raises challenges for the student and instructor alike. The Illustrated Book Tour that follows provides a guide to the rich features contributing to *Microsoft Official Academic Course* program's pedagogical plan. Following is a list of key features in each lesson designed to prepare students for success on the certification exams and in the workplace:

- Each lesson begins with a **Lesson Skill Matrix**. More than a standard list of learning objectives, the skill matrix correlates each software skill covered in the lesson to the specific MOS exam objective domain.

- Each lesson features a real-world **Business Case** scenario that places the software skills and knowledge to be acquired in a real-world setting.

- Every lesson opens with a **Software Orientation**. This feature provides an overview of the software features students will be working with in the lesson. The orientation will detail the general properties of the software or specific features, such as a ribbon or dialog box; and it includes a large, labeled screen image.

- Concise and frequent **Step-by-Step** instructions teach students new features and provide an opportunity for hands-on practice. Numbered steps give detailed, step-by-step instructions to help students learn software skills. The steps also show results and screen images to match what students should see on their computer screens.

- **Illustrations**: Screen images provide visual feedback as students work through the exercises. The images reinforce key concepts, provide visual clues about the steps, and allow students to check their progress.

- **Key Terms:** Important technical vocabulary is listed at the beginning of the lesson. When these terms are used later in the lesson, they appear in bold italic type with yellow highlighter and are defined. The Glossary contains all of the key terms and their definitions.

- Engaging point-of-use **Reader aids**, located throughout the lessons, tell students why this topic is relevant (*The Bottom Line*), provide students with helpful hints (*Take Note*), or show alternate ways to accomplish tasks (*Another Way*), or point out things to watch out for or avoid (*Troubleshooting*). Reader aids also provide additional relevant or background information that adds value to the lesson.

- **Certification Ready?** features throughout the text signal students where a specific certification objective is covered. They provide students with a chance to check their understanding of that particular MOS exam objective and, if necessary, review the section of the lesson where it is covered. MOAC provides complete preparation for MOS certification.

- **Workplace Ready.** These new features preview how the Microsoft Office 2013 system applications are used in real-world situations.

- Each lesson ends with a **Skill Summary** recapping the topics and MOS exam skills covered in the lesson.

- **Knowledge Assessment:** Provides a total of 20 questions from a mix of True/False, Fill-in-the-Blank, Matching or Multiple Choice testing students on concepts learned in the lesson.

- **Competency, Proficiency, and Mastery Assessment:** provide three progressively more challenging lesson-ending activities.

- **Circling Back:** These integrated projects provide students with an opportunity to renew and practice skills learned in previous lessons.

- **Online files:** The student companion website contains the data files needed for each lesson. These files are indicated by the file download icon in the margin of the textbook.

Conventions and Features Used in This Book

This book uses particular fonts, symbols, and heading conventions to highlight important information or to call your attention to special steps. For more information about the features in each lesson, refer to the Illustrated Book Tour section.

Convention	Meaning
Bottom Line	This feature provides a brief summary of the material to be covered in the section that follows.
CLOSE	Words in all capital letters indicate instructions for opening, saving, or closing files or programs. They also point out items you should check or actions you should take.
CERTIFICATION READY?	This feature signals the point in the text where a specific certification objective is covered. It provides you with a chance to check your understanding of that particular MOS objective and, if necessary, review the section of the lesson where it is covered.
Take Note	Reader aids appear in shaded boxes found in your text. Take Note provides helpful hints related to particular tasks or topics.
Another Way	Another Way provides an alternative procedure for accomplishing a particular task.
Cross Ref	These notes provide pointers to information discussed elsewhere in the textbook or describe interesting features that are not directly addressed in the current topic or exercise.
ALT + Tab	A plus sign (+) between two key names means that you must press both keys at the same time. Keys that you are instructed to press in an exercise will appear in the font shown here.
A **shared printer** can be used by many individuals on a network.	Key terms appear in bold italic.
Key My Name is	Any text you are asked to key appears in color.
Click OK	Any button on the screen you are supposed to click on or select will also appear in color.
	The names of data files will appear in bold, italic and red for easy identification. These data files are available for download from the Student Companion Site (www.Wiley.com/college/Microsoft).
	Step-by-step tutorial videos are available for many of the activities throughout this course. For information on how to access these videos, see the Student Companion Site (www.Wiley.com/college/Microsoft).
OPEN *BudgetWorksheet1*	The names of data files will appear in bold, italic and red for easy identification.

Instructor Support Program

The *Microsoft Official Academic Course* programs are accompanied by a rich array of resources that incorporate the extensive textbook visuals to form a pedagogically cohesive package. These resources provide all the materials instructors need to deploy and deliver their courses. Resources available online for download include:

- The **Instructor's Guide** contains Solutions to all the textbook exercises as well as chapter summaries and lecture notes. The Instructor's Guide and Syllabi for various term lengths are available from the Instructor's Book Companion site (www.wiley.com/college/microsoft).

- The **Solution Files** for all the projects in the book are available online from our Instructor's Book Companion site (www.wiley.com/college/microsoft).

- The **Test Bank** contains hundreds of questions organized by lesson in multiple-choice, true-false, short answer, and essay formats and is available to download from the Instructor's Book Companion site (www.wiley.com/college/microsoft). A complete answer key is provided.

- This title's test bank is available for use in Respondus' easy-to-use software. You can download the test bank for free using your Respondus, Respondus LE, or StudyMate Author software.

- Respondus is a powerful tool for creating and managing exams that can be printed to paper or published directly to Blackboard, WebCT, Desire2Learn, eCollege, ANGEL and other eLearning systems.

- **Test Bank Projects.** Two projects for each lesson are provided on the Instructor's Book Companion Site as well as solution files suitable for grading with OfficeGrader. These projects cover topics from within one specific lesson.

- **Comprehensive Projects:** Two comprehensive projects are provided on the Instructor's Book Companion Site for each Circling Back These projects cover topics from all lessons in the book up to that point. Solution files suitable for grading with OfficeGrader are also provided.

- **Capstone Projects:** Two capstone projects are provided with the final Circling Back on the Instructor's Book Companion Site. These projects are suitable for a final exam or final project for the course. These projects cover a range of topics from throughout the entire book. Solution files suitable for grading with OfficeGrader are also provided.

- **PowerPoint Presentations and Images**. A complete set of PowerPoint presentations is available on the Instructor's Book Companion site (www.wiley.com/college/microsoft) to enhance classroom presentations. Tailored to the text's topical coverage and Skills Matrix, these presentations are designed to convey key Microsoft .NET Framework concepts addressed in the text.

All figures from the text are on the Instructor's Book Companion site (www.wiley.com/ college/ microsoft). You can incorporate them into your PowerPoint presentations, or create your own overhead transparencies and handouts.

By using these visuals in class discussions, you can help focus students' attention on key elements of Windows Server and help them understand how to use it effectively in the workplace.

- **Office Grader** automated grading system allows you to easily grade student data files in Word, Excel, PowerPoint or Access format, against solution files. Save tens or hundreds of hours each semester with automated grading. More information on OfficeGrader is available from the Instructor's Book Companion site (www.wiley.com/college/microsoft).

- The **Student Data Files** are available online on both the Instructor's Book Companion Site and for students on the Student Book Companion Site.

Wiley **Faculty Network:** When it comes to improving the classroom experience, there is no better source of ideas and inspiration than your fellow colleagues. The Wiley Faculty Network connects teachers with technology, facilitates the exchange of best practices, and helps to enhance instructional efficiency and effectiveness. Faculty Network activities include technology training and tutorials, virtual seminars, peer-to-peer exchanges of experiences and ideas, personal consulting, and sharing of resources. For details visit www.WhereFacultyConnect.com.

IMPORTANT WEB ADDRESSES AND PHONE NUMBERS

To locate the Wiley Higher Education Rep in your area, go to the following Web address and click on the "*Contact Us*" link at the top of the page.

www.wiley.com/college

Or Call the MOAC Toll Free Number: 1 + (888) 764-7001 (U.S. & Canada only).

To learn more about becoming a Microsoft Certified Professional and exam availability, visit **www.microsoft.com/learning/mcp.**

DREAMSPARK PREMIUM
Free 3-Year Membership available to Qualified Adopters

DreamSpark Premium is designed to provide the easiest and most inexpensive way for schools to make the latest Microsoft developer tools, products, and technologies available in labs, classrooms, and on student PCs. DreamSpark Premium is an annual membership program for departments teaching Science, Technology, Engineering, and Mathematics (STEM) courses. The membership provides a complete solution to keep academic labs, faculty, and students on the leading edge of technology.

Software available through the DreamSpark Premium program is provided at no charge to adopting departments through the Wiley and Microsoft publishing partnership.

Contact your Wiley rep for details.

For more information about the DreamSpark Premium program, go to Microsoft's DreamSpark website

BOOK COMPANION WEBSITE (WWW.WILEY.COM/COLLEGE/MICROSOFT)

The students' book companion site for the MOAC series includes any resources, exercise files, and web links that will be used in conjunction with this course.

WILEY E-TEXT: POWERED BY VITALSOURCE

When you choose a Wiley E-Text you not only save money; you benefit from being able to access course materials and content anytime, anywhere through a user experience that makes learning rewarding.

With the Wiley E-Text you will be able to easily:
• Search
• Take notes
• Highlight key materials
• Have all your work in one place for more efficient studying

In addition, the Wiley E-Text is fully portable. Students can access it online and download to their computer for off line access and access read and study on their device of preference—computer, tablet, or smartphone.

WHY MOS CERTIFICATION?

Microsoft Office Specialist (MOS) 2013 is a valuable credential that recognizes the desktop computing skills needed to use the full features and functionality of the Microsoft Office 2013 suite.

In the worldwide job market, Microsoft Office Specialist is the primary tool companies use to validate the proficiency of their employees in the latest productivity tools and technology, helping them select job candidates based on globally recognized standards for verifying skills. The results of an independent research study show that businesses with certified employees are more productive compared to non-certified employees and that certified employees bring immediate value to their jobs.

In academia, as in the business world, institutions upgrading to Office 2013 may seek ways to protect and maximize their technology investment. By offering certification, they validate that decision—because powerful Office 2013 applications such as Word, Excel and PowerPoint can be effectively used to demonstrate increases in academic preparedness and workforce readiness.

Individuals seek certification to increase their own personal sense of accomplishment and to create advancement opportunities by establishing a leadership position in their school or department, thereby differentiating their skill sets in a competitive college admissions and job market.

PREPARING TO TAKE THE MICROSOFT OFFICE SPECIALIST (MOS) EXAM

The Microsoft Office Specialist credential has been upgraded to validate skills with the Microsoft Office 2013 system. The MOS certifications target information workers and cover the most popular business applications such as Word 2013, Excel 2013, PowerPoint 2013, Outlook 2013 and Access 2013.

By becoming certified, you demonstrate to employers that you have achieved a predictable level of skill in the use of a particular Office application. Employers often require certification either as a condition of employment or as a condition of advancement within the company or other organization. The certification examinations are sponsored by Microsoft but administered through exam delivery partners like Certiport.

To learn more about becoming a Microsoft Office Specialist and exam availability, visit http://www.microsoft.com/learning/en/us/mos-certification.aspx.

Preparing to Take an Exam

Unless you are a very experienced user, you will need to use a test preparation course to prepare to complete the test correctly and within the time allowed. The *Microsoft Official Academic Course* series is designed to prepare you with a strong knowledge of all exam topics, and with some additional review and practice on your own. You should feel confident in your ability to pass the appropriate exam.

After you decide which exam to take, review the list of objectives for the exam. This list can be found in the MOS Objectives Appendix at the back of this book. You can also easily identify tasks that are included in the objective list by locating the Lesson Skill Matrix at the start of each lesson and the Certification Ready sidebars in the margin of the lessons in this book.

To take the MOS test, visit http://www.microsoft.com/learning/en/us/mos-certification.aspx to locate your nearest testing center. Then call the testing center directly to schedule your test. The amount of advance notice you should provide will vary for different testing centers, and it typically depends on the number of computers available at the testing center, the number of other testers who have already been scheduled for the day on which you want to take the test, and the number of times per week that the testing center offers MOS testing. In general, you should call to schedule your test at least two weeks prior to the date on which you want to take the test.

When you arrive at the testing center, you might be asked for proof of identity. A driver's license or passport is an acceptable form of identification. If you do not have either of these items of documentation, call your testing center and ask what alternative forms of identification will be accepted. If you are retaking a test, bring your MOS identification number, which will have been given to you when you previously took the test. If you have not prepaid or if your organization has not already arranged to make payment for you, you will need to pay the test-taking fee when you arrive.

Test Format

MOS exams are Exams are primarily performance-based and conducted in a "live," or simulated, environment. Exam candidates taking exams for MOS 2007 or 2010 are asked to perform a series of tasks to clearly demonstrate their skills. For example, a Word exam might ask a user to balance newspaper column lengths or keep text together in columns. The new MOS 2013 exam format presents a short project the candidate must complete, using the specifications provided. This creates a real-world testing experience for candidates. All MOS exams must be completed in 90 minutes or less.

All of the practice files that you will use as you perform the exercises in the book are available for download on our student companion site. By using the practice files, you will not waste time creating the samples used in the lessons, and you can concentrate on learning how to use Microsoft Office 2013. With the files and the step-by-step instructions in the lessons, you will learn by doing, which is an easy and effective way to acquire and remember new skills.

COPYING THE PRACTICE FILES

Your instructor might already have copied the practice files before you arrive in class. However, your instructor might ask you to copy the practice files on your own at the start of class. Also, if you want to work through any of the exercises in this book on your own at home or at your place of business after class, you may want to copy the practice files.

1. OPEN Internet Explorer.
2. In Internet Explorer, go to the student companion site: www.wiley.com
3. Search for your book title in the upper right hand corner
4. On the Search Results page, locate your book and click on the Visit the Companion Sites link.
5. Select Student Companion Site from the pop-up box.
6. From the menu, select the arrow next to Browse By Resource and select Student Data Files from the menu.
7. A new screen will appear.
8. On the Student Data Files page, you can select to download files for just one lesson or for all lessons. Click on the file of your choice.
9. On the File Download dialog box, select Save As to save the data files to your external drive (often called a ZIP drive or a USB drive or a thumb drive) or a local drive.
10. In the Save As dialog box, select a local drive in the left-hand panel that you'd like to save your files to; again, this should be an external drive or a local drive. Remember the drive name that you saved it to.

Acknowledgments

We'd like to thank the many instructors and reviewers who pored over the outline and manu-script, providing invaluable feedback in the service of quality instructional materials.

ACCESS 2013

Catherine Bradfield, *DeVry University*

Mary Corcoran, *Bellevue College*

Cynthia Miller, *Harper College*

Aditi Mukherjee, *University of Florida—Gainesville*

Elizabeth Snow, *Southwest Florida College*

EXCEL 2013

Catherine Bradfield, *DeVry University*

DeAnnia Clements, *Wiregrass Georgia Technical College*

Dee Hobson, *Richland College*

Sandra Jolley, *Tarrant County College*

Joe Lamontagne, *Davenport University*

Edward Martin, *Kingsborough Community College-City University of New York*

Aditi Mukherjee, *University of Florida—Gainesville*

Linda Nutter, *Peninsula College*

Dave Rotherham, *Sheffield Hallam University*

POWERPOINT 2013

Mary Corcoran, *Bellevue College*

Rob Durrance, *East Lee County High School*

Phil Hanney, *Orem Junior High School*

Terri Holly, *Indian River State College*

Kim Hopkins, *Weatherford College*

Tatyana Pashnyak, *Bainbridge State College*

Michelle Poertner, *Northwestern Michigan College*

Theresa Savarese, *San Diego City College*

WORD 2013

Erik Amerikaner, *Oak Park Unified*

Sue Bajt, *Harper College*

Gregory Ballinger, *Miami-Dade College*

Andrea Cluff, *Freemont High School*

Caroline de Gruchy, *Conestoga College*

Donna Madsen, *Kirkwood Community College*

Lynn Mancini, *Delaware Technical Community College*

Denise Merrell, *Jefferson Community and Technical College*

Diane Mickey, *Northern Virginia Community College*

Robert Mike, *Alaska Career College*

Bettye Parham, *Daytona State College*

Barbara Purvis, *Centura College*

Janet Sebesy, *Cuyahoga Community College-Western*

Dorothy Weiner, *Manchester Community College*

Author Credits

KIM LINDROS

Kim Lindros is a full-time writer, content developer, and project manager who has worked around high technology and computing since the early 1990s. She co-authored *Introduction to Computers with Windows XP and Office 2007* (Kaplan, 2013), *MTA Microsoft Technology Associate Exam 98-349 Windows Operating System Fundamentals* (Wiley, 2012), *PC Basics with Windows 7 and Office 2010* (Jones & Bartlett Learning, 2010), and numerous courses focused on Windows and Microsoft Office.

RICK WINTER

Rick Winter has published over 50 computer and children's books and articles and has trained over 3,000 adults on computer software. He has a Bachelor's of Arts degree in International Environment from Colorado College and a Master of Public Administration from the University of Colorado at Denver. Rick has received awards that include Clear Creek School District Leadership and Service Award, Information Systems Trainers Distinguished Service Award, Rocky Mountain Chapter Society for Technical Communication Distinguished Award, Phi Beta Kappa, Eagle Scout, and is listed in "Who's Who in America."

JENNIFER FULTON

Jennifer Fulton, Senior Partner of Ingenus, LLC and iVillage's former "Computer Coach," is an experienced technical writer with over 20 years in the business. Jennifer has written and edited hundreds of online course materials for both college and middle school audience, and authored over 150 bestselling computer books for beginner, intermediate, and advanced users, including *Outlook 2010 All-in-One for Dummies*, *Windows 7 eLearning Kit for Dummies*, and *Outlook 2007 All-in-One Desk Reference for Dummies*. Jennifer is also a computer trainer for corporate personnel, teaching a variety of classes on Windows, Microsoft Office, Paint Shop Pro, Photoshop Elements, and others.

Brief Contents

www.wiley.com/college/microsoft
or call the MOAC Toll-Free Number: 1+(888) 764-7001 (U.S. & Canada only)

Contents

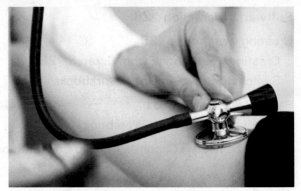

© webphotographeer / iStockphoto

Lesson 2: Working with Microsoft Excel 2013

©asiseeit / iStockphoto

Lesson 3: Using Office Backstage

© matthewwennisphotography / iStock photo

Lesson 4: Using Basic Formulas

© matthewennisphotography / iStock photo

Lesson 5: Using Functions

©MCCAIG / iStockphoto

Lesson 6: Formatting Cells and Ranges

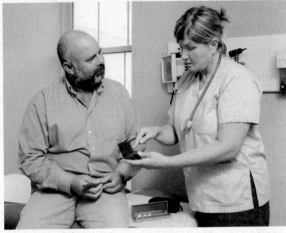
© Fertnig /iStockphoto

Lesson 7: Formatting Worksheets

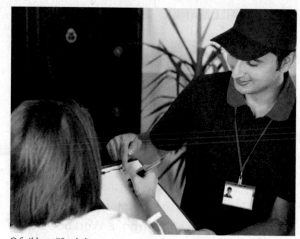
© fatihhoca /iStockphoto

Lesson 8: Managing Worksheets

© skynesher /iStockphoto

Lesson 9: Working with Data and Macros

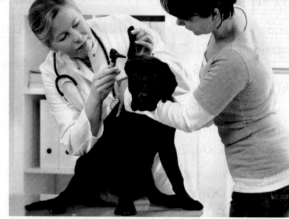

©AlexRaths /iStockphoto

Lesson 10: Using Advanced Formulas

©AtnoYdur /iStockphoto

Lesson 11: Securing and Sharing Workbooks

©spxChrome / iStockphoto

Lesson 12: Creating Charts

© kgelati1 / iStockphoto

Lesson 13: Adding Pictures and Shapes to a Worksheet

© kate_sept2004 / iStockphoto

www.wiley.com/college/microsoft
or call the MOAC Toll-Free Number: 1+(888) 764-7001 (U.S. & Canada only)

LESSON SKILL MATRIX

Skills	Exam Objective	Objective Number
Starting Excel	Create new Blank workbooks.	1.1.1
Working in the Excel Window	Customize the Quick Access Toolbar.	1.4.3
Changing Excel's View	Split the window.	1.4.13
	Change workbook views.	1.4.6
Working with an Existing Workbook	Demonstrate how to use Go To.	1.2.4
	Demonstrate how to use the Name Box.	1.2.5
Working with Excel's Help System		

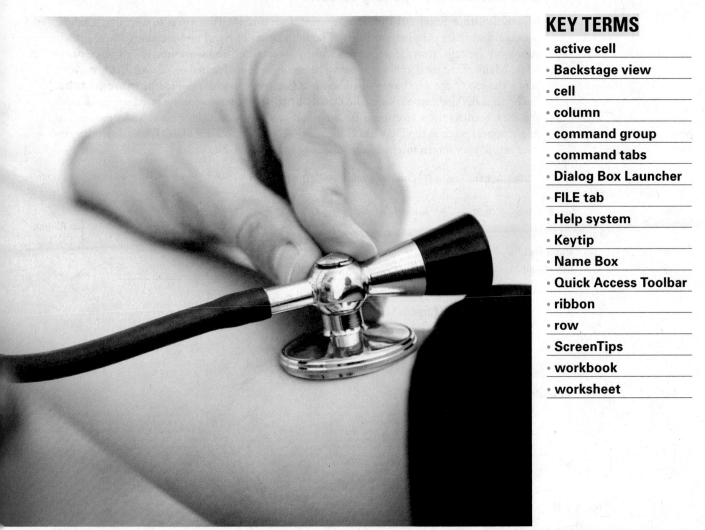

KEY TERMS

- **active cell**
- **Backstage view**
- **cell**
- **column**
- **command group**
- **command tabs**
- **Dialog Box Launcher**
- **FILE tab**
- **Help system**
- **Keytip**
- **Name Box**
- **Quick Access Toolbar**
- **ribbon**
- **row**
- **ScreenTips**
- **workbook**
- **worksheet**

© webphotographeer / iStockphoto

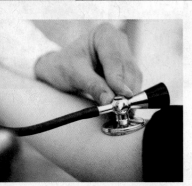

© webphotographeer / iStockphoto

Contoso, Ltd., provides specialty health care for the entire family—prenatal through geriatric care. The practice, owned by Dr. Stephanie Bourne, has an expanding patient list. It currently employs a staff of 36, which includes three additional family practice physicians. Each physician has unique patient contact hours; the office is open from 7 a.m. to 7 p.m. on Mondays and from 8 a.m. to 4 p.m. other weekdays. The office manager and the new assistant that she will hire must track revenue and expenses for the practice and maintain a large volume of employee data. The office manager will create simulation exercises to test the applicants and one of her target pools of applicants will be new college graduates. In this lesson, you learn how to enter text and numbers into an Excel worksheet to keep up-to-date employee records. By the end of the book, you should be able to accomplish simulation tasks that are required by the Microsoft Office User Specialist Test and the simulations requested by several jobs requiring Excel skills.

SOFTWARE ORIENTATION

Microsoft Excel's Opening Screen

Microsoft Office Excel 2013 provides powerful tools that enable users to organize, analyze, manage, and share information easily. The foundation of Excel and locations where you do your work are cells, rows, and columns within a worksheet, and worksheets as part of a workbook. Many of the tools you use while working in Excel are located on the **ribbon**, running across the top of the window. The ribbon is organized into task-oriented **command tabs**. Each tab is divided into task-specific **command groups** appropriate for the type of work the user is currently performing. Because you can customize the ribbon and new options might appear, such as the DEVELOPER, ADD-IN, and POWERPIVOT tabs depending on your setup, your screen might appear different than Figure 1-1.

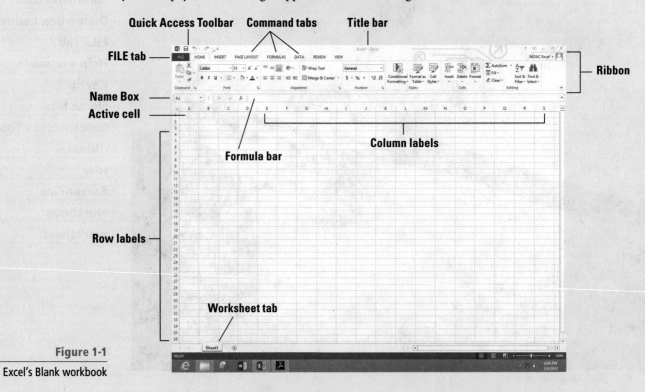

Figure 1-1

Excel's Blank workbook

STARTING EXCEL

To work efficiently in Microsoft Excel, you need to become familiar with its primary user inter-face. You can open Microsoft Excel 2013 in Windows 8 by moving to the bottom-left corner of your screen, clicking on Start, right-clicking a blank area of the Start screen, clicking All apps, and clicking Excel 2013.

Excel opens to a list of templates and in most cases you choose Blank workbook or open a previous file. A **workbook**, or spreadsheet file, is shown in Figure 1-1. Think of a workbook as a physical book with many pages. The filename (Book1) and the program name (Excel) appear in the title bar at the top of the screen. Book1 (or Book2, Book3, and so on) is a temporary title for your workbook until you save the workbook with a name of your choice. The new workbook contains one **worksheet** (Sheet1) by default—similar to the first page in a book—where you enter infor-mation. If a workbook has more pages (or worksheets), you use the sheet tabs that are located just above the Status bar and are identified as Sheet1, Sheet2, and Sheet3. You can rename worksheets to identify their content and add worksheets with the New sheet (+) button as needed.

Cross Ref   See Lesson 8, "Managing Worksheets," for more detail on how to add and rename worksheets.

Opening Excel

In this exercise, you learn to use the Start screen to open Excel and view the new workbook's first blank worksheet.

Start Excel

GET READY. Be sure Microsoft Excel is installed on your computer. Then, perform the following steps:

1. If the Windows desktop is displayed, click the Start screen thumbnail in the bottom left corner of the Windows 8 screen.
2. Right-click in a blank area of the screen and click All apps.
3. In the list of applications under Microsoft Office 2013, click Excel 2013. A window opens to recent Excel files you've opened and examples of templates you can use (see Figure 1-2).

Figure 1-2

Microsoft Excel's opening screen

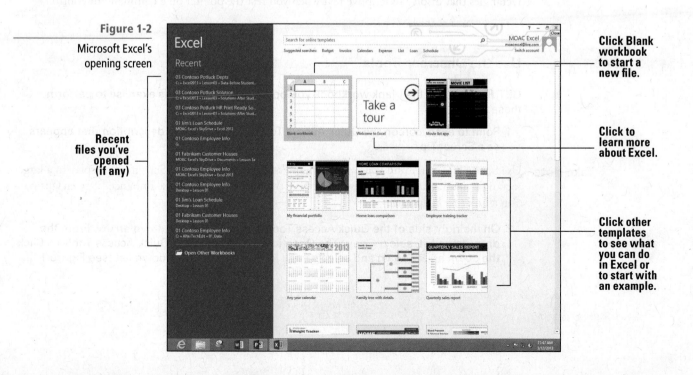

Recent files you've opened (if any)

Click Blank workbook to start a new file.

Click to learn more about Excel.

Click other templates to see what you can do in Excel or to start with an example.

Cross Ref   Templates are discussed in more detail in Lesson 3, "Using Office Backstage."

4. Click **Blank workbook**. A blank workbook opens, and the worksheet named *Sheet1* is displayed as shown previously, in Figure 1-1.

PAUSE. LEAVE the workbook open for the next exercise.

Take Note   If you use Excel repeatedly, you will want to pin your application to the Start screen. From the All Apps screen, right-click the app, and choose Pin to Start. You can also choose Pin to taskbar to allow you to click the icon on the bottom of the Windows Desktop screen to start Excel.

A worksheet is a grid composed of rows, columns, and cells. Each worksheet **column** starts at the top of the worksheet and goes to the bottom of the worksheet and is identified by a letter. Each **row** starts at the left edge of the worksheet and continues to the right and is identified by a number. Each box, or **cell**, on the grid is identified by the intersection of a column and a row. Thus, the first cell in an open worksheet is A1. You enter information by typing it into the selected or **active cell**, which is outlined by a bold rectangle. This is also called the *current* or *highlighted cell*.

WORKING IN THE EXCEL WINDOW

Bottom Line   When you launch Excel and click Blank workbook, the program opens a new workbook and displays a blank worksheet. You just learned about some of the most important components of the Excel worksheet such as rows, columns, and cells. In this section, you explore the Excel window and learn to identify and customize the Quick Access Toolbar, the ribbon, and other important onscreen tools and components. You also learn to open and use Backstage view, Microsoft's replacement for the Office button and File menu commands found in previous versions of Office.

Using the Onscreen Tools

The **Quick Access Toolbar** gives you fast and easy access to the tools you use most often in any given Excel session. It appears on the left side of the title bar, above the ribbon (although you can move the toolbar below the ribbon if you want it closer to your work area). You can add and remove commands to and from the toolbar so that it contains only those commands you use most frequently. In this lesson, you learn to move and customize the Quick Access Toolbar by adding and removing commands. You also learn how to use **ScreenTips**, which are small, onscreen rectangles that display descriptive text when you rest the pointer on a command or control.

STEP BY STEP   **Use the Onscreen Tools**

GET READY. USE the blank workbook you opened in the previous exercise to perform these steps:

1. Point to each icon on the Quick Access Toolbar and read the description that appears as a ScreenTip.

Take Note   Use ScreenTips to remind you of a command's function. Enhanced ScreenTips display in a larger rectangle that contains more descriptive text than a ScreenTip. Most Enhanced ScreenTips contain a link to a Help topic.

2. On the right side of the Quick Access Toolbar, click the drop-down arrow. From the drop-down list, select Open. The Open icon is added to the Quick Access Toolbar. Click the down arrow again and select Quick Print from the drop-down list (see Figure 1-3).

Figure 1-3

Customizing the Quick
Access Toolbar

Another Way
To add a command to the Quick Access Toolbar, you can also right-click any icon on the ribbon and then click Add to Quick Access Toolbar.

3. Next, right-click anywhere on the Quick Access Toolbar, and then select Show Quick Access Toolbar Below the Ribbon.

4. Right-click the HOME tab and click Collapse the Ribbon. Now, only the tabs remain on display, increasing the workspace area.

5. Right-click the HOME tab again and choose Collapse the Ribbon to uncheck the option and make the ribbon commands visible again.

6. On the right side of the Quick Access Toolbar, click the drop-down arrow. Click Show Above the Ribbon from the drop-down list.

7. Right-click the Open command, and select Remove from Quick Access Toolbar.

8. On the right side of the Quick Access Toolbar, click the drop-down arrow and click Quick Print to remove the checkmark from the menu and thus remove the Quick Print icon from the Quick Access Toolbar.

Take Note
To add commands to the Quick Access Toolbar that do not appear in the drop-down list, click More Commands on the drop-down list. The Excel Options dialog box opens. You can also right-click the Quick Access Toolbar or any ribbon tab and select Customize Quick Access Toolbar to open the Excel Options dialog box.

PAUSE. LEAVE the workbook open for the next exercise.

CERTIFICATION READY? 1.4.3

How do you manipulate the Quick Access Toolbar?

By default, the Quick Access Toolbar contains the Save, Undo, and Redo commands. As you work in Excel, customize the Quick Access Toolbar so that it contains the commands you use most often. Do not, however, remove the Undo and Redo commands. These commands are not available on the ribbon's command tabs.

Navigating the Ribbon

The ribbon organizes tools and commands into an intuitive and useful interface. Having commands visible on the work surface enables you to work quickly and efficiently and is especially helpful for new users. The ribbon in Microsoft Office Excel 2013 is made up of a series of tabs, each related to specific tasks that users perform in Excel. By pressing and releasing the Alt key, you can reveal **Keytips**, or small badges displaying keyboard shortcuts for specific tabs and commands on the ribbon and Quick Access Toolbar. In this exercise, you learn how to navigate between Excel tabs and use their commands and Keytips.

Take Note
Keytips are sometimes also referred to as *hotkeys*. Note, however, that when you use the Microsoft Office 2013 Help, no reference is listed for hotkeys. Only Keytips are referenced.

Within each tab on the ribbon, commands are organized into related tasks called *command groups*, or just *groups*, as shown in Figure 1-4. For example, consider the HOME tab. When the HOME tab is displayed, you see the Clipboard group, which contains the command buttons to cut, copy, and paste data. These commands allow you to revise, move, and repeat data in a worksheet. Similarly, you can use commands in the Editing group to fill adjacent cells, sort and filter data, find specific data in a worksheet, and perform other tasks related to editing worksheet data.

Some of the commands have an options arrow that displays additional options for the command. On some of the command groups are icons in the bottom-right corner of the group. These **Dialog Box Launchers** open a dialog box and give more options than display on the ribbon.

Figure 1-4

HOME tab command groups

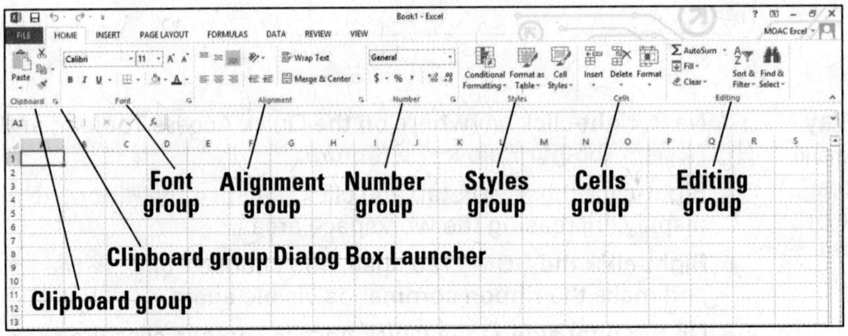

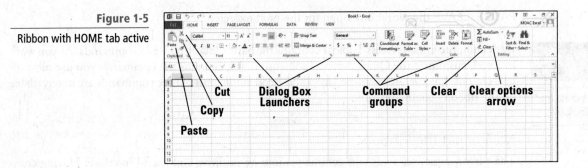

STEP BY STEP   **Navigate the Ribbon**

GET READY. LAUNCH Excel if necessary and open any workbook.

1. Click the HOME tab to make it active and click cell A1. Your ribbon should look similar to the one shown in Figure 1-5.

Figure 1-5

Ribbon with HOME tab active

2. In the Alignment group, click the Dialog Box Launcher to display the Alignment tab in the Format Cells dialog box.

3. Click the Cancel button to close the dialog box.

4. Click the INSERT tab.

   Your screen should now look similar to Figure 1-6. Commands on the INSERT tab enable you to add charts and illustrations and perform other functions that add items to enhance your Excel worksheets.

Figure 1-6

Ribbon with the INSERT tab
active

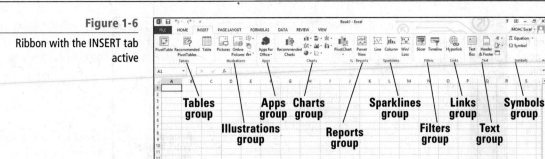

Figure 1-6

Ribbon with the INSERT tab
active

Tables group
Illustrations group
Apps group
Charts group
Reports group
Sparklines group
Filters group
Links group
Text group
Symbols group

5. Click the HOME tab.
6. Press and release the Alt key to display onscreen Keytips that show keyboard shortcuts for certain commands (see Figure 1-7).

Figure 1-7

Keytips on the ribbon

Alt key shortcuts for ribbon tabs
Quick Access Toolbar shortcuts

7. Type W to display the VIEW tab and then type Q to display the Zoom dialog box.
8. Click Cancel or press Esc to close the Zoom dialog box.
9. Press Alt + H to return to the HOME tab.
10. Press Alt to turn off the Keytips.
11. In the Editing group, click the Clear arrow to display the Clear options.
12. Press Esc to turn off the options.

PAUSE. CLOSE Excel.

Introducing Office Backstage

The most noticeable new feature in Microsoft Office 2010 and 2013 is Backstage. The **Backstage view** shows you behind-the-scenes options to manage files such as opening, saving, printing, and documenting files. Backstage view is covered in more depth in Lesson 3, but you need to know how to access it for simple commands in this lesson.

STEP BY STEP   **Open Backstage View**

GET READY. You should not have Excel running for this exercise.

1. LAUNCH Excel and click Blank workbook to start a new workbook. Notice that Book1 displays in the title bar at the top of the screen.
2. Click the FILE tab. This opens Backstage view (see Figure 1-8).

Figure 1-8

When you click a command in the left pane, the major portion of the Backstage screen changes to show options related to that command.

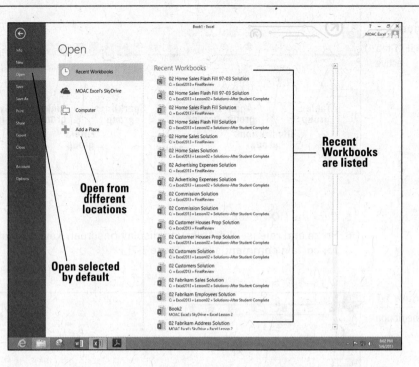

3. Notice that the Excel Backstage view and Excel icon on the taskbar are green. The Office suite has customized colors to designate which application you use.

Troubleshooting   Backstage defaults to different commands depending on what you're doing. When you are working in a blank workbook or with no workbooks open, Backstage defaults to the Open command, which shows different options for opening files. If you have started typing in a document, Backstage defaults to the Info.

4. The commands are on the left pane of the screen. Click Info and the right pane changes (see Figure 1-9). This shows information about the current file.

Figure 1-9

When the Info tab is selected, information about the current workbook displays.

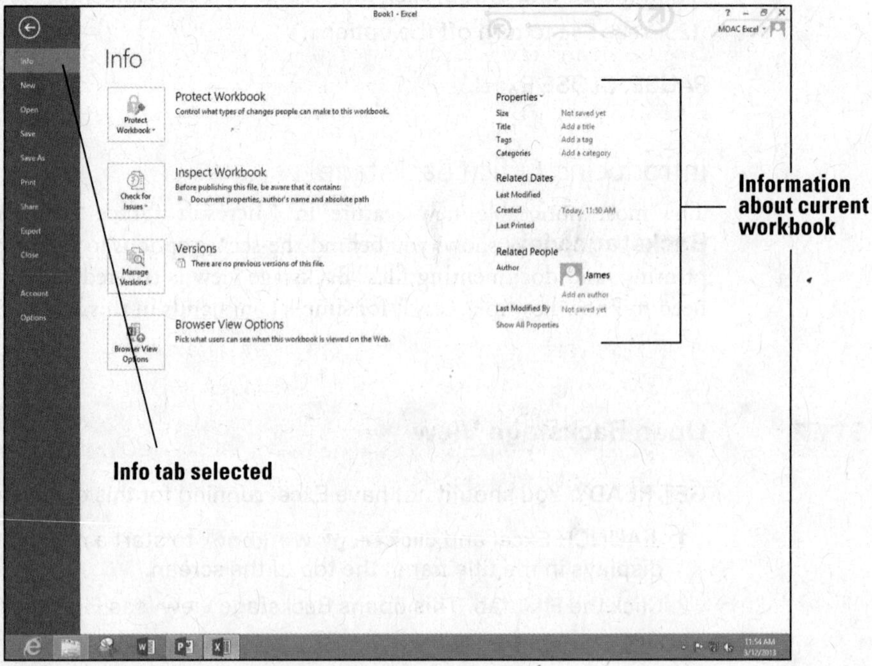

PAUSE. CLOSE Excel for the next exercise.

Using the Microsoft Office FILE Tab and Backstage View

In Microsoft Office 2013, clicking the **FILE tab** takes you to Backstage view, with its navigation bar of commands extending down the left side of the Excel window. Backstage view helps you access and use file management features, just as the ribbon offers commands that control Excel's authoring features. In this exercise, you learn to use the FILE tab to open Backstage view. You also use Backstage commands to create a new blank workbook.

STEP BY STEP	**Use the Microsoft Office FILE Tab and Backstage View**

GET READY. LAUNCH Excel and open a new blank workbook.

1. Click the FILE tab to open Backstage view.
2. In the left pane, click Close. Your worksheet disappears, but Excel remains open.
3. Click the FILE tab again, and then click New. The right pane shows the available options, which are the same as when you launch Excel.
4. Click Blank workbook. A new blank workbook is opened.

PAUSE. CLOSE Excel.

As you have seen, a new blank workbook in Excel 2013 contains one worksheet. You can enter data in the first worksheet and click the New sheet button to create another worksheet and then enter additional data. Excel saves the worksheets together in one workbook rather than as separate documents.

CHANGING EXCEL'S VIEW

Bottom Line

On the ribbon, the VIEW tab holds commands for controlling the appearance of the displayed document. You can also open and arrange new windows and split windows for side-by-side views of different parts of your document.

Change Excel's View

As mentioned in a previous section, some groups on the ribbon tabs have an arrow in their lower-right corner called a *Dialog Box Launcher*. Clicking the arrow opens a dialog box or a window containing more options for that particular group of commands. In this exercise, you learn how to use the VIEW tab commands to change Excel's view.

STEP BY STEP	**Change Excel's View**

GET READY. LAUNCH Excel and start a new workbook.

1. If necessary, click the HOME tab to activate it.
2. Select cell A1 to make it active. Then type 456 and press Tab.
3. In the lower-right corner of the Font group, click the Dialog Box Launcher arrow. The Format Cells dialog box shown in Figure 1-10 opens. In most cases, your default font in Excel will be Calibri, 11 point, without bold or italic.

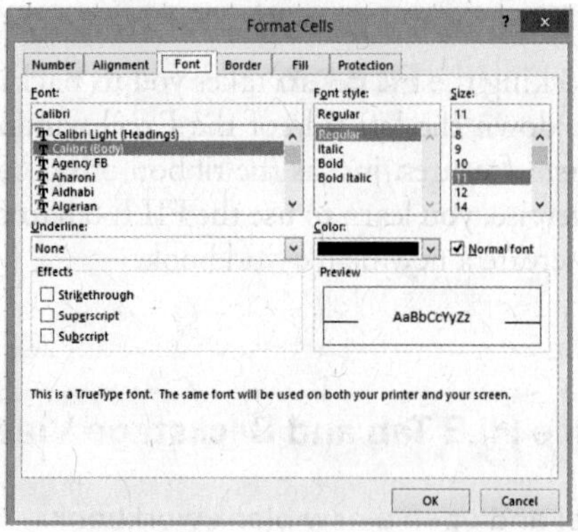

Figure 1-10

Format Cells dialog box

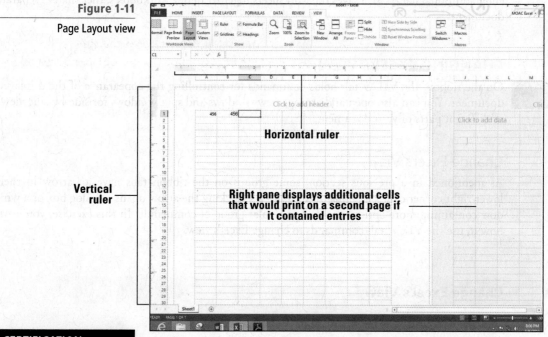

4. Notice that the Font tab of the dialog box is active. Scroll down in the Font list, click Arial, and then click OK. Cell B1 is the active cell now.

5. Type 456 in this cell, and then press Tab. Notice the difference in size and appearance between this number and the one you entered in cell A1.

6. Click the VIEW tab.

7. In the Workbook Views group, click Page Layout. In this view, you can see the margins, where pages break, and you can add a header or footer (see Figure 1-11).

CERTIFICATION READY? 1.4.6

How do you change to Page Layout view?

Figure 1-11

Page Layout view

Horizontal ruler

Vertical ruler

Right pane displays additional cells that would print on a second page if it contained entries

CERTIFICATION READY? 1.4.6

How do you change back to Normal view?

8. In the Workbook Views group, click Normal to return the worksheet to the view that no longer shows rulers, headers, footers, or page breaks.

PAUSE. LEAVE the workbook open for the next exercise.

Another Way
You can also change the view among Normal, Page Layout, Page Break Preview, and Zoom by using the icons in the status bar at the bottom of the screen.

As demonstrated in this exercise, you can preview your printed worksheet by clicking the ribbon's VIEW tab, and then clicking Page Layout in the Workbook Views group (first section). This view enables you to fine-tune pages before printing. You can change your worksheet's layout and format in both this view and Normal view. You can also use the rulers to measure the width and height of your window and determine whether you need to change its margins or print orientation.

Splitting the Window

When a worksheet contains a lot of data, you can see only a small portion of the worksheet in Excel's Normal and Page Layout views. The Split command enables you to overcome this limitation by viewing the worksheet in two panes or four quadrants. After issuing this command, you can use the scroll bars on the right and at the bottom of the window to display different sections of the worksheet at the same time so that you can more easily compare or contrast data or see what effect a change in one part of the worksheet might have on a distant part of the worksheet. In this exercise, you learn to split the Excel window and use the scroll bars to view different sections of a worksheet. You also practice entering data into cells in the split windows, and you learn how to remove the split to return to single-window view.

STEP BY STEP   **Split the Window**

GET READY. USE the worksheet you left open in the previous exercise or type 456 in cells A1 and B1 in a new workbook.

1. Click cell **F1** to make it active.

2. On the VIEW tab, click **Split**. Notice that the screen is split vertically in two different panes.

3. In the horizontal scroll bar of the right pane, hold down the **right arrow** until you see cell AA1. Notice that you can still see cells A1 and B1 in the left pane.

4. Click **Split** again. The screen is no longer split.

5. Click in cell **A17** and click **Split**. The screen is split horizontally in two different panes.

6. Click **Split** again. The screen is no longer split.

7. Click in cell **F14** and click **Split**. The screen is split into four panes this time.

8. Choose the lower-right quadrant by clicking any cell in that pane, and then scroll down to display row 40.

9. In cell H40, type **236** and press **Enter**. The data you entered in cells A1 and B1 should be visible along with what you just entered in cell H40 (see Figure 1-12).

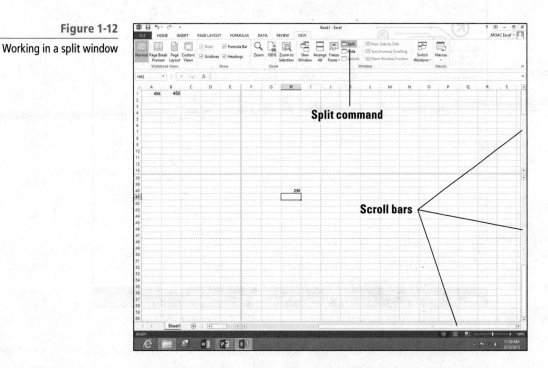

Figure 1-12

Working in a split window

10. Click **Split** to remove the split. The data in cell H40 is no longer visible.

PAUSE. LEAVE the workbook open to use in the next exercise.

Take Note   The Split command is especially useful when you need to compare various portions of a long worksheet.

When you use a worksheet that contains a small amount of data, it is easy to scroll through the worksheet and focus on specific cells. As you become experienced in working with Excel, however, you might find yourself working on much larger worksheets. The ability to view more than one section of a worksheet at the same time by using split windows is especially useful when you need to compare different sections of data.

Workplace Ready

LARGE WORKBOOKS

After you complete several of the lessons in this book, you might want to come back to this section on splitting the window. Excel is a great what-if tool for sales projections, assessments, and especially budgets. The following example shows a split workbook with assumptions on one pane and the final results in another pane.

For example, the following Figure represents a five-year school budget. The Net All and All Ending Fund Balance are formulas that depend on the assumptions shown and totals throughout the worksheet. Notice that with the current assumptions, the school loses money each year and eventually exhausts all of its fund balance. Therefore, something needs to change. The school has tried numerous marketing efforts, but because it is in a remote area of the state, the student growth rates are more dependent on the local economy compared to the efforts of the school. They only item on the assumption that is under the control of the school is the salary increase.

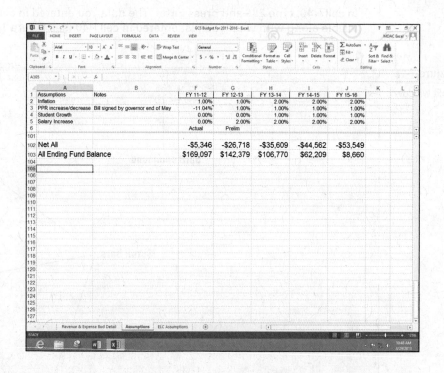

The only way to get a positive net balance with the available assumptions is to cut salaries by 6.5% in the next school year (FY 13-14). Luckily for you, you are just the one filling in the numbers in the model you are given. However, you may want to look deeper at the assumptions, add new assumptions, or start a list of recommendations for your boss. Using the split window gives you a tool to see how the changes might affect the bottom line before you make your presentation.

Opening a New Window

Splitting a window allows you to look at two sections of a worksheet side by side. You can also view two sections of a worksheet by using the New Window command. In this section, you learn to use the New Window command on the VIEW tab to open a new window in Excel. You also learn to use the Switch Window command to change the active window, and you learn how to close multiple windows.

STEP BY STEP	**Open a New Window**

GET READY. USE the worksheet you left open in the previous exercise or type 456 in cells A1 and B1 and 236 in cell H40 in a new workbook.

1. Press **Ctrl + Home** to make A1 the active cell.

2. With the VIEW tab active, in the Window group, click **New Window**. A new window titled *Book1:2* opens. If you have opened a different number of new workbooks, your title bar might show a different book number. The colon and 2 (:2) indicate that there are two windows from the same workbook open.

3. Scroll down in the window until cell H40 is visible (see Figure 1-13). Although cell A1 is not visible, it is still the active cell. It is important to note that you have opened a new view of the active worksheet—not a new worksheet.

Figure 1-13

A new window

Workbook title for new window

Close Window button

A1 is active but not visible.

Use Switch Windows command to view other open windows.

Another Way
You also can use the Arrange All command on the VIEW tab to display open windows side by side so that you can compare various parts of a large worksheet. Use the View Side by Side and Synchronous Scrolling commands to have both windows scroll together.

4. Click **Switch Windows**. A drop-down list of all open windows appears. Book 1:2 is checked, which indicates that it is the active window.

5. Click **Book 1:1**. You now see the original view of the worksheet with cell A1 active.

6. Click **Switch Windows** and make **Book1:2** active.

7. Click the **Close Window** button (in the upper-right corner of the workbook window) to close Book1:2. The window closes, and Book1 in the title bar tells you that you are now looking at the only open view of the workbook.

Take Note   Clicking the Close Window button closes only the new window opened at the beginning of this exercise. If you use the Close command on the FILE tab, you will close the entire workbook.

8. Click the **FILE** tab, and then click **Close**.

9. When asked if you want to save the changes in Book1, click **Don't Save**.

PAUSE. LEAVE Excel open for the next exercise.

WORKING WITH AN EXISTING WORKBOOK

Bottom Line

Many workbooks require frequent updating because existing data has changed or new data must be added. Workers frequently open an existing workbook, update information, and then save the workbook to be revised again at a later time. Often, files are created by one person, and then used or updated by others. Filenames should reflect the type of data contained in the file. A descriptive filename enables you to locate and retrieve files quickly. Filenames can be up to 255 characters long, including the filename extension. However, most workers use short descriptive filenames that clearly identify the content of the workbook.

Cross Ref   You can also use the File Properties, such as tags, to help you and others manage and find files. See Lesson 2, "Working with Microsoft Excel 2013," for more on File Properties.

Opening an Existing Workbook

When you save an Excel 2013 file, the program automatically adds the .xlsx extension to the end of the file's name. This extension identifies the program in which the file can be opened (for example, .xlsx is the file extension used in Excel). To open a file, you must also identify the location (such as network or SkyDrive), drive, and folder that contain the file. In your local computer environment, your local drive is usually designated as C:. Network, or flash drives can have other letters such as E: or S:.

STEP BY STEP | **Open an Existing Workbook**

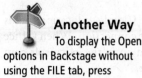

Another Way
To display the Open options in Backstage without using the FILE tab, press Ctrl+O. To display the Open dialog box, press Ctrl+F12.

GET READY. In this exercise, you use commands on the FILE tab to find and open an existing workbook.

1. In Excel, click the FILE tab and click Open. Documents you recently created or edited appear in the right pane, in the Recent Workbooks area.

2. Click Computer and then click Browse.

Take Note
Throughout this book, you see information that appears in brackets, such as [your e-mail address]. The information contained in the brackets is intended to be directions specific for you rather than something you actually type word for word. It instructs you to perform an action or substitute text. Do *not* type the actual text that appears within brackets.

3. In the Open dialog box, choose the location your Lesson01 data files.

Take Note
By default, the Open dialog box lists only the files that were created in the program you are using—in this case, Excel. To see files created in other programs, you can select All Files in the Files of type box (next to the File name box) at the bottom of the Open dialog box.

4. Select *01 Contoso Employee Info* from the listed files, and then click Open. The file opens as shown in Figure 1-14, with the workbook name displayed in the title bar.

Figure 1-14

Opening an existing workbook

	A	B	C	D
2			Contoso, Ltd.	
3	Last Name	First Name	Job Title	Hours
4	Bourne	Stephanie	Physician	36
5	Holliday	Nicole	Physician	36
6	Laszlo	Rebecca	Physician	36
7	Barnhill	Josh	Billing Clerk	36
8	Kane	John	Registered Nurse	30
9	Trenary	Jean	Registered Nurse	30
10	Da Silva	Sergio	Physician Assistant	36
11	Wang	Jian	Referral Specialist	36
12	Wilson	Dan	Physician	36
13	Valdez	Rachel	Receptionist	30
14	Giest	Jenny	Office Manager	40
15	Gottfried	Jim	Receptionist	30
16	Delaney	Aidan	Receptionist	20
17	Dellamore	Luca	Medical Assistant	36
18	Hamilton	David	Medical Assistant	36
19	Hoeing	Helge	Medical Assistant	36
20	Munson	Stuart	Referral Specialist	36
21	Murray	Billie Jo	Medical Assistant	36
22	Kenneth	Kevin	File Clerk	15
23	Hensien	Kari	File Clerk	20
24	Moore	Bobby	File Clerk	15
25	Moreland	Barbara	Billing Clerk	20
26	Metters	Susan	Billing Clerk	25
27	Poland	Carole	Nurse Practitioner	25

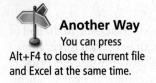

Another Way
You can press
Alt+F4 to close the current file
and Excel at the same time.

5. Click the FILE tab, and then click Close to close the Employee workbook.

PAUSE. LEAVE Excel open for the next exercise.

If you are familiar with Microsoft Word, you know that when you open a file, the program places your cursor and screen display at the beginning of the document. When you open an Excel workbook, however, the active cell is the same one that was active when you last saved the file. For example, when you open the Contoso Employee Info workbook, A22 is the active cell in Normal view, because A22 was the active cell displayed in Normal view when the file was last saved. This feature enables you to continue working in the same location when you return to the workbook.

Opening a Workbook from Your SkyDrive

SkyDrive is a Microsoft feature that allows you to work with files in the Cloud—a location that is available from any computer in the world as long as you have an Internet connection. When Office 2013 is installed, you have an option of installing SkyDrive or you can go to the Microsoft.com site, search for the SkyDrive download, and install it at a different time.

STEP BY STEP   **Open a Workbook from Your SkyDrive**

GET READY. Excel should be open. You need to have a SkyDrive account for this section.

1. Clicks the FILE tab.
2. If it is not selected, click Open.
3. If you do not have SkyDrive installed, click + Add a Place (see Figure 1-15), click SkyDrive, and go through the steps on the screen.
4. Click [Your Name] SkyDrive, and then click Browse.

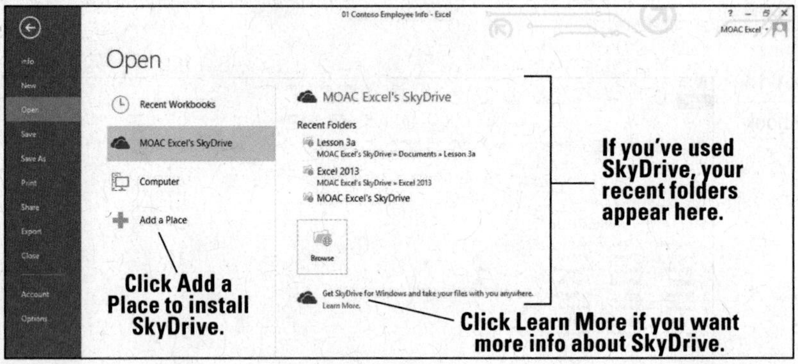

Figure 1-15

A computer with SkyDrive installed

5. If you have folders on the SkyDrive, double-click the folder where the file is located.
6. If there are subfolders, double-click the subfolder.
7. Continue to navigate to the folder where the file is located and click the file name.
8. Click Open. The file is displayed.

CLOSE the file and LEAVE Excel open for the next exercise.

Navigating a Worksheet

An Excel worksheet can contain more than one million rows and more than sixteen thousand columns. There are several ways to move through worksheets that contain numerous rows and columns. You can use the arrow keys, the scroll bars, or the mouse to navigate through a worksheet. In the following exercises, you explore the different methods for moving through a worksheet.

Take Note A worksheet can be very large or quite small depending on your needs. Available columns go from A through XFD, and available rows can go from 1 through 1,048,567.

STEP BY STEP	**Navigate a Worksheet**

GET READY. Click the File tab, and then click Open. In the Recent Workbooks area, click *01 Contoso Employee Info* or go to the class folder and open this file.

1. Press **Ctrl + End** to move to the end of the document (cell D27).
2. Press **Ctrl + Home** to move to the beginning of the document (cell A1).
3. Click in the **Name Box**, type **A3**, and press **Enter** to make the cell active.
4. Press **Ctrl + Down Arrow** to go to the last row of data (cell A27).

Take Note Ctrl + Arrow allows you to move to the start and end of ranges of data. The worksheet title, which spans all of the columns, is not considered part of the worksheet's data range.

5. Press **Ctrl + Right Arrow**. Cell D27, the last column in the range of data, becomes the active cell.
6. Press **Ctrl + Down Arrow**. The last possible row in the worksheet displays.
7. Press **Ctrl + Home**.
8. Press **Scroll Lock**. Then press the **Right Arrow** key. This moves the active column one column to the right, and the whole worksheet moves.
9. Use the vertical scroll bar (if necessary, refer to Figure 1-12) to navigate from the beginning to the end of the data.
10. If your mouse has a wheel button, roll the wheel button forward and back to quickly scroll through the worksheet.

CERTIFICATION READY?	1.2.5

Where is the Name Box located and what is it used for?

Take Note When Scroll Lock is on, SCROLL LOCK is displayed on the left side of the Status bar. To use the arrow keys to move between cells, you must turn off Scroll Lock. Some keyboards come equipped with an onboard Scroll Lock key, whereas others do not. This is an option, not a necessity.

PAUSE. Press **Scroll Lock** again to turn it off. LEAVE the workbook open for the next exercise.

Cross Ref You learn about ranges in more depth in Lesson 2.

Navigating Data with the Go To Command

The workbook used in these exercises is neither long nor particularly complicated. When you begin dealing with much larger databases, or longer sets of workbooks, you might wish you had some easier means to get around the data than just scrolling. The **Name Box** indicates the current cell you are in as well as gives you the opportunity to name the cell or a range. The Go To command can take you to particular points in a worksheet, including cells and cell ranges that you name yourself.

STEP BY STEP   **Navigate Data with the Go To Command**

CERTIFICATION
READY?   **1.2.4**

How do you name a range
and go to a cell or range
using the Go To dialog box?

USE the *01 Contoso Employee Info* workbook from the previous exercise.

1. Select cell A17.
2. In the Name Box to the left of the formula bar, select cell A17, as indicated in
   Figure 1-16.

Figure 1-16

Worksheet with A17 in the
Name Box selected

Name Box

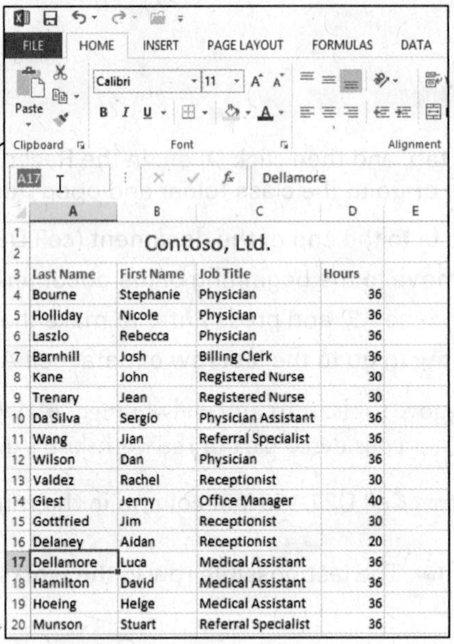

3. Delete A17, type MedAssts, and press Enter.
4. Select cell M11.
5. On the HOME tab, in the Editing group, click Find & Select. Click Go To. The Go To
   dialog box appears (see Figure 1-17).

Figure 1-17

Go To dialog box

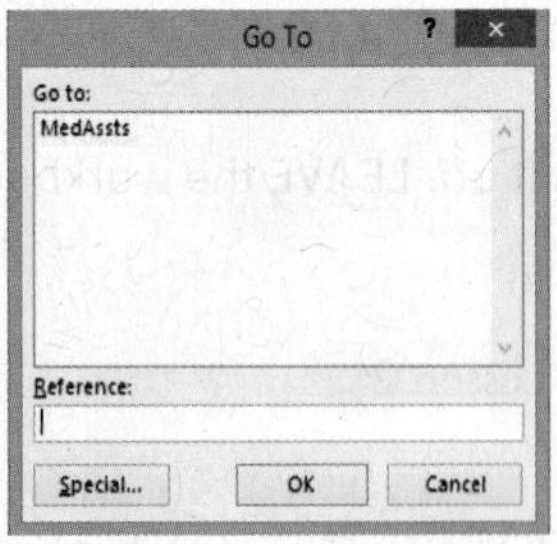

6. In the Go to list, click MedAssts, and then click OK. Cell A17 becomes the active cell.
7. Click Find & Select again, and then click Go To Special. The Go To Special dialog box
   appears (see Figure 1-18).

Figure 1-18

Go To Special dialog box

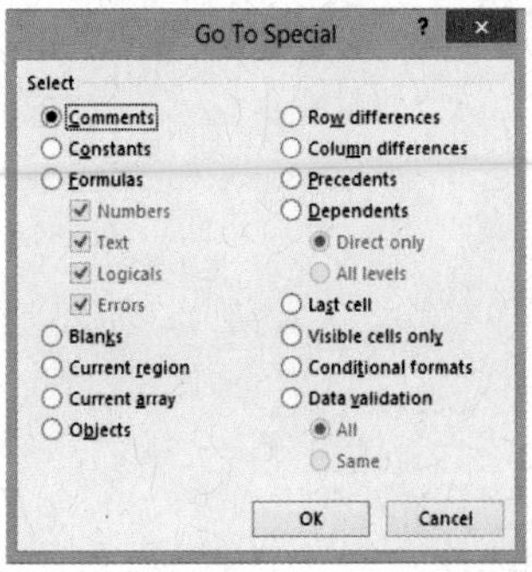

8. In the Go To Special dialog box, click Last cell.

9. Click OK. Cell D27 becomes the active cell. The last cell is the lower-right cell in the worksheet with contents or formatting.

CLOSE the workbook and do not save. LEAVE Excel open for the next exercise.

WORKING WITH EXCEL'S HELP SYSTEM

Bottom Line

The **Help system** in Excel 2013 is rich in information, illustrations, and tips that can help you complete any task as you create worksheets and workbooks. When you install Excel, you automatically install hundreds of help topics on your computer. Excel can also access thousands of additional help topics online.

Using the Help System

Finding the right information in Excel's Help system is easy: You can pick a topic from popular searches, see what's new, get training, or perform keyword searches by entering terms that best describe the task you want to complete. In this exercise, you learn to open the Help window and move between its online and offline topics.

Take Note   If you aren't sure what an onscreen tool does, just point to it. Once the mouse pointer rests on a tool, a box called a *ScreenTip* appears. A basic ScreenTip displays the tool's name and shortcut key (if a shortcut exists for that tool). Some of the ribbon's tools have enhanced ScreenTips, which also provide a brief description of the tool.

STEP BY STEP   **Use the Help System**

GET READY. OPEN a new workbook for this exercise.

1. Position your mouse pointer over the Help button, as shown in Figure 1-19, in the upper-right corner of the Excel window. A ScreenTip appears, telling you that this button enables you to access Excel's Help features and that you can click the button or press F1.

Figure 1-19

Help button

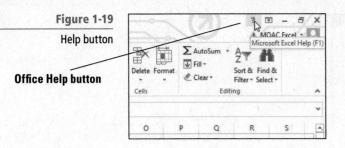

2. Click the Help button; the Help window opens, as shown in Figure 1-20.

Figure 1-20

Help window

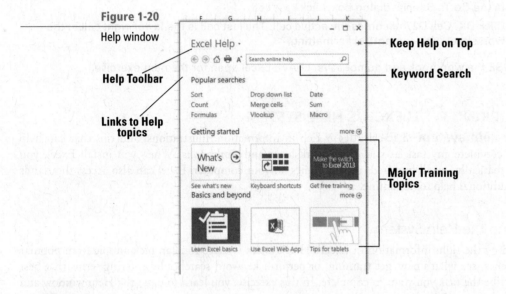

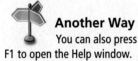

Another Way
You can also press
F1 to open the Help window.

3. In the Help window, click the What's New icon. The next screen gives you additional hyperlinked subcategories.

4. Navigate through three of the subtopics in the Help window.

5. In the Help window toolbar, click the Home button to return to the first screen.

6. Click the Excel Help drop-down arrow. This displays the Connection Status options shown in Figure 1-21. This feature enables you to choose whether the Help window displays content from files installed on your computer or from Office.com on the Internet.

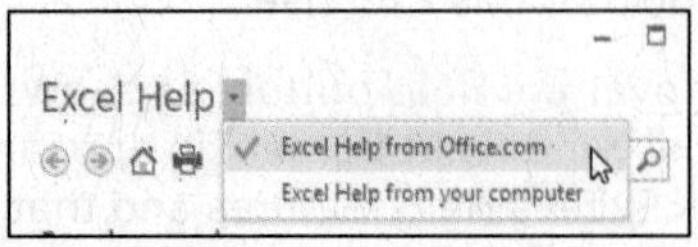

Figure 1-21

Connection Status options

7. Click in the workbook behind the Help window. Notice that the Help window is hidden and the workbook becomes the top window.

8. Click the Help button to display the Help window again.

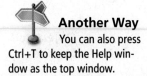

Another Way
You can also press Ctrl+T to keep the Help window as the top window.

9. Click the Keep Help on Top pin button.

10. Now click the workbook and notice that you can still see the Help window.

11. CLOSE the Help window.

CLOSE your workbook.

Excel's Help window gives you access to various help topics that offer information about specific Excel features or tools. Help topics can assist you with virtually any task, feature, or problem you encounter when working with Excel. The Help window is set up like a browser, with links to specific categories and topics, and it features some of the same tools you find in your web browser, including:

• **Back:** Jumps to the previously opened Help topic.

• **Forward:** Jumps to the next opened Help topic.

• **Home:** Returns to the initial Help window.

• **Print:** Allows you to print the current Help topic.

• **Use Large Text:** Shows larger text in the Help window.

Figure 1-22

The Excel Help Toolbar

Excel Help ▾

◉ ◉ ⌂ 🖶 A⁺ Search online help 🔍

Take Note Many Excel dialog boxes contain a Help button. When you click it, a Help window opens with information about that dialog box.

You can find help in several different ways. For example, you can click one of the links under *Popular searches* or click a topic listed under *Getting started* or *Basics and beyond*. You can also type a keyword or phrase in the Search box, and then press Enter. When you do this, related help topics appear in the Help window.

When you click the arrow next to Excel Help at the top of the Help window, the resulting menu lets you choose between searching help topics that are available online and just those topics installed on your computer (referred to as *offline help*). If your computer has an "always on" connection to the Internet, such as a cable modem or LAN connection, you might want to select Excel Help from Office.com, which is Microsoft's online-based built-in Help system. If your computer uses a dial-up modem, or if you simply choose not to access online help information, choose the Excel Help from your computer option to access the topics installed on your computer.

SKILL SUMMARY

In this lesson you learned how:	Exam Objective	Objective Number
To start Excel	Create new Blank workbooks.	1.1.1
To work in the Excel window	Customize the Quick Access Toolbar.	1.4.3
To change Excel's view	Split the window.	1.4.13
	Change workbook views.	1.4.6
To work with an existing workbook	Demonstrate how to use Go To.	1.2.4
	Demonstrate how to use Name Box.	1.2.5
To work with Excel's Help system		

Knowledge Assessment

Multiple Choice

Select the best response for the following statements.

1. An arrow in the bottom-right corner of a group on the ribbon tells you that which of the following is available?
   a. dialog box
   b. additional workbook
   c. list of worksheets
   d. additional part of the current range

2. Which of the following is a selected cell?
   a. current command
   b. default option
   c. active cell
   d. default cell

3. Which feature enables you to preview headers and footers, page breaks, and other features that will print?
   a. Page Layout
   b. Print Layout
   c. Synchronous Scrolling
   d. Window view

4. After a file has been opened, the filename appears in which of the following?
   a. title bar
   b. footer
   c. header
   d. Description pane

5. When you split a window, the window is divided into how many panes?
   a. two
   b. three
   c. four
   d. two or four

6. When you click the Help button, what opens?
   a. ScreenTips
   b. Keytips
   c. Help window
   d. dialog box

7. Which is the intersection of a row and column?
   a. range
   b. tab
   c. bar chart
   d. cell

8. Which of the following starts off with Save, Undo, and Redo and can be customized to contain the commands you use most frequently?
   a. A worksheet
   b. The Help window
   c. The Quick Access Toolbar
   d. The ribbon

9. How many worksheets does a new Excel 2013 workbook open with?
   a. one
   b. two
   c. three
   d. four

10. To get to the last cell on the worksheet, which of the following should you press?
    a. Ctrl + Home
    b. Ctrl + End
    c. Ctrl + Right
    d. Ctrl + Left

True / False

Circle T if the statement is true or F if the statement is false.

T F 1. Pressing the F1 key displays Backstage view.
T F 2. Pressing the Alt key activates Keytips that allow you to use the keyboard to choose ribbon tabs instead of clicking them with the mouse.
T F 3. Ctrl + O opens a new blank workbook.
T F 4. The Quick Access Toolbar appears on the right side of the title bar, above the ribbon.
T F 5. Ctrl + F displays Backstage view.
T F 6. Click the FILE tab to get to Backstage view.
T F 7. Press Ctrl + Home to go to cell A1.
T F 8. The columns in a worksheet are identified by numbers.
T F 9. The active cell in a worksheet is outlined by a bold rectangle.
T F 10. Page Layout view is useful when preparing your data for printing.

Competency Assessment

Project 1-1: Utilizing Help

Use this project to better familiarize yourself with the Help system.

GET READY. LAUNCH Excel if it is not already running.

1. On the right side of the title bar, click the Help button.
2. When the Help window opens, choose Learn Excel basics and read the first few topics displayed in the window.
3. Click the Home button.
4. Across from Getting started, click the more button and review the topics in the online help.
5. Close the browser window.

6. In the Excel Help window in the Search box, type select cells and read one of the topics.

7. Click the Close button is in the upper-right corner of the window to close the Help window.

LEAVE Excel open for the next project.

Project 1-2: **Printing Shortcuts**

GET READY. LAUNCH Excel if it is not already running.

Having a list of shortcuts can be helpful.

1. Click the Help button to display the Excel Help window.

2. Click the Keyboard shortcuts link and find the list of shortcuts.

3. If you have permission to print, click the Print icon to print the list. CLOSE the Help window.

LEAVE Excel open for the next project.

Proficiency Assessment

Project 1-3: **Utilizing the Ribbon**

GET READY. LAUNCH Excel if it is not already running and display a blank workbook.

1. Click the FILE tab. This is your instant access to Backstage view. Click several of the commands in Backstage view that are shown on the navigation bar in the left pane.

2. Click the Return to document arrow to return to the workbook. Click the HOME tab, if it isn't already displayed. Move the mouse pointer over the ribbon, reading the various ScreenTips that appear as the pointer rests over individual ribbon elements.

3. On the HOME tab, in the Font group, click the Font arrow. Note that the first font at the top of the font list is displayed. Click the arrow again to hide the list.

4. Click the Font arrow again, and choose Times New Roman. Note the corresponding change in font on the Font list.

5. Move the pointer to the Quick Access Toolbar and click the Undo button. Note that your font returns to the default font, usually Calibri.

6. Click the INSERT tab. Move the pointer over the ribbon and examine it while reading the ScreenTips.

7. Click the VIEW tab. Once again, point to the ribbon and examine its features.

8. Click the FILE tab again to display Backstage view.

9. Click the Close command at the bottom of the left pane to close the workbook. If prompted to save the document, choose Don't Save.

LEAVE Excel open for the next project.

Project 1-4: **Navigating a List of Homes for Sale**

Fabrikam, Inc., a realtor, has a list of homes for sale. You need to know how large the list is.

GET READY. LAUNCH Excel if it is not already running.

1. Open the *01 Fabrikam Customer Houses* file.
2. Press Ctrl + End to move to the last cell in the workbook.
3. Press Ctrl +Home to move to the first cell.
4. Click cell B6.
5. Press Ctrl + Right Arrow to go to the right edge of the active range.
6. Press Ctrl + Left Arrow to go to the left edge.
7. Press Ctrl + Up Arrow to go to the top edge of the active range.
8. CLOSE the workbook.

LEAVE Excel open for the next project.

Mastery Assessment

Project 1-5: **Viewing an Excel Training Video**

Use this project to better familiarize yourself with tutorials that come with Excel.

GET READY. LAUNCH Excel if it is not already running.

1. Press F1 to display the Excel Help window.
2. Click the Get free training icon.
3. Click the Download button.
4. If prompted, choose Open in the message bar to allow the application to load. This will launch a training exercise in Microsoft PowerPoint.
5. Follow the instructions in PowerPoint and go through the training. Press Esc when you are done.

CLOSE PowerPoint, the Web browser, and the Excel Help window. LEAVE Excel open for the next project.

Project 1-6: **Home Loan Calculator**

Excel can help you create a loan payment schedule for major purchases. However, to navigate within the workbook used in this project, you need to change the views.

GET READY. LAUNCH Excel if it is not already running.

1. OPEN the *01 Jim's Loan Schedule* file.
2. Go to Page Layout view and scroll to the end of the document to see how the pages will lay out.
3. Return to Normal view.
4. Split the screen into two windows and scroll so you can see the 360th payment as well as the top part of the worksheet (A1 through J17).

5. Change the Loan amount to 200,000 at 4.5% interest and edit the start date of the loan for the first of next month. Notice the change in scheduled payment and total interest.

6. Change the loan period to 15 years and notice that the payment numbers seem to disappear. Scroll up in the lower window until you see the last payments.

7. CLOSE Excel. If prompted to save the workbook, choose Don't Save.

Working with Microsoft Excel 2013 2

LESSON SKILL MATRIX

Skills	Exam Objective	Objective Number
Creating Workbooks	Create new blank workbooks.	1.1.1
Saving Workbooks	Save workbooks in alternate file formats.	1.5.2
	Maintain backward compatibility.	1.5.6
	Save files to remote locations.	1.5.8
Entering and Editing Basic Data in a Worksheet	Append data to a worksheet.	2.1.1
	Find and replace data.	2.1.2
	Adjust column width.	1.3.5
	Demonstrate how to use the Auto Fill tool.	2.1.4
	Expand data across columns.	2.1.5
	Delete cells.	2.1.6
Using Data Types to Populate a Worksheet	Apply Number formats.	2.2.6
Cutting, Copying, and Pasting Data	Copy and paste data.	2.1.3
Editing a Workbook's Properties	Add values to workbook properties.	1.4.8

©asiseeit / iStockphoto

KEY TERMS

- Auto Fill
- AutoComplete
- copy
- copy pointer
- cut
- fill handle
- Flash Fill
- formula bar
- keywords
- label
- move pointer
- natural series
- Office Clipboard
- paste
- range
- selecting text
- workbook properties

Purchasing a home is generally the biggest financial investment most people make in a lifetime. Real estate agents advise and assist those who want to buy a new home or sell their present home. Some real estate agents can also help people find rental homes. When people are ready to sell their homes, they often list with a real estate agent who earns a commission or percentage of the home's selling price when the home sells. Agents take an exam to be licensed by their state. Many licensed agents also become Realtors®. This is a trademarked name that an agent can use only when he or she joins the local, state, and national associations of Realtors®. Fabrikam, Inc., located in Columbus, Ohio, is a real estate firm owned by Richard Carey and David Ortiz. Fabrikam has five fulltime sales agents and a college intern. Fabrikam's intern uses Excel to help manage sales, expenses, and support the business. In this lesson, you continue to view, add, and manipulate data in an Excel 2013 spreadsheet similar to that used by Fabrikam, Inc.

©asiseeit / iStockphoto

SOFTWARE ORIENTATION

Excel's HOME Tab

The ribbon in Microsoft Office Excel 2013 is made up of a series of tabs, each related to specific kinds of tasks that you perform in Excel. The HOME tab, shown in Figure 2-1, contains the commands that people use the most when creating Excel documents. Having commands visible on the work surface enables you to see at a glance most tasks you want to perform. Each tab contains groups of commands related to specific tasks or functions.

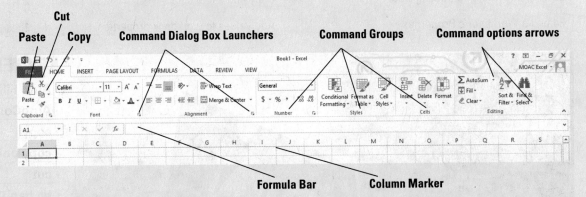

Figure 2-1

Ribbon, formula bar, and command options

Some commands have an arrow associated with them. In Figure 2-1, you see the option arrows associated with AutoSum and Find & Select. This indicates that in addition to the default task, other options are associated with the task. Similarly, some of the groups have Dialog Box Launchers associated with them. Clicking these displays additional commands not shown on the ribbon. In Figure 2-1, the Clipboard, Font, Alignment, and Number groups have associated dialog boxes, whereas Styles, Cells, and Editing do not.

CREATING WORKBOOKS

Bottom Line

There are three ways to create a new Microsoft Excel workbook. You can open a new, blank workbook using the FILE tab to access Backstage view or when you launch Excel. You can open an existing Excel workbook, enter new or additional data, and save the file with a new name, thus creating a new workbook. You can also use a template to create a new workbook. A template is a model that has already been set up to display certain kinds of data, such as sales reports, invoices, and so on.

Creating a Workbook from Scratch

To create a new workbook, launch Excel and select a blank workbook or another type of template. If you are working in Excel and want to begin a new workbook, click the FILE tab, click New, and then click Blank workbook. Worksheets often begin with text that describes the content of the worksheet. In this exercise, you create two Excel workbooks: one with a company address and one with a quick phone message.

STEP BY STEP | **Create a Workbook from Scratch**

 GET READY. LAUNCH Excel. Excel gives you options for starting a blank workbook, taking a tour, or using templates (see Figure 2-2).

Figure 2-2

Available options after Excel is launched

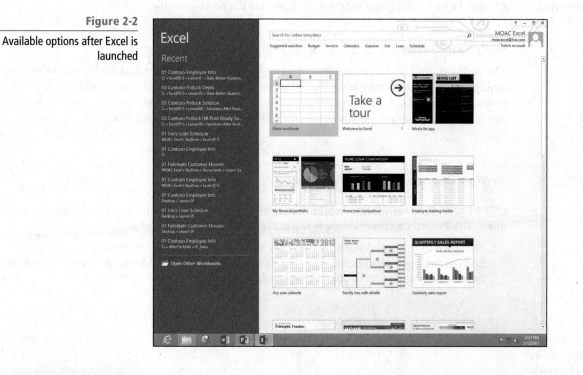

CERTIFICATION READY? **1.1.1**

How do you create a new workbook file?

1. Click **Blank workbook**. If you have just launched Excel, *Book1 – Excel* appears in the title bar at the top of the window. A blank workbook opens with A1 as the active cell.

2. In cell A1, type **Fabrikam Inc.** This cell is the primary title for the worksheet. Note that as you type, the text appears in the cell and in the formula bar (see Figure 2-3). See the definition of formula bar in the "Editing a Cell's Contents" section on page 37.

Figure 2-3

Typed text appears in both the active cell and the formula bar.

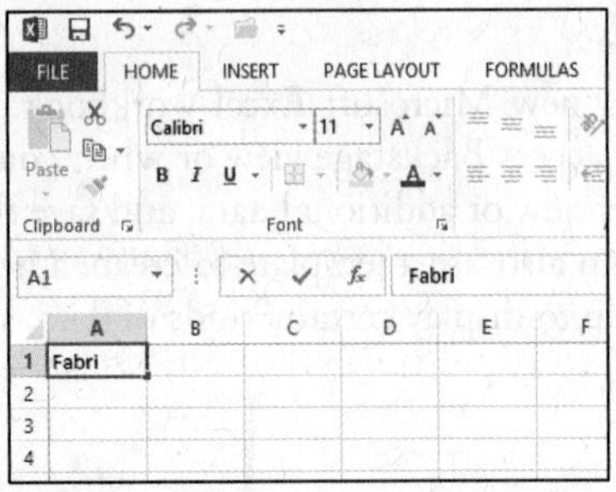

3. Press Enter. The text is entered into cell A1, but appears as if it flows into cell B1.

4. In cell A2, type 123 Fourth Street and press Enter.

5. In cell A3, type Columbus, OH 43204 and press Enter.

6. Sometimes you need a quick work area to complete another task while you are in the middle of a workbook. You can open another workbook as a scratch area. Click the FILE tab, and in the left pane, click New. The different templates available appear (refer to Figure 2-2).

7. In the Backstage view, click Blank workbook. A second Excel workbook opens and *Book2* appears in the title bar.

8. In cell A1, type Phone Calls and press Enter.

9. In cell A2, type David Ortiz UA flight 525 arriving 4:30 pm and press Enter.

PAUSE. LEAVE both Excel workbooks open for the next exercise.

Another Way
When you work in Excel, you can open a blank workbook with the shortcut combination Ctrl + N.

Switching Between Open Workbooks

The ability to multitask is prized by most employers. Windows and Excel enable you to work on multiple projects simultaneously. When the phone rings, you can quickly go to another area, make notes, or research a question, and then return to your work. If you have multiple workbooks open, you might need to move quickly between the workbooks to finish your tasks.

STEP BY STEP   **Switch Between Open Workbooks**

GET READY. Both temporary workbooks with the address and phone message should be open. The Phone Calls workbook is the current workbook in this case.

1. To return to the company address, click the Excel icon on the taskbar (see Figure 2-4). Each of the open workbooks appears in a preview window. When you move the mouse pointer over each workbook, it previews on the screen.

Figure 2-4

Open workbooks appear by clicking the Excel icon on the taskbar.

Excel icon (open)   Taskbar

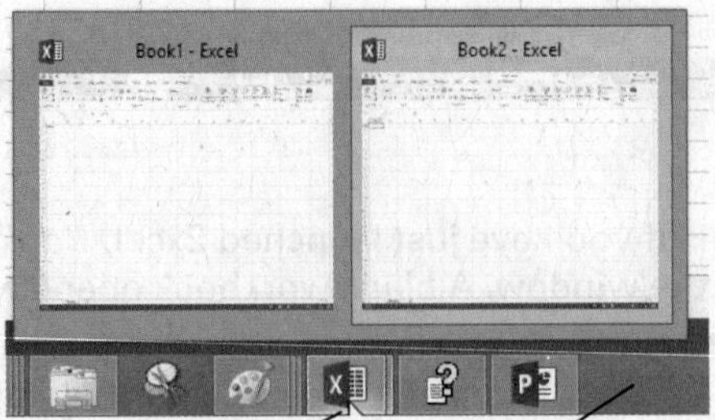

Another Way
You can also switch between two recent active workbooks with Ctrl + Tab.

2. Click Book1 - Excel. The unsaved company address becomes the active workbook.

Take Note   Unlike previous versions, Excel now displays each workbook in a separate window.

SAVING WORKBOOKS

Bottom Line

When you save a file, you can save it to a folder on your computer's hard drive, a network drive, disc, CD, USB drive, SkyDrive, or other storage location. You must first identify where the document is to be saved. The remainder of the Save process is the same, regardless of the location or storage device.

Naming and Saving a Workbook

When you save a file for the first time, you are asked two important questions: Where do you want to save the file? What name will you give to the file? In this lesson, you practice answering these questions for two different files. By default in all Office applications, documents are saved to the My Documents folder.

STEP BY STEP   **Name and Save a Workbook**

GET READY. USE the workbook from the previous exercise or type your name and address in a new workbook.

Another Way
You can also save the workbook with Ctrl + S.

1. Click the FILE tab to open Backstage view. In the left pane, click Save As to display the save options.
2. Double-click Computer to open the Save As dialog box (see Figure 2-5).

Figure 2-5

Save As dialog box

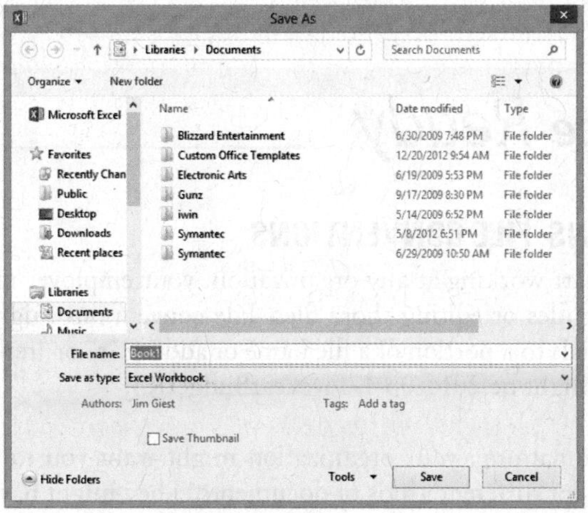

3. From the left-hand navigation pane, in the Save As dialog box, click Desktop. The Desktop becomes the new destination of your saved file.
4. In the Save As dialog box, click New folder. A folder icon appears with the words *New folder* selected (see Figure 2-6).

Save As
« My Documents › Excel2013 ›
Search Excel2013
Organize ▾
New folder
Documents
Music
Pictures
Videos
Homegroup
Computer
COMPAQ (C:)
FACTORY_IMAGI
DVD RW Drive (E:
Owner (owner-p
Name
Date modified
Type
Lesson01
1/8/2013 7:16 AM
File folder
Lesson02
1/8/2013 4:38 PM
File folder
Lesson03
1/13/2013 1:51 PM
File folder
Lesson10
12/31/2012 6:13 AM
File folder
Lesson11
1/14/2013 1:48 PM
File folder
Lesson12
1/14/2013 1:48 PM
File folder
Lesson14
1/14/2013 1:48 PM
File folder
New folder
1/14/2013 1:53 PM
File folder
Other
1/14/2013 1:33 PM
File folder
File name: Book1.xlsx
Save as type: Excel Workbook (*.xlsx)
Authors: Rick Winter
Tags: Add a tag
Save Thumbnail
Hide Folders
Tools
Open
Cancel

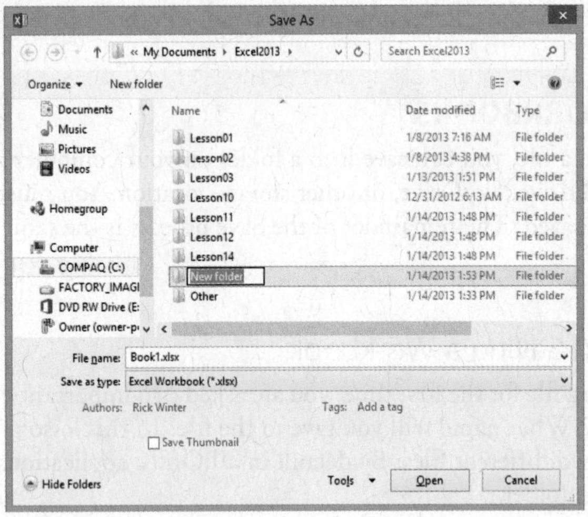

Figure 2-6

Type a new name in place of New folder.

CERTIFICATION READY? 1.5.2

How do you name and save a workbook to a specific location?

5. Type **Excel Lesson 2** and press **Enter**.
6. Click the **Open** button.
7. In the File name box, type ***02 Fabrikam Address Solution***.
8. Click the **Save** button.

PAUSE. LEAVE the workbook open to use in the next exercise.

Take Note Save your workbook often and especially before opening another workbook, printing, or after you enter information.

Workplace Ready

ORGANIZATIONS' FILE CONVENTIONS

When you first start working at any organization, your employer might give you conventions to use when naming files or editing those files. File conventions might include adding the date or your name or initials to a portion of a file name or adding "r" or "rev" followed by a revision number. An example might be 2014-03-17FiveYearBudgetR3.

In addition to file naming, your organization might want you to save files to specific network drives and folders for different kinds of documents. They might have rules for which files require passwords, when files should be destroyed, and frequencies required for backups. If you go into the business knowing how to manage files, you will be an asset to the organization. Even if there are no existing conventions, you might want to think about your own personal conventions to ensure you can find and protect your files.

Following is an example of a simple drive structure for a charter school.

Saving to Your SkyDrive

SkyDrive is a cloud-based application that allows you to store your files so you can retrieve them anywhere and share them with other people if desired. SkyDrive is also a great place to store backup files of important documents. SkyDrive comes with Windows 8 or you can install the free desktop app on Windows 7 and Windows Vista. This exercise assumes you have Windows 8 already loaded with SkyDrive.

STEP BY STEP   **Save to Your SkyDrive**

GET READY. USE the workbook from the previous exercise or type your name and address in a new workbook.

1. Click the **FILE** tab and then click Save As.
2. In the Backstage view, under Save As, click [Your name] SkyDrive (see Figure 2-7). You may need to sign in to SkyDrive if you haven't already.

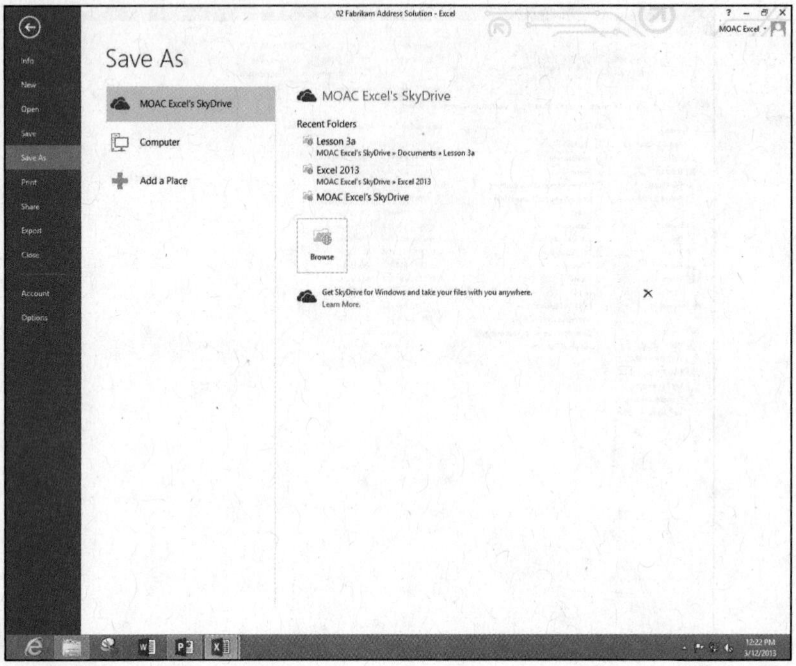

Figure 2-7

SkyDrive information on the Backstage view

CERTIFICATION READY? 1.5.8

How do you save a file to SkyDrive?

3. Click the **Browse** button.
4. Click the **New folder** button.
5. In the New folder text box, type **Excel Lesson 2** to save a folder for this lesson on your SkyDrive and press **Enter**.
6. Double-click the **Excel Lesson 2** icon to move to that folder.
7. Keep the file with the same name (or type ***02 Fabrikam Address Solution*** in the File name box), and then click the **Save** button.

PAUSE. LEAVE the workbook open to use in the next exercise.

Saving a Workbook Under a Different Name

You can rename an existing workbook to create a new workbook. For example, the address you created in the preceding exercise is current. When you have multiple offices, you can save the file with a new name and use it to enter data for another office. You can also use an existing workbook as a template to create new workbooks. In this exercise, you learn how to use the Save As dialog box to implement either of these options.

STEP BY STEP Save a Workbook Under a Different Name

GET READY. USE the workbook from the previous exercise or type **Fabrikam Inc.** in cell A1.

1. In cell A2, type **87 East Broad Street** and press **Enter**.
2. In cell A3, type **Columbus, OH 43215** and press **Enter**.
3. Click the **FILE** tab, and in the left pane, click **Save As**. The Backstage view shows that the Current Folder (see Figure 2-8) is Excel Lesson 2 on your SkyDrive, because it was the folder that was last used to save a workbook.

Figure 2-8

Current and Recent
folders used

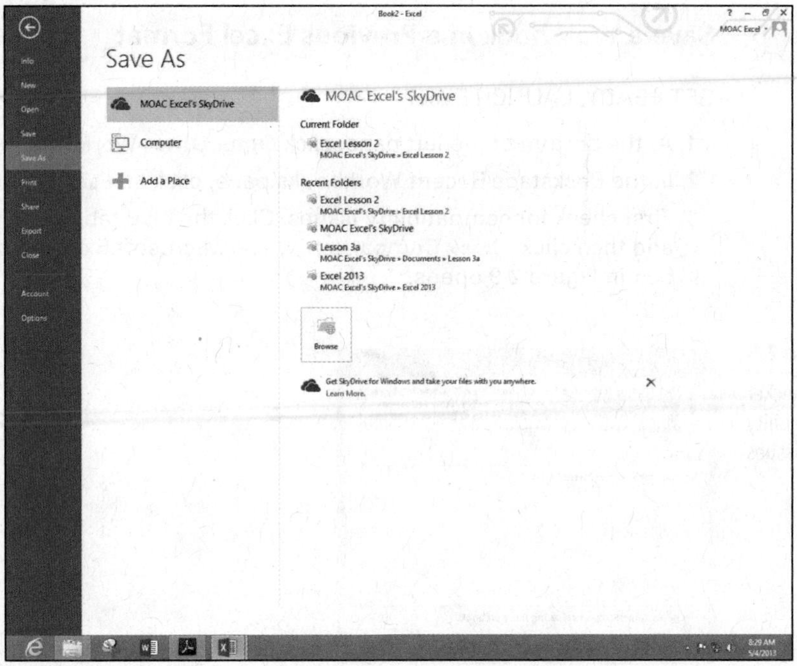

4. Click **Computer** to return to the drive you used before.

5. In the right pane, double-click **Excel Lesson 2**.

6. Click in the **File name** box, click after **Fabrikam**, and type **Broad** so the name reads **02 Fabrikam Broad Address Solution**.

7. Click **Save**. You created a new workbook by saving an existing workbook with a new name.

8. Click the **FILE** tab, click **Save As** in the left pane, and click Browse.

9. In the File name box, type **02 Fabrikam Address Template Solution**.

10. In the Save a type box, click the **drop-down arrow** and choose **Excel Template**. Click the **Save** button.

Take Note   Templates are automatically saved in another location so they can be opened with the FILE, New option.

CERTIFICATION READY?   1.5.2

How do you rename and save an existing workbook?

PAUSE. CLOSE Excel. Do not save the Phone Calls workbook.

Creating a template to use for each new workbook based on the example file eliminates the possibility that you might lose data because you might overwrite a file after you enter new data. To use the template, you choose FILE > New > Personal and select the template you saved. When you exit, you are prompted to save the file with a new name.

Cross Ref   For more information on templates, see the "Accessing and Using Excel Templates" section in Lesson 3.

Saving a Workbook in a Previous Excel Format

Files created in earlier Excel versions can be opened and revised in Excel 2013. However, if some of your users do not have the latest version or use other applications, they might not be able to open your file. You can save a copy of an Excel 2013 workbook (with the .xlsx file extension) to a version that is compatible with Excel 97 through Excel 2013 (with the .xls file extension) versions. The program symbol displayed with the filenames is different, but it is a good idea to give the earlier edition file a different name. It is also a good idea to check which issues might be lost with Excel's compatibility checker.

| **STEP BY STEP** | **Save a Workbook in a Previous Excel Format** |

GET READY. LAUNCH Excel.

1. At the bottom of the left pane, click Open Other Workbooks.
2. In the Backstage Recent Workbooks pane, click 02 Fabrikam Broad Address Solution.
3. First check for compatibility issues. Click the FILE tab, click Info, click Check for Issues, and then click Check Compatibility. The Microsoft Excel – Compatibility Checker dialog box in Figure 2-9 opens.

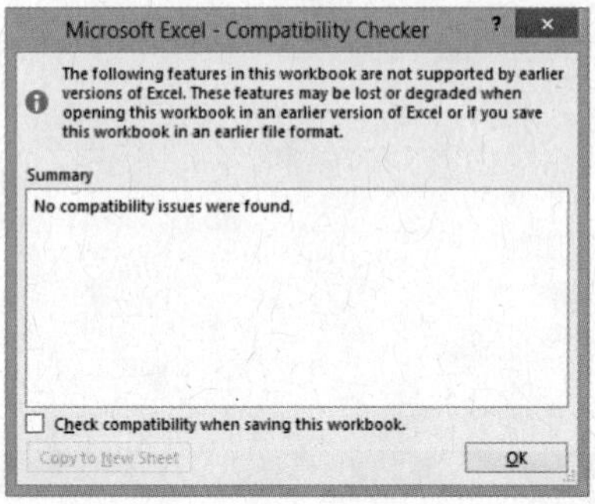

Figure 2-9

The Compatibility Checker showing no compatibility issues

4. Read the information in the Compatibility Checker dialog box and click OK.
5. Click the FILE tab, click Export, and then click Change File Type. The Backstage view shows the different file types (see Figure 2-10).

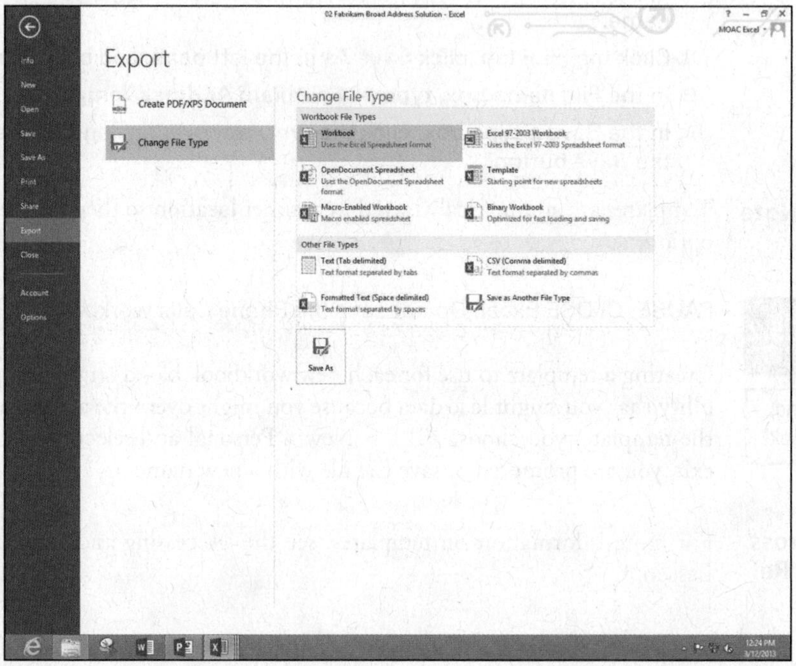

Figure 2-10

Change File Type options in Backstage view.

6. Click Excel 97-2003 Workbook (*.xls) and click Save As.
7. In the File name box, click before Solution and type 97-03, and then click Save.
8. Click the FILE tab, and then click Open. The Recent Workbooks pane in Backstage view shows the last set of documents that have been saved.
9. Click 02 Fabrikam Broad Address Solution.

PAUSE. LEAVE the workbook open to use in the next exercise.

| CERTIFICATION READY? | 1.5.6 |

How do you save a workbook for use in a previous version of Excel?

Saving in Different File Formats

You can save an Excel 2013 file in a format other than .xlsx or .xls. The file formats that are listed as options in the Save As dialog box or on the FILE tab depend on what type of file format the application supports. When you save a file in another file format, some of the formatting, data, and features might be lost.

STEP BY STEP   **Save in Different File Formats**

GET READY. USE the workbook from the previous exercise or type your name and address in a new workbook.

1. Click the **FILE** tab, and then click the **Export** button.
2. Click the **Change File Type** button. Excel explains the different file types (refer to Figure 2-10).
3. Click the **Create PDF/XPS Document** option. Figure 2-11 shows the reason for using this format.

Figure 2-11

Backstage preview giving you information about the PDF/XPS format

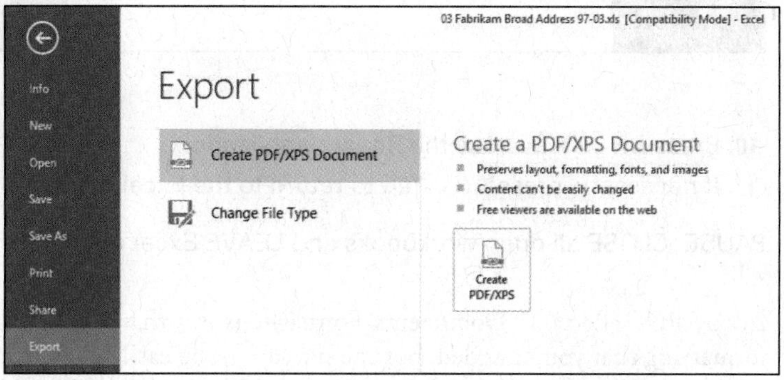

4. In the right pane, click the **Create PDF/XPS** button.
5. In the left navigation pane, click **Desktop**.
6. Double-click **Excel Lesson 2** to move to that folder.
7. The file name gives the last name with a PDF extension.
8. Click **Publish**.
9. The Reader application opens with the PDF file displayed (see Figure 2-12).

CERTIFICATION READY?   **1.5.2**

How do you save a workbook in PDF format?

Figure 2-12

PDF Reader

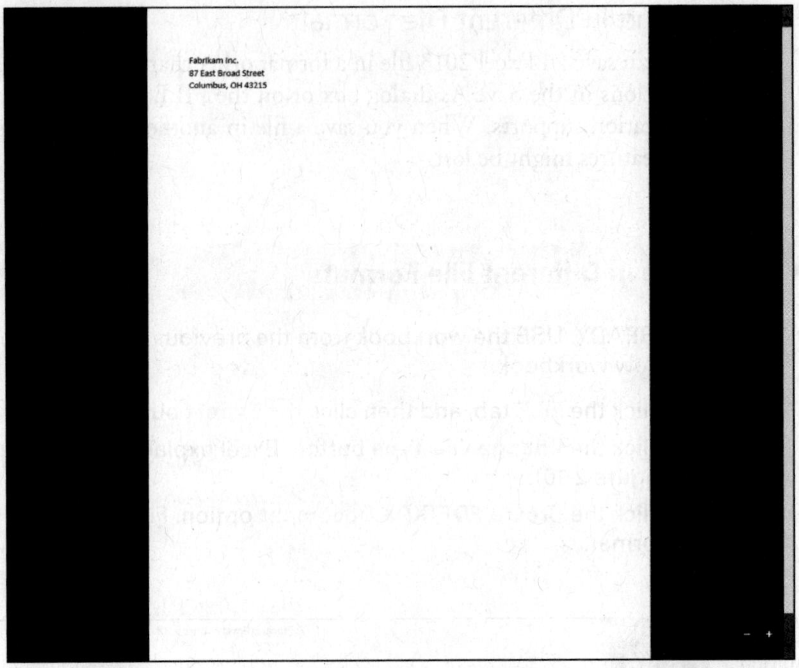

Fabrikam Inc.
87 East Broad Street
Columbus, OH 43215

10. Press **Alt + F4** to close the Reader application.
11. If necessary, press **Alt + Tab** to return to the Excel file.

PAUSE. CLOSE all open workbooks and LEAVE Excel open to use in the next exercise.

Take Note   Adobe PDF (Portable Documents Format) ensures that your printed or viewed file retains the formatting that you intended, but the file cannot be easily changed. You can also save your workbooks in a Web page format for use on websites with Single File Web Page or Web Page options. To import data into another format, you can also try Text (Tab delimited) or CSV (Comma delimited) formats. All of these options are available from the Save a type drop-down menu or the FILE tab.

ENTERING AND EDITING BASIC DATA IN A WORKSHEET

Bottom Line   You can type data directly into a worksheet cell or cells. You can also copy and paste information from another worksheet or from other programs. **Copy** takes the information from one location and duplicates it. You use **Paste** to put this information into another location. To enter data in a cell in a worksheet, you must make the desired cell active and then type the data. To move to the next column after text is entered, press Tab. Continue to press Tab to go to the next column.

Entering Basic Data in a Worksheet

When you finish typing the entries in a row, press Enter to move to the beginning of the next row. You can also use the arrow keys to move to an adjacent cell or click on any cell to make that cell active. Press Enter to accept the entry. In the following exercise, you create a list of people working in the office.

STEP BY STEP   **Enter Basic Data in a Worksheet**

GET READY. If necessary LAUNCH Excel and OPEN a new workbook.

1. Click cell **A1**, type **Fabrikam Inc.**, and press **Enter**. Notice that the active cell moves to the next row, to cell A2.

2. In cell A2, type Employee List and press Enter.

3. Click cell A4, type Name, and press Tab. Notice that the active cell moves to the next column, to cell B4.

Troubleshooting If you type the wrong data, you can click the cell and retype the entry. In the following sections, you see how to edit text.

CERTIFICATION
READY?   2.1.1

How do you add text and values to a workbook?

4. Type Extension and press Enter. Notice that the active cell moves to the first cell in the next row.

5. Type Richard Carey and press Tab.

6. Type 101 and press Enter. Richard Carey looks cut off.

7. Click cell A5 and notice that the complete entry for Richard Carey appears in the formula bar.

8. Click cell A6, type David Ortiz, and press Enter.

9. Type Kim Akers and press Enter.

10. Type Nicole Caron and press Enter.

11. SAVE the workbook in the Computer's Excel Lesson 2 folder as *02 Fabrikam Employees Solution.* Your file should look like Figure 2-13.

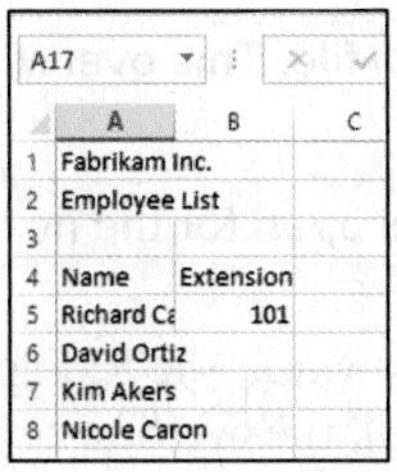

Figure 2-13

The completed 02 Fabrikam Employees workbook

CERTIFICATION
READY?   2.1.5

How do you display characters that extend longer than one column?

PAUSE. LEAVE the workbook open for the next lesson.

Take Note Text is stored in only one cell, even when it appears to extend into adjacent cells. If an entry is longer than the cell width and the next cell contains data, the entry appears in truncated form. To edit the data, you need to go to the cell where the text starts and not in the adjacent cells.

Changing the Column Width

In Excel, column width is established based on the existing data. When you add an entry in a column that extends beyond the column's width, it is necessary to adjust the column width to accommodate the entry.

STEP BY STEP   **Change the Column Width**

GET READY. Use the *02 Fabrikam Employees Solution* file from the previous exercise.

1. Move the mouse pointer between columns A and B, to the column markers at the top of the worksheet (see Figure 2-14). The mouse pointer changes to a double-headed arrow.

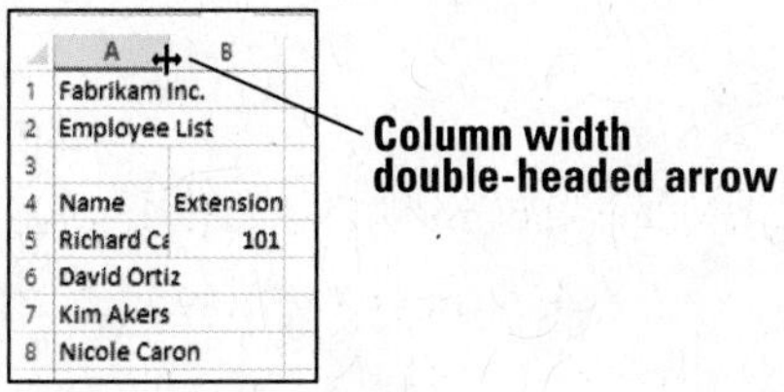

Figure 2-14

Column markers for columns A and B

Column width
double-headed arrow

2. Double-click the column marker between A and B. The width of the column changes to the widest entry in column A. In this case, the widest entries are Employee List and Richard Carey's name.

Take Note   To change the column width manually, point to the column marker between columns A and B and drag the pointer left or right instead of double-clicking.

3. Drag the double-headed arrow mouse pointer between columns B and C until the ScreenTip shows *Width: 20 (145 pixels)* or something close to this amount (see Figure 2-15).

Figure 2-15

By dragging the double-headed arrow the ScreenTip shows the width of the column

Clipboard	Font	
A17	Width: 19.14 (139 pixels)	
	A	B	C
1	Fabrikam Inc.		
2	Employee List		
3			
4	Name	Extension	
5	Richard Ca	101	
6	David Ortiz		
7	Kim Akers		
8	Nicole Caron		

CERTIFICATION READY?   **1.3.5**

How do you change the width of a column?

4. SAVE the *02 Fabrikam Employees Solution* file. This overwrites your previous version without the column width change.

PAUSE. CLOSE the workbook and LEAVE Excel open for the next exercise.

Take Note   When you type text that is longer than the cell's width, the text appears as if it extends into the next cell. However, when you type in the next cell, the overflow text does not display. The text is still there. It is often easier to proof your work if you have the column widths match the longest text. You can double-click on the column markers to automatically adjust to the widest entry or drag the column marker to adjust the column width to your desired width.

Editing a Cell's Contents

One advantage of electronic records versus manual records is that changes can be made quickly and easily. To edit information in a worksheet, you can make changes directly in the cell or edit the contents of a cell in the **formula bar**, located between the ribbon and the worksheet. When you enter data in a cell, the text or numbers appear in the cell and in the formula bar. You can also enter data directly in the formula bar. Before changes can be made, however, you must select the information that is to be changed. **Selecting text** means that you highlight the text that is to be changed. You can select a single cell or a portion of the cell's text in the formula bar before you make changes. You can also double-click in a cell to position the insertion point for editing.

STEP BY STEP   **Edit a Cell's Contents**

GET READY. OPEN a blank workbook.

1. Click cell **A1**, type Fabrikam, and press **Enter**. The insertion point moves to cell A2 and nothing appears in the formula bar.
2. Click cell **A1**. Notice that the formula bar displays *Fabrikam* (see Figure 2-16).

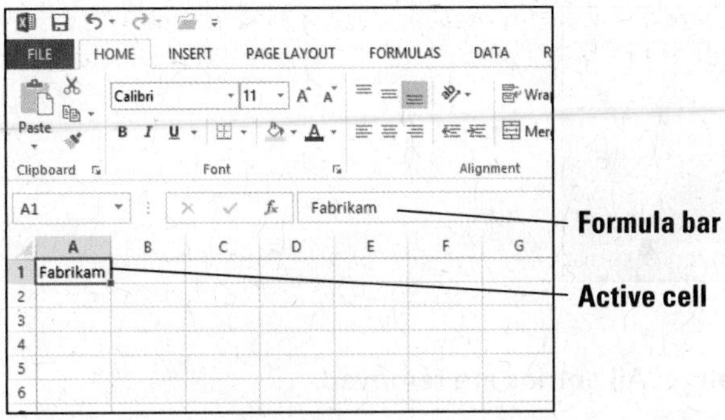

Figure 2-16

Active cell and formula bar displaying the same information

Formula bar

Active cell

3. Click after Fabrikam in the formula bar, type a space, type Incorporated, and press Tab. The insertion point moves to cell B1 and nothing appears in the formula bar (see Figure 2-17).

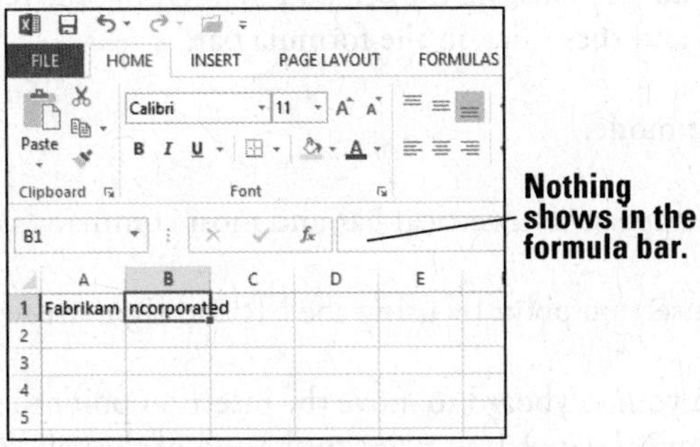

Figure 2-17

Although it looks like text is in B1, it is extended text from A1.

Nothing shows in the formula bar.

4. Click cell A1 and in the formula bar, double-click on Incorporated to select it. Type Inc. and press Enter.
5. Type Sales and press Enter.
6. Click cell A2 and click after Sales in the formula bar.
7. Press Home. The insertion point moves to the beginning of the formula bar.

Take Note While you are editing in the formula bar, you can press Home to move to the beginning, End to move to the end, or the left or right arrow keys to move one character at a time. Press Delete to delete characters after the insertion point. Press Backspace to delete characters before the insertion point.

CERTIFICATION READY? 2.1.2

How do you change a cell's data?

8. Type Monthly and then press the spacebar. Press Enter.
9. In cell A3, type January and press Enter.
10. Click cell A3, type February, and press Enter. Cell A3's original text is gone and February replaces January.
11. Click cell A3 and press Delete. The entry in A3 is removed.
12. Above row 1 and to the left of column A, click the Select All button (see Figure 2-18). All cells on the worksheet are selected.

Figure 2-18

The mouse pointer changes to
a white cross when moved to
the Select All button.

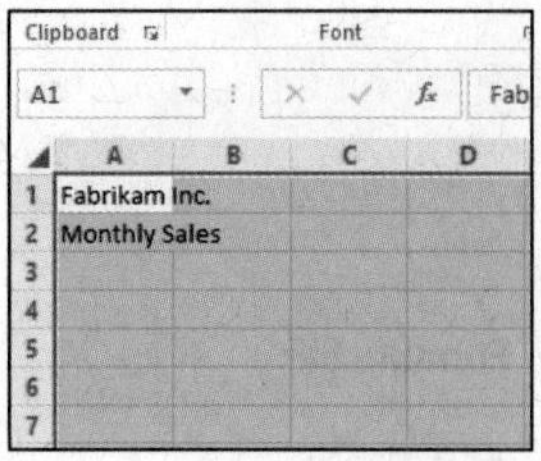

13. Press Delete. All entries are removed.

PAUSE. CLOSE the workbook without saving and LEAVE Excel open for the next exercise.

Take Note   If you edit a cell's contents and change your mind before you press Enter, press Esc and the original text will be restored. If you change the contents of a cell and then do not want the change, click the Undo button on the Quick Access Toolbar or press Ctrl + Z. The deleted text will be restored.

Another Way
You can right-click a cell or a selected range of cells and choose Delete from the shortcut menu that appears.

You can edit a cell by double-clicking the cell and then typing the replacement text in the cell. Or, you can click the cell and then click in the formula bar.

When you are in Edit mode:

• The insertion point appears as a vertical bar and most commands are inactive.

• You can move the insertion point by using the left and right arrow keys.

Use the Home key on your keyboard to move the insertion point to the beginning of the cell, and use the End key to move the insertion point to the end of the cell. You can add new characters at the location of the insertion point.

To select multiple characters while in Edit mode, press Shift while you press the arrow keys. You also can use the mouse to select characters while you are editing a cell. Just click and drag the mouse pointer over the characters that you want to select.

As in the preceding exercises, there are several ways to modify the values or text you enter into a cell:

• **Erase** the cell's contents.

• **Replace** the cell's contents with something else.

• **Edit** the cell's contents.

Deleting and Clearing a Cell's Contents

To erase the entire contents of a cell, click the cell and press Delete. This deletes what is in the cell rather than the cell itself. To erase the contents of more than one cell, select all the cells that you want to erase and on your keyboard, press Delete. Pressing Delete removes the cell's contents, but does not remove any formatting (such as bold, italic, or a different number format) that you might have applied to the cell.

CERTIFICATION READY?   **2.1.6**

How do you delete data in a workbook?

Delete and Clear a Cell's Contents

GET READY. OPEN a blank workbook.

1. In cell A1, type **1** and press **Enter**.
2. Type **2** and press **Enter**.

3. Type **3** and press **Enter**.

4. Type **4** and press **Enter**.

5. Highlight cells **A1** through **A4** (containing the numbers 1 through 4).

6. Press **Delete**. All the cells are erased.

7. On the Quick Access Toolbar, click the **Undo** button to return the cell entries.

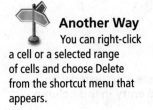

Another Way
You can right-click a cell or a selected range of cells and choose Delete from the shortcut menu that appears.

8. Click cell **B5**, type **$275,000**, and press **Enter**. The value and format are placed into the cell.

9. Click cell **B5** and press **Delete**.

10. Type **225000** without the dollar sign and comma and press **Enter**. Notice that $225,000 is formatted. Although the original entry is gone, the cell retains the previous format when you press **Delete**.

11. Click cell **B5** and on the HOME tab, in the Editing group, click **Clear** (see Figure 2-19).

Figure 2-19

The Clear menu

12. Click **Clear Formats**. *225000* displays without the dollar sign and comma.

Take Note   Clear displays a number of options. To remove both the entry and the format, choose Clear All.

PAUSE. CLOSE the workbook without saving and **LEAVE** Excel open for the next exercise.

USING DATA TYPES TO POPULATE A WORKSHEET

Bottom Line

You can enter three types of data into Excel: text, numbers, and formulas. In the following exercises, you enter text (labels) and numbers (values). You enter formulas in Lesson 4, "Using Basic Formulas." Text entries contain alphabetic characters and any other characters that do not have a purely numeric value. The strength of Excel is its capability to calculate and analyze numbers based on the numeric values you enter. Of course, if you enter the wrong numbers, you get the wrong calculations. For that reason, accurate data entry is crucial.

Entering Labels and Using AutoComplete

Labels are used to identify numeric data and are the most common type of text entered in a worksheet. Labels are also used to sort and group data. If the first few characters that you type in a column match an existing entry in that column, Excel automatically enters the remaining characters. This **AutoComplete** feature works only for entries that contain text or a combination of text and numbers.

STEP BY STEP   **Enter Labels and Use AutoComplete**

GET READY. OPEN a blank workbook.

Troubleshooting   To verify that AutoComplete is enabled, click the FILE tab accessing Backstage view, click Options, and then click Advanced in the navigation pane. In the Editing options section, click the Enable AutoComplete for cell values check box if it is not already checked. Click OK.

1. In cell A1, type **Fabrikam Inc.** and press **Enter**.

2. Type **Monthly Sales**.

3. Click cell **A4** and type **Agent** and press **Tab**.

4. In cell **B4**, type **Last Closing Date** and press **Tab**.

5. In cell **C4**, type **January** and press **Enter**.

6. In cell **A5**, type **Richard Carey**, and press **Enter**.

7. In cell **A6**, type **David Ortiz** and press **Enter**.

8. In cell **A7**, type **Kim Akers** and press **Enter**.

9. Type **Nicole Caron** and press **Enter**.

10. Click cell **A9** and type **R**. As shown in Figure 2-20, AutoComplete is activated when you type the R because it matches the beginning of a previous entry in this column. AutoComplete displays the entry for Richard Carey.

Figure 2-20

AutoComplete displaying a previous entry with matching first character

	A	B	C	D
1	Fabrikam Inc.			
2	Monthly Sales			
3				
4	Agent	Last Closir	January	
5	Richard Carey			
6	David Ortiz			
7	Kim Akers			
8	Nicole Caron			
9	Richard Carey			
10				

11. Type **y**. The AutoComplete entry disappears. Finish typing the entry for **Ryan Calafato** and press **Enter**.

12. Type **R**. Notice that no AutoComplete entry appears this time. Type **i** and notice that the AutoComplete entry shows **Richard Carey**.

13. Press **Esc** to undo the entry.

14. Increase the column widths for columns A and B so you can see the entries in row 4 and below (see Figure 2-21).

 Cross Ref See "Changing the Column Width" previously in this lesson for information on how to change the column widths.

Figure 2-21

Column widths for columns A and B adjusted to see items in all cells

	A	B	C
1	Fabrikam Inc.		
2	Monthly Sales		
3			
4	Agent	Last Closing Date	January
5	Richard Carey		
6	David Ortiz		
7	Kim Akers		
8	Nicole Caron		
9	Ryan Calafato		
10			
11			
12			

PAUSE. LEAVE the workbook open to use in the next exercise.

Take Note Excel bases the list of potential AutoComplete entries on the text in the rows above the current row. If different rows start with the same character, you might have to type more than one character for the AutoComplete entry to display.

To accept an AutoComplete entry, press Enter or press Tab. When you accept AutoComplete, the completed entry matches the pattern of uppercase and lowercase letters of the existing entry. To delete the automatically entered characters, press Backspace. Entries that contain only numbers, dates, or times are not automatically completed. If you do not want to use the AutoComplete option, the feature can be turned off by selecting FILE > Options > Advanced > Editing options section > Enable AutoComplete for cell values.

Entering Numeric Values

Numeric values are the foundation for Excel's calculations, analyses, charts, and graphs. Numbers can be formatted as currency, percentages, decimals, and fractions. By default, numeric entries are right-justified in a cell. Applying formatting to numbers changes their appearance but does not affect the cell value that Excel uses to perform calculations. The value is not affected by formatting or special characters (such as dollar signs) that are entered with a number. The true value is always displayed in the formula bar.

STEP BY STEP	Enter Numeric Values

GET READY. USE the workbook from the previous exercise.

1. Click cell C5, type $275,000, and press Enter.

2. Click cell C5 and notice that *275000* appears in the formula bar and the formatted value appears in the cell.

3. Click cell C6, type 125,000, and press Enter. Be sure to include the comma in your entry. The number is entered in C6 and C7 becomes the active cell. The number appears in the cell with the comma and no dollar sign (unlike the entry in C5); however, the formula bar displays the true value and disregards the special characters.

4. Type 209000 and press Enter. The number is entered with no dollar sign and no comma.

5. Type 258,000 and press Enter.

6. Type 145700 and then click cell C5. Figure 2-22 illustrates how your worksheet should look with the values you just typed.

Figure 2-22

The actual value of the cell entry in C5 is unaffected by formatting.

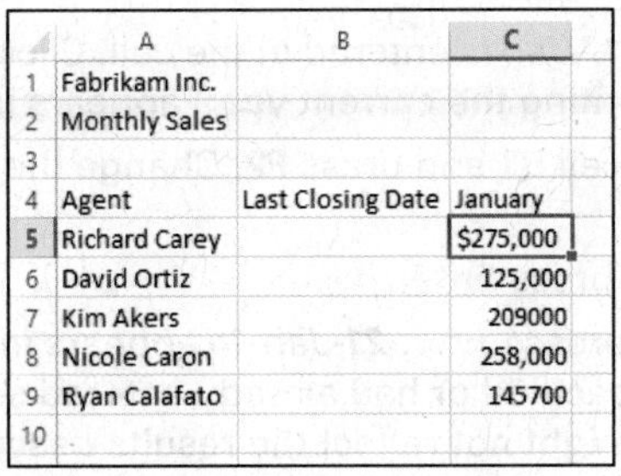

	A	B	C
1	Fabrikam Inc.		
2	Monthly Sales		
3			
4	Agent	Last Closing Date	January
5	Richard Carey		$275,000
6	David Ortiz		125,000
7	Kim Akers		209000
8	Nicole Caron		258,000
9	Ryan Calafato		145700
10			

PAUSE. LEAVE the workbook open to use in the next exercise.

Special characters that indicate the type of value can also be included in the entry. Table 2-1 illustrates special characters that can be entered with numbers.

	Character	Description
Table 2-1	+	Indicates a positive value.
Characters used to identify values	- or ( )	Indicates a negative value.
	$	Indicates a currency value.
	%	Indicates a percentage (typed after number).
	/	Indicates a fraction or a date.
	=	Indicates what follows is a number (or a formula). This is useful when there is an ambiguous entry. For example, 4/5 assumes April 5th of the current year, whereas =4/5 enters four-fifths or 0.8.
	.	Indicates a decimal.
	,	Separates the digits of an entry (thousands, millions, and so on).

Entering Dates

Dates are often used in worksheets to track data over a specified period of time. Like text, dates can be used as row and column headings. However, dates are considered serial numbers, which means that they are sequential and can be added, subtracted, and used in calculations. Dates can also be used in formulas and in developing graphs and charts. The way a date is initially displayed in a worksheet cell depends on the format in which you type the characters. In Excel 2013, the default date format uses four digits for the year. Also by default, dates are right-justified in the cells.

STEP BY STEP   **Enter Dates**

GET READY. Use the workbook from the previous exercise.

1. Click cell B5, type 1/4/2014, and press Enter.
2. Click cell B6, type 1/25/14, and press Enter. The date is entered in C6 as *1/25/2014* and B7 becomes the active cell.
3. Type 1/17 and press Enter. *17-Jan* is entered in the cell. Click cell B7, and notice that *1/17/20XX* (with XX representing the current year) appears in the formula bar.
4. If the year is not 2014, click cell B7 and press F2. Change the year to 2014 and press Enter.
5. In cell B8, type 1/28/14 and press Enter.
6. Type January 21, 2014 and press Enter. *21-Jan-14* appears in the cell. If you enter a date in a different format than specified or had already entered something in the cell and deleted it, your worksheet might not reflect the results described. The date formats in column B are not consistent (see Figure 2-23). You apply a consistent date format in the next section.

Figure 2-23

If you don't type dates the same way, the formats are inconsistent in a workbook.

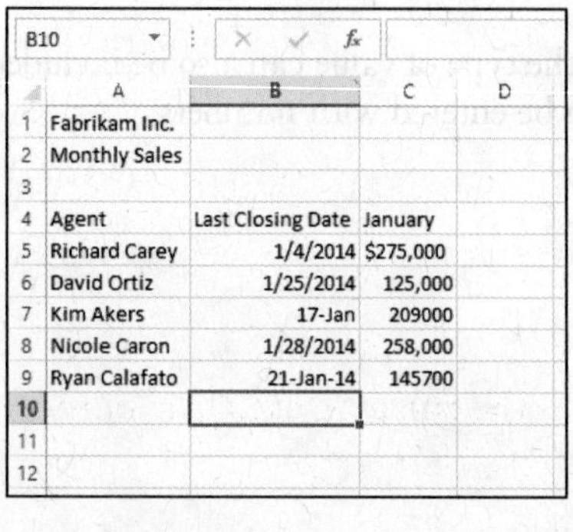

	A	B	C	D
		B10	fx	
1	Fabrikam Inc.			
2	Monthly Sales			
3				
4	Agent	Last Closing Date	January	
5	Richard Carey	1/4/2014	$275,000	
6	David Ortiz	1/25/2014	125,000	
7	Kim Akers	17-Jan	209000	
8	Nicole Caron	1/28/2014	258,000	
9	Ryan Calafato	21-Jan-14	145700	
10				
11				
12				

7. In cell B9, type **1/1/10** and press Enter. Notice that the value changes but the formatting remains the same.

8. Click the Undo button to return to the workbook shown in Figure 2-23.

PAUSE. LEAVE the workbook open to use in the next exercise.

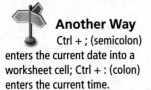

Another Way
Ctrl + ; (semicolon) enters the current date into a worksheet cell; Ctrl + : (colon) enters the current time.

Excel interprets two-digit years from 00 to 29 as the years 2000 to 2029; two-digit years from 30 to 99 are interpreted as 1930 to 1999. If you enter 1/28/28, the date will be displayed as 1/28/2028 in the cell. If you enter 1/28/37, the cell will display 1/28/1937.

If you type January 28, 2020, the date will display as 28-Jan-20. If you type 1/28 without a year, Excel interprets the date to be the current year. 28-Jan will display in the cell, and the formula bar will display 1/28/ followed by the current year. In the next section, you learn to apply a consistent format to a series of dates.

Take Note   When you enter a date into a cell in a particular format, the cell is automatically formatted even if you delete the entry. Subsequent numbers entered in that cell will be converted to the date format of the original entry.

Regardless of the date format displayed in the cell, the formula bar displays the date in month/day/four-digit-year format because that is the format required for calculations and analyses.

Filling a Series with Auto Fill

Excel provides **Auto Fill** options that automatically fill cells with data and/or formatting. To populate a new cell with data that exists in an adjacent cell, use the Auto Fill feature either through the command or the fill handle. The **fill handle** is a small green square in the lower-right corner of a selected cell or range of cells. A **range** is a group of adjacent cells that you select to perform operations on all of the selected cells. When you refer to a range of cells, the first cell and last cell are separated by a colon (for example, C4:H4). To use the fill handle, point to the lower-right corner of the cell or range until the mouse pointer turns into a +. Click and drag the fill handle from cells that contain data to the cells you want to fill with that data, or have Excel automatically continue a series of numbers, numbers and text combinations, dates, or time periods, based on an established pattern. In this exercise, you use the Auto Fill command and fill handle to populate cells with data. To choose an interval for your series, type the first two entries, select them, and then use the fill handle to expand the series using the pattern of the two selected cells.

STEP BY STEP   **Fill a Series with Auto Fill**

GET READY. USE the workbook from the previous exercise or type the text in Figure 2-23.

1. Select the range **C4:H4**. January is in the first cell.

2. On the HOME tab, in the Editing group, click the Fill button. The Fill menu appears (see Figure 2-24).

Figure 2-24

Fill drop-down menu

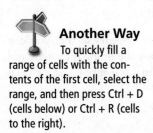

— **Fill button**

— **Fill options**

Another Way
To quickly fill a range of cells with the contents of the first cell, select the range, and then press Ctrl + D (cells below) or Ctrl + R (cells to the right).

3. From the menu, click Right. The contents of C4 (January) are filled into all the cells.

4. Click the Undo button.

5. Select the range C9:C13 and click the Fill button. Choose Down. The content of C9 is copied into the four additional cells.

6. Click the Undo button.

7. Click cell C4, point to the fill handle in the lower-right corner of the cell (see Figure 2-25), and drag it to E4 and release. The Auto Fill Options button appears, and January through March are displayed.

CERTIFICATION READY?   2.1.4

How do you copy a cell's contents using Auto Fill?

Figure 2-25

Mouse pointer changes to a black + in the bottom right of a selected range

C4	▼	:	×	✓	f_x	January		
	A		B			C		
1	Fabrikam Incorporated							
2	Monthly Sales							
3								
4	Agent		Last Closing Date			January		← **Fill handle**
5	Richard Carey		1/4/2014			$275,000		
6	David Ortiz		1/25/2014			125,000		

8. Click cell C5, point to the fill handle, and drag it to C9 and release. All the numbers turn to *$275,000* in column C. The Auto Fill Options button appears in D10 (see Figure 2-26).

Figure 2-26

You can fill numbers, formats, or other options.

	B	C	D
	Last Closing Date	January	February
	1/4/2014	$275,000	
	1/25/2014	$275,000	
	17-Jan	$275,000	
	1/28/2014	$275,000	
	21-Jan-14	$275,000	
			← **Auto Fill Options button**

9. Click the Auto Fill Options button, and choose Fill Formatting Only from the list that appears. All the numbers return to their previous values and are formatted with dollar signs and commas.

10. Repeat Steps 8 and 9 for the range B5:B9.

11. Click cell A9, and then drag the fill handle down to A15. Ryan Calafato's name is repeated.

12. Click the Undo button to return the spreadsheet to what is shown in Figure 2-27.

13. SAVE the workbook as *02 Fabrikam Sales Solution*.

CERTIFICATION READY?   2.2.6

How do you apply formatting with Auto Fill?

Figure 2-27

The completed sales workbook

	A	B	C	D	E
1	Fabrikam Inc.				
2	Monthly Sales				
3					
4	Agent	Last Closing Date	January	February	March
5	Richard Carey	1/4/2014	$275,000		
6	David Ortiz	1/25/2014	$125,000		
7	Kim Akers	1/17/2014	$209,000		
8	Nicole Caron	1/28/2014	$258,000		
9	Ryan Calafato	1/21/2014	$145,700		
10					

PAUSE. CLOSE Excel.

Take Note   When Excel recognizes a series, the default fill option is to complete the series. When you use the fill handle and a series is not present, the default is to copy the cell contents. The Auto Fill Options button also allows you to fill formatting only or to fill without formatting.

CERTIFICATION READY?   2.1.4

How do you fill a series using Auto Fill?

After you fill cells using the fill handle, the Auto Fill Options button appears so that you can choose how the selection is filled. In Excel, the default option is to copy the original content and formatting. With Auto Fill, you can select how the content of the original cell appears in each cell in the filled range.

Take Note   When you type sufficient data for Excel to recognize a series, the fill handle will do the rest. For example, to record daily sales, you might want to have consecutive columns labeled with the days of the week. If you type Monday in the first cell, you can fill in the rest of the days by dragging the fill handle from the Monday cell to complete the series.

Excel recognizes January as the beginning of a natural series and completes the series as far as you take the fill handle. By definition, a **natural series** is a formatted series of text or numbers that are in a normal sequence such as months, weekdays, numbers, or times. For example, a natural series of numbers could be 1, 2, 3, or 100, 200, 300, or a natural series of text could be Monday, Tuesday, Wednesday, or January, February, March. For different natural series, see Table 2-2.

Table 2-2

Examples of Auto Fill series

Initial Selection	Extended Series
1	1, 1, 1, 1, …
1, 2	3, 4, 5, …
2012, 2013	2014, 2015, 2016, …
8:00	9:00, 10:00, 11:00, …
6:00 PM	7:00 PM, 8:00 PM, …
Mon	Tue, Wed, Thu, …
Monday	Tuesday, Wednesday, Thursday, …
Jan	Feb, Mar, Apr, …
January	February, March, April, …
Qtr1	Qtr2, Qtr3, Qtr4, Qtr1, …
2/8/2014, 2/15/2014	2/22/2014, 3/1/2014, 3/8/2014, …
1st anytext	2nd anytext, 3rd anytext, 4th anytext, …
Anytext 1	Anytext 2, Anytext 3, Anytext 4, …

Take Note   Note that you might have to select two cells rather than one to continue some of the previous patterns. To create your own custom list, go to FILE > Options > Advanced > General section > Create lists for use in sorts and fill sequences > Edit Custom Lists.

Filling Cells with Flash Fill

Flash Fill is like Auto Fill, but Excel does more work. This is a new feature in Excel 2013. When Excel recognizes a pattern based on other information in your workbook, it will use the pattern. This is helpful in an example where you have typed first and last names in one column and later decide that you want to sort by last name and then first name. You can create two more columns to separate the names. After you start typing the first names, Excel completes the column. You can repeat with the last name column.

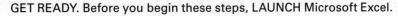

STEP BY STEP   **Fill Cells with Flash Fill**

GET READY. Before you begin these steps, LAUNCH Microsoft Excel.
1. Open the *02 Customers* file.
2. Click cell B1, type First, and press Tab.
3. Click cell C1, type Last, and press Enter.

4. Click cell **B2**, type **Kim**, and press **Enter**.

5. In cell **B3**, type **H**. Notice that Hazem shows in the rest of the cell and the other first names of the customers appear (see Figure 2-28).

Figure 2-28

Flash Fill showing a possible list for all first names

6. Press **Enter**.

7. Click cell **C2**, type **Abercrombie**, and press **Enter**.

8. In cell C3, type **A** and notice that *Abercrombie* is repeated with AutoComplete. Continue typing **bol** and notice that the last names all appear. Press **Enter**.

9. Double-click the right border of columns **B** and **C** to set the column width.

10. Scroll down and notice that the entire worksheet is filled in.

11. SAVE the file as *02 Customers Solution*.

PAUSE. CLOSE Excel.

CUTTING, COPYING, AND PASTING DATA

Bottom Line

After you enter data into a worksheet, you frequently need to rearrange or reorganize some of it to make the worksheet easier to understand and analyze. You can use Excel's Cut, Copy, and Paste commands to copy or move entire cells with their contents, formats, and formulas. These processes are discussed as the exercises in this section continue. You can also copy specific contents or attributes from the cells. For example, you can copy the format only without copying the cell value, or copy the resulting value of a formula without copying the formula itself. You can also copy the value from the original cell but retain the formatting of the destination cell.

Cut, copy, and paste functions can be performed in a variety of ways by using:

- The mouse

- Ribbon commands

- Shortcut commands, such as Ctrl + C (copy), Ctrl + X (cut), and Ctrl + V (paste)

- The Office Clipboard pane

Copying a Data Series with the Mouse

By default, drag-and-drop editing is turned on so that you can use the mouse to copy (duplicate) or move cells. Just select the cell or range of cells you want to copy and hold down Ctrl while you point to the border of the selection. When the pointer becomes a **copy pointer** (arrow with a plus), you can drag the cell or range of cells to the new location. As you drag, a scrolling ScreenTip identifies where the selection will be copied if you release the mouse button. In this exercise, you practice copying data with the mouse.

STEP BY STEP | **Copy a Data Series with the Mouse**

GET READY. Before you begin these steps, LAUNCH Microsoft Excel.

1. Open the *02 Customer Houses* file.
2. Select the range **A12:A22**.
3. Press **Ctrl** and hold the mouse button down as you point to the right border of the selected range. The copy pointer is displayed.

Troubleshooting Be sure to hold down the Ctrl key the entire time you are dragging a data series for copying with the mouse, or you will move the series instead of copying it.

4. With the copy pointer displayed, hold down the left mouse button and drag the selection to the right, until H12:H22 appears in the scrolling ScreenTip next to the selection.
5. Release the mouse button and then release **Ctrl**. The data in A12:A22 also appears in H12:H22.

PAUSE. LEAVE the workbook open to use in the next exercise.

CERTIFICATION READY? 2.1.3

How do you copy a data series with the mouse?

Moving a Data Series with the Mouse

Data can be moved from one location to another within a workbook in much the same way as copying. To move a data series, select the cell or range of cells and point to the border of the selection. When the pointer becomes a **move pointer**, you can drag the cell or range of cells to a new location. When data is moved, it replaces any existing data in the destination cells. In this exercise, you practice moving a data series from one range of cells to another.

STEP BY STEP | **Move a Data Series with the Mouse**

GET READY. USE the *02 Customer Houses* workbook from the previous exercise.

1. Select **E12:E22**.
2. Point to the right border of the selected range. The move pointer is displayed.
3. With the move pointer displayed, hold down the left mouse button and drag the selection to the right, until I12:I22 appears in the scrolling ScreenTip beside the selected range.

CERTIFICATION READY? 2.1.3

How do you move a data series with the mouse?

4. Release the mouse button. In your worksheet, the destination cells are empty; therefore, you are not concerned with replacing existing data. The data previously in E12:E22 is now in I12:I22.

5. Drag A1 to H12. Note that a dialog box warns you about replacing the contents of the destination cells.

6. Click Cancel.

7. Drag A1 to H11.

8. Drag E1 to I11. Your worksheet should look like the one shown in Figure 2-29.

PAUSE. LEAVE the workbook open to use in the next exercise.

Figure 2-29

02 Customer Houses

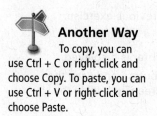

Take Note   When you attempt to move a selection to a location that contains data, a caution dialog box opens. *"There's already data here. Do you want to replace it?"* is a reminder that moving data to a new location replaces the existing data. You can click OK or cancel the operation.

Copying and Pasting Data

The **Office Clipboard** collects and stores up to 24 copied or cut items that are then available to be used in the active workbook, in other workbooks, and in other Microsoft Office programs. You can **paste** (insert) selected items from the Clipboard to a new location in the worksheet. **Cut** (moved) data is removed from the worksheet but is still available for you to use in multiple locations. If you copy multiple items and then click Paste, only the last item copied will be pasted. To access multiple items, you must open the Clipboard pane. In this exercise, you use commands in the Clipboard group and the Clipboard pane to copy and paste cell data.

STEP BY STEP   **Copy and Paste Data**

GET READY. USE the *02 Customer Houses* workbook from the previous exercise.

1. On the HOME tab of the ribbon, click the Clipboard Dialog Box Launcher. The Clipboard pane opens on the left side of the worksheet. The most recently copied item is always added at the top of the list in this pane, and it is the item that will be copied when you click Paste or a shortcut command.

Another Way

To copy, you can use Ctrl + C or right-click and choose Copy. To paste, you can use Ctrl + V or right-click and choose Paste.

2. Select A1:E22 and press Delete.

3. Select H11:I22 and in the Clipboard group, click the Copy button. The border around the selected range becomes a moving border.

4. Select **A1** and click the **Paste** button. The moving border remains active around H11:I22. A copied range does not deactivate until you type new text, issue another command, or double-click on another cell, or press **Esc**.

5. Select **A20** and click the down arrow on the **Paste** button. The Paste options menu appears (see Figure 2-30).

Figure 2-30

Paste options

CERTIFICATION READY? **2.1.3**

How do you copy and paste a data series?

6. Under Paste Values, select the first option. Notice that the values in column B are no longer formatted.

7. Click the **Undo** button.

8. Select **H11:I22** and press **Delete**.

9. Press **Ctrl + Home** to return to the top of the workbook.

10. SAVE the workbook as *02 Customer Houses Solution*.

PAUSE. LEAVE the workbook open to use in the next exercise.

Take Note Paste with Live Preview was new as of Office 2010. If you point to the Paste options in either the shortcut menu or the Paste command options in the Clipboard group, you will be able to view your changes before actually implementing them.

Cutting and Pasting Data

Most of the options for copying and pasting data also apply to cutting and pasting. The major difference is that data copied and pasted remains in the original location as well as in the destination cell or range. Cut and pasted data appears only in the destination cell or range. In this exercise, you cut and paste cell contents.

STEP BY STEP **Cut and Paste Data**

GET READY. USE the *02 Customer Houses Solution* workbook from the previous exercise.

1. Select **A1:B12** to highlight the Customer House Prices table.

2. In the Clipboard group, click the **Cut** button. The contents of A1:B12 are displayed in the Clipboard pane. Close the Clipboard pane.

Another Way
To cut, you can use Ctrl + X or right-click and choose Cut.

3. Click the **New sheet** button on the bottom of the worksheet. Sheet2 is created and cell A1 is the active cell.

4. Click **Paste** to move the former contents of Sheet1 to cell A1 into Sheet2.

PAUSE. CLOSE Excel and do not save the workbooks if requested.

Take Note When you delete text, it is not stored on the Clipboard. To remove data and use the text later, use Cut rather than Delete. By using the Cut feature, you are able to access the data or information from the Clipboard if needed. Deleted text can be restored only with Undo.

EDITING A WORKBOOK'S PROPERTIES

Bottom Line

The workbook has a number of properties that are associated with it to make managing it easier. The properties include items that you indirectly change such as file size and last edit date. The **workbook properties** also include items you directly change such as keywords. Assigning **keywords** to the document properties makes it easier to organize and find documents. You can also add more notes to your file for classification and document management.

Assigning Keywords

If you work for Fabrikam, Inc., you might assign the keyword *sales* to worksheets that contain data about revenue. You can then search for and locate all files containing information about sales. You can assign more than one keyword to a document.

STEP BY STEP   **Assign Keywords**

GET READY. Before you begin these steps, LAUNCH Microsoft Excel.

1. OPEN the *02 Customer Houses Solution* file you worked with in the previous exercises.
2. Click FILE. The Backstage view displays current properties on the right side of the window (see Figure 2-31).

Figure 2-31

Current document's properties

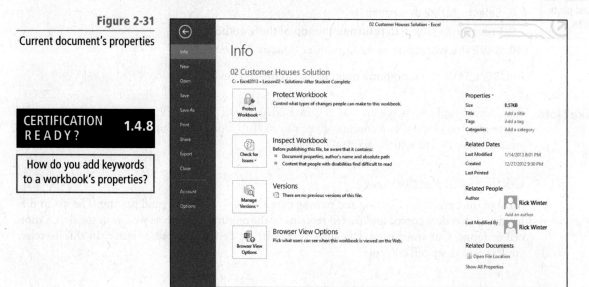

3. At the top of the right pane, click the Properties button. The Properties drop-down menu shows two options (see Figure 2-32). Click Show Document Panel.

Figure 2-32

Properties drop-down menu

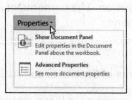

4. Click the Keywords field and type Customer, Sq Ft, Price.
5. Click the Category field and type Revenue.
6. Click the Author field and type your name.

7. Above the Author field, click the Document Properties drop-down arrow, and then click Advanced Properties. The Properties dialog box opens.

8. Click the Summary tab in the dialog box to see the properties you entered.

9. Click the Statistics tab to see the date you modified the file.

10. Click OK to close the Properties dialog box.

11. At the top right corner of the Document Information panel, click the Close button.

12. SAVE the workbook in the Lesson 2 folder as *02 Customer Houses Prop Solution*.

PAUSE. CLOSE Excel.

After a file is saved, the Statistics tab records when the file was accessed and when it was modified. It also identifies the person who last saved the file. After a workbook is saved, the Properties dialog box title bar displays the workbook name and location.

SKILL SUMMARY

In this lesson you learned how:	Exam Objective	Objective Number
To create workbooks	Create new blank workbooks.	1.1.1
To save workbooks	Save workbooks in alternate file formats.	1.5.2
	Maintain backward compatibility.	1.5.6
	Save files to remote locations.	1.5.8
To enter and edit basic data in a worksheet	Append data to a worksheet.	2.1.1
	Find and replace data.	2.1.2
	Adjust column width.	1.3.5
	Demonstrate how to use the Auto Fill tool.	2.1.4
	Expand data across columns.	2.1.5
	Delete cells.	2.1.6
To use data types to populate a worksheet	Apply Number formats.	2.2.6
To cut, copy, and paste data	Copy and paste data.	2.1.3
To edit a workbook's properties	Add values to workbook properties.	1.4.8

Knowledge Assessment

Multiple Choice

Select the best response for the following statements.

1. Which of the following consists of details that describe or identify a file, including the author?
   a. Paste
   b. Document properties
   c. Copy
   d. Range

2. Which command is used to insert a cut or copied selection to a cell or range of cells?
   a. Paste
   b. Document properties
   c. Copy
   d. Range

3. Which of the following is a group of adjacent cells that you select to perform operations on all of the selected cells?
   a. Paste
   b. Document properties
   c. Copy
   d. Range

4. Which of the following places a duplicate of a selection in the Office Clipboard?
   a. Paste
   b. Document properties
   c. Copy
   d. Range

5. If you want to use a workbook in another kind of document, you have the option to save as which of the following?
   a. File format
   b. Worksheet
   c. File sheet
   d. File range

6. Which is a small green square in the lower-right corner of a selected cell or range that you can use to copy one cell to adjacent cells or to create a series?
   a. Cell pointer
   b. Column marker
   c. Fill handle
   d. Formula bar

7. Which of the following is used to drag or double-click to change the width of a column?
   a. Cell pointer
   b. Column marker
   c. Fill handle
   d. Formula bar

8. Which of the following is a bar near the top of the Excel window where you can enter or edit cell entries or formulas?
   a. Cell pointer
   b. Column marker
   c. Fill handle
   d. Formula bar

9. Which Excel feature helps you quickly enter existing data into adjacent cells?
   a. AutoComplete
   b. AutoData
   c. QuickComplete
   d. QuickData

10. Which Excel feature automatically fills cells with data from another cell or range or completes a data series?
   a. Range Fill
   b. Auto Fill
   c. Data Fill
   d. Complete Fill

True / False

Circle T if the statement is true or F if the statement is false.

T F 1. When data is too wide for a cell, the part of the data that will not fit is automatically deleted.

T F 2. Using the Delete key removes both text and formats from a cell.

T F 3. Use Ctrl + : to enter the current date in a worksheet cell.

T F 4. You can assign keywords so that others can search for your documents online.

T F 5. To remove only the formats from a cell, you can use the Delete key.

T F 6. Dates can be displayed in only one way in Excel.

T F 7. All dates in Excel are actually stored in the serial date number system.

T F 8. The formula bar is found at the bottom of the Excel window.

T F 9. Use the fill handle to create a natural series, such as the months of the year.

T F 10. Workbooks can be saved as web pages, PDF files, and for use in previous versions of Excel.

Competency Assessment

Project 2-1: Creating a Highly Desired Housing Options Workbook

Create a new workbook for Fabrikam, Inc., that is a result of a focus group showing the most desired options for houses for first-time home buyers.

GET READY. LAUNCH Excel and start a new blank workbook.

1. Click cell **A1** and type **Fabrikam, Inc.** and press **Enter**.

2. Click cell **A2** and type **Focus Group Requests (Age 20-30)**.

3. Beginning in **A4**, type the following labels and values. Press **Tab** between each new cell and **Enter** to move to a new row:

Option	Priority	Cost
Gameroom	Low	25,000
Exercise equipment	Low	2500
Fenced yard for dog	Medium	$10,000
Flat screen HDTV	Medium	1000
Furnished	Medium	15000
Washer & dryer	High	1500
Dishwasher	Medium	1000
Near bike path	High	0
Basketball hoop	Low	100

4. If necessary, adjust the column widths to display all of the text in the columns.

5. Drag the fill handle from **C5** through **C13** and choose **Fill Formatting Only**.

6. SAVE the workbook as *02 Focus Group Solution* in the Excel Lesson 2 folder you created in a previous exercise.

PAUSE. LEAVE the workbook open for the next project.

Project 2-2: Setting Document Properties and Assigning Keywords

Use Document Properties to assign document properties to an existing workbook.

GET READY. If necessary, OPEN the *02 Focus Group Solution* workbook you created in the previous project.

1. Click the **FILE** tab.

2. Click **Properties**, and then click **Show Document Panel**.

3. Click the **Author** field, type **[your name]**, and press **Tab**.

4. In the Title field, type **Focus Group Requests** and press **Tab**.

5. In the Subject field, type **Sales** and press **Tab**.

6. In the Keywords field, type **20-30, options, priorities**.

7. Click the Status field, and type Needs to be formatted.
8. SAVE the file as *02 Focus Properties Solution*.
9. At the top of the Document Information Panel, click the Close (X) button.
10. CLOSE the file.

PAUSE. LEAVE Excel open for the next project.

Proficiency Assessment

Project 2-3: Creating a Commission Schedule

You have been asked to create a commission schedule in 5 minutes or less. Because you know how to use the fill handle, you should be able to quickly create the following workbook.

GET READY. OPEN a blank workbook.

1. Create the entries shown in Figure 2-33.

Figure 2-33

Create the worksheet in 5 minutes or less

	A	B	C	D	E	F	G
1	Sales	Jan	Feb	Mar	Apr	May	Jun
2	100,000	2.80%	2.80%	2.80%	2.80%	2.80%	3.00%
3	200,000	2.90%	2.90%	2.90%	2.90%	2.90%	3.10%
4	300,000	3.00%	3.00%	3.00%	3.00%	3.00%	3.20%
5	400,000	3.10%	3.10%	3.10%	3.10%	3.10%	3.30%
6	500,000	3.20%	3.20%	3.20%	3.20%	3.20%	3.40%
7							

2. Move the table so you can add text in cell A1, cell A2, and a blank cell in A3.
3. Click cell A1 and type Fabrikam Incorporated.
4. Click cell A2 and type Commission Schedule.
5. Add the following Document Properties:

Property	Value
Author	[Your Name]
Title	Commission Schedule
Keywords	Agent, Amount, Sales
Category	Revenue

6. SAVE the file as *02 Commission Solution* and CLOSE the workbook.

PAUSE. LEAVE Excel open for the next project.

Project 2-4: Advertising Expenditures

Fourth Coffee specializes in unique coffee and tea blends. Create a workbook to track and classify expenditures for January.

GET READY. OPEN a blank workbook.

1. Click cell A1 and type Fourth Coffee.
2. Click cell A2 and type January Expenditures.
3. Enter the following column headings in row 4: Date, Check No, Paid to, Category, and Amount.
4. Enter the following expenditures data in the appropriate columns:
   January 3, paid $3,000 to World Wide Importers for coffee, Check No. 4076
   January 20, paid $600 to Northwind Traders for tea, Check No. 4077

January 22, paid $300 to City Power and Light for utilities

January 28, paid $200 to A. Datum Corporation for advertising

January 29, paid $2,500 to World Wide Importers for coffee

5. Checks are written sequentially. Use the fill handle to enter the missing check numbers.

6. Adjust column widths as needed.

7. SAVE the workbook as *02 Advertising Expenses Solution*. CLOSE the workbook.

LEAVE Excel open for the next project.

Mastery Assessment

Project 2-5: Creating a Home Sales Workbook

Richard Carey asked you to keep track of the home sales for the Fabrikam staff. Each person sends you an e-mail with the home sales information.

GET READY. OPEN a blank workbook.

1. Create the workbook with the data in Figure 2-34.

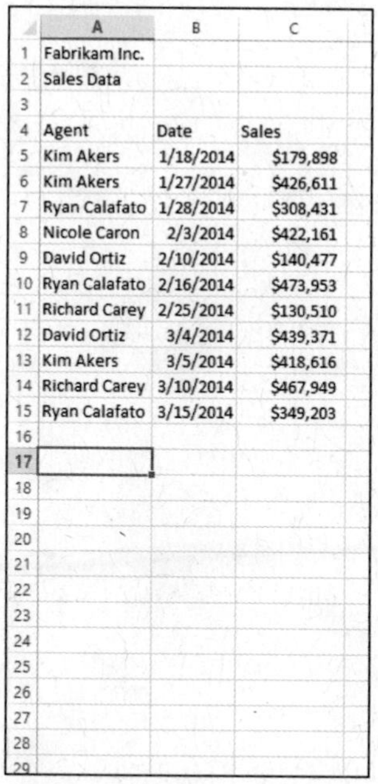

Figure 2-34

Create this workbook for Project 2-5

	A	B	C
1	Fabrikam Inc.		
2	Sales Data		
3			
4	Agent	Date	Sales
5	Kim Akers	1/18/2014	$179,898
6	Kim Akers	1/27/2014	$426,611
7	Ryan Calafato	1/28/2014	$308,431
8	Nicole Caron	2/3/2014	$422,161
9	David Ortiz	2/10/2014	$140,477
10	Ryan Calafato	2/16/2014	$473,953
11	Richard Carey	2/25/2014	$130,510
12	David Ortiz	3/4/2014	$439,371
13	Kim Akers	3/5/2014	$418,616
14	Richard Carey	3/10/2014	$467,949
15	Ryan Calafato	3/15/2014	$349,203
16			
17			
18			
19			
20			
21			
22			
23			
24			
25			
26			
27			
28			
29			

2. SAVE the workbook as *02 Home Sales Solution*.

3. Create a New workbook and copy the data and titles for the first quarter only.

4. Click cell A3 and type First Quarter 2014.

5. Move the Agent, Date, and Sales titles and data down so there is a blank row in row 4.

6. SAVE the new workbook as *02 Home Sales Q1 Solution*.

7. Repeat for the second quarter (4/9/2014-5/20/2014) and SAVE the workbook as *02 Home Sales Q2 Solution*.

CLOSE the workbooks and LEAVE Excel open for the next project.

Project 2-6: **Using Flash Fill**

Fabrikam's director has asked you to redo the workbook you created in Project 2-5 with separate columns for first name and last name and sequentially numbered sales. Save this as a PDF and Excel 1997-2003 file formats and with document properties in the new file.

1. OPEN the *02 Home Sales Solution* file.
2. Use Flash Fill to create columns for the First and Last name.
3. Delete the content of cells A4:A29.
4. In A4, type Item# and then use Auto Fill to create numbers starting with 1 that are sequential through 25.
5. Add a label in A3 that says 2014 To-Date.
6. Make sure there is a blank row 4.
7. Add your own Document Properties for Author, Title, Subject, Keywords, Category, and Status. In the Comments, type Project 2-6 final review.
8. SAVE the workbook as *02 Home Sales Flash Fill Solution*.
9. Create a PDF file and SAVE it with the same name.
10. Verify whether there are any compatibility issues for earlier versions of Excel.
11. Create an Excel 1997-2003 file and SAVE it as *02 Home Sales Flash Fill 97-03 Solution*.

CLOSE Excel.

LESSON SKILL MATRIX

Skills	Exam Objective	Objective Number
Accessing and Using Backstage View		
Printing with Backstage	Set a print area.	1.5.1
	Print individual worksheets.	1.5.3
	Set print scaling.	1.5.4
	Configure workbooks to print.	1.5.7
Changing the Excel Environment	Customize the Quick Access Toolbar.	1.4.3
	Customize the ribbon.	1.4.4
Accessing and Using Excel Templates	Create new workbooks using templates.	1.1.2

KEY TERMS

- **default settings**
- **group**
- **navigation pane**
- **print options**
- **tab**
- **template**

© matthewwennisphotography / iStock photo

© matthewennisphotography / iStock photo

Contoso, Ltd., employs hundreds of employees. The company rewards its employ-ees with monthly potluck dinners in their departments and between departments. In the past, there were too many drinks and desserts and not enough main dishes and salads. Contoso has asked the new assistant office manager to create some way of organizing the potlucks so the meals are balanced and still fun. In this lesson, you learn how to create the types of workbooks Contoso uses for this task. You also learn how to print these workbooks.

SOFTWARE ORIENTATION

Microsoft Excel 2013 Backstage View

The ribbon is a visual interface that allows you to work in a file and perform tasks such as changing fonts, creating charts, and formatting numbers. The Backstage view, on the other hand, is a visual interface that enables you to use and master Excel's file management fea-tures—functions that allow you to do things to a file rather than in a file. Backstage view's left-side *navigation pane* (see Figure 3-1) gives you access to workbook and file-related com-mands through a series of *tabs*, including Info, New, Open, Save, Save As, Print, Share, Ex-port, Close, Account, and Options. Some of the tabs give you additional tabs. Other tabs allow you to select from many different options or settings. Finally, some tabs accomplish a task and return you to the workbook.

Take Note   The Exit command is no longer available in Office 2013, at least in the same way it was avail-able in prior versions. In this case, the Close tab in Backstage view closes the workbook. The Close (X) button in the upper right corner of the Excel 2013 window closes Excel (see Figure 3-1).

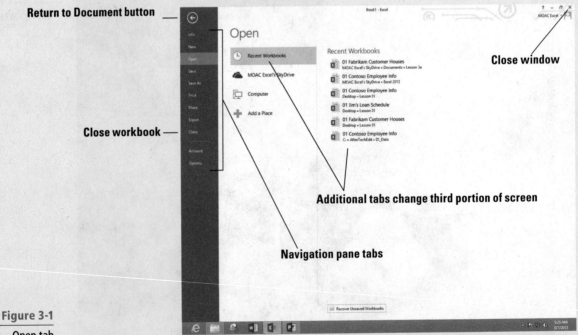

Figure 3-1

Backstage view—Open tab

ACCESSING AND USING BACKSTAGE VIEW

Bottom Line

In the Excel 2013 window, you see the green FILE tab in the upper left corner. This is your access to Backstage view. When you click the FILE tab to access Backstage view, you see the navigation pane containing many of the same commands that can be accessed through the Microsoft Office button in previous versions of Excel. In this section, you access Backstage view and use these commands to close a file.

STEP BY STEP **Access Backstage View**

Another Way
You can also press Alt + F to select FILE and go to the Backstage view.

GET READY. LAUNCH Excel and OPEN a blank workbook.

1. Click the FILE tab to display Backstage view with the Open tab selected (see Figure 3-1).
2. In the upper left corner of Backstage view, click the Return to document button.
3. In cell A1, type abc and press Enter.
4. Click the FILE tab. Backstage view, like the ribbon, is context-sensitive and changes to the Info tab (see Figure 3-2).

Figure 3-2

Backstage view—Info tab

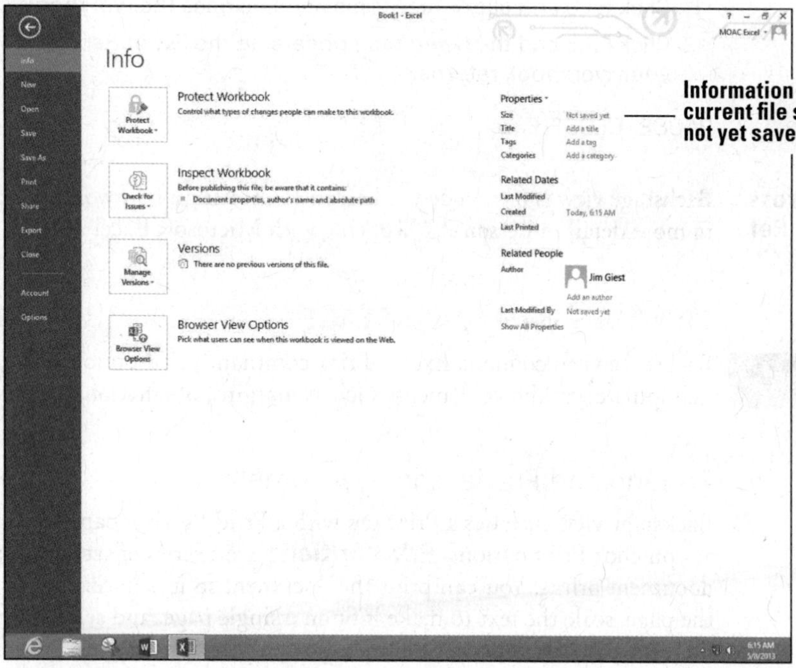

5. Click the Save tab. Notice that there are additional tabs depending on your setup. In this case, SkyDrive, Computer, and Add a Place appear.
6. Click the Save As tab. Notice that this looks identical to the Save tab. This is how it looks the first time you save the file.
7. Click Computer and notice that the Recent Folders section where you last saved your previous workbooks appears (see Figure 3-3).

Figure 3-3

Backstage view—Save As tab

Figure 3-3

Backstage view—Save As tab

Recent locations (drives and folders) that you have accessed

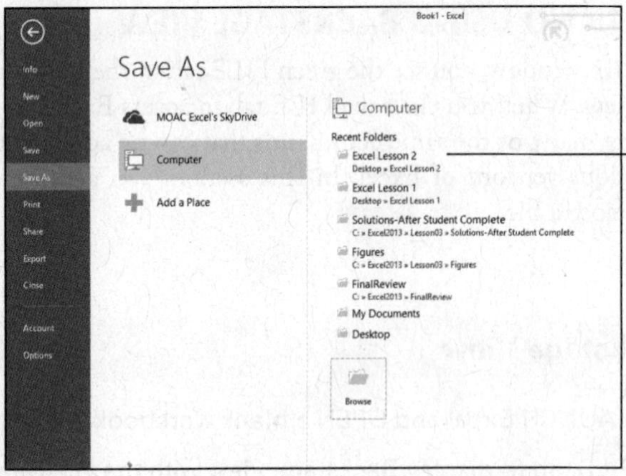

8. Click Browse. In the File name box, type Temp, and then click Save.

9. Click FILE. Notice the Info tab appears.

10. Click Save. Notice that you do not see the options shown in Figure 3-3 (and Step 5 previously), but that you return directly to the workbook.

11. Click FILE and click Close. This action closes the workbook, but not Excel.

12. Click FILE and the Open tab appears. In the list of Recent Workbooks, select Temp and your workbook returns.

PAUSE. CLOSE Excel.

Cross Ref   Backstage view is introduced in Lesson 1. Creating a new workbook and saving a file are discussed in more detail in Lesson 2, "Working with Microsoft Excel 2013."

PRINTING WITH BACKSTAGE

Bottom Line   Backstage view contains Excel's Print commands and options. You can use the Print settings to manipulate workbook elements such as margins, orientation, paper size, and so on.

Printing and Previewing a Document

Backstage view includes a Print tab with a Print Preview pane so you can preview your workbook as you click Print options. **Print options** are a series of settings that allow you to change how a document prints. You can print the document so it is horizontal or vertical, display gridlines on the page, scale the text to make it fit on a single page, and select from many other options. In this exercise, you create a form for a potluck and learn to use the Print and Print Preview features in Excel.

STEP BY STEP   **Print and Preview a Document**

GET READY. LAUNCH Microsoft Excel 2013.

1. Create a new workbook, enter the worksheet data shown in Figure 3-4, and save it as *03 Contoso Potluck solution* in a folder called Excel Lesson 3.

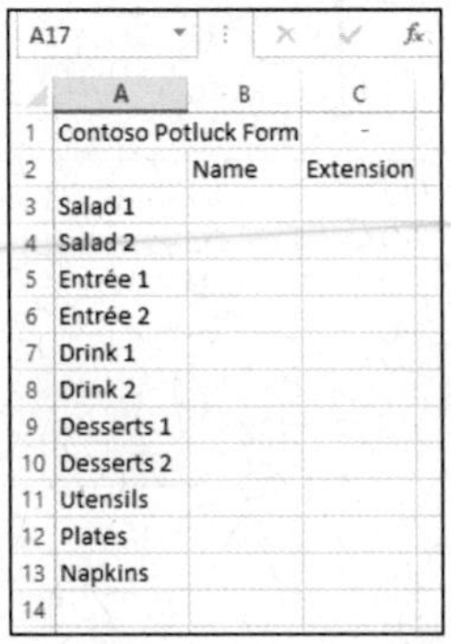

Figure 3-4

03 Contoso Potluck solution worksheet

	A	B	C
1	Contoso Potluck Form		
2		Name	Extension
3	Salad 1		
4	Salad 2		
5	Entrée 1		
6	Entrée 2		
7	Drink 1		
8	Drink 2		
9	Desserts 1		
10	Desserts 2		
11	Utensils		
12	Plates		
13	Napkins		
14			

Another Way
Another way to create a new workbook is with the Ctrl + N keyboard shortcut.

2. CLOSE Excel.

3. LAUNCH Excel again and notice that *03 Contoso Potluck Solution* appears in your Recent list. Click the file to bring it back up.

4. Click the FILE tab to automatically display the Info tab. As shown in Figure 3-5, the Properties area shows the size of the file, when it was last modified, and who the author is.

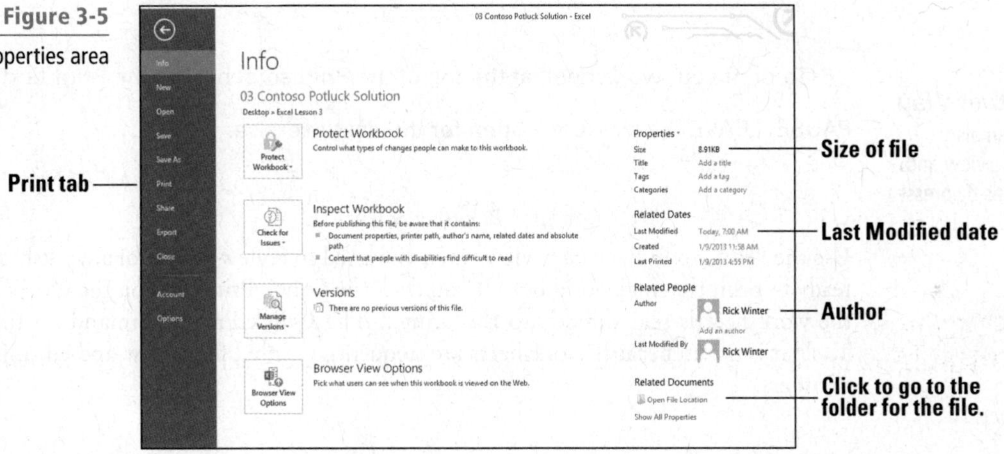

Figure 3-5

File Properties area

Take Note A handy feature, Open File Location, allows you to open the folder where the current file is located.

Cross Ref In Lesson 2, the "Editing a Workbook's Properties" section demonstrates how to make changes to some of the properties in a workbook.

5. Click the Print tab. Note that this displays the Print options in Backstage view. Take a moment to preview the workbook in the Print Preview section in the right pane and read through the Print options listed in the center section of the page (see Figure 3-6).

Figure 3-6

Document preview

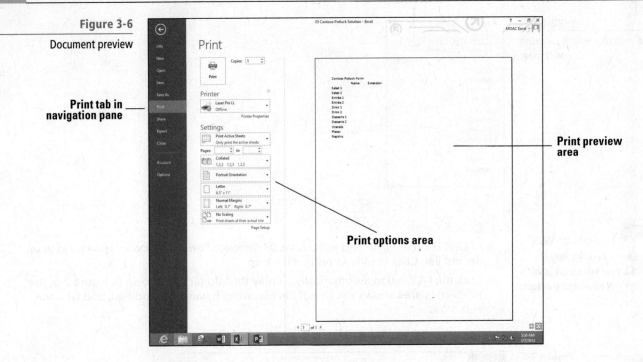

Print tab in
navigation pane

Print preview
area

Print options area

Another Way
You can also activate Backstage view and access Print options by pressing Ctrl + P.

6. To print your worksheet, at the top of the Print screen, click the Print button.

PAUSE. LEAVE the workbook open for the next exercise.

Using Quick Print to Print a Worksheet

Use the Print tab in Backstage view when you need to review a draft of a worksheet before you are ready to print the final workbook. If you click the Quick Print icon on the Quick Access Toolbar, the worksheet is sent directly to the printer. The Quick Print command on the Quick Access Toolbar is useful because worksheets are frequently printed for review and editing or distribution to others.

STEP BY STEP | **Use Quick Print to Print a Worksheet**

GET READY. USE the open workbook from the previous exercise or open *03 Contoso Potluck Solution*.

1. On the Quick Access Toolbar, if you do not see the Quick Print button, click the Customize Quick Access Toolbar arrow at the end of the toolbar, and select Quick Print (see Figure 3-7).

Figure 3-7

Customizing the Quick Access
Toolbar menu

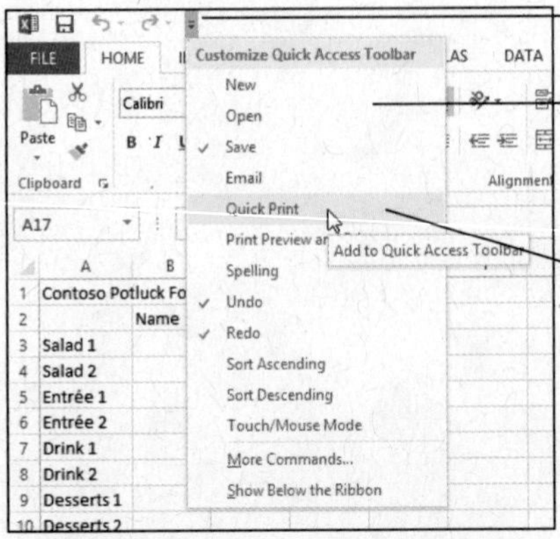

Arrow to access menu

Customize Quick Access Toolbar

Quick Print is not checked
so it needs to be selected.

Take Note   Discuss with your instructor whether you can print in the classroom. If you cannot, view all the documents in preview mode to see how the document would print whenever printing is mentioned in this book.

2. On the Quick Access Toolbar, click Quick Print (see Figure 3-8).

Figure 3-8

Quick Access Toolbar

3. Retrieve the printed copy of the worksheet from your printer.
4. Click the FILE tab, and then click Print. The preview pane should match what was printed.
5. Click the Return to document button.
6. Notice that a dotted vertical line appears in the middle of the screen. The line shows the right edge of the printed page. The line displays the first time you print or preview a page.

PAUSE. LEAVE the workbook open for the next exercise.

Setting the Print Area

You can use the Print options in Backstage view to print only a selected portion, or print area, of an Excel workbook. In this exercise, you learn to select an area of a workbook for printing. You print just the list of items and have a couple of people verify that these are items you should have people bring to the potluck.

STEP BY STEP   Set the Print Area

GET READY. USE *03 Contoso Potluck Solution* that is already open or create the workbook shown in Figure 3-4.

1. Click the PAGE LAYOUT tab.
2. In the Page Setup group, point to the Print Area button. Note the ScreenTip that displays and defines the task to be completed.
3. On the worksheet, click cell A3, hold the mouse button, and drag to cell A13. Your cell range should be highlighted in gray (see Figure 3-9).

Figure 3-9

Selecting a print area

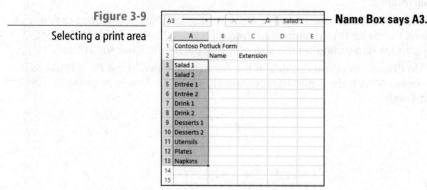

Name Box says A3.

4. With these cells highlighted, from the menu that appears, click the Print Area drop-down arrow and click Set Print Area. You have now set the print area. While the area is still selected, note that the Name Box now says *Print_Area* (see Figure 3-10).

Figure 3-10

Selected print area

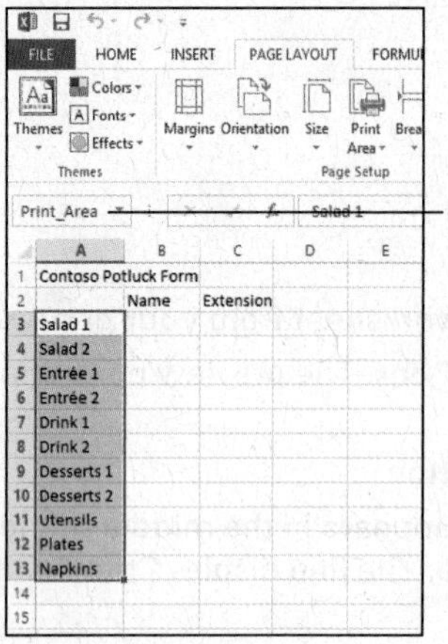

Name Box says Print_Area.

5. Click the FILE tab to open Backstage view.

6. Click Print and notice in the Print Preview pane that you can see only the list of items to bring and not the text in rows 1 and 2 and columns B and C.

7. Click the Return to document button. You will not print at this time.

PAUSE. SAVE the workbook in your Lesson 3 folder with the current name *03 Contoso Potluck Solution* and CLOSE Excel.

Printing Selected Worksheets

In this exercise, you learn to access the options for printing individual worksheets in a workbook. You can use these options to print the current worksheet only or to print multiple worksheets.

STEP BY STEP **Print Selected Worksheets**

GET READY. LAUNCH Excel 2013, and then perform these steps:

1. OPEN *03 Contoso Potluck Depts*. This is a modified version of the potluck workbook you created previously. In this case, there are three different worksheets for three different departments.

2. Click each of the three worksheet tabs: HR, Operations, and Finance. Notice that the title in C1 shows the department name and there are a different number of items to bring to each potluck depending on the size of the department. Click the HR tab.

3. Press Ctrl + P to display the Print options in the Backstage view. In the Print Preview pane, the entire worksheet does not display (see Figure 3-11). This is because of the selected print area.

Figure 3-11

The entire worksheet does not display because print area is selected.

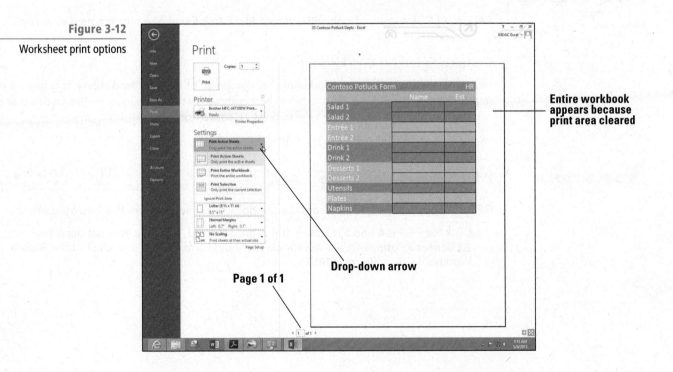

4. Press **Esc** or click the **Return to document** button.

5. Click the **PAGE LAYOUT** tab, click **Print Area**, and then select **Clear Print Area**.

6. Click the **FILE** tab and click **Print**. Notice that the entire worksheet for HR appears. Also notice that the page number shows 1 out of 1 indicating that only one of the worksheets will print, and it will all fit on one page.

7. In the Settings section of the center pane in Print options, click the **Print Active Sheets drop-down arrow**. In the drop-down menu that appears, as shown in Figure 3-12, you can select several printing options for your workbook or worksheet.

Figure 3-12

Worksheet print options

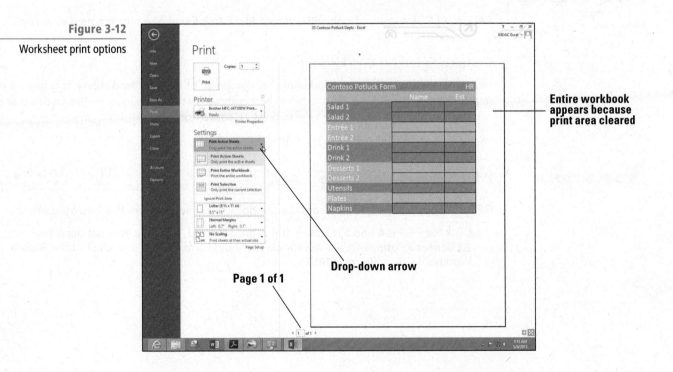

Entire workbook appears because print area cleared

Drop-down arrow

Page 1 of 1

8. Click the Return to document button.

9. While the HR worksheet is active, hold down **Ctrl** and click on the **Finance** tab. Now both the HR and Finance worksheets are selected.

10. Click the FILE tab and click Print. Now in the Print Preview area, the bottom of the screen shows 1 of 2 with the HR worksheet preview. Click the right arrow to go to the second page and notice that the Finance worksheet previews (see Figure 3-13).

Figure 3-13

Two worksheets will print this time.

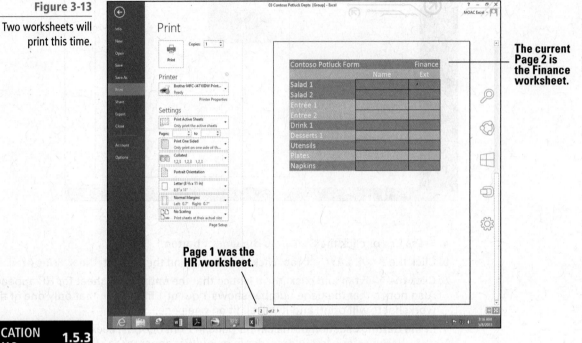

The current Page 2 is the Finance worksheet.

Page 1 was the HR worksheet.

CERTIFICATION READY?   **1.5.3**

How do you print selected worksheets?

11. Click the Return to document button to return to the workbook without printing.

PAUSE. CLOSE the workbook without saving. LEAVE Excel open for the next exercise.

Printing Selected Workbooks

In most scenarios in business, workbooks are composed of multiple worksheets. It is much easier to print an entire workbook than to print the workbook's worksheets individually. In this exercise, you use commands in Backstage view to print an entire workbook.

STEP BY STEP   **Print Selected Workbooks**

GET READY. With Excel open from the previous exercise, perform the following steps:

1. Click the FILE tab and click Open if it is not selected. Because you just used the *03 Contoso Potluck Depts* workbook, it should be at the top of the list of the Recent Workbooks (see Figure 3-14).

Figure 3-14

03 Contoso Potluck Depts
is the most recent
workbook used.

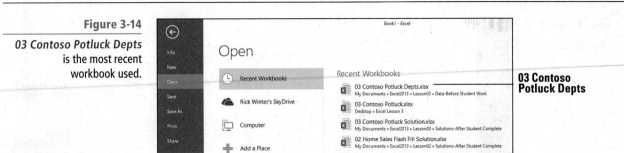

**03 Contoso
Potluck Depts**

2. Click *03 Contoso Potluck Depts* to open it.

3. Click the FILE tab and click Print.

4. Notice that the complete worksheet for HR does not display. This is because you did not save the workbook after you cleared the print area. Clear the print area as you did in Step 5 of the previous section and return to the Print tab of Backstage view.

5. In the Print window's Settings options, click the Print Active Sheets drop-down arrow and click Print Entire Workbook (see Figure 3-15). You will not print at this time.

Figure 3-15

Printing an entire workbook

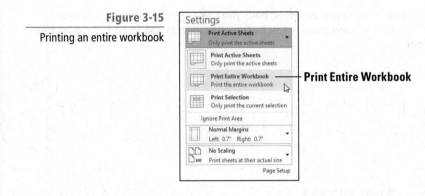

Print Entire Workbook

PAUSE. CLOSE Excel and do not SAVE the workbook.

CERTIFICATION
READY?   **1.5.7**

How do you print a
workbook?

Applying Printing Options

The Print command in Backstage view offers a number of options for customizing printed workbooks. This exercise prepares you to customize such options as page setup, scale, paper selection, and gridlines, all using the commands in Backstage view.

STEP BY STEP   **Apply Print Options**

GET READY. LAUNCH Excel, OPEN *03 Contoso Potluck HR*, and make sure the HR-P1 worksheet is selected.

1. Click the FILE tab and select Print (see Figure 3-16). Notice that the worksheet is small and it might be nice to have lines for people to write in on a printed page.

Figure 3-16

Print Settings area

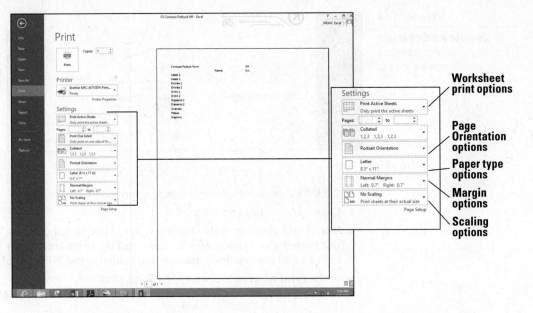

Figure 3-16

Print Settings area

2. In the Settings section of the Print window, click the Margins drop-down and click Wide (see Figure 3-17). The new margins will allow the worksheet to be hole-punched and put in a binder.

Figure 3-17

Normal margins are about ¾ of an inch. Wide margins are 1 inch.

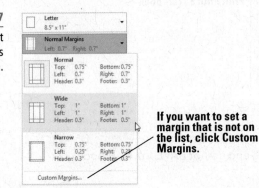

3. Click the Scaling drop-down and see the choices below (see Figure 3-18). The scaling options ensure that all columns, rows, or the entire worksheet fit on one page.

• Current choice is No scaling, so the document prints the same size as the screen.

• If you want to fit everything that is on the worksheet on one page, select Fit Sheet on One Page.

• If there are just a couple of columns extra, click Fit All Columns on One Page.

• If there are just a couple of rows extra, click Fit All Rows on One Page.

Figure 3-18

Print scaling options

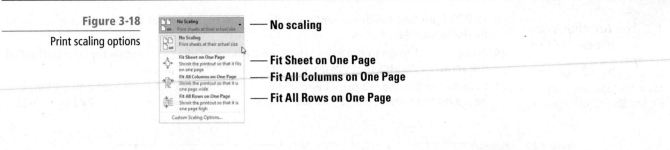

— No scaling

— Fit Sheet on One Page
— Fit All Columns on One Page
— Fit All Rows on One Page

4. In this case, you make the text larger without changing the font. Click **Custom Scaling Options**. The Page Setup dialog box opens.

5. Make sure that the **Page** tab is selected and select **Landscape** so the page prints horizontally.

6. In the Scaling area, type **200** for the % normal size (see Figure 3-19).

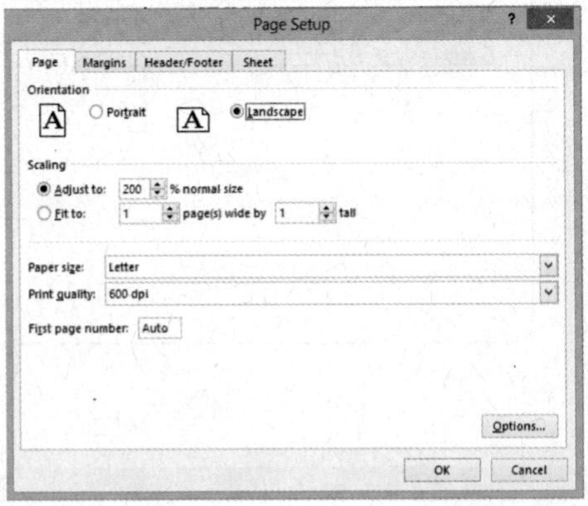

Figure 3-19

Page Setup dialog box

How do you set print scaling to make the entire document larger?

7. Click the **Sheet** tab and in the Print section, select the **Gridlines** box.

8. Click **OK** to return to Backstage view. Notice that the bottom of the screen still says, *1 of 1*, meaning that only one page will print and notice that Print Preview shows larger text with boxes around each cell (see Figure 3-20).

Figure 3-20

Final view of HR-P1 before printing

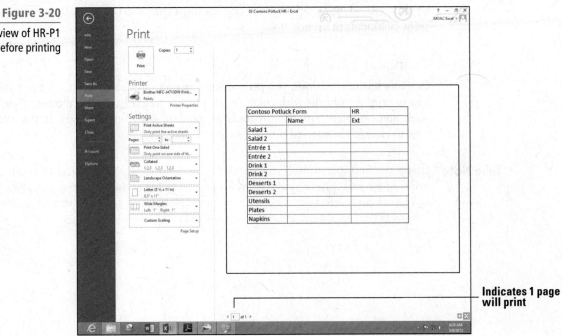

Indicates 1 page will print

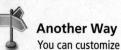

Another Way
You can customize the workbook settings and options from the PAGE LAYOUT tab in the Page Setup, Scale to Fit, and Sheet Options groups.

9. Without printing the document, click the Return to document button and then click the HR-P2 worksheet.

10. Press Ctrl + P to go to the Print tab of the Backstage view and notice that the bottom of the screen indicates that the document will print on two pages.

11. Change the Settings to print Landscape, to Fit Sheet on One Page, and add gridlines based on the previous steps in this section. Print Preview should look like Figure 3-21.

Figure 3-21

Final view of HR-P2 before printing

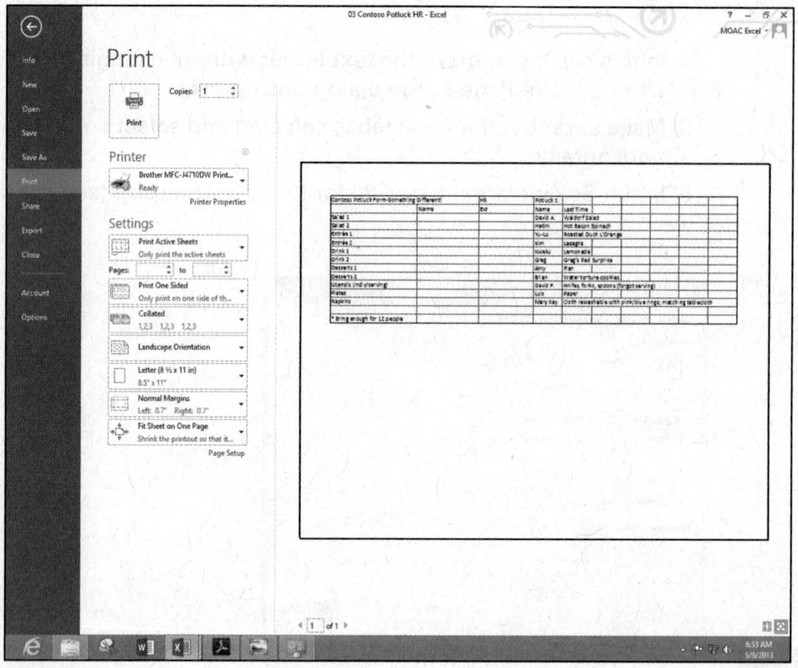

How do you apply printing options?

12. SAVE the workbook in your Lesson 3 folder as *03 Contoso Potluck HR Print Ready Solution*.

PAUSE. LEAVE the workbook open for the next exercise.

Cross Ref   See Lesson 7 for additional options for preparing a document for printing, including options for page breaks, margins, orientation, and scaling a worksheet to print on a page. See Lesson 11 to print comments in a workbook.

Changing a Printer

In many business settings, you print documents on multiple printers. Some of the printers allow you to print documents with color. Other printers might have special options such as large paper sizes. Some printers print quickly for large standard jobs of many pages. In this exercise, you learn how to change the selected printer using Backstage view.

Take Note   If you use multiple printers in your office, make sure you understand the costs associated with printing for each printer; some printers can print for around a penny per page, whereas others can be almost a dollar per page. Other Print options allow you to send a document by e-mail (see Lesson 11) or to a shared location (see Lesson 1).

STEP BY STEP   **Change a Printer**

GET READY. Continue with the previous workbook or if necessary, open *03 Contoso Potluck HR Print Ready Solution.*

1. Press **Ctrl + P** to display the Print tab of the Backstage view.

2. Your current default printer is displayed in the Printer options section of the Print tab. Click the **Printer drop-down arrow** to produce a menu of installed printers, similar to the one shown in Figure 3-22. Your printers will be either Ready or Offline.

Figure 3-22

Choosing a printer

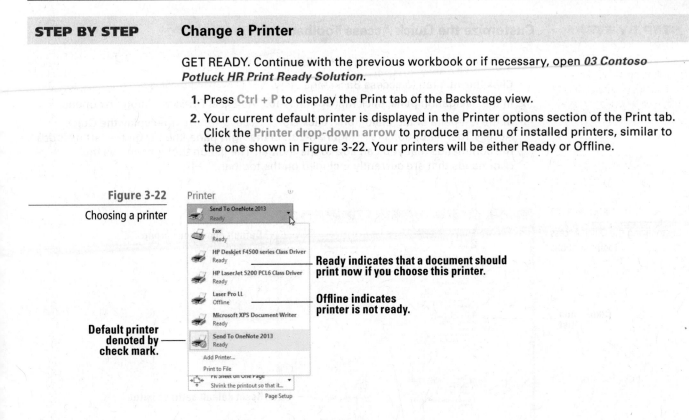

3. Click on a printer (other than your default printer) in the printer list. This printer should now be visible as your active printer. Should you attempt to print at this time with an inactive printer, you will get an error.

4. Once again, click the **Printer drop-down arrow**, and select your default printer (the one with the checkmark).

PAUSE. CLOSE your workbook and don't save if prompted.

Troubleshooting   To change a default printer in Windows 8, click the Start button, type devices and printers, click Settings, click Change Devices and Printers, right-click your printer, and select Set as default printer.

CHANGING THE EXCEL ENVIRONMENT

Bottom Line

Backstage view also offers a number of commands and options for changing the Excel work environment. In this section, you learn to manipulate various elements of the Excel environment, such as the ribbon, Quick Access Toolbar, Excel default settings, and workbook properties. **Default settings** are pre-set options that determine how Excel will behave when performing an action. For example, a default printer is the one your documents always print to unless you change the setting. By default, there is one worksheet in a workbook and the font is 11 points—but you can change those settings too.

Customizing the Quick Access Toolbar

You can't change the size of the Quick Access Toolbar, but you can customize it by adding and removing command buttons. In this exercise, you customize the Quick Access Toolbar by adding commands for functions you use most frequently in Excel, and by organizing the command buttons on the toolbar to best suit your working needs and style.

Take Note   After you change the Excel environment in these exercises, you return it to the defaults in the Resetting Default Settings, the Ribbon, and Quick Access Toolbar exercise.

STEP BY STEP   **Customize the Quick Access Toolbar**

GET READY. OPEN a blank workbook in Excel.

1. Click the FILE tab to access Backstage view.

2. In the navigation pane, click the Options tab. The Excel Options dialog box opens.

3. In the left pane of the dialog box, click Quick Access Toolbar to display the Quick Access Toolbar options (see Figure 3-23). In the right pane, the list on the left includes the commands that you can add to the toolbar. The list on the right shows the commands that are currently included on the toolbar.

Figure 3-23

Customizing the Quick Access Toolbar options

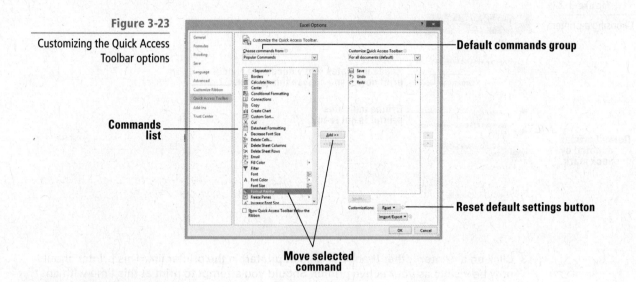

Commands list

Move selected command

Default commands group

Reset default settings button

CERTIFICATION READY?   1.4.3

How do you customize the Quick Access Toolbar?

4. In the list on the left, scroll down and click Format Painter, and then click the Add button in the center of the two lists to add the Format Painter to the Quick Access Toolbar.

5. Using the same process, move five more commands you use often to the Quick Access Toolbar. When you are done, click OK to apply your changes (the changes don't take effect until you click OK).

6. Your Quick Access Toolbar should now include additional command buttons, much like the example shown in Figure 3-24. Similarly, you can remove any command that you added to the toolbar. At any time, you can reset the toolbar to its default settings. See the Reset button in Figure 3-23.

Figure 3-24

Customized Quick Access Toolbar

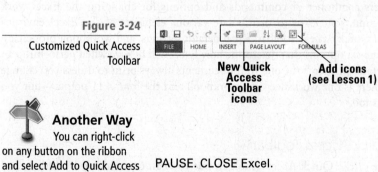

New Quick Access Toolbar icons

Add icons (see Lesson 1)

Another Way
You can right-click on any button on the ribbon and select Add to Quick Access Toolbar to instantly add it to the Quick Access Toolbar.

PAUSE. CLOSE Excel.

Customizing the Ribbon

As mentioned in Lesson 1, the ribbon is a visual interface that allows you to manipulate items on your worksheet. You can add a new ribbon tab, add a group on any ribbon tab, and add commands within a group. A **group** of commands on the default ribbon tabs are related in functionality. For example, on the HOME tab, the Font group allows you to change the font, font size, add bold, italic, or underline, or change the color of the cell or font. The Excel Options dialog box also offers selections for customizing the ribbon. You can add and remove commands, and you can change the location of ribbon commands to make accessing those you use most frequently more convenient. In this exercise, you use the commands in the Excel Options dialog box to create a new tab and command group to contain your frequently used commands.

STEP BY STEP   **Customize the Ribbon**

GET READY. OPEN a blank workbook in Excel.

1. Click the FILE tab to open Backstage view.

2. Click the Options tab.

3. In the Excel Options dialog box, click Customize Ribbon. The Customize the Ribbon options appear (see Figure 3-25). By default, Popular Commands is selected in the Choose Commands From drop-down box. The list of Popular Commands appears in the list below the drop-down box. Also, by default, the Main Tabs option appears in the Customize the Ribbon box on the right, with the ribbon's main tabs listed below.

Figure 3-25

Customize Ribbon options

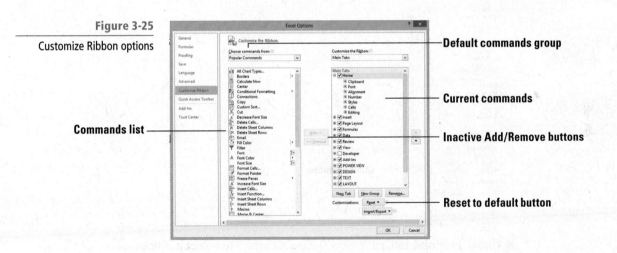

4. In the list of Popular Commands, click Format Painter. Note the Add button in the center of the dialog box is now active.

5. In the Customize the Ribbon list on the right, click the + preceding Home to expand the list of command groups within the Home tab if it isn't already expanded. You can use this method to display the current groups available on a ribbon tab.

6. Under the Customize the Ribbon options, click the New Tab button (see Figure 3-26) to insert a new blank tab into the Customize the Ribbon list. When you create a New Tab, New Group is automatically created inside that New Tab.

Figure 3-26

Customize the ribbon

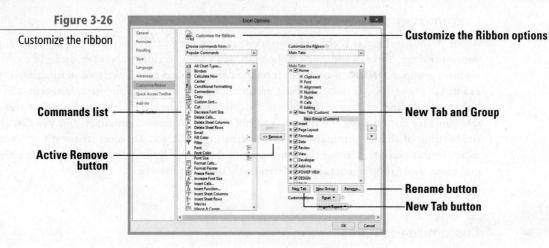

Commands list

Active Remove button

Customize the Ribbon options

New Tab and Group

Rename button

New Tab button

7. Click the New Tab (Custom) list item on the right to select it, and then click the Rename button. In the Rename dialog box that appears, type My New Tab (see Figure 3-27), and then click OK.

Figure 3-27

Rename dialog box and tab to be renamed

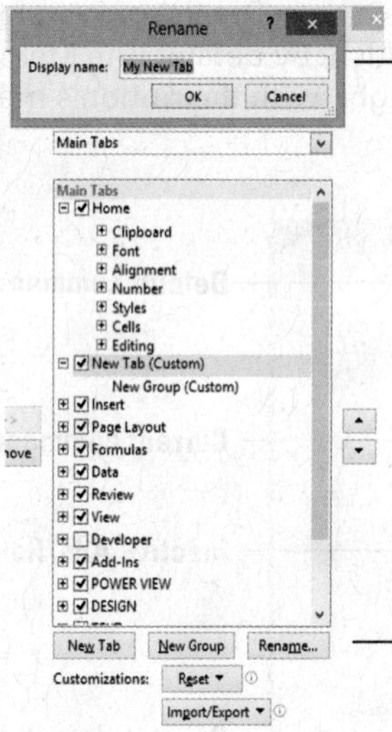

Rename dialog box

Click Rename.

8. Under your new tab, click New Group (Custom) to select it. Click the Rename button again. This time, the Rename dialog box allows you to select a symbol (see Figure 3-28). Select the hand symbol. In the Display name box, type My New Group, and then click OK. You see the New Group renamed.

Figure 3-28

Rename group dialog box

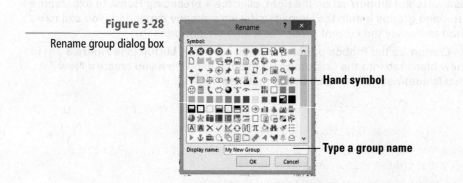

Hand symbol

Type a group name

9. In the Customize the Ribbon list on the right, click the My New Group list item. In the command list on the left, click on a command of your choice, and then click the Add button. The command appears on your new ribbon tab. In the *Choose commands from* list, select All Commands and then add another command from this list. In the Choose commands from list, select File Tab and then add another command. Your screen should look similar to Figure 3-29.

Figure 3-29

Added commands

Customize Ribbon option highlighted

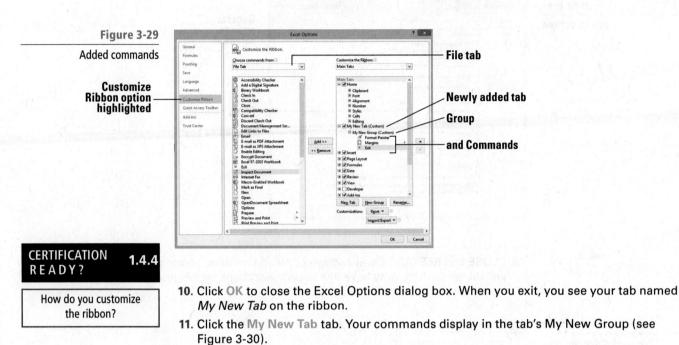

- File tab
- Newly added tab
- Group
- and Commands

10. Click OK to close the Excel Options dialog box. When you exit, you see your tab named *My New Tab* on the ribbon.
11. Click the My New Tab tab. Your commands display in the tab's My New Group (see Figure 3-30).

Figure 3-30

New tab and group on the ribbon

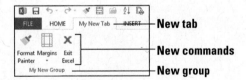

- New tab
- New commands
- New group

PAUSE. LEAVE the workbook open for the next exercise.

Customizing the Excel Default Settings

The Excel Options dialog box commands also enable you to modify the default settings in Excel. These defaults can include worksheet properties, printer settings, font style and size, and much more. By default, for example, Excel 2013 opens with one worksheet displayed in a new workbook and a default font size of 11pt. In this exercise, you change Excel's default settings using Backstage view.

STEP BY STEP   **Customize the Excel Default Settings**

GET READY. Continue with a blank workbook from the previous exercise.

1. Click the FILE tab to open Backstage view.
2. In the navigation pane, click Options. By default, the Excel Options dialog box opens with the General options displayed.
3. In the When creating new workbooks section, click in the Include this many sheets text box and type 5 to change the number of worksheets that appear by default in new workbooks.

Cross Ref

To insert or delete worksheets in one workbook, see "Organizing Worksheets" in Lesson 8.

4. In the Personalize your copy of Microsoft Office section, click the User name box and type [your first and last name] in the text box (see Figure 3-31). Click OK.

Figure 3-31

General options

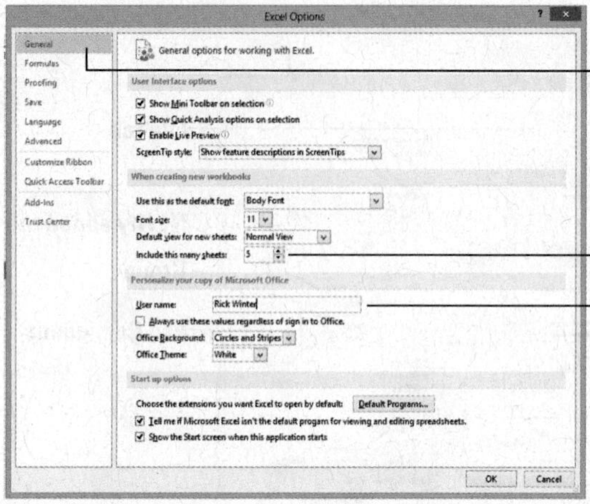

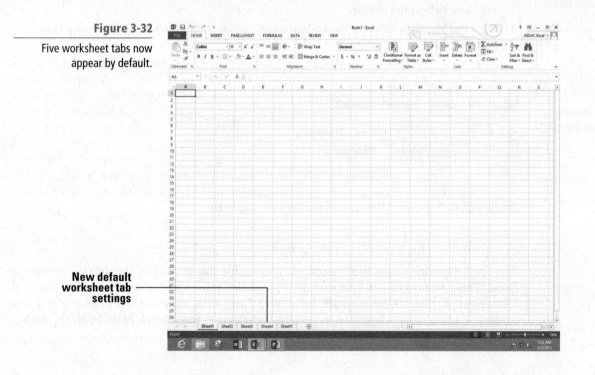

General options selected

Sheet settings

User name box

5. CLOSE and RESTART Excel and select Blank workbook. Note that instead of one worksheet tab, you now have five in your workbook (see Figure 3-32).

Figure 3-32

Five worksheet tabs now appear by default.

New default worksheet tab settings

PAUSE. LEAVE the workbook open for the next exercise.

Resetting Default Settings, the Ribbon, and Quick Access Toolbar

You should give some thought about how to be the most productive with Excel. Because this lesson shows you examples of how to change settings, you will want to return your settings to their normal state until you are ready to make changes.

STEP BY STEP   **Reset Default Settings, the Ribbon, and Quick Access Toolbar**

GET READY. Continue with a blank workbook from the previous exercise.

1. Click the FILE tab, and click Options.
2. On the General tab, in the When creating new workbooks section, in the Include this many sheets box, type 1.
3. Click the Customize Ribbon tab.
4. In the bottom right of the dialog box, click the Reset button, and then click Reset all customizations.
5. In the Confirmation dialog box, click Yes to clear all ribbon and Quick Access Toolbar customizations for this program.
6. Click OK to return to the workbook.

Take Note   The ribbon and Quick Access Toolbar changes are immediate, but you need to open a new, blank workbook to notice the change for the number of displayed workbooks.

PAUSE. LEAVE the workbook open for the next exercise.

ACCESSING AND USING EXCEL TEMPLATES

Bottom Line

Excel has several templates that are available when you start Excel or when you click the FILE tab and select New, and many more templates for which you can search. **Templates** are files that already include formatting and formulas complete with designs, tools, and specific data types. This exercise familiarizes you with where the templates are located and how to select and use them.

Selecting a Template from the New Tab

Templates allow you to create professional workbooks in a fraction of the time it would take you to develop them from scratch. Examples of these are budgets, loan models, invoices, calendars, and so on.

STEP BY STEP   **Select a Template from the New Tab**

CERTIFICATION READY?   1.1.2

How do you create a new workbook using a template?

GET READY. If necessary, OPEN a blank workbook.

1. Click the FILE tab and click New. The New window displays as shown in Figure 3-33, with a series of featured templates. You already used the Blank workbook template in this book.

Figure 3-33

Templates available in the New window

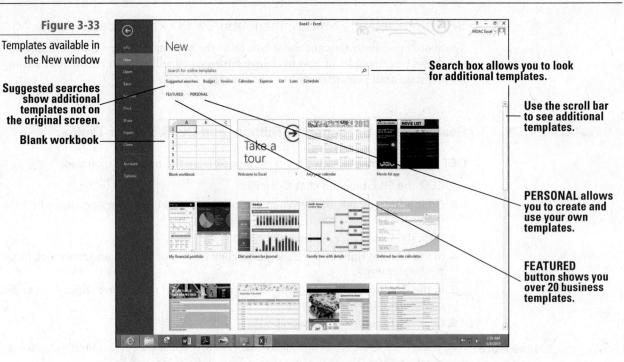

Suggested searches show additional templates not on the original screen.

Blank workbook

Search box allows you to look for additional templates.

Use the scroll bar to see additional templates.

PERSONAL allows you to create and use your own templates.

FEATURED button shows you over 20 business templates.

Cross Ref

In Lesson 2, the section, "Save a Workbook Under a Different Name," demonstrates how to save one of the workbooks as a template. If you completed this exercise, this template is shown by clicking on the PERSONAL screen. (Click FEATURED to return to Excel's templates.) To save any workbook as a template, go to the Save As dialog box (press F12) and change the Save as type setting to Excel Template.

2. Scroll down if necessary, and click the **Project Tracker** icon. Figure 3-34 shows a larger window with a larger picture and description of the template.

Troubleshooting

In some cases you will need to search for a template if it doesn't appear by default. If you can't find the Project Tracker template, type it in the Search box.

Figure 3-34

Project Tracker template preview

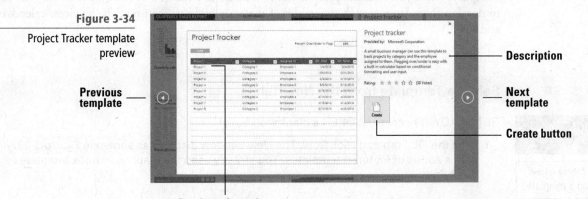

Previous template

Preview of template

Description

Next template

Create button

3. Click the **Create** button. Excel might take a moment to download the workbook.

4. Notice that there are two worksheets in this workbook: Project Tracker with the sample data you can change and Setup that allows you to input a list of categories and

employees. When you are finished looking at this template, click FILE and click Close. If prompted, do not save changes.

5. Click the FILE tab, click New.

6. Look for *Any year calendar* template and click the Create button..

7. Click on the year and use the up or down arrow to change to the current year if necessary.

8. Print the worksheet and put on your wall, if desired.

9. SAVE the workbook in your Lesson 3 folder as *03 My Calendar Solution*.

10. Click the FILE tab and click New. Notice that the *Any year calendar* template appears as the third item on your list of templates because it was recently used.

PAUSE. CLOSE the workbook and LEAVE Excel open for the next exercise.

Take Note   You can modify this new workbook with your name, company name, and favorite pictures to personalize your calendar and make it your own or use as a gift for others.

Searching for Additional Templates

There are thousands of online templates available to you, many more than are on the original New window.

STEP BY STEP   **Search for Additional Templates**

GET READY. If necessary, OPEN a blank workbook.

1. Click the FILE tab and click New. Notice the Suggested searches and Search for online templates box.

2. Click Budget on the Suggested searches row. As shown in Figure 3-35, the New window changes to show templates specifically related to working with budgets.

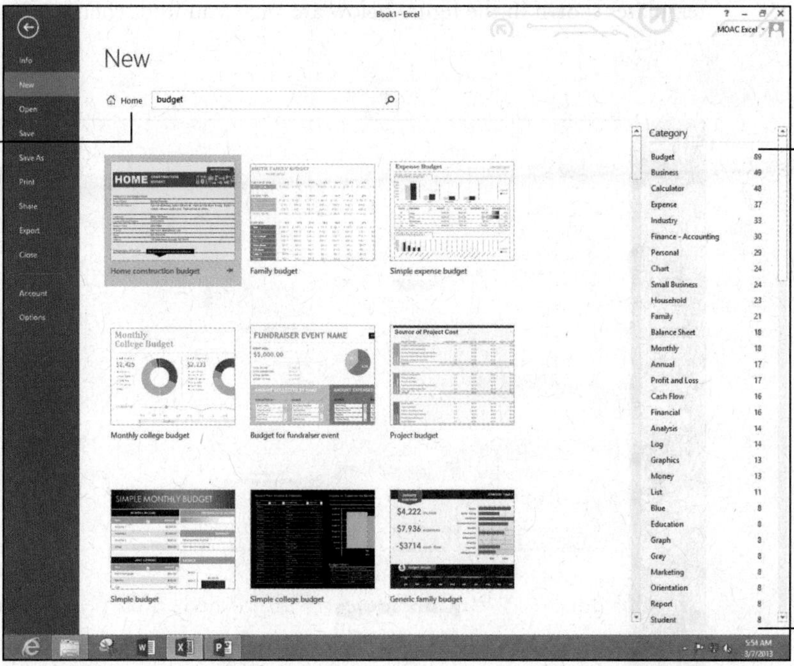

Figure 3-35

Budget templates

Home button returns to the original New window

Categories of templates

3. Scroll to the bottom of the window and click on a few templates to see their descriptions.

4. Scroll back to the top of the New window and click Home to return to the original templates screen.

5. In the Suggested searches row, click Calendars.

6. In the Category pane to the right, click Student.

7. Scroll to the Student assignment planner , click it, and read the description. Close the template description window.

8. In the Search box, type College and press Enter. Scroll through the list of suggested templates for college students and open the Weekly college schedule template.

9. In cell B1, type in [Monday's date], and then review the workbook.

10. SAVE the workbook in your Lesson 3 folder as *03 My Weekly Schedule Solution*. Click Yes when prompted to save this as a macro-free workbook.

Cross Ref   Macros allow you to automate your tasks. Some templates come with macros to make your work even quicker. Macros are discussed in Lesson 9, "Saving Work with Macros."

PAUSE. CLOSE Excel.

Workplace *Ready*

JOB INTERVIEW HINT

If Excel is a requirement for a job you are interviewing for, you can search for relevant templates. Open those that seem applicable to the job and study the important details for terms, how the office might be organized, and for some potential follow-up questions. Depending on your perceptions of the first interview, for the second interview you might print out two or three templates and ask if the office uses something similar to these documents. For example, if you are applying for a job in a doctor's office, medical supply warehouse, or pharmaceutical company, some of the templates shown in the figure below are what you find when you search for medical templates.

If you enjoy Excel, you might even use the templates for brainstorming related job opportunities that use Excel. For example in the figure, you can see that medical templates also relate to Youth sports (school or after-school activities), Babysitter checklists (part-time work while job searching or create your own business), and Fitness progress trackers (personal trainer, gyms, and recreation centers).

SKILL SUMMARY

In this lesson you learned how:	Exam Objective	Objective Number
To access and use Backstage View		
To print with Backstage	Set a print area.	1.5.1
	Print individual worksheets.	1.5.3
	Set print scaling.	1.5.4
	Configure workbooks to print.	1.5.7
To change the Excel environment	Customize the Quick Access Toolbar.	1.4.3
	Customize the ribbon.	1.4.4
To access and use Excel templates	Create new workbooks using templates.	1.1.2

Knowledge Assessment

Multiple Choice

Select the best response for the following statements.

1. Which of the following is where you can save, select a template, change document properties, and close or exit Excel?
   a. Backstage
   b. Print
   c. Edit
   d. Windows

2. To change printer, layout, or margin settings, you click the FILE tab and use which of the following options?
   a. Info
   b. Options
   c. Print
   d. Open

3. Which of the following can you customize for quicker access to the most commonly used commands?
   a. Print Preview
   b. Quick Access Toolbar
   c. Printer setup
   d. Workbook

4. Which feature enables you to create custom tabs and groups?
   a. ribbon
   b. Quick Access Toolbar
   c. view
   d. Tab

5. Which command in the Backstage view navigation pane enables you to view and open your most recently used workbooks or workbooks stored on SkyDrive or your computer?
   a. Info
   b. Options
   c. Print
   d. Open

6. Which dialog box in Backstage view should you access to view and alter your workbook's properties?
   a. Info
   b. Options
   c. Print
   d. Open

7. When you modify the ribbon, which of the following do you create?
   a. command
   b. tab
   c. button
   d. worksheet

8. Which of the following do you use to open Backstage view?
   a. Backstage menu
   b. FILE tab
   c. INSERT tab
   d. WORKBOOK tab

9. Which of the following do you click in the navigation pane to change Excel's default settings by accessing Backstage view?
   a. Info
   b. Options
   c. Print
   d. Open

10. What predesigned file already has a significant amount of formatting, text, and other features?
    a. Blank workbook
    b. Preset file
    c. Text file
    d. Template

True/False

Circle T if the statement is true or F if the statement is false.

T F 1. You do not have the ability to modify the number of default worksheets in a workbook.

T F 2. The Open dialog box enables you to access the Microsoft website for custom templates.

T F 3. Use Ctrl + N to create a new workbook.

T F 4. To access an Excel template, you can click the FILE tab and click New.

T F 5. You cannot have more than one worksheet in an Excel workbook.

T F 6. If you have too many columns on a page, the only option to see them all on a printed page is to decrease the column width.

T F 7. You can access Backstage view by pressing Ctrl + B.

T F 8. By default, Excel starts a new workbook with four worksheets.

T F 9. In Excel, you can add your most commonly used commands to the Quick Access Toolbar.

T F 10. You can create a completely new ribbon tab as well as groups on that ribbon.

Competency Assessment

Project 3-1: Search and Use a Template

In this project, you find a template for movies and add your own movie.

GET READY. LAUNCH Excel if it is not already running.

1. From Backstage view, click New and search for the movie list template.
2. Click the Create button.
3. Add an additional movie to the list.
4. SAVE the workbook as *03 My Movies Solution* and then close the file.

LEAVE Excel open for the next project.

Project 3-2: Print a Specific Area or Worksheet

You print a selected area in the worksheet and a specific worksheet.

GET READY. OPEN the file from the Lesson 3 folder titled *03 My Movies Solution*.

1. Select the range D5:L9.
2. OPEN Backstage view.
3. Click Print in the Backstage view navigation pane.
4. In the Settings section of the Print window, click the Print Active Sheets drop-down arrow, and click the Print Selection option in the drop-down menu.
5. Click the Print button to print the selected area of the worksheet.
6. From Backstage view, click lick the Print tab to return to the Settings options, open the Print Selection drop-down menu, and click Print Active Sheets.
7. Click the Print button to print the active worksheet.
8. CLOSE the workbook.

LEAVE Excel open for the next project.

Proficiency Assessment

Project 3-3: Change the Quick Access Toolbar

You customize the Quick Access Toolbar to add commands for users who are not familiar with Excel and the ribbon.

GET READY. LAUNCH Excel if it is not already running.

1. OPEN Backstage view. Click the Options tab.
2. In the left pane of the Excel Options dialog box, click Quick Access Toolbar.
3. In the Popular Commands list, add the Center button to the Quick Access Toolbar.
4. Repeating these steps as necessary, using the appropriate categories, add the following commands to the toolbar: Borders, Increase Indent, Copy, Cut, and Paste. Click OK. Note the changes to the toolbar in the upper-left portion of the screen.

LEAVE Excel open for the next project.

Project 3-4: Access a Template

You are in need of an invoice template for a client.

GET READY. LAUNCH Excel if it is not already running.

1. Click FILE to access Backstage view.
2. Click New.
3. On the Suggested searches row, click Invoice. If you are without an Internet connection, this process will not work.
4. Browse the results for invoices in the New window.
5. Click a template to preview it and read the description. Click the Create button.
6. After the download is complete, Excel automatically opens the template for you. Make note of what features the invoice you chose has to offer. Make changes to the template to see changes and actions.
7. SAVE the invoice as *03 My Invoice Solution*.

LEAVE Excel open for the next project.

Mastery Assessment

Project 3-5: Manage a Custom Ribbon

In order for your client to use and maintain the invoice you downloaded in the previous exercise, he has requested that you customize several tabs on the ribbon to make the worksheet easier to manage and edit.

GET READY. LAUNCH Excel if it is not already running.

1. OPEN *03 My Invoice Solution* from the Lesson 3 folder, if necessary.
2. OPEN Backstage view, and click Options.
3. In the Excel Options dialog box, click the Customize Ribbon tab.
4. Click the Reset button at the bottom right of the window and click Reset all customizations. When prompted to delete all customizations, click Yes.
5. Create a new tab named Invoice Edits.
6. Rename the new command group in Invoice Edits to Invoice Tools.
7. Select five commands to add to the Invoice Tools command group.
8. Create another new tab named My Edits.
9. Rename the new command group in My Edits to My Tools.
10. Add five commands to the My Tools command group.
11. Click OK.
12. Examine your changes to the ribbon.
13. OPEN Backstage view and click Options. Undo all the changes you just made to the ribbon. When prompted to delete all customizations, click Yes.

LEAVE Excel open for the next project.

Project 3-6: Create a List of the Five Templates You Most Likely Will Use

Because templates can make you look good in your current or a potential job, it's a good idea to explore them in more depth here and figure out which ones you will mostly likely use.

GET READY. LAUNCH Excel if it is not already running.

1. In a blank workbook, in cell A1, type Potential Templates.
2. In A2, type Template.
3. In B2, type Location.
4. In C2, type Priority (1=High, 5=Low).
5. Click the FILE tab and click the New tab. Navigate through the list of templates on the screen, the menu for the suggested templates, and the search box to select five templates.
6. Fill out rows 3 through 7 with templates you plan on using later.
7. Format the worksheet so you can read all text. An example of what your workbook should look like is shown in Figure 3-36. Do not use the same examples.

Figure 3-36

An example of a favorite templates list

	A	B	C
1	Potential Templates		
2	Template	Location	Priority (1=High, 5=Low)
3	Family Budget	Budgets	1
4	Personal Address Book	New	3
5	Loan Calculator	Loans	2
6	College Move Checklist	Search: College	3
7	Daily Work Schedule	Schedule	1
8			

8. SAVE the workbook as *03 My Favorite Templates Solution*.

CLOSE Excel.

4 Using Basic Formulas

LESSON SKILL MATRIX

Skills	Exam Objective	Objective Number
Understanding and Displaying Formulas	Display formulas.	1.4.10
Understanding Order of Operations	Define order of operations.	4.1.2
Building Basic Formulas		
Using Cell References in Formulas	Demonstrate how to use references (relative, mixed, absolute).	4.1.1
Using Cell Ranges in Formulas	Create named ranges.	2.3.4
	Reference cell ranges in formulas.	4.1.3

KEY TERMS

- absolute cell reference
- calculation operator
- cell reference
- constant
- external reference
- formula
- mixed cell reference
- named range
- nested parentheses
- operand
- order of operations
- relative cell reference
- scope
- value
- variable

© matthewwennisphotography / iStock photo

© matthewwennisphotography / iStock photo

When moving to a new rental home, you might need to make some up-front purchases for the new place, such as curtains, storage containers, and a few pieces of furniture. In addition, you have to pay rent each month, which generally is the same amount from one month to another (a recurring expense). Other monthly expenses change depending on usage and seasonal variations, such as electricity, water, and similar services. You can use Excel to track and budget for all of these expenses. In this lesson, you learn about the fundamentals of formulas and the order of operations. You then work on a simple household expenses worksheet, using simple formulas to summarize information from the data in the worksheet. Along the way, you find out how to make any worksheet more flexible by using cell references in formulas and naming cell ranges.

SOFTWARE ORIENTATION

Excel enables you to create many formulas by simply typing in a cell or using your mouse pointer to select cells to include in a formula. For example, you can create basic formulas for addition, subtraction, multiplication, and division using these methods. However, as you have discovered in previous lessons, the user interface offers tools that make it easier to work with data. In this lesson, you use a few command groups on the FORMULAS tab to display formulas and name ranges to be used in formulas.

Use Figure 4-1 as a reference throughout this lesson as you become familiar with some of the command groups on the FORMULAS tab and use them to work with formulas. You learn more about commands on the FORMULAS tab in the next lesson, which addresses functions.

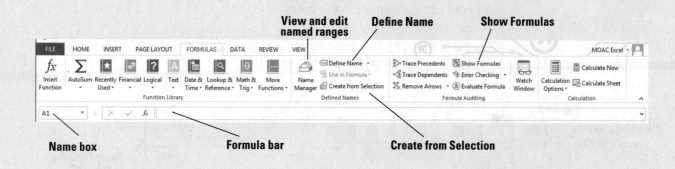

Figure 4-1

The FORMULAS tab in Excel 2013

UNDERSTANDING AND DISPLAYING FORMULAS

Bottom Line

The real strength of Excel is its capability to perform common and complex calculations. The formula is one of the essential elements of Excel, which enables you to add, subtract, multiply, and divide numbers. When you enter a formula in a cell, the formula is stored internally and the results are displayed in the cell. You can view the underlying formula in the formula bar when the cell is active, when you double-click the cell to edit it, and by using the FORMULAS tab.

STEP BY STEP   **Display Formulas**

GET READY. Before you begin these steps, LAUNCH Microsoft Excel and OPEN a new blank workbook.

1. Click cell **A1**.
2. Type =7+8*3/2-4 and press **Enter**. You just entered a formula.

Take Note   Formulas should be typed without spaces, but if you type spaces, Excel eliminates them when you press Enter.

3. Click cell **A1**. Notice that the result of the formula displays in the cell, but the formula itself appears in the formula bar (see Figure 4-2).

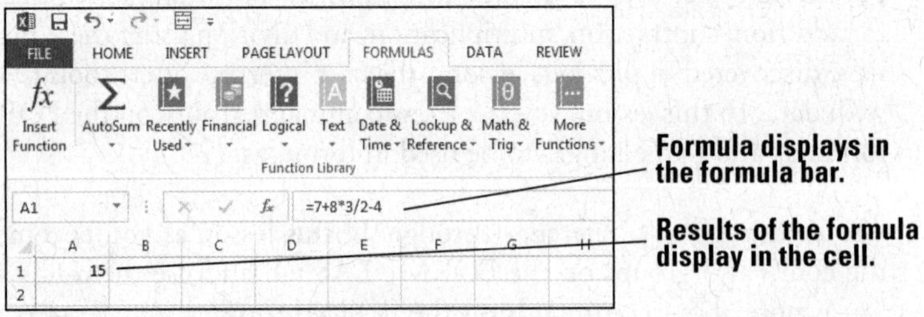

Figure 4-2

Viewing a formula in the formula bar

Formula displays in the formula bar.

Results of the formula display in the cell.

4. Double-click cell **A1**. The formula appears in both the active cell and the formula bar. You can edit the formula in this mode.
5. Press **Enter**.
6. On the FORMULAS tab, in the Formula Auditing group, click **Show Formulas**. The formula in cell A1 displays (see Figure 4-3).

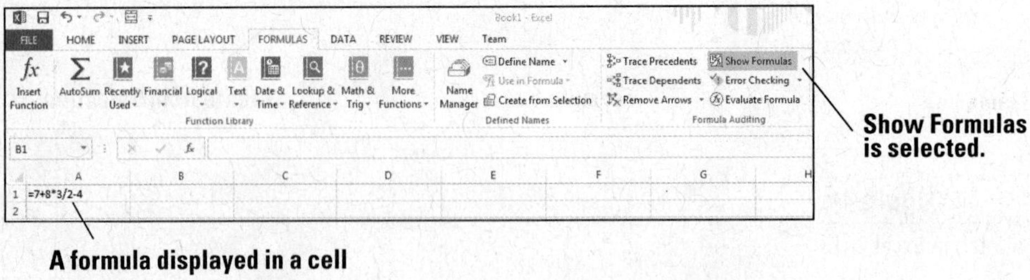

Figure 4-3

Displaying a formula using the Show Formulas command

Show Formulas is selected.

A formula displayed in a cell

Take Note   While you are displaying formulas, you will not see the results of those formulas.

7. Click **Show Formulas** again to turn off formula display.
8. SAVE the workbook in your Lesson 4 folder as *04 Formula Practice Solution*.

PAUSE. LEAVE the workbook open to use in the next exercise.

CERTIFICATION READY?   1.4.10

How do you display a formula in Excel?

A **formula** is an equation that performs calculations, such as addition, subtraction, multiplication, and division, on values in a worksheet. In Excel, a **value** can be a number, a cell address, a date, text, or Boolean data, but is usually a number or cell address in terms of formulas. A formula consists of two elements: operands and calculation operators. **Operands** identify the values to be used in the calculation. An operand can be a constant value, or a variable such as a cell reference, a range of cells, or another formula. A **constant** is a number or text value that is entered directly into a formula. A **variable** is a symbol or name that represents something else, which can be a cell address, a range of cells, and so on. **Calculation operators** specify the calculations to be performed. To allow Excel to distinguish formulas from data, all formulas begin with an equal sign (=).

Take Note   You can begin a formula with a plus (+) sign or a minus (–) sign as the beginning calculation operator, but Excel changes it to an equal sign when you press Enter. Excel doesn't recognize a construct like 3+4= as a legitimate formula. Excel treats it like an ordinary string of characters.

Excel uses four types of calculation operators: arithmetic, comparison, text concatenation, and reference. This lesson covers several arithmetic operators and the equal sign, which is a comparison operator. The arithmetic operators are listed in Table 4-1.

Table 4-1

Excel Arithmetic Operators

Arithmetic Operator	Name	Calculation	Example
+	Plus sign	Addition	5+2
–	Minus sign	Subtraction	5–2
		Negation	–5
*	Asterisk	Multiplication	5*2
/	Forward slash	Division	5/2
%	Percent sign	Percent	20%
^	Caret	Exponentiation	5^2

When you build a formula, it appears in the formula bar and in the cell itself. When you complete the formula and press Enter, the value displays in the cell and the formula displays in the formula bar if you select the cell. You can edit a formula in the cell or in the formula bar the same way you can edit any data entry.

When you click the Show Formulas button on the FORMULAS tab, all formulas in your worksheet display. Click the Show Formulas button again to toggle off display of formulas.

UNDERSTANDING ORDER OF OPERATIONS

Bottom Line   If you use more than one operator in a formula, Excel follows a specific order—called the **order of operations**—to calculate the formula. Parentheses play an important role in controlling the order of operations.

STEP BY STEP   **Understand Order of Operations**

GET READY. USE the worksheet from the previous exercise.

1. Click cell A1 to make it the active cell.
2. Click in the formula bar.
3. Insert parentheses around 7 + 8.

4. Insert parentheses around 3 / 2.

5. Insert parentheses around (7 + 8) * (3 / 2), as shown in the formula bar in Figure 4-4. Press Enter. The result in A1 changes to *18.5*.

Figure 4-4

Parentheses added to the formula

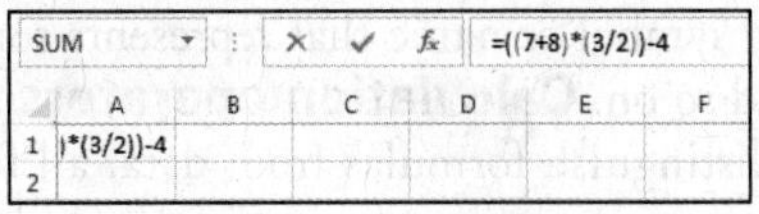

6. SAVE the workbook in your Lesson 4 folder as *04 Order of Operations Solution* and CLOSE it.

PAUSE. LEAVE Excel open to use in the next exercise.

Excel applies the rules of mathematics to determine how formulas are calculated. The following is the order in which arithmetic operators are applied:

• Negative number (–)

• Percent (%)

• Exponentiation (^)

• Multiplication (*) and division (/) (left to right)

• Addition (+) and subtraction (–) (left to right)

For example, consider the original equation:

7 + 8 * 3 / 2 – 4 = 15

CERTIFICATION
READY?   **4.1.2**

How do you determine
the order of operations for
arithmetic operators in an
Excel formula?

Following arithmetic operator priorities, the first operation is 8 multiplied by 3 and that result is divided by 2. Then 7 is added and 4 is subtracted.

You can use parentheses in a formula to override the standard order of operations. Excel performs calculations on formulas inside parentheses first. Parentheses inside of parentheses are called **nested parentheses**. Calculations are performed on formulas in the innermost set of parentheses first, and from left to right if nested parentheses are at the same level. Therefore, the result of the following equation with parentheses is different from the previous one:

((7 + 8) * (3 / 2)) – 4 = 18.5

Following arithmetic operator priorities, the first operation is the sum of 7 + 8 multiplied by the quotient of 3 divided by 2. Then, 4 is subtracted.

Troubleshooting While modifying a complex formula, if you decide to revert back to the original formula and start over, just press Esc. If you've already pressed Enter, you'll need to click the Undo button on the Quick Access Toolbar.

BUILDING BASIC FORMULAS

Bottom Line You do basic math in your head or using scratch paper every day. Excel is handy for performing basic calculations also. Although you probably won't use Excel to add or subtract a few numbers, it's important to learn how to create simple formulas in Excel, which serve as the building blocks for more complex calculations. This section shows you how to create basic formulas that let you perform addition, subtraction, multiplication, and division.

Creating a Formula that Performs Addition

You can add two or more numbers in Excel using the plus sign between each number. To use proper Excel format, you must include the equal sign at the beginning of the formula.

STEP BY STEP **Create a Formula that Performs Addition**

GET READY. LAUNCH Microsoft Excel if it is not already open.

1. OPEN the *04 Budget Start* data file for this lesson.
2. In cell A18, type January Rent plus Deposit and press Enter.
3. In cell B18, type the equal (=) sign, type 1200+500, and press Enter. This is the simplest way to enter an addition formula. Excel adds the values in the formula and displays the result, *1700*, which is your first month's rent plus a $500 deposit. Your worksheet now looks like that shown in Figure 4-5.

Figure 4-5

The result of an addition formula

	A	B	C	D	E	F	G	H	I	J	K	L	M	N
1	2013 Housing Expenses													
2	Expense Category	Jan	Feb	Mar	Apr	May	June	July	Aug	Sept	Oct	Nov	Dec	Total
3	Rent	1200	1200	1200	1200	1200	1200	1200	1200	1200	1200	1200	1200	14400
4	Renter's Insurance	40	40	40	40	40	40	40	40	40	40	40	40	480
5	Furnishings	500												500
6	Miscellaneous													
7	Utilities													
8	Electricity	180	180	180	150	150	180	220	230	160	150	160	170	2110
9	Gas	120	120	110	90	80	70	70	70	80	90	100	120	1120
10	Water	35	35	35	35	35	35	35	35	35	35	35	35	420
11	Garbage Service	50	50	50	50	50	50	50	50	50	50	50	50	600
12	Phone	50	50	50	50	50	50	50	50	50	50	50	50	600
13	Internet	65	65	65	65	65	65	65	65	65	65	65	65	780
14	Cable TV	135	135	135	135	135	135	135	135	135	135	135	135	1620
15	Monthly Subtotals	2375	1875	1865	1815	1805	1825	1865	1875	1815	1815	1835	1865	
16	Utilities Subtotals	635	635	625	575	565	585	625	635	575	575	595	625	
17														
18	January Rent plus Deposit	1700												

The result of =1200+500

4. SAVE the workbook in your Lesson 4 folder as *04 Budget Basic Formulas Solution*.

PAUSE. LEAVE the workbook open to use in the next exercise.

When entering formulas that perform addition, if a positive number is entered first, it is not necessary to enter a plus sign.

If you make a mistake in your data entry, you can select the cell with the erroneous formula, press F2 to enter cell editing mode, and edit your formula. Once you make your corrections, press Enter to revise.

Creating a Formula that Performs Subtraction

Subtraction works the same way as addition, except that you enter a minus (–) sign rather than a plus (+) sign between the values in the formula.

STEP BY STEP **Create a Formula that Performs Subtraction**

GET READY. USE the worksheet you modified in the previous exercise.

1. Double-click cell A18.
2. Click after the word "Deposit," type , minus Discount, and press Enter.
3. Right-click cell A18, select Format Cells, click the Alignment tab, select the Wrap text check box, and click OK. Now you can see all of the new text added to A18.

Cross Ref You learn about different kinds of formatting techniques in Lesson 6.

4. Click cell B18 to make it the active cell.
5. Click in the formula bar.

6. Position the cursor immediately after =1200+500, type -100, and press Enter. Your landlord gave you a $100 discount for moving into your rental home early, so you are subtracting $100 from your first month's rent. The value in cell B18 changes to *1600* to reflect the new formula (see Figure 4-6).

Figure 4-6

The result of a subtraction formula

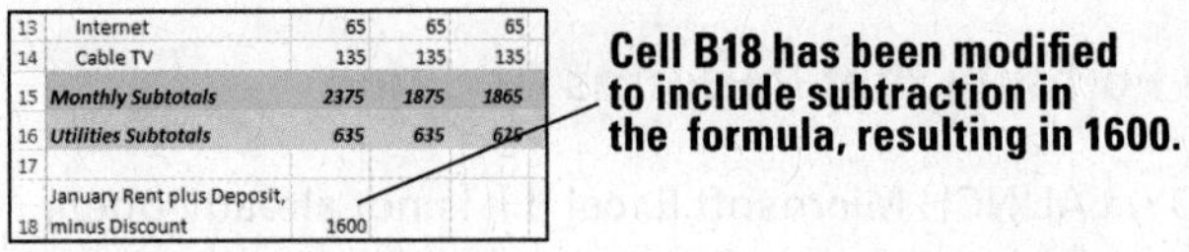

13	Internet	65	65	65
14	Cable TV	135	135	135
15	*Monthly Subtotals*	2375	1875	1865
16	*Utilities Subtotals*	635	635	625
17				
18	January Rent plus Deposit, minus Discount	1600		

Cell B18 has been modified to include subtraction in the formula, resulting in 1600.

7. SAVE the workbook.

PAUSE. LEAVE the workbook open to use in the next exercise.

When you modified the formula to subtract 100 from 1700, you could have entered =1200+500–100 or = –100+1200+500. Either formula yields a positive 1600.

Creating a Formula that Performs Multiplication

Multiplication not only uses the values in cells, but other numbers that you enter. The symbol for multiplication is the asterisk (*).

STEP BY STEP   **Create a Formula that Performs Multiplication**

GET READY. USE the worksheet you modified in the previous exercise.

1. In cell A19, type Annual Rent per Lease and press Enter.
2. In cell B19, type =1200*12 and press Enter. The result displays in cell B19, which is the total amount of rent you will pay in one year (see Figure 4-7).

Figure 4-7

The result of a multiplication formula

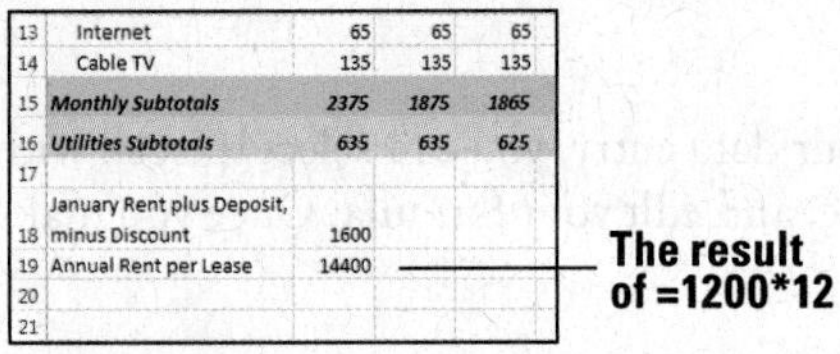

13	Internet	65	65	65
14	Cable TV	135	135	135
15	*Monthly Subtotals*	2375	1875	1865
16	*Utilities Subtotals*	635	635	625
17				
18	January Rent plus Deposit, minus Discount	1600		
19	Annual Rent per Lease	14400		
20				
21				

The result of =1200*12

3. SAVE the workbook.

PAUSE. LEAVE the workbook open to use in the next exercise.

Creating a Formula that Performs Division

Division works the same way as multiplication, except that the symbol for division is the forward slash (/).

STEP BY STEP   **Create a Formula that Performs Division**

GET READY. USE the worksheet you modified in the previous exercise.

1. In cell A20, type Average Electricity and press Enter.
2. In cell B20, type =N8/12 and press Enter. The result displays in cell B20, which is the average monthly amount you will pay for electricity in one year (see Figure 4-8).

Figure 4-8

The result of a division formula

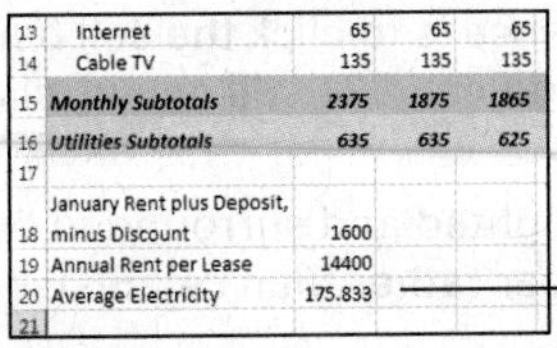

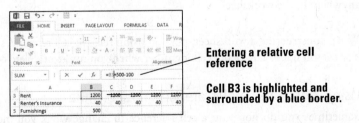

The result of =N8/12

3. SAVE the workbook and CLOSE it.

PAUSE. LEAVE Excel open to use in the next exercise.

USING CELL REFERENCES IN FORMULAS

Bottom Line

As you learned in Lesson 1, "Overview," each cell in an Excel worksheet has a unique identifier indicating its column and row, such as A1 (column A, row 1) or E4 (column E, row 4). When you create a formula, you can reference a cell's identifier rather than typing the number that appears in that cell. A **cell reference** identifies a cell's location in the worksheet, based on its column letter and row number. Using a cell reference rather than the data displayed in a cell gives you more flexibility in your worksheet. If the data in a cell changes, any formulas that reference the cell change as well. For example, if cell E1 contains the number 12 but is later changed to 15, any formula that references cell E1 updates automatically. The same principle applies to a cell that contains a formula and is referenced in another formula.

Using Relative Cell References in a Formula

A **relative cell reference** is one that adjusts the cell identifier automatically if you insert or delete columns or rows, or if you copy the formula to another cell. A relative cell reference is, therefore, one whose references change "relative" to the location where it is copied or moved.

STEP BY STEP   **Use Relative Cell References in a Formula**

GET READY. OPEN the *04 Budget Cell References* data file for this lesson.

1. Click cell B18.
2. Click in the formula bar and replace 1200 with cell B3. Notice that cell B3 is highlighted and surrounded by a blue border while you're modifying the formula (see Figure 4-9).

Figure 4-9

Entering a relative cell reference

Entering a relative cell reference

Cell B3 is highlighted and surrounded by a blue border.

Take Note   You can use either uppercase or lowercase when you type a cell reference in a formula. For example, it does not matter whether you type B4 or b4 in the formula you enter.

3. Press **Enter**. The formula in cell B18 now uses a relative cell reference to cell B3.
4. Copy cell B18 to cell B21. The displayed result changes to *400*.
5. Notice in the formula bar that the formula in cell B21 is =B6+500-100, but the formula you copied is =B3+500-100. That's because the original cell reference of cell B3 changed to cell B6 when you copied the formula down three cells, and cell B6 is blank. The cell reference is adjusted relative to its position in the worksheet.

6. An alternate way to use a cell reference is to click the cell being referenced while creating or modifying a formula. With cell B21 still active, click in the formula bar and select B6.

7. Click cell B3. Cell B3 becomes highlighted and surrounded by a blue dashed border, and cell B3 appears in the formula bar rather than cell B6 (see Figure 4-10). Press Enter.

Figure 4-10

Using the mouse to enter a relative cell reference

Entering a relative cell reference

Cell B3 is highlighted and surrounded by a blue dashed border.

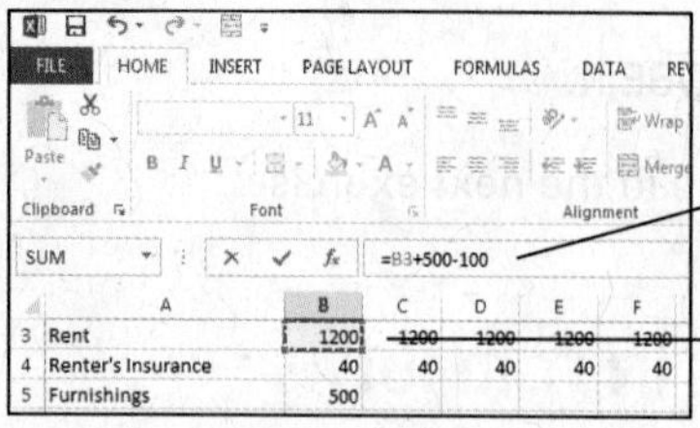

CERTIFICATION READY?   4.1.1

How do you use a relative cell reference in a formula?

---

8. SAVE the workbook in your Lesson 4 folder as *04 Budget Cell References Solution*.

PAUSE. LEAVE the workbook open to use in the next exercise.

You use relative cell references when you want the reference to automatically adjust when you copy or fill the formula across rows or down columns in ranges of cells. By default, new formulas in Excel use relative references.

In this exercise, you learn two methods for creating formulas using relative references:

• By typing the formula directly into the cell

• By clicking a cell to include in the formula rather than typing the cell reference

The second method is usually quicker and eliminates the possibility of typing an incorrect cell identifier, especially if you need to create a formula with many cell references. For example, it might be easy to make a mistake typing =D2+D7+D9+D12+D14 rather than just clicking each cell to add it to the formula.

You can also reference a range of cells in a formula, which you learn about later in this lesson.

Cell referencing raises another important point about Excel. When you perform math on a series of numbers on paper, they're usually right next to each other in a column or a single row. In a worksheet, the numbers don't have to be adjacent: You can create formulas that reference cells anywhere in the worksheet.

Take Note   When constructing a worksheet, plan on using relative cell references unless you know there will be a reason not to adjust the cell identifier when you insert or delete columns and rows.

Using Absolute Cell References in a Formula

Sometimes you do not want a cell reference to change when you move or copy it. To make an absolute cell reference, use the dollar sign ($) before the column and row of the cell you want to reference.

STEP BY STEP   Use an Absolute Cell Reference in a Formula

GET READY. USE the worksheet you modified in the previous exercise.

1. Click cell **B18**.
2. Click in the formula bar and insert dollar signs in the B3 cell reference so it looks like **$B$3**.
3. Press **Enter**. The formula in cell B18 now uses an absolute cell reference to cell B3.
4. Copy cell **B18** to cell **B21**. The displayed result is *1600*, which matches B18.
5. Copy cell **B21** to cell **C21**. The displayed result is still *1600*.
6. Notice in the formula bar that the formulas in cells B21 and C21 are both =$B$3+500-100. Figure 4-11 shows the formula for cell C21. Regardless of where you copy the formula in the worksheet, the formula still refers to cell B3.

Figure 4-11

An absolute cell reference

C21			✗ ✓	f_x	=$B$3+500-100		An absolute cell reference contains dollar signs.

	A	B	C	D	E
2	Expense Category	Jan	Feb	Mar	Apr
3	Rent	1200	1200	1200	1200
4	Renter's Insurance	40	40	40	40
5	Furnishings	500			
6	Miscellaneous				
7	Utilities				
8	Electricity	180	180	180	150
9	Gas	120	120	110	90
10	Water	35	35	35	35
11	Garbage Service	50	50	50	50
12	Phone	50	50	50	50
13	Internet	65	65	65	65
14	Cable TV	135	135	135	135
15	Monthly Subtotals	2375	1875	1865	1815
16	Utilities Subtotals	635	635	625	575
17					
18	January Rent plus Deposit, minus Discount	1600			
19	Annual Rent per Lease	14400			
20	Average Electricity	175.833			
21		1600	1600		

Cells B21 and C21 show the results of the same absolute cell reference.

7. SAVE the workbook.

PAUSE. LEAVE the workbook open to use in the next exercise.

CERTIFICATION READY?   4.1.1

How do you use an absolute cell reference in a formula?

An **absolute cell reference** refers to a specific cell or range of cells regardless of where the formula is located in the worksheet. Absolute cell references include two dollar signs in the formula, preceding the column letter and row number. The absolute cell reference $B$3, for example, refers to column (B) and row (3). When you copy the formula to any other cell in the worksheet, the absolute reference will not adjust to the destination cells.

Workplace Ready

ABSOLUTE CELL REFERENCES FOR PAYROLL TRACKING

Assume you work for a company that hires seasonal workers. All seasonal employees are paid the same hourly wage, but the number of hours each person works each week may vary. You are responsible for creating weekly payroll reports.

You can enter the hourly wage in one cell, and then use absolute cell references in calculations to refer to the hourly wage. In the following figure, each employee's gross pay is calculated using an absolute cell reference to the hourly wage in cell B1, which is $13.17. You could substitute 13.17 for $B$1 in each formula, but if the hourly wage changes, you would need to modify every formula.

Using an absolute cell reference lets you change just the value in cell B1, and then all formulas that reference that cell would change automatically.

In addition, if you add columns for taxes and deductions, regardless of where the Gross Pay column is located, all formulas in that column would still reference cell B1.

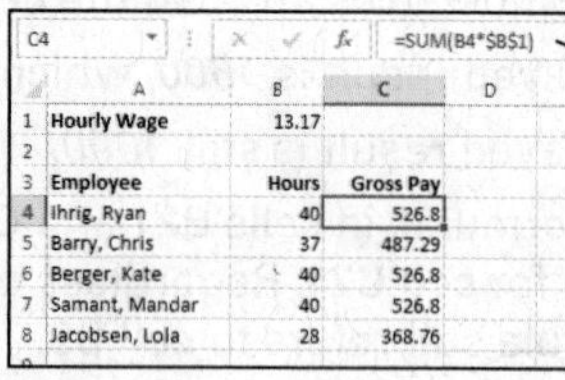

Absolute cell reference

Using Mixed Cell References in a Formula

You can also create a mixed reference in which a column or a row is absolute, and the other is relative. For example, if the cell reference in a formula is $A5 or A$5, you would have a mixed reference in which one component is absolute and one is relative.

STEP BY STEP   **Use a Mixed Cell Reference in a Formula**

GET READY. USE the worksheet you modified in the previous exercise.

1. Click cell **B21**.
2. Click in the formula bar and delete the dollar sign before 3 in the formula so it looks like $B3.
3. Press **Enter**. The formula in cell B21 now uses a mixed cell reference.
4. Copy cell **B21** to cell **C22**. The displayed result is *440*, which is different from the result in B21. That's because the formula in C22 references cell B4 (see Figure 4-12). The dollar sign before the B in the formula is absolute, but the row number is relative.

Figure 4-12

A mixed cell reference

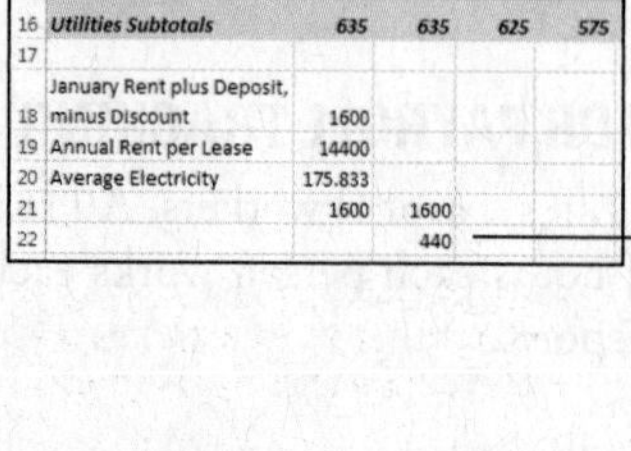

A mixed cell reference contains one dollar sign.

Cell C22 shows the result of a mixed cell reference.

5. Delete the contents of cell **B21**, cell **C21**, and cell **C22**.
6. SAVE the workbook.

PAUSE. LEAVE the workbook open to use in the next exercise.

A **mixed cell reference** is a cell reference that uses an absolute column or row reference, but not both.

In the exercise, the column portion of the cell reference is absolute and remains unchanged in the formula regardless of where the formula is copied. The row portion of the formula is relative (no dollar sign precedes the row number of 3), so that part of the cell reference changes when the cell is copied.

If you copy a formula across rows or down columns, the relative reference automatically adjusts, and the absolute reference does not adjust. For example, when you copied the formula containing the mixed reference $B3 to a different cell in column C, the reference in the destination cell changed to $B4. The column reference remained the same because that portion of the formula is absolute. The row reference adjusted because it is relative.

Using External Cell References

You've been creating or modifying cell references that refer to cells in the same worksheet. However, you can also refer to cells in another worksheet in the same workbook or to another workbook entirely. References to cells located in a separate workbook are considered *external references*. Unless you specify another worksheet or workbook, Excel assumes your cell references are to cells in the current worksheet.

Referring to Data in Another Worksheet

An **external reference** refers to a cell or range in a worksheet in another Excel workbook, or to a defined name in another workbook. (You learn how to define range names later in this lesson.) You might need to use this strategy, for example, to create a summary of data in one worksheet based on data in another worksheet. The basic principles for building these formulas are the same as those for building formulas referencing data within a worksheet.

STEP BY STEP | **Refer to Data in Another Worksheet**

GET READY. USE the worksheet you modified in the previous exercise.

1. Click the Summary sheet tab in the *04 Budget Cell References Solution* workbook.

2. Click cell D8. You want the average payment for electricity to appear in this cell, similar to the content that appears in B20 in the Expense Details worksheet. However, your formula must reference the Expense Details worksheet to gather the data.

3. Type =SUM('Expense Details'!N8)/12 and press Enter. This formula divides the value of cell N8 in the Expense Details worksheet by 12. The result is *176*, rounded due to cell formatting applied to the worksheet (see Figure 4-13).

Figure 4-13

Creating a link to a worksheet in the same workbook

The formula includes a reference to the Expense Details worksheet, which is in the same workbook as the Summary worksheet.

Cell D8 shows the result of a cell reference to a cell in the Expense Details worksheet.

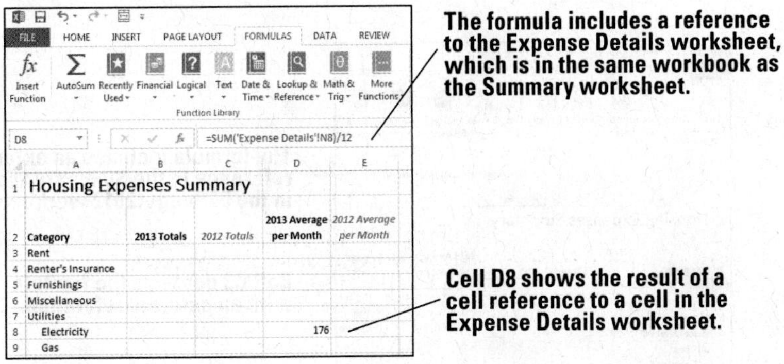

Cross Ref — You learn about cell formatting in Lesson 6, "Formatting Cells and Ranges."

4. SAVE the workbook.

PAUSE. LEAVE the workbook open to use in the next exercise.

The general format of a formula that references a cell in a different worksheet is *SheetName!CellAddress*. That is, you enter the external worksheet name followed by an exclamation point, and then the cell address in the external worksheet. For worksheet names that include one or more spaces, you need to enclose the name in single quotation marks, similar to 'Sheet Name'!CellAddress.

You can also refer to a range of cells in an external worksheet. For example, in the exercise, you can use a similar formula, =SUM('Expense Details'!B8:M8)/12, to accomplish the same task. The portion B8:M8 is called a *range*, as you learned in Lesson 2, "Working with Microsoft Excel 2013." This formula adds the values in the range B8:M8 and then divides them by 12 to produce the average monthly payment for electricity over one year. You see how to work with cell ranges after the next section.

Microsoft calls references to cells in another worksheet or in another workbook *links* because you are essentially linking to data in those remote locations.

Excel provides several functions to help you create formulas more easily. One of the most common functions, SUM, adds the values in a series of cells specified in a range. The construct =SUM(D2:D5) is the same as specifying =D2+D3+D4+D5.

🔍 **Cross Ref**   You learn about basic functions in Lesson 5, "Using Functions" and advanced formulas and functions in Lesson 10, "Using Advanced Formulas."

Referencing Data in Another Workbook

The procedure for referencing data in another workbook is nearly the same as referencing data in another worksheet in the same workbook. The difference is that, when creating a reference to cells in another workbook, you must enclose the other workbook name in square brackets ([ ]) and both workbooks must be open.

STEP BY STEP   **Reference Data in Another Workbook**

GET READY. USE the worksheet you modified in the previous exercise.

1. Open a second workbook, the data file named *04Budget2012*.
2. In *04 Budget Cell References Solution*, on the Summary sheet, click cell C3.
3. Type =([04Budget2012.xlsx]Summary!B3), as shown in Figure 4-14, and press Enter. The formula links to cell B3 on the Summary sheet in the workbook named *04Budget2012*.

Figure 4-14

An external reference to a cell in another workbook

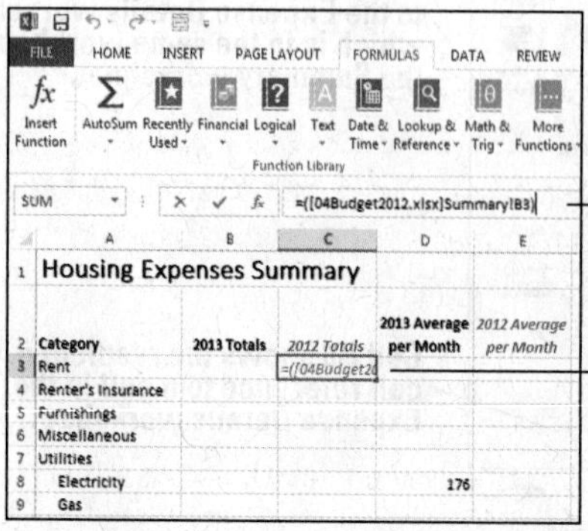

The formula includes an external reference to the Summary Worksheet in the 04Budget2012 workbook.

Cell C3 contains the formula with an external reference.

4. SAVE the workbook and CLOSE it.
5. CLOSE *04Budget2012*.

PAUSE. LEAVE Excel open to use in the next exercise.

The paired brackets [ ] identify the name of the workbook file, and Summary! identifies the worksheet within that file.

If the data in the referenced cell in the 04Budget2012 worksheet changes, so will the data in the corresponding cell on the Summary worksheet in 04 Budget Cell References Solution. This holds true even if you save 04 Budget Cell References Solution under a different file name.

If you don't have the external workbook open when creating the formula, the Update Values dialog box appears. You must navigate to the location of 04Budget2012.xlsx, select the file, and click OK.

If you close both workbooks and reopen only 04 Budget Cell References Solution , the full path to the 04Budget2012 workbook displays in the formula bar (see Figure 4-15).

Figure 4-15

The full path to the linked workbook

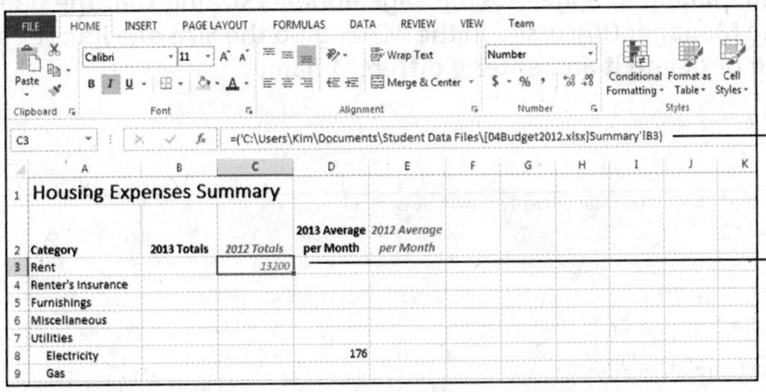

The formula includes the full path to the external workbook.

The result of the formula

If you close and then reopen the workbook that contains the cell reference to the external workbook, a message appears prompting you to update your links (see Figure 4-16).

Figure 4-16

A message dialog box prompting you to update links

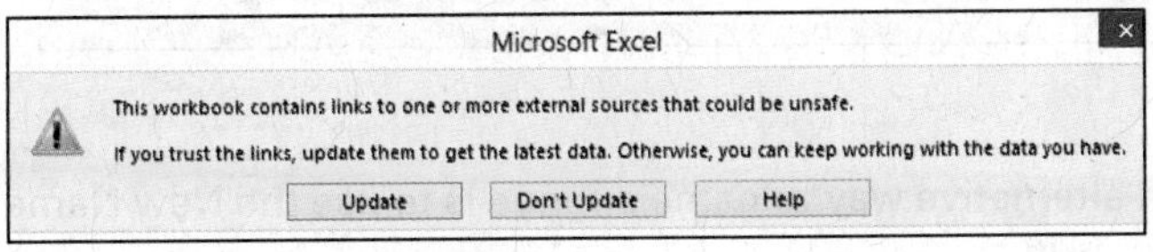

USING CELL RANGES IN FORMULAS

Bottom Line

In Excel, groups of cells are called *ranges*. The cell groups are either contiguous or non-contiguous. You can name (define) ranges, change the size of ranges after you define them, and use named ranges in formulas. The Name box and the Name Manager help you keep track of named ranges and their cell addresses. You can also use the Paste Names command to create a list of named ranges and their addresses in a worksheet.

Naming a Range

When you refer to the same cell range over and over, it might be more convenient to give it a name. Excel recognizes the name as the cell range and uses the values in those cells to do what you specified. For instance, if you have a series of sales figures in a column, instead of referring to them as the range *C4:C10*, you can name them *SalesQ3*. Any time you use the name *SalesQ3* in a formula,

Excel would then use the values in those cells.

STEP BY STEP   Name a Range of Cells

GET READY. OPEN the *04 Budget Ranges* data file for this lesson.

1. Click Enable Content, if prompted. Click the Expense Details sheet tab.
2. Select B3:B14. These are the cells to be named.
3. To the left of the formula bar, click the Name box.
4. Type a one-word name for the list, such as Q1Expenses, and press Enter. The range name appears in the Name box (see Figure 4-17). Excel saves this name and uses it in any subsequent reference to this range. (Don't worry about the apparent misnaming of the range. You modify this range to include additional months in an exercise later in this lesson.)

Troubleshooting   When naming a range, if a message appears stating that the name already exists, display the Name Manager (discussed in the "Changing the Size of a Range" section) and edit the existing name or delete it and enter a different name.

Figure 4-17

Using the Name box to name a range

The range name appears in the Name box.

The highlighted cells that are part of the range

5. An alternative way to name a range is to use the New Name dialog box. Select B16:M16.
6. On the FORMULAS tab, in the Defined Names group, click Define Name. The New Name dialog box appears (see Figure 4-18).

Figure 4-18

Using the New Name dialog box to name a range

7. Excel uses the row heading as the range name, shown in the Name text box. You can change the name if you like. For this exercise, leave the default name.
8. Open the Scope drop-down list. Your options are Workbook, Expense Details, and Summary. The last two entries correspond to individual sheets in the workbook. Close the drop-down list, leaving Workbook selected.

9. Enter comments in the Comments text box, if you like.

10. Leave the cell address that appears in the Refers to text box. This is the range you selected. Notice that the sheet name is also included automatically.

11. Click OK. The name *Utilities_Subtotals* is saved for the range B16:M16.

12. A third way to name a range is to use the Create Names from Selection dialog box. Select **N2:N14**. This selection includes the column heading label.

13. On the FORMULAS tab, in the Defined Names group, click Create from Selection. The Create Names from Selection dialog box appears (see Figure 4-19).

Figure 4-19

Using the Create Names from Selection dialog box to name a range

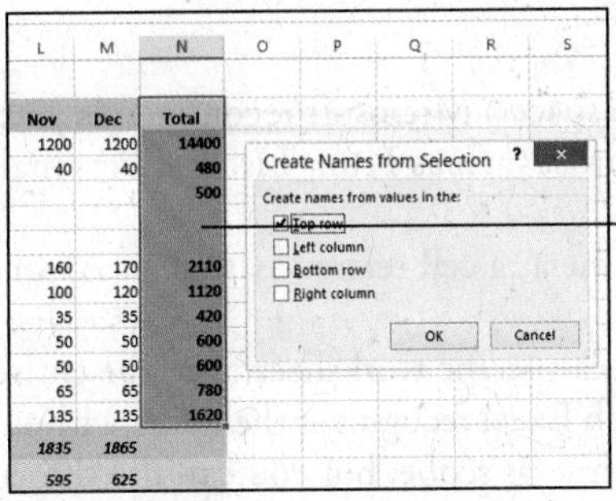

14. Excel determines that you want to use the column heading label as the range name. Click OK. The range is saved with the name *Total*.

15. Open the Name box drop-down list (see Figure 4-20). You have three named ranges from which to select.

Figure 4-20

Three named ranges appear in the Name box drop-down list

The Name box drop-down list displays the newly created range names.

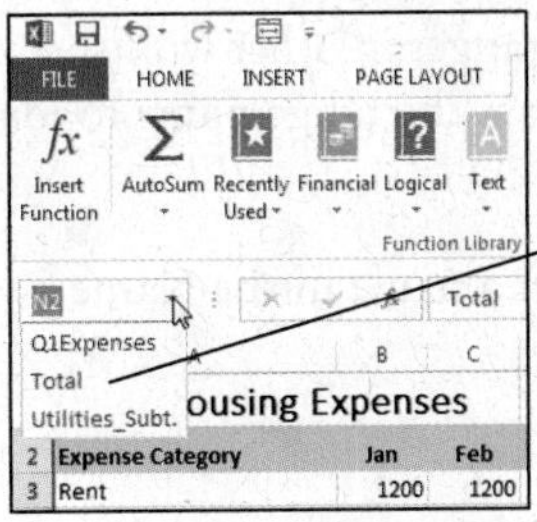

CERTIFICATION
READY?   2.3.4

How do you name ranges in a worksheet?

16. SAVE the workbook in your Lesson 4 folder as *04 Budget Ranges Solution*.

PAUSE. LEAVE the workbook open to use in the next exercise.

As you learned in Lesson 2, a range is a group of adjacent cells that you select to perform operations on all of the selected cells. You refer to a cell range by separating the first and last cell in the range by a colon, such as B1:B9 and D4:G9. The totals and subtotals in 04 Budget Ranges use cell ranges in their formulas.

A **named range** is a group of cells, and occasionally a single cell, with a designated name. The most common reason to name a range is to refer to it in formulas and functions. Naming ranges or an individual cell according to the data they contain is a time-saving technique, even though it might not seem so when you work with limited data files in practice exercises. However, naming a range in a large or complex worksheet enables you to go to the location quickly, similar to a bookmark.

After selecting a range of cells, you can name the range using three different methods:

• By typing a name in the Name box next to the formula bar

• By using the New Name dialog box

• By using the Create Names from Selection dialog box

Rules and guidelines for naming ranges include the following:

• Range names can be up to 255 characters in length.

• Range names may begin with a letter, the underscore character (_), or a backslash (\). The rest of the name may include letters, numbers, periods, and underscore characters, but not a backslash.

• Range names may not consist solely of the letters "C", "c", "R", or "r", which are used as shortcuts for selecting columns and rows.

• Range names may not include spaces. Microsoft recommends you use the underscore character (_) or period (.) to separate words, such as Fruit_List and Personal.Budget.

• Range names cannot be the same as a cell reference, such as A7 or $B$3.

All names have a scope, either to a specific worksheet or to the entire workbook. The **scope** of a name is the location within which Excel recognizes the name without qualification. Excel requires that a name must be unique within its scope, but you can use the same name in different scopes. In the New Name dialog box, if you select a worksheet name from the Scope list, the scope is at the local worksheet level. If you select Workbook, the scope is at the global workbook level.

If you defined a named range after you entered a cell reference in a formula, you might want to update the existing cell reference to the defined name. Select an empty cell, click the arrow next to Define Name, and click Apply Names. In the Apply Names dialog box, click one or more names, and click OK.

Take Note   You can use the same name for equivalent ranges in other worksheets within a workbook. Include the name of the worksheet in brackets before the range name to identify which worksheet you're referring to.

After creating named ranges, you can select a name in the Name box drop-down list to select the named range on the worksheet.

Changing the Size of a Range

You might want to change the size of a range to include or exclude data that you didn't consider when you created the range.

STEP BY STEP   **Change the Size of a Range**

GET READY. USE the worksheet you modified in the previous exercise.

1. Click the Expense Details sheet, if it's not already active.
2. On the FORMULAS tab, in the Defined Names group, click Name Manager.
3. Select Q1Expenses.
4. At the bottom of the dialog box, highlight everything in the Refers to box (see Figure 4-21).

Figure 4-21

The Refers to box
in the Name Manager

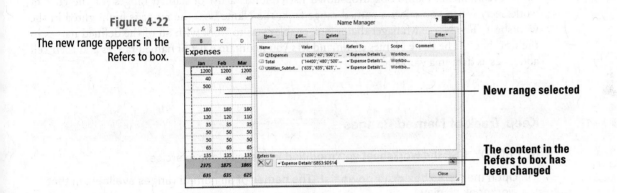

——— The Refers to box

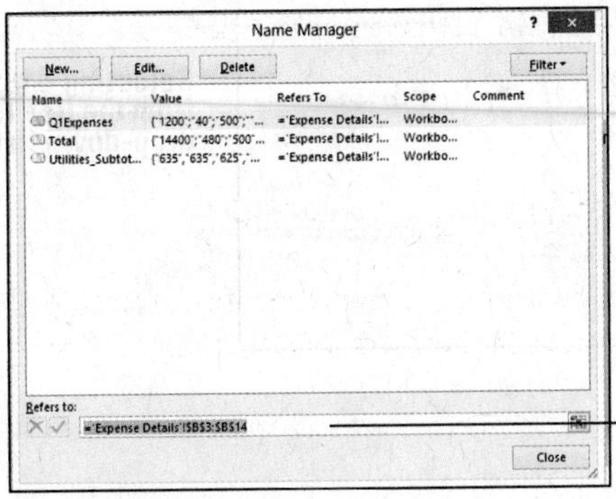

5. In the Expenses Details worksheet, select B3:D14. The content in the Refers to box in the Name Manager dialog box reflects the new range (see Figure 4-22).

Figure 4-22

The new range appears in the
Refers to box.

——— New range selected

——— The content in the
Refers to box has
been changed

6. Click Close, and then click Yes when asked if you want to save your changes.
7. SAVE the workbook.

PAUSE. LEAVE the workbook open to use in the next exercise.

To change the parameters of a named range, you can easily redefine the range by using the Name Manager on the FORMULAS tab. The Name Manager contains all the information about named ranges.

Creating a Formula that Operates on a Named Range

You can use the name of any range in a formula, just as you can use a cell identifier.

STEP BY STEP   **Create a Formula that Operates on a Named Range**

Another Way
You can just enter
the formula and range name,
such as =sum(Q1Expenses)
directly into the cell.

GET READY. USE the worksheet you modified in the previous exercise.

1. In the Expense Details sheet, click A21.
2. Type First Quarter Expenses and press Enter.
3. In cell B21, type =SUM(.
4. On the FORMULAS tab, in the Defined Names group, click Use in Formula.
5. Select Q1Expenses from the list (see Figure 4-23), type) to close the equation, and press Enter. The total amount of expenses for January through March appears in cell B21.

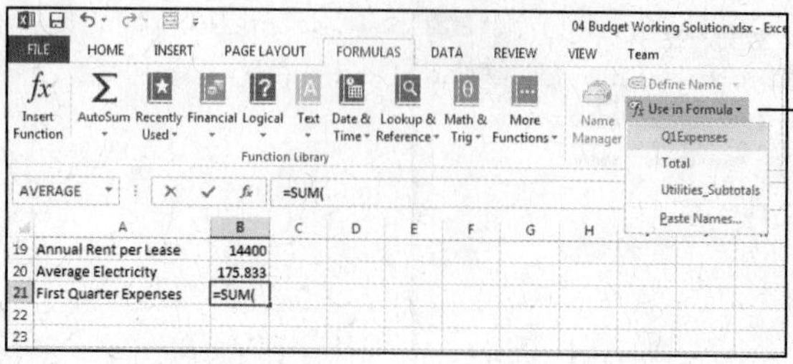

Figure 4-23

Using a named range in a formula

Selecting Q1Expenses from the Use In Formulas drop-down list

CERTIFICATION READY? 4.1.3

How do you reference named ranges in a formula?

6. SAVE the workbook.

PAUSE. LEAVE the workbook open to use in the next exercise.

Keeping Track of Named Ranges

As you've seen, the Name box drop-down list contains a list of named ranges for the current worksheet. When you select a named range from the Name box, the range is highlighted in the worksheet. The Name Manager dialog box enables you to work with all of the defined names in the workbook. The Paste Names command lets you maintain a list of named ranges and their cell addresses as data in a worksheet.

STEP BY STEP **Keep Track of Named Ranges**

GET READY. USE the worksheet you modified in the previous exercise.

1. Open the Name box drop-down list. The names of all named ranges available in that workbook display.

2. To verify your change to the size of the Q1Expenses range in a previous exercise, select Q1Expenses. The range B3:D14 appears highlighted.

3. On the FORMULAS tab, in the Defined Names group, click Name Manager. Each named range is listed in the dialog box. You can use Name Manager to create a new range, rename a range, delete a range, and verify the scope of a range, among other tasks.

4. Click Close to close the Name Manager.

5. To display range names and their cell ranges as data in the worksheet, select a cell with blank cells to the right and below it, such as cell P2.

6. On the FORMULAS tab, in the Defined Names group, click Use in Formula and then select Paste Names. The Paste Name dialog box opens.

7. Click Paste List. Widen the width of column P to display all range names fully. Range names display in column P and their cell ranges display in column Q (see Figure 4-24).

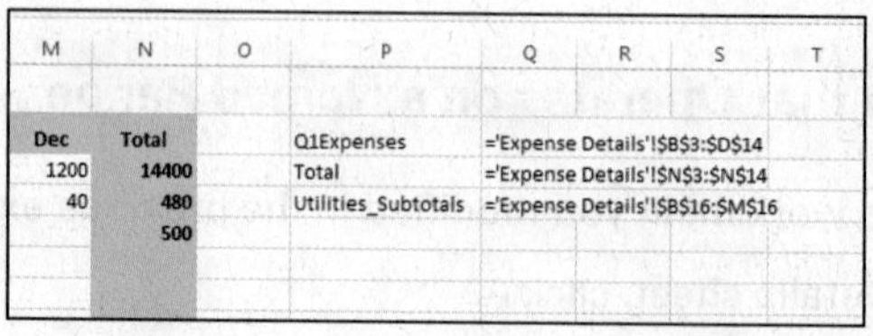

Figure 4-24

Range names and cell addresses pasted into a worksheet

8. SAVE the workbook and CLOSE it.

CLOSE Excel.

You can use the Name Manager as a convenient way to confirm the value and reference of a named range or to determine its scope. In addition, you can add, change, or delete names.

It is easier to remember names than to memorize cells and cell ranges. You can create a list of defined names in a workbook using the Paste List command. Doing so makes it simpler to keep track of your data.

SKILL SUMMARY

In this lesson you learned how:	Exam Objective	Objective Number
To display formulas.	Display formulas.	1.4.10
To follow the order of operations.	Define order of operations.	4.1.2
To build basic formulas.		
To use relative, mixed, and absolute cell references in formulas.	Demonstrate how to use references (relative, mixed, absolute).	4.1.1
To create named ranges in worksheets.	Create named ranges.	2.3.4
To reference cell ranges in formulas.	Reference cell ranges in formulas.	4.1.3

Knowledge Assessment

Multiple Choice

Select the best response for the following statements.

1. Which of the following is *not* an arithmetic operator?
   a. +
   b. –
   c. *
   d.]

2. In Excel, what is the result of =1 + 3 * 2 / 2 - 1?
   a. 2
   b. 3
   c. 4
   d. 6

3. Per the order of operations, which of the following is calculated first?
   a. Addition (+) and subtraction (–) (left to right)
   b. Exponentiation (^)
   c. Percent (%)
   d. Negative number (–)

4. Which of the following refers to an unnamed range in the current worksheet?
   a. =SUM(C2:E12)
   b. =Q3Expenses!A19
   c. =[Media.xlsx]MasterList!$D$10
   d. =SUM(budget.summary)

5. Which of the following shows a formula for a reference to another worksheet in the same workbook?
   a. =SUM(C2:E12)
   b. =Q3Expenses!A19
   c. =[Media.xlsx]MasterList!$D$10
   d. =SUM(budget.summary)

6. Which of the following shows a formula for a reference to another workbook?
   a. =SUM(C2:E12)
   b. =Q3Expenses!A19
   c. =[Media.xlsx]MasterList!$D$10
   d. =SUM(budget.summary)

7. Which of the following is an acceptable name for a named range?
   a. C7
   b. subtotal_west
   c. subtotal west
   d. subtotal/west

8. Which of the following is an example of an absolute cell reference?
   a. A9
   b. A$9
   c. $A$9
   d. A9:E9

9. Which of the following is an example of a mixed cell reference?
   a. A9
   b. A$9
   c. $A$9
   d. A9:E9

10. Which of the following can you *not* do using the Name Manager?
   a. Enter values into a range.
   b. Change a range name.
   c. Delete a named range.
   d. Verify the scope of a range.

True / False

Circle T if the statement is true or F if the statement is false.

T F 1. To allow Excel to distinguish formulas from data, all formulas begin with an equal sign (=).

T F 2. Regarding a named range, the scope of a name is the location within which Excel recognizes the name without qualification.

T F 3. Excel recognizes a construct like 3+4= as a legitimate formula.

T F 4. Range names may begin with the caret (^) character.

T F 5. You cannot use a named range in a formula that references another worksheet.

T F 6. Range names cannot be the same as a cell reference, such as C10 or $D$8.

T F 7. Once you name a range, you can change the size of the range using the Name Manager.

T F 8. You can create a new range by selecting the cells and typing a name in the Name box next to the formula bar.

T F 9. The order of operations determines which parts of a formula are calculated before other parts of the formula.

T F 10. The formula = 6 * 2 / 3 produces the same result as =6 * (2 / 3).

Competency Assessment

Project 4-1: Create Basic Formulas

Practice creating addition, subtraction, multiplication, and division formulas.

GET READY. Before you begin these steps, LAUNCH Microsoft Excel and OPEN a blank workbook.

1. Click cell **A1** and type **=20+15**. Press **Enter**. Excel calculates the value in A1 and displays *35* in the cell.

2. In A2, type =34+51+22. Press Tab. The sum of the three numbers, *107*, appears in the cell.

3. Click A2 to display the formula for that cell in the formula bar.

4. With A2 selected, click the formula bar. Select 51 and type 15. Press Enter. Notice that the formula result changes to *71*.

5. In A3, type =35.3+41.6+17.4. Press Enter. The value *94.3* appears in A3.

6. In B1, type =375−68. Press Enter. The value *307* appears in the cell.

7. In B2, type =45−13−8. Press Enter. The value in B2 should be *24*.

8. In B3, create a formula to subtract 125 from 189. The value in B3 should be *64*.

9. In C1, type =125*4 and press Enter. The value that appears in C1 is *500*.

10. In C2, type =2*7.50*2 and press Enter. The value in C2 is *30*.

11. In C3, type =5+2*8. The value in C3 is *21*.

12. In D1, create the formula =795/45 and press Enter. Excel returns a value of *17.66667* in D1.

13. In D2, create the formula =65−29*8+97/5 and press Enter. The value in D2 is *−147.6*.

14. In D3, create the formula =-12+10+20.5/3 and press Enter. Excel returns a value of *4.833333* in D3.

15. In E1, type =2^4 and press Enter. The value *16* displays in E1. This formula calculated 2 raised to the 4th power.

16. In E2, type =25*(1+35%) and press Enter. Excel returns a value of *33.75*. The formula increased 25 by 35%.

17. In E3, type =3^2*(1+25%) and press Enter. Excel returns a value of *11.25* in E3.

18. SAVE the workbook in your Lesson 4 folder as *04 Project Math Solution* and CLOSE it.

PAUSE. LEAVE Excel open to use in the next project.

Project 4-2: **Work with the Order of Operations**

Practice working with the order of operations.

 GET READY. Before you begin these steps, OPEN the *04 Project Operations Practice* workbook.

1. Select C3 and modify the formula by inserting parentheses around 5+2. Press Enter. The new formula should be =(5+2)*8. The value in C3 changes from *21* to *56*.

2. Select D2. Click in the formula bar and place parentheses around 65−29. Press Enter. The new formula should be =(65−29)*8+97/5. The value in D2 changes from *−147.6* to *307.4*.

3. Select D2. Click in the formula bar and place parentheses around 97/5. Press Enter. The new formula should be =(65−29)*8+(97/5). The value in D2 remains the same at *307.4*.

4. Select D2. Click in the formula bar and change the parentheses so the formula looks like =(65−(29*8)+97)/5. Press Enter. The value in D2 changes to *−14*.

5. SAVE the workbook in your Lesson 4 folder as *04 Project Operations Solution* and CLOSE it.

LEAVE Excel open to use in the next project.

Proficiency Assessment

Project 4-3: Link to Data in Other Worksheets within a Workbook

You work for A. Datum Corporation as an accountant. You have a workbook with several sheets that contain budgets for western division offices located in Alaska, Washington, Oregon, and California. You created a summary sheet and named the sheet tab WesternSummary. You will link to information in the four other worksheets to present summary data in one place. Each area worksheet is organized the same way to make it easy to find the same kind of data for each area.

GET READY. Before you begin these steps, OPEN the *04_ADatum_Start* workbook.

1. On the WesternSummary sheet, click cell B3 and enter the formula =Alaska!B8. The formula links to the data in cell B8 (the Gross Sales total) on the Alaska worksheet and displays it in cell B3 of the WesternSummary worksheet.
2. In B4, enter the formula =Washington!B8 to link to the Washington office gross sales total.
3. Create similar formulas to display the Oregon and California gross sales data on the WesternSummary sheet.
4. Compare the figures in column B on the WesternSummary sheet to the appropriate cells in the other worksheets to verify that your formulas are correct. If not, adjust the formulas on the WesternSummary sheet to correct them.
5. Create similar formulas to display the COGS totals in column C, the commissions totals in column D, and the net sales totals in column E on the WesternSummary sheet. (To save time, you can select B3:B6 and drag the fill handle to the right to fill all additional totals.)
6. Compare the figures on the WesternSummary sheet to the other worksheets to verify that your formulas are correct. If not, adjust the formulas to correct them.
7. SAVE the workbook in your Lesson 4 folder as *04_ADatum_USWest Solution* and CLOSE it.

LEAVE Excel open to use in the next project.

Project 4-4: Use External References

You now want to create a summary in a workbook named *04_ADatum_GlobalSales* and link to information in the 04_ADatum_USWest workbook.

GET READY. LAUNCH Excel if it is not already running.

1. OPEN *04_ADatum_USWest* and *04_ADatum_GlobalSales* from your data files.
2. In *04_ADatum_GlobalSales*, on the GlobalSummary sheet, click cell B4 to make it active.
3. Enter the formula =([04_ADatum_USWest]WesternSummary!B8). The formula links to the data in cell B8 on the WesternSummary sheet in the 04_ADatum_USWest workbook.
4. Copy B4 to C4.
5. SAVE the *04_ADatum_GlobalSales* workbook and leave it open.
6. In *04_ADatum_USWest*, on the California tab, change the data in cell B6, which is the Gross Sales figure for Release 3.4, to 284,125.
7. Check the WesternSummary sheet to verify that the linked cell updated automatically.
8. Save the *04_ADatum_USWest* workbook and close it.
9. CLOSE *04_ADatum_GlobalSales* without saving the workbook.
10. Reopen *04_ADatum_GlobalSales*.
11. Click Enable Content, if prompted.

12. Click Update if the message window appears.

13. OPEN *04_ADatum_USWest*.

14. Verify that the data in cell B4 in *04_ADatum_GlobalSales* matches the corresponding data in *04_ADatum_USWest*.

15. SAVE *04_ADatum_USWest* in your Lesson 4 folder as *04_ADatum_USWestSales Solution*.

16. SAVE *04_ADatum_GlobalSales* in your Lesson 4 folder as *04_ADatum_GlobalSales Solution*.

17. CLOSE both workbooks.

LEAVE Excel open for the next project.

Mastery Assessment

Project 4-5: Name a Range and Use the Range in a Formula

Blue Yonder Airlines wants to analyze the sales and expense data from its four-year history.

GET READY. LAUNCH Excel if it is not already running.

1. OPEN the *04 Income Analysis* workbook for this lesson.

2. On the Sales sheet, select B4:E4 and use the Define Name command on the FORMULAS tab to name the range. Accept the defaults in the dialog box.

3. Select B5:E5 and use the Name box to name the range. Use the row heading as the range name using an underscore to separate the words.

4. Select A6:E6. Use the Create from Selection command on the FORMULAS tab to name the range. Use the default option in the dialog box.

5. Create a named range for A7:E7 using the method of your choice.

6. Create a formula in cell F4 that sums the values in B4:E4 using the range name.

7. Repeat Step 6 for the other three income sources.

8. Create range names on the Expenses sheet using the method of your choice.

9. Total the four expense categories on the Expenses sheet as you did on the Sales sheet. Be careful to select the worksheet range name rather than the workbook range name in each case. You use this workbook again in Lesson 5 and create formulas with functions on the Analysis sheet.

10. SAVE the workbook in your Lesson 4 folder as *04 Income Analysis Solution* and then CLOSE the file.

LEAVE Excel open to use in the next project.

Project 4-6: Create a Personal Budget

Most people agree that it is vitally important for a business to have a realistic budget. It is equally important for an individual to have a personal budget—a plan for managing income and expenses. Using a personal budget worksheet prepopulated with data, create range names to identify specific blocks of data, and then use those range names in formulas you create to compare budgeted to actual costs.

GET READY. LAUNCH Excel if it is not already running.

1. OPEN the *04 Personal Budget Start* workbook for this lesson.

2. On the Expenses sheet, name cell B7 Income_Total. If you use the Define Name command, use the defaults in the New Name dialog box.

3. Name cells B10:B14 Home_Total.

4. Create named ranges similar to Step 3 for budgeted amounts for the Daily Living Total, Transportation Total, and Entertainment Total categories.

5. Create a formula in cell D4 that subtracts the actual amount from the budgeted amount. The cells in column D are formatted to display a dash if the budgeted amount and the actual amount are the same. Copy the formula in D4 to D5:D6.

6. Create a formula in cell D7 that subtracts the actual amount from the budgeted amount using the Income_Total range name.

7. Beginning with the Home section, create a formula in the non-Total cells in column D that subtracts the actual amount from the budgeted amount using the range name for the budgeted amount. For example, the formula in cell D10 would be =Home_Total-C10. Be aware that the formulas might result in a positive number, no difference, or negative numbers.

8. Beginning with the Home section, create a formula in the Total cells in column D that subtracts the actual amount from the budgeted amount. Use the cell address for the budgeted amount.

9. In cells E10 through E14, create a formula that divides the budgeted amount by the income total. Use the range names Home_Total and Income_Total in the formula.

10. In cell E15, create a formula that divides the budgeted amount by the income total using a cell reference to the Home total and the range name Income_Total.

11. Complete column E per Steps 9 and 10 for the remaining cells.

12. The figure that displays in cell B36 is based on a named range, but part of the range is incorrect. Use the Name Manager or the Show Formulas command to analyze the formula for the Expenses range and correct it.

13. SAVE the workbook in your Lesson 4 folder as *04 Personal Budget Solution* and then CLOSE the file.

CLOSE Excel.

LESSON SKILL MATRIX

Skills	Exam Objective	Objective Number
Exploring Functions		
Displaying Dates and Times with Functions		
Summarizing Data with Functions	Demonstrate how to apply the SUM function.	4.2.1
	Demonstrate how to apply the COUNT function.	4.2.3
	Demonstrate how to apply the AVERAGE function.	4.2.4
	Demonstrate how to apply the MIN and MAX functions.	4.2.2
Using a Financial Function		
Using Formulas to Create Subtotals		
Uncovering Formula Errors		
Displaying and Printing Formulas		

KEY TERMS

- argument
- AutoSum
- AVERAGE function
- COUNT function
- COUNTA function
- function
- MAX function
- MIN function
- NOW function
- PMT function
- SUBTOTAL function
- SUM function
- TODAY function
- trace arrow

Creating and maintaining a personal budget requires more than simply estimating and tracking expenses. You often want to see subtotals of certain data, for example, to determine how much you spend quarterly. Sometimes you want to know your average payment per month for expenses that vary throughout the year. Budgets are also working documents—they change over time and might require modifications to the structure. Creating proper formulas builds flexibility into your worksheets. Excel provides a wealth of predefined functions to help you enter formulas quickly and accurately. In this lesson, you learn how to use simple Excel functions by working on an annual budget of household expenses.

©MCCAIG / iStockphoto

SOFTWARE ORIENTATION

FORMULAS Tab

The FORMULAS tab in Excel 2013, shown in Figure 5-1, provides access to a library of formulas and functions. On this tab, you can use commands for quickly inserting functions, inserting totals, and displaying a visual map of cells that are dependent on a formula.

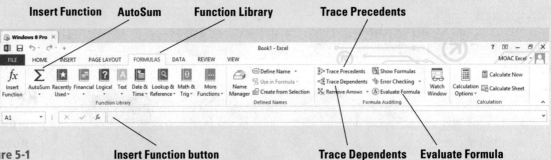

Figure 5-1

The FORMULAS tab in Excel 2013

In this lesson, you learn how to use a variety of simple functions to perform calculations in a budgeting worksheet. You also learn subtotaling techniques, how to work with formula errors, and how to print formulas.

EXPLORING FUNCTIONS

Bottom Line

A **function** is a predefined formula that performs a calculation. Excel's built-in functions are designed to perform different types of calculations—from simple to complex. When you apply a function to specific data, you eliminate the time involved in manually constructing a formula. Using functions ensures the accuracy of the formula's results. You can type functions directly into Excel or use the tools on the FORMULAS tab to help you fill in formulas with the correct syntax.

STEP BY STEP   **Explore Functions**

GET READY. LAUNCH Excel and open a new, blank workbook.

1. To become familiar with the tools available to build formulas and insert functions, click the FORMULAS tab. Excel arranges functions by category in the Function Library group, such as Financial, Logical, Text, and so on. Click the Financial button arrow to display a drop-down list of functions (see Figure 5-2). If you create a financial function, you can simply scroll through the list and select the function you want.

Figure 5-2

The Financial group menu of functions

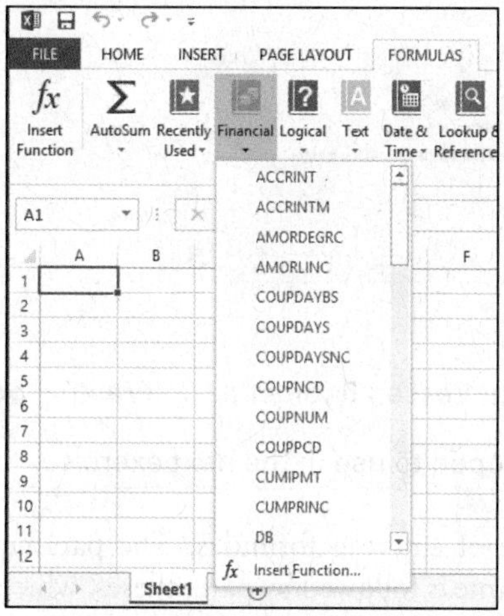

2. You can also find a function using the Insert Function dialog box. On the FORMULAS tab or on the formula bar, click the Insert Function button. The buttons are shown in Figure 5-3.

Figure 5-3

The Insert Function buttons

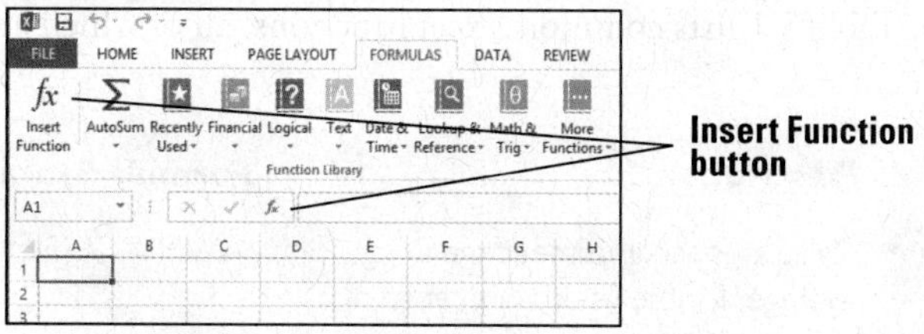

Insert Function button

3. In the Insert Function dialog box, type a description of what you want to do. For example, type date and click Go. Excel returns a list of functions that most closely match your description (see Figure 5-4).

Function	Description	Formula Syntax
SUBTOTAL	Returns a subtotal for a list	=SUBTOTAL(function number,ref1,[ref2],...)
SUM	Takes all of the values in each of the specified cells and totals their values.	=SUM(first value, second value,...)
TODAY	Returns the current date.	=TODAY()

DISPLAYING DATES AND TIMES WITH FUNCTIONS

Bottom Line

In Excel, dates are numbers. When you see a date in a worksheet, it's actually a numeric value formatted to look like a date. The same principle applies to time. Two functions display the current date and/or time in a worksheet: NOW and TODAY. NOW returns the current date and time, whereas TODAY returns the current date but not the time. Neither of these functions uses arguments, so you insert blank parentheses after them. With NOW and TODAY, you can create automatically updated dates and times in worksheets that you frequently revisit and update.

Exploring Dates

Excel stores dates as sequential serial numbers. By default, January 1, 1900 is serial number 1, January 2, 1900 is serial number 2, and so on. Each date is a number that represents the number of days that have elapsed since January 1, 1900. You can add, subtract, multiply, and divide using a date, just as you can with any other number. How the date is displayed depends on the format you assign to it.

STEP BY STEP   **Explore Dates**

GET READY. USE the workbook you created in the previous exercise.

1. In cell A2, type **1/10/1900** and press **Enter**.
2. Select cell **A2**.
3. On the HOME tab, in the Number group, open the Number Format menu and select General. The value in A2 changes to *10* (see Figure 5-6). When you enter a date manually into Excel, the format of the cell automatically changes to Date. Because the date 1/10/1900 is the tenth day after (and including) January 1, 1900, the value is 10. Excel's Date format displays the value as a date, and the General format displays the value as a number.

Figure 5-6

In Excel, a date is actually a serial number.

A date displayed as a serial number

4. With A2 still selected, change the number format to Short Date using the Number Format menu. The cell displays *1/10/1900*.
5. Click cell **A3**, type **40000** and press **Enter**. Because the cell is formatted as General by default, the value appears as a number.
6. Click cell **A2**.
7. On the HOME tab, in the Clipboard group, click the Format Painter, and then click cell **A3**. The formatting of A2 is copied to A3. The value in A3 now appears as a date: *7/6/2009*.
8. In cell A4, type **=A3-A2** and press **Enter**. The result is *39990*, which is the number of days between the two dates.

9. SAVE the workbook.

PAUSE. LEAVE the workbook open to use in the next exercise.

Using TODAY

The **TODAY function** returns the current date in a worksheet. The value returned by the TODAY function automatically updates every time you change the worksheet. To specify a date that doesn't change, enter the date you want to use manually.

STEP BY STEP   **Use the TODAY Function**

GET READY. USE the workbook you modified in the previous exercise.

1. In cell A5, type =TODAY() and press Enter. The current date displays (see Figure 5-7).

Figure 5-7

The result of the TODAY function

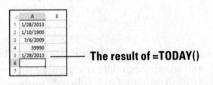

The result of =TODAY()

2. SAVE the workbook.

PAUSE. LEAVE the workbook open to use in the next exercise.

The default format for the TODAY function is mm/dd/yyyy, but you can have it appear in any date format.

You can also use TODAY to calculate an interval. For example, you can enter a formula to calculate the number of years you have lived by creating a formula to subtract your birth date from today's date, like this: =YEAR(TODAY())-1993.

Using NOW

The **NOW function** returns today's date and the current time, in the default format of mm/dd/yyyy hh:mm. You can apply any date or time format to values returned by the NOW function.

STEP BY STEP   **Use the NOW Function**

GET READY. USE the workbook you modified in the previous exercise.

1. In cell A6, type =NOW() and press Enter. The column width automatically expands, and the current date and time display (see Figure 5-8).

Figure 5-8

The result of the NOW function

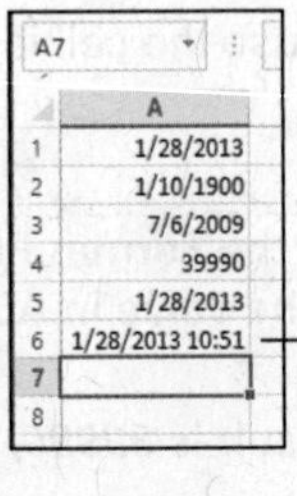

The result of =NOW()

2. Copy cell **A6** to **A7**.

3. Select cell **A7**.

4. On the HOME tab, in the Number group, from the Number Format menu, select Time. The current time without the date appears in A7 (see Figure 5-9).

Figure 5-9

The result of the NOW function with the Time format applied

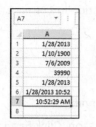

	A
1	1/28/2013
2	1/10/1900
3	7/6/2009
4	39990
5	1/28/2013
6	1/28/2013 10:52
7	10:52:29 AM
8	

5. SAVE the workbook and CLOSE it.

PAUSE. LEAVE Excel open to use in the next exercise.

Like TODAY, the NOW function also updates automatically every time you change the worksheet. However, because it also reports the time, its value changes every time you save the worksheet, even if that is several times during a single day.

In addition to simply displaying the current date and time, you might use the NOW function in a calculation that requires a value based on the current date and time.

Workplace *Ready*

USING DATES AT WORK

The Excel TODAY and NOW functions are handy when you simply want to display the current date, the date and time, or the date in a calculation. However, using TODAY or NOW means the date changes every time someone opens the workbook. Sometimes it's important that the date remains static. For example, you create an invoice with the invoice date at the top. You also have a line that says, "Terms: Net 30." A Net 30 term means you expect your customer to pay your invoice within 30 days of the date of your invoice. It's important that your invoice date never changes to avoid confusing your customer and so you get paid on time.

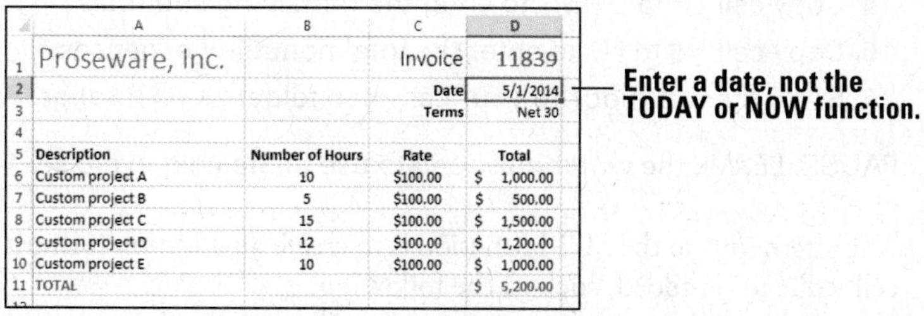

	A	B	C	D	
1	Proseware, Inc.		Invoice	11839	
2			Date	5/1/2014	— Enter a date, not the **TODAY or NOW function.**
3			Terms	Net 30	
4					
5	Description	Number of Hours	Rate	Total	
6	Custom project A	10	$100.00	$ 1,000.00	
7	Custom project B	5	$100.00	$ 500.00	
8	Custom project C	15	$100.00	$ 1,500.00	
9	Custom project D	12	$100.00	$ 1,200.00	
10	Custom project E	10	$100.00	$ 1,000.00	
11	TOTAL			$ 5,200.00	

SUMMARIZING DATA WITH FUNCTIONS

Bottom Line

Functions provide an easy way to perform mathematical work on a range of cells, quickly and conveniently. This section shows you how to use some of the basic functions in Excel: SUM, COUNT, COUNTA, AVERAGE, MIN, and MAX.

Using the SUM Function

Adding a range of cells is one of the most common calculations performed on worksheet data. The **SUM function** totals all of the cells in a range, easily and accurately. **AutoSum** makes that even easier by calculating (by default) the total from the adjacent cell through the first nonnumeric cell, using the SUM function in its formula. SUM is usually the first function most people learn how to use in Excel. In fact, you already saw it in action in Lesson 4, "Using Basic Formulas."

STEP BY STEP | **Use the SUM Function**

GET READY. LAUNCH Excel if it is not already running.

1. OPEN the *05 Budget Start* data file for this lesson. Click **Enable Editing**, if prompted. This workbook is similar to the *04 Budget Start* workbook used in Lesson 4, but with modifications to accommodate the current lesson.

2. In cell B7, type **=SUM(B3:B6)** and press **Enter**. The result, 2140, is the sum of January nonutility expenses.

⚠️ **Troubleshooting** | If you get an error message when entering a basic Excel formula, remember that all formulas must start with an equal sign (=). A function is simply a predefined formula, so you must use the equal sign.

3. Click in cell **C7**. Click the **FORMULAS** tab and then click the top part of the **AutoSum** button. The SUM function appears with arguments filled in, but only C6 is included. Type **C3:** before C6 to correct the range (see Figure 5-10). Press **Enter**. The result, 1340, is the sum of February nonutility expenses.

Figure 5-10

Using the SUM function

	A	B	C	D	E	F
1	2013 Housing Expenses					
2	Expense Category	Jan	Feb	Mar	Apr	May
3	Rent	1200	1200	1200	1200	1200
4	Renter's Insurance	40	40	40	40	40
5	Furnishings	500				
6	Miscellaneous	400	100	200		100
7	Nonutility Subtotals	2140	=SUM(C3:C6)			
8	Utilities		SUM(number1, [number2], ...)			
9	Electricity	180	180	180	150	150
10	Gas	120	120	110	90	80
11	Water	35	35	35	35	35

Expense Details | Summary | ⊕

CERTIFICATION READY? 4.2.1

How do you create a formula with the SUM function?

4. Copy cell **C7** to **D7:M7** to enter the remaining subtotals.

5. Copy cell **N6** to **N7** to enter the total nonutility expenses.

6. SAVE the workbook to your Lesson 5 folder as *05 Budget Math Solution*.

PAUSE. LEAVE the workbook open to use in the next exercise.

The alternative to the SUM function is to create an addition formula using cell references for every cell value to be added, such as the following:

=B7+C7+D7+E7+F7+G7+H7+I7+J7+K7+L7+M7

The easier way to achieve the same result is to use the SUM function or AutoSum. AutoSum is a built-in feature of Excel that recognizes adjacent cells in rows and columns as the logical selection to perform the AutoSum.

Using the COUNT Function

Statistical functions, such as SUM and COUNT, compile and classify data to present significant information. Use the **COUNT function** when you want to determine how many cells in a range contain a number.

STEP BY STEP

Use the COUNT Function

1. USE the workbook you modified in the previous exercise.
2. In cell O5, type Count and press Enter. This is the label identifying the formula you will enter in the next step.
3. In cell O6, type =COUNT(B6:M6) and press Enter. The result, *9*, is the number of months in which you budgeted for miscellaneous expenses (see Figure 5-11).

Figure 5-11

Result of the COUNT function

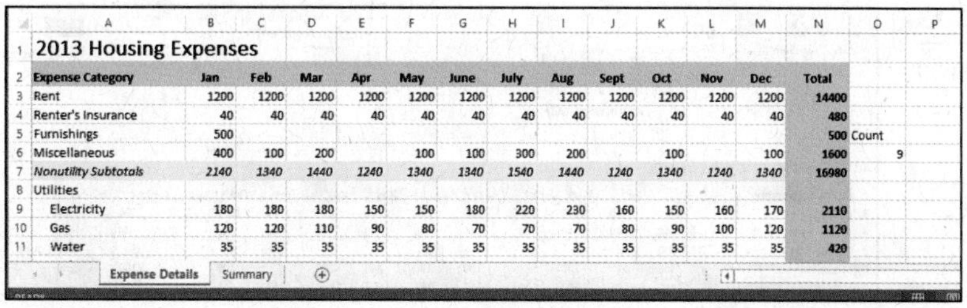

	A	B	C	D	E	F	G	H	I	J	K	L	M	N	O	P
1	2013 Housing Expenses															
2	Expense Category	Jan	Feb	Mar	Apr	May	June	July	Aug	Sept	Oct	Nov	Dec	Total		
3	Rent	1200	1200	1200	1200	1200	1200	1200	1200	1200	1200	1200	1200	14400		
4	Renter's Insurance	40	40	40	40	40	40	40	40	40	40	40	40	480		
5	Furnishings	500												500	Count	
6	Miscellaneous	400	100	200		100	100	300	200		100		100	1600	9	
7	*Nonutility Subtotals*	*2140*	*1340*	*1440*	*1240*	*1340*	*1340*	*1540*	*1440*	*1240*	*1340*	*1240*	*1340*	16980		
8	Utilities															
9	Electricity	180	180	180	150	150	180	220	230	160	150	160	170	2110		
10	Gas	120	120	110	90	80	70	70	70	80	90	100	120	1120		
11	Water	35	35	35	35	35	35	35	35	35	35	35	35	420		

CERTIFICATION READY? 4.2.3

How do you create a formula with the COUNT function?

4. SAVE the workbook.

PAUSE. LEAVE the workbook open to use in the next exercise.

In this exercise, you could have included the row heading—Nonutility Subtotals—in the formula range, along with the data in cells B6 through M6. The COUNT function disregards A6 because it doesn't contain a number, and the function disregards blank cells. You'll see this effect using COUNTA in the next exercise.

Using the COUNTA Function

The **COUNTA function** returns the number of cells in the selected range that contain text or values, but not blank cells. In this exercise, you use the Insert Function button on the formula bar to enter the function.

STEP BY STEP

Use the COUNTA Function

GET READY. USE the workbook you modified in the previous exercise.

1. In cell P5, type CountA and press Enter. This is the label identifying the formula you will enter in the next step.
2. In cell P6, on the formula bar, click the Insert Function button.
3. In the Insert Function dialog box, in the Search for a function text box, type counta and then click Go.
4. Select COUNTA in the results list and click OK. The Function Arguments dialog box opens.
5. Click Collapse Dialog (see Figure 5-12). The box collapses to a single entry box.

Figure 5-12

The Function Arguments dialog box

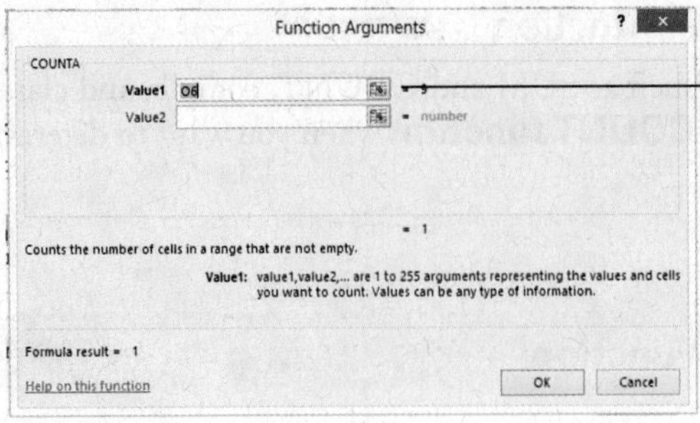

Collapse Dialog

6. Select A6:M6. The new range appears in the dialog box.
7. Click Expand Dialog shown in Figure 5-13, and click OK to close the dialog box. The result, *10*, is the number of nonblank cells in the range.

Figure 5-13

Expand Dialog

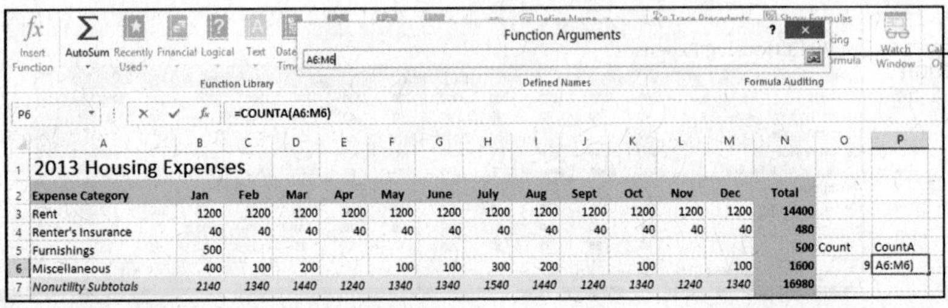

Expand Dialog

8. SAVE the workbook.

PAUSE. LEAVE the workbook open to use in the next exercise.

Using the AVERAGE Function

The **AVERAGE function** adds a range of cells and then divides by the number of cell entries, determining the mean value of all values in the range. Regarding your personal budget, because the cost of electricity and gas fluctuates seasonally, it might be interesting to know the average monthly amount you might spend over the course of an entire year.

STEP BY STEP **Use the AVERAGE Function**

GET READY. USE the workbook you modified in the previous exercise.

1. In cell O8, type Average and press Enter.
2. In cell O9, type =AVERAGE(B9:M9) and press Enter. The result, *175.8333*, is your average expected monthly electricity bill.
3. In cell O10, type =AVERAGE(B10:M10) and press Enter. The result, *93.33333*, is your average expected monthly gas bill (see Figure 5-14).

Figure 5-14

The results of the AVERAGE function

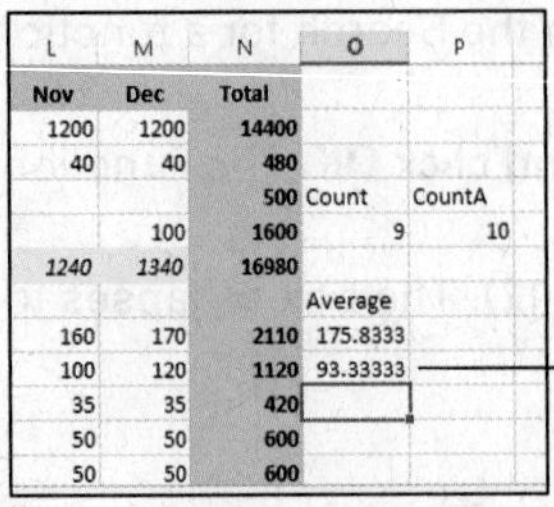

AVERAGE function results

CERTIFICATION READY? 4.2.4

How do you create a formula with the AVERAGE function?

4. SAVE the workbook.

PAUSE. LEAVE the workbook open to use in the next exercise.

Using the MIN Function

The **MIN function** allows you to determine the minimum value in a range of cells. Let's use this function to determine what your minimum electricity and gas bills will be. Instead of entering the formula manually, you'll use the Function Library group on the FORMULAS tab to build the formula.

STEP BY STEP   **Use the MIN Function**

GET READY. USE the workbook you modified in the previous exercise.

1. In cell P8, type **Min** and press **Enter**.
2. Click in cell **P9** and then click the **FORMULAS** tab.
3. Click the **AutoSum** button arrow, and then select **Min** from the menu. The range B9:O9 is automatically selected (see Figure 5-15). This range is incorrect, so you need to edit it.

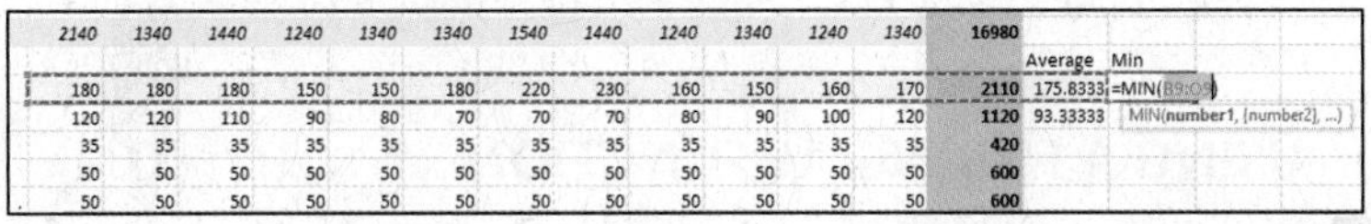

Figure 5-15

The wrong range is selected for the MIN function.

4. Click cell **B9**, hold down the **Shift** key, and click cell **M9**. The range B9:M9 appears in the function, which now looks like =MIN(B9:M9). See Figure 5-16. Press **Enter**. The result, *150*, appears, which is the lowest expected electricity bill for the year.

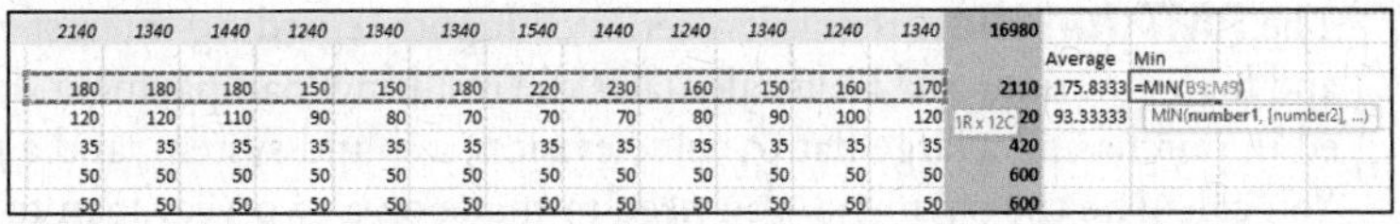

Figure 5-16

Modifying the MIN function

CERTIFICATION READY? 4.2.2

How do you create a formula with the MIN function?

5. Copy cell **P9** to cell **P10**. The result, *70*, is the lowest expected gas bill for the year.
6. SAVE the workbook.

PAUSE. LEAVE the workbook open to use in the next exercise.

Using the MAX Function

The **MAX function** returns the largest value in a set of values. The MAX function works the same way as MIN, except MAX determines the maximum value in a range of cells. To use MAX in a formula, let's enter the function manually.

STEP BY STEP	Use the MAX Function

CERTIFICATION
READY?   4.2.2

How do you create a formula
with the MAX function?

GET READY. USE the workbook you modified in the previous exercise.

1. In cell Q8, type **Max** and press **Enter**.

2. In cell Q9, type **=MAX(B9:M9)** and press **Enter**. The result, *230*, is the highest monthly electricity bill that you expect to receive.

3. Copy cell **Q9** to **Q10**. The result, *120*, is the highest monthly gas bill that you expect to receive (see Figure 5-17).

Figure 5-17

The results of the MAX function

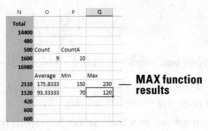

MAX function results

4. SAVE the workbook to your Lesson 5 folder and CLOSE it.

PAUSE. LEAVE Excel open to use in the next exercise.

USING A FINANCIAL FUNCTION

Bottom Line

Functions provide a wide variety of pre-determined calculations for you to choose from, allowing you to easily perform a complex calculation and use it in your worksheet. So far, you have worked with mathematical and statistical functions. Financial functions, in contrast, are designed specifically for various finance tasks that you might want to work on.

Use PMT

The **PMT function** requires a series of inputs regarding interest rate, loan amount (principal), and loan duration, and then calculates the resulting loan payment. In this exercise, you're interested in purchasing a large flat-panel television, a sound system, and a game box with several games. You calculate the payments you need to make on a two-year loan to purchase the equipment.

STEP BY STEP	Use the PMT Function

GET READY. LAUNCH Excel if it is not already running.

1. OPEN the *05 Budget PMT* data file for this lesson.

2. In cell R2, type **Electronics** and press **Enter**.

3. In cell R3, type **Interest** and press **Enter**.

4. In cell R4, type **Years** and press **Enter**.

5. In cell R5, type **Loan Amt** and press **Enter**.

6. In cell R6, type **Payment** and press **Enter**.

7. In cell S3, type **7.5%** and press **Enter**. This is the interest rate on the loan.

8. In cell S4, type **2** and press **Enter**. This is the number of years in which the loan will be repaid.

9. In cell S5, type **2500** and press **Enter**. This is the loan amount, which will cover the total cost of the equipment.

10. In cell S6, type **=-PMT(S3/12,S4*12,S5)** and press **Enter**. The result, *$112.50*, is your calculated monthly payment (see Figure 5-18).

Figure 5-18

The result of the PMT function

R	S
Electronics	
Interest	7.50%
Years	2
Loan Amt	2500
Payment	$112.50

11. SAVE the workbook to your Lesson 5 folder as *05 Budget PMT Solution* and CLOSE it.

PAUSE. LEAVE Excel open to use in the next exercise.

The PMT function calculates a loan payment and uses the syntax =PMT(*rate, nper, pv, [fv], [type]*). The three required arguments for the PMT function are:

- **Rate:** The interest rate charged per period (for example, per month)

- **Nper:** The total number of payments for the loan

- **Pv:** The present value of the loan—in other words, how much you owe; also known as the *principal*

Optional arguments include the future value (fv), which is a cash balance you want to attain after the last payment is made, and type, which indicates when payments are due using the number 1 (due at the beginning of a period) or 0 (due at the end of a period).

When functions take more than one argument, you enter them in a single set of parentheses, separated by commas.

For the purposes of your budget, you include the negative sign (–) at the beginning of the PMT function (=–PMT(S3/12, S4*12,S5)) because the function calculates a payment as a negative value by default. By including the negative sign, the payment appears as a positive number. This follows a basic rule of mathematics: The negative of a negative is a positive.

You divide the first set of values by 12 because 7.5% is the annual interest rate, and dividing it by 12 gives you the monthly interest rate. You multiply the second set of values by 12 to convert the loan term from years to months.

USING FORMULAS TO CREATE SUBTOTALS

Bottom Line

Many Excel veterans use formulas to create subtotals. Subtotaling lets you more easily analyze large sets of data. You can specify ranges for subtotals even if the ranges are not contiguous. In this section, you learn how to use the SUBTOTAL function applied to cell ranges and named ranges.

Selecting and Creating Ranges for Subtotaling

You learn how to select ranges and name them in Lesson 4. You use those skills in this section to prepare to subtotal parts of your budget worksheet.

STEP BY STEP **Select and Create Ranges for Subtotaling**

GET READY. LAUNCH Excel if it is not already running.

1. OPEN the *05 Budget Subtotals* data file for this lesson.
2. Select **B7:M7**.
3. On the FORMULAS tab, in the Defined Names group, click the **Define Name** button. The New Name dialog box opens.

4. In the Name text box, verify that Nonutility_Subtotals appears (see Figure 5-19). Click OK. This names a range for the nonutility subtotal figures.

Figure 5-19

The New Name dialog box

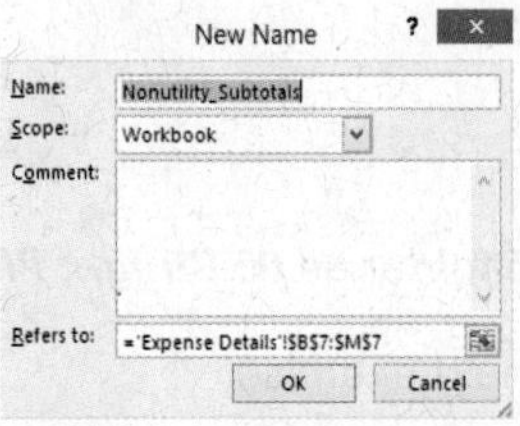

5. SAVE the workbook to your lesson 5 folder   as *05 Budget Subtotals Solution.*

PAUSE. LEAVE the workbook open to use in the next exercise.

Building Formulas for Subtotaling

You can calculate subtotals using the **SUBTOTAL function**, which returns a subtotal for a list. This function recognizes values, cell references, ranges, and named ranges, and totals values created using SUM, AVERAGE, COUNT, and many other functions. This exercise shows you how to use the SUBTOTAL function to sum ranges of cells, both named and unnamed.

STEP BY STEP   **Build Formulas to Subtotal**

GET READY. USE the workbook you modified in the previous exercise.

🔍 **Cross Ref**   This lesson shows you how to build subtotals using the SUBTOTAL function. Lesson 9 , "Working with Data and Macros," covers grouping and outlining to produce subtotals.

1. In cell B17, type **=SUBTOTAL(9,B7,B16)**, as shown in Figure 5-20. Press **Enter**. This formula adds the nonutility subtotal and utility subtotal for January.

Figure 5-20

Entering the SUBTOTAL formula to add two cells that include SUM functions

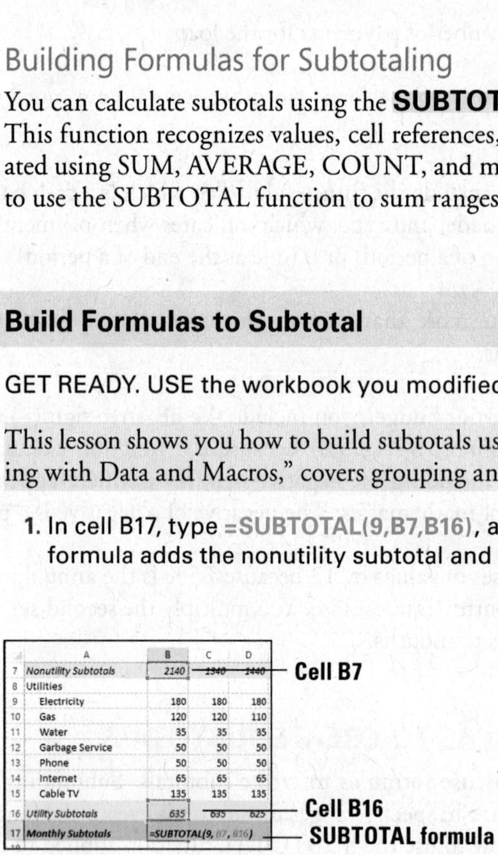

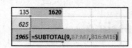

⟵ **Cell B7**

⟵ **Cell B16**
SUBTOTAL formula

2. Copy cell **B17** to **C17:M17**. All monthly subtotals are entered.
3. In cell N17, type **=SUBTOTAL(9,B7:M7,B16:M16)**, as shown in Figure 5-21. Press **Enter**. This formula adds all nonutility and utility expenses for the year.

Figure 5-21

Entering the SUBTOTAL function to add two cell ranges

4. SAVE the workbook.

PAUSE. LEAVE the workbook open to use in the next exercise.

The SUBTOTAL function uses the syntax =SUBTOTAL(*function_num,ref1*,[*ref2*],...).

As you enter the SUBTOTAL function, Excel, displays a list of the function numbers for the first argument. The function number for SUM is 9. You can learn the function numbers for other functions, such as AVERAGE, COUNT, and COUNTA, when entering the SUBTOTAL function or by searching for SUBTOTAL in Excel Help.

Ref1 is the first cell reference, cell range, or named range you want to subtotal. You can include additional cells or ranges by separating them with commas.

In the exercise, you also used the SUBTOTAL function to calculate the total for the budget in cell N17. Creating a total is a standard bookkeeping technique, and allows you to track and adjust subtotals while keeping the final total current.

Modifying Ranges for Subtotaling

Once you create a range in a subtotal, you can easily modify it by editing the range in the formula. You can also modify ranges that are already used in formulas that include the SUBTOTAL function.

STEP BY STEP

Modify Ranges for Subtotaling

GET READY. USE the workbook you modified in the previous exercise.

1. In cell N17, notice that the result of the current formulas is *24,230*.
2. Use the formula bar to modify the formula in N17 like this: **=SUBTOTAL(9,Nonutility_Subtotals,Utility_Subtotals)**. See Figure 5-22. Press **Enter**. This formula replaces the cell ranges with named ranges to add all nonutility and utility expenses for the year, and the result remains the same at *24,230*.

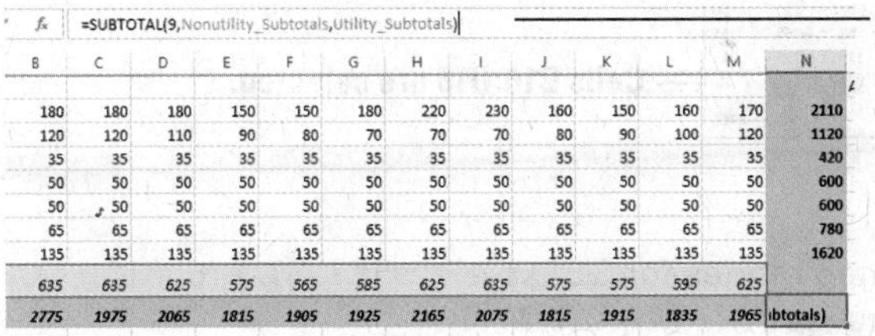

B	C	D	E	F	G	H	I	J	K	L	M	N
180	180	180	150	150	180	220	230	160	150	160	170	2110
120	120	110	90	80	70	70	70	80	90	100	120	1120
35	35	35	35	35	35	35	35	35	35	35	35	420
50	50	50	50	50	50	50	50	50	50	50	50	600
50	50	50	50	50	50	50	50	50	50	50	50	600
65	65	65	65	65	65	65	65	65	65	65	65	780
135	135	135	135	135	135	135	135	135	135	135	135	1620
635	635	625	575	565	585	625	635	575	575	595	625	
2775	1975	2065	1815	1905	1925	2165	2075	1815	1915	1835	1965	btotals)

Modifying the formula

Figure 5-22
Modifying the SUBTOTAL function to use named ranges

3. Click in cell **B19** and then click in the formula bar. Change the formula from =SUM(Q1Expenses) to **=SUBTOTAL(9,Q1Expenses)**. This cell sums the named range Q1Expenses. Because the named range includes monthly data and subtotals, you need to correct the range to include only subtotal figures.
4. On the FORMULAS tab, in the Defined Names group, click **Name Manager**.
5. Select **Q1Expenses** in the list and click **Edit**. The Edit Name dialog box opens (see Figure 5-23).

Figure 5-23

The Edit Name dialog box

Figure 5-23

The Edit Name dialog box

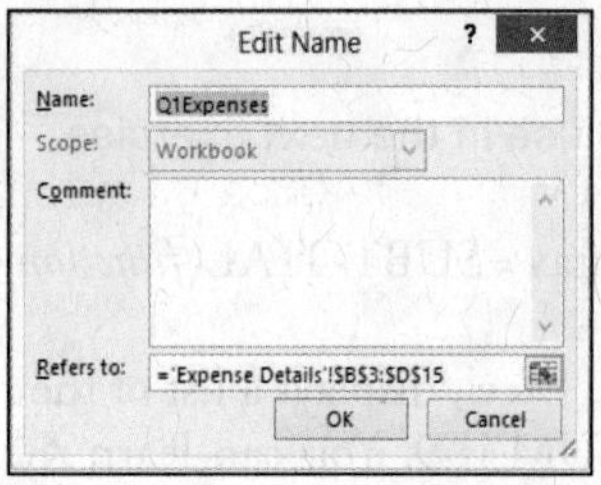

6. Highlight everything in the Refers to text box and press Backspace to delete it.

7. Click cell B7, press and hold the Shift key, and click D7. The range B7:D7 is highlighted.

8. Press and hold the Ctrl key while clicking cells B16, C16, and D16. The selections are shown in Figure 5-24.

Figure 5-24

Selecting multiple ranges to include in the Q1Expenses named range

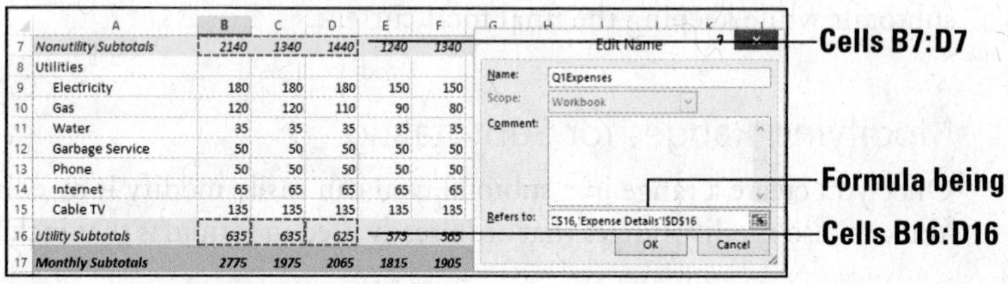

9. In the Edit Name dialog box, click OK.

10. In the Name Manager dialog box, click Close.

11. To verify that you selected the proper ranges for the Q1Expenses range, open the Name box drop-down list (to the left of the formula bar) and select Q1Expenses. The ranges B7:D7 and B16:D16 are selected (see Figure 5-25).

Figure 5-25

Verifying the new ranges for Q1Expenses

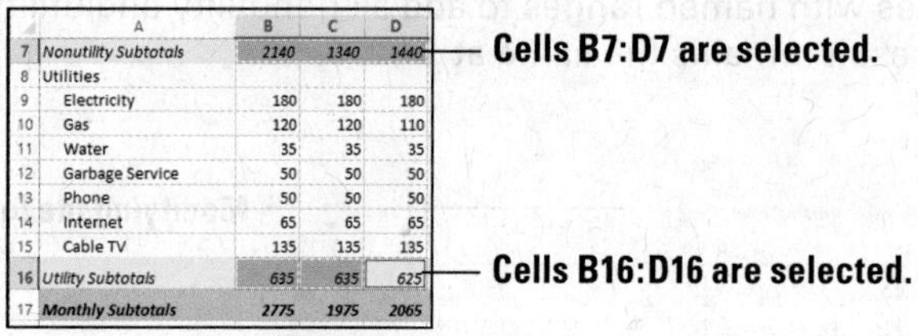

12. Create named ranges for Q2Expenses (E7:G7, E16:G16), Q3Expenses (H7:J7, H16:J16), and Q4Expenses (K7:M7, K16:M16).

13. Copy the formula from cell B19 to B20:B22. Edit the formulas in cells B20, B21, and B22 to use the appropriate named range. For example, the formula in cell B20 should be =SUBTOTAL(9,Q2Expenses).

14. SAVE the workbook to your Lesson 5 folder and CLOSE it.

PAUSE. LEAVE Excel open to use in the next exercise.

UNCOVERING FORMULA ERRORS

Bottom Line

Formulas, because of the sometimes-complex mathematics behind them, are prone to errors when you enter them manually. Fortunately, Excel provides easy-to-use tools to find and correct problems. In this exercise, you intentionally create an error, and then learn how to correct that error.

Reviewing Error Messages

The best way to resolve an error is to analyze, or audit, the error message Excel provides for you. A warning icon appears to the left of cell errors, and clicking that icon provides a pop-up menu with formula evaluation and formula editing commands, and access to Excel Help.

STEP BY STEP	Review an Error Message

GET READY. LAUNCH Excel if it is not already running.

1. OPEN the *05 Budget Error* data file for this lesson.
2. Click in cell **S6**.
3. Edit the formula to change S3 to **R3** and press **Enter**. The first cell reference in the PMT formula now points to the wrong cell. A #VALUE! error displays in cell S6 (see Figure 5-26).

Figure 5-26

An error displays in cell S6.

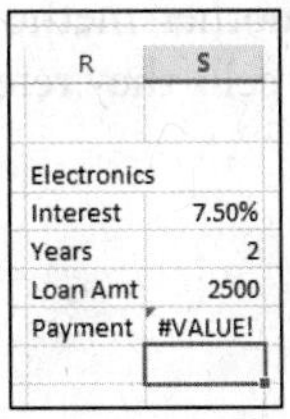

4. Click in cell **S6**. Click the small, yellow warning icon to the left of the cell. A pop-up menu appears (see Figure 5-27). The first item tells you that there is a value error in the function.

Figure 5-27

The pop-up menu for the error

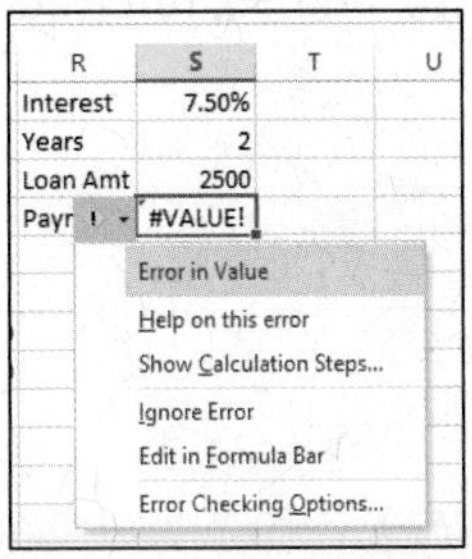

5. In the menu, select **Help on this error**. Excel Help opens to a page on information regarding formula errors. Browse the help topics to see if any of the potential solutions apply to your situation.
6. CLOSE the Excel Help window.
7. SAVE the workbook to your Lesson 5 folder as *05 Budget Error Solution*.

PAUSE. LEAVE the workbook open to use in the next exercise.

Notice the small green triangle in the upper-left corner of cell S6. This means the cell contains a formula error.

To evaluate the error in the formula, select the Show Calculation Steps option from the pop-up menu that appears after you click the warning icon. The Evaluate Formula dialog box, shown in Figure 5-28, indicates the first part of the function is incorrect. In this case, the reference to cell R3 points to a cell containing text. The cell reference should be S3, which contains the interest figure.

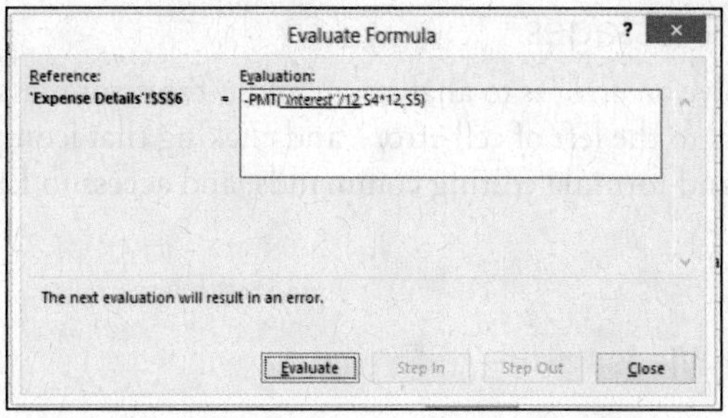

Figure 5-28

The Evaluate Formula
dialog box

Evaluate Formula

Reference: Evaluation:
'Expense Details'!$S$6   = -PMT(Interest/12,S4*12,S5)

The next evaluation will result in an error.

Evaluate   Step In   Step Out   Close

Once you know how to correct an error, you can click the warning icon and select Edit in Formula Bar from the pop-up menu. Make the necessary corrections directly in the formula.

Tracing and Removing Trace Arrows

It's not always easy to resolve a formula error, even using the Show Calculation Steps command, the Evaluate Formula dialog box, and Excel Help. Another method is to use **trace arrows**, which show the relationship between formulas and the cells they refer to.

STEP BY STEP   **Trace a Formula and Remove Trace Arrows**

GET READY. USE the workbook you modified in the previous exercise.

1. Select cell **S6** if it's not already selected.

2. On the FORMULAS tab, in the Formula Auditing group, click Trace Precedents. Two arrows appear (see Figure 5-29). One arrow extends from cell R3 to cell S6, and another (combined) arrow extends from cells S4 and S5 to S6. The arrows indicate that the formula in cell S6 refers to cells R3, S4, and S5, referred to as *precedent cells*.

Figure 5-29

The worksheet showing
trace precedents

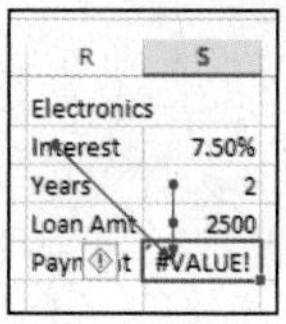

R	S
Electronics	
Interest	7.50%
Years	2
Loan Amt	2500
Payment	#VALUE!

3. On the FORMULAS tab, in the Formula Auditing group, click Remove Arrows. The trace arrows disappear from the worksheet.

4. Click cell **S4**. On the FORMULAS tab, in the Formula Auditing group, click Trace Dependents. One arrow appears from cell S4 to cell S6 (see Figure 5-30). The arrow indicates that cell S4 is part of the formula in cell S6.

Figure 5-30

The worksheet showing
trace dependents

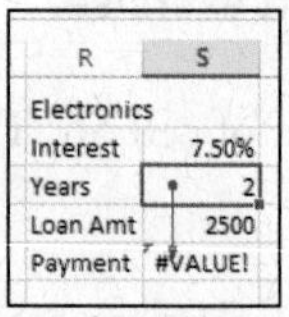

R	S
Electronics	
Interest	7.50%
Years	2
Loan Amt	2500
Payment	#VALUE!

5. SAVE the workbook and CLOSE it.

PAUSE. LEAVE Excel open to use in the next exercise.

You can use trace precedents and trace dependents for formulas that reference cells in another workbook. However, the external workbook must be open before you use the trace commands.

DISPLAYING AND PRINTING FORMULAS

Bottom Line

When you audit the formulas in a worksheet, you might find it useful to print the worksheet with the formulas displayed. In this exercise, you display formulas for printing.

STEP BY STEP | **Print Formulas**

GET READY. LAUNCH Excel if it is not already running.

1. OPEN *05 Budget Print* from your Lesson 5 folder.
2. On the FORMULAS tab, in the Formula Auditing group, click Show Formulas. The formulas appear in the worksheet (see Figure 5-31).

Figure 5-31

Formulas displayed in the worksheet

	A	B	C	D	E	F	G	H	I
1	2013 Housing Expenses								
2	Expense Category	Jan	Feb	Mar	Apr	May	June	July	Aug
3	Rent	1200	1200	1200	1200	1200	1200	1200	1200	1
4	Renter's Insurance	40	40	40	40	40	40	40	40	4
5	Furnishings	500							
6	Miscellaneous	400	100	200		100	100	300	200	
7	Nonutility Subtotals	=SUM(B3:B6)	=SUM(C3:C6)	=SUM(D3:D6)	=SUM(E3:E6)	=SUM(F3:F6)	=SUM(G3:G6)	=SUM(H3:H6)	=SUM(I3:I6)	=
8	Utilities								
9	Electricity	180	180	180	150	150	180	220	230	1
10	Gas	120	120	110	90	80	70	70	70	8
11	Water	35	35	35	35	35	35	35	35	3

Expense Details | Summary

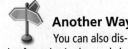

Another Way

You can also display formulas in the worksheet by pressing Ctrl + ` (the grave accent mark). The grave accent mark is usually located on a key on the upper-left part of the keyboard.

3. Click the FILE tab. Click Print and view the Print Preview.
4. Click the Portrait Orientation button and select Landscape Orientation.
5. At the bottom of the print settings, click the Page Setup link to open the Page Setup dialog box.
6. On the Page tab of the dialog box, click Fit to: and leave the defaults as 1 page(s) wide by 1 tall (see Figure 5-32). Click OK to close the dialog box.

Figure 5-32

Settings in the Page Setup dialog box

Print

Copies: 1

Print

Pages: [ ] to [ ]

Print One Sided
Only print on one side of...

Collated
1,2,3 1,2,3 1,2,3

Landscape Orientation

Letter
8.5" x 11"

Normal Margins
Left: 0.7" Right: 0.7"

No Scaling
Print sheets at their actual...

Page Setup

Page Setup

Page | Margins | Header/Footer | Sheet

Orientation

○ Portrait   ● Landscape

Scaling

○ Adjust to: 100 % normal size
● Fit to: 1 page(s) wide by 1 tall

Paper size: Letter
Print quality: 600 dpi

First page number: Auto

Options...

OK | Cancel

1 of 4

7. At the top-left corner of the Backstage view window, click the **Print** button to print the worksheet with formulas displayed.

Cross Ref   You learn more about print options in Lesson 7 , "Formatting Worksheets."

8. On the FORMULAS tab, in the Formula Auditing group, click Show Formulas again to stop displaying formulas in the worksheet.

9. SAVE the workbook to your Lesson 5 folder as *05 Budget Print Solution* and CLOSE it.

CLOSE Excel.

SKILL SUMMARY

In this lesson you learned how:	Exam Objective	Objective Number
To find tools for building functions on the FORMULAS tab.		
To display dates and times with functions.		
To use the SUM function.	Demonstrate how to apply the SUM function.	4.2.1
To use the COUNT function.	Demonstrate how to apply the COUNT function.	4.2.3
To use the AVERAGE function.	Demonstrate how to apply the AVERAGE function.	4.2.4
To use the MIN and MAX functions.	Demonstrate how to apply the MIN and MAX functions.	4.2.2
To use the PMT financial function.		
To use formulas to create subtotals.		
To respond to formula errors.		
To display and print formulas.		

Knowledge Assessment

Multiple Choice

Select the best response for the following statements.

1. Which of the following calculates the total from the adjacent cell through the first nonnumeric cell by default, using the SUM function in its formula?
   a. AVERAGE
   b. AutoSum
   c. COUNTA
   d. MAX

2. The arguments of a function are contained within which of the following?
   a. brackets
   b. asterisks
   c. commas
   d. parentheses

3. When using the SUBTOTAL function, which is the function number for the SUM function?
   a. 1
   b. 4
   c. 9
   d. 11

4. You want to add a range of cells and then divide by the number of cell entries, determining the mean value of all values in the range. Which function do you use?
   a. SUBTOTAL
   b. AVERAGE
   c. COUNT
   d. PMT

5. Which of the following is *not* a required argument for the PMT function?
   a. Fv
   b. Rate
   c. Nper
   d. Pv

6. You want to calculate the number of nonblank cells in your worksheet. Which function do you use?
   a. SUM
   b. COUNT
   c. COUNTA
   d. MAX

7. You want to create a formula that calculates the number of years you have lived. You were born in 1991. Which of the following formulas is correct?
   a. =YEAR(TODAY())-1991
   b. =YEAR(TODAY())+1991
   c. =YEAR(COUNT())-1991
   d. =YEAR(COUNT())+1991

8. Which of the following statements accurately describes the default selection for AutoSum?
   a. You must make the selection before clicking AutoSum.
   b. By default, AutoSum totals all entries above the cell in which the formula is located, even if the cells contain a mix of numeric and nonnumeric content.
   c. By default, AutoSum calculates the total from the adjacent cell through the first nonnumeric cell.
   d. AutoSum does not have a default selection.

9. You want to sum multiple noncontiguous cell ranges that are named. Which of the following is best to use?
   a. AutoSum
   b. SUBTOTAL
   c. MAX
   d. MIN

10. The COUNT and MIN functions are examples of which category of functions?
   a. text
   b. statistical
   c. financial
   d. logical

True / False

Circle T if the statement is true or F if the statement is false.

T F   1. All functions require arguments within parentheses.

T F   2. Using functions helps to ensure the accuracy of a formula's results.

T F   3. The TODAY function returns the current date in a worksheet.

T F   4. The AVERAGE function returns the number of cells in the selected range that contain text or values, but not blank cells.

T F   5. When functions take more than one argument, you should enter them in multiple sets of nested parentheses, separated by commas.

T F 6. In the PMT function, the Nper argument is the total number of payments for the loan.

T F 7. You can use a range in the SUBTOTAL function, but you cannot modify the range once it's in use.

T F 8. A cell cannot be a trace dependent and a trace precedent for the same formula.

T F 9. You can refer to the TODAY and NOW functions in other formulas to perform calculations.

T F 10. To evaluate the error in the formula, select the Edit in Formula Bar option from the pop-up menu that appears after you click the warning icon.

Competency Assessment

Project 5-1: Use Statistical Functions to Analyze Game Wins and Losses

You work for Wingtip Toys and have been playing three new games each day to master them, hoping to demo the games in the retail store. You've been keeping track of your wins and losses in a worksheet. A "1" indicates a win, and a "0" indicates a loss.

GET READY. LAUNCH Excel if it is not already running.

1. OPEN the *05 Game Stats* data file for this lesson.
2. In cell E3, type =AVERAGE(B3:D3) and press Enter.
3. Copy the formula in E3 to E4:E12.
4. Click cell G2.
5. On the FORMULAS tab, in the Function Library group, click the AutoSum button arrow and select Count Numbers.
6. Click cell B3 and drag the mouse pointer to cell D12.
7. Release the mouse and press Enter to accept the range B3:D12. The result, *30*, is the total number of times you played the games in 10 days.
8. In cell G3, type =SUM(B3:D12) and press Enter. The result, *17*, represents the total number of times you won the games.
9. In cell G4, type =G2-G3 and press Enter. The result, *13*, represents the total number of times you lost the games.
10. On the FORMULAS tab, in the Formula Auditing group, click Show Formulas. The formulas appear in the worksheet.
11. Click the Show Formulas button again to turn off the display of formulas.
12. SAVE the workbook to your Lesson 5 folder as *05 Game Stats Solution* and then CLOSE the file.

LEAVE Excel open to use in the next project.

Project 5-2: Create Formulas to Calculate Totals and Averages

An employee at Wingtip Toys has entered second quarter sales data into a worksheet. You will enter formulas to calculate monthly and quarterly totals and average sales.

GET READY. LAUNCH Excel if it is not already running.

1. OPEN *05 Wingtip Toys Sales* from the data files for this lesson.
2. Click cell B11, type =SUM(B4:B10), and press Enter.

3. Click cell C11. On the FORMULAS tab, in the Function Library group, click Insert Function.

4. In the Insert Function dialog box, select SUM and click OK.

5. In the Function Arguments dialog box, click Collapse Dialog and select C4:C10, if it's not already entered.

6. Click the Expand Dialog button and click OK to close the dialog box.

7. Copy the formula from C11 to D11.

8. Click cell E4. On the FORMULAS tab, in the Function Library group, click the AutoSum button. Press Enter to accept B4:D4 as the cells to total.

9. Click cell E5 and then in the Function Library group click Insert Function. In the Insert Function dialog box, SUM will be the default. Click OK.

10. The range B5:D5 should appear in the Number1 box in the Function Arguments dialog box. Click OK to close the dialog box.

11. Click cell E5 and use the fill handle to copy the formula to E6:E10.

12. Click cell E11. In the Function Library group click AutoSum. Press Enter to accept the range as E4:E10.

13. Click cell F4. Click the Insert Function button. Select AVERAGE in the Insert Function dialog box and click OK. In the Function Arguments dialog box, click OK.

14. Click in the formula bar and change E4 to D4. Click OK.

15. Click cell F4 and use the fill handle to copy the formula to F5:F11.

16. SAVE the workbook to your Lesson 5 folder as *05 Wingtip Toys Sales Solution* and then CLOSE the file.

LEAVE Excel open to use in the next project.

Proficiency Assessment

Project 5-3: Compare Payments

Monica recently graduated from college and needs to replace her current vehicle. She wants to use Excel 2013 to help her decide whether she should buy a lower priced vehicle or something newer.

GET READY. LAUNCH Excel if it is not already running.

1. OPEN *05 Compare Payments* from the data files for this lesson.

2. Enter a formula that displays today's date in cell B2.

3. Enter a formula in cell B4 that calculates a monthly interest rate based on the rate displayed in B3. Be sure to use an absolute cell reference to B3.

4. Use the PMT function to calculate loan payments for each dollar amount below the Amount Borrowed heading. Be sure to use absolute cell references for the rate and nper arguments, and add a minus sign before PMT in the formula so the result is a positive value.

5. SAVE the workbook to your Lesson 5 folder as *05 Compare Payments Solution* and then CLOSE the file.

LEAVE Excel open for the next project.

Project 5-4: Resolve Formula Errors

You work for the School of Fine Arts and have been asked to correct errors in a student GPA worksheet.

GET READY. LAUNCH Excel if it is not already running.

1. OPEN *05 Fine Art Formulas* from the data files for this lesson.
2. An error occurs in cell F4. Examine the formula in the formula bar and correct the error manually.
3. For the error in cell F6, click the warning icon and use one of the options in the pop-up list to correct the error.
4. For the error in cell F12, use the Show Calculation Steps command to determine the source of the error and then correct the error using the formula bar.
5. One of the formulas at the bottom of the worksheet needs to be corrected. Use trace arrows to determine which formula's range includes an extra cell and correct the formula.
6. SAVE the workbook to your Lesson 5 folder as *05 Fine Art Formulas Solution* and then CLOSE the file.

LEAVE Excel open for the next project.

Mastery Assessment

Project 5-5: Build Formulas to Track Merchandise Stock Levels

Wide World Importers sells a variety of fine wool rugs, textiles, ceramics, furniture, and statues from the Middle East. The company tracks levels of stock in nine different categories, and keeps several units of each type of stock in five warehouses spread across the region. You have been asked to track all 45 stock levels.

GET READY. LAUNCH Excel if it is not already running.

1. OPEN *05 Importers Stock* from the data files for this lesson.
2. Use the SUM formula to total the number of stock units in each warehouse.
3. Calculate the number of stock units that are at zero (0) across all six warehouses in cell B14.
4. Calculate the maximum number of stock units in any warehouse in cell B15.
5. Calculate the minimum number of stock units in any warehouse in cell B16.
6. SAVE the workbook to your Lesson 5 folder as *05 Importers Stock Solution* and then CLOSE the file.

LEAVE Excel open for the next project.

Project 5-6: Complete the Analysis Sheet in the Budget Workbook

Blue Yonder Airlines wants to analyze the sales and expense data from its four-year history. You will complete the Analysis sheet to summarize the data.

GET READY. LAUNCH Excel if it is not already running.

1. OPEN *05 Income Analysis Start* from the data files for this lesson.

2. On the Analysis sheet, calculate average sales for each of the four service categories using range names. Use Name Manager to examine range names in the workbook before you enter the formulas.

3. Calculate the average expenses for each of the four service categories.

4. Calculate the maximum sales for each of the four service categories.

5. Calculate the maximum expenses for each of the four service categories.

6. SAVE the workbook to your Lesson 5 folder as *05 Income Analysis Solution* and then CLOSE the file.

CLOSE Excel.

The Graphic Design Institute offers associate's and bachelor's degrees in graphic design, with a full slate of in-classroom and online classes. Students from the United States and several other countries attend the Institute as full-time students during fall and spring semesters, or by participating in accelerated programs offered twice a year.

As an employee in the organization's home office, you create workbooks related to the Institute's programs and fundraising efforts.

Project 1: Creating a Workbook and Entering Data

Your first task is to create a workbook that can serve as the initial structure for recording students' GPAs. The student names you type in the worksheet are in an accelerated program and work with a specific instructor.

GET READY. LAUNCH Excel if it is not already running.

1. Open a new, blank workbook.
2. In cell A1, type Graphic Design Institute and press Enter.
3. In cell A2, type Instructor: Sachin Karnik and press Enter.
4. In cells A3:F3, type the following:

   Name
   ID
   GD1
   DM1
   Type1
   GPA

5. In cells A4:A14, type the following:

   Con, Aaron
   Cunha, Goncalo
   Byham, Richard A.
   Klimov, Sergey
   Chopra, Manish
   Davison, Eric
   Hensien, Kari
   Levitan, Michal
   Paschke, Dorena
   Wang, Tony
   Ribaute, Delphine

6. Double-click the right border of column A to expand the column width.
7. In cell B4, type 13001.
8. Copy cell B4 to B5. In cell in B5, change 13001 to 13002.
9. Highlight cells B4:B5, point to the fill handle in the lower-right corner of cell B5, drag it to cell B14, and release the mouse.
10. Click the FILE tab to open Backstage view. In the left pane, click Save As to display the save options.
11. Under Save As, click Computer, and then click Browse.
12. Use the left navigation pane in the Save As dialog box to navigate to your student data folder.

13. In the toolbar near the top of the Save As dialog box, click New folder. A folder icon appears with the words *New folder* selected.

14. Type Circling Back and press Enter.

15. Double-click the Circling Back folder.

16. In the File Name box, type *GPA Solution*.

17. Click the Save button.

18. CLOSE the file.

LEAVE Excel open for the next project.

Project 2: Using Basic Formulas and Functions

The Graphic Design Institute is supported in part by individual and corporate tax-deductible contributions. Contributors are asked to select a fund to which their contribution applies. It is your responsibility to create some simple statistics to help senior management understand the number of contributors, the average amount contributed per organization and per individual, and the minimum and maximum dollar amounts of all contributions.

GET READY. LAUNCH Excel if it is not already running.

1. Open *Contributions* from the student data files.

2. In cell A33, type Total Contributions and press Enter.

3. In cell C33, type =SUM(C4:C32) and press Enter.

4. Select cells C4:C32. On the FORMULAS tab, in the Defined Names group, click the Define Name button arrow and select Define Name.

5. In the New Name dialog box, accept the defaults and click OK. A range named Amount is created.

6. In cell B35, type =COUNT(C4:C32) and press Enter. The result represents the number of contributions made to Graphic Design Institute.

7. Click in B36. On the FORMULAS tab, in the Function Library group, click Insert Function. In the Insert Function dialog box, search for AVERAGE, select it in the Select a function list box, and click OK.

8. In the Function Arguments dialog box, click Collapse Dialog and select C4:C21.

9. Click the Expand Dialog button and click OK to close the dialog box. A triangle appears in the upper left corner of B36 and an error message button is displayed. Click the button arrow, and then click Ignore Error. The result in B36 represents the average dollar amount contributed by organizations.

10. Copy the formula in cell B36 to B37.

11. With B37 selected, change the range in the formula to C22:C32. A triangle appears in the upper left corner of B37 and an error message button is displayed. Click the button arrow, and then click Ignore Error. The result in B37 represents the average dollar amount contributed by individuals.

12. In cell B38, type =MIN(Amount) and press Enter. This formula uses the named range and displays the minimum dollar amount contributed by an organization or individual.

13. In cell B39, type =MAX(Amount) and press Enter. This formula displays the maximum dollar amount contributed by an organization or individual.

14. SAVE the workbook to your Lesson 5 folder as *Contributions Solution* in the Circling Back folder.

LEAVE the workbook open for the next project.

Project 3: Configuring a Workbook for Printing

You have prepared a workbook with data related to contributions to the Institute and have been asked to print copies for a meeting to be attended by senior management.

GET READY. USE the workbook you saved in the previous project.

1. Select cells A1:C39.
2. Click the PAGE LAYOUT tab, and in the Page Setup group, click the Print Area button and select Set Print Area.
3. Click the FILE tab to access Backstage view.
4. Click Print and view the document in the Print Preview pane.
5. Click the Scaling button arrow, and then click Custom Scaling Options.
6. In the Page Setup dialog box, in the Adjust to box, type 110. This action makes the text a little larger without having to change the font in the document. Click OK.
7. Click Print.
8. Click anywhere in the worksheet to remove highlighting from the selection.
9. Check the Quick Access Toolbar. If you do not see the Quick Print button, click the Customize Quick Access Toolbar arrow at the end of the toolbar and select Quick Print. The Quick Print button appears on the toolbar, which you can use to print any Excel document in the future.
10. SAVE the workbook to your Lesson 5 folder as *Contributions Print Solution* in the Circling Back folder, and then CLOSE the file.

CLOSE Excel.

LESSON SKILL MATRIX

Skills	Exam Objective	Objective Number
Inserting and Deleting Cells	Insert and delete cells.	2.1.6
Manually Formatting Cell Contents	Modify cell alignment and indentation.	2.2.2
	Change font and font styles.	2.2.3
	Apply highlighting.	2.2.7
	Apply Number formats.	2.2.6
	Wrap text within cells.	2.2.5
	Merge cells.	2.2.1
Copying Cell Formatting with the Format Painter	Use Format Painter.	2.2.4
Understanding Paste Special Options		
Formatting Cells with Styles	Apply cell styles.	2.2.8
Working with Hyperlinked Data	Insert hyperlinks.	1.2.2
Applying Conditional Formatting to Cells	Apply conditional formatting.	2.3.1
Clearing a Cell's Formatting		

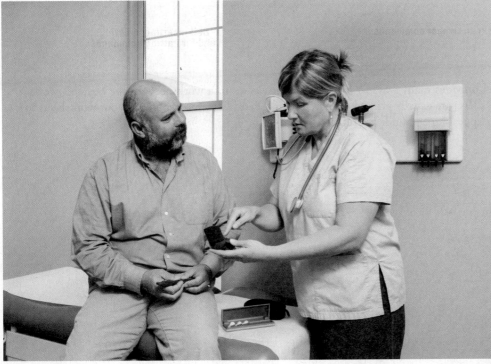

© Fertnig /iStockphoto

KEY TERMS

- align
- attribute
- conditional formatting
- font
- Format Painter
- hyperlink
- merged cells
- Mini toolbar
- Paste Special
- Rules Manager
- style
- wrap

Contoso, Ltd.'s income is

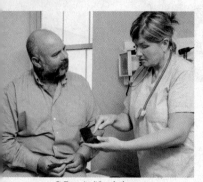

© Fertnig /iStockphoto

generated by four physicians and a physician's assistant (PA). Working in collaboration with the physicians, the PA sees patients who need an appointment when all the physicians' schedules are full. Many chronically ill patients whose conditions require frequent monitoring are scheduled with the PA. Because the firm often experiences hectic schedules and overtime, management is considering adding a nurse practitioner (NP) to balance the patient load. An NP is a registered nurse who provides some of the same care as a physician. For instance, in most states, an NP can prescribe medications. In this lesson, you use Excel to manage the relevant data associated with Contoso's physicians and their assistants to determine whether an NP should be added to the staff.

SOFTWARE ORIENTATION

Formatting Excel Worksheets

The Excel HOME tab shown in Figure 6-1 contains formatting and editing commands that help you enhance the appearance and readability of your worksheets. You will use commands from almost every group on this tab as you learn to apply formatting to data, copy formatting, and apply styles.

Character attributes   **Number formats**   **Style commands**

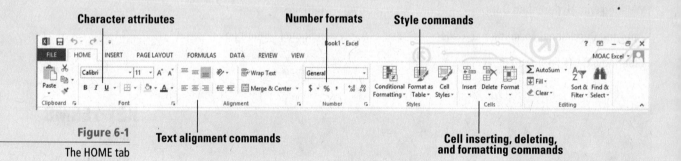

Figure 6-1

The HOME tab

Text alignment commands   **Cell inserting, deleting, and formatting commands**

Excel provides many ways to format text and values in a worksheet. In the business world, worksheets are usually printed or shared with others. Therefore, you want your worksheets to be as appealing and understandable as possible.

INSERTING AND DELETING CELLS

Bottom Line

After creating a worksheet, you might decide to add more data or delete unnecessary data. Although you can insert or delete entire rows and columns, sometimes you just need to work with a single cell or a range of cells. You can insert or delete single cells or ranges of cells, but be aware that doing so affects the location of other cells.

Inserting Cells into a Worksheet

When you insert a cell in a column, you force the other cells in the same column to move down. Inserting a cell into a row shifts the other cells in the same row to the right.

STEP BY STEP   **Insert Cells into a Worksheet**

GET READY. Launch Microsoft Excel.

1. OPEN the *06 Patient Visits Insert Delete* data file for this lesson.
2. Click in cell **G5** to make it the active cell.
3. On the HOME tab, in the Cells group, click the top part of the Insert button, as shown in Figure 6-2. All cells in column G beginning with G5 shift down one cell.

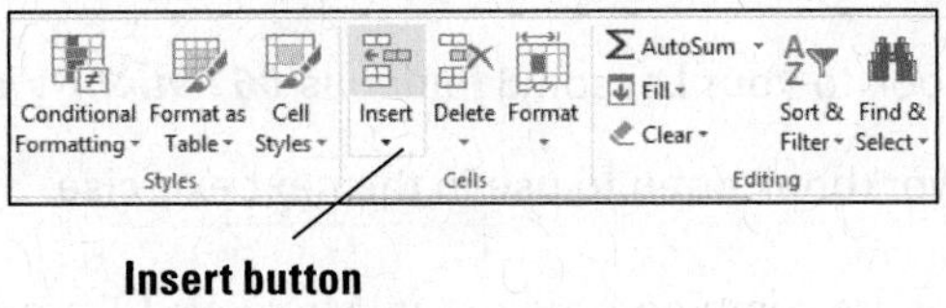

Figure 6-2

The Insert button in the Cells group on the HOME tab

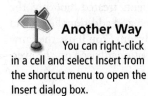

Insert button

Another Way
You can right-click in a cell and select Insert from the shortcut menu to open the Insert dialog box.

4. Type **590** and press **Enter**.
5. Select cells **O3:O9**.
6. On the HOME tab, in the Cells group, click the **Insert** button arrow and then select **Insert Cells**.
7. In the Insert dialog box, ensure the **Shift cells right** option is selected, as shown in Figure 6-3. Click **OK**.

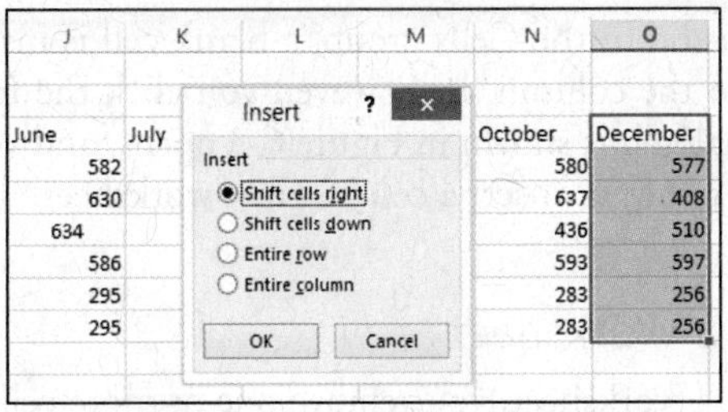

Figure 6-3

The Insert dialog box

8. Notice that the cells formerly in O3:O9 shift one cell to the right. The worksheet should look similar to Figure 6-4.

Figure 6-4

The worksheet after inserting cells

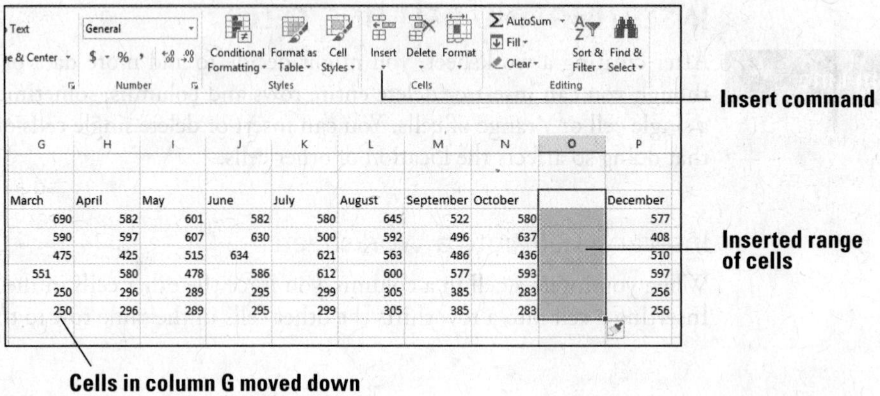

Insert command

Inserted range of cells

Cells in column G moved down

CERTIFICATION READY?   2.1.6

How do you insert cells into a worksheet?

9. In cell O3, type November.

10. Enter the following numbers in cells O4 through O9:

480

502

446

577

302

302

11. SAVE the workbook to your Lesson 6 folder as *06 Patient Visits Insert Delete Solution*.

PAUSE. LEAVE the workbook open to use in the next exercise.

Additions and changes are common activities in Microsoft Office Excel 2013 workbooks. After creating and saving an Excel workbook that tracks the number of patients treated monthly, the Contoso administrative assistant discovered that corrections were needed and additional data had to be added. In the previous exercise, you made the corrections and additions. You'll use the same worksheet later in this lesson to determine whether to hire a nurse practitioner based on the average number of hours worked by employees.

When you click the Insert command arrow in the Cells group on the HOME tab, the menu indicates you can easily insert cells, worksheet rows, worksheet columns, or even a new worksheet into a workbook.

If you click the Insert button in the Cells group, a blank cell is inserted and, by default, the existing cells move down in the column. If, however, you click the Insert button arrow and select Insert Cells, the Insert dialog box shown in Figure 6-3 opens, and you can choose to shift cells to the right or down, insert a row, or insert a column in a worksheet.

Deleting Cells from a Worksheet

When you delete cells in a worksheet, you remove one or more cells, forcing other cells to move up or to the left.

STEP BY STEP   **Delete Cells from a Worksheet**

GET READY. USE the workbook you modified in the previous exercise.

1. Click cell P7 to make it the active cell.

2. On the HOME tab, in the Cells group, click the Delete button arrow, and then select Delete Cells.

Another Way
You can right-click in a cell and select Delete from the shortcut menu to open the Delete dialog box.

3. In the Delete dialog box, select the Shift cells left option and click OK. The content in cell Q7 shifts to the left and appears in cell P7.

4. Highlight the range A8:P8.

CERTIFICATION
READY?   2.1.6

How do you delete a cell
from a worksheet?

5. Right-click the selection, which is a duplicate of the next row of data, and select Delete from the shortcut menu.

6. In the Delete dialog box, ensure Shift cells up is selected and click OK.

7. To delete a range of cells in a column, highlight the range D3:D8, and on the HOME tab, in the Cells group, click the Delete button arrow and then select Delete Cells. Ensure Shift cells left is selected, and click OK. The worksheet should look similar to Figure 6-5.

Figure 6-5

The worksheet after deleting cells

	A	B	C	D	E	F	G	H	I	J	K	L	M	N	O
1	Contoso, Ltd.														
2															
3	Last Name	First Name	Job Title	January	February	March	April	May	June	July	August	September	October	November	December
4	Carey	Cynthia	Physician	602	605	690	582	601	582	580	645	522	580	480	577
5	Garcia	Debra	Physician	579	550	590	597	607	630	500	592	496	637	502	408
6	Laszlo	Rebecca	Physician	604	594	475	425	515	634	621	563	486	436	446	510
7	Wilson	Dan	Physician	575	325	551	580	478	586	612	600	577	593	577	600
8	Koska	Tomas	PA	326	311	250	296	289	295	299	305	385	283	302	256
9															

8. SAVE the workbook and CLOSE the file.

PAUSE. LEAVE Excel open to use in the next exercise.

When you click the arrow below the Delete command in the Cells group on the HOME tab, notice that you can delete a cell, a worksheet row, a worksheet column, or an entire worksheet.

Deleting a cell is not the same as clearing a cell's content, which you learned about in Lesson 2, "Working with Microsoft Excel 2013." Think of an Excel worksheet being similar to several stacks of boxes. The boxes are lined up alongside one another and on top of one another to form a grid. The open side of every box is facing you. You can take contents out of a box, thus emptying the box, but the box still remains in the stack. This is equivalent to clearing a cell's content. The same principle applies when you press Delete on the keyboard—you're simply removing the cell's content. However, when you pull a box out of the stack, the entire box is gone. This is the same as deleting a cell using the Delete Cells command.

Cross Ref   For more information about clearing a cell's content, refer to Lesson 2.

MANUALLY FORMATTING CELL CONTENTS

Bottom Line

Excel provides many different tools to help you format cell content. Applying formatting can make your worksheets easier to understand, draw attention to important information, and provide a professional touch. The tools you need to make your worksheets look outstanding are located in various groups on the ribbon's HOME tab.

Aligning and Indenting Cell Contents

Excel enables you to align text and numbers horizontally and vertically. To **align** means to arrange in a line or bring into alignment. Horizontal alignment includes left, right, and center. Vertical alignment includes top, middle, and bottom. You can use Alignment commands in the Alignment group on the HOME tab or commands in the Format Cells dialog box to change the alignment of cell contents. Indentation moves cell contents closer to the right border of a cell.

STEP BY STEP   Align Cell Contents

GET READY. LAUNCH Excel if it is not already running.

1. OPEN the *06 Patient Visits Format Cells* data file for this lesson.
2. Select **A3:O3**.

Troubleshooting Manual formatting is applied only to selected cells. Therefore, you need to select the cell or a range of cells before applying the formatting.

3. On the HOME tab, in the Alignment group, click the Center button, as shown in Figure 6-6. The column labels are now horizontally centered.

Figure 6-6

The Alignment buttons

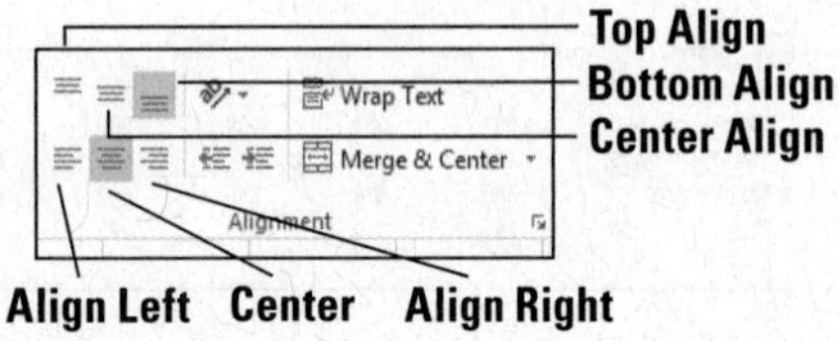

Top Align
Bottom Align
Center Align

Align Left   Center   Align Right

CERTIFICATION
READY?   2.2.2

How do you align cell content in a worksheet?

4. Select **D4:O8**, and then on the HOME tab, in the Alignment group, click the Align Right button. All numbers in the months columns are now right-aligned.
5. SAVE the workbook to your Lesson 6 folder as *06 Patient Visits Format Cells Solution*.

PAUSE. LEAVE the workbook open to use in the next exercise.

By default, when you enter alphabetic characters or alphabetic characters combined with numbers or symbols, the cell content is left-aligned horizontally, which means it lines up along the left side of the cell. When you enter numbers, the content is right-aligned—that is, it lines up with the right side of the cell. When you center content, it lines up with the midpoint of a cell.

Another Way
You can access the Format Cells dialog box by right-clicking in a cell or on a column or row label and selecting Format Cells.

Vertical alignment affects the location of content vertically within a cell. Your options in the Alignment group on the HOME tab are Top Align, Middle Align, and Bottom Align. You can also select Justify or Distributed, which are available in the Format Cells dialog box, shown in Figure 6-7. To access the dialog box, click the Dialog Box Launcher in the lower-right corner of the Alignment group on the HOME tab.

Figure 6-7

The Format Cells dialog box

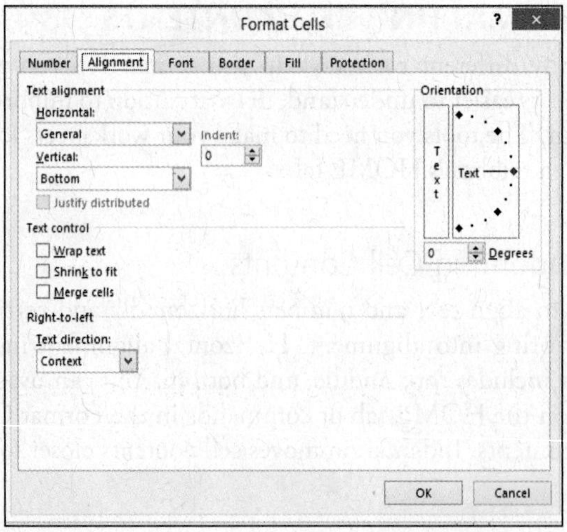

The following describes each type of vertical alignment:

- **Top (or Top Align):** The top line of text appears at the top of the cell.

- **Center (or Middle Align):** Text is centered halfway between the top and bottom of the cell.

- **Bottom (or Bottom Align):** Text appears at the bottom of the cell. This is the default vertical alignment.

- **Justify:** Text is spread evenly throughout the cell. Excel will wrap text and automatically adjust the row height, if necessary.

- **Distributed:** Text is spread evenly between the top of the cell and the bottom, separated by blank space.

STEP BY STEP	**Indent Cell Contents**

GET READY. USE the workbook you saved in the previous exercise.

Another Way
You can press the Alt key and press H, and then press 6 to indent a cell's content.

1. Select C4:C8.
2. On the HOME tab, in the Alignment group, click the Increase Indent button, as shown in Figure 6-8. The cell content moves toward the right cell border.

Figure 6-8

Indentation button options

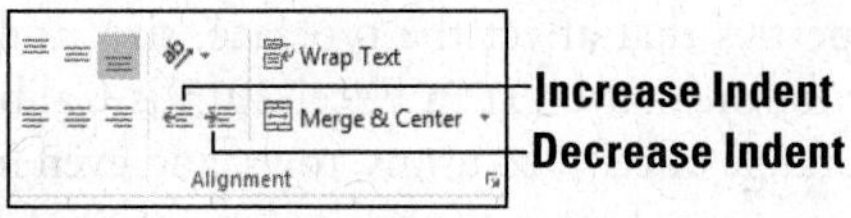

Increase Indent
Decrease Indent

3. Click the Decrease Indent button. The cell content moves back toward the left cell border.

PAUSE. LEAVE the workbook open to use in the next exercise.

Indenting data in an Excel worksheet is often performed on subordinate text to enhance readability.

Changing Text Orientation

Changing the orientation of text can help you fit long column or row headings into a small space without changing the font size or column width. You can find the Orientation tool in the Alignment group on the HOME tab.

STEP BY STEP	**Change Text Orientation**

GET READY. USE the workbook from the previous exercise.

1. Select A3:O3.
2. Click the Orientation button to open the menu, as shown in Figure 6-9.

Figure 6-9

The Orientation menu

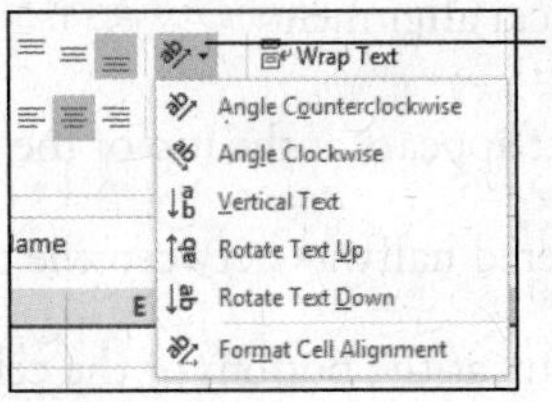

**Orientation button opens
the Orientation menu**

3. Select **Angle Counterclockwise**. The column heading labels appear angled from lower left to upper right within each cell.
4. Click the **Orientation** button, and select **Angle Clockwise**. The column heading labels appear angled from upper left to lower right.
5. Click the **Orientation** button, and select **Vertical Text**. The column heading labels appear in a vertical line from top to bottom.
6. Click the **Orientation** button, and select **Rotate Text Up** and then **Rotate Text Down** to see how these settings affect the text.
7. Click the **Orientation** button, and select **Format Cell Alignment**. In the Format Cells dialog box, in the Degrees box, enter **0** and click **OK**. The column heading labels return to their original orientation.

PAUSE. LEAVE the workbook open to use in the next exercise.

Choosing Fonts and Font Sizes

A **font** is a set of text properties that affect the typeface, size, and similar aspects of text. The default, or predefined, font for ordinary text in Excel 2013 is Calibri, 11 point. You can change the font for a selected cell, a range of cells, columns, rows, and even for specific characters within a cell. To change the font, select a new font in the Font menu in the Font group on the HOME tab. You can also change the size in the Font Size box or click Increase Font Size or Decrease Font Size until the size you want is displayed in the Font Size box.

STEP BY STEP   **Choose Fonts and Font Sizes**

GET READY. USE the workbook from the previous exercise.

1. Click **A1**.
2. On the HOME tab, in the Font group, open the **Font** menu and select the first option under Theme Fonts at the top, **Calibri Light**, as shown in Figure 6-10. Only the text in cell A1 changes to the new font.

Figure 6-10

The Font menu

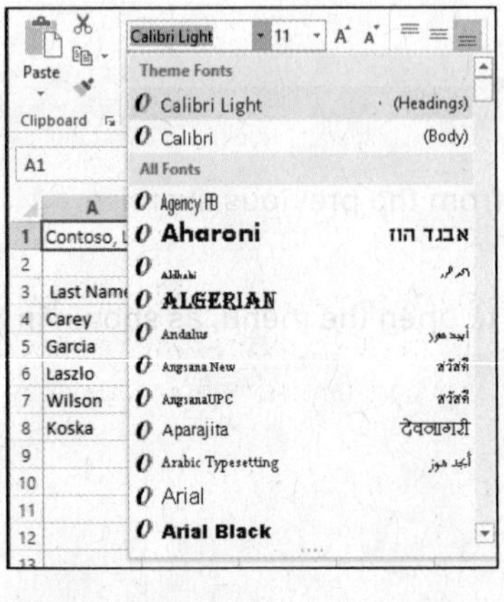

3. With cell A1 still selected, open the Font Size menu indicated in Figure 6-11. Select 18. The font size of the text changes to 18 point.

Figure 6-11

The font-related options in the Font group

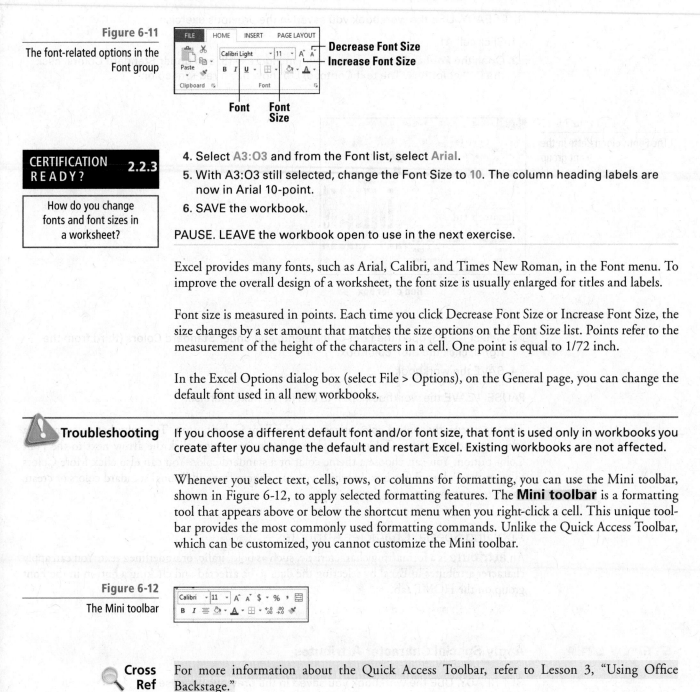

CERTIFICATION READY?   **2.2.3**

How do you change fonts and font sizes in a worksheet?

4. Select A3:O3 and from the Font list, select Arial.

5. With A3:O3 still selected, change the Font Size to 10. The column heading labels are now in Arial 10-point.

6. SAVE the workbook.

PAUSE. LEAVE the workbook open to use in the next exercise.

Excel provides many fonts, such as Arial, Calibri, and Times New Roman, in the Font menu. To improve the overall design of a worksheet, the font size is usually enlarged for titles and labels.

Font size is measured in points. Each time you click Decrease Font Size or Increase Font Size, the size changes by a set amount that matches the size options on the Font Size list. Points refer to the measurement of the height of the characters in a cell. One point is equal to 1/72 inch.

In the Excel Options dialog box (select File > Options), on the General page, you can change the default font used in all new workbooks.

Troubleshooting   If you choose a different default font and/or font size, that font is used only in workbooks you create after you change the default and restart Excel. Existing workbooks are not affected.

Whenever you select text, cells, rows, or columns for formatting, you can use the Mini toolbar, shown in Figure 6-12, to apply selected formatting features. The **Mini toolbar** is a formatting tool that appears above or below the shortcut menu when you right-click a cell. This unique toolbar provides the most commonly used formatting commands. Unlike the Quick Access Toolbar, which can be customized, you cannot customize the Mini toolbar.

Figure 6-12

The Mini toolbar

Cross Ref   For more information about the Quick Access Toolbar, refer to Lesson 3, "Using Office Backstage."

Changing Font Color

Excel enables you to pick from thousands of colors to apply to data in worksheets. Open the Font Color menu in the Font group on the HOME tab to work with theme colors and the standard color palette, or click More Colors to access a much wider selection of colors.

STEP BY STEP   **Change Font Color**

GET READY. USE the workbook you saved in the previous exercise.

1. Click cell **A1**.
2. Open the Font Color menu, as shown in Figure 6-13, and under Standard Colors, click the Red color box. The text Contoso, Ltd. now has a red font color.

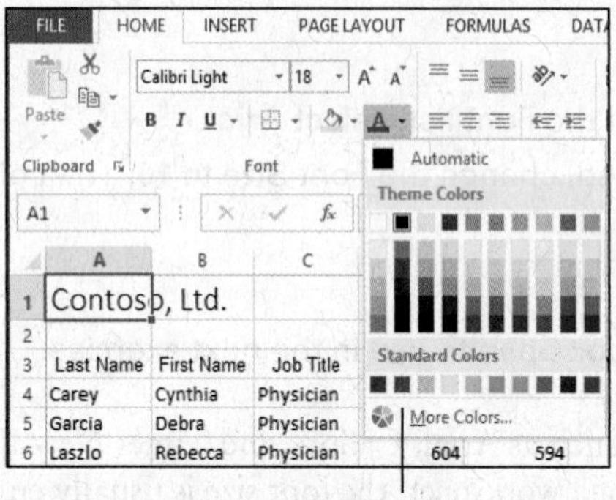

Figure 6-13

The Font Color palette in the Font group

Red color box

3. Select **A3:O3**, open the Font Color menu, and under Standard Colors (third from the right), click the Blue color box.
4. SAVE the workbook.

PAUSE. LEAVE the workbook open to use in the next exercise.

The most recently applied color appears on the Font Color button. To apply that color, make a selection and click Font Color. To apply a different text color, click the arrow next to the Font Color button. You can choose a theme color or a standard color. You can also click More Colors to open the Colors dialog box, in which you can choose from additional standard colors or create colors to your own specifications.

Applying Special Character Attributes

An **attribute** is a formatting characteristic, such as bold, italic, or underlined text. You can apply character attributes in Excel by selecting the data to be affected and clicking a button in the Font group on the HOME tab.

STEP BY STEP   **Apply Special Character Attributes**

GET READY. USE the workbook you saved in the previous exercise.

1. Select **A3:O3**.
2. In the Font group, click the Bold button, and then click the Italic button, as shown in Figure 6-14. The column labels appear in bold and italics.

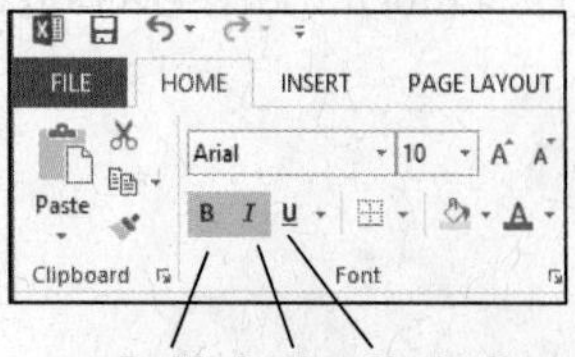

Figure 6-14

The Bold, Italic, and Underline buttons in the Font group

Bold Italic Underline

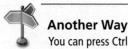
Another Way
You can press Ctrl + B to apply boldface, Ctrl + I to apply italics, or Ctrl + U to apply underlining to selected text.

3. Select A4:B8 and click the **Bold** button. The first and last names are now bolded.

4. SAVE the workbook.

PAUSE. LEAVE the workbook open to use in the next exercise.

Special character attributes provide visual appeal beyond changing the font and font size. You can also call attention to specific data by applying these special characteristics.

To apply underlining, click the Underline button in the Font group. You can also click the arrow next to the Underline button and select Double Underline from the list.

When you apply underlining to cells, only the cell contents appear underlined, as shown in Figure 6-15. To create the appearance of a continuous rule, or underline, across the bottom of a cell, you need to apply a border. You'll learn about borders later in this lesson.

Figure 6-15

Underlined cells

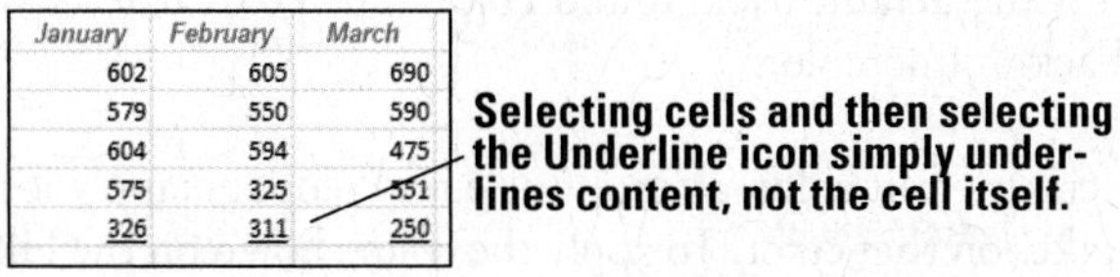

January	February	March
602	605	690
579	550	590
604	594	475
575	325	551
326	311	250

Selecting cells and then selecting the Underline icon simply underlines content, not the cell itself.

Filling Cells with Color

When formatting worksheets, you'll find you often want to apply a colored shading, or highlighting, to the background of cells to make them stand out from the rest of the cells around them. Use the Fill Color tool in the Font group on the HOME tab to achieve this type of highlighting.

STEP BY STEP **Fill Cells with Color**

GET READY. USE the workbook you saved in the previous exercise.

1. Select A3:O3.

2. In the Font group, click the **Fill Color button arrow**, as shown in Figure 6-16. The Theme Colors and Standard Colors palettes appear.

Figure 6-16

The Fill Color button in the Font group

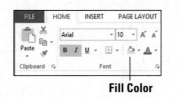

Fill Color

3. Select the **Blue, Accent 1, Lighter 80%** color box, as shown in Figure 6-17. A light blue background is applied to the column heading row.

Figure 6-17

The Blue, Accent 1,
Lighter 80% color box in
the Fill Color tool

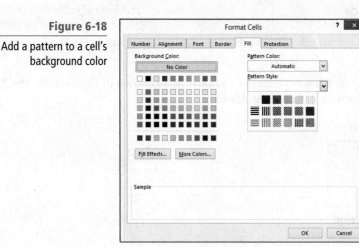

CERTIFICATION
READY?   2.2.7

How do you apply a
background fill color, or
highlighting, to cells in
a worksheet?

4. SAVE the workbook and CLOSE the file.

PAUSE. LEAVE Excel open to use in the next exercise.

No Fill (clear) is the default background color. The color palette you used to apply font color is also used for background color.

Much like selecting a font color, after you select a color and apply it to a cell's background, the Fill Color button takes on that color. To apply the color shown on the Fill Color button, simply make a selection and click the button. To apply a different fill color, click the arrow next to Fill Color and apply either a theme color or a standard color. You can also click More Colors to open the Colors dialog box and custom blend colors.

You can apply a pattern effect to cells as well as a background color. To do so, first select the range of cells to which you want to apply a background color with fill effects, then click the Font group's Dialog Box Launcher. The Format Cells dialog box opens. Click the Fill tab. As shown in Figure 6-18, make a selection in the Pattern Style box to add a pattern to the background color.

Figure 6-18

Add a pattern to a cell's
background color

Applying Number Formats

Normally, values you enter into cells are unformatted—they consist of a string of numerals. You should format the numbers so they are easier to read or are consistent in terms of the number of decimal places shown. You can use tools in the Number group on the HOME tab to apply a wide variety of number formats, from currency to dates and times to scientific notation.

STEP BY STEP   **Apply Number Formats**

GET READY. With Excel running, perform these actions:

1. OPEN the *06 Contoso Revenue* data file for this lesson.
2. Ensure that Sheet1 is the active sheet.
3. Select B4:D8. This data should be formatted as General, without commas or decimal places.
4. On the HOME tab, in the Number group, open the Number Format menu as shown in Figure 6-19.

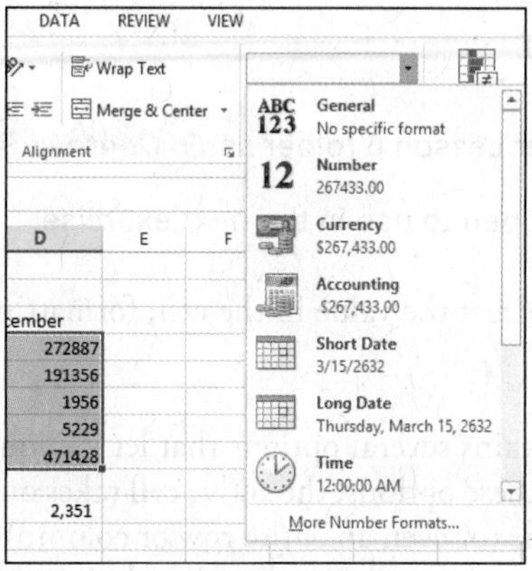

Figure 6-19

The Number Format menu

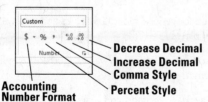

Another Way

You can also apply number formats using the Format Cells dialog box. Just right-click a cell or range of cells and select Format Cells from the shortcut menu. In the Format Cells dialog box, click the Number tab.

5. Select Currency. The numbers are now formatted as dollars, with two decimal places to represent cents.
6. With B4:D8 still selected, in the Number Format menu, select Accounting. This format left-aligns the dollar sign in each cell.
7. In the Number group, click the Decrease Decimal button twice to display no decimal places. The Increase Decimal and Decrease Decimal buttons are shown in Figure 6-20. The numbers are now rounded to whole dollars.

Figure 6-20

The buttons in the Number group

8. Click in a blank cell, such as A11.
9. Click Sheet2.
10. Select B6:B11.
11. In the Number group, click the Comma Style button. Notice that the numbers are formatted with a thousands separator and two decimal places but no dollar sign.
12. With B6:B11 still selected, in the Number group, click the Accounting Number Format button, and then click the Decrease Decimal button twice. These actions make the current range consistent with the number format on Sheet1.
13. Select C6:C11.
14. In the Number Format menu, select Short Date. The dates are now displayed in the mm/dd/yyyy format.

CERTIFICATION READY?   2.2.6

How do you apply number formatting in a worksheet?

15. Manually decrease the width of column C to eliminate extra space, similar to Figure 6-21.

Figure 6-21

Sheet2 after applying number and date formats and decreasing the width of column C

	A	B	C
1	Contoso, Ltd		
2	Accounts Receivable		
3	Outstanding Balances as of December 31		
4			
5	Patient	Amount	Invoice Date
6	Strande, Amy	$ 2,830	11/20/2012
7	Samant, Mandar	$ 3,890	10/10/2012
8	Allen, Michael	$ 587	10/25/2012
9	Bonifaz, Luis	$ 621	12/4/2012
10	Combel, Craig	$ 354	10/30/2012
11	Gaffney, Lawrie	$ 875	11/8/2012

16. SAVE the workbook to your Lesson 6 folder as *06 Contoso Revenue Solution*.

PAUSE. LEAVE the workbook open to use in the next exercise.

Formatting a number does not affect the value in the cell; formatting simply changes the appearance of the number.

The Number Format menu contains several options that let you quickly apply common number formats. When you click one of these options, the active cell takes on the specified number format. You also can select a range of cells (or even an entire row or column) before clicking a number format option. If you select more than one cell, Excel applies the number format to all of the selected cells. Table 6-1 summarizes the various formats available in the Number Format menu.

Table 6-1

Excel number format preset options available in the Number Format menu

Number Format	Description
General	This is the default format that Excel applies when you enter text or a number in a cell.
Number	This format is used for the general display of numbers, with two decimal places by default.
Currency	This format is used for general monetary values and displays the default currency symbol with two decimal places.
Accounting	This format is also used for monetary values. Currency symbols and decimal points are aligned in this format.
Short Date	This format displays days, months, and years in the mm/dd/yyyy style by default.
Long Date	This format displays dates in a long format, such as Sunday, January 10, 2014.
Time	This format applies a single format: 12:00:00 AM. If you want to choose another time format, you must use the Format Cells dialog box.
Percentage	This format displays the number with a percent sign and two decimal places.
Fraction	This format displays the number as a fraction.
Scientific	This format displays numbers in exponential notation (with an E): for example, 2.00E+05 = 200,000; 2.05E+05 = 205,000.

In most cases, the number formats provided in the Number Format menu are adequate. However, you may occasionally want more control over how your values appear. Excel offers control over number formats through the Format Cells dialog box.

The Number tab of the Format Cells dialog box displays 12 categories of number formats from which to choose, most of which are also available from the Number Format menu. However, when you select a category from the list box in the Format Cells dialog box, the right side of the tab changes to display options.

For example, the Number category has three options that you can control:

• The number of decimal places to display

• Whether to use a thousand separator

• How to display negative numbers

Notice that the Negative Numbers list box has four choices, two of which display negative values in red. These choices change depending on the number of decimal places and whether you choose to separate thousands. Also, notice that a Sample section near the top of the dialog box previews how the active cell will appear with the selected number format. After you make your choices, click OK to apply the number format to all of the selected cells.

The number format categories that are unique to the Number tab in the Format Cells dialog box are described in Table 6-2.

Table 6-2 Additional Number format categories	**Number Format**	**Description**
	Special	Contains additional number formats specific to your country. In the United States, there are four (Zip Code, Zip Code+4, Phone Number, and Social Security Number); in Canada, there are two (Phone Number and Social Insurance Number); in most other countries, there are none.
	Custom	Enables you to define custom number formats that are not included in any of the other categories.
	Text	When applied to a value, causes Excel to treat the value as text (even if it looks like a number). This feature is useful for items such as part numbers.

Wrapping Text in a Cell

When a cell is formatted to **wrap** text, data that's too long to display within the cell's width automatically displays on the next line within the cell. Wrapped text also increases row height automatically. If you later change the column width, the text wrapping and row height adjust automatically.

STEP BY STEP   **Wrap Text in a Cell**

GET READY. USE the workbook you saved in the previous exercise.

CERTIFICATION READY? 2.2.5	1. Click **Sheet1**. Notice that the content in two cells in column A cannot be fully displayed because of length.
How do you wrap text in a cell?	2. Click **A4**, and then hold down the **Ctrl** key and click **A7**. Both cells—A4 and A7—are selected.
	3. On the HOME tab, in the Alignment group, click the **Wrap Text** button. The text in both cells wraps to a second line without affecting the column width, as shown in Figure 6-22. Notice that the Wrap Text button takes on a green background, indicating that the text in the selected cells is wrapped.

Figure 6-22

The formatted worksheet with text wrapping

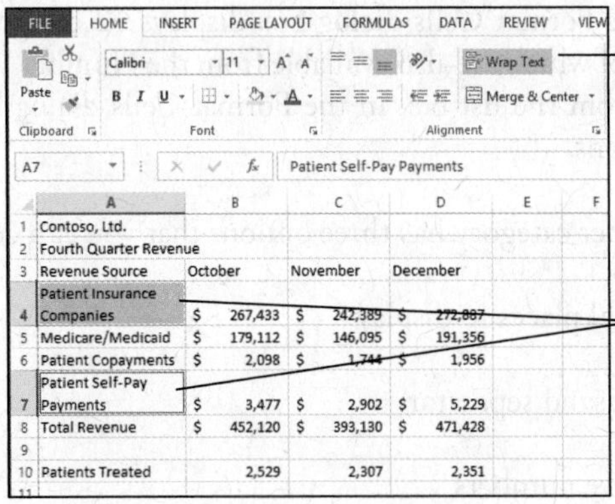

4. SAVE the workbook.

PAUSE. LEAVE the workbook open to use in the next exercise.

You can remove text wrapping by selecting the appropriate cell or cells and clicking the Wrap Text button again.

Troubleshooting   If you choose a different default font and/or font size, that font is used only in workbooks you create after you change the default and restart Excel. Existing workbooks are not affected.

Merging Cells and Splitting Merged Cells

Merging is a useful tool when combining data from other sources, and as a means of centering a heading across multiple columns. A **merged cell** combines two or more cells into a single cell. Splitting cells, or unmerging them, separates previously merged cells. The Merge & Center button in the Alignment group on the HOME tab provides several merge commands and the Unmerge Cells command.

STEP BY STEP   **Merge and Split Cells**

GET READY. USE the workbook you saved in the previous exercise.

1. On Sheet1, select **A1:D1**.
2. On the HOME tab, in the Alignment group, click the main part of the Merge & Center button. The company name remains in a single cell, which is now centered across the columns.
3. Select **A2:D2**.
4. On the HOME tab, in the Alignment group, open the Merge & Center menu. Select Merge & Center. The heading remains in a single cell, which is now centered across the columns. This step has the same effect on A2:D2 as Step 2 had on A1:D1.
5. Select **A3:D3**.
6. From the Merge & Center menu, click Merge & Center.
7. Read the error message that appears and click OK.
8. Only the heading in the first column remains, which is not the effect we want. Press Ctrl + Z to undo the last change and restore the headings. See Figure 6-23.

CERTIFICATION READY?   **2.2.1**

How do you merge two or more cells in a worksheet?

Figure 6-23

The formatted worksheet
with cells in the first two rows
merged and centered

Figure 6-23

The formatted worksheet
with cells in the first two rows
merged and centered

	A	B	C	D	
1		Contoso, Ltd.			Merged and
2		Fourth Quarter Revenue			centered
3	Revenue Source	October	November	December	
4	Patient Insurance Companies	$ 267,433	$ 242,389	$ 272,887	
5	Medicare/Medicaid	$ 179,112	$ 146,095	$ 191,356	
6	Patient Copayments	$ 2,098	$ 1,744	$ 1,956	
7	Patient Self-Pay Payments	$ 3,477	$ 2,902	$ 5,229	
8	Total Revenue	$ 452,120	$ 393,130	$ 471,428	
9					
10	Patients Treated	2,529	2,307	2,351	
11					

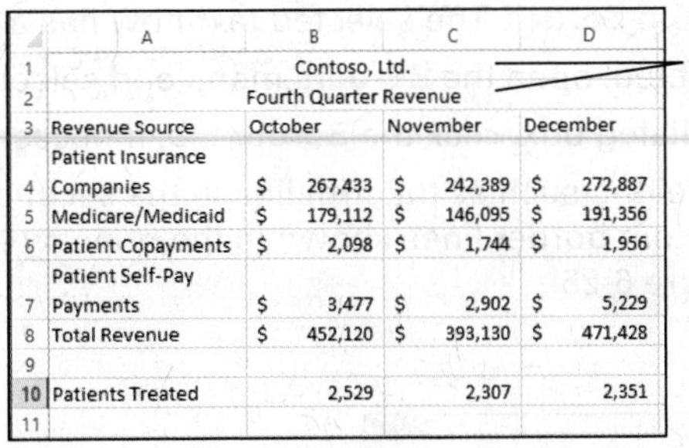

9. SAVE the workbook.

PAUSE. LEAVE the workbook open to use in the next exercise.

A merged cell is created by combining two or more horizontally or vertically adjacent cells. When you merge cells, the selected cells become one large cell that spans multiple columns or rows.

To split, or unmerge, cells right after merging them, press Ctrl + Z. Otherwise, open the Merge & Center menu and select Unmerge Cells to split merged cells. You can split cells that have been merged into separate cells again, but you cannot split a single worksheet cell that has not been merged.

Placing Borders around Cells

You can use borders to enhance a worksheet's visual interest and to make it easier to read. You can either apply Excel's predefined border styles, or you can customize borders by specifying a line style and color of your choice.

STEP BY STEP   **Place Borders around Cells**

GET READY. USE the workbook you saved in the previous exercise.

1. On Sheet1, select **A3:D3**.
2. On the HOME tab, in the Font group, click the **Borders** button arrow to open the Borders menu, as shown in Figure 6-24.

Figure 6-24

The Borders menu in the Font group

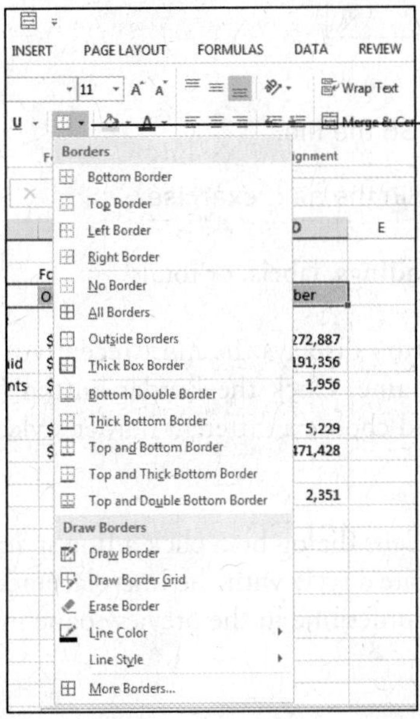

The Borders button opens the Borders menu.

3. Select **Top and Bottom Border**. The selected text now has a top and bottom border.

4. With **A3:D3** still selected, open the **Borders** menu and select **More Borders**.

5. In the Format Cells dialog box, click the **Border** tab, if necessary.

6. Click a thicker line weight, such as the fifth line in the second column under Style. Then click the top and bottom border lines shown in the preview to the right to apply the thicker line. See Figure 6-25.

Figure 6-25

Applying a border option

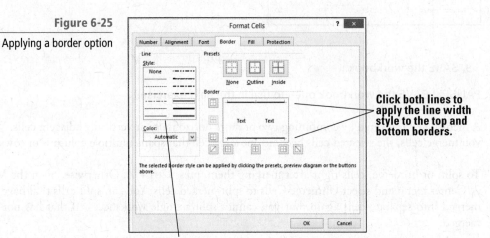

Click both lines to apply the line width style to the top and bottom borders.

Selected line width style

7. Open the **Color** list and under Standard Colors, select the **Blue** color box (third from right under Standard Colors), and then click the top and bottom border lines shown in the preview to the right to apply the color. Click **OK** and then click in a blank cell so you can view the result. See Figure 6-26.

Figure 6-26

The worksheet with a colored border above and below column heading labels

	A	B	C	D
1		Contoso, Ltd.		
2		Fourth Quarter Revenue		
3	Revenue Source	October	November	December
4	Patient Insurance Companies	$ 267,433	$ 242,389	$ 272,887
5	Medicare/Medicaid	$ 179,112	$ 146,095	$ 191,356
6	Patient Copayments	$ 2,098	$ 1,744	$ 1,956
7	Patient Self-Pay Payments	$ 3,477	$ 2,902	$ 5,229
8	Total Revenue	$ 452,120	$ 393,130	$ 471,428
9				
10	Patients Treated	2,529	2,307	2,351

8. SAVE the workbook and CLOSE the file.

PAUSE. LEAVE Excel open to use in the next exercise.

Borders are often used to set off headings, labels, or totals.

In the Font group, the Borders button displays the most recently used border style, and the button's name changes to that style name. Click the Border button (not the arrow) to apply that style, or you can click the arrow and choose a different border style. Click More Borders to apply a custom or diagonal border.

On the Border tab of the Format Cells dialog box, click a line style and a color. You can select a border style from the presets or create a style with the line-placement options in the Border area. To remove a border, just click the border line in the preview pane in the Format Cells dialog box.

COPYING CELL FORMATTING WITH THE FORMAT PAINTER

Bottom Line

Format Painter is a feature found in most Office applications that allows you to quickly copy formatting attributes that you have already applied and "paint" those attributes onto other text, shapes, pictures, and worksheet cells. You can use Format Painter to copy font, font size, font color, character attributes like bolding and underlining, alignment, indentation, number formats, and borders and shading. Format Painter is located in the Clipboard group on the HOME tab and on the Mini toolbar.

STEP BY STEP **Use the Format Painter to Copy Formatting**

GET READY. LAUNCH Excel if it is not already running.

1. OPEN the *06 Contoso Painter Paste Special* data file for this lesson.
2. Click Sheet2.
3. Click in cell A5.

Another Way
Format Painter is available on the Mini toolbar as well as in the Clipboard group.

4. On the HOME tab, in the Alignment group, click the Center button.
5. On the HOME tab, in the Clipboard group, click the Format Painter button. The mouse pointer changes to a plus sign with a paint brush, as shown in Figure 6-27.

Figure 6-27

The Format Painter pointer

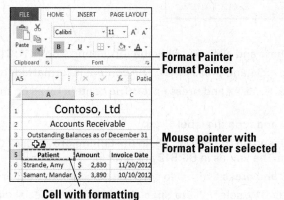

6. Drag over B5:C5. The formatting from A5 is applied to B5 and C5.
7. If Format Painter is still active, click the Format Painter button again or press Esc to turn off the Format Painter.
8. SAVE the workbook to your Lesson 6 folder as *06 Contoso Painter Paste Special Solution*.

CERTIFICATION READY? 2.2.4

How do you use Format Painter to copy formatting from one cell to another?

PAUSE. LEAVE the workbook open to use in the next exercise.

You can double-click the Format Painter if you want to apply formats to multiple selections.

UNDERSTANDING PASTE SPECIAL OPTIONS

Bottom Line

Excel gives you another tool, called **Paste Special,** that enables you to control specifically what you want to paste after using the Copy or Cut command, such as cell content, formulas, values, formatting, and much more. Paste Special is available in the Clipboard group on the HOME tab, or in the shortcut menu that appears after right-clicking a cell.

STEP BY STEP **Understand Paste Special Options**

GET READY. USE the workbook you saved in the previous exercise.

1. Ensure you are on Sheet2.
2. In cell A12, type **Jacobsen, Lola**.
3. Select **B11:C11**.
4. Press **Ctrl + C** to copy the selection to the Clipboard.
5. Right-click in cell **B12** and select **Paste Special** from the shortcut menu. The Paste Special dialog box opens, as shown in Figure 6-28.

Figure 6-28

The Paste Special dialog box

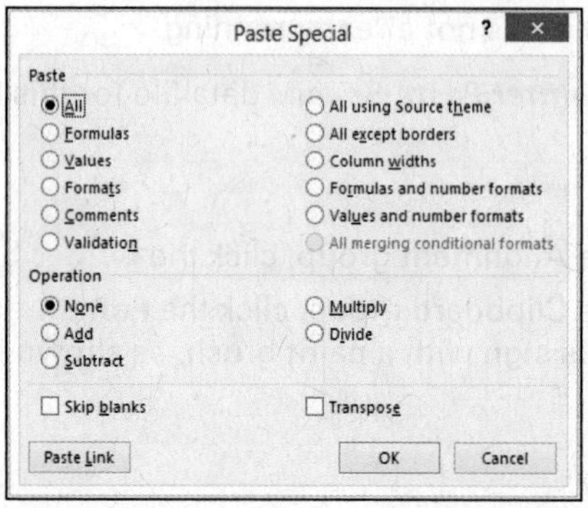

6. Select **Formats** and click **OK**. Only the formatting from B11:C11 is applied to B12:C12.
7. In B12, type **1534** and press **Enter**. The content is formatted the same as B11.
8. In C12, type **12/15/12** and press **Enter**. The content takes on the same date format as C11.
9. Click in **A13** and type the label **Total**.
10. Click in **B13**, and on the HOME tab, in the Editing group, click the **AutoSum** button, and press **Enter**. The values in B6:B12 are totaled.
11. Click in **B13** and press **Ctrl + C** to copy the selection to the Clipboard.
12. Right-click in **B14**, select **Paste Special**, in the Paste Special dialog box, select **Values**, and then click **OK**. Press **Esc** to cancel the moving border in cell B13. Only the value of the formula in B13 was copied to B14, not the formula itself or any cell formatting.
13. Delete the content in cell **B14**. See Figure 6-29.

Figure 6-29

The worksheet after applying Paste Special

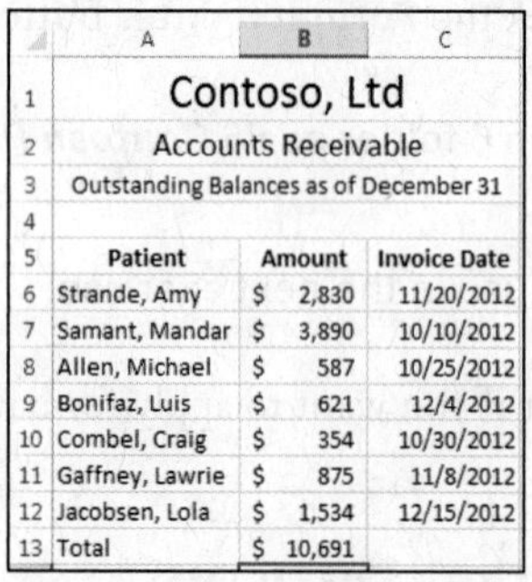

	A	B	C
1	Contoso, Ltd		
2	Accounts Receivable		
3	Outstanding Balances as of December 31		
4			
5	Patient	Amount	Invoice Date
6	Strande, Amy	$ 2,830	11/20/2012
7	Samant, Mandar	$ 3,890	10/10/2012
8	Allen, Michael	$ 587	10/25/2012
9	Bonifaz, Luis	$ 621	12/4/2012
10	Combel, Craig	$ 354	10/30/2012
11	Gaffney, Lawrie	$ 875	11/8/2012
12	Jacobsen, Lola	$ 1,534	12/15/2012
13	Total	$ 10,691	

14. SAVE the workbook and CLOSE the file.

PAUSE. LEAVE Excel open to use in the next exercise.

With Paste Special, you select a cell or range of cells with the content or formatting you want to copy, issue the Copy or Cut command, and then select Paste Special. Using either the buttons in a menu or the Paste Special dialog box, you can choose what you want to paste into a different cell or range. Some of the paste options include formulas, only the values displayed as a result of formulas, cell formatting, column widths, everything except cell borders, values and number formats, and links.

 Cross Ref   Lesson 7, "Formatting Worksheets," covers transposing rows and columns using the Paste Special command.

FORMATTING CELLS WITH STYLES

Bottom Line   Excel provides a gallery of preset cell styles you can apply to greatly enhance the appeal of your worksheets. You can duplicate and modify styles to create your own custom styles, and you can easily remove styles if you no longer want to use that particular formatting.

Applying a Cell Style

A **style** is a set of formatting attributes that you can apply to a cell or range of cells more easily than by setting each attribute individually. To apply a cell style to an active cell or range, click Cell Styles in the Styles group on the HOME tab, then choose the cell style that you want to apply. You can apply more than one style to a cell or range.

STEP BY STEP   **Apply Cell Styles**

GET READY. LAUNCH Excel if it is not already running.

1. OPEN the *06 Contoso Cell Styles* data file for this lesson.
2. Click Sheet1.
3. Select cell A1.
4. On the HOME tab, in the Styles group, open the Cell Styles menu. The Cell Styles gallery appears, as shown in Figure 6-30.

Figure 6-30

The Cell Styles gallery

[Figure showing the Cell Styles gallery with sections: Custom (Currency 2, Normal 2); Good, Bad and Neutral (Normal, Bad, Good, Neutral); Data and Model (Calculation, Check Cell, Explanatory..., Input, Linked Cell, Note, Output, Warning Text); Titles and Headings (Heading 1, Heading 2, Heading 3, Heading 4, Title, Total); Themed Cell Styles (20%-Accent1 through 20%-Accent6, 40%-Accent1 through 40%-Accent6, 60%-Accent1 through 60%-Accent6, Accent1 through Accent6); Number Format (Comma, Comma [0], Currency, Currency [0], Percent); New Cell Style...; Merge Styles...]

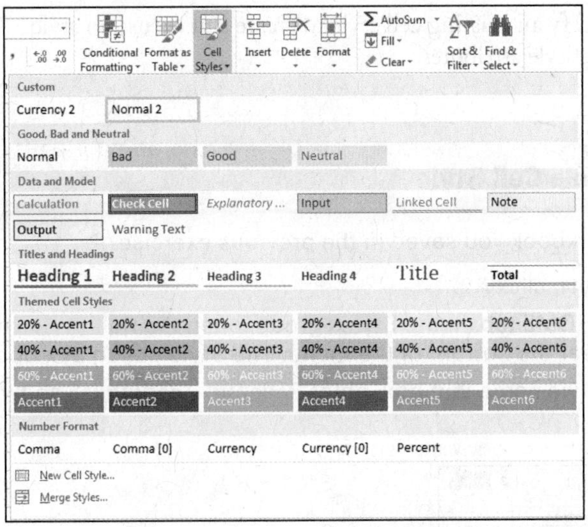

5. In the Titles and Headings section, select the Heading 1 style to apply it to the first cell of the worksheet.
6. Select cell A2.
7. Open the Cells Styles gallery and in the Themed Cell Styles section, select Accent1. A blue background with white text is applied to cell A2.
8. Select A8:D8.
9. Open the Cells Styles gallery and in the Titles and Headings section, select Total. A thin blue border appears above A8:D8, and a double underline appears under the range of cells. Select a blank cell to see the results. See Figure 6-31.

Figure 6-31

The worksheet with cell styles applied

	A	B	C	D
1		Contoso, Ltd.		
2		Fourth Quarter Revenue		
3	Revenue Source	October	November	December
4	Patient Insurance Companies	$ 267,433	$ 242,389	$ 272,887
5	Medicare/Medicaid	$ 179,112	$ 146,095	$ 191,356
6	Patient Copayments	$ 2,098	$ 1,744	$ 1,956
7	Patient Self-Pay Payments	$ 3,477	$ 2,902	$ 5,229
8	Total Revenue	$ 452,120	$ 393,130	$ 471,428
9				
10	Patients Treated	2,529	2,307	2,351

CERTIFICATION READY?   2.2.8

How do you apply cell styles to one or more cells in a worksheet?

10. SAVE the workbook to your Lesson 6 folder as *06 Contoso Cell Styles Solution*.

PAUSE. LEAVE the workbook open to use in the next exercise.

Style attributes include fonts and font sizes, number formats, and borders and shading. Excel has several predefined styles that you can apply; you can also modify or duplicate a cell style to create a custom cell style.

When you point to defined styles in the Cell Styles gallery, you can see the formatting that will be used when you apply each style. This feature allows you to assess the formatting without actually applying it.

Experiment with combining styles to achieve your desired effect. For example, you can click a themed cell style, which will apply shading to the cell. Then, you can click Cell Styles again and click Heading 1, which applies a larger font size, bold, and a thick bottom border.

If you are not satisfied with a style you apply, you can use the Undo command immediately after applying the style, remove the style by applying the Normal style, or apply another style to the cell or range.

Customizing Cell Styles

You can modify an existing cell style to create a new custom style. When doing so, you can either add or delete style attributes.

STEP BY STEP   **Customize a Cell Style**

USE the workbook you saved in the previous exercise.

1. On Sheet1, click A2.
2. On the HOME tab, in the Styles group, open the Cell Styles menu and select New Cell Style near the bottom of the menu. The Style dialog box opens.
3. In the Style name text box, enter Revenue Heading, as shown in Figure 6-32.

Figure 6-32

The Style dialog box

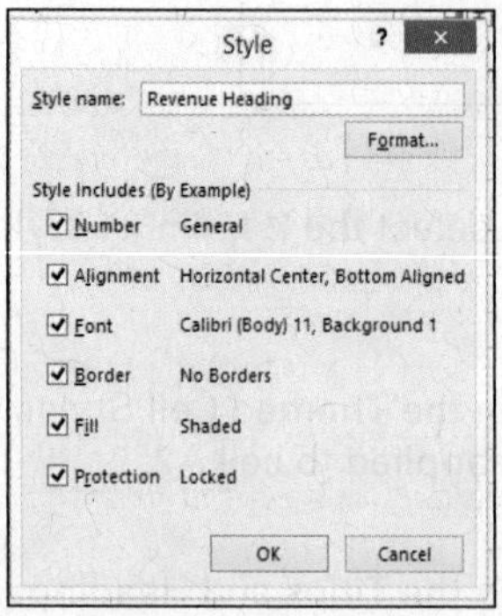

Style	? ✕
Style name:	Revenue Heading
	Format...

Style Includes (By Example)

☑ Number	General
☑ Alignment	Horizontal Center, Bottom Aligned
☑ Font	Calibri (Body) 11, Background 1
☑ Border	No Borders
☑ Fill	Shaded
☑ Protection	Locked

OK   Cancel

4. Click the Format button.

5. Click the Font tab, in the Font style list, select Bold Italic, and click OK.

6. Click OK to close the Style dialog box.

7. With A2 still selected, open the Cell Styles menu and click Revenue Heading to apply the new style, as shown in Figure 6-33.

Figure 6-33

The new style applied to the worksheet cell

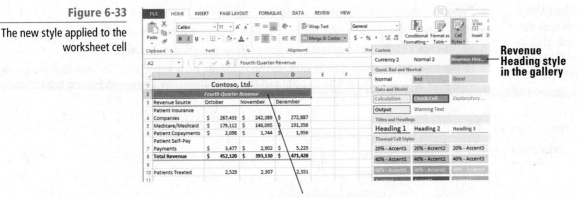

Revenue Heading style in the gallery

Revenue Heading style applied to cell A2

8. SAVE the workbook and CLOSE the file.

PAUSE. LEAVE Excel open to use in the next exercise.

In this exercise, you created a new custom style by renaming (and thus duplicating) an existing cell style and then modifying the style. Your custom style was added to the Cell Styles gallery.

When creating a new style based on an existing style, you can uncheck options in the Style dialog box that you want to remove from your new style.

To simply modify an existing style, click Cell Styles in the Styles group. When the Styles gallery is displayed, right-click the cell style you want to change and select Modify. The Styles dialog box opens with the current style name displayed but not accessible. This tells you that any changes you make to the style will be made to the existing style rather than a customized style.

You can delete styles from the Cells Styles gallery. Doing so also removes the style from all cells that are formatted with it. To remove a style from the Cell Styles gallery, right-click the style in the gallery and select Delete from the shortcut menu. Although you can delete most preset styles from the Cell Styles gallery, it's not recommended.

Take Note You cannot delete the Normal cell style.

WORKING WITH HYPERLINKED DATA

Bottom Line

For quick access to related information in another file or on a web page, you can insert a hyperlink in a worksheet cell. A **hyperlink** is a shortcut of sorts that enables you to navigate to a web page or a location in another file in just one click of the mouse. Hyperlinks enable you to supplement worksheet data with additional information and resources.

Inserting a Hyperlink into a Worksheet

You can add a hyperlink to your document by right-clicking a cell and selecting Hyperlink from the shortcut menu.

STEP BY STEP Insert a Hyperlink in a Cell

GET READY. LAUNCH Excel if it is not already running.

1. OPEN the ***06 Contoso Hyperlink*** data file for this lesson.
2. Click Sheet2.
3. Click in cell A15.
4. Type Company website: and press Enter.
5. Manually widen column A until all content displays properly in cell A15.
6. Right-click cell B15 and select Hyperlink from the shortcut menu.
7. In the Insert Hyperlink dialog box, in the Address box, type http://www.contoso.com/ and click OK. The hyperlink appears in the worksheet, as shown in Figure 6-34.

Another Way
You can open the Insert Hyperlink dialog box by clicking the Hyperlink command in the Links group on the INSERT tab.

Figure 6-34

A hyperlink inserted into a worksheet

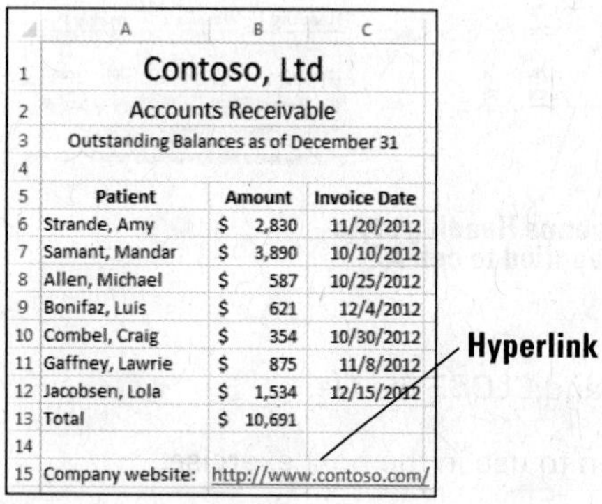

	A	B	C
1	Contoso, Ltd		
2	Accounts Receivable		
3	Outstanding Balances as of December 31		
4			
5	Patient	Amount	Invoice Date
6	Strande, Amy	$ 2,830	11/20/2012
7	Samant, Mandar	$ 3,890	10/10/2012
8	Allen, Michael	$ 587	10/25/2012
9	Bonifaz, Luis	$ 621	12/4/2012
10	Combel, Craig	$ 354	10/30/2012
11	Gaffney, Lawrie	$ 875	11/8/2012
12	Jacobsen, Lola	$ 1,534	12/15/2012
13	Total	$ 10,691	
14			
15	Company website:	http://www.contoso.com/	

CERTIFICATION READY? 1.2.2

How do I insert a hyperlink into a worksheet?

8. SAVE the workbook to your Lesson 6 folder as ***06 Contoso Hyperlink Solution.***

PAUSE. LEAVE the workbook open to use in the next exercise.

Using a Hyperlink

Using a hyperlink refers to clicking the link to navigate to the location that's embedded in the hyperlink.

STEP BY STEP Use a Hyperlink

GET READY. USE the workbook you saved in the previous exercise.

1. Click the hyperlink in cell B15. Because the hyperlink points to a website, your default web browser opens.
2. Close the browser window.

PAUSE. LEAVE the workbook open to use in the next exercise.

Clicking a hyperlink brings you to a new location. To select the cell that contains a hyperlink, click and hold the mouse.

Removing a Hyperlink from a Worksheet

You can remove a hyperlink from a cell using the Remove Hyperlink command. Doing so does not delete the text linked to the hyperlink.

STEP BY STEP **Remove a Hyperlink from a Cell**

GET READY. USE the workbook you worked on in the previous exercise.

1. Right-click cell **B15** and select **Remove Hyperlink** from the shortcut menu, as shown in Figure 6-35. The hyperlink is removed from the URL, but the URL text remains.

Figure 6-35

The Remove Hyperlink menu item

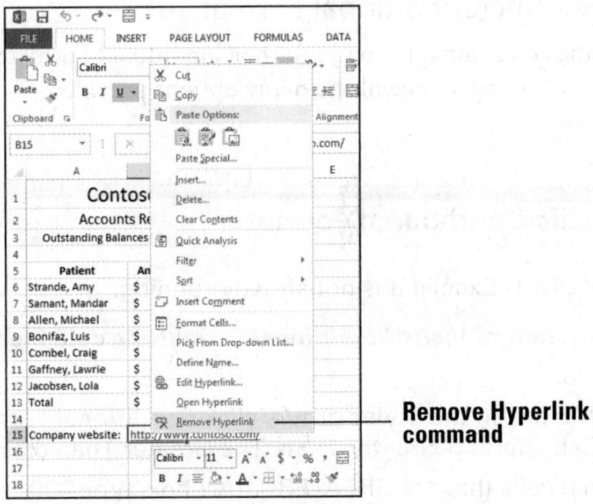

Remove Hyperlink command

2. CLOSE the workbook without saving your changes.

PAUSE. LEAVE Excel open to use in the next exercise.

Workplace *Ready*

THE VERSATILITY OF HYPERLINKS

A hyperlink is typically associated with accessing a web page, but Excel provides a lot more uses for hyperlinks. For example, inserting a hyperlink composed of the name of a file lets you open the file from a worksheet. You can create a hyperlink that lets you navigate to a specific location within the current worksheet, based on a cell reference or a named range.

Want to set up a hyperlink that automatically opens an email window? Just use the E-mail Address option in the insert Hyperlink dialog box, and enter an email address and Subject line text. When you click the resulting hyperlink, your default email program opens automatically, enabling you to type a message and attach files (if you want) and then send the message.

You can insert a hyperlink directly into an Excel worksheet, or attach the hyperlink to an object, such as a shape, chart, or photo.

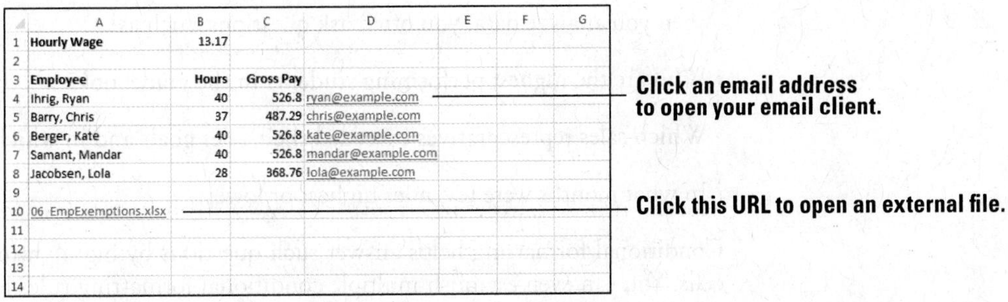

	A	B	C	D	E	F	G
1	Hourly Wage	13.17					
2							
3	Employee	Hours	Gross Pay				
4	Ihrig, Ryan	40	526.8	ryan@example.com			
5	Barry, Chris	37	487.29	chris@example.com			
6	Berger, Kate	40	526.8	kate@example.com			
7	Samant, Mandar	40	526.8	mandar@example.com			
8	Jacobsen, Lola	28	368.76	lola@example.com			
9							
10	06_EmpExemptions.xlsx						
11							
12							
13							
14							

Click an email address to open your email client.

Click this URL to open an external file.

APPLYING CONDITIONAL FORMATTING TO CELLS

Bottom Line

The Excel conditional formatting feature enables you to apply formatting according to rules. You can apply a single rule or multiple rules, and you can use the preset rules provided by Excel or customize them for your particular needs. The Excel **Rules Manager** gives you even greater control over rules by enabling you to set the order of multiple rules, fine-tune rule settings, and more.

Applying a Specific Conditional Format

To apply a specific conditional format, use the Conditional Formatting menu in the Styles group on the HOME tab and select one of the many options provided.

STEP BY STEP   **Apply a Specific Conditional Format**

GET READY. LAUNCH Excel if it is not already running.

1. OPEN the *06 Patient Visits Conditional Formatting* data file for this lesson.
2. Select D4:O8.
3. On the HOME tab, in the Styles group, click Conditional Formatting, and then select Highlight Cells Rules > Greater Than. The Greater Than dialog box appears.
4. In the Format cells that are GREATER THAN box, type 600.
5. Leave the default fill color, as shown in Figure 6-36. Click OK. Cells that contain a value greater than 600 are formatted with a light red background color and a dark red text color. This data represents the months in which the physicians were seeing more than the ideal number of patients.

Figure 6-36

The Greater Than dialog box and cells displaying conditional formatting

Last Name	First Name	Job Title	January	February	March	April	May	June	July	August	September	October	November	December
Carey	Cynthia	Physician	602	605	690	582	601	582	580	645	522	580	480	577
Garcia	Debra	Physician	579	550	590	597	607	630	500	592	496	637	502	408
Laszlo	Rebecca	Physician	604	594	475	425	515	634	621	563	486	436	446	510
Wilson	Dan	Physician	575								577	593	577	600
Koska	Tomas	PA	326								385	283	302	256

Contoso, Ltd.

Greater Than

Format cells that are GREATER THAN:

600 with Light Red Fill with Dark Red Text

OK   Cancel

CERTIFICATION READY?   2.3.1

How do you apply a single criterion for conditional formatting?

6. SAVE the workbook to your Lesson 6 folder as *06 Patient Visits Conditional Formatting Solution*.

PAUSE. LEAVE the workbook open to use in the next exercise.

Conditional formatting is a powerful Excel feature that enables you to specify how cells that meet a given condition should be displayed. Thus, conditional formatting means that Excel applies formatting automatically, based on established criteria.

When you analyze data, you often ask questions, such as:

• Who are the highest performing students in the gradebook?

• Which sales representatives exceeded their sales goals and in which quarters?

• In what months were revenues highest or lowest?

Conditional formatting helps answer such questions by highlighting pertinent cells or ranges of cells. You can even establish multiple conditional formatting rules for a data range.

Applying Conditional Formatting for Multiple Criteria

To see the effect of two or more criteria on a set of data, you can apply multiple conditional formatting rules one on top of the other. This exercise shows you how to set two different conditional formatting rules on the same range of data.

STEP BY STEP   **Apply Multiple Conditional Formatting Rules**

GET READY. USE the workbook you saved in the previous exercise.

1. Select D4:O8.
2. On the HOME tab, in the Styles group, open the Conditional Formatting menu, and then select Highlight Cells Rules > Less Than.
3. In the Format cells that are LESS THAN box, type 300.
4. In the drop-down menu, click the Yellow Fill with Dark Yellow Text option. Click OK. All values of less than 300 appear with a yellow background and dark yellow text color, along with values over 600 indicated by a light red background and dark red text, as shown in Figure 6-37.

Figure 6-37

The worksheet with two sets of conditional formatting applied

	A	B	C	D	E	F	G	H	I	J	K	L	M	N	O
1	Contoso, Ltd.														
2															
3	Last Name	First Name	Job Title	January	February	March	April	May	June	July	August	September	October	November	December
4	Carey	Cynthia	Physician	602	605	690	582	601	582	580	645	522	580	480	577
5	Garcia	Debra	Physician	579	550	590	597	607	630	500	592	496	637	502	408
6	Laszlo	Rebecca	Physician	604	594	475	425	515	634	621	563	486	436	446	510
7	Wilson	Dan	Physician	575	325	551	580	478	586	612	600	577	593	577	600
8	Koska	Tomas	PA	326	311	250	296	289	295	299	305	385	283	302	256

5. SAVE the workbook.

PAUSE. LEAVE the workbook open to use in the next exercise.

In this lesson's exercises, you have worked with data related to the number of patients treated each month at Contoso, Ltd. The chapter-opening scenario indicated that you are trying to determine whether you should hire a nurse practitioner. With both sets of conditional formatting applied, you can see at a glance which staff members see more than 600 patients or less than 300 patients in a month.

Using the Rules Manager to Apply Conditional Formats

Excel's Rules Manager enables you to choose from preset specific conditional formats that provide a visual analysis of a worksheet or selected range of data. You can apply a single rule or multiple rules, and you can modify preset rules to display formats however you like.

STEP BY STEP   **Use the Rules Manager to Apply Conditional Formats**

GET READY. USE the workbook you saved in the previous exercise.

1. Select D4:O8.
2. On the HOME tab, in the Styles group, open the Conditional Formatting menu, and select Clear Rules > Clear Rules from Selected Cells.
3. Open the Conditional Formatting menu again and select Manage Rules. The Conditional Formatting Rules Manager dialog box appears.
4. Click the New Rule button. In the New Formatting Rule dialog box, select Format only top or bottom ranked values. The dialog box changes as shown in Figure 6-38.

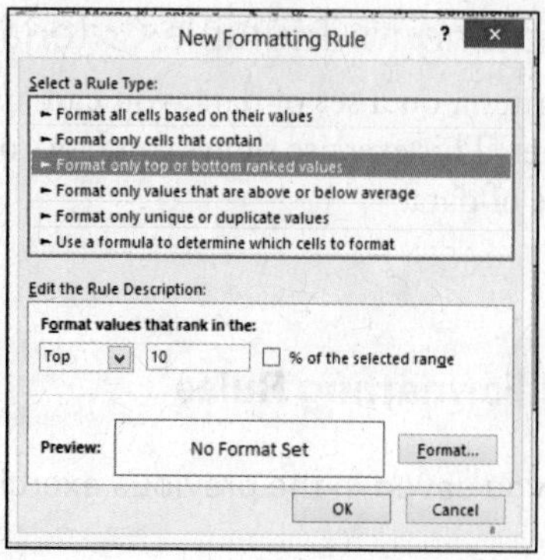

Figure 6-38

The New Formatting Rule
dialog box

CERTIFICATION
READY?   **2.3.1**

How do you use the
Rules Manager to apply
conditional formatting?

5. In the Edit the Rule Description section, click the % of the selected range checkbox.
6. Click the Format button. The Format Cells dialog box opens.
7. Click the Fill tab if it's not already selected, and then select the light red (pink) color box, as shown in Figure 6-39. Click OK twice.

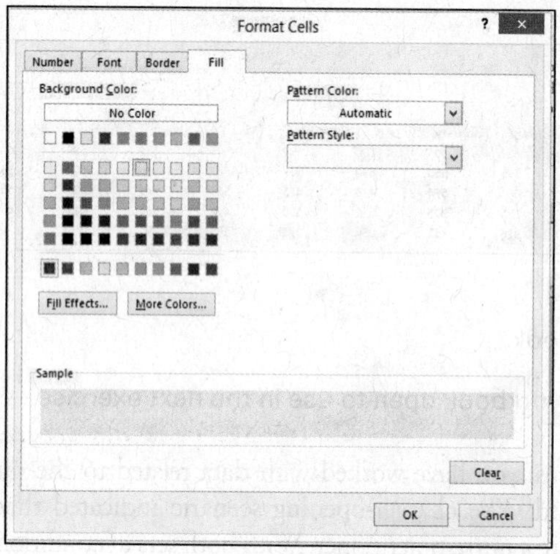

Figure 6-39

Selecting a background color
for the rule

8. In the Conditional Formatting Rules Manager dialog box, click the New Rule button.
9. In the New Formatting Rule dialog box, select Format only top or bottom ranked values.
10. In the Edit the Rule Description section, in the first drop-down list on the left, select Bottom, and then click the % of the selected range checkbox.
11. Click the Format button.
12. In the Format Cells dialog box, click a yellow background color on the Fill tab, and then click OK twice. The Conditional Formatting Rules Manager dialog box should look similar to Figure 6-40.

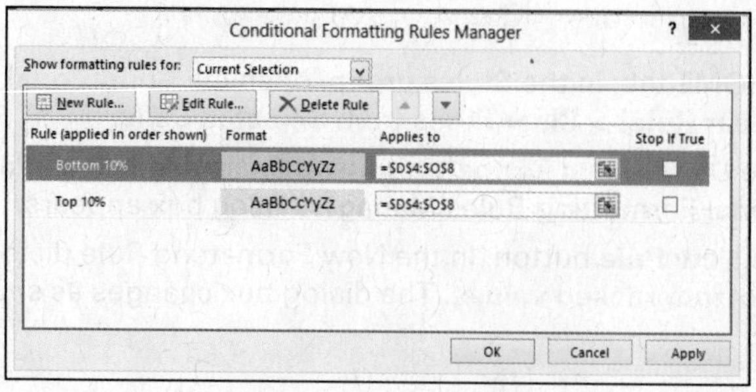

Figure 6-40

The Conditional Formatting
Rules Manager dialog box with
two rules configured

13. Click **OK**. The Rules Manager applies the rules to the selected cells, as shown in Figure 6-41. This view enables you to see the top 10 percent and bottom 10 percent values in the range.

Figure 6-41

The worksheet with the top 10% and bottom 10% rules applied

	A	B	C	D	E	F	G	H	I	J	K	L	M	N	O
1	Contoso, Ltd.														
2															
3	Last Name	First Name	Job Title	January	February	March	April	May	June	July	August	September	October	November	December
4	Carey	Cynthia	Physician	602	605	690	582	601	582	580	645	522	580	480	577
5	Garcia	Debra	Physician	579	550	590	597	607	630	500	592	496	637	502	408
6	Laszlo	Rebecca	Physician	604	594	475	425	515	634	621	563	486	436	446	510
7	Wilson	Dan	Physician	575	325	551	580	478	586	612	600	577	593	577	600
8	Koska	Tomas	PA	326	311	250	296	289	295	299	305	385	283	302	256

14. SAVE the workbook to your Lesson 6 folder as *06 Patient Visits Conditional Formatting Revised Solution*.

PAUSE. LEAVE the workbook open to use in the next exercise.

The Excel **Rules Manager** enables you to create, modify, apply, remove, and manage conditional formatting, including multiple criteria, all in one dialog box.

In addition, you can display the Rules Manager to see what rules are in effect for the worksheet and apply those rules at an appropriate time. From the Conditional Formatting Rules Manager dialog box, you can add new rules, edit existing rules, or delete one or all of the rules. The rules are applied in the order in which they are listed in the Rules Manager. You can apply all the rules, or you can apply specific rules to analyze the data. Formatting is visible when the Conditional Formatting Rules Manager dialog box is open. Thus, you can experiment with the formats you want to apply and the order in which they are applied.

CLEARING A CELL'S FORMATTING

Bottom Line

Although cell formatting can greatly improve the aesthetics and readability of your worksheets, sometimes you may need to remove the formatting, either to start over again or to use the data in another worksheet. Excel makes it easy to remove formatting from a single cell, a range of cells, or the entire worksheet.

STEP BY STEP   **Clear a Cell's Formatting**

GET READY. USE the workbook you saved in the previous exercise.

1. Select **A3:O3**.

2. On the HOME tab, in the Editing group, open the Clear menu, and select Clear Formats. The formatting for the range A3:O3 is removed.

3. In the upper-left corner of your worksheet, at the intersection of the column and row headings, click the Select All button, or press **Ctrl+A**.

4. From the Clear menu, click Clear Formats. All worksheet formatting disappears.

5. Close the workbook without saving your changes.

CLOSE Excel.

As you saw in this exercise, clearing formatting from cells or an entire worksheet does not affect the text, numbers, or formulas in the worksheet.

SKILL SUMMARY

In this lesson you learned how:	Exam Objective	Objective Number
To insert and delete cells.	Insert and delete cells.	2.1.6
To manually format cell contents.	Modify cell alignment and indentation.	2.2.2
	Change font and font styles.	2.2.3
	Apply highlighting.	2.2.7
	Apply Number formats.	2.2.6
	Wrap text within cells.	2.2.5
	Merge cells.	2.2.1
To copy cell formatting with the Format Painter.	Use Format Painter.	2.2.4
To use Paste Special options.		
To format cells with styles.	Apply cell styles.	2.2.8
To work with hyperlinked data.	Insert hyperlinks.	1.2.2
To apply conditional formatting to cells.	Apply conditional formatting.	2.3.1
To clear a cell's formatting.		

Knowledge Assessment

Multiple Choice

Select the best response for the following statements.

1. You want to insert a cell into your worksheet. Which command do you use?
   a. The Insert command in the Cells group on the HOME tab
   b. The Format command in the Cells group on the HOME tab
   c. The Format Painter command in the Clipboard group on the HOME tab
   d. The Format command in the shortcut menu when you right-click a cell

2. You want to format a cell so the text is spread evenly throughout the cell, wrapping automatically and adjusting the row height, if necessary. Which alignment option do you choose?
   a. Center
   b. Middle Align
   c. Justify
   d. Distributed

3. You want to fit a long column heading into a small space without changing the font size or column width. Which of the following is the best choice?
   a. Adjust text orientation.
   b. Use the Center alignment command.
   c. Use the Merge & Center command.
   d. Apply a special character attribute.

4. How do you display the Mini toolbar?
   a. Left-click a cell.
   b. Right-click a cell.
   c. Select Format > Mini toolbar.
   d. Select View > Mini toolbar.

5. Which of the following can you *not* copy using Format Painter?
    a. Font color
    b. Bold
    c. Font size
    d. Cell content

6. Which Paste Special option pastes only the result of a formula rather than the formula itself?
    a. Formulas
    b. Values
    c. Formats
    d. Formulas and number formats

7. You don't like the cell style you just applied. Which of the following is the least effective way to remove or replace the style?
    a. Apply another style to the cell.
    b. Use the Undo command.
    c. Clear the cell's content.
    d. Apply the Normal style to the cell.

8. How do you remove a hyperlink?
    a. Delete the cell.
    b. Edit the cell's style.
    c. Reformat the cell.
    d. Right-click the cell and select Remove Hyperlink.

9. In which group on the HOME tab is the Clear Formats command located?
    a. In the Editing group
    b. In the Clipboard group
    c. In the Font group
    d. In the Cells group

10. Which of the following is *not* useful for changing the font size?
    a. Font Size drop-down list
    b. Increase Font Size button
    c. Decrease Font Size button
    d. Orientation button

True / False

Circle T if the statement is true or F if the statement is false.

T F 1. When you delete cells in a worksheet, you remove one or more cells, forcing other cells to move down or to the right.

T F 2. When selecting a font color, you can choose a themed color but not a standard color from the palette.

T F 3. When you point to defined styles in the Cell Styles gallery, you can see the formatting that will be used when you apply each style.

T F 4. Underlining a cell's content is the same as adding a border.

T F 5. You can apply multiple conditional formatting criteria or rules to the same set of data.

T F 6. Deleting a cell is the same as clearing a cell's content.

T F 7. A hyperlink enables you to navigate to a web page, another file, or to a specific location in another file.

T F 8. Style attributes include fonts and font sizes, number formats, and borders and shading.

T F 9. You cannot split a single worksheet cell that has not been merged.

T F 10. After you select a color and apply it to a cell's background, the Fill Color button takes on that color.

Competency Assessment

Project 6-1: Apply Basic Formatting

Apply basic formatting to a worksheet listing regional sales figures for a sports equipment reseller.

GET READY. Launch Excel if it is not already running.

1. OPEN *06 Regional Sales*.
2. Select A1:E1.
3. Merge and center the worksheet title.
4. Select A2:E2.
5. Bold and center the headings.
6. Select B3:E6.
7. Apply the Currency number format.
8. Decrease the decimal places by two, so no decimal places appear.
9. SAVE the workbook to your Lesson 6 folder as *06 Regional Sales Solution*.

LEAVE the workbook open for the next project.

Project 6-2: Apply Cell Styles to a Worksheet

Total sales figures and apply styles to enhance the appearance of a worksheet listing regional sales figures for a sports equipment reseller.

GET READY. Launch Excel if it is not already running.

1. OPEN *06 Regional Sales Solution* if it's not already open.
2. In cell A7, type the word Total.
3. Select B7:E7.
4. AutoSum each cell.
5. Click A1.
6. In the Cell Styles menu, apply the Title style.
7. Select A2:E2.
8. In the Cell Styles menu, apply the Accent6 style.
9. Select A3:A7.
10. Apply the 40% - Accent6 cell style.
11. Select B3:E7.
12. Apply the 20% - Accent6 cell style.
13. Select A7:E7.
14. Bold all cells in the range.
15. SAVE the workbook to your Lesson 6 folder as *06 Regional Sales Formatted Solution* and CLOSE the file.

LEAVE Excel open for the next project.

Proficiency Assessment

Project 6-3: **Format a Student List for Readability**

Use a variety of techniques to improve the readability of a School of Fine Arts student list. Techniques include Merge & Center, applying italics, wrapping text, and using the Decrease Decimal command.

GET READY. LAUNCH Excel if it is not already running.

1. OPEN *06 Fine Art*.
2. Merge and center A1:E1.
3. Apply Calibri Light, 16-point, Blue to the cell A1 content.
4. Center and italicize the content in cells A2:E2.
5. Widen column C so all text displays in its entirety.
6. Wrap the text in cell D2.
7. Decrease the width of column D to fit the longest date.
8. Format row 2 to autofit the row height.
9. Format the content in E3:E12 so that only two decimal places display.
10. Decrease the width of column E to eliminate unnecessary whitespace.
11. SAVE the workbook to your Lesson 6 folder as *06 Fine Art Solution*.

LEAVE the file open for the next project.

Project 6-4: **Use Pasting Techniques to Add Entries to a Worksheet**

Add rows of data to a worksheet, and use Format Painter and Paste Special to apply formatting and copy formulas.

GET READY. LAUNCH Excel if it is not already running.

1. OPEN *06 Fine Art Solution* if it's not already open.
2. Add two more rows of data, as follows:

First	Last	Discipline	Enrollment Date	GPA
Cassie	Hicks	Painting	1/14/2013	
Jeff	Price	Computer Art	1/14/2013	

3. Use the Format Painter to format cells A13:D14 in the same style as A12:D12.
4. Use the Copy command to copy the new enrollment date (1/14/2013) to replace the 1/3/2013 dates in rows 11 and 12.
5. Use Paste Special to copy the GPA formula and number format from a cell that display a GPA to the two new cells that do not have GPAs entered.
6. Modify the formula in the GPA column for Cassie Hicks to total 3.3, 3.5, and 3.7.
7. Modify the formula in the GPA column for Jeff Price to total 2.9, 3.4, and 3.5.
8. Format A2:E2 as 20% - Accent1 and reapply italics.
9. SAVE the workbook to your Lesson 6 folder as *06 Fine Art Revised Solution* and (the file.

LEAVE Excel open for the next project.

Mastery Assessment

Project 6-5: Create a Custom Style

Create a new style and configure its settings, apply the style, and then modify the style settings.

GET READY. LAUNCH Excel if it is not already running.

1. OPEN a new, blank workbook.
2. Create a new cell style using your first name as the style name. Include the following formats in the style:
   Alignment: Horizontal Center, Vertical Center
   Font: Arial Narrow, 16-point, Italic
   Border Style: Solid line (your choice), Bottom
   Border Color: Dark Blue
   Fill Color: Light Blue
   Pattern Style: 6.25% Gray
3. Type your first name in cell A1 and apply the style to your name.
4. Modify the style to remove the pattern style. Widen column A, if necessary.
5. SAVE the workbook to your Lesson 6 folder as *06 My Style Solution* and then CLOSE the file.

LEAVE Excel open for the next project.

Project 6-6: Analyze Trends in Sales

Apply conditional formatting to regional sales figures to determine dollar amounts above and below specific levels.

GET READY. LAUNCH Excel if it is not already running.

1. OPEN *06 Regional Sales Formatted Solution* from a previous project.
2. Use conditional formatting to indicate which sales figures exceeded $24,000.
3. Use conditional formatting to indicate, in a different color, which sales figures were below $20,000.
4. SAVE the workbook to your Lesson 6 folder as *06 Regional Sales Trends Solution* and then CLOSE the file.

CLOSE Excel.

LESSON SKILL MATRIX

Skills	Exam Objective	Objective Number
Working with Rows and Columns	Insert and delete columns and rows.	1.3.3
	Adjust row height and column width.	1.3.5
	Hide columns and rows.	1.4.2
	Transpose columns and rows.	2.3.3
Using Themes	Change workbook themes.	1.3.4
Modifying a Worksheet's Onscreen and Printed Appearance	Modify page setup.	1.3.2
Inserting Headers and Footers	Insert headers and footers.	1.3.7
	Insert watermarks.	1.3.6
	Repeat headers and footers.	1.5.5
Preparing a Document for Printing	Set print scaling.	1.5.4
	Configure workbooks to print.	1.5.7

© fatihhoca /iStockphoto

KEY TERMS

- boundary
- column heading
- column width
- document theme
- effects
- footer
- gridlines
- header
- orientation
- page break
- Page Break Preview
- Print Preview
- row heading
- row height
- scaling
- transposing
- watermark
- white space

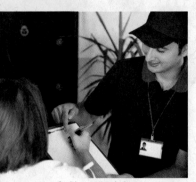

© fatihhoca /iStockphoto

Consolidated Messenger is a same-day and rush delivery service to more than 500 attorneys in New York City. The company offers foot, bike, and vehicle deliveries to provide court filings, process serving, document and small package delivery, and records retrieval. Consolidated Messenger dispatchers use Excel worksheets to track daily deliveries. The accounting department combines worksheets from all dispatchers to process invoices and payroll, and to provide reports to management. The management reports must look professional and be highly readable whether viewed onscreen or printed. In this lesson, you learn how to work with rows and columns in a worksheet, apply themes, modify a worksheet's onscreen and printed appearance, insert headers and footers, and prepare a document for printing.

SOFTWARE ORIENTATION

Formatting Excel Worksheets

Excel 2013 provides many tools to enhance the look of your worksheets whether viewed on-screen or in print. To improve how a worksheet displays on a computer monitor or to prepare a worksheet for printing, you will use commands mainly on the HOME tab and the PAGE LAYOUT tab, shown in Figure 7-1. Using and applying formatting options from the command groups on these tabs ensures that your worksheets are more useful, more readable, and more attractive.

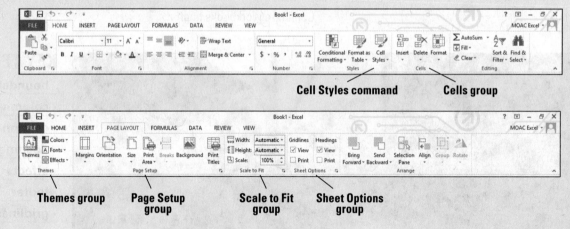

Figure 7-1

HOME tab and PAGE LAYOUT tab command groups

WORKING WITH ROWS AND COLUMNS

Bottom Line

Microsoft designed Excel worksheets for flexibility, enabling you to insert or delete rows and columns in an existing worksheet, increase or decrease row height and column width, and apply all kinds of formatting to entire rows and columns. You can also hide and unhide rows and columns, and even transpose data so that data in a row appears in a column and vice versa.

Inserting or Deleting a Row or Column

Many times, after you've already entered data in a worksheet, you will need to insert additional rows or columns. To insert a row, select the row or a cell in the row *below* which you want the new row to appear. The new row is then inserted *above* the selected cell or row. To insert multiple rows, select the same number of rows as you want to insert. Inserting columns works the same way, except columns are inserted to the *left* of the selected cell or column. By default, the inserted column is formatted the same as the column to the left. Deleting a row or column is just as easy—just select and delete.

STEP BY STEP   **Insert and Delete Rows and Columns**

GET READY. Before you begin these steps, be sure to launch Microsoft Excel.

1. Open the workbook named *07 Messenger Row-Column*.
2. Click the row **14** heading to select the entire row.
3. On the HOME tab, in the Cells group, click the Insert button arrow and select Insert Sheet Rows, as shown in Figure 7-2. A new blank row appears as row 14.

Figure 7-2

The Insert menu

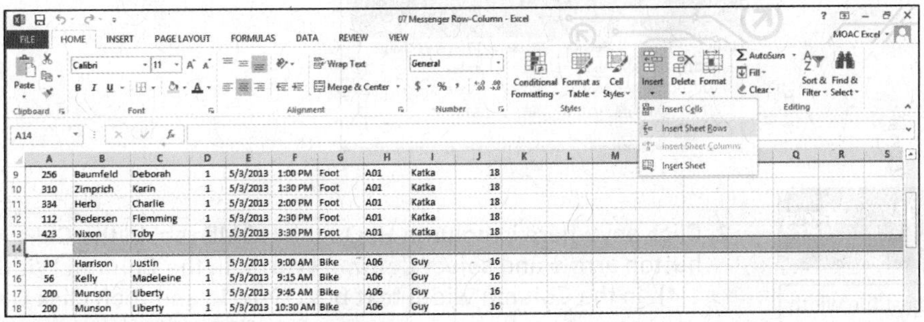

4. To insert several rows at once, click the row **25** heading, hold down the **Ctrl** key, and then click row headings **34** and **43**. Right-click any of the selected rows and select Insert from the shortcut menu. Blank rows appear above the selected rows, so that data for each messenger is separated by a blank row.
5. Click the column **D** heading to select the entire column. This column contains the delivery zone.
6. On the HOME tab, in the Cells group, click the Delete button arrow and select Delete Sheet Columns. The Zone column disappears.
7. Right-click the row **3** heading and select Insert from the shortcut menu. In cell A3, type Zone 1.
8. Select A3:I3. On the HOME tab, in the Alignment group, click the Merge & Center button. The "Zone 1" text is centered across the data columns.
9. SAVE the workbook as *07 Messenger Row-Column Solution*.

PAUSE. LEAVE the workbook open to use in the next exercise.

CERTIFICATION READY? 1.3.3
How do you insert a row in a worksheet?

Another Way
To delete an entire row, select the row or rows to be deleted, right-click the selection, and select Delete from the shortcut menu.

CERTIFICATION READY? 1.3.3
How do you delete a row from a worksheet?

The **row heading** or **column heading** is its identifying letter or number. You select an entire row or column by clicking its heading. To select multiple adjacent rows or columns, click the first row or column heading, hold the Shift key, and then click the last heading. You can also select multiple nonadjacent rows or columns. Just click the first row or column heading, and then hold down the Ctrl key while clicking other headings.

Modifying Row Height and Column Width

By default, all columns in a new worksheet are the same width and all rows are the same height. In most worksheets, you will want to change some column or row defaults to accommodate the worksheet's data. Modifying the height of rows and width of columns can make a worksheet's contents easier to read and increase its visual appeal. You can set a row or column to a specific height or width or change the height or width to fit the contents. To change height and width settings, use the Format commands in the Cells group on the HOME tab, use the shortcut menu that appears when you right-click a selected row or column, or double-click or drag the **boundary**, which is the line between rows or columns.

STEP BY STEP   **Modify Row Height and Column Width**

GET READY. USE the workbook from the previous exercise.

1. Double-click the boundary to the right of the column G heading (see Figure 7-3), which adjusts the column width to show all content in column G.

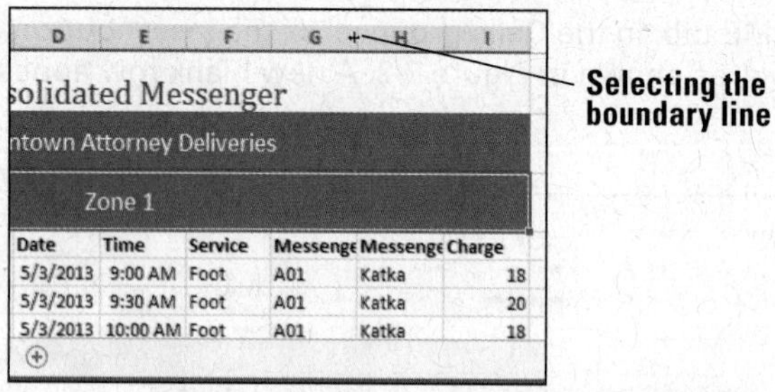

Figure 7-3

Double-clicking the boundary line between columns G and H

Selecting the boundary line

CERTIFICATION READY?   **1.3.5**

How do you adjust the width of a column in a worksheet?

2. Click anywhere in column H. On the HOME tab, in the Cells group, click the Format button arrow and select Column Width. In the Column Width dialog box (see Figure 7-4), in the Column width text box, type 16 and then click OK. All content in column H appears.

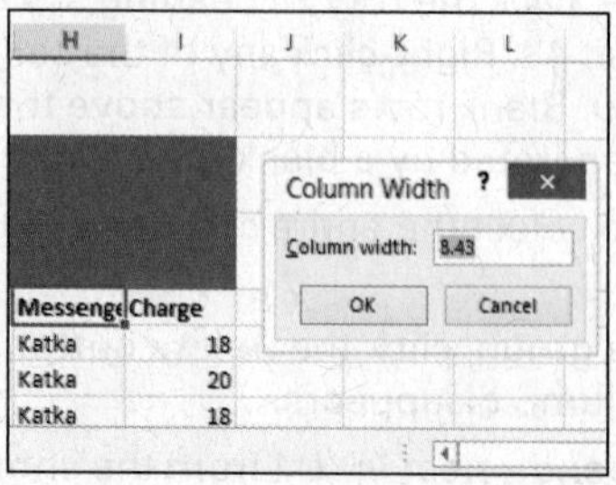

Figure 7-4

The Column Width dialog box

3. Click and hold the boundary under the row 3 heading. Drag the line up to decrease the height of row 3 to 18, as shown in Figure 7-5. Notice that a ScreenTip appears as you drag the boundary line, showing you the height of the row in points (the first number) and pixels.

Figure 7-5

Decreasing a row's height by
dragging the boundary line

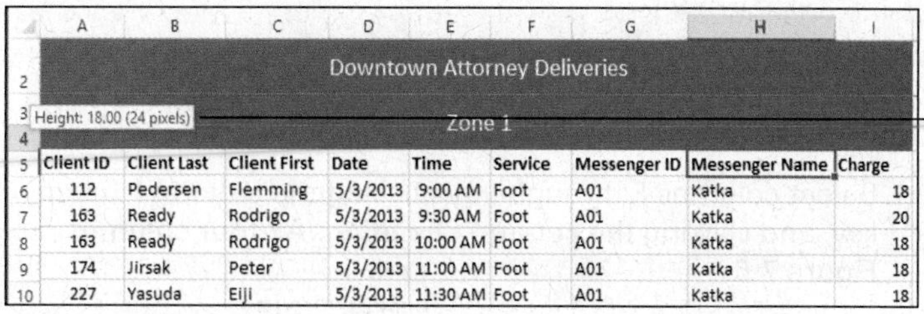

ScreenTip
showing
row height

Another Way

To access the
Column Width dialog box to
change a column's width, select the column, right-click the
selection, and select Column
Width from the shortcut menu.

4. Select row 2. On the HOME tab, in the Cells group, click the Format button arrow and select AutoFit Row Height. With the row still selected, click the Format button arrow again and select Row Height. The Row Height dialog box indicates that the row is 18.75 points in height. Click OK.

5. SAVE the workbook.

PAUSE. LEAVE the workbook open to use in the next exercise.

Row height, or the top-to-bottom measurement of a row, is measured in points; one point is equal to 1/72 inch. The default row height is 15 points, but you can specify a row height of 0 to 409 points. **Column width** is the left-to-right measurement of a column. Although you can specify a column width of 0 to 255 characters, the default column width is 8.43 characters (based on the default font and font size). If a column width or row height is set to 0, the corresponding column or row is hidden.

As you learned in Lesson 2, when the text you enter exceeds the column width, the text overflows to the next column, or it is truncated when the next cell contains data. Similarly, if the value entered in a column exceeds the column width, the #### symbols appear, which indicate the number is larger than the column width.

Take Note   To quickly AutoFit the entries in all rows on a worksheet, click the Select All icon in the upper-left corner of your worksheet (at the intersection of column and row headings), then double-click one of the row boundaries.

Depending on the alignment of the data in your columns, worksheet data may appear crowded or too loose when you use the AutoFit Column Width option because this option adjusts column width to the exact width of the longest entry in the column. Therefore, after using this option, you may want to use the mouse to drag the right column boundary for any columns that seem crowded or have too much white space. **White space** is the empty area of a document, in which no content appears.

Take Note   You can use the Format Painter to copy the width of one column to other columns. To do so, select the heading of the first column, click the Format Painter, and then click the heading of the column or columns to which you want to apply the column width.

In Excel, you can change the default width for all columns on a worksheet or a workbook. To do so, click Format and then select Default Width. In the Standard Width dialog box, type a new default column measurement. Note that when changing the default column width or row height, columns and rows that contain data or that have been previously formatted retain their formatting.

Formatting an Entire Row or Column

To save time, achieve a consistent appearance, and align cell contents in a consistent manner, you often want to apply the same format to an entire row or column. To apply formatting to a row or column, click the row heading or column heading to select it, and then apply the appropriate format or style.

STEP BY STEP   **Format an Entire Row or Column**

GET READY. USE the workbook from the previous exercise.

1. Select columns F through I by clicking the column F heading, pressing the Shift key, and clicking the column I heading. All four columns are selected, as shown in Figure 7-6.

Figure 7-6

Four columns selected

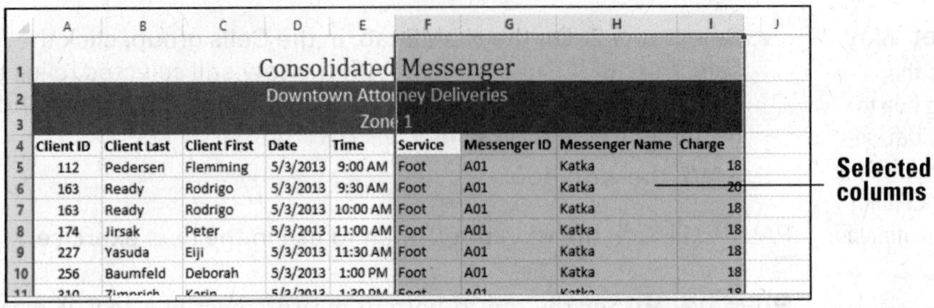

Selected columns

2. On the HOME tab, in the Alignment group, click the Center icon, as shown in Figure 7-7. The content in columns F through I is centered.

Figure 7-7

The Center icon in the Alignment group

Center icon

3. Click the column I heading. The Charge column is selected.

4. On the HOME tab, in the Number group, select Currency from the Number Format menu. Only the values in column I are styled as currency.

5. Select row 4 and center the column headings using the Center icon.

6. SAVE the workbook.

PAUSE. LEAVE the workbook open to use in the next exercise.

In this exercise, you could have selected data ranges and then applied formatting. For example, you could have selected A4: I4 and centered the headings. However, formatting rows and columns rather than applying formatting to a range of cells that contain data has an advantage: When you insert rows or columns or add additional data to a worksheet in the future, the new data will be formatted correctly.

Some formatting shouldn't be applied to an entire row or column. For example, when you apply a cell style with an underline effect, such as the Heading 1 cell style, to an entire row, you will see the underline in all blank cells to the end of the row (cell XFD1).

Hiding or Unhiding a Row or Column

You may not want or need all rows and columns in a worksheet to be visible all the time, particularly if the worksheet contains a large number of rows or columns. You can hide a row or a column by using the Hide command or by setting the row height or column width to zero. When rows are hidden, they do not appear onscreen or in printouts, but the data remains and can be unhidden.

STEP BY STEP   **Hide or Unhide a Row or Column**

GET READY. USE the workbook from the previous exercise.

1. Select **columns D** and **E**. The columns for Date and Time are selected.
2. Right-click the column D or E heading and select **Hide**. The Date and Time columns are hidden from view, and a green line appears, indicating hidden content, as shown in Figure 7-8.

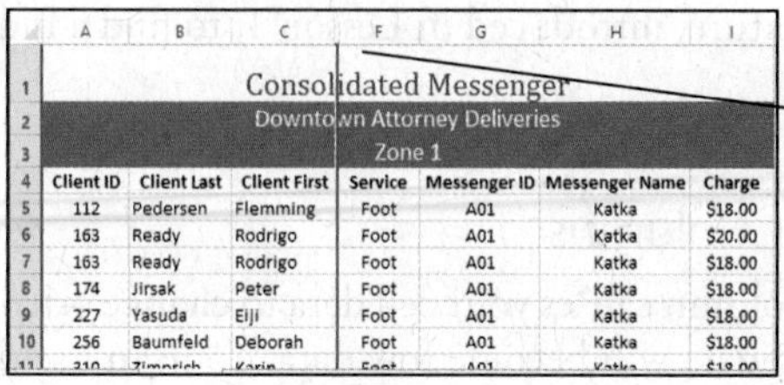

Figure 7-8

The Date and Time columns
are no longer visible in the
worksheet.

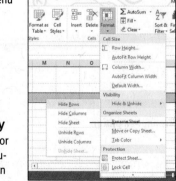

Green line indicates
hidden content.
Columns D and E
no longer appear.

3. Click in any cell. The green line disappears, and the boundary between columns C and F is a double vertical line (see Figure 7-9), which indicates hidden columns.

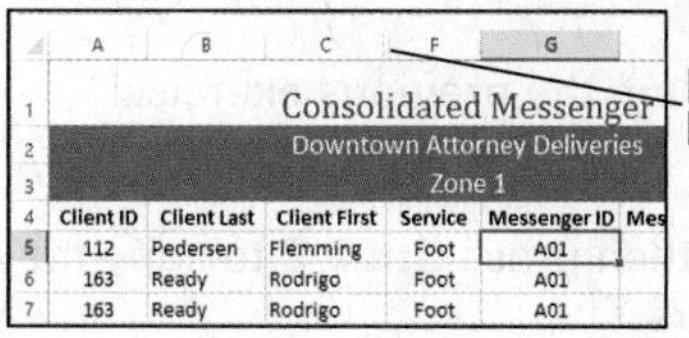

Figure 7-9

The double vertical boundary
line indicates hidden columns.

Double vertical
boundary line

4. Select **row 3**. On the HOME tab, in the Cells group, click the **Format button arrow**, point to **Hide & Unhide**, and select **Hide Rows**, as shown in Figure 7-10. Row 3 is now hidden.

Figure 7-10

The Hide & Unhide menu

Hide & Unhide
commands

Another Way
To unhide a row or
column, double-click the double lines in the row or column
heading that indicate hidden
content.

5. Select **rows 2** and **4**. Right-click the selection and select **Unhide**. Row 3 is now visible.

Troubleshooting   When you select rows 2 and 4 to unhide the hidden row, you must select them in a way that includes the hidden rows. Press Shift when you select row 4 or select row 2 and drag to include row 4. If you select row 2, press Ctrl, and click row 4, the hidden row will not unhide. Additionally, selecting only the data in the rows will not release the hidden row.

6. SAVE the workbook.

PAUSE. LEAVE the workbook open to use in the next exercise.

A worksheet may contain rows or columns of sensitive or extraneous data that you are not using or do not want to be visible while you are working in other areas of the worksheet. Using the Hide command simply hides them from view, but they still exist in the worksheet.

To make hidden rows visible, select the row above and the row below the hidden row or rows and use the Unhide Rows command. To display hidden columns, select the adjacent columns and follow the same steps used for displaying hidden rows.

You can use the Go To feature, introduced in Lesson 1, to find a hidden row or column and then make it visible.

Transposing Rows or Columns

Transposing a row or column causes your cell data to change orientation. Row data will become column data, and column data will become row data. You can use the Paste Special command to perform this type of irregular cell copying. In the Paste Special dialog box, select the Transpose check box to transpose row or column data.

STEP BY STEP   **Transpose Rows or Columns**

GET READY. USE the workbook from the previous exercise.

1. Click the Sheet2 tab.
2. Select rows 2 through 7, and then press Ctrl + C to copy the data to the Clipboard. A green marquee border appears.
3. Click cell A10.
4. On the HOME tab, in the Clipboard group, click the Paste button arrow and select Paste Special. The Paste Special dialog box opens.
5. Check the Transpose check box, as shown in Figure 7-11.

Figure 7-11

The Paste Special dialog box

Transpose option

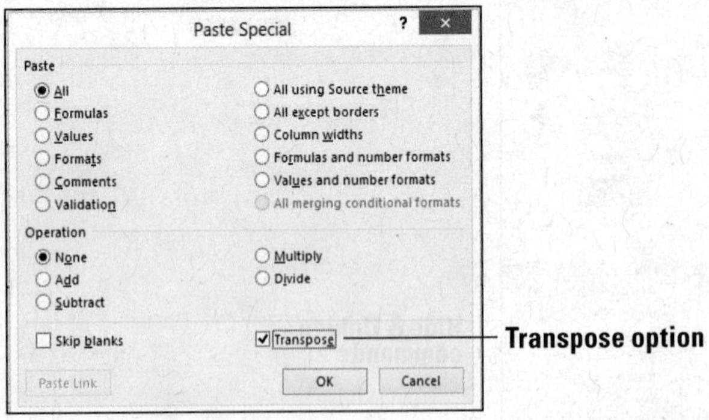

6. Click OK. The data appears with the row data in columns and the column data in rows, as shown in Figure 7-12.

Figure 7-12

Transposed data

	A	B	C	D	E	F
2	Messenger Name	January	February	March	April	
3	Bill	$4,105	$3,875	$3,900	$4,075	
4	Guy	$3,850	$3,790	$4,205	$4,090	
5	Jenny	$3,260	$3,680	$3,575	$3,700	
6	Katka	$3,125	$2,960	$2,940	$3,325	
7	Stuart	$3,860	$3,975	$3,850	$3,725	
8						
9						
10	Messenger Name	Bill	Guy	Jenny	Katka	Stuart
11	January	$4,105	$3,850	$3,260	$3,125	$3,860
12	February	$3,875	$3,790	$3,680	$2,960	$3,975
13	March	$3,900	$4,205	$3,575	$2,940	$3,850
14	April	$4,075	$4,090	$3,700	$3,325	$3,725
15						

— Original data

— Transposed data

◄ ► Sheet1 | Sheet2 | ⊕

CERTIFICATION READY?   2.3.3

How do you transpose a row or column?

7. Click the **Sheet1** tab to return to the main worksheet.

8. SAVE the workbook and CLOSE the file.

PAUSE. LEAVE Excel open to use in the next exercise.

USING THEMES

Bottom Line

A **document theme** is a predefined set of colors, fonts, and effects that can be applied to an entire workbook or to specific items within a workbook, such as charts or tables. You can use document themes to easily format an entire document and give it a fresh, professional look. Themes can be shared across other Office applications, such as Microsoft Office Word and Microsoft Office PowerPoint, enabling you to give all your Office documents a uniform look in terms of colors, fonts, and effects. (**Effects**, such as shadows or bevels, modify the appearance of an object.)

Choosing a Theme for a Workbook

Excel has several predefined document themes. When you apply a theme to a workbook, the colors, fonts, and effects contained within that theme replace any styles that were already applied to cells or ranges.

STEP BY STEP   **Choose a Theme for a Workbook**

GET READY. LAUNCH Excel if it is not already running.

1. OPEN the *07 Messenger Theme* data file for this lesson.

2. With Sheet1 active, click cell **A3**.

3. On the HOME tab, in the Styles group, click the **Cell Styles** button arrow and select **20% - Accent 4**. A light purple background is applied to the cell range, the font size is reduced, and the font color changes to black.

4. On the PAGE LAYOUT tab, in the Themes group, click the **Themes** button arrow to open the Themes gallery. Several built-in themes appear in the gallery. Move your mouse pointer over each theme to see its effect on the underlying worksheet, which is referred to as Live Preview.

5. Find and select the **Facet** theme, as shown in Figure 7-13. You just changed the default document theme to the Facet theme. The font for subheadings and general data changed from Calibri to Trebuchet MS, and the background of cells A3:I3 is now a light pink color.

Figure 7-13

The Themes gallery

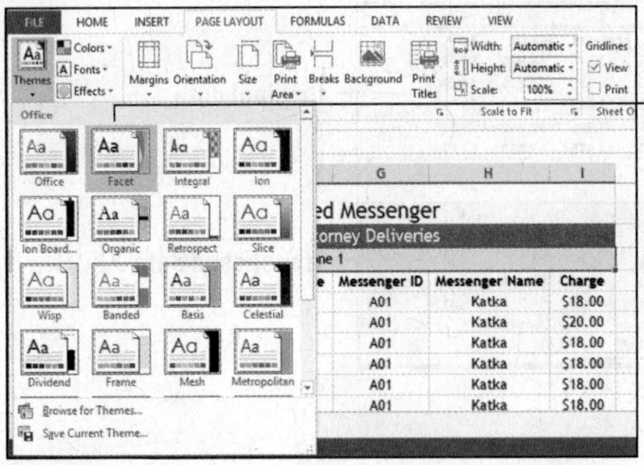

The Facet theme

CERTIFICATION READY?   **1.3.4**

How do you change a workbook theme?

6. Click Sheet2. Notice that the font changed on that sheet as well.

7. Click Sheet1 to return to the main worksheet. On the HOME tab, in the Styles group, click the Cell Styles button arrow to display the Styles gallery. Notice that the color schemes for the various groups have changed. This is because a new document theme has been applied, and several built-in cell styles were created using theme fonts and colors.

8. SAVE the workbook as *07 Messenger Theme Solution*.

PAUSE. LEAVE the workbook open to use in the next exercise.

The default document theme in Excel 2013 is named Office. Document themes are consistent in all Microsoft Office 2013 programs.

Applying a new theme changes fonts and colors, and the color of shapes and SmartArt, tables, charts, and other objects.

Cross Ref   You'll learn about tables in Lesson 9, charts in Lesson 12, and shapes, SmartArt, and other graphics in Lesson 13.

Remember that cell styles are used to format specific cells or ranges within a worksheet; document themes are used to apply sets of styles (colors, fonts, lines, and fill effects) to an entire document.

Many built-in cell styles use theme-aware formatting, so applying a new theme determines which fonts and colors are used by styles. That's why you noticed a change in the Styles gallery after applying the new theme in the exercise. However, styles are independent from themes in that you can change styles regardless of the theme that's applied to a document.

Take Note   When you apply a heading cell style to text and then increase the font size of that cell, the font size will not change after applying a new document theme. If you don't change the font size of heading text, apply a heading cell style, and then apply a new theme, the heading text will display in the default font size for the new theme.

Customizing a Theme

You can create a customized theme by making changes to one or more of an existing theme's components—colors, fonts, or effects (line and fill effects). The changes you make to one or more of a theme's components immediately affect the styles that you have applied in the active document. Many companies create a customized document theme and use it consistently. You can experiment by applying various predefined themes until you decide on the "look" that appeals to you.

Customizing a Theme by Selecting Colors

Although Excel provides several themes you can apply to your workbook, you can modify the color scheme for any theme. You can then save the new color scheme and use it in a custom theme.

STEP BY STEP   **Customize a Theme by Selecting Colors**

GET READY. USE the workbook from the previous exercise.

1. Ensure Sheet1 is active.
2. On the PAGE LAYOUT tab, in the Themes group, click Colors. Figure 7-14 illustrates the color array for some of the built-in themes. You have to scroll through the entire list to see them all. Each theme has an array of accent colors that are the same as the accents in the Styles group.

Figure 7-14

Theme colors

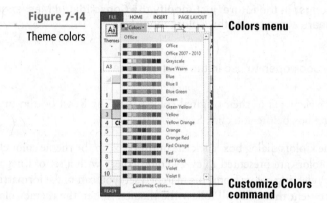

3. Scroll down and select Violet II.
4. Open the Colors menu again and click Customize Colors at the bottom of the menu. The Create New Theme Colors dialog box opens (see Figure 7-15), showing the colors used with the Violet II color scheme currently applied to the Facet theme. Move the dialog box so you can see the worksheet more clearly, if necessary.

Figure 7-15

Create New Theme Colors dialog box

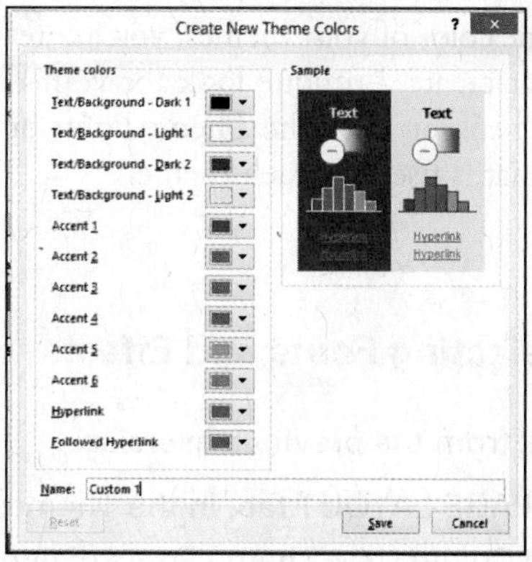

5. Open the Text/Background - Dark 2 drop-down list. The current color is highlighted under Theme Colors. Click Black, Background 1, Lighter 15% as shown in Figure 7-16 to change the color to dark gray.

Figure 7-16

Selecting a new theme color

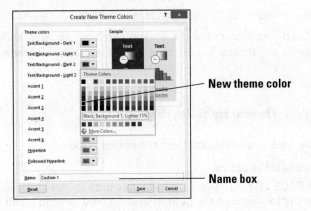

New theme color

Name box

6. In the Name box at the bottom of the dialog box, type Consolidated Messenger and click Save. The new text color is reflected in row 1. If you want to modify colors for Consolidated Messenger in the future, just modify the Consolidated Messenger color scheme, which appears at the top of the Colors menu.

7. SAVE the workbook.

PAUSE. LEAVE the workbook open to use in the next exercise.

Take Note To return all theme color elements to their original colors, click the Reset button in the Create New Theme Colors dialog box before you click Save.

In the Create New Theme Colors dialog box, click the button next to the theme color element you want to change. Theme colors are presented in every color gallery with a set of lines and shades based on those colors. By selecting colors from this matched set, you can make formatting choices for individual pieces of content that will still follow the themes. When the theme colors change, the gallery of colors changes and so does all document content using them.

Theme colors (referred to as color schemes) contain four text and background colors, six accent colors, and two hyperlink colors. It is easy to create your own theme that can be applied to all of your Excel workbooks and other Office 2013 documents. You can choose any of the color schemes shown in Figure 7-14, or you can create your own combination of colors.

Customizing a Theme by Selecting Fonts and Effects

Now that you have customized the color of your themes, you are ready to choose the font for your theme. Use fonts and effects that create a unique look for your documents. Themes contain a heading font and a body font. When you click the Theme Fonts button, you see the name of the heading font and the body font that is used for each theme.

STEP BY STEP **Customize a Theme by Selecting Fonts and Effects**

GET READY. USE the workbook from the previous exercise.

1. With Sheet1 active, on the PAGE LAYOUT tab, in the Themes group, click Fonts.

2. Click Customize Fonts. The Create New Theme Fonts dialog box opens.

3. Open the Heading font drop-down menu, locate the Arial font, and select it.

4. In the Body font box, locate and select Arial Narrow. The preview in the Sample box is updated with the fonts that you selected.

5. In the Name box, type Consolidated Messenger as the name for the new theme fonts and click Save. Your customized theme fonts will be available for you to use to customize any of the built-in themes or to use the next time you click Cell Styles on the HOME tab. (See Figure 7-17.)

Figure 7-17

Cell styles that use built-in themes reflect any changes you make to theme fonts.

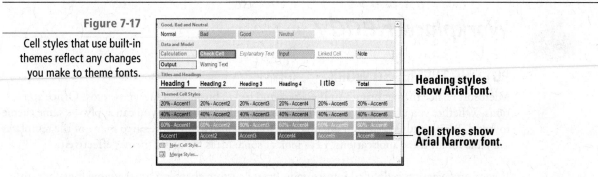

Heading styles show Arial font.

Cell styles show Arial Narrow font.

⚠ **Troubleshooting** If your customized theme font is not automatically applied, click Cell Styles and click the customized heading font to apply it. For example, click A1, go to Cell Styles on the HOME tab, and select Title.

6. On the PAGE LAYOUT tab, in the Themes group, click Themes and then click Save Current Theme. The Save Current Theme dialog box opens.

7. In the File name box, type Consolidated Messenger and click Save. Your customized document theme is saved in the Document Themes folder, and it is automatically added to the list of custom themes that now appears at the top of the Themes gallery, as shown in Figure 7-18.

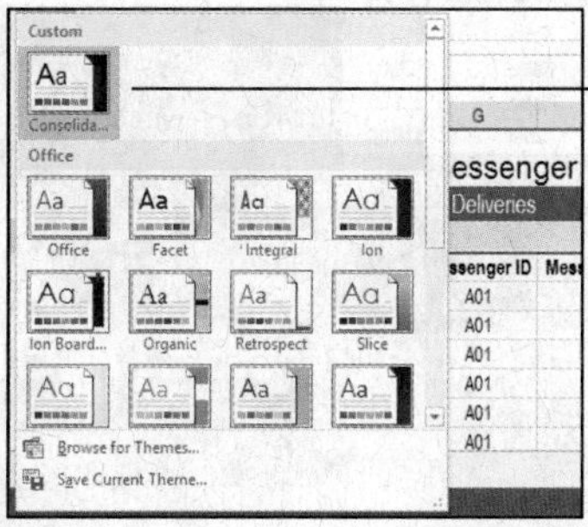

Figure 7-18

Custom theme appears at the top of the Themes gallery.

New custom theme

8. On the PAGE LAYOUT tab, in the Themes group, click Effects. Theme effects are sets of lines and fill effects. Hovering your mouse over the effects might show subtle changes in the cells; however, you will notice the result of changing an effect only if you have charts, shapes, SmartArt, or similar graphics in your workbook.

9. Click the Reflection effect to apply it to the workbook. In the Quick Access Toolbar, click Undo to undo the theme effect.

10. SAVE the workbook and CLOSE the file.

PAUSE. LEAVE Excel open to use in the next exercise.

You can customize any of the built-in themes by changing the attributes of the theme. For example, say you like the colors in the Organic theme but you want to use a different font. In this situation, first apply the Organic theme, then click Theme Fonts and apply the font of your choice.

You can then save the resulting theme and apply it to other documents. You cannot change the built-in theme effects, but you can apply a different built-in effect to modify the appearance of the theme you are editing, which can include changing the shading, beveling, or other effects.

If you want to delete a customized theme, open the Themes gallery, right-click the custom theme at the top of the gallery, and select Delete from the shortcut menu. The same principle applies to customized color schemes, font schemes, and effects schemes.

Workplace Ready

PUTTING THEMES TO WORK

Microsoft Office themes bring a unified look and feel to business documents across Office applications. Whether you use a ready-made theme or customize your own, you can apply the same theme to Excel, Word, and PowerPoint documents. You can also apply a theme to many of the templates available for all three applications. Let's look at some ideas for using themes effectively.

If your organization is divided into regions, create custom themes with the same fonts but different color schemes for each group. Apply the themes to each group's financial reports to know at a glance which report is for which group.

Prepare professional-looking meeting materials in Excel, Word, and PowerPoint with the same design elements by simply applying the same theme.

Create proposals, estimates, invoices, and project plans using the same theme, and include your organization's logo. Your prospects and customers will easily recognize your materials.

MODIFYING A WORKSHEET'S ONSCREEN AND PRINTED APPEARANCE

Bottom Line

You can draw attention to a worksheet's onscreen appearance by displaying a background picture. **Gridlines** (the lines that display around worksheet cells), row headings, and column headings also enhance a worksheet's appearance. Onscreen, these elements are displayed by default, but they are not printed automatically.

Formatting a Worksheet Background

You can use a picture as a worksheet background for display purposes only. A worksheet background is saved with your worksheet, but it is not printed by default and it is not retained in a worksheet or as an item that you save as a web page.

STEP BY STEP   Format a Worksheet Background

GET READY. LAUNCH Excel if it is not already running.

1. OPEN the *07 Messenger Appearance* data file for this lesson.

2. Ensure Sheet1 is active.

3. On the PAGE LAYOUT tab, in the Page Setup group, click the Background button. The Insert Pictures dialog box opens.

4. Click Browse next to From a file. The Sheet Background dialog box opens.

5. Navigate to the student data files folder, select *07 bike_courier.jpg*, and then click Insert. The selected picture is displayed behind the text and fills the worksheet, as shown in Figure 7-19.

Figure 7-19

The worksheet with a background image

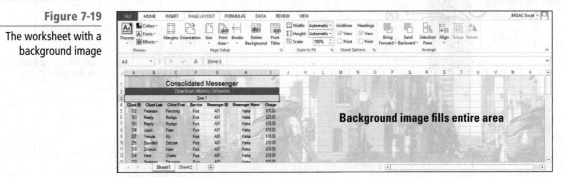

© Mike Clarke / iStockphoto

6. On the PAGE LAYOUT tab, in the Page Setup group, click Delete Background. The background is removed.

7. SAVE the workbook as *07 Messenger Appearance Solution*.

PAUSE. LEAVE the workbook open to use in the next exercise.

You should carefully consider the use of background images and use them judiciously. An image can detract from the readability of a worksheet if the wrong image is selected. You can lighten an image, or apply a light color cell shading, to make a background image work well. It's also best to remove gridlines when a sheet background is used. You'll learn about gridlines in the next section.

Viewing and Printing a Worksheet's Gridlines

You can choose to show or hide gridlines in your worksheet. By default, gridlines are present when you open a worksheet. You can also choose whether gridlines are printed. A printed worksheet is easier to read when gridlines are included.

STEP BY STEP   View and Print a Worksheet's Gridlines

GET READY. USE the workbook from the previous exercise.

1. Ensure Sheet1 is active.

2. On the PAGE LAYOUT tab, in the Sheet Options group, uncheck the Gridlines View check box. The gridlines disappear from the worksheet.

3. Check the Gridlines View check box to restore viewable gridlines.

4. Check the Gridlines Print check box, as shown in Figure 7-20. This action will force gridlines to appear in your printed worksheet.

Figure 7-20

The Gridlines check boxes

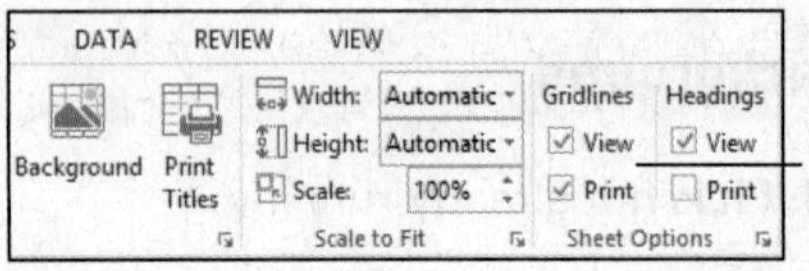

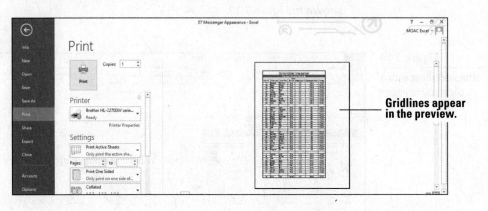

View and Print check boxes for gridlines

5. Click the Dialog Box Launcher in the Sheet Options group to open the Page Setup dialog box.

6. On the Sheet tab, notice that the Gridlines check box is checked. Click the Print Preview button. Gridlines appear in the preview, as shown in Figure 7-21.

Figure 7-21

Print Preview showing gridlines

Gridlines appear in the preview.

7. In the upper-left corner of the Print window, click the Back button to return to the worksheet.

8. SAVE the workbook.

PAUSE. LEAVE the workbook open to use in the next exercise.

CERTIFICATION READY?   1.3.2

How do you modify page setup?

Lesson 3 introduced you to Backstage, Print Preview, and some printing options. **Print Preview** is the screen that appears when you click the FILE tab and then click Print, or if you click Print Preview in a dialog box that provides the button. In Print Preview, you can see what your document will look like before sending it to the printer.

Viewing and Printing Column and Row Headings

You can choose whether to view row and column headings in your worksheet and to have them appear in printed worksheets. This exercise shows you how.

STEP BY STEP   **View and Print Column and Row Headings**

GET READY. USE the workbook from the previous exercise.

1. Ensure Sheet1 is active.

2. On the PAGE LAYOUT tab, in the Sheet Options group, uncheck the Headings View check box. The row and column headings disappear from the worksheet.

3. Check the Headings View check box to restore the row and column headings.

4. Check the Headings Print check box. This action forces row and column headings to appear in your printed worksheet.

5. In the Sheet Options group, click the Dialog Box Launcher to open the Page Setup dialog box.

6. On the Sheet tab, notice that the Row and column headings check box is checked. Click the Print Preview button. Row and column headings appear in the preview, as shown in Figure 7-22.

Figure 7-22

Print Preview showing row and column heading.

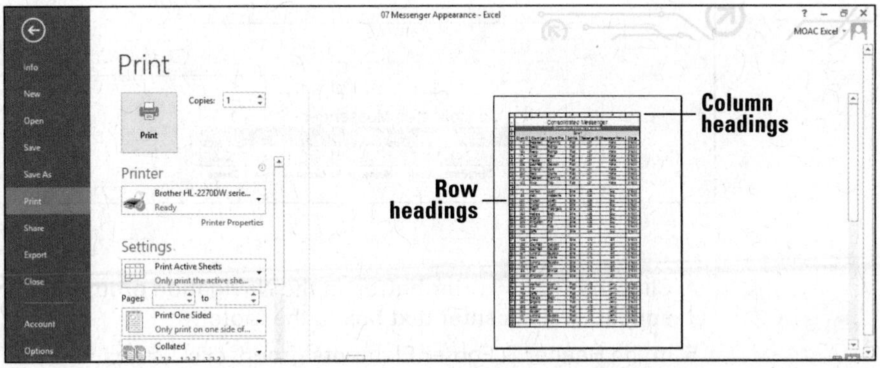

7. In the upper-left corner of the Print window, click the Back button to return to the worksheet.
8. On the PAGE LAYOUT tab, in the Sheet Options group, uncheck the Headings Print check box.
9. SAVE the workbook.

PAUSE. LEAVE Excel open to use in the next exercise.

INSERTING HEADERS AND FOOTERS

Bottom Line

You can add headers or footers to your worksheets to provide useful information about the worksheet, such as who prepared it, the date it was created or last modified, the page number, and so on. Headers and footers are visible in Page Layout view and appear on printouts. A **header** is a line of text that appears at the top of each page of a printed worksheet. **Footers** are lines of text that appear at the bottom of each page. You can add predefined header or footer information to a worksheet; insert elements such as page numbers, date and time, and filename; or add your own content to a header or footer.

Adding Page Numbers to a Worksheet

Page numbers are handy, and often necessary, for large worksheets that will print with multiple pages. The most common way to incorporate page numbers in a worksheet is to insert the page number code in the header or footer.

STEP BY STEP   **Add Page Numbers to a Worksheet**

GET READY. LAUNCH Excel if it is not already running.

1. OPEN the *07 Messenger Header-Footer* data file for this lesson.
2. Ensure Sheet1 is active.
3. On the INSERT tab, in the Text group, click the Header & Footer button. The worksheet is now displayed in Page Layout view. Note that the center Header text box is active and the DESIGN tab is added to the ribbon, as shown in Figure 7-23. The Header & Footer DESIGN tab command groups are thus available for you to use in the worksheet. By default, your cursor will appear in the center Header section.

Formatting W

Figure 7-23

Page Layout view displaying the DESIGN tab

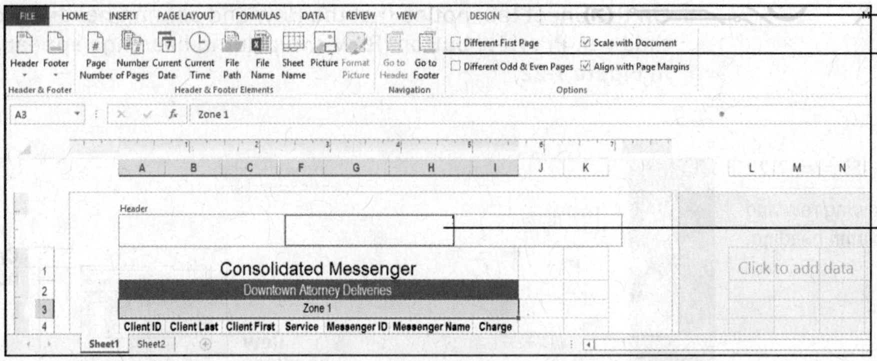

DESIGN tab
Go to Footer button

Three header text boxes: left, center, and right

4. Click the Go to Footer button in the Navigation group on the ribbon. The cursor appears in the center text box in the footer.

5. In the Header & Footer Elements group, click Page Number. The code &[Page] appears in the text box, as shown in Figure 7-24. The ampersand symbol (&) indicates that the appropriate page number will be added to each page of the printed worksheet.

Figure 7-24

The page number code

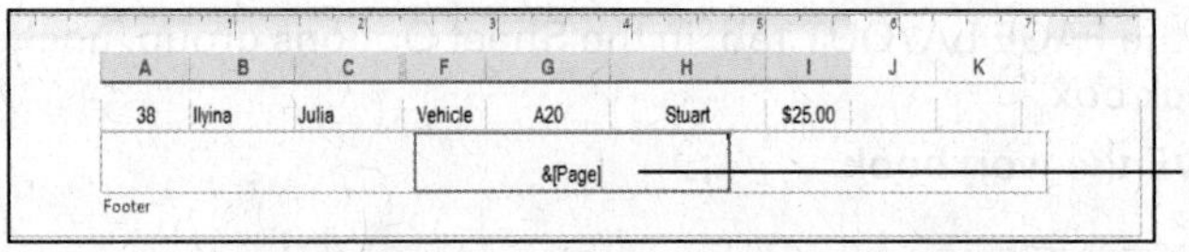

Excel inserts a page number code

6. Click in a worksheet cell that's not part of the footer, and then click the Normal view icon on the right side of the status bar.

7. SAVE the workbook as *07 Messenger Header-Footer Solution*.

PAUSE. LEAVE the workbook open to use in the next exercise.

Take Note The addition of the DESIGN contextual tab illustrates one advantage of Excel's ribbon interface. With the ribbon, instead of every command being available all the time, some commands appear only in response to specific user actions.

Inserting a Predefined Header or Footer

On the DESIGN tab, the Header & Footer group contains predefined headers and footers that allow you to automatically add text to the header or footer, such as the date, page number, number of pages, name of the sheet, and so on.

STEP BY STEP **Insert a Predefined Header or Footer**

GET READY. USE the workbook from the previous exercise.

1. Ensure Sheet1 is active. Click cell A1.

2. On the VIEW tab, in the Workbook Views group, click the Page Layout view button to view headers and footers.

3. Click the center header text box (which displays the "Click to add header" placeholder text). Click the Header & Footer Tools DESIGN tab now that it has become active. In the Header & Footer Elements group, click Sheet Name. &[Tab] appears in the text box.

4. In the Navigation group, click Go to Footer. Click the right footer text box.

5. In the Header & Footer group , click the Footer button arrow, and click the last option in the list, which combines Prepared by *username*, Current Date, and Page Number.

CERTIFICATION
R E A D Y ?   1.3.7

How do you insert predefined headers and footers?

Because the footer is wider than the right text box, the majority of the footer is moved to the center text box, and the page number appears in the right text box, as shown in Figure 7-25.

Figure 7-25

The predefined footer

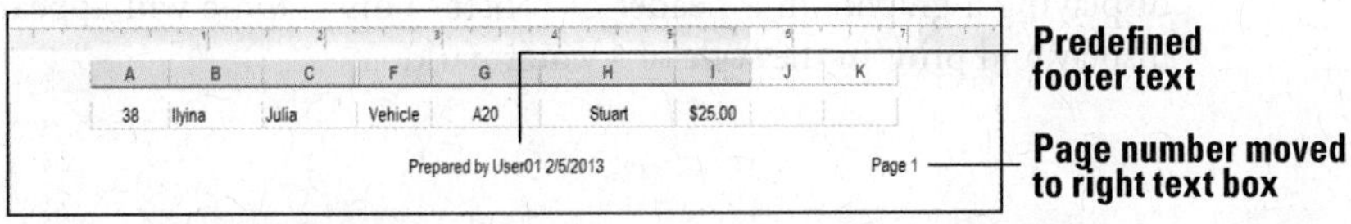

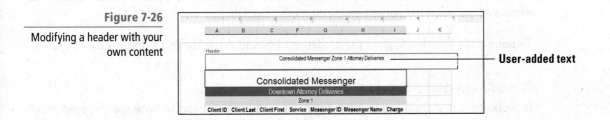

Predefined footer text

Page number moved to right text box

6. SAVE the workbook.

PAUSE. LEAVE the workbook open to use in the next exercise.

You can populate headers and footers by selecting one or more predefined elements in Excel, which inserts codes into the header or footer. When your workbook is printed, Excel replaces these codes with the current date, current time, and so on. You can view how the headers and footers will look by using Print Preview in Backstage view.

Many of Excel's predefined headers and footers combine one or more elements. In the previous exercise, you inserted a combined entry by clicking it. You can then customize the appearance of your header or footer in Page Layout view. Within this view, once you have the header or footer selected, you can modify the appearance of the text it contains using the Font group on the HOME tab. In this way, you can change font type or size, add special effects, or add other options to your text.

Adding Content to a Header or Footer

Excel's predefined headers and footers will not always meet your needs. When this happens, you can simply enter text into any of the header or footer text boxes.

STEP BY STEP **Add Content to a Header or Footer**

GET READY. USE the workbook from the previous exercise.

1. With Sheet1 active and in Page Layout view, click the center header text box and delete the existing header. You can click the DESIGN tab and then click Go to Header to move to the header quickly.

2. Type **Consolidated Messenger Zone 1 Attorney Deliveries**, as shown in Figure 7-26. When you preview your worksheet for printing or print the worksheet, you will see the header text.

Figure 7-26

Modifying a header with your own content

User-added text

3. SAVE the workbook.

PAUSE. LEAVE the workbook open to use in the next exercise.

Inserting a Watermark

In most documents, a **watermark** is text or a picture that appears behind a document, similar to a sheet background in Excel. However, Excel doesn't print sheet backgrounds, so it cannot be used as a watermark. Excel 2013 doesn't provide a watermark feature, but you can mimic one by displaying a graphic in a header or footer. This graphic will appear behind the text, and it will display and print in the style of a watermark.

STEP BY STEP	Insert a Watermark

GET READY. USE the workbook from the previous exercise.

1. Ensure Sheet1 is active and in Page Layout view.
2. Click the left header text box.
3. On the DESIGN tab in the Header & Footer Elements group, click Picture. Click the Browse button, navigate to the student data files folder, select *07 watermark.gif,* and then click Insert. Excel inserts an *&[Picture]* code into the left header text box.
4. Click outside of the header area, and then click the Normal view icon on the status bar.
5. Click the FILE tab and then click Print. The preview shows the watermark in your worksheet, as shown in Figure 7-27. Click the Back button to exit Print Preview.

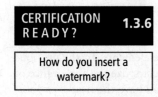

CERTIFICATION READY? 1.3.6

How do you insert a watermark?

Figure 7-27

The worksheet with a watermark

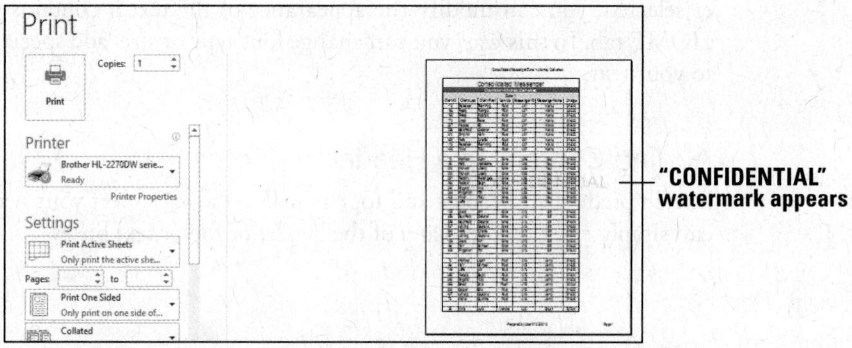

"CONFIDENTIAL" watermark appears

6. SAVE the workbook.

PAUSE. LEAVE the workbook open to use in the next exercise.

The watermark in this exercise was created using a simple graphic program and saved as a transparent GIF file, so only the text and not the background of the image displays as a watermark.

You can resize or scale the picture using the Format Picture button on the DESIGN tab in the Header & Footer Elements group. Clicking the button opens the Format Picture dialog box, where you can select the options you want on the Size tab.

To remove the watermark, go to the header text box and delete the &[Picture] code.

Repeating Headers and Footers

In worksheets that span two or more pages, you can instruct Excel to print specific rows or columns on each page to give your readers a better perspective of the data they are viewing. They won't have to go back to the first page to see column or row headings or labels, which are also referred to as titles. Titles help to give your worksheet a uniform look from the first to the last page.

STEP BY STEP   Repeat Headers and Footers

GET READY. USE the workbook from the previous exercise.

1. Ensure Sheet1 is active and in Normal view.

2. On the PAGE LAYOUT tab, in the Page Setup group, click the Print Titles button. The Page Setup dialog box opens to the Sheet tab.

3. Type A1:I54 in the Print area text box. This is the range of all data on Sheet1 to be printed.

Cross Ref   You learned how to set the print area and some other print features in Lesson 3.

4. In the Rows to repeat at top text box, type 1:4, as shown in Figure 7-28. This will repeat the first four rows of the worksheet, which includes column headings, on every page.

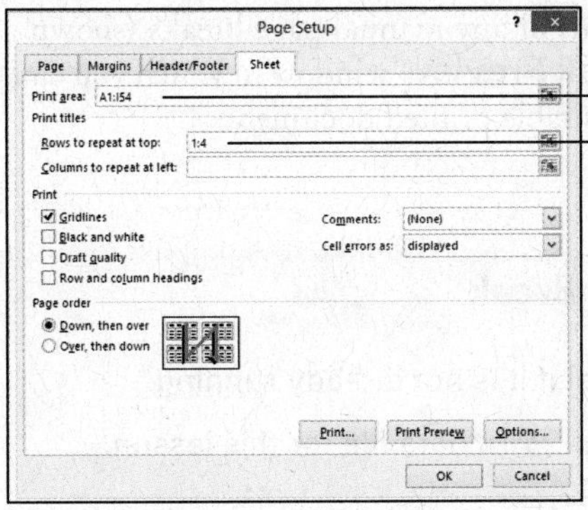

Figure 7-28

The Page Setup dialog box, Sheet tab

	→ Print area text box
	→ Rows to repeat at top (also called print titles)

CERTIFICATION READY?   1.5.5

How do you repeat headers and footers?

5. Click Print Preview. The Print Preview window appears. Click the right-facing arrow at the bottom of the screen to advance to the second page. The first four rows of the worksheet appear on the second page (see Figure 7-29). Click the left-facing arrow to return to the preview of page 1.

Figure 7-29

Print Preview shows that the first four rows of the worksheet appear on the second page.

	→ The first four rows of the worksheet repeat
	→ Navigation arrows

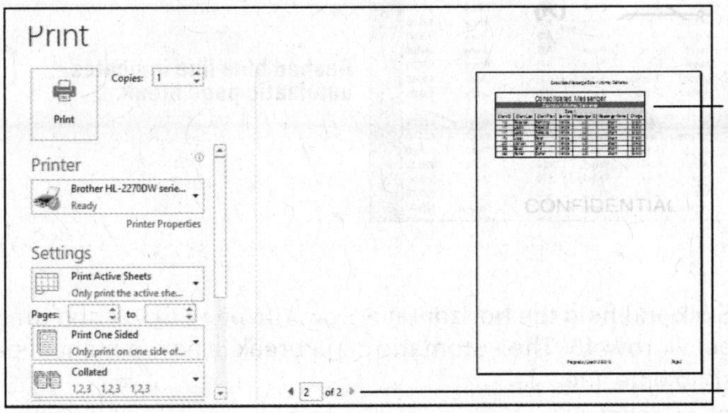

6. Click the Back button to return to the worksheet.

7. SAVE the workbook and CLOSE the file.

PAUSE. LEAVE Excel open to use in the next exercise.

PREPARING A DOCUMENT FOR PRINTING

When worksheet data prints on more than one page, you can use several commands to set up your document to print in a well-organized and easy-to-read manner. The Page Break Preview command on the VIEW tab controls where page breaks occur, enabling you to break data where it is most logical. You can also change page margins, change the orientation of the worksheet, and scale the worksheet to fit more data on a single page.

Adding and Moving a Page Break

CERTIFICATION READY?   **1.5.7**

How do you prepare a workbook for printing?

The Print window in Backstage displays a full-page preview of a worksheet just as it will be printed. With Print Preview, you can check the format and overall layout of a worksheet before actually printing it. You cannot make changes to the document in Print Preview, however.

A **page break** is a divider that breaks a worksheet into separate pages for printing. Excel inserts automatic vertical page breaks (shown as a dashed line) based on paper size, margin settings, scaling options, and the positions of any manual page breaks (shown as a solid line) that you insert. Excel provides a **Page Break Preview** window in which you can quickly adjust automatic page breaks to achieve a more desirable printed document.

STEP BY STEP   **Add and Move a Page Break**

GET READY. LAUNCH Excel if it is not already running.

1. OPEN the *07 Messenger Print* data file for this lesson.

2. Ensure Sheet1 is active.

3. On the VIEW tab, in the Workbook Views group, click Page Break Preview. Scroll down to view the entire print area. Notice that a dashed blue line appears after row 47 (see Figure 7-30). The dashed line is an automatic page break inserted by Excel.

Figure 7-30

Page Break Preview showing a horizontal page break

	A	B	C	F	G	H	I	J
35	349	Ringstrom	Titti	Bike	A13	Bill	$16.00	
36								
37	10	Harrison	Justin	Foot	A15	Jenny	$18.00	
38	88	Yair	Shmuel	Foot	A15	Jenny	$18.00	
39	148	Jaffe	Jon	Foot	A15	Jenny	$18.00	
40	262	Hadaya	Sagiv	Foot	A15	Jenny	$18.00	
41	290	Brigandi	Nick	Foot	A15	Jenny	$18.00	
42	395	Bassli	Shai	Rush	A15	Jenny	$40.00	
43	302	Gruber	Eric	Foot	A15	Jenny	$18.00	
44	437	Achong	Gustavo	Foot	A15	Jenny	$18.00	
45	72	Mohan	Suchitra	Foot	A15	Jenny	$18.00	
46								
47	38	Ilyina	Julia	Vehicle	A20	Stuart	$25.00	
48	112	Pedersen	Flemming	Vehicle	A20	Stuart	$25.00	
49	117	Laszlo	Rebecca	Vehicle	A20	Stuart	$25.00	
50	117	Laszlo	Rebecca	Vehicle	A20	Stuart	$25.00	
51	174	Jirsak	Peter	Vehicle	A20	Stuart	$18.00	
52	200	Munson	Liberty	Vehicle	A20	Stuart	$25.00	
53	395	Bassli	Shai	Vehicle	A20	Stuart	$25.00	

Dashed blue line indicates automatic page break.

4. Click and hold the horizontal automatic page break and drag it upward so it is now below row 46. The automatic page break is now a manual page break represented by a solid blue line.

5. On the VIEW tab, in the Workbook Views group, click Normal.

6. SAVE the workbook as *07 Messenger Print Solution*.

PAUSE. LEAVE the workbook open to use in the next exercise.

Use manual page breaks to control page break locations. You can drag an automatic page break to a new location to convert it to a manual page break.

Another way to insert a manual page break is to click a cell in the row where you want a page break to occur, then click the PAGE LAYOUT tab. In the Page Setup group, click Breaks and then click Insert Page Break. A horizontal page break appears.

Setting Margins

Margins are an effective way to manage and optimize the white space on a printed worksheet. Achieving balance between data and white space adds significantly to the readability and appearance of a worksheet. In Excel, you can choose one of three built-in margin sets, or you can create customized margins using the Page Setup dialog box.

STEP BY STEP	Set Margins

GET READY. USE the workbook from the previous exercise.

1. Ensure Sheet1 is active and in Normal view.
2. On the PAGE LAYOUT tab, in the Page Setup group, click the Margins button arrow to open the Margins menu.
3. At the bottom of the menu, click Custom Margins. The Page Setup dialog box opens to the Margins tab, as shown in Figure 7-31.

Figure 7-31

The Page Setup dialog box, Margins tab

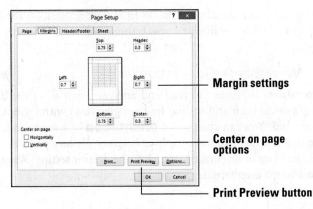

4. Change the left and right margins to 1.4. This will make the margins slightly wider than normal.
5. Check the Center on page Horizontally check box. The content in your worksheet will print centered.
6. Click Print Preview. The page is centered horizontally, as shown in Figure 7-32.

Figure 7-32

Print Preview shows the page centered horizontally

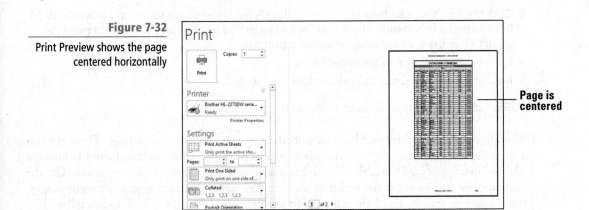

7. Click the Back button to leave Backstage.

8. SAVE the workbook.

PAUSE. LEAVE the workbook open to use in the next exercise.

The Margins menu includes predefined Normal, Wide, and Narrow settings. The Normal margin setting is the default for a new workbook. Narrower margins allow more area for data when you print a workbook, where wider margins will introduce more white space. You can also set custom margins in Excel.

When you click Custom Margins at the bottom of the Margins menu, the Page Setup dialog box opens with the settings that have been applied to the active worksheet. You can change any of the settings to create a custom margin setting. Header and footer margins automatically adjust when you change the page margins.

Worksheets that do not fill an entire page can be centered vertically and horizontally, thereby evenly distributing the page's white space. Use the Margins tab of the Page Setup dialog box to set these features.

To quickly remove all manual page breaks from a worksheet, on the PAGE LAYOUT tab, in the Page Setup group, click the Breaks arrow button and select Reset All Page Breaks.

Setting a Worksheet's Orientation

Printed worksheets are easiest to read and analyze when all of the data appears on one piece of paper. Excel's orientation and scaling features give you control over the number of printed pages of worksheet data. You can change the **orientation** of a worksheet, which is the position of the content, so that it prints either vertically or horizontally on a page. A worksheet that is printed vertically uses the Portrait orientation, which is the default setting. A worksheet printed horizontally uses the Landscape orientation.

STEP BY STEP   **Set a Worksheet's Orientation**

GET READY. USE the workbook from the previous exercise.

1. Ensure Sheet1 is active and in Normal view.
2. On the PAGE LAYOUT tab, in the Page Setup group, click Orientation and then click Landscape.
3. Click the FILE tab, and then click Print. Click through the pages to see the worksheet in Landscape orientation. If you decided to keep this orientation, you would need to adjust page breaks to display all content properly.
4. Click the Back button to leave Backstage.
5. Repeat Step 2 to change the orientation back to Portrait.

PAUSE. LEAVE the workbook open to use in the next exercise.

Orientation is the way your workbook or worksheet appears on the printed page. There are two settings: Portrait and Landscape. Portrait is a vertical printing of the workbook, and Landscape is the horizontal aspect. By default, all workbooks and worksheets are printed in Portrait. Use the Landscape orientation when the width of the area you want to print is greater than the height. Data is easier to read when all the columns fit on one page. This can often be accomplished by changing a worksheet's orientation to Landscape. When you can't fit all of the data on one printed page by changing the orientation, you can shrink or reduce it using Excel's scaling options, as described in the next exercise.

Scaling a Worksheet to Fit on a Printed Page

Scaling refers to shrinking or stretching printed output to a percentage of its actual size. One use for scaling is to resize a document so that it fits on a single page. Before attempting to change the scaling for a worksheet's output, the maximum width and height must be set to Automatic.

STEP BY STEP	Scale a Worksheet to Fit on a Printed Page

GET READY. USE the workbook from the previous exercise.

1. Ensure Sheet1 is active and in Normal view.
2. On the PAGE LAYOUT tab, in the Page Setup group, click Orientation and verify that Portrait is selected.
3. In the Scale to Fit group, click the Height arrow and select 1 page. The scale of the worksheet is reduced so that all rows fit on the same page.
4. Click the FILE tab, and then click Print. Notice that all rows appear on the page and that the content is smaller than it was previously, as shown in Figure 7-33. When output is reduced, it shrinks the height and width proportionally.

Figure 7-33

Viewing the worksheet after scaling it to fit on one page

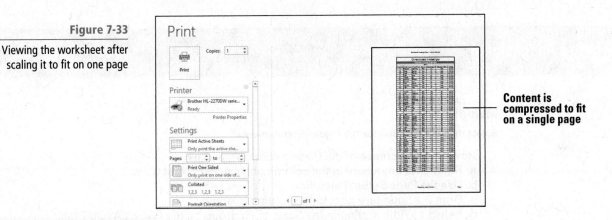

Content is compressed to fit on a single page

5. SAVE the workbook and CLOSE the file.

CLOSE Excel.

CERTIFICATION READY?	1.5.4

How do you set print scaling?

The most common reason for scaling a worksheet is to shrink it so that you can print it on one page. You can also enlarge the sheet so that data appears bigger and fills up more of the printed page. When the Width and Height boxes are set to Automatic, you can click the arrows in the Scale box to increase or decrease scaling of the printout. Each time you click the arrow, the scaling changes by 5%.

Take Note   The Width and Height settings must be set to Automatic if you want to specify a scale, such as 75%.

SKILL SUMMARY

In this lesson you learned how:	Exam Objective	Objective Number
To work with columns and rows.	Insert and delete columns and rows.	1.3.3
	Adjust row height and column width.	1.3.5
	Hide columns and rows.	1.4.2
	Transpose columns and rows.	2.3.3
To use themes.	Change workbook themes.	1.3.4
To modify a worksheet's onscreen and printed appearance.	Modify page setup.	1.3.2
To insert headers and footers.	Insert headers and footers.	1.3.7
	Insert watermarks.	1.3.6
	Repeat headers and footers.	1.5.5
To prepare a document for printing.	Set print scaling.	1.5.4
	Configure workbooks to print.	1.5.7

Knowledge Assessment

Multiple Choice

Select the best response for the following statements.

1. How do you increase or decrease a column's width?
   a. Right-click anywhere in the column and select Format Cells.
   b. Use the Page Setup dialog box.
   c. Drag the boundary next to the column heading.
   d. Select a Width setting in the Scale to Fit group on the PAGE LAYOUT tab.

2. Which should you do before formatting an entire row or column?
   a. Click the row heading or column heading to select it.
   b. Open Print Preview.
   c. Go into Page Layout view.
   d. Select a cell range.

3. Which dialog box do you use to transpose rows and columns?
   a. Page Setup
   b. Paste Special
   c. Column Width
   d. Row Height

4. Which of the following can you *not* modify when customizing a document theme?
   a. Colors
   b. Fonts
   c. Effects
   d. Page orientation

5. Where are check boxes you can select to view or print gridlines?
   a. In Print Preview
   b. On the HOME tab, in the Cells group
   c. On the PAGE LAYOUT tab, in the Sheet Options group
   d. On the PAGE LAYOUT tab, in the Page Setup group

6. Which Excel feature or view lets you drag automatic page breaks, converting them to manual page breaks, to achieve a more desirable printed document?
   a. Print Preview
   b. Page Break Preview
   c. Page Layout view
   d. Normal view

7. Which feature do you use to repeat column A on every page when printing a multiple-page worksheet?
   a. Print Titles
   b. Page Break Preview
   c. A header
   d. Custom margins

8. Which is *not* a predefined margin setting?
   a. Normal
   b. Large
   c. Narrow
   d. Wide

9. How do you unhide a hidden row or column?
   a. Select a range of cells in the row or column, right-click, and select Unhide.
   b. Use the Page Setup dialog box.
   c. Remove all page breaks.
   d. Select the rows/columns before and after the hidden rows/columns and then right-click and select Unhide.

10. A worksheet is a little too wide to print on one page. Which feature can you use to force all data to print on one page?
    a. A page break
    b. The Wide margin setting
    c. Scale to Fit
    d. Commands in the Sheet Options group on the PAGE LAYOUT tab

Fill in the Blank

Complete the following sentences by writing the correct word or words in the blanks provided.

1. _____ are the lines that display around worksheet cells.

2. The _____ is the line between rows or columns.

3. A(n) _____ is a line of text that appears at the top of each page of a printed worksheet.

4. _____ a row or column causes your cell data to change orientation. Row data will become column data, and column data will become row data.

5. _____ is the top-to-bottom measurement of a row, measured in points.

6. The identifying letter at the top of a column is called the _____.

7. _____ refers to shrinking or stretching printed output to a percentage of its actual size.

8. A(n) _____ is a predefined set of colors, fonts, and effects that can be applied to an entire workbook or to specific items within a workbook, such as charts or tables.

9. You can change the _____ of a worksheet, which is the position of the content, so that it prints either vertically or horizontally on a page.

10. A(n) _____ is a divider that breaks a worksheet into separate pages for printing.

Competency Assessment

Project 7-1: Practice Working with Rows and Columns

Use the worksheet for the School of Fine Arts to practice working with rows and columns.

GET READY. LAUNCH Excel if it is not already running.

1. OPEN *07 Fine Art* from the data files for this lesson.
2. Click the column D heading to select the entire column.
3. On the HOME tab, in the Cells group, click the Format button arrow, point to Hide & Unhide, and select Hide Columns. Column D is now hidden.
4. Click the column B heading to select the entire column.
5. On the HOME tab, in the Cells group, click the Format button arrow and select Column Width. In the Column Width dialog box, type 11 in the Column width text box and click OK.
6. Double-click the double boundary between column headings C and E. Column D appears.
7. Click the row 11 heading, right-click, and select Insert.
8. Enter the following in the blank row:

First	Last	Discipline	Enrollment Date	GPA
Bruce	Keever	Sculpture	10/15/2012	=SUM(3.4+3.5+3.7)/3

9. Click the plus (+) sign to the right of Sheet1 to create a new, blank worksheet.
10. Click Sheet1, select A2:E15, and press Ctrl + C to copy the content to the Clipboard.
11. Click Sheet2, and then click cell A1.
12. On the HOME tab, in the Clipboard group, click the Paste button arrow and select Paste Special. The Paste Special dialog box opens.
13. Check the Transpose check box, and click OK.
14. In Sheet2, select all content.
15. On the HOME tab, in the Cells group, click the Format button arrow, and select AutoFit Column Width.
16. Click Sheet1.
17. SAVE the workbook as *07 Fine Art Solution* and CLOSE the file.

LEAVE Excel open for the next project.

Project 7-2: Change and Customize a Theme

You work for Wingtip Toys and have been asked to modify a sales worksheet to make it match the company color and font scheme.

GET READY. LAUNCH Excel if it is not already running.

1. OPEN *07 Wingtip Toys* from the data files for this lesson.
2. On the PAGE LAYOUT tab, in the Themes group, click the Themes button arrow to open the Themes menu.
3. Find and select the Slice theme.
4. In the Themes group, click Colors.
5. Scroll down and select the Slipstream color scheme.
6. On the PAGE LAYOUT tab, in the Themes group, click Fonts.
7. Locate the Gill Sans MT font and select it.
8. Click Fonts in the Themes group and select Customize Fonts.

9. Open the Heading font drop-down menu and select Arial. Click Save.
10. On the PAGE LAYOUT tab, in the Themes group, click Themes and then click Save Current Theme. The Save Current Theme dialog box opens.
11. In the File name box, type WingTipToys and click Save.
12. SAVE the workbook as *07 Wingtip Toys Solution* and CLOSE the file.

LEAVE Excel open for the next project.

Take Note Remember, you can delete a customized theme by opening the Themes gallery, right-clicking the custom theme at the top of the gallery, and then selecting Delete from the shortcut menu. Similar steps apply to customized color schemes and font schemes. However, it's recommended that you don't delete customizations until you're finished with the course.

Proficiency Assessment

Project 7-3: Modify the Appearance of a Worksheet

Albert, the CEO's administrative assistant at A. Datum, asked you to help him prepare documents to email to board members. Albert wants to enhance the appearance of the A. Datum sales worksheet, which will be viewed onscreen and may be printed.

GET READY. LAUNCH Excel if it is not already running.

1. OPEN *07 ADatum Appearance* from the data files for this lesson.
2. On the PAGE LAYOUT tab, in the Page Setup group, click the Background button. The Insert Pictures dialog box opens.
3. Next to From a file, click Browse. The Sheet Background dialog box opens.
4. Navigate to the student data files folder, select *07 confidential.png*, and then click Insert.
5. On the PAGE LAYOUT tab, in the Sheet Options group, uncheck the Gridlines View check box. The gridlines disappear from the worksheet.
6. Check the Gridlines View check box to restore viewable gridlines.
7. On the PAGE LAYOUT tab, in the Page Setup group, click the Dialog Box Launcher. The Page Setup dialog box opens.
8. Click the Margins tab.
9. Check the Center on page Horizontally check box and the Vertically check box.
10. Click Print Preview. Verify that the content is centered horizontally and vertically, and then click the Back button to exit Print Preview.
11. SAVE the workbook as *07 ADatum Appearance Solution* and CLOSE the file.

LEAVE Excel open for the next project.

Project 7-4: Insert Headers and Footers

Albert has returned for additional help with the A. Datum sales worksheet. He wants to make a few formatting changes and add a header and footer to the worksheet.

GET READY. LAUNCH Excel if it is not already running.

1. OPEN *07 ADatum Header-Footer* from the data files for this lesson.
2. Select A1:E1, and then on the HOME tab, in the Alignment group, click Merge & Center.
3. Select columns B through E. Center all content. You might have to click Center

twice because some of the selected data is already centered. The first click removes centering for those cells, and the second click applies it to all selected cells.

4. On the PAGE LAYOUT tab, in the Page Setup group, click the Dialog Box Launcher. In the Page Setup dialog box, click the Margins tab.

5. Uncheck the Center on page Vertically check box. Click OK.

6. Click in row 10. On the PAGE LAYOUT tab, in the Page Setup group, click Breaks and select Insert Page Break.

7. On the INSERT tab, in the Text group, click Header & Footer. Type the text A. Datum March 2013 Board Meeting in the center header text box.

8. Click the Go to Footer button in the Navigation group. With the cursor in the center footer text box, click Footer in the Header & Footer group and select Confidential, <date>, Page 1.

9. Click outside of the header area, on the status bar, click the Normal view icon.

10. Preview the worksheet for printing.

11. SAVE the workbook as *07 ADatum Header-Footer Solution* and CLOSE the file.

LEAVE Excel open for the next project.

Mastery Assessment

Project 7-5: Enhance a Worksheet and Prepare for Printing

Margie's Travel is an agency that sells travel-related products and services to clients on behalf of third parties such as airlines, hotels, and cruise lines. You are preparing a worksheet that lists a variety of cruises for Fabrikam, an important client.

GET READY. LAUNCH Excel if it is not already running.

1. OPEN *07 Cruises* from the data files for this lesson.
2. Remove the background image from the worksheet.
3. Change the orientation of the worksheet to Landscape.
4. Change the margin setting to Narrow.
5. Change the document theme to Banded.
6. Center the worksheet horizontally for printing.
7. Preview the worksheet for printing.
8. SAVE the workbook as *07 Cruises Solution* and CLOSE the file.

LEAVE Excel open for the next project.

Project 7-6: Formatting a Payroll Worksheet

Contoso, Ltd. is a busy family practice clinic that recently expanded its operations to a second location. You are formatting a payroll worksheet.

GET READY. LAUNCH Excel if it is not already running.

1. OPEN *07 Payroll* from the data files for this lesson.
2. AutoFit all columns so that all data is viewable.
3. Change the row height of rows 3 through 33 to 18.
4. Change the theme to Wisp.

5. Set rows 1 through 3 to repeat on every page, anticipating that additional rows will be added to a future revision of the worksheet.

6. Insert a footer that includes the file name and page number.

7. Configure gridlines to appear in printed worksheets.

8. Scale the width of the worksheet to fit on one page.

9. Preview the worksheet for printing.

10. SAVE the workbook as *07 Payroll Solution* and CLOSE the file.

CLOSE Excel.

8 Managing Worksheets

LESSON SKILL MATRIX

Skills	Exam Objective	Objective Number
Organizing Worksheets	Copy and move worksheets.	1.1.6
	Change worksheet order.	1.2.3
	Change worksheet tab color.	1.3.1
	Hide worksheets.	1.4.1
	Add worksheets to existing workbooks.	1.1.5
Using Zoom and Freeze to Change the Onscreen View	Demonstrate how to use zoom.	1.4.9
	Freeze panes.	1.4.11
Finding and Replacing Data	Search for data within a workbook.	1.2.1
	Find and replace data.	2.1.2
	Demonstrate how to use Go To.	1.2.4

KEY TERMS

- **Find command**
- **freeze**
- **hide**
- **pane**
- **Replace command**
- **unhide**
- **zoom**

© skynesher /iStockphoto

© skynesher /iStockphoto

You work for an office management service whose clients include a local athletic club. Inside the club is a spa, which maintains its books separately from the rest of the club. The way the spa organizes its records, each day's clients are recorded on an individual Excel worksheet, and each week's transactions are recorded in a workbook file. Each new week begins with a kind of "template," containing one form for Monday's clients. Your job is to record the transactions for each client on its own line of a worksheet, so that the totals for that sheet reflect the final totals for the day. For each new day of the week, it's up to you to add new sheets to the workbook using Monday's sheet as a form. So you need to know how to add, move, and change the components of an Excel workbook, as well as change your view of the data in the worksheets of that workbook, to make them easier for you to manage.

SOFTWARE ORIENTATION

Worksheet Management

Think of an Excel workbook as a collection of the types of things you used to see recorded on paper and stored in a folder that was then filed in a cabinet. A workbook does not have to include the contents of the entire cabinet, just the records that pertain to one subject. Business transactions that take place during a period of time, such as a specific week or month, might make up a workbook. If you're keeping track of time that clients spend, you might create a workbook that breaks down how your clients spend their time into categories, and have one tab for each category. If your clients are billed on different cycles, then you might need a workbook that shows you when each client should be billed.

(continued on next page)

Figure 8-1

Commands to organize worksheets

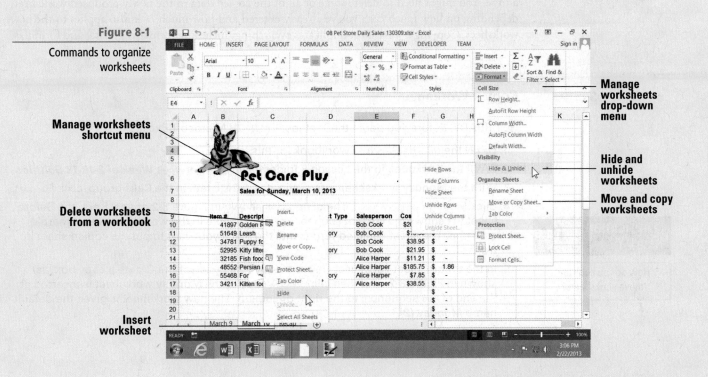

One good way to divide that workbook into sheets is to subcategorize transactions into days, such as the records for a spa. Another option is to have each sheet represent a certain sales department. This assumes your workbook is used as a ledger, and Excel can also be used for many other purposes besides keeping track of business accounts.

In this lesson, you become familiar with how a workbook contains worksheets, and how you manipulate those worksheets within a workbook the way you might reorganize the contents of a folder in your desk drawer. Unlike the old desk drawer, though, you have a few tools that will remind you that you're using a computer, such as the Find command to help you search for certain contents. You find the commands for this lesson located in the Cells group and Editing group, which are both located on the HOME tab (see Figure 8-1).

ORGANIZING WORKSHEETS

Bottom Line

When you create a new Excel workbook, by default, it has one blank worksheet. You might need only one, though you can add more when you need multiple worksheets that pertain to the same topic. There's no practical limit to how many worksheets a workbook can contain. The order of worksheets in a workbook is determined by the sequence of tabs along the bottom of the Excel window. You use these tabs to switch between worksheets in the window. In this way, you can arrange worksheets in a sensible order that helps you find them easier and keep related content grouped together.

Copying a Worksheet

There's a clear difference between copying the contents of a worksheet into another worksheet and copying worksheets in their entirety. This objective covers the latter task, and one big reason you'd want to do this is to create a new form that's identical in style and format to an existing one, so you can enter new data. Imagine a kind of ledger form that you publish for yourself, one sheet at a time. You might need to delete some or all of the copied data in the newly produced worksheet, depending on how much data you've already entered and how much of it also applies to the new worksheet. Copying a worksheet duplicates everything, including formatting, data, and formulas.

STEP BY STEP   **Copy a Worksheet**

GET READY. Before you begin these steps, **LAUNCH** Microsoft Excel.

1. OPEN the *08 Spa Services* workbook for this lesson.

2. SAVE the workbook in the Lesson 8 folder as *08 Spa Services Week of 2-18-13 Solution*.

3. With the Monday worksheet active, click the HOME tab, in the Cells group, click Format.

4. Click Move or Copy Sheet. The dialog box shown in Figure 8-2 opens. Here, the Before sheet list shows the current sequence of worksheets in the workbook even if there's only one. The sheet selected represents the place you want to put the copied sheet in front of.

5. In the Before sheet list, select (move to end). Next, select the Create a copy box, as shown in Figure 8-2, and then click OK. A copy of the Monday worksheet is inserted at the end of the sequence, to the right of Lookup. The new worksheet is given the default name *Monday (2)*.

CERTIFICATION READY?   **1.1.6**

How do you copy and move worksheets?

Figure 8-2

Move or Copy dialog box

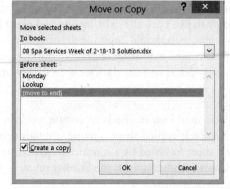

Another Way
You can also right-click a worksheet's tab to display the shortcut menu, and then click Move or Copy to display the Move or Copy dialog box.

6. Click the Monday worksheet tab. Next, click and hold the Monday tab, and then press and hold Ctrl. The pointer changes from an arrow to a paper with a plus sign in it.

7. Drag the pointer to the right until the down-arrow just above the tabs bar points to the divider to the right of Monday (2). Release the mouse button and Ctrl key. A new worksheet is created, with its tab located just to the right of where the down-arrow was pointing. Its name is Monday (3).

8. With Monday (3) active, click cell B4 and type the date 2/19/2013.

9. Select cells B8:H13.

10. Beginning in cell B8, type the following data, skipping over cells without an "x" or a number (see Figure 8-3):

Sarah	351	x		x		0.5
Elena	295	x	x	x	x	1
Clarisse	114			x		
Genevieve	90	x	x	x		1
Abhayankari	205	x	x	x	x	1
Regina	34			x		

Figure 8-3

The completed Spa Services worksheet

	A	B	C	D E F G	H	I	J	K	L	M	N
1											
2	Michigan Avenue Athletic Club Spa Services										
3											
4	Date:	2/19/2013									
5											
6											
7		Client Name	Member #	M HW F R	Massage Duration	Massage Cost	Herbal Wrap	Facial	Revitalizer	Invoice Total	
8		Sarah	351 x	x	0.5	50	0	75	0	125	
9		Elena	295 x x	x x	1	100	65	75	175	415	
10		Clarisse	114	x		0	0	75	0	75	
11		Genevieve	90 x x	x	1	100	65	75	0	240	
12		Abhayankari	205 x x	x x	1	100	65	75	175	415	
13		Regina	34	x		0	0	75	0	75	
14						0	0	0	0	0	
15						0	0	0	0	0	
16						0	0	0	0	0	
17						0	0	0	0	0	

◀ ▶ ... | Lookup | Monday (2) | **Monday (3)** | ⊕

11. SAVE the workbook.

PAUSE. LEAVE it open to use in the next exercise.

When you need a new worksheet that has the styles, formatting, and formulas that work well in an existing worksheet, it's easy to just copy the existing one and place it where it needs to go in the workbook. When it's convenient, you should copy the existing one before you add data to it, but that's not always possible. Your copied worksheet contains a duplicate of whatever data the existing one contains, but you can easily delete just the data without removing the formatting you wanted to copy in the first place.

In the preceding exercise, you used two methods to copy a worksheet, resulting in a workbook with three sheets. Excel gives each copied sheet a name, though probably just a temporary one with the name of the copied sheet followed by a number in parentheses, such as Monday (3). Selecting the Move or Copy Sheet command from the Format menu is more explicit, showing you a dialog box with all your options.

The second method is more of a shortcut, where you hold the pointer down over the worksheet tab while pressing Ctrl, and move the copied sheet to its new location. In Figure 8-4, you can see how the mouse pointer helps you by signaling to you symbolically that you're copying a worksheet. You can use whichever method you prefer.

Figure 8-4

Copying a worksheet using the mouse

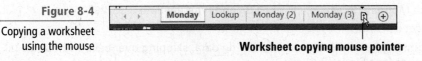

Worksheet copying mouse pointer

Renaming a Worksheet

The name Excel gives a newly copied worksheet is supposed to be temporary, because Excel can't guess the name you intend for it to be. In the example, obviously we don't want multiple Mondays, and the day for which you just entered transactions happens to be Tuesday.

STEP BY STEP   **Rename a Worksheet**

GET READY. USE the workbook from the previous exercise.

1. Double-click the Monday (3) worksheet tab to select its name.
2. Type Tuesday and press Enter. The new name appears on the tab.

Another Way
You can also right-click a worksheet's tab to display the shortcut menu, and then click Rename.

3. Repeat this process for the Monday (2) worksheet tab, renaming it Wednesday.
4. With the Wednesday worksheet active, select cell B4 and type the date 2/20/2013.
5. Select cells B8:H15.
6. Beginning in cell B8, enter the following data, skipping over cells without an "x" or a number (see Figure 8-5):

Regina	210		x			
Angela	44		x	x	x	1.5
Ariel	191		x	x	x	x	1
Micaela	221		x	x		x	1
Julie	118			x	x	
Yolanda	21		x	x	x	x	1
Gwen	306		x	x	x		1
Elizabeth H.	6		x	x	x	x	1

Figure 8-5

The completed Wednesday worksheet

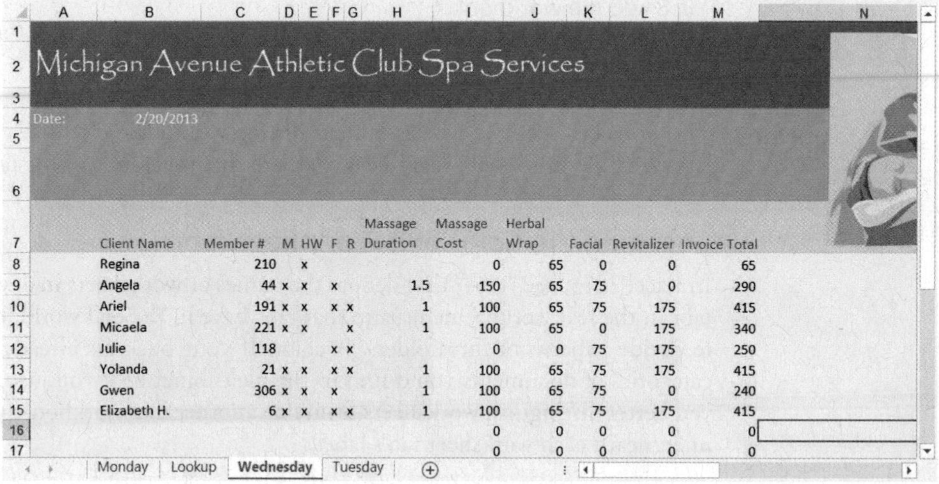

	Client Name	Member #	M	HW	F	R	Massage Duration	Massage Cost	Herbal Wrap	Facial	Revitalizer	Invoice Total
8	Regina	210	x					0	65	0	0	65
9	Angela	44	x	x		x	1.5	150	65	75	0	290
10	Ariel	191	x	x	x	x	1	100	65	75	175	415
11	Micaela	221	x	x		x	1	100	65	0	175	340
12	Julie	118			x	x		0	0	75	175	250
13	Yolanda	21	x	x	x	x	1	100	65	75	175	415
14	Gwen	306	x	x	x		1	100	65	75	0	240
15	Elizabeth H.	6	x	x	x	x	1	100	65	75	175	415
16								0	0	0	0	0
17								0	0	0	0	0

Date: 2/20/2013

Michigan Avenue Athletic Club Spa Services

Monday | Lookup | **Wednesday** | Tuesday

PAUSE. SAVE the workbook and LEAVE it open to use in the next exercise.

Repositioning the Worksheets in a Workbook

If you were to hand a manila file folder full of important documents to someone important, such as your boss, the sequence of papers in that folder would be important. You wouldn't want to just shove a bunch of papers in the folder, because your boss might be the type of person who reads the folder's contents from top to bottom or in chronological order. The same principle applies to organizing worksheets in a workbook. Not having a proper sequence of organization, even if it's not obvious at first and you had to come up with such a sequence on your own, doesn't really help you.

STEP BY STEP   **Reposition the Worksheets in a Workbook**

GET READY. USE the workbook from the previous exercise.

1. Click the Tuesday worksheet tab. On the HOME tab, in the Cells group, click Format.
2. Click Move or Copy Sheet. The Move or Copy dialog box opens.
3. To make sure Tuesday appears before Wednesday, in the Before sheet list, click Wednesday and then click OK.
4. Click and hold the Lookup worksheet tab. The pointer changes from an arrow to a paper without a plus sign.
5. Drag the pointer to the right until the down-arrow just above the tabs bar points to the divider to the right of Wednesday. Release the mouse button. The Lookup worksheet is repositioned at the end of the sequence, and nothing inside the worksheet itself is changed.
6. Click the Monday worksheet tab.
7. Select cells B8:H11.
8. Beginning in cell B8, enter the following data, skipping over cells without an "x" or a number:

Barbara C.	15	x	x		x	x	1
Regina	210	x			x		1
Ellen	301		x		x		
Genevieve	213	x	x		x	x	1

9. SAVE the workbook.

PAUSE. LEAVE it open to use in the next exercise.

Take Note The worksheet you see when you first open a workbook is whichever sheet was active when you last saved the workbook, regardless of where that sheet falls in the tab order.

Changing the Color of a Worksheet Tab

In Excel 2013, the "tabs" that denote the names of worksheets in a workbook don't quite look like tabs in the real world. One feature that tabs have in the real world, especially when you use them to divide paperwork into folders, is color. If your business already uses color coding to denote categories of documents you'd find in the file cabinet or if you just need a splash of color to help you better distinguish worksheets from one another in a workbook, you can apply a stripe of color underneath each worksheet tab's label.

STEP BY STEP **Change the Color of a Worksheet Tab**

GET READY. USE the workbook from the previous exercise.

1. Right-click the Monday worksheet tab.
2. In the shortcut menu, click Tab Color.
3. In the popup menu, under Standard Colors, click Red. Excel gives a slightly red tint to the Monday worksheet tab.
4. Click the Tuesday worksheet tab. Notice the Monday worksheet tab is now the bold red color you chose. Excel applies only the gradient tint to the tab for the currently visible worksheet to make it stand out above the others.
5. Repeat the color selection process for the Tuesday and Wednesday worksheet tabs, choosing Orange and Yellow, respectively.
6. Click the Lookup worksheet tab. Your tabs bar should now appear as shown in Figure 8-6.

Figure 8-6

Colored worksheet tabs

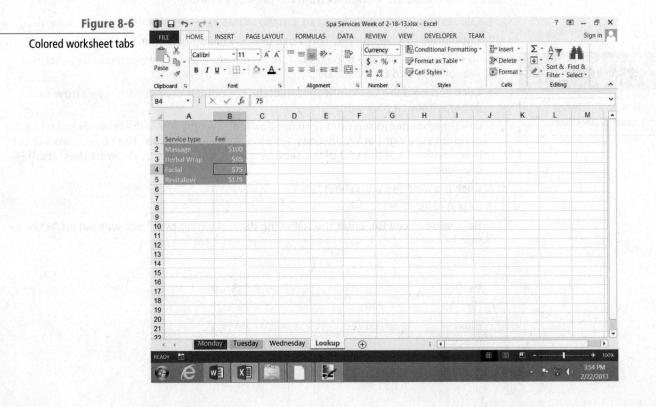

PAUSE. SAVE the workbook and LEAVE it open to use in the next exercise.

Take Note   When you copy a worksheet whose tab has been given a color, that color is copied to the new worksheet along with its contents and formatting.

Hiding and Unhiding Worksheets

Not every element of data in a workbook is something you need to be visible to every user, especially if you're training a new computer user to work with Excel and you don't want to confuse that person. For example, many workbooks contain lookup tables and other auxiliary data. It might need to be updated from time to time, but it doesn't need to always display to those using the workbook. For this reason, you can **hide** a worksheet and **unhide** it to work with it again. Hiding a worksheet does not make it confidential, because all worksheets are easy to unhide, and certainly Excel knows it's still in the workbook. Hiding simply gets stuff out of your way just as filing something away in a desk drawer keeps it out of sight.

STEP BY STEP   **Hide and Unhide a Worksheet**

GET READY. USE the workbook from the previous exercise.

CERTIFICATION READY?   1.4.1

How do you hide a worksheet?

1. With the Lookup worksheet tab active, on the HOME tab, in the Cells group, click Format.
2. Click Hide & Unhide and then click Hide Sheet. The Lookup worksheet is no longer visible.
3. Click Format, click Hide & Unhide, and then click Unhide Sheet. The Unhide dialog box appears (see Figure 8-7).

Figure 8-7

Unhide dialog box

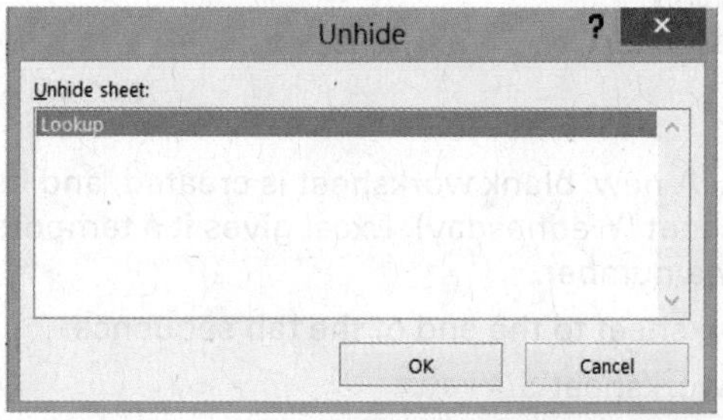

4. Make sure Lookup is chosen in the Unhide sheet list, and then click OK. The Lookup worksheet reappears and is activated.
5. In the Lookup worksheet, select cell B3.
6. Type 70 and press Enter.
7. Right-click the Lookup worksheet tab, and click Hide. The Lookup worksheet disappears again, although the change you made to one price is reflected in the other sheets that refer to it.

PAUSE. SAVE the workbook and LEAVE it open to use in the next exercise.

Take Note   When a workbook contains hidden worksheets, the Unhide Sheet command is enabled in the Format menu, and the Unhide command is enabled in the shortcut menu when you right-click any tab.

To hide several worksheets at the same time, hold down Ctrl, click the tab for each sheet you want to hide, then right-click any of these tabs and click Hide in the shortcut menu. However, you can unhide only one worksheet at a time. You can right-click any visible tab and click Unhide to bring up the Unhide dialog box with the Unhide sheet list, where you choose a worksheet to make visible.

Inserting a New Worksheet into a Workbook

When you create a new workbook, the latest version of Excel inserts only one worksheet. For most everyday tasks, you'll be surprised how often you need more than one. There's no way a workbook can become too full, at least from Excel's perspective. You could keep adding worksheets forever, though in practice, you'll find it easier to keep the number down to a handful. If your tasks become so complex that you need dozens of worksheets at a time, you might consider dividing sheets among multiple workbooks. Excel recognizes cell references that cross workbook boundaries, so your workbooks are not limited to worksheets that relate just to one another.

STEP BY STEP   **Insert a New Worksheet into a Workbook**

CERTIFICATION READY? **1.1.5**	GET READY. USE the workbook from the previous exercise.

How do you add worksheets to an existing workbook?

1. Click the Wednesday tab.
2. On the HOME tab, in the Cells group, click the down-arrow next to Insert (see Figure 8-8).

Figure 8-8

Insert menu

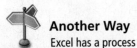

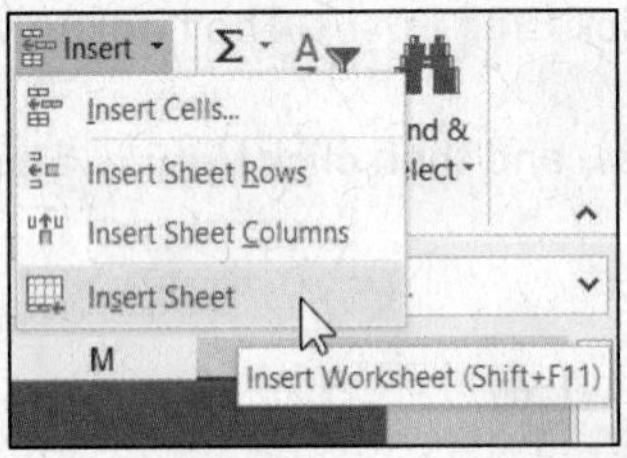

Another Way

Excel has a process for inserting a number of different things into a workbook, with a worksheet being one of the selections. Right-click the tab to the right of the spot you want the new worksheet, and then click Insert. To insert a blank worksheet (as opposed to an existing sheet with something in it), choose Worksheet from the Insert dialog box as shown in Figure 8-9. Some examples of preconfigured worksheets appear under the Spreadsheet Solutions tab.

3. Click Insert Sheet. A new, blank worksheet is created, and its tab is inserted before the tab of the active sheet (Wednesday). Excel gives it a temporary name, beginning with *Sheet* followed by a number.
4. Move the new worksheet to the end of the tab sequence.
5. Rename the new worksheet Survey.
6. Click the Wednesday worksheet tab again.
7. Click the + button to the right of the worksheet tabs. Another new worksheet is created with a temporary name, and this time, its tab is inserted after Wednesday.
8. Rename this new worksheet Totals.

PAUSE. SAVE the workbook and LEAVE it open to use in the next exercise.

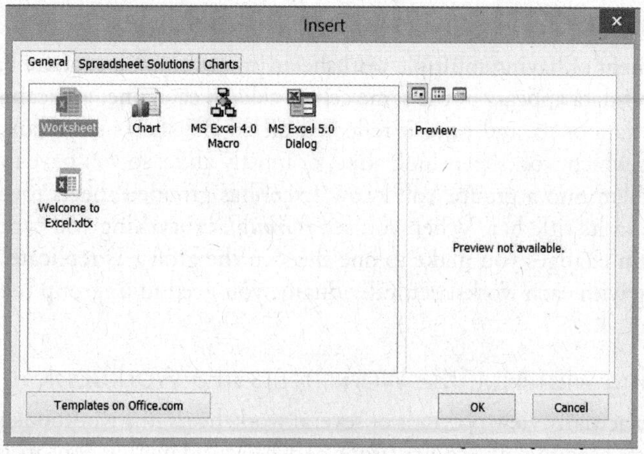

Figure 8-9

Insert dialog box

Figure 8-9

Insert dialog box

Take Note   In addition to common elements of Excel such as a worksheet and chart, the Insert dialog box might also contain templates you have created yourself or downloaded from online. This way, if you build a worksheet into a reusable form, you can save that form as a template and insert new copies of that form into a workbook as you need them.

Deleting a Worksheet from a Workbook

Removing a worksheet from a workbook and its sequence of tabs is a simple process, at least up front. Any problems will likely come later, if you have to reconcile formulas that might have referred to data on the deleted sheet. Be certain the contents of a worksheet you're about to delete are not referred to or required by any element inside another worksheet.

STEP BY STEP   **Delete a Worksheet from a Workbook**

GET READY. USE the workbook from the previous exercise.

1. Click the Totals worksheet tab.
2. On the HOME table, in the Cells group, click the down-arrow next to Delete.
3. Click Delete Sheet. The Totals worksheet is removed and its tab disappears.
4. Right-click the Survey tab, and click Delete. The Survey worksheet is removed and its tab disappears.

Take Note   You can use the tabs bar to delete more than one worksheet at a time. To select a block of worksheets whose tabs are adjacent to one another, click the tab at one end of the block, then while holding down the Shift key, click the tab at the other end. To select a group of worksheets that might not be adjacent, click one worksheet's tab, then while holding down the Ctrl key, click each tab for the others. Once all the tabs you want to delete are highlighted, right-click any of those tabs and in the shortcut menu, and then click Delete.

5. SAVE the workbook.

PAUSE. LEAVE it open to use in the next exercise.

Troubleshooting   Although Excel offers a reliable way to undo many of the things you do to workbooks by accident (press Ctrl + Z to step back over mistakes you made, for instance), you cannot undo the deletion of a worksheet from a workbook. To protect yourself against losing hours of work, save your workbook often. That way, if you do accidentally delete a worksheet, you can at least recover a slightly older version from a saved file.

WORKING WITH MULTIPLE WORKSHEETS

Bottom Line

One benefit of having multiple worksheets in a workbook that are based on the same form is that whenever data appears in the same cell or cells in each one, you can select them all, make changes to that data once, and have it reflected on all the sheets simultaneously. Excel doesn't know in advance which worksheets look alike, or mostly alike, so you have to select them yourself first and enroll them into a group. You know Excel has grouped sheets together when the word *[Group]* appears in its title bar. When you see *[Group]*, everything you type into one sheet in the group, or certain changes you make to one sheet in the group, is replicated to all the others. To resume working with each worksheet individually, you need to ungroup the worksheets first.

Working with Multiple Worksheets in a Workbook

You can actually view portions of several worksheets in a workbook simultaneously. This is handy when you need to make comparisons between the data that appears on these sheets. You don't have to close one window and open the other, go back and forth, and rely on your memory to fill in the details of what you don't see. In this next exercise, you group a handful of worksheets together in preparation to make changes that affect all of them, and you arrange them onscreen to compare contents.

STEP BY STEP   **Work with Multiple Worksheets in a Workbook**

GET READY. USE the workbook from the previous exercise.

1. SAVE the workbook in the Lesson 8 folder as *08 Spa Services Week of 2-18-13 Solution 2*.

2. Right-click any worksheet's tab and click Select All Sheets. The title bar now reads *Spa Services Week of 2-18-13 Solution 2.xlsx [Group]*. All visible worksheets are enrolled in this group, whereas hidden worksheets are excluded. Although all the worksheets' tabs are now boldface, the active worksheet remains highlighted in green.

3. Select cells I8:M33.

4. On the HOME tab, in the Number group, click $ (Accounting Number Format). The cell formats for the range switch to a currency style where the dollar sign is aligned left, and the value aligned right with dollars and cents. Column K (Facial) is too narrow for its contents, so its values currently read ####.

Take Note   You can paste data from the Clipboard to multiple worksheets simultaneously when they're grouped like this. You cannot, however, paste linked or embedded data (see Lesson 6, "Formatting Cells and Ranges") to multiple worksheets, only to one.

5. Adjust the width of column K to fit its contents (see Lesson 7, "Formatting Worksheets").

6. Select column M.

7. In the Font group, click B (Bold). All cells in column M are now boldfaced.

8. Click the tab for a worksheet other than Wednesday. The worksheets are now ungrouped, but the changes you made to the previous sheet are reflected in all three worksheets, as demonstrated by the reformatted Wednesday worksheet in Figure 8-10.

Figure 8-10

Reformatted worksheet

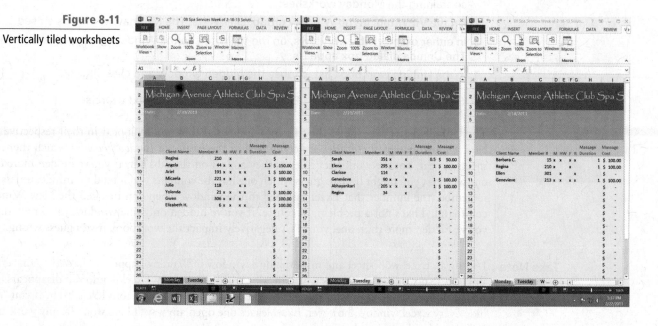

Client Name	Member #	M	HW	F	R	Massage Duration	Massage Cost	Herbal Wrap	Facial	Revitalizer	Invoice Total
Regina	210	x					$ -	$ 70.00	$ -	$ -	$ 70.00
Angela	44	x	x	x		1.5	$ 150.00	$ 70.00	$ 75.00	$ -	$ 295.00
Ariel	191	x	x	x	x	1	$ 100.00	$ 70.00	$ 75.00	$ 175.00	$ 420.00
Micaela	221	x	x		x	1	$ 100.00	$ 70.00	$ -	$ 175.00	$ 345.00
Julie	118			x	x		$ -	$ -	$ 75.00	$ 175.00	$ 250.00
Yolanda	21	x	x	x	x	1	$ 100.00	$ 70.00	$ 75.00	$ 175.00	$ 420.00
Gwen	306	x	x	x		1	$ 100.00	$ 70.00	$ 75.00	$ -	$ 245.00
Elizabeth H.	6	x	x	x	x	1	$ 100.00	$ 70.00	$ 75.00	$ 175.00	$ 420.00

Another Way

Another way to un-group a group of worksheets is to right-click any tab in the group, and then click Ungroup Sheets.

9. Select the Monday worksheet.

10. On the VIEW tab, in the Window group, click New Window. A new Excel window appears, also containing the Monday worksheet.

11. With the new window active, select the Tuesday worksheet.

12. Click the View tab and click New Window again. Another window appears.

13. With this new window active, select the Wednesday worksheet.

14. On the VIEW tab, in the Windows group, click Arrange All. The Arrange Windows dialog box opens.

15. In the dialog box, click Vertical, and then click OK. Excel rearranges your three windows to appear as shown in Figure 8-11.

Figure 8-11

Vertically tiled worksheets

PAUSE. LEAVE the workbook open to use in the next exercise.

Suppose you grouped several worksheets together, as you learned previously. When you try to copy or cut data from any one worksheet in a group, Excel assumes you're trying to extract that data from the entire group. So when you try to paste that data into a single, ungrouped worksheet—perhaps in another book—you can't. The reason is because Excel expects the area to which you're pasting data to be the same size as the cut or copied data, which in this case comes from multiple sheets. Now, if you try to paste into a *group* of worksheets that's the same number as the cut or copied area comes from, you can.

Take Note   When there is too little space for all the visible worksheet tabs to appear in the tabs bar, as is the case in Figure 8-11, left and right scroll arrows appear next to one another in the lower left corner of each window. Use these arrows to slide the tabs left and right until you find the one you're looking for.

When you save a workbook that has a number of windows open, and then close the workbook, when you reopen that workbook later, it will open the same number of windows. So you don't have to create multiple windows with the New Window command all over again.

Hiding and Unhiding Worksheet Windows in a Workbook

There are two ways to think about the elements you're working with in this lesson: as worksheets in an Excel workbook and as windows on your Desktop. You've already seen how to hide worksheets, and the reason for doing that might be to get data that doesn't need to be seen all the time out of the way. The difference in this exercise is that you're simply changing your view of the workbook at the present time, not the contents of the workbook itself.

STEP BY STEP   **Hide and Unhide Worksheet Windows in a Workbook**

GET READY. USE the workbook from the previous exercise.

1. With all three non-hidden worksheets visible, click the title bar of the window containing the Monday worksheet.
2. On the VIEW tab, in the Window group, click Hide. The Monday window is closed.
3. In either of the visible windows, on the VIEW tab, in the Window group, click Unhide. The Unhide dialog box appears.
4. In the Unhide workbook list, choose the hidden window and click OK.

PAUSE. SAVE the workbook and LEAVE it open to use in the next exercise.

The Unhide dialog box shows the titles of windows as they would appear in their respective title bars. Unfortunately, these titles are comprised of the names of the *workbook* in which the worksheets appear, not the worksheet titles as they appear on the tabs bar. If you've hidden more than one window, you might have to guess which one has the contents you intend to unhide, unless you remember the number that Excel assigned to the window when you invoked the New Window command. That's not a problem, of course, if you've hidden only one window. Just know that if you've hidden more than one, you can't negatively impact the workbook if you guess wrong.

Take Note   Hiding an Excel worksheet and minimizing a window in Windows appear to have the same effect. But they're not quite the same act. Specifically, when you hide an Excel window, it disappears from the Windows Taskbar, and you cannot restore it from there—only from Excel itself. If you try to hide every Excel window, however, Excel leaves one open anyway. There won't be any worksheets in it, but it will contain the ribbon tabs so you can still operate the program. You need at least the VIEW tab to eventually unhide a window.

Workplace Ready

IDEAS FOR ARRANGING WORKSHEETS IN EXCEL

You've seen how to build a workbook so that it includes multiple worksheets and how to arrange the worksheets like pages in a folder. What arrangements do certain people—especially office managers—expect to see in a workbook? You may know how to arrange the contents of a written report, but which workbook arrangements are considered "right" and which ones are considered "wrong?"

There's no set of answers that hold true for every professional office, although there are certain guidelines you can follow, depending on the type of work your Excel workbooks are designed to perform.

For example, not all Excel workbooks are digital versions of old, written ledgers. Assume you've been asked to assemble a financial report for your boss, or the boss of your boss. Executives typically do not like to scroll down or wade through pages and pages of data just to find the results they're looking for, someplace along the end. Granted, many of the formulas you'll enter will refer to cells that happen to be above them, but that's for when you're creating the formulas. When you *present* them, you might consider moving or copying the results to a special page at the "front" (the far left side of the tabs). This way, when the boss opens the file, the summary data is right in front of her.

Perhaps a workbook you're working on is a special assignment, something that may help you to produce a one-time report. The data you might be demonstrating at a meeting may not necessarily be the entire workbook, especially if you plan to add charts (see Lesson 12). In such a situation, it might be preferable for you to create one separate worksheet in your workbook that contains all the presentable data, including the charts, so you can keep track of what you're copying. It's easy to locate copies of your charts in PowerPoint, but it's not always easy to find the original charts in Excel if they're scattered throughout the workbook.

USING ZOOM AND FREEZE TO CHANGE THE ONSCREEN VIEW

Bottom Line

Microsoft Windows has a general approximation of how big your screen is. Most of the time, it tries to render the contents of documents such as Excel worksheets at relatively the same size as it would appear if you printed it onto a piece of paper from your printer. That approximate size is what Excel calls "100%." So, 50% magnification equals roughly half the size that your worksheet would appear if printed, whereas 200% equals twice the size. You can adjust or **zoom** this display magnification at any time to make contents easier for you to read, or to fit more contents onto the screen at one time, without impacting the size of the worksheet when you print it. When you save the workbook, Excel saves the magnification of each of its worksheets.

You're familiar with a pane of glass on the window of your house. In some Windows applications, including Excel, a **pane** is a portion of a divided window. Oftentimes with worksheets that are serving as forms, you reserve a row of cells for use as labels. But when the amount of data you add to that form gets too big, you can lose sight of that labels row when you need to scroll down. Excel gives you a way to **freeze** portions of a worksheet onscreen so that when you do scroll down, or even when you change magnification, you don't lose track of which elements the labels refer to.

STEP BY STEP **Use Zoom and Freeze to Change the Onscreen View**

GET READY. USE the workbook from the previous exercise.

1. SAVE the workbook in the Lesson 8 folder as *08 Spa Services Week of 2-18-13 Solution 3*.

CERTIFICATION READY? 1.4.9

How do you use zoom?

2. Maximize the window containing the Monday worksheet.
3. Select cell **B8**.
4. To increase magnification, click and hold the zoom control in the lower right corner (see Figure 8-12) and slide the pointer to the right. The maximum zoom is 400%. Notice the window zooms in on the cell you select.

Figure 8-12

Maximum zoom on a worksheet

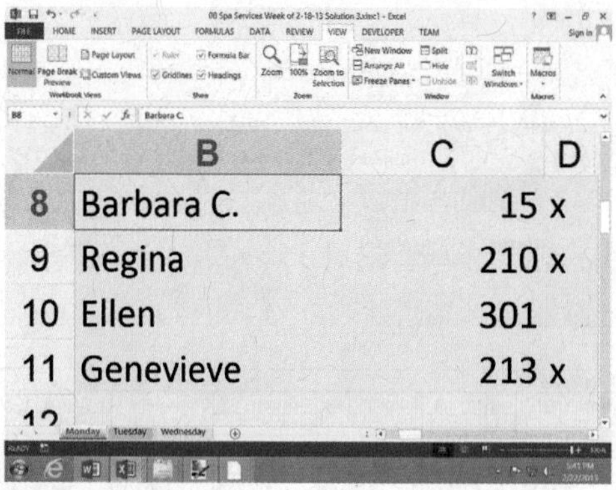

Another Way
To choose a precise screen magnification, rather than just eyeballing it, click Zoom on the View tab, and in the Zoom dialog box, under Magnification, in the Custom box, type a number, and click OK.

5. Click the VIEW tab, and in the Zoom group, click 100%. The worksheet returns to standard magnification. Scroll to the top of the worksheet so that row 1 is visible again. If you need to, scroll left so you can also see column A again.
6. On the VIEW tab, in the Window group, click Freeze Panes, and then click Freeze Panes in the menu that appears. Cells above and to the left of the selected cell (B8) are now frozen in place for scrolling.
7. Scroll down so that row 33 comes close to the labels in row 7. Notice that rows 1 through 7 remain in place (see Figure 8-13).

Figure 8-13

Worksheet with frozen panes

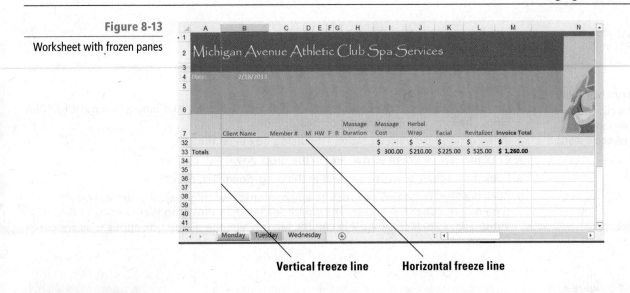

Vertical freeze line   **Horizontal freeze line**

8. Press **Ctrl + Home** to scroll the worksheet to the top. In the Window group, click Freeze Panes, and then click Unfreeze Panes. The thin lines denoting the frozen borders of the worksheet disappear.

PAUSE. LEAVE the workbook open to use in the next exercise.

If you're accustomed to using the wheel of your mouse to scroll up and down, you can use the same wheel while holding down the Ctrl key to zoom in (up) and out (down) of a worksheet.

Take Note   The Freeze Top Row and Freeze First Column commands in the Freeze Panes menu of the Window group do not work in complement to one another. Choosing Freeze First Column, for instance, unfreezes anything that was frozen previously, including the top row with Freeze Top Row.

FINDING AND REPLACING DATA

Bottom Line   If you've used a word processor before, such as Microsoft Word, then you've probably used the **Find command**, which locates a passage of text. And if you've written a letter or a memo, maybe you've used Find and Replace to change the spelling of a word throughout a document. Excel has a Find command and a Replace command that work similarly, only they navigate through cells instead of paragraphs.

Locating Data with the Find Command

With Excel, you can use the Find command to search for text you've entered as data, such as a person's name, as well as values that happen to be the results of formulas. That's important, because if you're certain that $10,000 comes up in a cell someplace but you've never typed those digits into the system directly, you can still find it, even if it's the sum of a column or the result of a formula.

Take Note   The Find command does not match contents in a hidden worksheet.

Locate Data with the Find Command

Another Way
You can also open the Find and Replace dialog box with the keyboard shortcut Ctrl+F.

GET READY. USE the workbook from the previous exercise.

1. Select the Monday worksheet. Select cell B8.
2. On the HOME tab, in the Editing group, click Find & Select (the binoculars button). Click Find. The Find and Replace dialog box appears.
3. In the dialog box, click Options. The dialog box expands.
4. Click the Within down arrow, and in the drop-down list, click Workbook.
5. Click the Look in down arrow, and in the drop-down list, click Values.
6. Click the Find what text box, delete any contents that might appear there, and type Angela. Click Find Next. The workbook window moves to Wednesday, and automatically selects *Angela* in cell B9. Meanwhile, the dialog box appears as shown in Figure 8-14.

Figure 8-14

Find and Replace dialog box

	A	B	C	D E F G	H	I	J	K	L	M	N
1											
2	Michigan Avenue Athletic Club Spa Services										
3											
4	Date:	2/20/2013									

Find and Replace

Find | Replace
Find what: Angela | No Format Set | Format...
Within: Workbook | Match case
Search: By Rows | Match entire cell contents
Look in: Values | Options <<
Find All | Find Next | Close

7	Client Name	Member #
8	Regina	210
9	Angela	44
10	Ariel	191
11	Micaela	221
12	Julie	118
13	Yolanda	21
14	Gwen	306
15	Elizabeth H.	6 x x x x	1 $ 100.00 $ 70.00 $ 75.00 $ 175.00 $ 420.00
16			$ - $ - $ - $ - $ -
17			$ - $ - $ - $ - $ -

Monday Tuesday Wednesday

How do you search for data within a workbook?

7. Double-click the Find what text box, press Delete, and then type Beth. Click Find Next. Excel highlights cell B15, whose contents include "beth" in the middle of the cell and in a non-matching case.
8. Select cell B9.
9. In the dialog box, click Match case, and then click Find Next. This time, Excel reports the text can't be found, because it's looking for a name that begins with a capital "B." Click OK to dismiss the message.
10. Double-click the Find what text box, press Delete, and then type 420. Click Find All. The dialog box shows a detailed report listing all the cells in the workbook that contain the value 420 (see Figure 8-15). In this case, it points to all the locations where customers paid "the works" for all the services together.

Figure 8-15

Find and Replace dialog box
after Find All

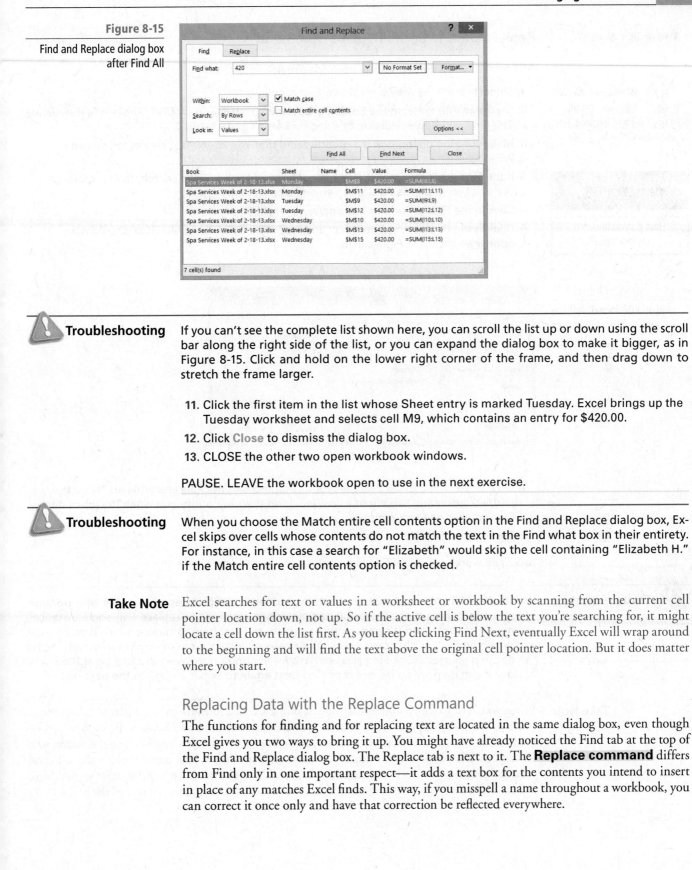

Figure 8-15

Find and Replace dialog box after Find All

⚠️ **Troubleshooting** If you can't see the complete list shown here, you can scroll the list up or down using the scroll bar along the right side of the list, or you can expand the dialog box to make it bigger, as in Figure 8-15. Click and hold on the lower right corner of the frame, and then drag down to stretch the frame larger.

11. Click the first item in the list whose Sheet entry is marked Tuesday. Excel brings up the Tuesday worksheet and selects cell M9, which contains an entry for $420.00.

12. Click **Close** to dismiss the dialog box.

13. CLOSE the other two open workbook windows.

PAUSE. LEAVE the workbook open to use in the next exercise.

⚠️ **Troubleshooting** When you choose the Match entire cell contents option in the Find and Replace dialog box, Excel skips over cells whose contents do not match the text in the Find what box in their entirety. For instance, in this case a search for "Elizabeth" would skip the cell containing "Elizabeth H." if the Match entire cell contents option is checked.

Take Note Excel searches for text or values in a worksheet or workbook by scanning from the current cell pointer location down, not up. So if the active cell is below the text you're searching for, it might locate a cell down the list first. As you keep clicking Find Next, eventually Excel will wrap around to the beginning and will find the text above the original cell pointer location. But it does matter where you start.

Replacing Data with the Replace Command

The functions for finding and for replacing text are located in the same dialog box, even though Excel gives you two ways to bring it up. You might have already noticed the Find tab at the top of the Find and Replace dialog box. The Replace tab is next to it. The **Replace command** differs from Find only in one important respect—it adds a text box for the contents you intend to insert in place of any matches Excel finds. This way, if you misspell a name throughout a workbook, you can correct it once only and have that correction be reflected everywhere.

STEP BY STEP   **Replace Data with the Replace Command**

GET READY. USE the workbook from the previous exercise.

Another Way
You can also display the Find and Replace box by pressing Ctrl + H.

CERTIFICATION READY?   **2.1.2**

How do you find and replace data?

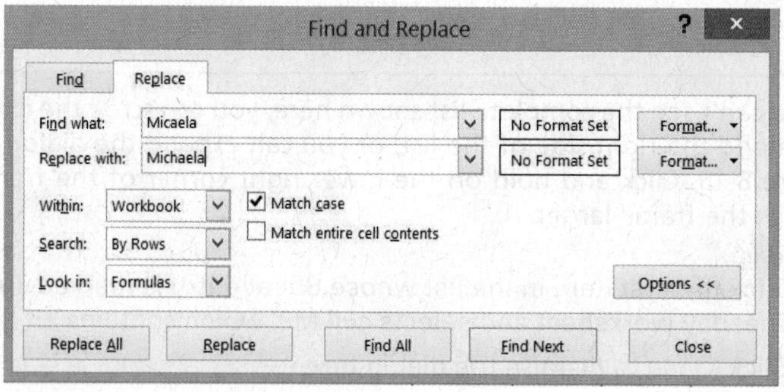

1. Select the Wednesday worksheet. Select cell B8.
2. On the HOME table, in the Editing group, click Find & Select. Click Replace in the menu. The Find and Replace dialog box appears (see Figure 8-16).
3. Make sure the dialog box is expanded and that Workbook is the selected option for Within.
4. If the Find what text box shows the contents of the previous search, then double-click the text box and press Delete to erase its contents.
5. Click in the Find what text box and type Micaela.
6. Click in the Replace with text box and type Michaela. The dialog box should now appear as shown in Figure 8-16.

Figure 8-16

Find and Replace dialog box with Replace tab chosen

7. Click Replace All. Excel searches for all instances of *Micaela* and adds an "h" to the middle (correcting this client's spelling), and then will notify you when the job is done. Excel makes one replacement.
8. Click OK, and then click Close.

SAVE the workbook. CLOSE Excel.

Troubleshooting   Use Replace All only when you are certain you need to replace every instance of a passage of text or an item of data. There will be times when you need to replace only some instances but not all of them, and it's impossible to explain to Excel how to choose which ones change and which don't. In such a case, you can review each instance one-by-one in a list, and make the decision yourself. Click Find Next to have Excel bring up the next instance, and then click Replace if you do need to replace it or Find Next again to skip it and go to the next one.

Take Note   When you need to search and replace only text or parts of a formula within a part of a worksheet, select the range of cells to search first. When you open the Find and Replace dialog box, do not use Replace All—that will search the entire worksheet or workbook (depending on the option set). Instead, click Replace to have Excel replace the instance of the matched text in the active cell, and then automatically search for the next instance within the block. Watch the location of the active cell carefully. Keep clicking Replace only until the current cell reaches the end of the block.

SKILL SUMMARY

In this lesson you learned how:	Exam Objective	Objective Number
To organize worksheets	Copy a worksheet.	1.1.6
	Rename a worksheet.	1.2.3
	Reposition the worksheets in a workbook.	1.3.1
	Change the color of a worksheet tab.	1.4.1
	Hide and unhide a worksheet.	1.1.5
	Insert a new worksheet into a workbook.	
	Delete a worksheet from a workbook.	
To work with multiple worksheets	Work with multiple worksheets in a workbook.	
	Hide and unhide worksheet windows in a workbook.	1.4.1
To use Zoom and Freeze to change the onscreen view	Use Zoom and Freeze to change the onscreen view.	1.4.9
	Freeze Panes	1.4.11
To find and replace data	Locate data with the Find command.	1.2.1
	Replace data with the Replace command.	2.1.2
	Navigate data with the Go To command.	1.2.4

Knowledge Assessment

Multiple Choice

Select the best response for the following statements.

1. Which of the following procedures is *not* a way to delete a worksheet from a workbook?
   a. Right-click a worksheet tab and click Delete.
   b. Press Ctrl + A to select all cells in the worksheet and press Delete.
   c. Click the down arrow next to Delete on the HOME menu tab and click Delete Sheet.
   d. Select a group of worksheets, right-click the group, and click Delete.

2. Which of the following statements about hidden and unhidden worksheets is correct?
   a. Unhidden worksheets cannot contain formulas that refer to hidden worksheets.
   b. When you click Find All, the Find and Replace dialog box will show matched contents within hidden worksheets as well as unhidden ones.
   c. A hidden worksheet cannot be inadvertently deleted.
   d. Excel creates a minimized window for each hidden worksheet.

3. Why would you need to copy a worksheet within a workbook?
   a. It's the easiest way to make a backup before making changes.
   b. It lets you repeat formats and working formulas into a new sheet.
   c. It helps Excel learn where your data ranges are located.
   d. You should keep one worksheet hidden in case of an error.

4. To render twice the normal amount of worksheet for any given area of the screen, what would you change the Zoom to?
   a. 200%
   b. 120%
   c. 75%
   d. 50%

5. How do you change the color of a worksheet tab?
   a. On the PAGE LAYOUT tab, in the Themes group, select Colors.
   b. Right-click the tab and select Tab Color.
   c. Use the Fill Color tool on the HOME tab.
   d. You cannot change the color of a worksheet tab.

6. Which of the following steps is required for hiding a worksheet window?
   a. On the VIEW tab, in the Window group, click Hide.
   b. Select the visible area of the worksheet.
   c. Right-click the worksheet's tab and click Hide.
   d. Enter the name of the worksheet in the Hide dialog box.

7. Which of the following steps is *not* a method for inserting a worksheet into a workbook?
   a. Right-click the tab to the right of the spot where you want to insert a worksheet, and then click Insert.
   b. On the HOME tab, click Insert, and then click Insert Sheet.
   c. On the INSERT tab, click Worksheet.
   d. In the Insert dialog box, click Worksheet, and then click OK.

8. In order for you to freeze the first column of a worksheet into a frozen pane:
   a. The entire contents of the column must be visible.
   b. The first row of the column must be non-blank.
   c. Duplicate worksheets must also be able to have their first columns frozen.
   d. You can click Freeze First Column in the Freeze Panes menu.

9. You just created a copy of a worksheet named *August*. Which name does Excel gives it?
   a. September
   b. August (2)
   c. Sheet2
   d. July

10. When you click the + button (New Sheet) on the tabs bar, where is a worksheet always inserted?
    a. At the beginning of the tabs sequence
    b. Before the active worksheet
    c. After the active worksheet
    d. At the end of the tabs sequence

True / False

Circle T if the statement is true or F if it is false.

T F 1. The Arrange All command lets you stack Excel's open windows horizontally or vertically.

T F 2. The Find and Replace button displays the Find and Replace dialog box.

T F 3. When you insert a new worksheet into a workbook, a new window appears.

T F 4. You unhide a hidden worksheet window with the Unhide Sheet command.

T F 5. Find & Select, by default, locates Carol in a search for Caroline, but will not locate Mike in a search for Michael.

T F   6. Freezing a row or column creates what Windows calls a *pane*.

T F   7. Changing the magnification of the display does not change the magnification for printing.

T F   8. Select all the cell blocks in each worksheet of a group individually, before changing the formatting for those blocks.

T F   9. You can use the Insert dialog box to insert forms you created in advance.

T F   10. When searching for dollar amounts, use a dollar sign in the Find What text box.

Competency Assessment

Project 8-1: Music Store Annual Sales Sheet

You are performing accounting for a chain of sheet music and collectable CD stores throughout the state. In this project, you rename a worksheet, use the Name box to navigate a worksheet, and copy an existing worksheet.

GET READY. LAUNCH Excel if it is not already running.

1. OPEN *08 Brooks Music Annual Sales* from the data files for this lesson.w

2. SAVE the workbook as *08 Brooks Music Annual Sales 2013 Solution*.

3. On the HOME tab, in the Cells group, click Format. Click Rename Sheet.

4. Type Q1 and press Enter.

5. Click Format again, and then click Move or Copy Sheet.

6. In the Move or Copy dialog box, click (move to end), click Create a copy, and then click OK.

7. Rename the Q1 (2) sheet as Q2.

8. In the Q2 worksheet, select cell C5.

9. Delete the text Jan and replace it with Apr.

10. Use AutoFill to change the next two months' column headings, and then change Qtr 1 to Qtr 2.

11. Click the Name box, and then enter the cell reference C6:E10. Press Enter, and then press Delete.

12. For the months in the second quarter, enter the following values:

$22,748.00	$21,984.00	$20,194.00
$22,648.00	$21,068.00	$21,698.00
$24,971.00	$23,498.00	$23,011.00
$23,400.00	$24,681.00	$23,497.00
$21,037.00	$20,960.00	$19,684.00

13. If necessary, adjust the width of each column so that the entries are legible.

SAVE and CLOSE the workbook. LEAVE Excel open for the next project.

Project 8-2: Photo Store Accessory Sales Tracker

You're helping a photo development kiosk at a local office supplies store to keep track of the extra sales its employees have to produce in order to keep a development shop open in the digital camera era. In this lesson, you rename worksheets, unhide a hidden form worksheet, arrange windows onscreen, and make changes.

GET READY. LAUNCH Excel if it is not already running.

1. OPEN *08 Photo Weekly Product Tracker* from the data files for this lesson.

2. SAVE the workbook as *08 Photo Weekly Product Tracker 130407 Solution* .

3. Click the Sheet1 worksheet tab.

4. On the HOME tab, in the Cells group, click Format. In the menu, click Rename Sheet.

5. In the worksheet tab for Sheet1, type Akira (the first name of the sales associate in cell A7) and press Enter.

6. Repeat this process for the sales associates in Sheet2 and Sheet3.

7. On the HOME tab, in the Cells group, click Format. In the menu, click Hide & Unhide, and click Unhide Sheet.

8. In the Unhide dialog box, choose Form and click OK.

9. With the Form sheet active, click Format again, and then click Move or Copy Sheet.

10. In the Move or Copy dialog box, in the Before sheet list, click Form. Click Create a copy. Click OK.

11. Click cell A7. Type the name Jairo Campos.

12. Edit cell B4 to reflect the date shown in the other worksheets.

13. Rename the Form (2) worksheet Jairo.

14. Right-click the Form tab. Click Hide.

15. In the Jairo worksheet, select cells B9:H13 and type the following values for each of the days shown in the following table, skipping blank cells as indicated:

Sunday	Monday	Tuesday	Wednesday	Thursday	Friday	Saturday
2		3		4		2
10	1		2		6	
		4			2	
400		75		150		200
3	4			2	1	2

16. Select the Akira worksheet.

17. On the VIEW tab, in the Window group, click New Window.

18. In the new window, select the Taneel worksheet.

19. Again, on the VIEW tab, in the Window group, click New Window.

20. In the new window, select the Kere worksheet.

21. Once again, on the VIEW tab, in the Window group, click New Window.

22. In this new window, select the Jairo worksheet.

23. In the Jairo worksheet, on the VIEW tab, in the Window group, click Arrange All.

24. In the Arrange Windows dialog box, click Tiled. Click Windows of active workbook. Click OK.

SAVE this workbook and CLOSE all windows related to it. LEAVE Excel open for the next project.

Proficiency Assessment

Project 8-3: Pet Store Daily Sales Tally, Part 1

You have been asked to build a daily accounting system for a pet supplies store, which has been keeping its receipt records on paper. In this project, you insert one new worksheet, make a copy of another, and adjust the view to show multiple worksheets at one time.

GET READY. LAUNCH Excel if it is not already running.

1. OPEN *08 Pet Store Daily Sales* from the data files for this lesson.
2. SAVE the workbook as *08 Pet Store Daily Sales 130309 Solution*.
3. Right-click the Sheet1 tab on the tabs bar. Click Rename.
4. Type March 9 and press Enter.
5. On the HOME tab, in the Cells group, click the down arrow next to Insert. Click Insert Sheet.
6. In the tabs bar, drag the new worksheet to the end of the sequence after March 9.
7. Click the March 9 tab. Use the Name box to select cells B52:E67.
8. On the HOME tab, in the Clipboard group, click Cut.
9. Click the tab for the new worksheet. On the HOME tab, click Paste.
10. Adjust the width of columns A through D to fit their contents (see Lesson 7).
11. Rename the new worksheet Recap.
12. Click the March 9 tab. On the HOME tab, in the Cells group, click Format. Click Move or Copy Sheet.
13. In the Move or Copy dialog box, in the Before sheet list, click Recap.
14. Click Create a copy. Click OK.
15. Rename March 9 (2) to March 10.
16. Right-click the Recap tab. Click Hide in the menu.
17. Click the March 9 tab.
18. On the VIEW tab, in the Window group, click New Window.
19. In the newly opened window, click the March 10 tab.
20. On the VIEW tab, click Arrange All.
21. In the Arrange Windows dialog box, click Vertical. Click OK.
22. In the March 10 worksheet, edit the date to reflect Sunday, March 10.
23. Select cells B10:F49 and press Delete.
24. Select cells B10:F17 and type the following data:

41897	Golden Retriever puppy	Dog	Bob Cook	$201.50
51649	Leash	Accessory	Bob Cook	$13.95
34781	Puppy food	Feed	Bob Cook	$38.95
52995	Kitty litter	Accessory	Bob Cook	$21.95
32185	Fish food	Feed	Alice Harper	$11.21
48552	Persian kitten	Cat	Alice Harper	$185.75
55468	Food bowl	Accessory	Alice Harper	$7.85
34211	Kitten food	Feed	Alice Harper	$38.55

SAVE this workbook and LEAVE it and Excel open for the next project.

Project 8-4: Pet Store Daily Sales Tally, Part 2

You have a handful of worksheets to work with now, but they look a bit dull. In this project, you make changes to one worksheet and have them reflected in another, and then copy formulas in one worksheet to another range of the worksheet and use Find and Replace to edit those formulas to reflect a different day.

GET READY. LAUNCH Excel if it is not already running.

1. SAVE the workbook as *08 Pet Store Daily Sales 130309 Solution 2*.
2. Arrange separate windows for the March 9 and March 10 worksheets, if they are not already arranged this way.
3. In any open window, right-click any worksheet's tab and click Select All Sheets in the shortcut menu.
4. Select column A in its entirety.
5. On the HOME tab, in the Cells group, click Delete.
6. Select rows 1 through 6.
7. On the HOME tab, in the Font group, click the Fill Color arrow button. In the palette, click the swatch of color labeled Blue, Accent 1, Lighter 60%.
8. Right-click a worksheet tab on either worksheet. Click Ungroup Sheets.
9. Right-click a worksheet tab again, and this time click Unhide. In the Unhide dialog box, choose Recap. Click OK.
10. Click cell B1. Type Saturday and press Enter.
11. In the Name box, type B1:D16 and press Enter.
12. On the HOME tab, in the Clipboard group, click the Copy button.
13. Select cell B20.
14. Click the Paste button.
15. Select cell B20 again. Type Sunday and press Enter.
16. Select cells B21:D35.
17. On the HOME tab, in the Editing group, click Find & Select. Click Replace.
18. In the Find and Replace dialog box, if the options are not showing, click Options. Click the Within list box down arrow and choose Sheet. For the Look in list box, choose Formulas.
19. In the Find what box, type March 9. In the Replace with box, type March 10.
20. Click Find Next. When C21 is the active cell, click Replace.
21. Keep clicking Replace until after cell D35 has been processed. (The cell contents should change from $35.90 to $163.45.) Close the dialog box at that point.

SAVE this workbook and CLOSE all windows associated with it.

Mastery Assessment

Project 8-5: Bakery Sales Template

You've been given the task of bookkeeping for a not-for-profit bakery. It has one location but is soon to open a second. You've been handed a workable format for a daily retail tally sheet. Your instructions are to create a daily form that employees can use for an entire week's worth of daily sales tallies. In this project, you take one day's worksheet, hide rows that need to be seen only on occasion, and create enough copies for an entire work week.

GET READY. LAUNCH Excel if it is not already running.

1. OPEN *08 Whole Grains Daily Sales 130520* from the data files for this lesson.

2. Open a blank workbook.

3. Use the VIEW tab to adjust the view so that both windows appear in the workspace side-by-side.

4. Adjust the magnification of the original workbook window so that you can see columns A through R all at once.

5. Adjust the magnification of the blank workbook window (which probably has Book1 in its title bar) to the same value.

6. In the original workbook window, copy the entire sheet's contents to the Clipboard.

7. In the blank workbook window, click cell A1 and paste the entire contents.

8. In the Book1 window, delete cells A22:L45, cells N22:N45, and cells Q22:R45.

9. In the Book1 window, click the File tab. Click Save As, and then in Backstage, click Browse.

10. In the Save As dialog box, click the Save as type box, and choose Excel Template (*.xltx).

11. Click New folder. Type Whole Grains and press Enter.

12. Click in the File name box, and SAVE the template as *08 Whole Grains Daily Sales Solution.xltx*.

13. In the template workbook, hide rows 11 through 18.

14. Rename Sheet1 to Monday.

15. Make five copies of the Monday worksheet within the workbook template, and name them Tuesday through Saturday.

16. Arrange the worksheets by days of the week if necessary.

SAVE the workbook template and LEAVE both windows open for the next project.

Project 8-6: Bakery Sales Error Correction

Something's not tallying properly with the workbooks you've been given by your contact with the bakery. You learn that there's an error in the formula used to calculate sales throughout an entire column. In this project, you use Find and Replace to make a complex formula correction, and you test the results on a daily worksheet made from your template.

GET READY. LAUNCH Excel if it is not already running.

1. OPEN *08 Whole Grains Daily Sales Form Solution.xltx* and *08 Whole Grains Daily Sales 130520.xlsx* if they are not already open.

2. Arrange the two files in side-by-side vertical windows, if they are not already so arranged.

3. In the template window (the one with blank worksheets), group the six worksheets together, and then select cells M22:M45.

Troubleshooting The nature of the error here is that the formula confuses "wheat rolls" with "white rolls," and vice versa. Though you study much more about formulas in the lessons to follow, here all you need to know is that the terms for these pastries are juxtaposed with one another, and you can use Find and Replace to make them switch places.

4. Open the Find and Replace dialog box.

5. Set the options so that the search process looks through formulas in the entire workbook.

6. Make sure Match entire cell contents is deselected.

7. Click in the Find what box, and then type whiteroll.

8. Click in the Replace with box, and then type XXXXX.

9. Click Replace All. Some 144 replacements should have been made. Click OK to dismiss the notice.

10. Repeat the process, this time replacing wheatroll with whiteroll.

11. Repeat one more time, replacing XXXXX with wheatroll. Click Close.

12. Ungroup the worksheets in the workbook template.

13. SAVE and CLOSE the workbook template.

14. Click the File tab, and then click New.

15. In Backstage, click Personal. Double-click the Whole Grains folder.

16. Double-click the Whole Grains Daily Sales Form Solution template. A new workbook opens with the title "Whole Grains Daily Sales Form1 Solution."

17. SAVE the new workbook in the Lesson 8 folder as *08 WG Sales 130520 Solution*.

18. Arrange the two open workbooks to be side-by-side.

19. In the new workbook, open the Monday tab.

20. Copy the contents of cells A22:L45 from the original worksheet, to the new Monday worksheet. Cell M46 should read $453.29 (correct), not $452.93 (incorrect) as in the original worksheet.

21. Select the Saturday worksheet.

22. Select rows 10 through 19, including the hidden rows. Right-click the selection and click Unhide.

23. Change the price for a cinnamon bagel for Saturday to 75¢.

24. Hide rows 11 through 18 again.

SAVE the *08 WG Sales 130520 Solution* workbook and CLOSE both workbooks. CLOSE Excel.

LESSON SKILL MATRIX

Skills	Exam Objective	Objective Number
Importing Data	Open non-native files directly in Excel.	1.1.4
	Import files.	1.1.3
	Append data to worksheets.	2.1.1
Ensuring Your Data's Integrity	Set data validation.	1.3.8
Sorting Data		
Filtering Data		
Outlining and Subtotaling Data	Create outlines.	2.3.5
	Collapse groups of data in outlines.	2.3.6
	Insert subtotals.	2.3.7

(continued on next page)

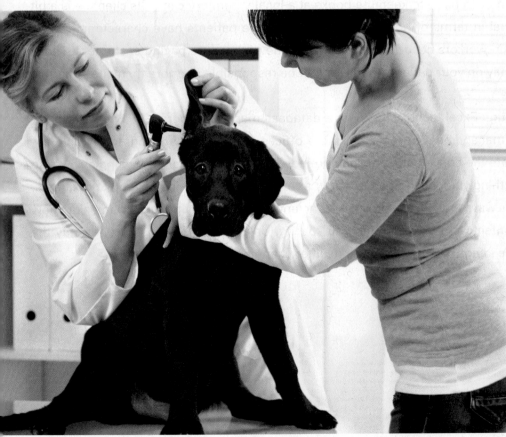

©AlexRaths /iStockphoto

KEY TERMS

- auto-outline
- AutoFilter
- collapse
- criterion
- data file
- database
- delimiter
- filter
- grouping
- macro
- outline
- outline symbol
- parse
- quick format
- slicer
- subtotal
- table
- validation

LESSON SKILL MATRIX (*continued*)

Skills	Exam Objective	Objective Number
Setting Up Data in a Table Format	Apply styles to tables.	3.2.1
	Band rows and columns.	3.2.2
	Remove styles from tables.	3.2.4
	Define titles.	3.1.3
	Insert total rows.	3.2.3
	Add and remove cells within tables.	3.1.2
	Filter records.	3.3.1
	Sort data on multiple columns.	3.3.2
	Change the sort order.	3.3.3
	Remove duplicates.	3.3.4
	Move between tables and ranges.	3.1.1
Saving Work with Macros	Assign shortcut keys.	1.4.12
	Record simple macros.	1.4.7
	Manage macro security.	1.4.5

©AlexRaths /iStockphoto

You've been hired to keep the books at a local veterinary clinic. Its clientele is a bit unusual in terms of bookkeeping. Although the patients have characteristics that your co-workers need to keep track of, none of them are paying customers. Those who pay on your patients' behalf might be responsible for more than one patient at a time.

Although Excel technically is not a database manager program, it's used for database management purposes in more offices than any other program. People appreciate the convenience of keeping individual records aligned by single rows, so everything you need to record about a certain feline or canine patient, for example, is recorded in a single row. This way, you can have Excel sort an entire database by patients' names or show only certain records whose contents meet criteria that you specify (only the cats, for instance, or only the spaniels) without disrupting the integrity of the database itself or changing the workbook.

SOFTWARE ORIENTATION

Data Tab

Most of the exercises in this lesson use the DATA tab. Although spreadsheet programs such as Excel were originally intended to serve as calculation engines, it's often convenient to have recordkeeping and calculation in the same program. Although you might imagine data entry tasks as about as dull and repetitive as a marathon of city council meetings on public access television, Excel actually makes data easy to import from sources other than your own fingertips, and it makes it easy to arrange and manage that data properly once you bring it into a workbook.

Figure 9-1

The DATA tab

Figure 9-1 shows the DATA tab on a maximized Excel window, with many of the features you use in this lesson pointed out.

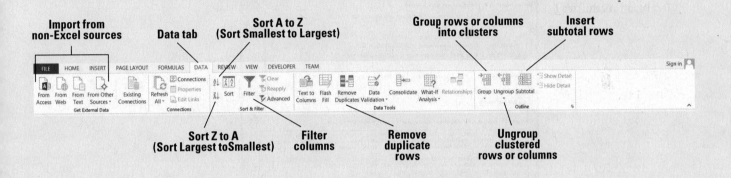

IMPORTING DATA

Bottom Line

When you work with a workbook that requires a large amount of data, one thing you can fervently wish for is that the data already exists in some form and that you don't have to type it manually. If the data you need for a workbook is sourced outside of Excel, then what Excel needs is to be able to receive that data in such a way that it can make sense of where cells begin and end and where records begin and end. Even simple text files where values are separated (delimited) by commas can be imported, because commas act like fence posts, and Excel recognizes fence posts. Complex relational databases are comprised of multiple tables, and thus can't be imported directly. So the trick is to be able to open a connection to the database (such as a communications channel) and stream the specific tables you need into Excel, in a manner that Excel can readily **parse** (interpret character-by-character).

Opening Non-Native Files Directly in Excel

Excel has two main data formats: an older one that was owned and operated by Microsoft and whose files end with the .XLS extension and a newer, XML-based .XLSX format whose specifications have been shared publicly. Because the newer format is public, there are more programs and services now that publish data to a format that Excel accepts. But not all of them do; many services provide data in a basic XML format that Excel can import. In that case, there's no guarantee that the columns will all be aligned properly or that the headings will be in the place Excel expects them to be for a table. The "lowest common denominator" for file compatibility is the .CSV file, which is straight text that uses certain characters, such as commas and quotation marks, as **delimiters**—characters that separate data entries from one another—and that Excel will not interpret as part of a cell entry.

STEP BY STEP   Open a Non-Native File Directly in Excel

GET READY. Before you begin these steps, LAUNCH Microsoft Excel.

1. If the active workbook is not a new, blank workbook, then click the FILE tab. In Backstage, click New, and then click the thumbnail marked Blank workbook.

2. On the DATA tab, in the Get External Data group, click From Text.

3. In the Import Text File dialog box, locate and click *09 NA-EST2012-01.csv*. Click Import.

4. In Step 1 of the Text Import Wizard, notice the preview at the bottom (see Figure 9-2). This is Excel's best guess, for the moment, as to how the data should be formatted. There are population figures rendered in "quotation marks" with commas between each figure. Here, each comma acts as the delimiter, and it's difficult to judge whether each figure between the commas will be the same length. Under Choose the file type that best describes your data, choose Delimited, and select My data has headers.

Figure 9-2

Text Import Wizard, step 1

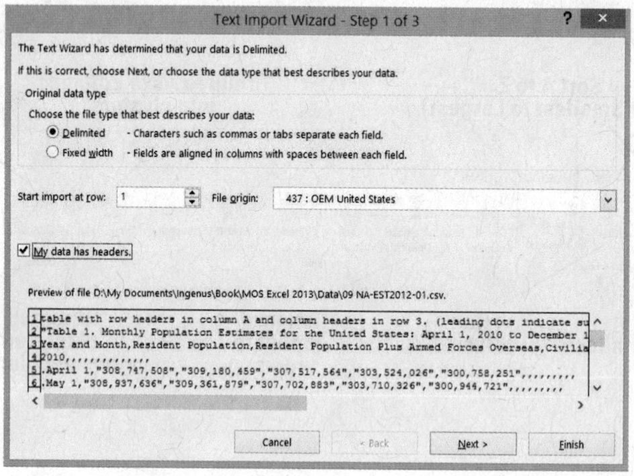

5. The preview shows the headers starting on row 3. Thus, for the Set import at row option, choose 3. Click Next.

6. In Step 2 of the wizard, shown in Figure 9-3, uncheck Tab because the preview does not indicate long spaces between the figures. Check Comma. Set Text qualifier to " (quotation mark). Scroll down the Data preview pane, and notice now that Excel has found the column separations between figures. Click Next.

Figure 9-3

Text Import Wizard, step 2

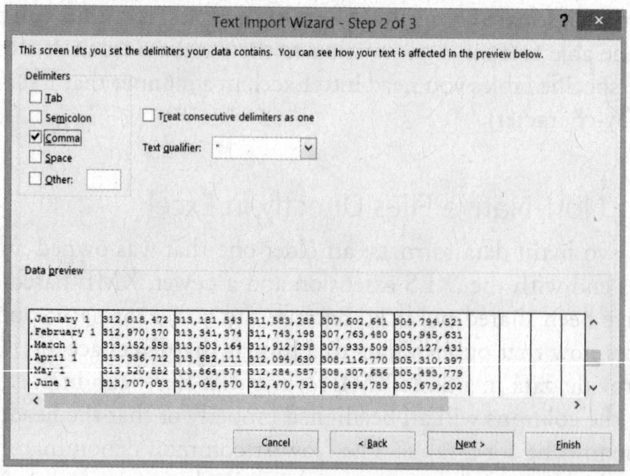

7. Step 3 of the wizard, shown in Figure 9-4, lets you establish the data type for each discovered column. Click the first column in the Data preview pane. Then, under Column data format, click Date. Click Finish.

Figure 9-4

Text Import Wizard, step 3

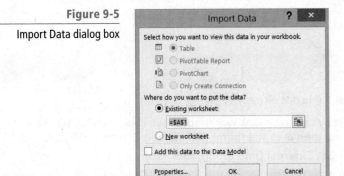

8. In the Import Data dialog box that appears next (see Figure 9-5), leave Where do you want to put the data? set to **Existing worksheet**. Click **OK**.

Figure 9-5

Import Data dialog box

9. Shorten the width of column A to **16**.

10. The worksheet that Excel has generated, shown in Figure 9-6, shows United States population estimates for each month from April 2010 to December 2012. Excel could not make sense of the dates in column A, so it left the data type set to General for most of the cells. However, it did make an error in attempting to convert the year in cell A25. To correct it, begin by deleting rows **2**, **12**, and **25**.

Figure 9-6

Freshly imported census data worksheet

	A	B	C	D	E	F
1	Year and Month	Resident Population	Resident Population Plus Armed Forces Overseas	Civilian Population	Civilian Noninstitutionalized Population	Household Population
2	2010					
3	.April 1	308,747,508		309,180,459	307,517,564	303,524,026	300,758,251
4	.May 1	308,937,636		309,361,879	307,702,883	303,710,326	300,944,721
5	.June 1	309,122,451		309,544,899	307,889,928	303,898,353	301,125,879
6	.July 1	309,326,225		309,745,660	308,091,141	304,100,547	301,325,995
7	.August 1	309,540,608		309,956,285	308,313,027	304,322,798	301,538,796
8	.September 1	309,768,270		310,173,518	308,531,330	304,541,466	301,764,876
9	.October 1	309,994,453		310,395,556	308,761,399	304,771,900	301,989,477
10	.November 1	310,179,397		310,589,914	308,957,140	304,968,006	302,172,839
11	.December 1	310,353,742		310,774,403	309,141,425	305,152,656	302,345,602
12	2011					
13	.January 1	310,544,109		310,951,978	309,326,771	305,338,367	302,534,387
14	.February 1	310,704,719		311,109,109	309,479,260	305,491,221	302,693,415
15	.March 1	310,851,993		311,268,198	309,638,124	305,650,450	302,839,107
16	.April 1	311,035,995		311,444,450	309,811,745	305,824,436	303,021,527
17	.May 1	311,220,789		311,624,208	309,994,764	306,007,820	303,204,739
18	.June 1	311,387,209		311,805,500	310,171,775	306,185,196	303,369,577
19	.July 1	311,587,816		312,004,661	310,370,316	306,384,095	303,568,593
20	.August 1	311,794,537		312,210,438	310,578,786	306,593,494	303,774,526
21	.September 1	312,017,861		312,422,810	310,794,410	306,810,047	303,997,062
22	.October 1	312,232,049		312,640,035	311,021,669	307,038,235	304,210,462
23	.November 1	312,427,243		312,829,503	311,211,110	307,228,605	304,404,868
24	.December 1	312,619,619		313,009,235	311,394,871	307,413,295	304,596,456
25	2/1/2021					
26	.January 1	312,818,472		313,181,543	311,583,288	307,602,641	304,794,521
27	.February 1	312,970,370		313,341,374	311,743,198	307,763,480	304,945,631
28	.March 1	313,152,958		313,503,164	311,912,298	307,933,509	305,127,431
29	.April 1	313,336,712		313,682,111	312,094,630	308,116,770	305,310,397
30	.May 1	313,520,882		313,864,574	312,284,587	308,307,656	305,493,779

Sheet1 ⊕

11. Click cell **A2**, type **April 2010**, and press **Enter**.

12. Drag the fill handle from cell **A2** down to cell **A34** and release. Excel changes the entries in column A to proper months.

13. Delete rows **35** through **40**.

14. SAVE the workbook in the Lesson 9 folder as *09 Monthly Census Data Solution*.

CLOSE the workbook and leave Excel open for the next exercise.

Getting External Data

In the world of computers, there are databases and data files. Because databases are typically stored in files, a rational question is, "What's the difference?" A **data file** stores a series of records in a relatively simple format, and Excel is a program that uses data files in this manner. A **database** is a comparatively complex system that can store a large amount of related data, which requires a program to be able to assess and render that data. So when Excel imports data from a database as opposed to a data file (as in the previous exercise), it actually launches a program, begins a communications process with that program, and instructs the program to stream the data it requires.

Take Note   In this exercise, you use a file from Microsoft Access, although you do not need Access installed on your computer to follow along.

STEP BY STEP   **Get External Data**

CERTIFICATION
R E A D Y ?   **1.1.3**

How do you import files?

GET READY. LAUNCH Excel if it is not already running.

1. If the active workbook is not a new, blank workbook, then click the **FILE** tab. In Backstage, click **New**, and then click the thumbnail marked **Blank workbook**.

2. On the DATA tab, in the Get External Data group, click **From Access**.

3. In the Select Data Source dialog box, locate the *09 GMcC Customer contacts.accdb* database file. Select it and click **Open**.

4. In the Select Table dialog box shown in Figure 9-7, click **Customers** (the table we want to import), and then click **OK**.

Figure 9-7

Select Table dialog box

Name	Description	Modified	Created
Customers		10/4/2003 7:41:49 PM	3/17/2001 12:
Invoices		10/4/2003 9:36:16 PM	10/4/2003 9:3
Product Inventory		10/4/2003 9:36:16 PM	10/4/2003 9:3

Select Table

☐ Enable selection of multiple tables

OK   Cancel

5. In the Import Data dialog box (refer to Figure 9-5), click **Table**. Under Where do you want to put the data, click **Existing Worksheet** and ensure the text box reads **=!$A$1**.

6. Click **OK**. Excel takes a moment to query the database. Soon, it displays a fully formatted table (see Figure 9-8), complete with AutoFilter buttons in the headers, which you learn more about later in this lesson in "Using AutoFilter."

Figure 9-8

Mismatched, freshly imported XML data

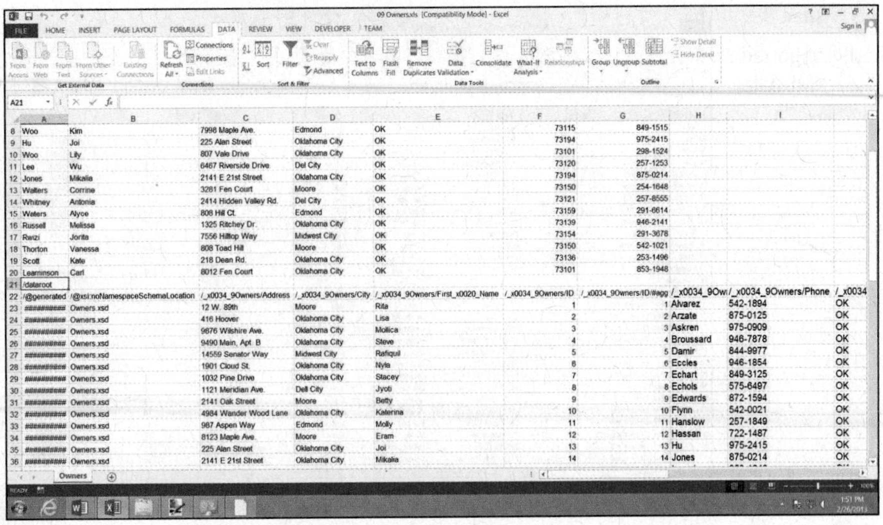

7. SAVE the workbook in the Lesson 9 folder as *09 2005 Customers Solution*.

CLOSE the workbook and leave Excel open for the next exercise.

Appending Data to a Worksheet

After you import data from another format or database into a worksheet, you'll probably spend a good deal of time reconciling that data with existing records. In the previous two exercises, you were lucky enough to import data into blank worksheets. In a more real-life situation, you'll bring data from other sources into a full worksheet and make the effort to make it fit somehow.

STEP BY STEP **Append Data to a Worksheet**

GET READY. OPEN the *09 Owners.xls* workbook for this lesson.

1. Click cell A21.
2. On the DATA tab, in the Get External Data group, click **From Other Sources**, and then click **From XML Data Import**.
3. In the Select Data Source dialog box, locate and select the *09 2010_Owners.xml* data file. Click **Open**.
4. In the Import Data dialog box, click **Existing worksheet**, and then click **OK**. Although a list of customers is appended to the end of the worksheet, the columns don't line up, as Figure 9-9 clearly indicates. This is typical of appended data. A dialog marked Error in XML might appear at this point. If so, click OK to dismiss the dialog box and proceed.

CERTIFICATION READY? 2.1.1

How do you append data to a worksheet?

⚠ **Troubleshooting** In the course of history, the folders where old data files used to reside may cease to exist. This is indeed the case with the original XML file from which you imported data into the worksheet. Some versions of the Microsoft XML parser will see this as an "error," and others will not. Any number of factors may contribute to which XML parser your PC actually has. In either case, it isn't really an error, and you don't need to worry about it.

Figure 9-9

Mismatched, freshly imported
XML data

5. To correct the problem, begin by moving the first names from cell range E23:E75 to B23:B75. Overwrite the existing contents in column B.

6. Move the last names from cell range H23:H75 to A23:A75. Overwrite the existing contents in column A.

7. Repeat the process for the states in column J that should be in column E, the ZIP codes in column K that should be in column F, and the phone numbers in column I that should be in column G.

8. Delete columns H through L.

9. Delete rows 21 and 22.

10. Replace all 11 instances of Dell City in column D with Del City.

SAVE the workbook in the Lesson 9 folder as *09 Car Owners Solution.xlsx*. CLOSE the workbook and leave Excel open for the next exercise.

Workplace *Ready*

WORKING WITH DATABASES

The most commonly distributed definition for the word "database" is "an organized collection of data." Technically, that's wrong. If this definition was correct, any book could be a database because books contain data—even blank books.

The reason why this matters is because you will likely acquire data from multiple sources for use in the worksheets you produce. To be accurate, a database is anything you can use as a *source* for data. When you import data from a database into an Excel spreadsheet, if that data is stored by a relational database manager, it might not actually exist as a file yet. So the file you "import" into Excel might communicate with the database manager to produce the data that ends up appearing in your worksheet.

This is important, because a financial database manager usually produces information in real-time—meaning, as close to "right now" as possible. So you might import data into a worksheet that's actually accurate up-to-the-second.

However, depending on how the database is set up, it might produce separate files that serve as "snapshots" of the data's state for a given point in time. When you import this type of data, you need to know if it's old and just how old it is. On occasion, you might not actually be able to import files because the database manager program has locked them to prevent inadvertent loss of data. In these situations, you might need to have the person overseeing the database export a separate file for you to import. While you're at it, you can ask for that export file to be in a regular format, such as comma-separated values (CSV) or even a worksheet format such as Excel's old XLS.

The example you used in "Getting External Data" involves a kind of snapshot file produced by Microsoft Access, a database manager that's part of some versions of Office. In a real-world setting, even though such a file exists, it might not always be available, for the reasons just explained. In these cases, you need to ask for help—perhaps for someone in the IT department to produce an export file and meet you halfway.

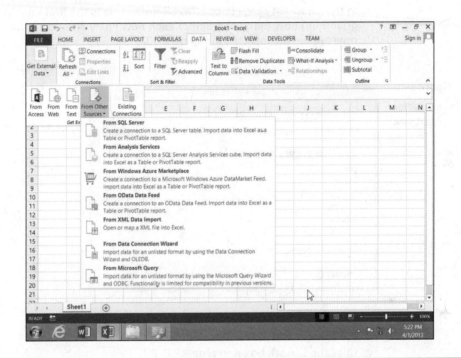

ENSURING YOUR DATA'S INTEGRITY

Bottom Line

It isn't obvious on the surface, but an Excel workbook is actually a kind of program in itself. You don't just feed it data, run off a few formulas, and tabulate the result. You actually can create rules for each workbook, which Excel might enforce, helping you and others to enter the right data properly. When typing in new data from paper—especially several records at once—it's easy for anyone to type the wrong digits or characters, especially in a field where a single character denotes a *type*, such as a senior citizen or a child, or such as a dog or a cat. Quickly, ask yourself this: Should "C" in a vet clinic stand for "cat" or "canine?" **Validation** ensures data gets entered correctly, before it gets processed incorrectly. Excel's data validation tools can help you set up rules that keep you or anyone else from entering invalid or unusable data, or from failing to enter data when it's required.

Restricting Cell Entries to Certain Data Types

Perhaps the most common form of rule you'll create for Excel workbooks will set certain expectations for data being typed in. For example, in North America (where local business clients will tend to reside anyway), a telephone area code has three digits. You can set up a rule that pings the user whenever he types a two- or four-digit code by mistake. The user may then respond by dismissing the message and starting over, or cancelling altogether if the problem is that the user didn't mean to type anything into this cell in the first place.

STEP BY STEP   **Restrict Cell Entries to Certain Data Types**

GET READY. OPEN the *09 Vet Clinic Patients* workbook for this lesson.

1. Click the FILE tab and select Save As. SAVE the workbook in the Lesson 9 folder as *09 Vet Clinic Patients (Active) Solution*.
2. Freeze rows 1 through 5 in both worksheets in the workbook.
3. In the Client list worksheet, select column L (Area Code).
4. On the DATA tab, in the Data Tools group, click Data Validation. The Data Validation dialog box opens.
5. Click the Settings tab.
6. In the Allow list box, choose Text length. This is the first step in the creation of a rule governing how many characters each new entry should contain. The dialog box should now appear as depicted in Figure 9-10.

Figure 9-10

Set up validation rules for input data

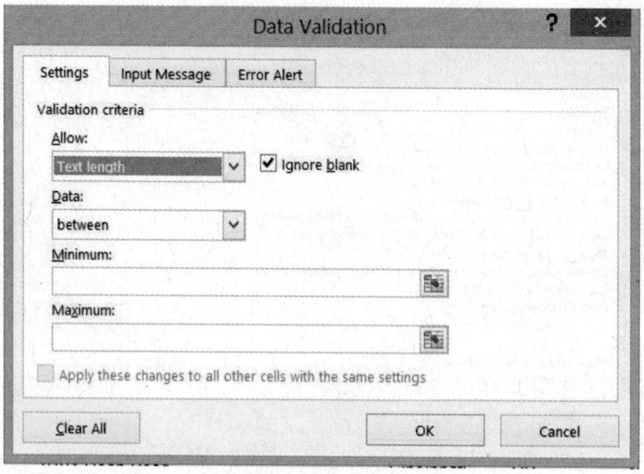

7. In the Data list box, choose equal to.
8. Click the Length box and type 3.
9. Click the Input Message tab. This tab displays a ScreenTip whenever you select a cell in this specially validated area.
10. Click the Title box and type Rule:
11. Click the Input message box and type Three-digit area codes only, please. The Data Validation dialog box should now appear as shown in Figure 9-11.

CERTIFICATION READY?   **1.3.8**

How do you set data validation?

Figure 9-11

Have Excel notify the user about your validation rule

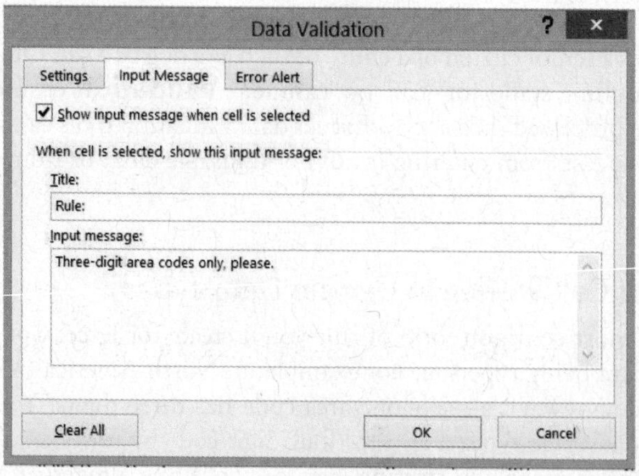

12. Click the Error Alert tab. Excel notifies a user who missed your ScreenTip that the data he has entered is invalid.

13. Click the Title box and type Data Entry Error.

14. Click the Error message box and type Only three-digit area codes are recognized. This message is displayed in a dialog box whenever an invalid entry is made in column L. The dialog box should now appear as shown in Figure 9-12.

Figure 9-12

Set up a warning for when the validation rule is violated.

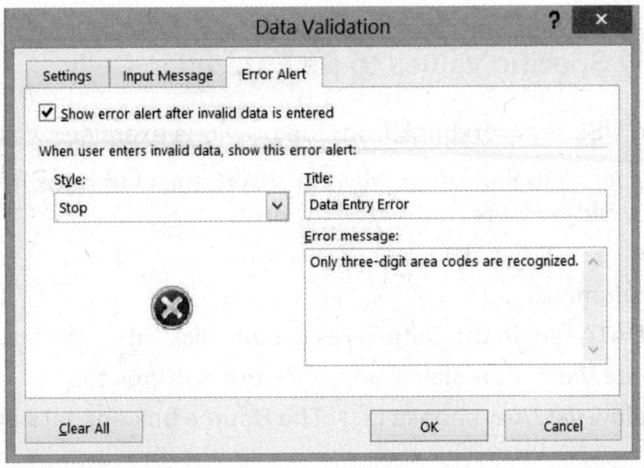

15. Click OK.

16. To test the new validation rule, click cell L58. You should see the notification message you typed into the Input Message tab.

17. Type 40 and press Enter. Excel displays an alert dialog box with the message you created (see Figure 9-13).

Figure 9-13

Worksheet with validation rule enforced

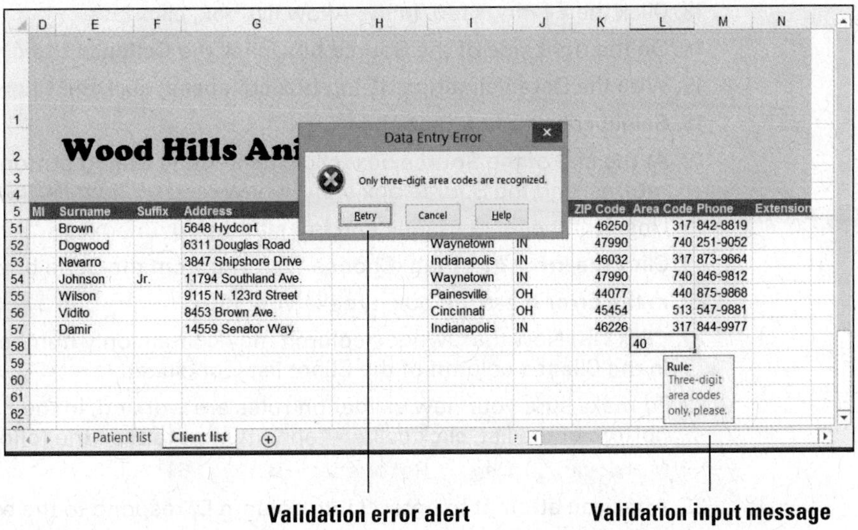

Validation error alert   Validation input message

18. Click Cancel. The partial entry in cell L58 is erased.

PAUSE. SAVE the workbook and leave it open to use in the next exercise.

Take Note   Excel's validation rules pertain to only new data as you enter it into the workbook, not to data that existed in the workbook prior to creating the rules. Don't rely on validation rules to correct errors that might already exist, but to catch any new errors that might arise.

Allowing Only Specific Values to Be Entered in Cells

A typical piece of information you'll find in a database is often a single letter that represents a characteristic, such as gender or political party affiliation or the work shift to which one is assigned. In data entry, it's easy for someone to slip and enter an invalid character. If that error isn't caught and the person who entered the data is replaced, would her replacement be able to rectify it? You can preempt events like this by building a rule that restricts entry to a handful of valid characters.

STEP BY STEP   **Allow Only Specific Values to Be Entered in Cells**

GET READY. USE the workbook from the previous exercise.

1. Click the FILE tab and select Save As. SAVE the workbook in the Lesson 9 folder as *09 Vet Clinic Patients (Active) Solution 2*.
2. Click the Patient list tab.
3. Select column D.
4. On the DATA tab, in the Data Tools group, click Data Validation.
5. In the Data Validation dialog box, click the Settings tab.
6. In the Allow list box, choose List. The Source box appears at the bottom of the dialog box.
7. Click the Source box. Type M,F,N being careful to include the commas.
8. Uncheck the Ignore blank box.
9. Click the Input Message tab. Click the Input message box and type Male, Female, or Neutered.
10. Click OK. Now anyone entering a new patient into the database must specify the animal's gender.
11. Select column E (Owner #).
12. In the Data Tools group, click Data Validation.
13. Click the Settings tab. In the Allow list box, click List.
14. On the right side of the Source box, click the Collapse Dialog button.
15. With the Data Validation dialog box collapsed, click the Client list worksheet tab.
16. Select column A (Client #).
17. At the end of the Source box, click the Expand Dialog button. The full dialog box returns, and the Source box should now read ='Client list'!$A:$A.
18. Unselect the Ignore blank and In-cell dropdown boxes.
19. Click the Error Alert tab. Choose Warning from the Style box.
20. In the Error message box, type Owner must be the number for a pre-existing client.
21. Click OK. Now the Owner # column may contain only numbers for clients who appear in the Client # column of the Client list worksheet.
22. To make sure your new validation rules are working, in the Patient list worksheet, at the bottom of the list, click cell A58 and attempt to type the following data:
Murdock   Dog   Rottweiler   B   61
23. After you attempt to enter B into column D, respond to the error dialog box by clicking Retry and by typing M.
24. After you attempt to enter 61 into column E, respond to the error dialog box shown in Figure 9-14 by clicking No and typing 31.

Figure 9-14

Excel attempts to enforce a validation rule.

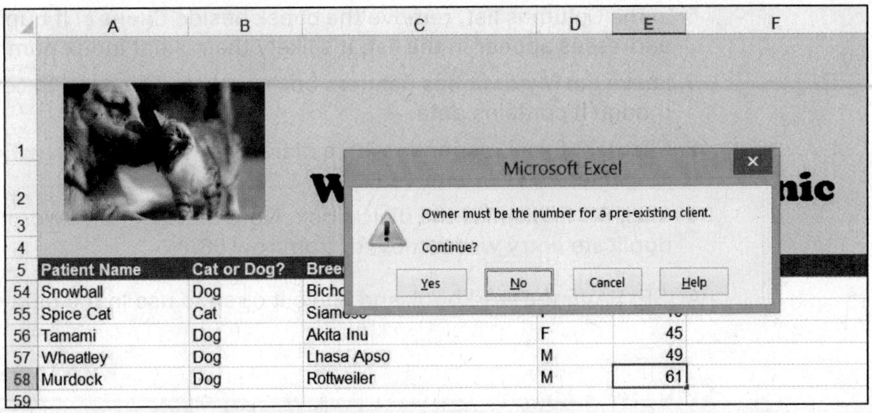

PAUSE. SAVE the workbook and leave it open to use in the next exercise.

Take Note   It's still feasible for an invalid value to remain in a worksheet after the user has been warned that it's invalid. For example, in the previous step if you were to click Yes instead of No, the value 61 would remain in column E, even though there is no client numbered 61 in column A of the Client list worksheet. Conceivably, this way you can purposefully enter a new canine patient into the list without an owner, if you intend to add the owner's information later.

Removing Duplicate Rows from a Worksheet

In many databases, it's important that each record (each row of an Excel database table) is unique. If an entry appears twice, Excel might treat them as separate entries even if they somehow (especially by accident) contain identical information. The difficulty then comes when you try to reconcile any other records or subsequent data that might refer to either of these duplicate entries. As a means of cleansing your database, you can have Excel search for duplicate entries and purge them before too much damage is done.

STEP BY STEP   **Remove Duplicate Rows from a Worksheet**

GET READY. USE the workbook from the previous exercise.

1. SAVE the current workbook as *09 Vet Clinic Patients (Active) Solution 3*.
2. Click the Client list worksheet tab.
3. Click cell A58 and in row 58, type the following data in the appropriate columns:
   Mrs.   Mary Jane   Brink   704 Fairway Drive   Cincinnati   OH   255-1655
4. Select the cell range A5:N58.
5. On the DATA tab, in the Data Tools group, click Remove Duplicates. The Remove Duplicates dialog box appears (see Figure 9-15).

Figure 9-15

Remove Duplicates dialog box

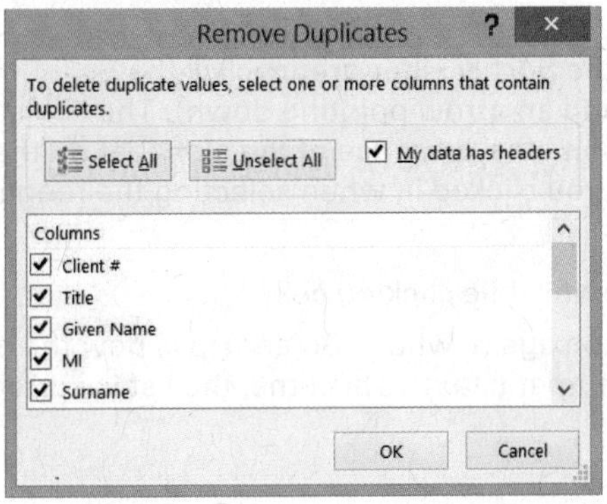

6. In the Columns list, remove the check beside Client #. If duplicate names and addresses appear in the list, it's likely their client index numbers were not duplicated.

7. Leave the My data has headers box checked. This way, Excel won't treat row 5 as though it contains data.

8. Click OK. Excel responds with a dialog box stating one duplicate value set (the one you just entered) was removed.

9. Click OK to dismiss the dialog box. Note the second (lowermost) instance of the duplicate entry was removed, from row 58.

PAUSE. SAVE the workbook and leave it open to use in the next exercise.

SORTING DATA

Bottom Line

After you enter data into a data range or, as you see later in this lesson, a formal database table, the number of the row each record appears on doesn't matter at all. In fact, it's important for you to remember that data entries in Excel are not indexed by their row numbers, because they're subject to change. Sorting a data range helps *you* to locate the precise data you need. In a few respects, it can also help Excel to look up certain data for inputs into formulas (see Lesson 5), but for the most part sorting is for your benefit. You might want, for example, to keep people sorted in a table by their surname rather than some arbitrary customer number you won't remember. So when you enter a new customer whose surname begins with something earlier than "Z," you might find it easier to enter the name at the bottom of the list, and then resort alphabetically. This way, you don't have to manually insert a blank row in the middle of the worksheet, at the appropriate alphabetical location.

Sorting Data on a Single Criterion

You've probably heard the word "criteria" more often than its singular form, **criterion**. Both words relate to elements that are referred to in the course of executing a function. For instance, the White Pages of a telephone directory is sorted by phone owners' last names (or rather, in this more culturally expansive society, by their surnames). The surname is one criterion of the sort. Because many people share the same surname, lists of surname-sharing phone owners are then sorted by their first names (given names), and then by their middle initials when they're used. This leads to three different criteria for such a sort. When individuals in a database are indexed by number, however, and that number is guaranteed to be unique, it forms a single criterion for a common sort operation.

STEP BY STEP | **Sort Data on a Single Criterion**

GET READY. USE the workbook from the previous exercise.

1. SAVE the current workbook as *09 Vet Clinic Patients (Active) Solution 4*.

Another Way
You can also quickly sort the data in a range in alphabetical order, even without selecting the entire range first, by right-clicking one cell in the column you want to sort, clicking Sort, and then clicking Sort A to Z (or Sort Smallest to Largest).

2. In the Patient list worksheet, click cell E6. Note this is the top row of the Owner # column and its entries are all numerical.

3. Hold the Shift key down while clicking cell A58. This selects the entire range you wish to sort.

4. On the DATA tab, in the Sort & Filter group, click the Sort Smallest to Largest button (with A on top of Z, and an arrow pointing down). The list is now sorted in ascending numerical order (despite the presence of the alphabet on the button) by Order #, which was the first column you clicked in when selecting the range.

5. Click cell A6.

6. Hold the Shift key down while clicking cell E58.

7. Click the sorting button again, whose ScreenTip is now the Sort A to Z button (because you're sorting alphanumeric text). This time, the list is sorted by Patient Name, and

again, the first column you clicked in when selecting the range. Murdock the Rottweiler, which you previously added to row 58, now appears on row 45.

PAUSE. SAVE the workbook and leave it open to use in the next exercise.

Take Note   The Sort A to Z button (also known as Sort Smallest to Largest) and Sort Z to A button (also known as Sort Largest to Smallest) assume that the column you wish to use as your sorting criterion is the one that contains the active cell. In selecting a range, whether you hold down Shift to select the opposite corner (as you did in this exercise) or whether you drag the pointer from one corner to the opposite corner, the (or Sort Smallest to Largest) the cell that you clicked on first.

Troubleshooting   Before sorting a range, make sure you select the entire range first, including the rightmost column(s). Excel leaves any contents outside the selected sort range exactly as they are, which leaves you with out-of-order contents should you fail to select the entire width of the range.

Sorting Data on Multiple Criteria

A proper database containing records of people divides each element of their names into, at the very least, last and first names, and preferably includes optional elements such as middle initials and prefixes and suffixes. For this reason, any time you sort a database, range, or table by names, you want to sort by multiple criteria.

STEP BY STEP   **Sort Data on Multiple Criteria**

GET READY. USE the workbook from the previous exercise.

1. Click the Client list tab.
2. Select the range A5:N57.
3. Name the range Clients.
4. On the DATA tab, in the Sort & Filter group, click Sort. The Sort dialog box appears.
5. In the Sort by list box, under Column, choose Surname.
6. Click Add Level.
7. In the Then by list box that appears, choose Given Name.
8. Click Add Level.
9. In the next Then by list box, choose MI (middle initial).
10. Click Add Level again.
11. In the next Then by list box, choose Suffix. The dialog box should now appear as depicted in Figure 9-16.

Figure 9-16

Sort dialog box

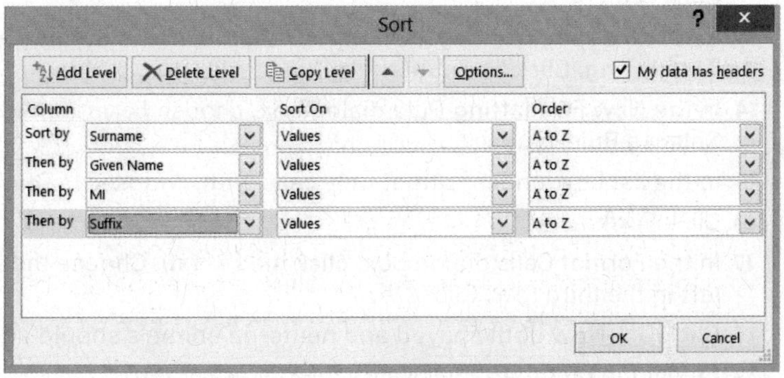

12. Leave My data has headers checked, so that Excel won't treat the headers row as a data entry.

13. Click OK. The clients list is now sorted alphabetically, with people sharing the same surname sorted alphabetically by first name. Although the client numbers appear all out of sort, the data is unchanged and the database itself retains its full integrity.

PAUSE. SAVE the workbook and leave it open to use in the next exercise.

Sorting Data Using Cell Attributes

In Lesson 6, you saw how Excel can apply special formatting to cells based on their ascertained contents (for example, shading a temperature column extra-red when the number climbs above 90 degrees). Excel is capable of sorting records based on the conditional formatting that is applied to their cells. This is important because Excel does not have a "conditional sort" feature, where you create a rule or a formula that Excel evaluates to group or arrange rows. Instead, you create rules that apply specific formats or graphics to cells based on their contents. Then Excel can sort and group those records whose cells have these special formats applied to them.

| STEP BY STEP | Sort Data Using Cell Attributes |

GET READY. USE the workbook from the previous exercise.

1. On the Patient list worksheet, select column E.
2. Right-click the column, and then click Insert in the shortcut menu.
3. With column E selected, on the DATA tab, in the Data Tools group, click Data Validation.
4. In the Data Validation dialog box, click Clear All. Click OK.

Troubleshooting When creating a new column to the right of one governed by a data validation rule, the new column acquires that same rule even if it's intended for a different purpose. To clear this rule, select the new column, bring up the Data Validation dialog box, and click Clear All as demonstrated previously.

5. Click cell E5 and type Spayed/Neutered.
6. In column E, type S for the following row numbers: 7, 22, 23, 26, 35, 38, 47, and 51.
7. In column E, type N for the following row numbers: 6, 8, 9, 10, 11, 13, 14, 16, 17, 18, 20, 21, 25, 28, 30, 31, 32, 33, 36, 37, 39, 42, 43, 44, 46, 48, 49, 50, 53, 55, 56, 57, and 58.
8. Select column E.
9. On the DATA tab, in the Data Tools group, click Data Validation.
10. In the Data Validation dialog box, click the Settings tab. Under Allow, choose List.
11. In the Source box, type N,S.
12. Click the Input Message tab. In the Input message box, type S = Spayed, N = Neutered. Click OK.
13. Select the range E6:E100. On the HOME tab, in the Styles group, click Conditional Formatting. Click New Rule.
14. In the New Formatting Rule dialog box, choose Format only cells that contain in the Select a Rule Type list.
15. In the list box, under Format only cells with, choose No Blanks.
16. Click Format.
17. In the Format Cells dialog box, click the Fill tab. Choose the sixth color swatch from the left in the third row. Click OK.
18. Click OK. Now both spayed and neutered animals should appear shaded.
19. Select the range A5:F58. Name the range Patients.
20. On the DATA tab, in the Sort & Filter group, click Sort.
21. In the Sort dialog box, in the Sort by list, choose Spayed/Neutered.
22. In the Sort On list, choose Cell Color.

23. Click the down arrow next to No Cell Color. As Figure 9-17 shows, the list box that appears shows only those colors that are actually in use for conditional formatting—in this case, only one swatch. Click the color swatch.

Figure 9-17

Sort dialog box showing conditional format color choice

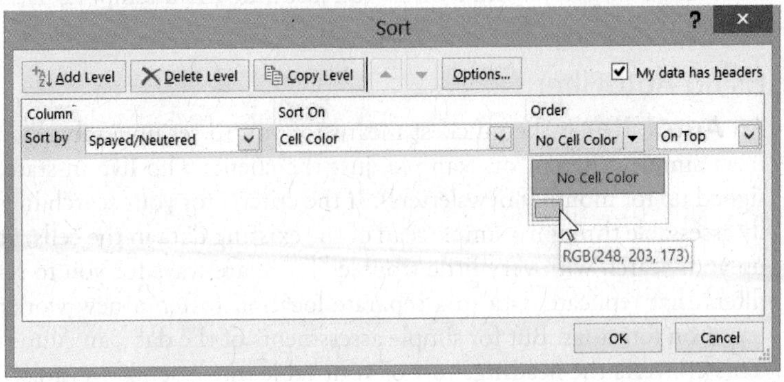

24. Click OK. The sorted worksheet should now appear as shown in Figure 9-18. All the "N" and "S" animals are grouped together at the top, with the two types mingling among each other. All the non-operated-on animals are bunched toward the bottom.

Figure 9-18

Worksheet with conditional format-based sort applied

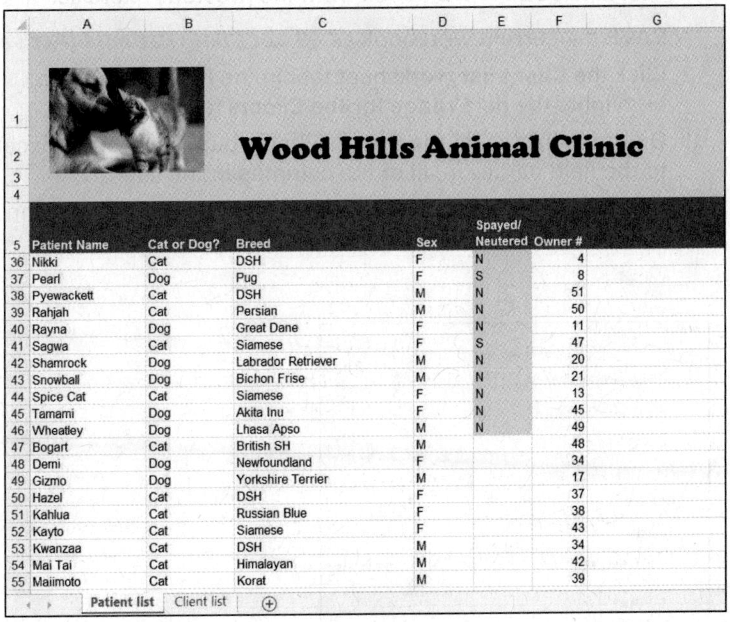

PAUSE. SAVE the workbook and leave it open to use in the next exercise.

Troubleshooting

Any table you intend for Excel to sort must not contain merged cells (see Lesson 6). For Excel to be able to exchange cell contents between positions evenly, each row must have an identical number of cells. Each of the cells in a column may be formatted differently, though their widths may not vary.

FILTERING DATA

Bottom Line

When you search for information online, what you expect to happen is for the search engine to return the most relevant data to your search at the top of the list. Similarly with any database, when you make a request or a query for just the records that meet particular criteria, you expect to see only the relevant data, and for irrelevant or non-matching data to be filtered out. With Excel, there's a way for you to formally specify the boundaries of your database table—to say, "*This* part of my worksheet is to be treated like a database" —and to then have Excel **filter** out just those rows that don't pertain to what you're searching for. This does not change the database, and you don't delete any rows with a filter. You just hide them temporarily.

Using AutoFilter

An **AutoFilter** is the quickest means for you to set up a table so that it displays only rows that meet simple criteria (for example, just the clients who live in-state, or just the clients who have signed up for monthly newsletters). If the criteria for your search involves information that is readily assessable through a simple read of the existing data in the cells, you can use an AutoFilter to set up your search with very little trouble. There are ways for you to set up more complex, advanced filters that replicate data to a separate location (often a new worksheet) using advanced criteria based on formulas. But for simple assessments of the data, an AutoFilter requires much less effort. This converts the headings row of your table into a set of controls, which you then use to choose your criteria and select the data you want to see.

STEP BY STEP   **Use AutoFilter**

GET READY. USE the workbook from the previous exercise.

1. SAVE the current workbook as *09 Vet Clinic Patients (Active) Solution 5*.
2. Click the Client list worksheet tab. In the Name box, type Clients and press Enter. Excel highlights the data range for the Clients table.
3. On the DATA tab, in the Sort & Filter group, click Filter. Excel adds down arrow buttons to the field names in all of the columns in the list.
4. Click the down arrow beside the Client # heading in column A. Excel displays the AutoFilter menu shown in Figure 9-19.

Figure 9-19

AutoFilter menu for a numeric column

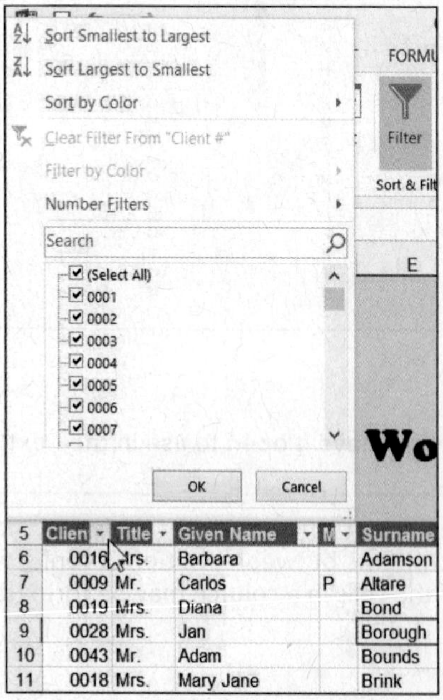

5. To sort the table by client number, click Sort Smallest to Largest. This gives you a shortcut for sorting that bypasses the menu.

6. To show just the clients with addresses in Ohio, click the down arrow beside State. In the AutoFilter menu that appears (shown in Figure 9-20), uncheck the (Select All) box to clear all check boxes, and then check OH and click OK.

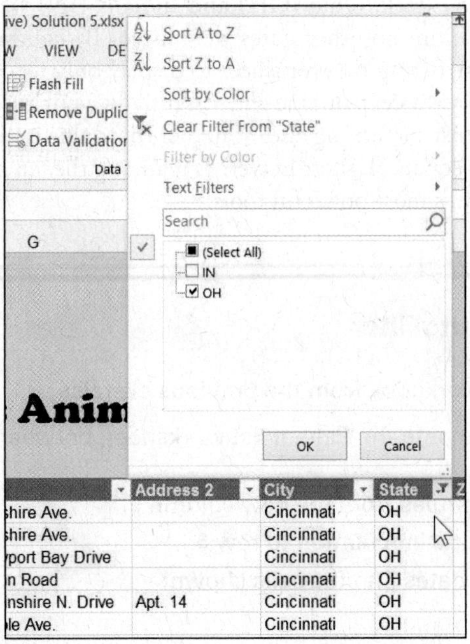

Figure 9-20

AutoFilter menu for a text column

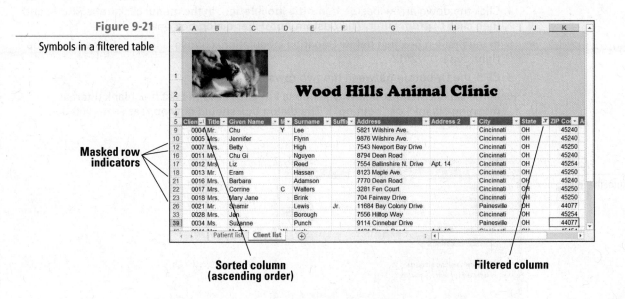

PAUSE. SAVE the workbook and leave it open to use in the next exercise.

When an AutoFilter is active, so that you see filtered results rather than the complete table, Excel applies special notation to the AutoFilter buttons and to the row numbers. As Figure 9-21 shows, the button for the column used in the sort now contains a long up-arrow, whereas the button for the column used in the filter contains a funnel symbol, like the thing you pour motor oil through.

Figure 9-21

Symbols in a filtered table

Also, notice the row numbers are colored blue and are not consecutive. If you look closely, you'll see that where nonmatching rows are hidden, Excel puts a double-border between the numbers for matching rows—for instance, between rows 18 and 21 and between 47 and 55.

Creating a Custom AutoFilter

A custom AutoFilter uses a rule that you create, instructing Excel how to evaluate the entries in each row. The result of that evaluation determines whether rows are displayed or filtered out. With a simple AutoFilter, Excel looks for contents based on actual samples from the column. For example, with the previous task, Ohio (OH) and Indiana (IN) were choices because both were featured in the State column; no other states were listed. By contrast, with a custom AutoFilter, you can devise a rule instructing the worksheet to display only records whose values in one given column are above or below a certain amount. Essentially, your rule tells Excel to compare each value in the column against something else. Whether that value is displayed depends on the terms of the comparison—is it equal? Higher? Lower? Is it among the ten highest or lowest? The custom AutoFilter is among Excel's most powerful tools.

STEP BY STEP **Create a Custom AutoFilter**

GET READY. USE the workbook from the previous exercise.

1. Insert a new column into the Patient list worksheet, between the existing columns D and E.
2. Clear the validation rules from the new column E.
3. Add the title Hepatitis inoculation to row 5.
4. Type the following dates into the cells shown:

E9	1/18/2012
E12	8/16/2011
E14	5/15/2012
E19	3/1/2009
E23	10/19/2010
E27	7/5/2012
E33	2/2/2011
E38	8/15/2012
E39	7/14/2011
E44	9/1/2012

5. Select the Patients data range. The range should have automatically stretched to include the new column.
6. On the DATA tab, in the Sort & Filter group, click Filter.
7. Click the down arrow beside Hepatitis inoculation. In the menu, click Date Filters, and then click Custom Filter. The Custom AutoFilter dialog box opens.
8. In the first list box just below Hepatitis inoculation, choose is before. In the box to the right, type 1/1/2012.
9. Click the Or button between the two rows of list boxes.
10. In the second list box below Or, choose equals. Leave the list box blank (literally meaning "blank" or "nothing"). The dialog box should now appear as depicted in Figure 9-22.

Figure 9-22

Custom AutoFilter dialog box

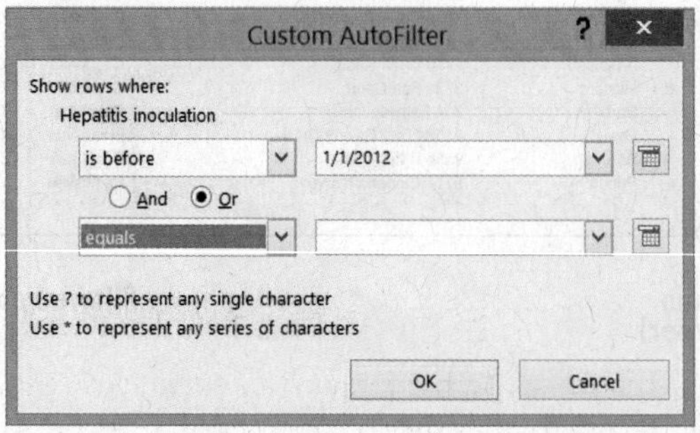

11. Click OK. After the dialog box disappears, Excel filters out all entries in the patient list where the patient is known to have had a hepatitis inoculation in 2012 or later. What

remains are both the animals known to have been inoculated in 2011 or earlier, or whose inoculation dates are not known.

12. Click the filter button beside Hepatitis inoculation again. In the menu, click Date Filters, and then click Custom Filter.

13. In the second list box that currently reads equals, choose the blank entry at the top of the list. The box should now be empty.

14. Click OK. The list should now show only the five animals known to have been inoculated in 2011 or earlier (see Figure 9-23).

Figure 9-23

Worksheet with custom filter applied

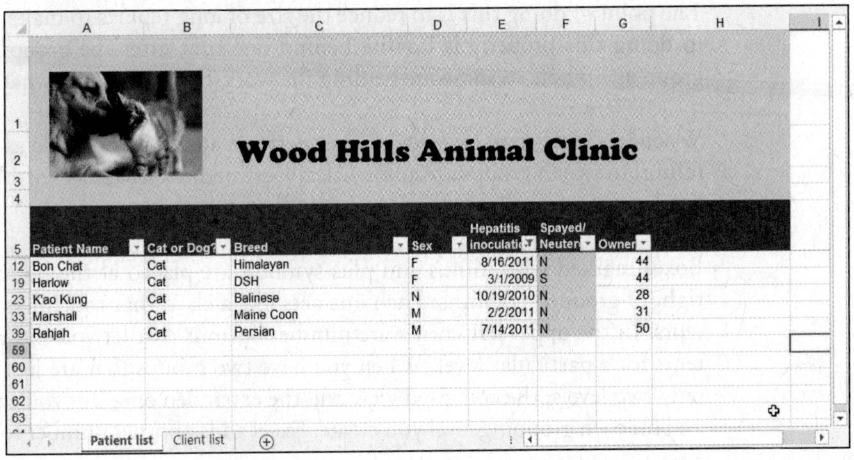

	Patient Name	Cat or Dog?	Breed	Sex	Hepatitis inoculation	Spayed/ Neutered	Owner
12	Bon Chat	Cat	Himalayan	F	8/16/2011	N	44
19	Harlow	Cat	DSH	F	3/1/2009	S	44
23	K'ao Kung	Cat	Balinese	N	10/19/2010	N	28
33	Marshall	Cat	Maine Coon	M	2/2/2011	N	31
39	Rahjah	Cat	Persian	M	7/14/2011	N	50

Patient list | Client list

15. Click the filter button beside Hepatitis inoculation again. In the menu, choose Clear Filter from "Hepatitis inoculation".

PAUSE. SAVE the workbook and leave it open to use in the next exercise.

Filtering Data Using Cell Attributes

When conditional formatting is applied to a column of cells, that formatting is something that Excel can "get a handle on." In other words, it's just as good as a value in giving the filtering system something to look for. So you can easily have a filter hide rows where cells in a column don't have a particular format, such as a shaded background or a font color.

STEP BY STEP | **Filter Data Using Cell Attributes**

GET READY. USE the workbook from the previous exercise.

1. In the Patient list worksheet, click the Spayed/Neutered button down arrow.

2. In the menu, click Filter by Color.

3. In the popup menu, choose the pink swatch. Excel now shows only those animals that have been spayed or neutered.

PAUSE. SAVE the workbook and leave it open for the next exercise.

OUTLINING AND SUBTOTALING DATA

Bottom Line

Up to this point, you've been working with data that's arranged as tables full of records, where each row represents an entry of related elements. Another purpose for worksheets is to serve as lists of values and their related descriptions. Imagine an inventory list showing the sale price of items arranged by department. In its most basic form, you need only two columns: one for the description and the other for the price. For this list to be useful to you, however, you'll want a way to break down items into their respective departments—for example, by listing their location on the shelf. These descriptive categories help subdivide data into groups, and then **collapse** those groups into single-row headings called **outlines**. Excel uses outlines to generate reports that provide you with meaningful data about the items in each group collectively. The most important, and probably the most frequently used of these reports shows you **subtotals** for the values that are grouped together.

Grouping and Ungrouping Data

The simplest form of data **grouping** involves taking a row of cells that have one related attribute, clustering them together, and then collapsing the cluster like a folder that can be reopened later. The point of doing this is to reduce the size of long reports to make them easier to read. The trick to doing this properly is leaving behind one row, after the group is collapsed, to represent the group as a whole so someone reading the worksheet will know what to open later.

Whenever you group rows together or perform an operation (such as auto-outlining or auto-subtotaling) in which groups are automatically created, Excel adds controls next to the row and column headings. Excel calls these controls **outline symbols**.

Boxes marked with minus and plus symbols are placed at the bottom of grouped rows or to the right of grouped columns. Each one acts like a clasp that can collapse or expand the group's contents. In the upper left corner are number buttons that let you show or hide all of the group contents for a particular level. When you have two groups that are just beside one another, you have only two levels: the collapsed view and the expanded one. But you can have groups within groups, and for each grouping level you create, Excel adds another number to this bank of outline symbols.

Take Note   The rows and columns that you enroll into a group should be those that you do *not* want to see when the group is collapsed. Field name rows that identify cells and total rows that include subtotals should not be included in groups.

STEP BY STEP   **Group and Ungroup Data**

GET READY. USE the workbook from the previous exercise.

1. SAVE the current workbook as *09 Vet Clinic Patients 130114 Solution*. Grouping data is best reserved for final reports and not for active databases where new data might be entered later.

Take Note   Enrolling a set of records into a group changes the behavior of AutoFilters that might incorporate that group. For example, when you try to sort a column, only the records that are not members of a group are sorted. Once records are grouped, their order is fixed and their usefulness as parts of an active database is reduced, especially if you add subtotal rows to the middle. For this reason, you should reserve grouping and outlining for workbooks that are presented as final (unchanging) reports for a particular point in time.

2. With the Patient list worksheet active, on the DATA tab, in the Sort & Filter group, click Clear.

3. Next to Cat or Dog?, click the down arrow button. In the menu, click Sort A to Z. Now, all the cats are clustered together at the top, and dogs at the bottom.

4. Right-click the heading for row 30, the row where the first dog appears. Click Insert in the shortcut menu.

5. Select cell H30. Type Number of cats.

6. Select cell G30. On the HOME tab, in the Font group, click the Bold button. This makes this particular number stand out.

7. On the HOME tab, in the Editing group, click the AutoSum down arrow. In the menu, click Count Numbers, and then press Enter. Excel inserts a function into the cell that counts the number of contiguous cells in the column just above it that contains numbers—in this case, the owner numbers for clients.

8. Add a similar function for counting the number of dogs to row **60**. (Bypass the validation rule by clicking **Yes** in the dialog box.)

9. Select rows **6** through **29** (all the cats).

10. On the DATA tab, in the Outline group, click the **Group** button. A group indicator line is added to the left of the row markers and an outline symbol on the row just below the end of the group (see Figure 9-24).

Figure 9-24

Worksheet with groups applied

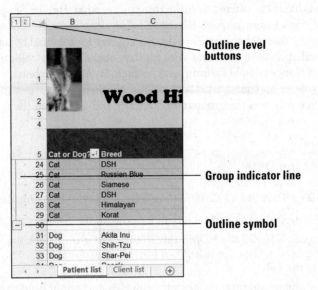

Outline level buttons

Group indicator line

Outline symbol

> **Another Way**
>
> To collapse all the groups in a worksheet, select the entire worksheet first, and then click Hide Detail in the Outline group of the DATA menu tab. To expand all groups, click Show Detail.

11. Repeat the process in Steps 9 and 10 for the dogs in rows **31** through **59**. Format cell **G60** as **Bold**. In cell **H60,** type **Number of dogs**.

12. To collapse the cats group, click the minus box (shown in Figure 9-24) beside row **30**, which contains the cats count. The control becomes a plus box, indicating that when you click on it, it expands to show hidden rows.

13. Collapse the dogs group with the minus box in row **60**. The worksheet now appears fully collapsed (see Figure 9-25).

Figure 9-25

Worksheet with collapsed groups

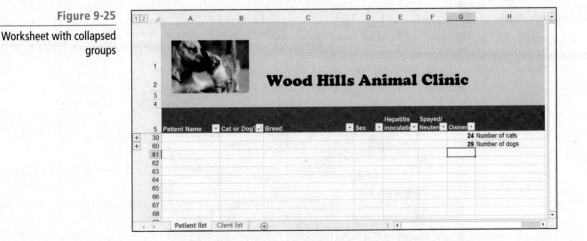

14. Click the **Select All** button. On the DATA tab, in the Outline group, click **Show Detail**.

15. Select columns **B** through **F**.

16. In the Outline group, click the **Group** button. A new column group is created.

17. Click the minus box over column **G** to collapse the column group. Click the plus box that takes its place to expand it.

18. Select columns **B** through **G**.

19. In the Outline group, click the **Ungroup** button. The columnar group disappears.

SAVE and CLOSE the workbook. Leave Excel open for use in the next exercise.

Auto-Outlining Data

Grouping data is an easy process when you have only a few groups in your worksheet that really matter, such as cats and dogs. For a complex report, such as a balance sheet with assets and liabilities broken down into departments and sub-departments, the task gets much more tedious. For this reason, Excel has offered to make things somewhat simpler. Suppose you inserted total value cells along the bottom rows of related cells, or along the right column beside related cells—or perhaps both. You probably need to do this anyway for a formal balance sheet, or for a table with names of salespeople in rows and sales for days of the week in columns—here, you total for each salesperson along the right column, and for each day along the bottom row. Excel can detect when and why you set up your worksheet like this, so when you **auto-outline** a table or a worksheet full of tables, it creates the groups automatically and spares you the trouble.

STEP BY STEP   **Auto-Outline Data**

GET READY. OPEN the *09 Critical Care Expenses* workbook for this lesson.

1. SAVE the workbook in the Lesson 9 folder as *09 Critical Care Expenses 0315 Solution*.
2. Select cell **H18**. On the HOME tab, in the Font group, click the Bold button. Then, in the Editing group, click the AutoSum button and press Enter. The grand total appears as bold in the cell.
3. Repeat the grand total process for cell **H28** and apply Bold to the cell.
4. Select the cell range **B10:H28**, covering both groups of expenses in their entirety.
5. On the DATA tab, in the Outline group, click the down arrow next to Group. In the menu, click Auto Outline. As Figure 9-26 shows, Excel automatically groups rows 12 through 17 and rows 22 through 27, having spotted the Total Expenses row along the bottom of each cluster. Excel also groups together the columns for March 15 through 19, having spotted the weekly totals columns along the right.

CERTIFICATION READY?   **2.3.5**

How do you create outlines?

Figure 9-26

Outlined worksheet

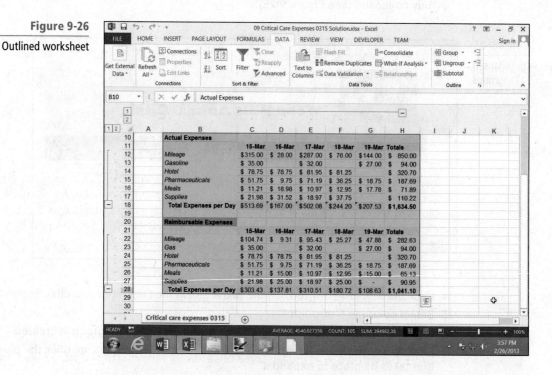

SAVE the workbook and LEAVE Excel open for the next exercise.

Collapsing Groups of Data in an Outline

When you create an outline around groups of data in a worksheet, outline symbols appear for each group of rows and columns. You use these devices to collapse and then expand the outline, thus switching between summary and detailed views of the worksheet.

STEP BY STEP **Collapse Groups of Data in an Outline**

GET READY. USE the workbook from the previous exercise.

1. Click all three minus boxes to collapse their respective groups. The worksheet should now appear shrunken to just the grand totals cells you created with the appropriate labels (see Figure 9-27).

Figure 9-27

Outlined worksheet with collapsed groups

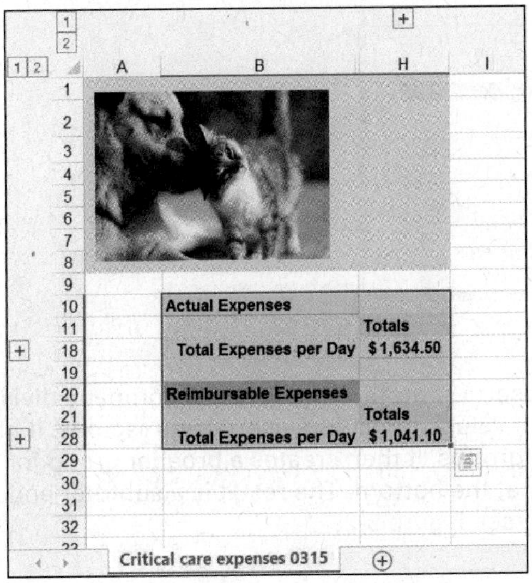

2. Click any of the plus boxes (which replaced the minus boxes) to expand the group to which it's attached.
3. To remove the outline entirely, on the DATA tab, in the Outline group, click the Ungroup button arrow. In the menu, click Clear Outline.

SAVE and CLOSE the workbook. Leave Excel open for the next exercise.

CERTIFICATION READY? **2.3.6**

How do you collapse groups of data in an outline?

Subtotaling Data in Outlines

Suppose a worksheet serves as a report of certain activity that takes place on given days with respect to specific divisions of the company in particular regions of the country. These three categories represent levels of information. When you sort a worksheet so that these levels are in a precise order, as you've already seen how to do, then Excel can accept each of these levels as tiers in an outline. An outline gives you the complete summary while hiding the details until you request them.

STEP BY STEP **Subtotal Data in Outlines**

GET READY. OPEN the *09 Server Usage Stats* workbook for this lesson.

1. SAVE the workbook in the Lesson 9 folder as *09 Server Usage Stats 130831 Solution*.
2. Select the range A5:G140.
3. On the DATA tab, in the Sort & Filter group, click Sort.

CERTIFICATION READY? 2.3.7

How do you insert subtotals?

4. In the Sort dialog box, in the Sort by line, choose **Date, Oldest to Newest**. Click **OK**.
5. On the DATA tab, in the Outline group, click **Subtotal**. The Subtotal dialog box appears.
6. In the At each change in list box, click **Department**.
7. If necessary, in the Use function list box, choose **Sum**.
8. In the list of columns marked Add subtotal to, select the boxes for **Avg. Bandwidth**, **Data In**, **Data Out**, and **Transactions**.
9. Check the **Summary below data** and **Replace current subtotals** check boxes, if necessary. The dialog box should now appear as depicted in Figure 9-28.

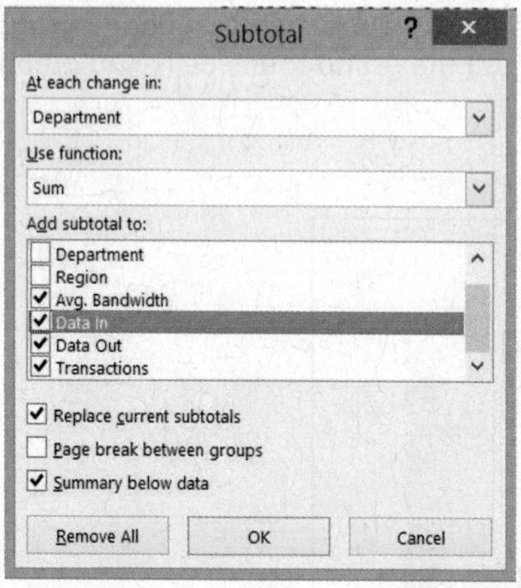

Figure 9-28
Subtotal dialog box

10. Click **OK**. Excel inserts subtotal rows for each company division, grouping together data consumption values for all three corporate regions. It places each of these division row clusters into groups. It then creates a broader group for the entire range and adds a grand total row at the bottom. The result is a subtotal-endowed worksheet with a three-tier outline (see Figure 9-29).

	A	B	C	D	E	F	G
4				Kb/sec	Mb	Mb	
5	Date	Department	Region	Avg. Bandwidth	Data In	Data Out	Transactions
6	1 Jul	Accounting	Central	214.7	3169	21661	81355
7	1 Jul	Accounting	North	114.5	2601	12359	64135
8	1 Jul	Accounting	South	84.6	1684	9467	46810
9		Accounting Total		413.8	7454	43487	192300
10	1 Jul	Distribution	Central	12.4	674	943	4121
11	1 Jul	Distribution	North	38.6	1551	2064	9102
12	1 Jul	Distribution	South	16.4	876	1643	8460
13		Distribution Total		67.4	3101	4650	21683
14	1 Jul	Merchandising	Central	51.6	495	2943	9103
15	1 Jul	Merchandising	North	56.5	518	3106	10312
16	1 Jul	Merchandising	South	48.5	406	2674	8513
17		Merchandising Total		156.6	1419	8723	27928
18	1 Jul	Point of sale	Central	109.9	1974	15464	65467
19	1 Jul	Point of sale	North	213.9	3164	26492	103454
20	1 Jul	Point of sale	South	184.0	2649	19733	78669
21		Point of sale Total		507.8	7787	61689	247590
22	1 Jul	Purchasing	Central	89.1	1064	3946	29431
23	1 Jul	Purchasing	North	110.4	1304	6103	35406
24	1 Jul	Purchasing	South	59.8	964	4766	25164
25		Purchasing Total		259.3	3332	14815	90001
26	8 Jul	Accounting	Central	205.6	3024	20461	79404
27	8 Jul	Accounting	North	106.4	2564	11643	62164
28	8 Jul	Accounting	South	88.5	1794	9501	46795
29		Accounting Total		400.5	7382	41605	188363

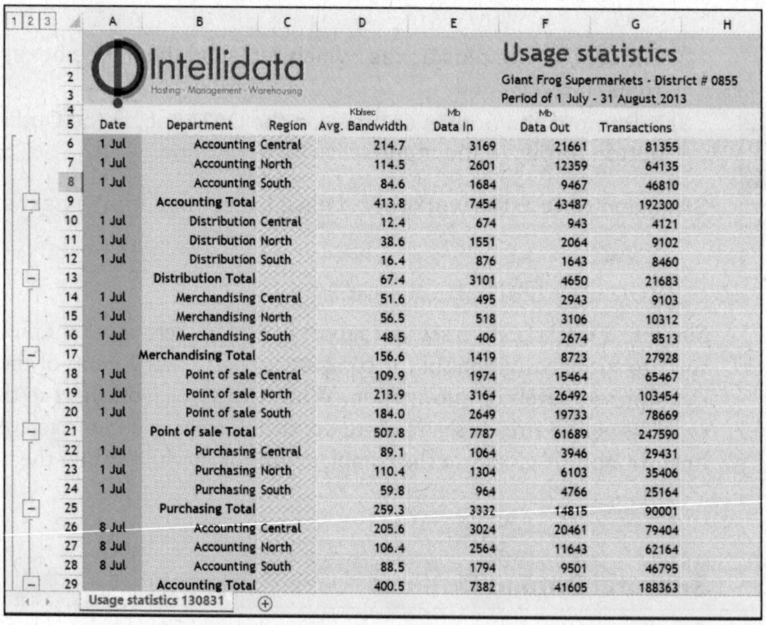

Figure 9-29
Automatically subtotaled worksheet with three-tier outline

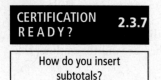

SAVE and CLOSE the workbook. Leave Excel open for the next exercise.

Take Note   When you remove an outline from an automatically subtotaled range, the subtotal rows that Excel inserted automatically remain. So to return a worksheet to its pre-subtotaled state, you must delete each subtotal row manually.

SETTING UP DATA IN A TABLE FORMAT

Bottom Line

Up to now in this lesson, you might think most of the data you used in worksheets has been, for all intents and purposes, tables. How could they not be tables? They have headings along the top, they have unique entries that identify rows, and some even have indexes. From a typesetting perspective, they're certainly tables. But Excel has a special relevance for a class of data that it formally calls a **table**. When you format a single, rectangular range with a row of headers along the top, and columns beneath the headers, converting that range to a table enables Excel to treat it like a database. Processing a table's data is faster, including for sorting. And Excel can apply an elaborate **quick format** that makes the table look sleek and professional. When you compose formulas, formal tables let you refer to field names explicitly (for example, "Price" and "Markup") rather than by their cell reference (for example, B7).

Formatting a Table with a Quick Style

Let's be honest: Big worksheets are hard to read. When you look at a well-laid out document that contains a table full of figures, you can see how typesetters apply graphic tools to make the table easier to read—tools such as alternating bands across every other line. You can (meticulously) apply such a style to a normal range, but what would happen when you sorted the range? The cell formatting would move along with the cells, and your alternating bands would be jumbled up. By denoting which part of a worksheet is a table, Excel can apply some formatting independently of contents. So a properly banded table *stays* properly banded when you sort the table, or when you insert and delete rows.

STEP BY STEP   **Format a Table with a Quick Style**

GET READY. OPEN the *09 Pet Pharma Sales* workbook for this lesson.

1. SAVE the workbook in the Lesson 9 folder as *09 Pet Pharma Sales August Solution*.
2. In the August Sales worksheet, select the data range A6:K93.
3. On the HOME tab, in the Styles group, click **Format as Table**. Excel brings up a colorful menu full of sample layouts (see Figure 9-30).

Figure 9-30

Table format menu

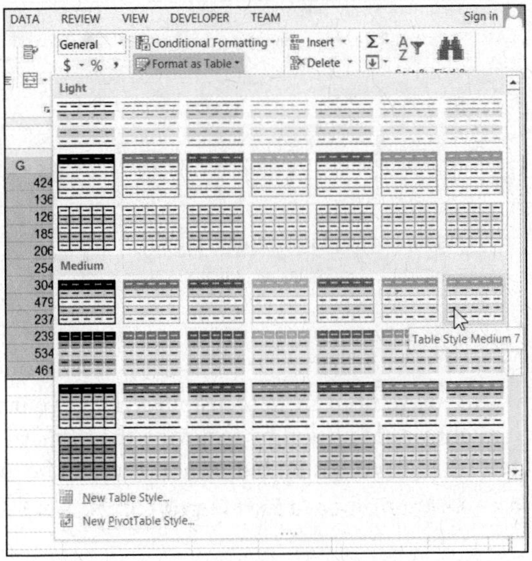

CERTIFICATION READY?   **3.2.1**

How do you apply styles to tables?

4. Click the sample in row 4, column 7 (**Table Style Medium 7**). The Format As Table dialog box appears (see Figure 9-31).

Figure 9-31

Format As Table dialog box

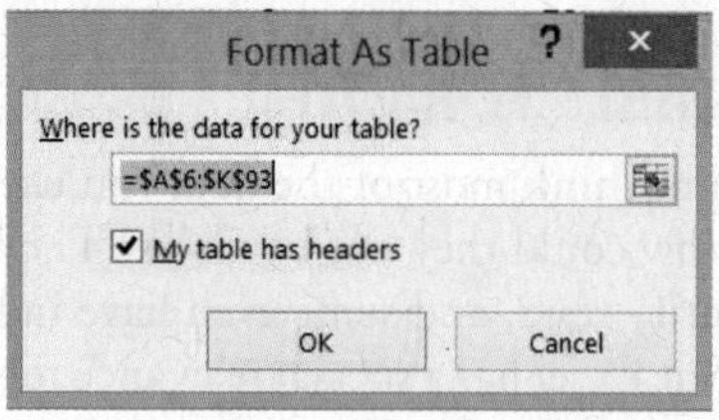

Take Note You can change the format of a table at any time using the Format as Table command. You only see the Format As Table dialog box the *first* time you format a table, which effectively changes a standard range to a table. Afterwards, you only need to select a cell inside the table to tell Excel which table you want to reformat.

CERTIFICATION READY? 3.2.2

How do you band rows and columns?

5. Because the cell reference under Where is the data for your table? is accurate, don't make any changes and click **OK**. Excel converts the data range into a formal table and applies the style you chose, which includes automatically banded rows that maintain their banding even when rows become sorted. AutoFilter controls are also added to the field names row.

6. To automatically boldface the rightmost column in the table (Total Sales), click any cell inside the table. On the DESIGN tab, in the Table Style Options group, click **Last Column**.

Take Note The Table Style Options group also contains an option for banding columns instead of rows. Uncheck Banded Rows from this group, and then check Banded Columns.

SAVE the workbook and LEAVE it open for the next exercise.

Take Note When you scroll down a data table so that the field names row disappears, as long as the active cell stays within the table area, the usual column headings (A, B, C, and so on) are replaced with the complete field names, as Figure 9-32 depicts. The AutoFilter buttons also move to the headings row. This way, you don't need to freeze the field names row in place to keep the names themselves visible. When you move the active cell outside the table area, the standard column headings reappear.

Figure 9-32

Field names display in the headings row.

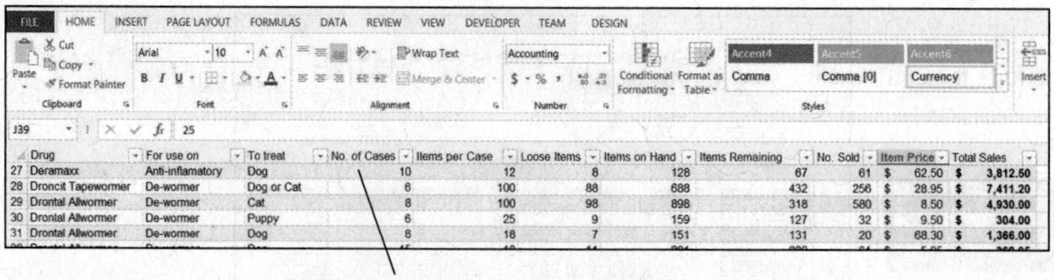

Field names replace column labels

Removing Styles from a Table

If you're at a point where you want to create a custom style for your table, or for multiple tables in your workbook, you might want to begin by removing the formatting that's already present. The table style removal feature in Excel is a bit buried and needs to be uncovered to be used.

STEP BY STEP Remove Styles from a Table

GET READY. USE the workbook from the previous exercise.

1. SAVE the workbook in the Lesson 9 folder as *09 Pet Pharma Sales August Solution 2*.

2. In the August Sales worksheet, click anywhere inside the table.

3. On the DESIGN tab, in the Table Styles group, click the More down arrow button. (Or if you see only the Quick Styles button, click that instead.)

4. In the menu, as indicated in Figure 9-33, click Clear. The automatic formatting is removed.

CERTIFICATION READY? 3.2.4

How do you remove styles from tables?

Figure 9-33

Table Styles menu on the DESIGN tab

Troubleshooting There are two places to find the table styles menu in Excel. One is under the Format as Table button on the HOME tab. The other is in the Table Styles group of the DESIGN menu tab. At first, both menus look the same. But only the one on the DESIGN tab has the Clear button to remove styles from a table.

5. To change the table style to something that contrasts against the others in this series, bring up the Quick Styles menu again, and this time, choose Table Style Light 6 (upper right corner).

6. To automatically apply boldface to the rightmost column, in the Table Style Options group, ensure Last Column is checked. To do the same for the leftmost column, check First Column.

SAVE the workbook and LEAVE it open for the next exercise.

Defining a Title for a Table

Up to now, you've seen some nuanced and subtle differences between tables and ordinary data ranges. The one big difference between the two lay with the table's ability to be given a title, so that it and its constituent columns can be referred to by name instead of by reference location. This changes everything when you write formulas that refer to parts of the table, because now you don't have to know where they're located, just what they're called.

Once a table is given a title, all the names of its columns can be used in place of cell references in a formula. The result is not only a formula that's easier to conceive, but easier to read and even easier to type. So instead of an absolute cell reference such as $B$2:$B$55 (which starts on the second row, of course, because the headers are always on the first row), you can use a reference such as Inventory[Sale Price]. Excel already knows not to treat the first row as values, and whenever records are added to the table, the results of the formula are adjusted without the formula itself even having to change its appearance.

The syntax of a reference to fields in an Excel table is as follows:

TableName[FieldName]

Component	Meaning
TableName	An arbitrary name you give to a table, in place of its reference as a range. You can have more than one table on a worksheet, although it might not always be convenient. Examples: Customers, Back Orders, Comics issues
FieldName	The field name from the header row of the table. The name refers to the set of all cells that comprise the named column in the table. You do not need to specify the start and end cell. The field name is always denoted with [square brackets]. Examples: Surname, Issue date, Sale price

Note: Excel recognizes four constants that refer to the same general area of a table, which you may use here when applicable to replace the field name:

#All	The set of all cells in the table
#Data	The set of all cells that contain data, excluding the header row at the top and any total or subtotal rows that might appear at the bottom
#Headers	The set of all cells in the first row in the table
#Totals	The set of all cells where totals appear, usually the rightmost column of the table where a SUM function is employed

When you type a table-style reference inside a formula, Excel gives you a shortcut. After you type the second character of the table name, Excel displays a list of names you can add to the formula (including named ranges). Figure 9-34 shows you what it looks like. Instead of typing in the rest of the name, you can use the arrow keys on the keyboard to navigate this menu until the name you want (the table name) is highlighted, and then you press Tab. The entire name is entered into the formula, saving you a few seconds of time.

Figure 9-34

IntelliSense menu for the table name

Menu pops up here

With the table name entered, when it's time to refer to a field name in the table, you can start with the left square bracket ([ ). Excel displays a list of all the field names already in the table. You use the arrow keys to highlight the one you're looking for, and then press Tab. Then type the right square bracket ( ]) to complete the reference.

Similarly, whenever you want to use one of the four constants (#All, #Data, #Headers, or #Totals), you just start with the pound sign #. Excel displays the list, and then you highlight the one you want and press Tab. Microsoft markets this feature as *IntelliSense*, and you see it referred to as such in the Help system.

Troubleshooting When you highlight the entry you want on the IntelliSense menu, make sure to press Tab, not Enter. The Enter key tells Excel the formula is complete, and at this point, it's often not.

Take Note When referring to a field name by name in a formula that's used inside the same table as the field name, you can omit the table name. For example, the reference Customers[Surname] can be substituted with just Surname when the reference is inside the Customers table.

STEP BY STEP | **Define a Title for a Table**

GET READY. USE the workbook from the previous exercise.

1. SAVE the workbook in the Lesson 9 folder as *09 Pet Pharma Sales August Solution 3*.
2. In the August Sales worksheet, click anywhere inside the table.
3. On the DESIGN tab, in the Properties group, click the text box under Table Name.

CERTIFICATION READY? **3.1.3**

How do you define titles in a table?

4. Type DrugSales (all one word) and press Enter. You have given a name to the table. Now you can replace the strange-looking formulas at the bottom of the August Sales worksheet with formulas that are easier to read, yet yield the same results.
5. Select cell D97 (Total Sales).
6. Type =sum(Dr
7. When DrugSales appears in the list, press Tab.
8. Type [(left square bracket).
9. Use the arrow keys to select Total Sales from the list, and then press Tab.
10. Type] (right square bracket), followed by) (right parenthesis) and Enter. If you enter the formula properly, the result should be identical to what was there before.
11. Replace the formula in cell D98 with the following:
    =SUMIF(DrugSales[To treat],"Dog",DrugSales[Total Sales])
12. Replace the formula in cell D99 with one based on the formula in D98, but searching for Cat instead of Dog.

SAVE the workbook and leave it open for the next exercise.

Using the Total Row Command in a Table

Once Excel recognizes a formal table, it can automatically place an automatic totals row along the bottom. It's not the same as a subtotal row that falls after a group. However, once you choose a table style, Excel automatically applies boldface to the totals row to make it stand out—so it's obvious from a distance that it contains totals, and so it serves as a "bookend" for all the data in the middle.

STEP BY STEP | **Use the Total Row Command in a Table**

CERTIFICATION READY? **3.2.3**

How do you insert total rows in a table?

GET READY. USE the workbook from the previous exercise.

1. Select any cell in the table. Excel adds the DESIGN tab to the ribbon.
2. With the August Sales worksheet active, on the DESIGN tab, in the Table Style Options group, select the Total Row box. Excel adds a total row to the bottom, as shown in

Figure 9-35, with a label in the leftmost column and the grand total in the rightmost column.

Figure 9-35

Total row added below table

Total row —

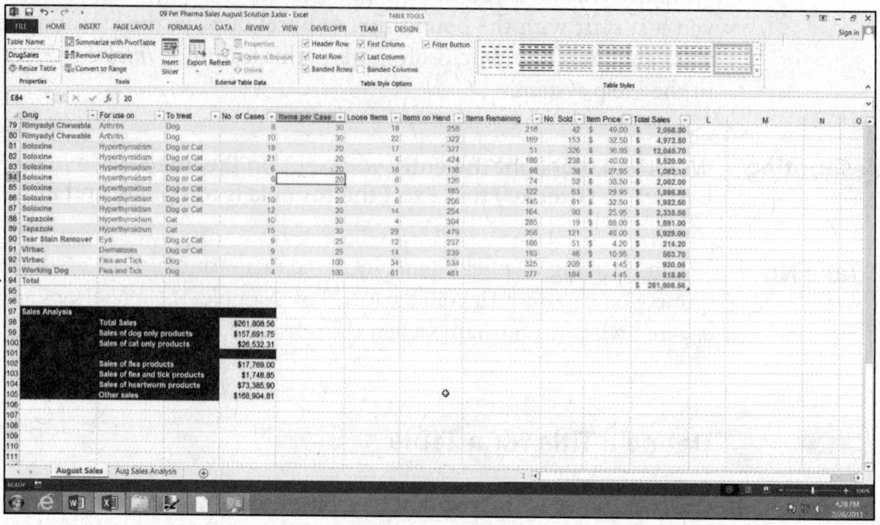

Figure 9-35

Total row added below table

3. To add other subtotals or formulas to the Total Row, you can choose one from a drop-down menu. Click the cell in the total row at the bottom of the Item Price column.

4. Click the down arrow that appears to the right of the blank cell. In the popup menu (see Figure 9-36), click **Average**. Excel calculates the average price per sales item.

Figure 9-36

Adding formulas to the total row

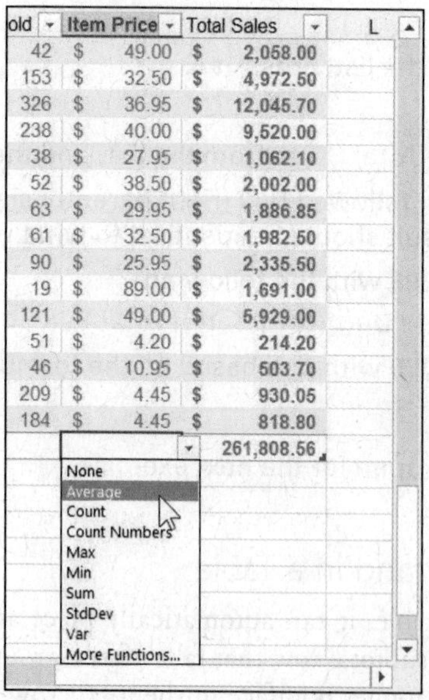

5. Repeat the process to find the maximum number of items sold in one order by choosing the **Max** function for the **No. Sold** column.

SAVE the workbook and leave it open for the next exercise.

Adding and Removing Rows or Columns in a Table

Databases are never *finished*. When you maintain data in an ordinary range, one problem you frequently face is how and where to insert a new row. There's no rule that says you have to insert a new record in alphabetical order, when the range is sorted alphabetically. You can add it to the end and sort again. Here's the problem: If you've named your range already, when you add the record to the end, you might need to reassign the range name. With a formal table, not only does the range for the table stay named properly, but when you insert rows (as well as delete them) the named range covered by the table is adjusted to fit automatically. And any formulas you use inside each of the rows in the table are copied and adjusted to the new rows you add.

STEP BY STEP   **Add and Remove Rows and Columns in a Table**

GET READY. USE the workbook from the previous exercise.

1. SAVE the workbook in the Lesson 9 folder as *09 Pet Pharma Sales August Solution 4*.
2. In the August Sales worksheet, select cell **A88** (in the Drug column).
3. On the HOME tab, in the Cells group, click the Insert down arrow. In the menu, click Insert Table Rows Above.
4. Type the following values into cells **A88:F88**:

   Soloxine   Hyperthyroidism   Dog or Cat   7   20   2

5. Note that the value in the Items on Hand column is automatically updated, because Excel copied the formula into the new row.
6. Select cell **H88** (in the Items Remaining column) and type the value 41. Cell I88 is updated.
7. Select cell **J88** (in the Item Price column) and type the value 25.95. Cell K88 is updated.
8. Select any cell in row 32.
9. On the HOME tab, in the Cells group, click the Delete down arrow. In the menu, click Delete Table Rows. Row 32 is deleted, and the table shrinks to fit.
10. Select any cell in column I (No. Sold).
11. On the HOME tab, in the Cells group, click the Delete down arrow, and then click Delete Table Columns. Column I is removed, and for the time being, #REF! errors are generated throughout the Total Sales column, which contain formulas that referred to No. Sold.
12. With a cell in column I still selected, click the down arrow next to Insert in the Cells group, and in the menu, click Insert Table Columns to the Left.
13. Change the header in cell **I6** to read No. Sold.
14. Click cell **I7** and enter the formula =[Items on Hand]-[Items Remaining]. Use the "IntelliSense" menus when you type each left bracket [to expedite your entry. Notice when you press Enter that Excel automatically copies the formula down the remainder of the column. You normally don't have to do this manually for a table.
15. Click cell **K7** and enter the formula =[No. Sold]*[Item Price]. This time when you press Enter, Excel does *not* fill the formula down the column, because it will not autofill over nonblank cells.
16. Fill the new Total Sales formula down to row 93, making sure to stop short of the total row. The grand total formula in cell K94 is now fixed.
17. Click cell **L7**, outside the table.
18. Enter the formula =[Total Sales]/AVERAGE([Total Sales]). Notice you don't get the "IntelliSense" menus this time, because the active cell is not inside the table. After you press Enter, Excel not only creates the formula but extends the table one column to the right, and copies the formula down the entire column L. For now, Excel gives the new column the temporary name *Column1* (see Figure 9-37).

Another Way
To insert multiple contiguous rows in a table, start by selecting a block of cells that's as tall as the number of rows you want to insert.

CERTIFICATION READY?   3.1.2

How do you add and remove cells within tables?

Figure 9-37

Appended column to a table

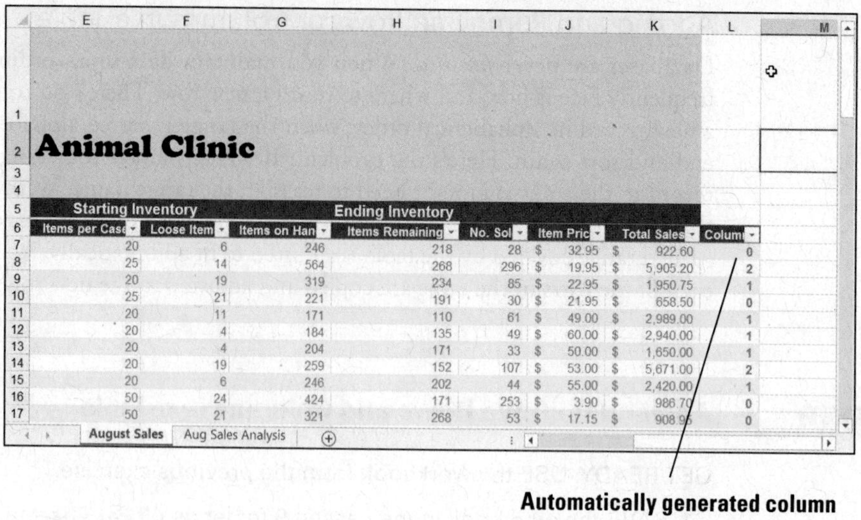

Automatically generated column

Take Note   Excel doesn't apply its autofill IntelliSense feature for table field names while you enter data outside the table.

19. Rename the new column % of Avg.

20. Select cell range L7:L93 and give the range a percent style. Excel does not automatically copy custom cell styles down a column, so you must select the range manually first. Note how Excel has moved the last column's boldfaced format from Total Sales to % of Avg.

21. Click any cell in % of Avg., and then click the down arrow next to Delete. Click Delete Table Columns. As the appended column disappears, the boldfacing is returned to Total Sales.

SAVE the workbook and leave it open for the next exercise.

Filtering Records in a Table

The filtering/sorting buttons that appear beside the field names at the top row of a table work the same way as the filtering/sorting buttons for a range where AutoFilter is applied. The big difference with tables concerns the total row. The values in a subtotal row change to reflect only what's visible in the table after the filter is applied.

STEP BY STEP	Filter Records in a Table

GET READY. USE the workbook from the previous exercise.

1. In the August Sales worksheet, click the Total Sales down arrow.

2. In the menu (see Figure 9-38), click Number Filters, and then click Top 10. The Top 10 AutoFilter dialog box appears.

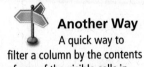

Figure 9-38

AutoFilter menu for records in a table

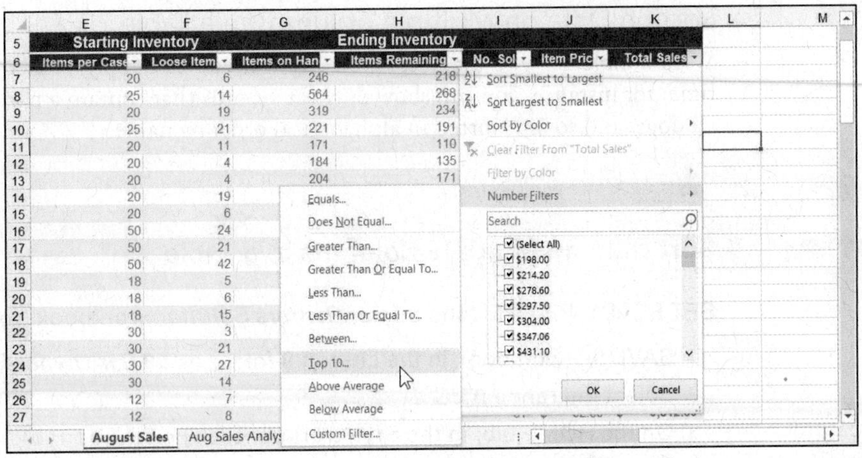

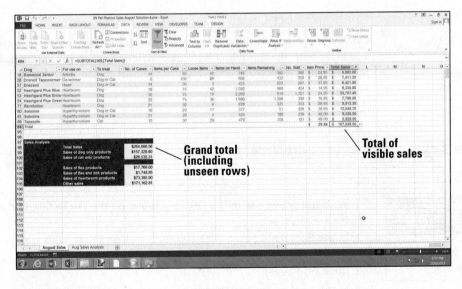

Another Way
A quick way to filter a column by the contents of one of the visible cells in that column is to right-click that cell, click Filter in the menu, and then click Filter by Selected Cell's Value.

3. Leave the choices set at *Top 10 items*, and then click *OK*. The table is filtered down to the 10 items with the highest sales.

SAVE and CLOSE the workbook and leave Excel open for the next exercise.

Take Note The Top 10 items filter always results in 10 items displayed (unless the table has fewer than 10 records to begin with). By comparison, the Top 10 percent filter displays however many records comprise the top 10 percent of the values in the filtered column.

The total row of a filtered table adjusts its contents so that its formulas reflect only the visible (filtered) cells. As Figure 9-39 demonstrates, the averaging formula in cell J94 is adjusted to show the average item price among just the top 10. However, look further down at the analysis section. The formulas for Total Sales, Sales of dog only products, and so on, still refer to the *entire table*, not just the filtered portion. So any analysis you want to perform using filtering should be entered on a total row, which is included within the filtered area.

Figure 9-39

Changed and unchanged filtered table

Troubleshooting The exceptions to the rule about references to a table outside a filtered table are the # constants. If the formula in cell D98 of the example is =SUM(DrugSales[#Totals]) instead of =SUM(DrugSales[Total Sales]), the formula would adjust itself to tally only the visible, filtered records.

Sorting Data on Multiple Columns in a Table

With a table, as with an AutoFiltered range, you can apply a filter and a sort order at the same time; for instance, you can show only the records that contain a particular entry (all motorcycles, all dogs, and so on), sorted in alphabetical order by name.

STEP BY STEP   **Sort Data on Multiple Columns in a Table**

GET READY. RE-OPEN the *09 Car Owners Solution* workbook from earlier in this lesson.

1. SAVE the workbook in the Lesson 9 folder as *09 Car Owners Solution 2*.
2. Select the range A1:G73.
3. On the HOME tab, in the Styles group, click Format as Table. In the menu, click Table Style Medium 14.
4. In the Format As Table dialog box, click OK.
5. Because this range contains data appended from an outside source (see the "Appending Data to a Worksheet" section earlier in this lesson), the query data related to that outside source is still attached to the range. Click Yes in the dialog box to have Excel remove those connections.
6. Click the Name box and rename the table Owners.
7. Resize columns B, E, and F to more appropriately fit their contents.
8. Change the font for the entire table to Cambria, 11 pt.
9. Left-justify column G.
10. With the Owners table selected, on the DATA tab, in the Sort & Filter group, click Sort. The Sort dialog box appears (refer to Figure 9-16).
11. In the Sort by list box under Column, choose Last Name.
12. Click Add Level.
13. In the Then by list box that appears under Column, choose First Name. Click OK.

SAVE the workbook and leave it open for the next exercise.

CERTIFICATION READY?   3.3.2

How do you sort data on multiple columns in a table?

Changing Sort Order in a Table

Once you set the sort order for a table, you can change it in two ways. First, any sorting choice you make with the AutoFilter buttons override the current sort order, including when the table is sorted by multiple columns. Second, in the Sort dialog box, delete the existing order and enter a new one.

STEP BY STEP   **Change Sort Order in a Table**

GET READY. USE the workbook from the previous exercise.

1. With the active cell in the Owners table, on the DATA tab, in the Sort & Filter group, click Sort.
2. In the Sort dialog box, click Delete Level, and then click Delete Level again, to remove the existing sort order.
3. Click Add Level.
4. In the Sort by list box that appears, click ZIP. Click OK.

SAVE the workbook and leave it open for the next exercise.

CERTIFICATION READY?   3.3.3

How do you change the sort order in a table?

Removing Duplicates in a Table

When you import data and append it to the end of an existing table or range, you might end up with duplicate entries—cases where a person appears twice, or perhaps more. Rather than go through the list by hand, Excel has a way to excise duplicate entries from a table more intelligently.

STEP BY STEP | **Remove Duplicates in a Table**

GET READY. USE the workbook from the previous exercise.

1. Click any cell inside the table.
2. On the DESIGN tab, in the Tools group, click Remove Duplicates.
3. The Remove Duplicates dialog box (refer to Figure 9-15) lets you determine how much of a record needs to be duplicated before it qualifies as a duplicate. For instance, two or more customers might have the same name, though they probably don't share the same address or phone number. In the Columns list, uncheck City, State, and ZIP.
4. Click OK. Excel shows a dialog box reporting how many duplicate entries were removed. Click OK to dismiss.

SAVE and CLOSE the workbook and leave Excel open for the next exercise.

CERTIFICATION READY? 3.3.4

How do you remove duplicates in a table?

 Another Way

After Excel finds duplicate rows, it removes the lowermost duplicates from the table, leaving the row on top. This is important when you remove rows based on some, not all, the fields in the rows. Excel does not automatically reconcile the contents of rows deemed to be duplicates, so any data in the lowermost rows that does not appear in the uppermost duplicate row will be deleted without asking you first.

Using a Slicer to View Table Data

There are two ways to filter a table so that it shows only records containing a certain object. One way is through the AutoFilter. Another makes the table more easily accessible to a novice user. It's called the **slicer**, and it's a selection panel that floats above a worksheet (the way a chart does). This panel includes buttons labeled with each of the contents of one of the columns in the table. When you click a button, the table is filtered to show only rows that match the selection. When designing the worksheet, each slicer is like a window with a title bar. You can relocate a slicer by dragging it by its title bar, which you need to do because it begins its life in the middle of the worksheet. Each slicer also has white handles along its edges. You drag one of these handles to resize the slicer in the direction you're dragging.

STEP BY STEP | **Use a Slicer to View Table Data**

GET READY. RE-OPEN the *09 Pet Pharma Sales August Solution 4* workbook for this lesson.

1. SAVE the workbook in the Lesson 9 folder as *09 Pet Pharma Sales August Solution 5*.
2. On the DATA tab, in the Sort & Filter group, click Clear. Click any cell inside the table.
3. On the DESIGN tab, in the Tools group, click the Insert Slicer button.
4. The Insert Slicers dialog box contains empty check boxes for each of the fields for which you can create buttons (see Figure 9-40). Click For use on and To treat.

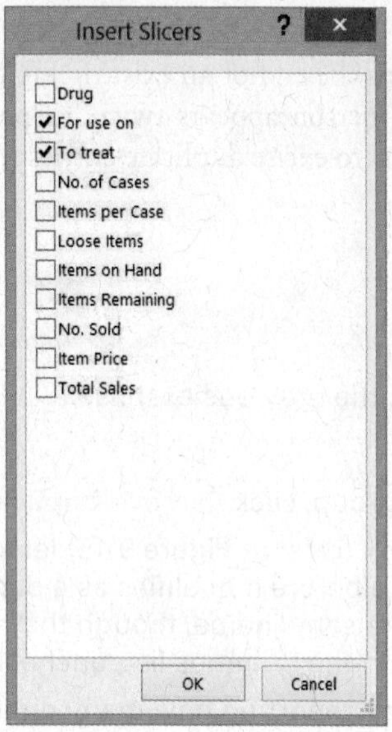

Figure 9-40

Insert Slicers dialog box

5. Click **OK**. As the dialog box disappears, the two slicer tools appear as graphic objects in the center of the worksheet. They're not actually inside the table.

6. Relocate the **For use on** slicer by dragging its title bar toward the upper right of the worksheet. As you drag toward the edge of the window, the worksheet automatically scrolls to reveal space where you can drop the slicer. Drop the slicer when it's to the right of the table, just beneath the headers row.

7. Repeat the process with the **To treat** slicer, dragging it below the For use on slicer. The worksheet should look similar to Figure 9-41.

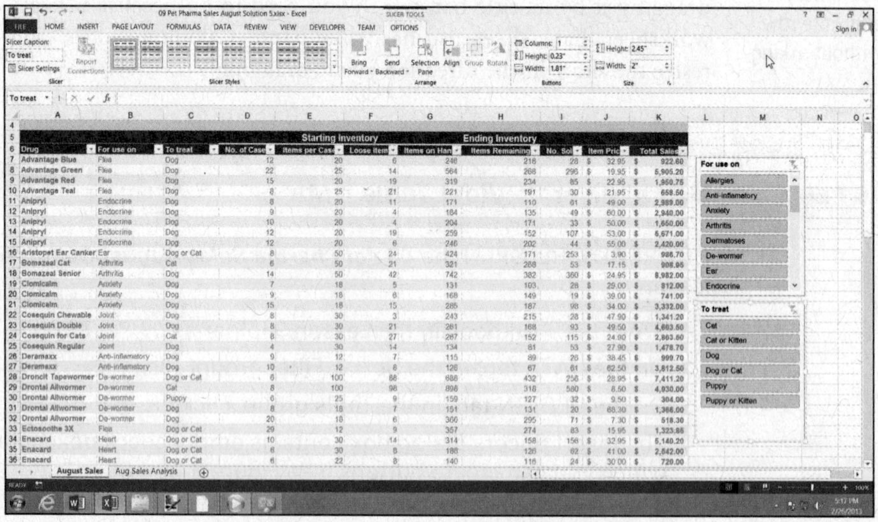

Figure 9-41

Worksheet with slicers added

8. To see just the treatments that apply to dogs only, click **Dog** on the To treat slicer. Note that the AutoFilter button for the To treat column shows a filter has been applied.

9. To show just the treatments that apply to the endocrine system, click **Endocrine** on the For use on slicer. Note that the filters from both slicers apply simultaneously, so you should see endocrine system treatments for dogs only. The slicer highlights only the criterion in use for the current filter.

10. To clear the filters using the slicers, click the **Clear Filter** button in the upper right corner of each slicer.

SAVE and CLOSE the workbook and leave Excel open for the next exercise.

Troubleshooting When an AutoFilter button for a column is used to filter a table and a slicer exists for that same column, the slicer shows the criteria currently in use for that filter. However, the Clear Filter button for the slicer is disabled. To clear this filter, you have to use the AutoFilter button.

Converting a Table into a Range

To append more data to a table from an outside source, it might be convenient for you to remove the "table-ness" from the table, if only temporarily, and reapply it once the new data is imported and the data is cleaned up. Also, before you export a workbook file to a new format (for instance, for importing by someone else into a database), you might need to convert tables to ranges, because Excel treats data stored in tables differently than data stored in ordinary worksheets.

STEP BY STEP	**Convert a Table to a Range**

GET READY. RE-OPEN the *09 2005 Customers Solution* workbook for this lesson.

CERTIFICATION READY? 3.1.1

How do you move between tables and ranges?

1. Near the top of the Excel window, respond to the security warning by clicking Enable Content.
2. SAVE the workbook in the Lesson 9 folder as *09 2005 Customers Solution 2*.
3. Click any cell inside the table.
4. On the DESIGN tab, in the Tools group, click Convert to Range.
5. Excel opens a dialog box to verify this conversion is what you want. Click OK. The AutoFilter buttons are removed from the header row and entries are left sorted as they were. Subtotals and total rows remain (if applicable), and formatting is left as it was. The DESIGN tab is no longer displayed.

SAVE and CLOSE the workbook and leave Excel open for the next exercise.

SAVING WORK WITH MACROS

Bottom Line

Some of the first spreadsheet programs used lists of functions, typed down some tucked away column in an unseen edge of the sheet as multiple-step calculations that had the added virtue of executing commands automatically. These were the first macros, and the fact that they were considered "big functions" is how they got their name. Over the years, the number of different categories of macros that Excel can execute has grown, and the categories themselves vary so widely that a complete discussion of them would require another book. For the purposes of this lesson, we concentrate on one type: a recording of a sequence of commands and typed entries that you can then replay elsewhere in the worksheet. This way, you can perform the same sequences of commands in different places, cutting down the time it takes to complete redundant work.

Recording a Basic Macro

What makes a recorded macro useful is the fact that it can be replayed on whatever cell is the active cell. A recorded **macro** is a series of steps that can be repeated and that you might want to repeat frequently to save you time. As you've seen, there are ways to automate the formatting of cells that are actually easier than recording and playing back macros. So the kinds of steps you want to record are the repetitive kind that you would otherwise have to repeat yourself dozens of times or more.

Troubleshooting Excel records only those steps that have a direct impact on the contents of the worksheet. To be accurate, it records the impact those steps have, not actually the commands that led to the impact. For example, if you select several rows and columns, Excel records the act of the rows and columns being grouped. But if you expand or collapse that group, it does not record that fact because doing so does not impact the worksheet itself. Exceptions include filtering and sorting ranges and tables, which Excel does record.

Workplace Ready

PLANNING TO RECORD A MACRO

To ensure that the macro you record is useful to you in a variety of situations, you should consider whether you need it to record absolute or relative cell references. This is because Excel keeps track of every change in the position of the active cell during macro recording. When that change is made, Excel needs to know whether it's more important for it to know the exact address of the new cell's location (absolute) or the number of cells left or right or up or down that the pointer was moved from its previous location (relative).

When you're recording absolute references, record a macro, and then click on cell A5, the recording always moves to A5. But if you use the arrow keys on the keyboard to move to another cell instead, the recording takes note of each arrow key pressed. So if you record the macro on A5 and use the down arrow key to move two cells down, and the macro replays from cell Y5, the macro moves to Y7.

By comparison, when you record relative references and then click a new location on the worksheet, Excel records the distance to the new cell. This makes the starting cell location critical to the macro. If you start with a cell selected in column D, and you click on a cell on the same row in column A, Excel records a movement three cells to the left. That is *not* the same thing as moving to the leftmost column, which you normally can do by pressing the Home key. However, in relative recording mode, pressing Home records the distance covered in getting to column A. So when you replay this macro, you could end up starting in a cell in column F and end up moving to column C when you expect to move to column A. Or, you can start in column B and trip an error condition when Excel tries to move too far to the left of column A.

For this reason, it's important to map out your precise cell movements (if any) prior to recording a macro, and then slowly repeat that sequence during the recording process. The recording does not account for how much time you take, so if you're nice and slow, the playback won't be any slower.

```
Microsoft Visual Basic for Applications - 09 4Strong Tour Revenues Solution.xlsm - [Module1 (Code)]
File  Edit  View  Insert  Format  Debug  Run  Tools  Add-Ins  Window  Help

Project - VBAProje          (General)                              CustomSubtotals

VBAProject (09 4Str          Sub CustomSubtotals()
Microsoft Excel Obje        '
   SheetM (Revenue           ' CustomSubtotals Macro
   ThisWorkbook              '
Modules                      ' Keyboard Shortcut: Ctrl+Shift+S
   Module1                   '
VBAProject (Nov-De               Application.WindowState = xlMinimized
                                 Application.WindowState = xlNormal
                                 ActiveCell.Range("A1:A2").Select
                                 Selection.EntireRow.Insert
Properties - Modu                Application.WindowState = xlMinimized
                                 Application.WindowState = xlNormal
Module1 Module                   ActiveCell.Select
Alphabetic  Categorized          Application.WindowState = xlMinimized
Module1                          Application.WindowState = xlNormal
                                 ActiveCell.FormulaR1C1 = "=SUM(R[-16]C:R[-1]C)"
                                 ActiveCell.Offset(0, 1).Range("A1").Select
                                 Application.WindowState = xlMinimized
                                 Application.WindowState = xlNormal
                                 ActiveCell.FormulaR1C1 = "=MAX(R[-16]C[-1]:R[-1]C[-1])"
                                 ActiveCell.Offset(0, 1).Range("A1").Select
                                 Application.WindowState = xlMinimized
                                 Application.WindowState = xlNormal
                                 ActiveCell.Offset(0, -1).Range("A1").Select
                                 Selection.Style = "Currency"
                                 Application.WindowState = xlMinimized
                                 Application.WindowState = xlNormal
                             End Sub
```

STEP BY STEP **Record a Basic Macro**

GET READY. OPEN the *09 4Strong Tour Revenues* workbook for this lesson.

1. Click the FILE tab, and then click Options.
2. In the Excel Options dialog box, click Customize Ribbon.
3. In the Main Tabs list on the right, check the Developer box if it is not already checked. This adds the DEVELOPER tab to Excel, enabling you to record macros. Click OK.
4. The macro that you record creates a custom subtotal row at the place you define, rather than at some place Excel determines. The rule you follow is that the user (you) must select the cell where you want the subtotal to appear, and then run the macro. So to prepare for recording, click cell D21.
5. On the DEVELOPER tab, in the Code group, find Use Relative References. If it is not highlighted, click to select it. You want relative references for this macro.
6. In the Code group, click Record Macro.
7. In the Record Macro dialog box, click the Macro name box and type CustomSubtotals.
8. In the Shortcut key box beside Ctrl +, type the capital S. This changes the shortcut key to Ctrl + Shift + S. Leave Store macro in set to This Workbook. The dialog box should now appear as depicted in Figure 9-42.

CERTIFICATION READY? | 1.4.12

How do you assign a shortcut key?

Figure 9-42

Record Macro dialog box

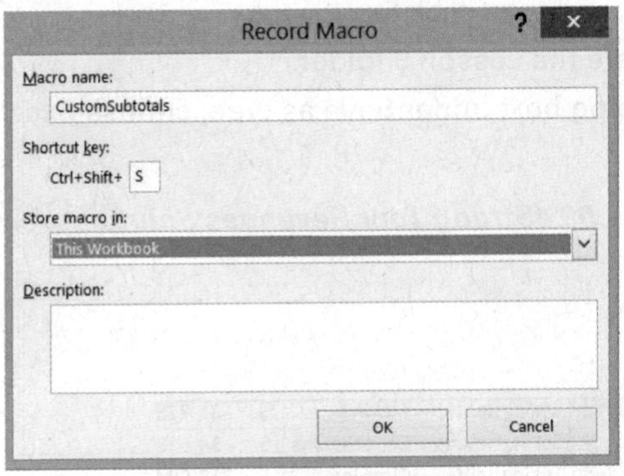

9. Click OK. You are now recording a macro.

⚠ **Troubleshooting** If you mess up a step during the macro recording, don't worry. Click Stop Recording in the Code group of the DEVELOPER tab. Then start again from Step 6. Use the same name, and when Excel asks whether you want to overwrite the existing macro with the same name, respond with Yes.

10. Press Shift + Down Arrow.
11. On the HOME tab, in the Cells group, click the Insert arrow. In the menu, click Insert Sheet Rows.
12. Press Shift + Up Arrow.
13. In the Editing group, click AutoSum. Do not press Enter yet.
14. In the Clipboard, click Copy.
15. Press Tab.
16. Type the partial formula =max(.
17. In the Clipboard group, click Paste.
18. Type) (end parenthesis) and press Tab.
19. Press Left Arrow.
20. Click $ (Accounting Number Format) in the Number group.
21. On the DEVELOPER tab, in the Code group, click Stop Recording.

CERTIFICATION READY? | 1.4.7

How do you record a simple macro?

22. Now that you're not recording, adjust the width of column **E** to fit its contents. As Figure 9-43 shows, the macro generates a total for the bottom of the arbitrary cluster of records, and also tabulates the highest value in that cluster in the cell adjacent to the subtotal.

Figure 9-43

Custom subtotals generated with macro

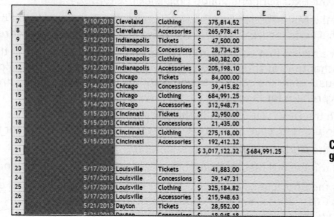

Custom subtotals generated with macro

23. Click the **FILE** tab, and then click Save As.

24. In Backstage, locate the Lesson 9 folder.

25. In the Save As dialog box, under Save as type, choose Excel Macro-Enabled Workbook (*.xlsm).

SAVE the workbook as *09 4Strong Tour Revenues Solution.xlsm* and leave it open for the next exercise.

Another Way

In the green status bar along the bottom of the Excel window, there's an icon that looks like a worksheet with a dot in the upper left corner, as shown in Figure 9-44. Click this to bypass the ribbon and immediately start recording a new macro. Click the same spot again to stop recording.

Figure 9-44

Alternate record macro button

31		5/23/2013	Springfield	Tickets	$	31,775
32		5/23/2013	Springfield	Concessions	$	34,615
33		5/23/2013	Springfield	Clothing	$	318,994

Revenues ⊕

READY

No macros are currently recording. Click to begin recording a new macro.

Record macro

For security reasons, Excel no longer saves macros in its regular .XLS and .XLSX files. This is due to how often the macros feature was maliciously used by people sending Excel workbooks to others via e-mail attachments. Now, the only way to save a macro-enabled workbook is to give it the special .XLSM file type. This way, companies that want to avoid any possibility of spreading malware can enforce policies preventing .XLSM files from being attached to or received within e-mails.

Running a Macro

A recorded macro follows the steps you gave Excel during the recording process. For that reason, it's up to you to prepare the worksheet and select the cell you want before you begin. You can play back any macro by selecting it from the Macro dialog box. But it's generally easier to assign it to a keystroke, as you did in the previous exercise, and simply launch it from the keyboard.

STEP BY STEP **Run a Macro**

GET READY. USE the workbook from the previous exercise.

1. Click cell **D39**.
2. On the DEVELOPER tab, in the Code group, click **Macros**.
3. In the Macro dialog box, click **CustomSubtotals**. Click **Run**. The custom subtotals row is added immediately, with a one-row gap between the clusters.
4. Click cell **D57**.
5. Press **Ctrl + Shift + S**. The custom subtotals row appears here immediately.

SAVE the workbook and leave it open for the next exercise.

Managing Macro Security

Because of the proliferation of malicious software, Microsoft has set up Excel so that after it's installed, you cannot execute macros from a file you open (even an explicitly macro-enabled workbook) until you read the notification and click Enable Content. If you never plan to run macros or if you're skeptical about your office colleagues, you can turn off macros completely. You can also turn off the notifications and enable all macros, if you work in an office such as a financial services provider where macros are in use constantly, you trust the source of the Excel workbooks, and notifications would only get in the way.

STEP BY STEP **Manage Macro Security**

CERTIFICATION READY? **1.4.5**

How do you manage macro security?

GET READY. USE the workbook from the previous exercise.

1. On the DEVELOPER tab, in the Code group, click **Macro Security**.
2. In the Trust Center dialog box (see Figure 9-45), click **Disable all macros with notification** to have Excel warn you whenever an opened workbook contains macros, enabling you to turn those macros on or off based on your decision.

Figure 9-45

Trust Center with macro protection settings

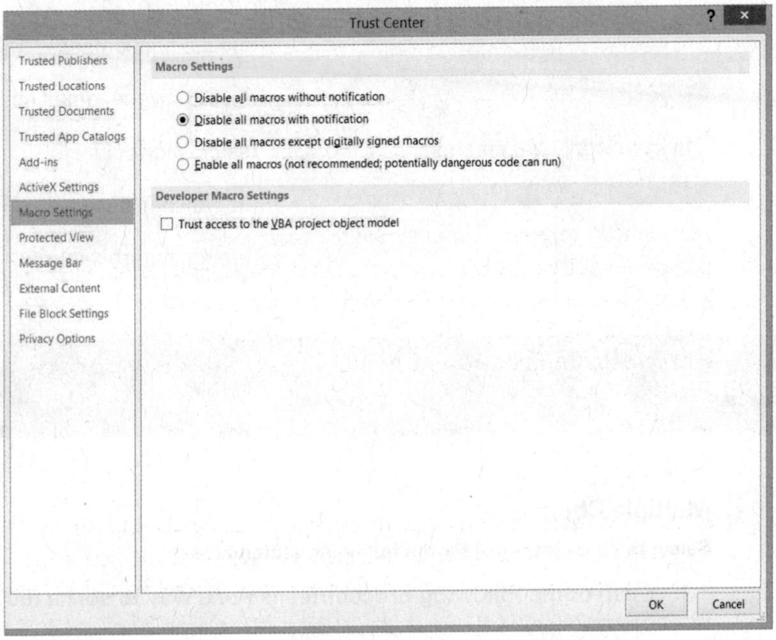

3. Click **OK**.

CLOSE the workbook. CLOSE Excel.

SKILL SUMMARY

In this lesson you learned how:	Exam Objective	Objective Number
To import data.	Open non-native files directly in Excel.	1.1.4
	Import files.	1.1.3
	Append data to worksheets.	2.1.1
To ensure your data's integrity.	Set data validation.	1.3.8
To sort data.		
To filter data.		
To outline and subtotal data.	Create outlines.	2.3.5
	Collapse groups of data in outlines.	2.3.6
	Insert subtotals.	2.3.7
To set up data in a table format.	Apply styles to tables.	3.2.1
	Band rows and columns.	3.2.2
	Remove styles from tables.	3.2.4
	Define titles.	3.1.3
	Insert total rows.	3.2.3
	Add and remove cells within tables.	3.1.2
	Filter records.	3.3.1
	Sort data on multiple columns.	3.3.2
	Change sort order.	3.3.3
	Remove duplicates.	3.3.4
	Move between tables and ranges.	3.1.1
To save work with macros.	Assign shortcut keys.	1.4.12
	Record simple macros.	1.4.7
	Manage macro security.	1.4.5

Knowledge Assessment

Multiple Choice

Select the best response for the following statements.

1. Which of the following procedures is *not* a way to sort a table by the contents of one column?
   a. Click the Sort button in the Sort & Filter group of the DATA tab.
   b. Click an AutoFilter button in the total row.
   c. Click an AutoFilter button in the field names row.
   d. Click the Filter button in the Sort & Filter group of the DATA tab.

2. Which is a valid reason you'd want to convert a table to a range?
   a. To clear the sorting criteria and start over.
   b. To prepare for deleting a column.
   c. To prepare for importing new data from a non-Excel file.
   d. To prepare to change its conditional formatting.

3. Which of the following is the difference between an Auto Outlined worksheet and a worksheet with multiple groups?
   a. None.
   b. Only an Auto Outlined worksheet may contain total rows.
   c. An Auto Outlined worksheet contains only one button for collapsing and expanding.
   d. Only a multi-grouped worksheet can cluster rows and columns.

4. Which of the following is a correct reference to the cell in the Total Sale column on the rightmost side of a table called Auction Items?
   a. Table[Auction Items(Total Sale)]
   b. Auction Items(Total Sale)
   c. Auction Items[#Totals]
   d. #Totals[Total Sale]

5. Which of the following procedures is *not* a way to filter a table by the contents of one column?
   a. Click the criterion button on the slicer.
   b. Right-click the cell whose contents you want for the criterion, and click Filter in the menu.
   c. Click the Filter button in the Sort & Filter group of the DATA tab.
   d. Click the AutoFilter button in the total row at the bottom.

6. Which of the following attributes is *not* a potential criterion for an AutoFilter sort?
   a. Font color
   b. Font style
   c. Cell color
   d. Cell icon

7. Which is the difference between an AutoFiltered range of records in a list and a table?
   a. None.
   b. A table maintains its sort order after you close and then open it again.
   c. A table given a title enables its field names to be used in formulas in place of cell references.
   d. A table enables special subtotal functions for total rows.

8. Which characters may not be used to begin a field name in a table?
   a. = @ -
   b. $ = (
   c. % { [
   d. $ % @

9. Which is the reason you would want to record a macro with absolute references rather than relative?
   a. You want to preserve the integrity of any cells referenced by formulas in the macro.
   b. You want the values of any cells copied to the macro to be accurate.
   c. You want the results of any formulas produced by the macro to be accurate.
   d. You want the macro to reproduce its results in the same place each time.

10. From which of the following does Excel *not* have features for importing data?
    a. An active database
    b. A Web page
    c. A Web search
    d. An XML file

True / False

Circle T if the statement is true or F if the statement is false.

T F 1. You remove duplicate rows from a table the same way you would for a named range of AutoFiltered records.

T F 2. You cannot sort a table in alphabetical or numerical order for one column and by conditional formatting for another column at the same time.

T F 3. When importing data from a text file, you can tell Excel to recognize a character other than a comma as a field delimiter.

T F 4. You can have no more than two criteria in a custom AutoFilter.

T F 5. Immediately after you group together a cluster of adjacent rows, Excel prompts you to create a total row beneath it.

T F 6. Once you remove an automatic style from a table, it is no longer a table.

T F 7. The title given to a table appears above the field names row.

T F 8. The @ character is required before any reference to a specific value in a named row.

T F 9. Field names in a table, as opposed to a named range, must begin with an alphabetic character.

T F 10. Excel will not let any macro run in a worksheet without the user's direct approval, unless the option for that notification is explicitly turned off.

Competency Assessment

Project 9-1: Home Buying Comparison

You've created a list of homes available for sale in your neighborhood with some important characteristics you want to compare with one another. You're wondering whether your realtor is asking as much for your house as she could be asking. In this project, you'll generate a table, filter the table by multiple criteria, and calculate the average asking price for homes in the neighborhood that meet the criteria.

GET READY. LAUNCH Excel if it is not already open.

1. OPEN *09 Homes for Sale* from the files for this lesson.
2. SAVE the workbook as *09 Homes for Sale 3-19 Solution*.
3. Click any cell in the data range. On the HOME tab, in the Styles group, click Format as Table. Give the table the style Table Style Light 19. Click OK.
4. On the DESIGN tab, in the Table Style Options group, click First Column.
5. Click cell A23.
6. On the HOME tab, in the Editing group, click the down arrow button next to AutoSum. In the menu, click Average.
7. Click the filter button for Fireplace. In the menu, clear the checked boxes and then check the box for Y. Click OK.
8. Repeat this process for the Great Room column.
9. Click the down arrow beside Sq. Ft. In the menu, click Number Filters, and then click Greater Than Or Equal To.
10. In the Custom AutoFilter dialog box, next to is greater than or equal to, type 1900. Click OK. The table now shows all homes for sale in the neighborhood with a fireplace and a great room, and with 1,900 square feet or more. The total row shows the average asking price for only the six houses shown.

SAVE and CLOSE this workbook. Leave Excel open for the next project.

Project 9-2: Fundraising Revenue Summary

You're a volunteer for a charity that generates money for worthwhile causes by gathering together famous athletes for public events. In this project, you will generate collapsible subtotal rows for a list of moneys raised at various tour stops.

GET READY. LAUNCH Excel if it is not already open.

1. OPEN *09 4Strong Tour Revenues.xlsx* from the files for this lesson. Note that this is *not* the *.xlsm* solution file you created during the Recording a Basic Macro exercise.
2. SAVE the workbook as *09 4Strong Tour Revenues Summary Solution.xlsx*.
3. Select the range A4:D232.
4. On the DATA tab, in the Outline group, click Subtotal.
5. In the Subtotal dialog box, set At each change in to Tour Stop Date. Set Use function to Sum. Check only the Sales box under Add subtotal to. Check Summary below data. Click OK.
6. After the groups are all added, in the Outline group, click Hide Detail.
7. Expand column D if necessary to make room for the Grand Total at the bottom.

SAVE and CLOSE this workbook. Leave Excel open for the next project.

Proficiency Assessment

Project 9-3: Hot Sauce Sales Report

You work in the accounting department of a nonprofit organization that manufactures jars of various recipes of homemade hot sauce, for resale by charity groups. In this project, you combine three sheets worth of data into a single sheet that can be expanded and collapsed, and that shows subtotals for each month.

GET READY. LAUNCH Excel if it is not already open.

1. OPEN *09 Hot Sauce Sales Q1* from the files for this lesson.
2. SAVE the workbook as *09 Hot Sauce Sales Q1 Report Solution*.
3. Click the February tab.
4. Select cell range A6:J30.
5. Copy the range to the January worksheet starting at cell A32.
6. Adjust the formulas in Gross Sales for the copied region to point to the correct cells in the Unit Prices worksheet, starting with cell B9.
7. Repeat the process, copying the range in the March worksheet to January, with the top left cell in A58. Be sure to correct the Gross Sales formulas.
8. Adjust the height of rows with column headers to more appropriately fit their contents.
9. Click cell B4 and type First quarter 2013.
10. Click cell A6 and type January. Repeat this for the respective cells in the other two months' tables.
11. Delete the February and March worksheets.
12. Rename the January worksheet First quarter.
13. Select row 17 and insert a new row.
14. Create AutoSum formulas for January Unit Sales columns B through J, giving a special boldface to J17.
15. Copy row 17 and insert it below the Unit Sales tables for the other two months.
16. Create AutoSum formulas for January Gross Sales columns B through I. Copy these formulas to February and March.
17. Select rows 8 through 16. On the DATA tab, in the Outline group, click the Group button.
18. Repeat this process for the remaining five tables.
19. Select columns B through I. Click the Group button.

20. Select the entire worksheet. In the Outline group, click Hide Detail. Both rows and columns are collapsed to reveal just the sales summaries. Widen column J, if necessary.

SAVE and CLOSE this workbook. Leave Excel open for the next project.

Project 9-4: Employee Archive Rescue

You're helping a colleague to restore some lost data, by reconstructing it from old backups. One of these backup files is an .MDB format database file. In this project, you'll import the data from that file into an Excel table, and correcting the formulas inside that table.

GET READY. LAUNCH Excel if it is not already open.

1. OPEN a Blank workbook.

2. On the DATA tab, in the Get External Data group, click From Access.

3. In the Select Data Source dialog box, locate and select 09CMKPAY.mdb. Click Open.

4. In the Import Data dialog box, leave the settings for a new Table in an Existing worksheet. Set the target location to the upper left corner cell. Click OK.

5. After the table is imported, use the Name Manager dialog box to rename the table from Table__09_CMKPAY to Employees.

6. Change all the contents of columns D through L to Accounting number format.

7. Insert a new column between LTD and NET_PAY and name it Total Deductions.

8. Click cell L2 and type the following formula:
   =SUM(Employees[@[FED_TAX]:[LTD]])

9. Note how the colon in-between the two field names FED_TAX and LTD makes this reference into a range, just as it would if you entered D2:K2. The formula you entered automatically fills down the rest of the column.

10. For cell M2, type the following formula:
    =[GROSS_PAY]-[Total deductions]

11. Note that when the formula is used *inside* the table, which is the case here, you can omit the @ prefix from the reference, which otherwise means "on this row."

12. Because the rest of the column is nonblank, use the fill handle to fill the new formula down to cell M11.

13. Group columns E through K together and collapse them.

SAVE the workbook as *09 Charter Employees Solution*. Leave the workbook open for the next project.

Mastery Assessment

Project 9-5: Macro for Table Reconciliation

The remainder of the employees file you're trying to reconstruct resides in an old Excel worksheet. The problem is that the data in that worksheet is all comprised of totals from consolidation formulas, and each employee record is a header for a collapsed group. When you copy the records, you end up copying everything except the data used in the consolidation, resulting in a sheet full of #REF! errors. You need a copying function that Excel doesn't have. In this project, you'll record a macro that fulfills the job of copying just the data you need, saving you the hassle of copying all the errors and weeding them out.

GET READY. USE the workbook from the previous project.

1. OPEN *09 2006+ Employees.xls* from the data files for this lesson. Dismiss the usual security warning.

2. Arrange the 2006+ Employees and Charter Employees windows side-by-side.

3. In the 2006+ Employees window, click the Sheet1 tab. Click cell A7 (ID).

4. In the Charter Employees window, create a new worksheet Sheet2. Click cell A1.

5. In the Charter Employees window, on the DEVELOPER tab, click the Code group to ensure Use Relative References is highlighted.

6. In the Code group, click Record Macro.

7. In the Record Macro dialog box, name the macro CopyValRecord. Assign it the keystroke Ctrl + Shift + C. Click OK to begin recording.

8. Switch to the 2006+ Employees window.

9. Hold down Shift and click cell P7 to select the entire row.

10. On the HOME tab, in the Clipboard group, click Copy.

11. Switch to the Charter Employees window.

12. In the Clipboard group, click Paste Values. The headings row should appear in the worksheet.

13. Press Left Arrow, and then press Down Arrow. Cell A2 should be the active cell.

14. Switch to the 2006+ Employees window. Press Left Arrow, and then press Down Arrow.

15. Switch to the Charter Employees window. On the DEVELOPER tab, in the Code group, click Stop Recording.

16. To test the macro's effectiveness, leave the same cells selected in both worksheets, and press Ctrl + Shift + C. In a moment, Excel should have copied over the next row, ID# 38448, which is actually three rows down in the old employees' worksheet.

17. Keep pressing Ctrl + Shift + C until the last customer, ID #55412, has been copied into row 36.

SAVE the newly loaded workbook as *09 Charter Employees Solution.xlsm*. CLOSE the 2006+ Employees workbook and leave Charter Employees open for the next project.

Project 9-6: **Reconciling Tables**

You now have two employee tables of different ages imported into separate worksheets. You need to reconcile them into a single table, but the problem is that you need to keep some aspects of both tables and discard certain aspects of others. The solution is to make the tables structurally equivalent to one another, copy the data from one into the other, and then trim any unwante parts from the product.

GET READY. USE the *09 Charter Employees Solution.xlsm* workbook from the prev project.

1. OPEN Sheet2. Change the number formats for cell ranges F2:L36 and Accounting. Change the number formats for M2:M36 to Percentag places.

2. OPEN Sheet1 and expand the group. Change the heading a new column to the left of 401K named 401K rate. Add Employee Name called Title, First name, and Last B. Rename the REGULAR_HO column Hours. A Rate. Delete the Total Deductions column.

3. Copy the contents of Sheet2 to the en fields align with one another.

4. Relocate the rows with full-na of the table in Sheet1, so t format.

5. Click any cell in th Duplicates.

6. In the Re numb

7. Because all the old employees were apparently duplicated, delete the Employee Name column.

8. Re-insert the Total deductions column and just before the NET_Pay column, type its formula, this time being careful to omit 401K rate from the calculation.

9. Enter a new formula for the NET_PAY column starting at the top row and filling down, subtracting Total deductions from GROSS_PAY.

10. Widen any partly-visible columns if necessary.

11. Apply boldface to the final column of the table.

SAVE the workbook as *09 Charter Employees Solution 2.xlsm*. CLOSE Excel.

Circling Back 2

The Graphic Design Institute tracks many different types of data on its students, such as name, country of origin, the general type of program (accelerated or regular), tuition costs, and the month in which the student starts his or her program. In addition, instructors must maintain grade books, which track grades for each student for each course taken. In this set of projects, you apply formatting to cells and entire worksheets, search and replace text in individual worksheets and across a workbook, and sort, filter, and subtotal data tables.

Project 1: Formatting Cells and Ranges

In this project, you format cells using character attributes, cell styles, and a number of other techniques to give the Student Roster workbook a professional finish.

GET READY. LAUNCH Excel if it is not already running.

1. OPEN *Student Roster*.
2. Select cells A1:E1. On the HOME tab, in the Alignment group, click the Merge & Center button.
3. Select cells A2:E2. On the HOME tab, in the Alignment group, click the Merge & Center button.
4. Select cells A3:E3. Right-click and select Delete. In the Delete dialog box, ensure Shift cells up is selected and click OK.
5. Select cells A3:E3. On the HOME tab, in the Font group, click the Bold button.
6. Select columns C and D. On the HOME tab, in the Alignment group, click the Center button.
7. Click cell A1. On the HOME tab, in the Styles group, click the Cell Styles button arrow to display the gallery.
8. Select the Title style.
9. Select cell A2. On the HOME tab, in the Styles group, click the Cell Styles button arrow, and then under Themed Cell Styles, select Accent1.
10. Apply bold to cell A2.
11. Select cells D4:D46. On the HOME tab, in the Number group, open the Number Format drop-down menu and select Accounting.
12. In the Number group, click the Decrease Decimal button until no decimal places display.
13. Click cell A4. Click the VIEW tab, and in the Window group, click the Freeze Panes button arrow and select Freeze Panes.
14. SAVE the workbook as *Student Roster 1 Solution* in the Circling Back folder.

LEAVE the workbook open for the next project.

Project 2: Formatting Worksheets

Apply the formatting skills you learned in Lesson 6 to adjust the size of rows and columns in the Student Roster worksheet, add a header and footer, and fix the formatting of a repeated word using the Replace feature.

GET READY. USE the workbook you saved in the previous project.

1. Double-click the border between the rows 1 and 2 headings to automatically resize row 1 to fit the contents.

2. Select row 2. On the HOME tab, in the Cells group, click the Format button arrow, select Row Height, in the Row Height text box, type 18.75, and then click OK.

3. Double-click the border between the columns D and E headings to automatically resize column D to fit the contents.

4. Click the PAGE LAYOUT tab, and in the Themes group, click the Themes button arrow to open the gallery. Select the Integral theme.

5. Click cell A1. Click the HOME tab, and in the Font group, change the font size to 24.

6. Change the font size of the content in cell A2 to 14.

7. Select cells A3:E46. Change the font size to 12.

8. Adjust the size of each column as follows:

    Column A: 20

    Column B: 15

    Column C: 12

    Column D: 10

    Column E: 13

9. Click the VIEW tab, and in the Window group, click the Freeze Panes button arrow, and then select Unfreeze Panes.

10. Click the INSERT tab, and in the Text group, click the Header & Footer button.

11. Click the HEADER & FOOTER TOOLS DESIGN tab, in the Header & Footer group, click the Header button arrow, and then select Sheet1, Confidential, Page 1.

12. Click anywhere in the header. On the HEADER & FOOTER TOOLS DESIGN tab, in the Navigation group, click the Go to Footer button.

13. In the Header & Footer group, click the Footer button arrow and select the file name option, which is the sixth option in the list.

14. Press Ctrl + H to open the Find and Replace dialog box to the Replace tab. In the Find What box, type accelerated and press Tab. In the Replace With box, type Accelerated. Click the Options button and select the Match case checkbox. Click the Replace All button. After the words are replaced, click OK, and then click Close.

15. On the status bar, click the Normal view button to return to Normal view.

16. SAVE the workbook as *Student Roster 2 Solution* in the Circling Back folder, and then CLOSE the file.

LEAVE Excel open for the next project.

Project 3: Managing Worksheets

In this project, you help an instructor add the GPA worksheet to a grade book and reorganize the worksheets within the grade book. You will also show the instructor how easy it is to find and replace data across worksheets in a workbook.

GET READY. LAUNCH Excel if it is not already running.

1. OPEN *Grade Book* and *GPA*.

2. In the *GPA* workbook, right-click Sheet1 and select Move or Copy.

3. In the Move or Copy dialog box, open the To Book drop-down menu and select Grade Book.xlsx.

4. Under Before Sheet, select (move to end) and click OK. The GPA worksheet is added to the Grade Book workbook, and the GPA workbook closes.

5. In the *Grade Book* workbook, right-click the Sheet1 tab, select Rename, and type Graphic Design 1.

6. Rename the Sheet2 tab to Digital Media 1.

7. Rename the Sheet3 tab to Typography 1.

8. Rename the last sheet tab to GPA.

9. Click and hold the Digital Media 1 tab. Drag and drop it after the Typography 1 tab.

10. Right-click the GPA sheet tab, point to Tab Color, and under Standard Colors, select the Purple color box.

11. You must replace every instance of Herp in the Last Name column and Jesper in the First Name column with Byham and Richard A., respectively. The change must be made to the first three worksheets. To do so, select the Graphic Design 1, Typography 1, and Digital Media 1 sheet tabs. You can select all of them by pressing the Shift key while you click each sheet tab.

12. Press Ctrl + H to open the Find and Replace dialog box to the Replace tab.

13. In the Find What box, type Herp. In the Replace With box, type Byham. Click Replace All and then click OK.

14. In the Find and Replace dialog box, in the Find What box, type Jesper and in the Replace With box, type Richard A. Click Replace All and then click OK. Click Close to close the Find and Replace dialog box.

15. Right-click any of the grouped sheet tabs and select Ungroup Sheets.

16. Click each of the three sheet tabs and verify that the names were replaced appropriately.

17. SAVE the workbook as *Grade Book Solution* in the Circling Back folder, and then CLOSE the file.

LEAVE Excel open for the next project.

Project 4: **Working with Data**

The chief financial officer created a new worksheet based on the Contributions worksheet. She would like you to create two groups—one for organizations and another for individuals. In each group, she wants you to sort by the type of fund and then the contribution amount (highest to lowest), and provide subtotals for each fund in both groups.

GET READY. LAUNCH Excel if it is not already running.

1. OPEN *Contributions 2*.

2. Before row 4, insert a blank row. In cell A4, type Organizations and press Enter.

3. Insert two blank rows before row 23 (just before the row that contains "Voss, Florian"). In cell A24, type Individuals and press Enter.

4. Bold the content in cell A24. Select A24:C24. If necessary, click the HOME tab, in the Clipboard group, click the Format Painter button. Copy the formatting from cells A24:C24 to A4:C4.

5. Select rows 4:22.

6. Click the DATA tab, and in the Outline group, click the Group button. A group indicator line is added to the left of the row markers and an outline symbol on the row just below the end of the group.

7. Select rows 24 through 35 (all of the individuals in the Contributions worksheet).

8. On the DATA tab, in the Outline group, click the Group button.

9. Select rows 5:22.

10. On the DATA tab, in the Sort & Filter group, click Sort.

11. In the Sort dialog box, clear the My Data has Headers check box if it is selected. In the Sort By drop-down menu, select Column B. In the Order drop-down menu, ensure A to Z appears. Click the Add Level button. In the Then By drop-down menu, select Column C, and in the Order drop-down menu, select Largest to Smallest. Click OK.

12. Select rows 25:35 and repeat steps 10 and 11.

13. Select rows 3:35. Be sure the column headings (in row 3) are included in the selection.

14. On the DATA tab, in the Outline group, click Subtotal. The Subtotal dialog box appears.

15. In the At Each Change In list box, select Fund.

16. In the Use Function list box, verify that Sum appears.

17. In the Add Subtotal To list box, verify that only Amount is selected.

18. Near the bottom of the dialog box, verify that only Replace Current Subtotals and Summary Below Data are selected.

19. Click OK. Excel inserts subtotal rows after each type of fund in both groups.

20. Highlight row 45 (the Total Contributions row). Use the Format Painter to copy formatting from row 45 to row 44.

21. Delete row 45.

22. SAVE the workbook as *Contributions Sorted Solution* in the Circling Back folder, and then CLOSE the file.

CLOSE Excel.

LESSON SKILL MATRIX

Skills	Exam Objective	Objective Number
Using Formulas to Conditionally Summarize Data	Demonstrate how to apply the SUMIF function.	4.3.1
	Demonstrate how to apply the COUNTIF function.	4.3.3
	Demonstrate how to apply the AVERAGEIF function.	4.3.2
Using Formulas to Look up data in a workbook		
Adding Conditional Logic Functions to Formulas		
Using Formulas to Modify Text	Demonstrate how to use the RIGHT, LEFT, and MID functions.	4.4.1
	Demonstrate how to use the TRIM function.	4.4.2
	Demonstrate how to use the UPPER and LOWER functions.	4.4.3
	Demonstrate how to use the CONCATENATE function.	4.4.4

©AtnoYdur /iStockphoto

KEY TERMS

- **arguments**
- **conditional formula**
- **criteria**
- **lookup functions**
- **table**
- **table array**

©AtnoYdur /iStockphoto

Fabrikam, Inc. uses several of Excel's analytical tools to review sales data during strategic planning activities. Fabrikam's owners created a bonus program as part of the company's employee-retention efforts and to encourage individual sales agents and all employees to support the total sales goals. The bonus is based on years of service and when an agent reaches his or her sales goal for the year. Fabrikam realizes that all back office employees support the sales agents and so it gives a bonus to the entire staff if the total sales goal is met. To determine which agents and employees will receive the performance bonus, Fabrikam's accountants must create formulas to analyze the company's sales data. Excel's built-in formulas are the perfect solution to compute and display all the calculations the accountants need. You learn to apply these formulas in the exercises in this lesson.

SOFTWARE ORIENTATION

The FORMULAS Tab

In this lesson, you use commands on the FORMULAS tab to create formulas to conditionally summarize data, look up data, apply conditional logic, and modify text. The FORMULAS tab is shown in Figure 10-1.

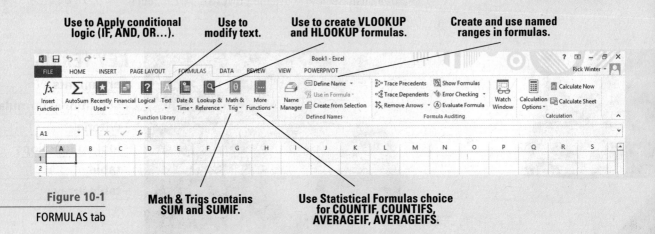

Figure 10-1

FORMULAS tab

USING FORMULAS TO CONDITIONALLY SUMMARIZE DATA

Bottom Line

As you learn in Lesson 4, "Using Basic Formulas," a formula is an equation that performs calculations—such as addition, subtraction, multiplication, and division—on values in a worksheet. When you enter a formula in a cell, the formula is stored internally and the results are displayed in the cell. Formulas give results and solutions that help you assess and analyze data. As you learned in Lesson 6, "Formatting Cells and Ranges," you can use a conditional format—which changes the appearance of a cell range based on a criterion—to help you analyze data, detect critical issues, identify patterns, and visually explore trends.

Conditional formulas add yet another dimension to data analysis by summarizing data that meets one or more criteria. **Criteria** can be a number, text, or expression that tests which cells to sum, count, or average. A conditional formula is one in which the result is determined by the presence or absence of a particular condition. Conditional formulas used in Excel include the functions SUMIF, COUNTIF, and AVERAGEIF that check for one criterion, or their counterpoints SUMIFS, COUNTIFS, and AVERAGEIFS that check for multiple criteria.

Using SUMIF

The SUMIF function calculates the total of only those cells that meet a given criterion or condition. The syntax for the SUMIF function is SUMIF(Range, Criteria, *Sum_range*). The values that a function uses to perform operations or calculations in a formula are called **arguments**. Thus, the arguments of the SUMIF function are Range, Criteria, and Sum_range, which, when used together, create a conditional formula in which only those cells that meet a stated Criteria are added. Cells within the Range that do not meet the criterion are not included in the total. If you use the numbers in the range for the sum, the *Sum_range* argument is not required. However, if you are using the criteria to test which values to sum from a different column, then the range becomes the tested values and the *Sum_range* determines which numbers to total in the same rows as the matching criteria. In this chapter, optional arguments will be in italics.

STEP BY STEP   **Use the SUMIF Function**

Table 10-2 explains the meaning of each argument in the SUMIF syntax. Note that if you omit Sum_range from the formula, Excel evaluates and adds the cells in the range if they match the criterion.

Table 10-2

Arguments in the
SUMIF syntax

Argument	Explanation
Range	The range of cells that you want the function to evaluate. Also add the matched cells if the Sum_range is blank.
Criteria	The condition or criterion in the form of a number, expression, or text entry that defines which cells will be added.
Sum_range	The cells to add if the corresponding row's cells in the Range match the criteria. If this is blank, use the Range for both the cells to add and the cells to evaluate the criteria against.

GET READY. LAUNCH Excel.

1. OPEN the *10 Fabrikam Sales* file for this lesson, and SAVE it to the Lesson 10 folder as *10 Fabrikam Sales Solution*.

2. Select **C20**. Click the **FORMULAS** tab and in the Function Library group, click **Math & Trig**. Scroll and click **SUMIF**. The Function Arguments dialog box opens with text boxes for the arguments, a description of the formula, and a description of each argument.

3. In the Function Arguments dialog box, click the **Collapse Dialog** button for the Range argument. This allows you to see more of the worksheet. Select the cell range **C5:C16**. Press **Enter**. By doing this, you apply the cell range that the formula will use in the calculation.

4. In the Criteria box, type **>200000** and press **Tab**. Figure 10-2 shows that the Sum_range text box is not bold. This means that this agrument is optional. If you leave the Sum_range blank, Excel sums the cells you enter in the Range box. You now applied your criteria to sum all values that are greater than $200,000.

Figure 10-2

The Function Arguments dialog box guides you in building SUMIF formulas.

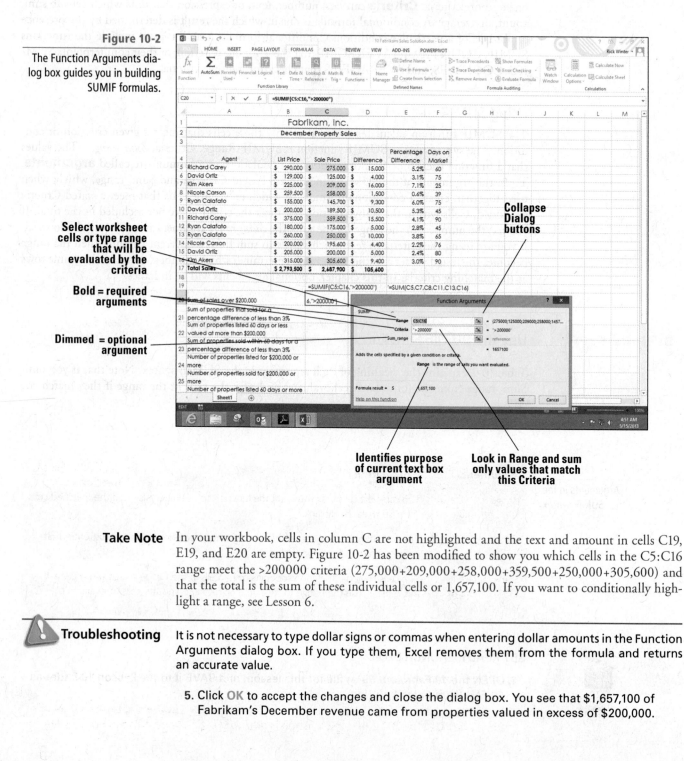

Take Note   In your workbook, cells in column C are not highlighted and the text and amount in cells C19, E19, and E20 are empty. Figure 10-2 has been modified to show you which cells in the C5:C16 range meet the >200000 criteria (275,000+209,000+258,000+359,500+250,000+305,600) and that the total is the sum of these individual cells or 1,657,100. If you want to conditionally highlight a range, see Lesson 6.

Troubleshooting   It is not necessary to type dollar signs or commas when entering dollar amounts in the Function Arguments dialog box. If you type them, Excel removes them from the formula and returns an accurate value.

5. Click **OK** to accept the changes and close the dialog box. You see that $1,657,100 of Fabrikam's December revenue came from properties valued in excess of $200,000.

6. If for some reason you need to edit the formula, select the cell that contains the function, and on the FORMULAS tab, or in the Formula Bar, click the Insert Function button to return to the Function Arguments dialog box (see Figure 10-3).

Figure 10-3

Insert Function buttons allow you to return to the Function Arguments dialog box.

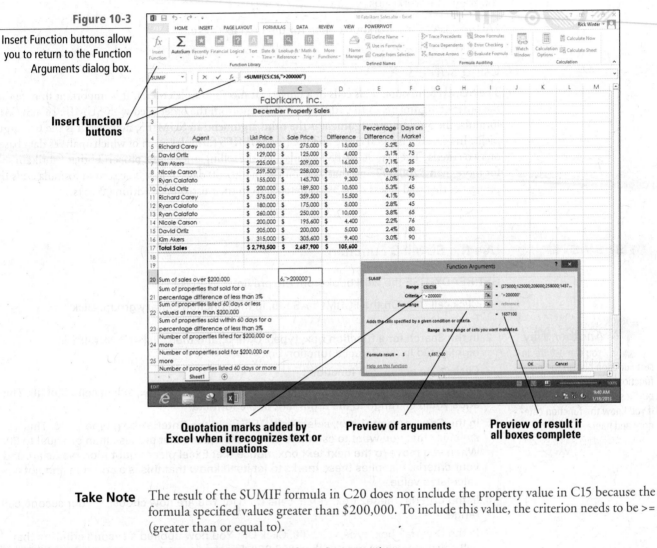

Insert function buttons

Quotation marks added by Excel when it recognizes text or equations

Preview of arguments

Preview of result if all boxes complete

Take Note   The result of the SUMIF formula in C20 does not include the property value in C15 because the formula specified values greater than $200,000. To include this value, the criterion needs to be >= (greater than or equal to).

7. Click OK or press Esc if you have no changes.

8. Select cell C21, and in the Function Library group, click Recently Used, and then click SUMIF to once again open the Function Arguments dialog box. The insertion point should be in the Range box.

Take Note   When you click Recently Used, the last function that you used appears at the top of the list. Similarly, when you click Insert Function, the Insert Function dialog box opens with the last used function highlighted.

9. In the Range field, select cells E5:E16. The selected range is automatically entered into the text box. Press Tab.

Take Note   You do not need to collapse the dialog box as you did in Step 3. You can directly highlight the range if the dialog box is not in the way. Another option is to move the dialog box by dragging the title bar.

10. In the Criteria box, type <3% and press Tab. You enter the criteria to look at column E and find values less than 3%.

11. In the Sum_range field, select cells C5:C16. The formula in C21 is different that the formula in C20. In C21, the criteria range is different than the sum range. In C20, the

criteria range and the sum range are the same. In C21, SUMIF checks for values in column E that are less than 3% (E8 is the first one) and finds the value in the same row and column C (C8 in this case) and adds this to the total. Click **OK** to accept your changes and close the dialog box. Excel returns a value of $1,134,200.

12. SAVE the workbook.

PAUSE. LEAVE the workbook open for the next exercise.

Using SUMIFS

The SUMIFS function adds cells in a range that meet multiple criteria. It is important to note that the order of arguments in this function is different from the order used with SUMIF. In a SUMIF formula, the Sum_range argument is the third argument; in SUMIFS, however, it is the first argument. In this exercise, you create and use two SUMIFS formulas, each of which analyzes data based on two criteria. The first SUMIFS formula adds the selling price of the properties that Fabrikam sold for more than $200,000 and that were on the market 60 days or less. The second formula adds the properties that sold at less than 3% difference from their listed price within 60 days.

STEP BY STEP   **Use the SUMIFS Function**

GET READY. USE the workbook from the previous exercise.

1. Click cell **C22**. On the FORMULAS tab, in the Function Library group, click **Insert Function**.

Another Way
You can use the Insert Function button to find a function or one of the function buttons in the Function Library if you know the function category and name.

2. In the Search for a function box, type **SUMIFS**, and then click **Go**. SUMIFS is highlighted in the Select a function box.

3. Click **OK** to accept the function.

4. In the Function Arguments dialog box, in the Sum_range box, select cells **C5:C16**. This adds your cell range to the argument of the formula.

5. In the Criteria_range1 box, select cells **F5:F16**. In the Criteria1 box, type **<=60**. This specifies that you want to calculate only those values that are less than or equal to 60. When you move to the next text box, notice that Excel places quotation marks around your criteria. It applies these marks to let itself know that this is a criterion and not a calculated value.

6. In the Criteria_range2 box, select cells **C5:C16**. You are now choosing your second cell range.

7. In the Criteria2 box, type **>200000**. Click **OK**. You now applied a second criterion that will calculate values greater than 200,000. Excel calculates your formula, returning a value of $742,000.

8. Select **C23** and in the Function Library group, click **Recently Used**.

9. Select **SUMIFS**. In the Sum_range box, select **C5:C16**.

10. In the Criteria_range1 box, select cells **F5:F16**. Type **<=60** in the Criteria1 box.

11. In the Criteria_range2 box, select cells **E5:E16**. Type **<3%** in the Criteria2 box and press **Tab**. To see all arguments, scroll back to the top of the dialog box. The Function Arguments dialog box should look like Figure 10-4.

Figure 10-4

SUMIFS formula applies two or more criteria.

Function Arguments	? ×
SUMIFS	
Sum_range C5:C16	= {275000;125000;209000;258000;1457...
Criteria_range1 F5:F16	= {60;75;25;39;75;45;90;45;65;76;80;90}
Criteria1 "<=60"	= "<=60"
Criteria_range2 E5:E16	= {0.0517241379310345;0.0310077519...
Criteria2 "<3%"	= "<3%"
	= 433000

Preview indicates total will be 433000.

Adds the cells specified by a given set of conditions or criteria.

Sum_range: are the actual cells to sum.

Formula result = $ 433,000

Help on this function   OK   Cancel

Troubleshooting   It is a good idea to press Tab after your last entry and preview the result of the function to make sure you entered all arguments correctly.

12. Click OK. After applying this formula, Excel returns a value of $433,000.

13. SAVE the workbook.

PAUSE. LEAVE the workbook open for the next exercise.

The formulas you use in this exercise analyze the data on two criteria. You can continue to add up to 127 criteria on which data can be evaluated.

Because the order of arguments is different in SUMIF and SUMIFS, if you want to copy and edit these similar functions, be sure to put the arguments in the correct order (first, second, third, and so on).

Using COUNTIF

In a conditional formula, the COUNTIF function counts the number of cells in a given range that meet a specific condition. The syntax for the COUNTIF function is COUNTIF(Range, Criteria). The Range is the range of cells to be counted by the formula, and the Criteria are the conditions that must be met in order for the cells to be counted. The condition can be a number, expression, or text entry. In this exercise, you practice using the COUNTIF function twice to calculate values of homes sold and listed >=200,000. The ranges you specify in these COUNTIF formulas are prices of homes. The criterion selects only those homes that are $200,000 or more.

STEP BY STEP   **Use the COUNTIF Function**

GET READY. USE the workbook from the previous exercise.

Another Way
You can also choose Insert Function and Search for the function by

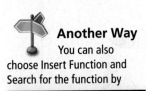

CERTIFICATION READY?   4.3.3

How do you create a formula that counts the number of cells within a range that meets a criterion?

1. Select C24. In the Function Library group, click More Functions, select Statistical, and click COUNTIF.

2. In the Function Arguments dialog box, in the Range box, select cells B5:B16.

3. In the Criteria box, type >=200000 and press Tab. Preview the result and click OK. You set your criteria of values greater than or equal to $200,000. Excel returns a value of 9.

4. Select C25 and in the Function Library group, click Recently Used.

5. Select COUNTIF. In the Functions Arguments box, in the Range box, select cells C5:C16.

6. In the Criteria box, type >=200000 and press Tab. Preview the result and click OK. Excel returns a value of 7 when the formula is applied to the cell.

7. SAVE the workbook.

PAUSE. LEAVE the workbook open for the next exercise.

Using COUNTIFS

The COUNTIFS formula counts the number of cells within a range that meet multiple criteria. The syntax is COUNTIFS(Criteria_range1, Criteria1, Criteria_range2, Criteria2, and so on). You can create up to 127 ranges and criteria. In this exercise, you perform calculations based on multiple criteria for the COUNTIFS formula.

STEP BY STEP　　**Use the COUNTIFS Function**

GET READY. USE the workbook from the previous exercise.

1. Select **C26**. In the Function Library group, click **Insert Function**.
2. In the Search for a function box, type **COUNTIFS** and then click **Go**. COUNTIFS is highlighted in the Select a function box.
3. Click **OK** to accept the function and close the dialog box.
4. In the Function Arguments dialog box, in the Criteria_range1 box, type **F5:F16**. You selected your first range for calculation.
5. In the Criteria1 box, type **>=60** and press **Tab**. The descriptions and tips for each argument box in the Function Arguments dialog box are replaced with the value when you navigate to the next argument box (see Figure 10-5). The formula result is also displayed, enabling you to review and make corrections if an error message occurs or an unexpected result is returned. You now set your first criterion. Excel shows the calculation up to this step as a value of 8.

Another Way
In previous examples, you collapse the dialog box and select the range, select the range without collapsing the dialog box, and you can also type the range as in this example.

Figure 10-5

Arguments and results for COUNTIFS formula

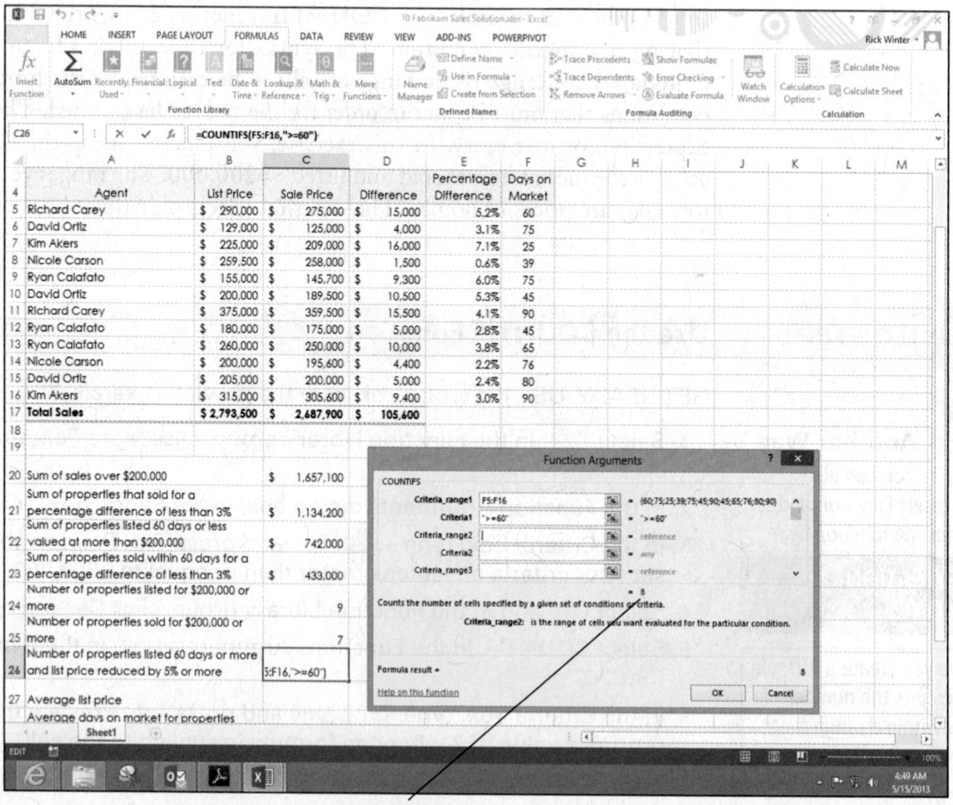

Preview formula result. Watch this change as each criterion is added.

6. In the Criteria_range2 box, select cells E5:E16. You selected your second range to be calculated.

7. In the Criteria2 box, type >=5% and press Tab to preview. Click OK. Excel returns a value of 2.

8. SAVE the workbook.

PAUSE. LEAVE the workbook open for the next exercise.

A cell in the range you identify in the Function Arguments dialog box is counted only if all of the corresponding criteria you specified are TRUE f or that cell. If a criterion refers to an empty cell, COUNTIFS treats it as a 0 value.

Take Note When you create formulas, you can use the wildcard characters, question mark (?) and asterisk (*), in your criteria. A question mark matches any single character; an asterisk matches any sequence of characters. If you want to find an actual question mark or asterisk, type a grave accent (`) preceding the character. You apply this technique later in the lesson.

Using AVERAGEIF

The AVERAGEIF formula returns the arithmetic mean of all the cells in a range that meet a given criteria. The syntax is similar to SUMIF and is AVERAGEIF(Range, Criteria, *Average_range*). In the AVERAGEIF syntax, Range is the set of cells you want to average. For example, in this exercise, you use the AVERAGEIF function to calculate the average number of days that properties valued at $200,000 or more were on the market before they were sold. The range in this formula is B5:B16 (cells that contain the listed value of the homes that were sold). The criterion is the condition against which you want the cells to be evaluated, that is, >=200000. Average_range is the actual set of cells to average—the number of days each home was on the market before it was sold. As in the SUMIF formula, the last argument, Average_range, is optional if the range contains the cells that both match the criteria and are used for the average. In this exercise, you first find the average of all cells in a range and then find a conditional average.

STEP BY STEP **Use the AVERAGEIF Function**

GET READY. USE the workbook from the previous exercise.

1. Select C27 and in the Function Library group, click More Functions. Select Statistical and click AVERAGE.

2. In the Number1 box, type B5:B16 and click OK. A mathematical average for this range is returned.

3. Select C28 and in the Function Library group, click Insert Function.

CERTIFICATION READY? **4.3.2**

How do you create a formula that averages the number of cells within a range that meets a criterion?

4. Select AVERAGEIF from the function list or use the function search box to locate and accept the AVERAGEIF function. The Function Arguments dialog box opens.

5. In the Function Arguments dialog box, in the Range box, select cells B5:B16.

6. In the Criteria box, type >=200000.

7. In the Average_range box, select F5:F16 and press Tab to preview the formula. In the preview, Excel returns a value of 63.33 (see Figure 10-6).

Figure 10-6

Results for AVERAGEIF formula

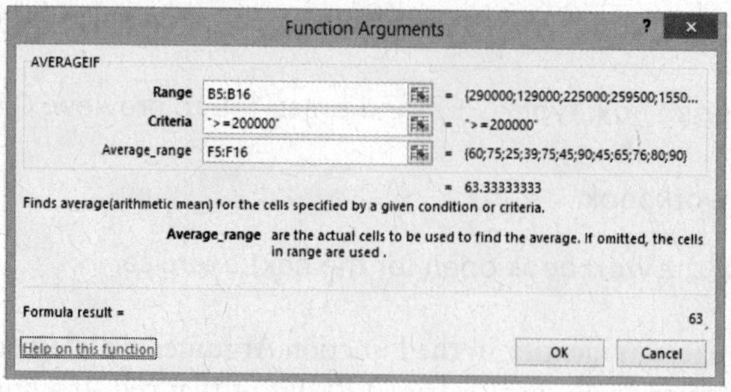

8. Click **OK** to close the dialog box.

9. SAVE the workbook.

PAUSE. LEAVE the workbook open for the next exercise.

Using AVERAGEIFS

An AVERAGEIFS formula returns the average (arithmetic mean) of all cells that meet multiple criteria. The syntax is AVERAGEIFS(Average_range, Criteria_range1, Criteria1, Criteria_range2, Criteria2, and so on). You learn to apply the AVERAGEIFS formula in the following exercise to find the average of a set of numbers where two criteria are met.

STEP BY STEP | **Use the AVERAGEIFS Function**

GET READY. USE the workbook from the previous exercise.

1. Click cell **C29**. In the Function Library group, click **Insert Function**.

2. Type **AVERAGEIFS** in the Search for a function box and click **Go**. AVERAGEIFS is highlighted in the Select a function box.

3. Click **OK** to accept the function and close the dialog box.

4. In the Function Arguments dialog box, in the Average_range box, select cells **F5:F16**. Press **Tab**.

5. In the Criteria_range1 box, select cells **B5:B16** and press **Tab**. You selected your first criteria range.

6. In the Criteria1 box, type **<200000**. You set your first criteria.

7. In the Criteria_range2 box, select cells **E5:E16** and press **Tab**. You have selected your second criteria range.

8. In the Criteria2 box, type **<=5%** and press **Tab**. Click **OK**. Excel returns a value of 60.

9. SAVE the *10 Fabrikam Sales Solution* workbook, and then close it.

PAUSE. LEAVE Excel open for the next exercise.

You entered only two criteria for the SUMIFS, COUNTIFS, and AVERAGEIFS formulas you created in the previous exercises. However, in large worksheets, you often need to use multiple criteria in order for the formula to return a value that is meaningful for your analysis. You can enter up to 127 conditions that data must match in order for a cell to be included in the conditional summary that results from a SUMIFS, COUNTIFS, or AVERAGEIFS formula.

The following statements summarize how values are treated when you enter an AVERAGEIF or AVERAGEIFS formula:

- If Average_range is omitted from the function arguments, the range is used.

- If a cell in Average_range is an empty cell, AVERAGEIF ignores it.

- If the entire range is blank or contains text values, AVERAGEIF returns the #DIV0! error value.

- If no cells in the range meet the criteria, AVERAGEIF returns the #DIV/0! error value.

USING FORMULAS TO LOOK UP DATA IN A WORKBOOK

Bottom Line

When worksheets contain long and sometimes cumbersome lists of data, you need a way to quickly find specific information within these lists. This is where Excel's lookup functions come in handy. **Lookup functions** are an efficient way to search for and insert a value in a cell when the desired value is stored elsewhere in the worksheet or even in a different workbook. VLOOKUP and HLOOKUP are the two lookup formulas that you use in this section. These functions can return the contents of the found cell. As you work through the following exercises, note that the term **table** refers to a range of cells in a worksheet that can be used by a lookup function.

Using VLOOKUP

The "V" in VLOOKUP stands for vertical. This formula is used when the comparison value is in the first column of a table. Excel goes down the first column until a match is found and then looks in one of the columns to the right to find the value in the same row. The VLOOKUP function syntax is vwLOOKUP(Lookup_value, Table_array, Col_index_num, Range_lookup). See Figure 10-7 for a graphical explanation of the function.

Figure 10-7

Vertical lookup (VLOOKUP)

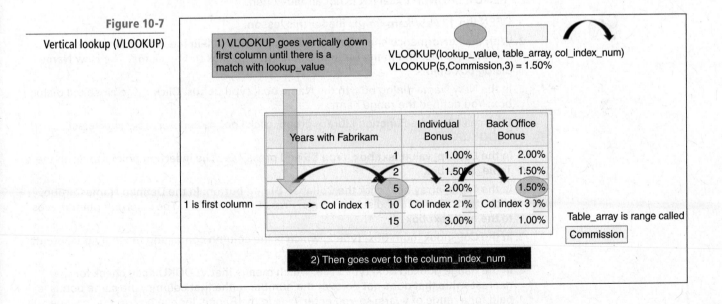

Table_array is a table of text, numbers, or values that you use for the formula. It can either be a range of cells (A1:D5) or a range name (Commission). The data in a **table array** must be arranged in rows and columns. In the next exercise, you apply this formula to calculate employee bonuses. When working with VLOOKUP functions and arguments, there are several key points to keep in mind:

- If Lookup_value is smaller than the smallest value in the first column of Table_array, VLOOKUP returns the #N/A error value.

- Table_array values can be text, numbers, or logical values. Uppercase and lowercase text is equivalent.

- The values in the first column of the Table_array selection must be placed in ascending sort order; otherwise, VLOOKUP might not give the correct value. The lookup table you use in this exercise lists years of service in ascending order.

- Range_lookup is an optional fourth argument not shown in Figure 10-7.

- If the Range_lookup argument is True or omitted, an exact or approximate match is returned. If VLOOKUP cannot find an exact match, it returns the next largest value that is less than the value you specified in Lookup_value.

- If Range_lookup is False, VLOOKUP finds only an exact match. If an exact match is not found, the error value #N/A is returned.

Take Note Range names or cell references used in VLOOKUP or HLOOKUP are not case sensitive, so you can type them in uppercase, lowercase, or any combination of uppercase and lowercase characters. Also, the VLOOKUP and HLOOKUP function names are not case sensitive.

STEP BY STEP   Use the VLOOKUP Function

GET READY. LAUNCH Excel if it is not already open.

1. OPEN the *10 Fabrikam Bonus* file for this lesson.

2. With the Performance sheet active, select cells A15:C20 in the worksheet. Click the FORMULAS tab, and in the Defined Names group, click Define Name. The New Name dialog box opens.

3. In the New Name dialog box, in the Name box, type Bonus. Click OK to close the dialog box. You defined the range name.

4. Click cell E5, in the Function Library group, click Lookup & Reference, and select VLOOKUP.

5. In the Lookup_value text box, type B5 and press Tab. The insertion point moves to the Table_array box.

6. In the Table_array box, click the Collapse Dialog button. In the Defined Names group, click Use in Formula and select Bonus. Press Enter and Tab. The insertion point moves to the next text box.

7. In the Col_index_num box, type 2, which is the column containing the individual bonus amounts. Press Tab.

8. In the Range_lookup box, type True, which means that VLOOKUP can check for the nearest value that does not go over the number in the first column; the same bonus is paid for a range of years, so you enter True in the Range_lookup box so that a value will be returned for all agents. The Function Arguments dialog box should look similar to the one shown in Figure 10-8. Click OK. Excel returns a value of 2.5%.

Figure 10-8

VLOOKUP Function Arguments
dialog box

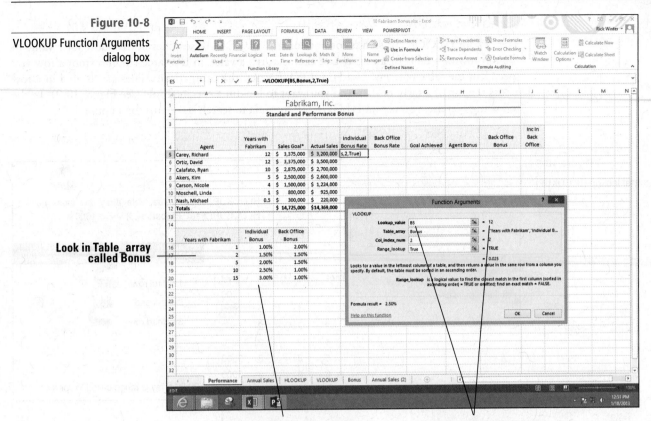

**Look in Table_array
called Bonus**

**Find in column number 2 value
is in same row as 10 (closest
without going over 12). Answer
is 0.025 or 2.5%.**

Lookup_value is B5 (which is 12)

9. Using the fill handle in cell E5, copy the formula to the range E6:E11. This calculates bonus rates for the other sales agents. The #N/A error message appears in cell E11 because a value is not available for agents who have been employed for less than one year. (Agents become eligible for a bonus only after a full year of service.) You change this error message in another exercise.

10. Click in cell F5 and type =VLOOKUP(B5,Bonus,3). Notice that the ScreenTip gives you information and help as you go. This looks up values in the third column of the Bonus range. Press Enter.

11. Copy the formula from F5 to the range F6:F11.

12. SAVE the workbook as *10 Fabrikam Bonus Solution*.

PAUSE. LEAVE the workbook open for the next exercise.

Take Note   Entering True in the Range_lookup box returns the closest value. False returns only an exact value. If you leave the Range_lookup box empty as it is in Step 10 in the previous exercise, Excel enters True when you click OK.

Using HLOOKUP

The "H" in HLOOKUP stands for horizontal. HLOOKUP searches horizontally for a value in the top row of a table or an array and then returns a value in the same column from a row you specify in the table or array. Use HLOOKUP when the comparison values are located in a row across the top of a table of data and you want to look in a specified row (see Figure 10-9). In the following exercise, you use an HLOOKUP formula to search standards for a house.

Figure 10-9

Horizontal lookup (HLOOKUP)

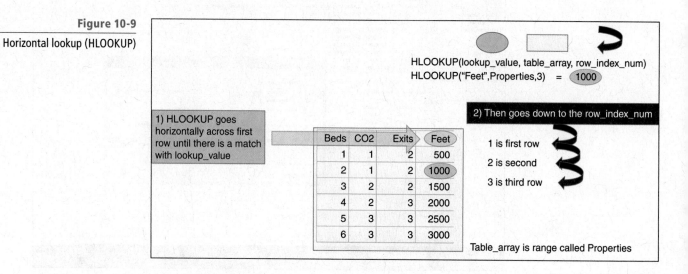

HLOOKUP and VLOOKUP are similar in format. Figure 10-10 and Table 10-3 compare the syntax of the two functions.

Figure 10-10

Comparing VLOOKUP and HLOOKUP

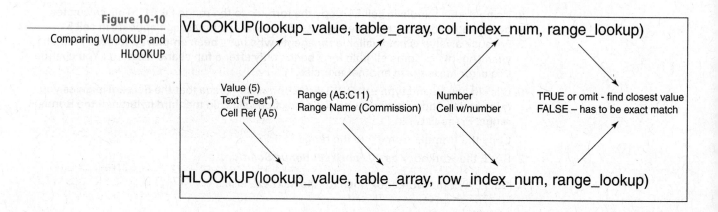

Table 10-3

Function Syntax for VLOOKUP
and HLOOKUP

Argument	Notes
Lookup_value	The value to be found in the first column or row; this can be a constant value, a text value enclosed in quotation marks, or the address or name of a cell that contains a numeric or text constant.
Table_array	Two or more columns of data. Use a reference to a range or a range name. The values in the first column of Table_array are the values searched by Lookup_value in VLOOKUP. The values in the first row are values searched by Lookup_value in HLOOKUP.
Col_index_num	The numeric position of the column that is to be searched for by VLOOKUP. The column number in Table_array from which the matching value must be returned. A Col_index_num of I returns the value in the first column in Table_array; a Col_index_num of 2 returns the value in the second column in Table_array, and so on.
Row_index_num	The numeric position of the row that is to be searched for by HLOOKUP.
Range_lookup	A logical value that specifies whether it is ready for VLOOKUP or HLOOKUP to find an approximate match. If the function is to return the nearest value, even when there is no match, this value should be set to True; if an exact match is required, this value should be set to False; if this argument is not included, the function assumes the value to be True.

STEP BY STEP Use the HLOOKUP Function

GET READY. USE the workbook from the previous exercise.

1. Click on the Standards worksheet tab to move to the Standards worksheet.
2. Click cell F11, and in the Function Library group, click Lookup & Reference, and select HLOOKUP.
3. In the Lookup_value text box, type E11. This is the cell you will change and the box previews to Feet because that is what is currently typed in cell E11.
4. In the Table_array text box, type A1:D7. This will be the range of cells you will look in.
5. In the Row_index_num, type D11+1. This currently evaluates to 3. If you just do the number of beds that is in D11, you don't come down enough rows because of the labels in the first row of the Table_array. The number of beds is actually one row more than the number of beds because the labels (Beds, CO2, Exits, and Feet) count as the first row and row 2 is for 1 bed.
6. In Range_lookup, type FALSE because you want an exact match. The screen should look like Figure 10-11. Click OK. In the following steps, you will change the values in D11 and D11 and see what happens when there are different values and when there is not an exact match.

Figure 10-11

HLOOKUP Function Arguments

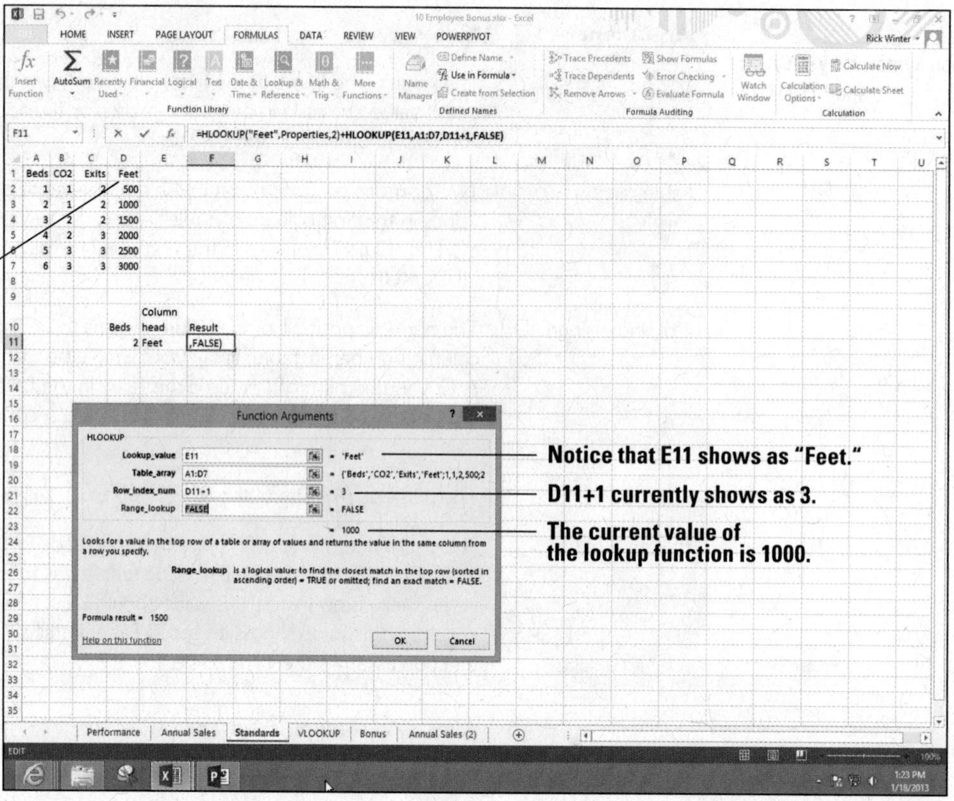

Go to column headed by Feet and count down starting with the first row and you get 1000.

Notice that E11 shows as "Feet."

D11+1 currently shows as 3.

The current value of the lookup function is 1000.

7. In cell D11, type 5 and notice that the result in F11 changes to 2500.

8. In cell E11, type CO2 and notice that the result changes to the result for the CO2 column for 5 beds, which is 3.

9. Click cell D11, and then type 7. Notice that you get a #REF! error because the table goes up to five beds.

10. In cell D11, type 1. Cell F11 displays a result of 1.

11. SAVE the workbook.

PAUSE. LEAVE the workbook open for the next exercise.

It might be difficult to remember the syntax for an HLOOKUP or VLOOKUP function. You can always use the Function Arguments dialog box to help you remember the order of the arguments for any and all formulas. When you click in each field, review the tips that appear on the right side of each box, as well as the explanation below the argument boxes that tells the purpose of each argument in the formula.

ADDING CONDITIONAL LOGIC FUNCTIONS TO FORMULAS

Bottom Line

You can use the AND, OR, and NOT functions to create **conditional formulas** that result in a logical value, that is, True or False. Such formulas test whether a series of conditions evaluate to true or false. In addition, you can use the IF conditional formula that checks if a calculation evaluates as true or false. You can then tell IF to return one value (text, number, or logical value) if the calculation is true or a different value if it is false.

Using IF

The result of a conditional formula is determined by the state of a specific condition or the answer to a logical question. An IF function sets up a conditional statement to test data. An IF formula returns one value if the condition you specify is true and another value if it is false. The IF function requires the following syntax: IF(Logical_test, Value_if_true, Value_if_false). In this exercise, you use an IF function to determine who achieved his goal and is eligible for the performance bonus.

STEP BY STEP

Use the IF Function

GET READY. USE the workbook from the previous exercise.

1. Click the **Performance** worksheet tab to make it the active worksheet.
2. Click cell **G5**. In the Function Library group, click **Logical** and click **IF**. The Function Arguments dialog box opens.
3. In the Logical_test box, type **D5>=C5**. This component of the formula determines whether the agent has met his or her sales goal.
4. In the Value_if_true box, type **Yes**. This is the value returned if the agent met his or her goal.
5. In the Value_if_false box, type **No** and click **OK**.
6. With G5 still selected, use the fill handle to copy the formula to **G6:G12**. Excel returns the result that three agents earned the performance award by displaying Yes in the cells (see Figure 10-12).

Figure 10-12

Using the IF function

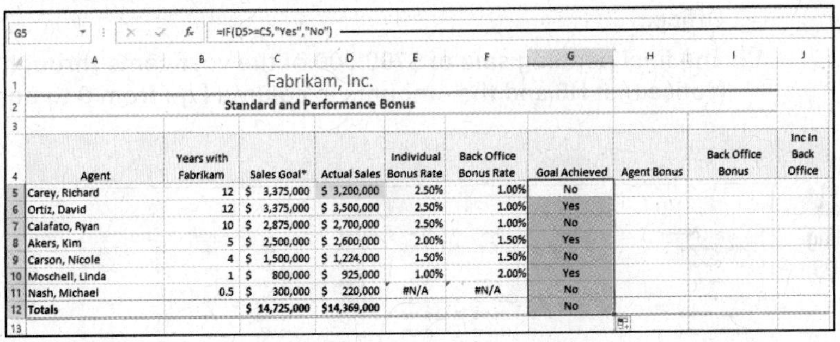

Agent	Years with Fabrikam	Sales Goal*	Actual Sales	Individual Bonus Rate	Back Office Bonus Rate	Goal Achieved	Agent Bonus	Back Office Bonus	Inc In Back Office
Carey, Richard	12	$ 3,375,000	$ 3,200,000	2.50%	1.00%	No			
Ortiz, David	12	$ 3,375,000	$ 3,500,000	2.50%	1.00%	Yes			
Calafato, Ryan	10	$ 2,875,000	$ 2,700,000	2.50%	1.00%	No			
Akers, Kim	5	$ 2,500,000	$ 2,600,000	2.00%	1.50%	Yes			
Carson, Nicole	4	$ 1,500,000	$ 1,224,000	1.50%	1.50%	No			
Moschell, Linda	1	$ 800,000	$ 925,000	1.00%	2.00%	Yes			
Nash, Michael	0.5	$ 300,000	$ 220,000	#N/A	#N/A	No			
Totals		$ 14,725,000	$14,369,000			No			

The IF formula in the Formula bar

Take Note The entire company is evaluated on making the goal, and bonuses are awarded to the back office staff if the company goal is met. The result in G12 is used for the formulas in column I. When you copy, the formatting is included.

7. Click the **Auto Fill Options** button in the bottom right corner of the range and choose **Fill Without Formatting**.
8. In cell H5, type **=IF(G5="Yes",E5*D5,0**. Before you complete the formula, notice the ScreenTip, the cells selected, and the colors (see Figure 10-13). Move the mouse pointer to each of the arguments and they become a hyperlink. E5 is the individual bonus rate and D5 is the actual sales. The bonus is the rate times the sales.

Figure 10-13

Help items as you type a formula

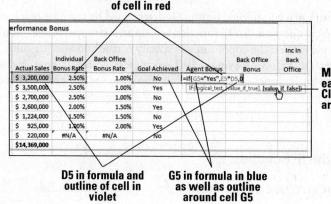

E5 in formula and outline of cell in red

Mouse pointer highlights each argument in ScreenTip. Click on highlight to move to argument in formula.

D5 in formula and outline of cell in violet

G5 in formula in blue as well as outline around cell G5

9. Press **Enter** to finish the formula.

Take Note In some cases, Excel completes the formula. In Step 8, the closing parenthesis was not added, and Excel was able to complete the formula.

10. Use the fill handle in H5 to copy the formula from to H6:H11.

11. In I5, type **=IF($G$12="Yes",F5*D5,0)**, and then press **Enter**.

 Cross Ref Remember that dollar signs before the column and row indicate an absolute reference. When you copy the formula, $G$12 remains the same in every cell.

12. Use the fill handle in I5 to copy the formula from cto I6:I11. Notice that Richard Carey, the Senior Partner, did not receive an Agent Bonus and there was no bonus for Back Office.

13. The final pending sale of $700,000 of the year came through. In D5, type **$3,900,000**. Notice that H5 and the amounts in column I go from 0 to bonuses (see Figure 10-14).

Figure 10-14

Bonuses change by adding sales to D5.

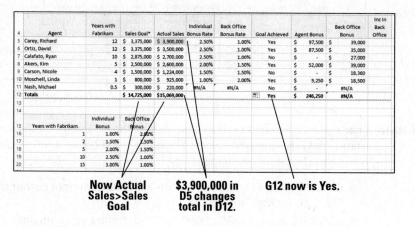

Now Actual Sales>Sales Goal

$3,900,000 in D5 changes total in D12.

G12 now is Yes.

14. SAVE the workbook.

PAUSE. LEAVE the workbook open for the next exercise.

Using AND

The AND function returns True if all its arguments are true, and False if one or more arguments are false. The Syntax is AND(Logical1, Logical2, and so on). In this exercise, you use the AND function to determine whether Fabrikam's total annual sales met the strategic goal and whether the sales goal exceeded the previous year's sales by 5 percent.

STEP BY STEP   Use the AND Function

GET READY. USE the workbook from the previous exercise.

1. Click the Annual Sales worksheet tab. Click the FORMULAS tab if necessary.
2. Click cell B6. In the Function Library group, click Logical and click the AND option. The Function Arguments dialog box opens with the insertion point in the Logical1 box.
3. Click cell B3, type <=, select cell B16, and press Enter. This argument represents the first condition: Did actual sales equal or exceed the sales goal? Because this is the first year, only one logical test is entered.
4. Select cell C6, click the Recently Used button, and click AND. In the Logical1 box, type C3<=C16. This is the same as the condition in Step 3 (sales exceed or equals sales goal).
5. In the Logical2 box, type C16>=B16*1.05 and press Tab. The preview of the formula returns True, which means that both conditions in the formula have been met. The AND function arguments are illustrated in Figure 10-15.

> **Another Way**
>
> Because you type only one condition in this formula, another option is to type =B3<=B16 directly in the cell without the AND function.

Figure 10-15

AND function arguments

AND condition

Result to be returned

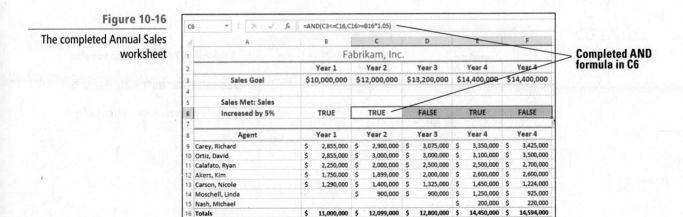

Formula description

6. Click OK to complete the formula.
7. Select cell C6 and copy the formula to D6:F6 (see Figure 10-16).

Figure 10-16

The completed Annual Sales worksheet

Completed AND formula in C6

	A	B	C	D	E	F
1			Fabrikam, Inc.			
2		Year 1	Year 2	Year 3	Year 4	Year 4
3	Sales Goal	$10,000,000	$12,000,000	$13,200,000	$14,400,000	$14,400,000
4						
5	Sales Met: Sales					
6	Increased by 5%	TRUE	TRUE	FALSE	TRUE	FALSE
7						
8	Agent	Year 1	Year 2	Year 3	Year 4	Year 4
9	Carey, Richard	$ 2,855,000	$ 2,900,000	$ 3,075,000	$ 3,350,000	$ 3,425,000
10	Ortiz, David	$ 2,855,000	$ 3,000,000	$ 3,000,000	$ 3,100,000	$ 3,500,000
11	Calafato, Ryan	$ 2,250,000	$ 2,000,000	$ 2,500,000	$ 2,500,000	$ 2,700,000
12	Akers, Kim	$ 1,750,000	$ 1,899,000	$ 2,000,000	$ 2,600,000	$ 2,600,000
13	Carson, Nicole	$ 1,290,000	$ 1,400,000	$ 1,325,000	$ 1,450,000	$ 1,224,000
14	Moschell, Linda		$ 900,000	$ 900,000	$ 1,250,000	$ 925,000
15	Nash, Michael				$ 200,000	$ 220,000
16	Totals	$ 11,000,000	$ 12,099,000	$ 12,800,000	$ 14,450,000	$ 14,594,000
17						

C6 formula: =AND(C3<=C16,C16>=B16*1.05)

8. SAVE the workbook.

PAUSE. LEAVE the workbook open for the next exercise.

Again, the AND function returns a True result only when both conditions in the formula are met. For example, consider the results you achieved in the preceding exercise. Sales in the second year exceeded sales for the previous year; therefore, the first condition is met. Year 2 sales also exceeded Year 1 sales by 5 percent. Because both conditions are met, the formula returns a True result.

Now consider the arguments for the logical tests for Year 3 (the formula in D6). Sales did not exceed the sales goal; therefore, the first argument returns a False value. However, sales did exceed the previous year's sales by 5 percent. When only one condition is met, the formula returns False.

Using OR

Although all arguments in an AND function have to be True for the function to return a True value, only one of the arguments in the OR function has to be True for the function to return a True value. The syntax for an OR formula is similar to that for an AND formula. With this formula, the arguments must evaluate to logical values such as True or False or references that contain logical values. In this exercise, you create a formula that evaluates whether sales agents are eligible for the back office bonus when they are new or when they did not get the sales bonus (less than 4 years with the company or did not get the agent bonus). The OR formula returns True if either of the conditions are True.

STEP BY STEP   **Use the OR Function**

GET READY. USE the workbook from the previous exercise.

1. Click on the **Performance** worksheet tab to activate this worksheet. Select **J5** and in the Function Library group, click **Logical** .

2. Click **OR**. The Function Arguments dialog box opens. You create a formula that answers the following question: Has Carey worked with the company for less than 4 years?

3. In the Logical1 box, type **B5<4** and press **Tab**.

4. In the Logical2 box, type **G5="No"** and press **Tab**. This argument answers the second question: Did Carey not achieve the sales goal? Each of the arguments evaluates to false and so the entire function evaluates to false.

5. Click **OK** to close the dialog box.

6. Select cell **J5** and copy the formula to **J6** through **J11**.

7. Cell J7 is the first in the column that returns a True value. To see each of the arguments, click cell **J7** and then click the **Insert Function** button and you return to the Function Arguments dialog box (see Figure 10-17).

Figure 10-17

OR Function Arguments

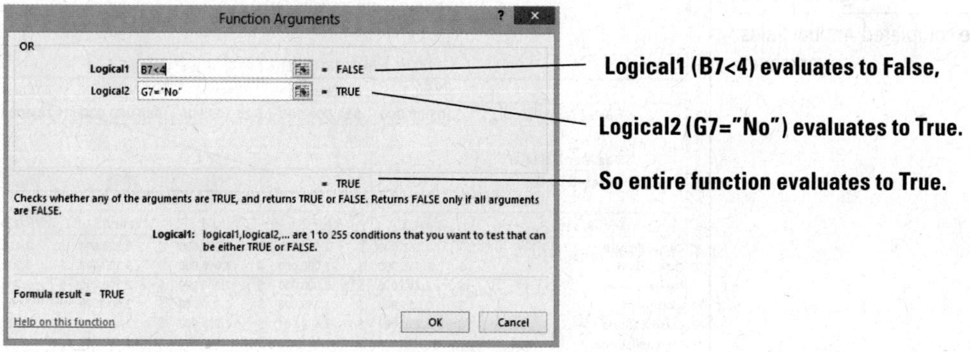

Logical1 (B7<4) evaluates to False,

Logical2 (G7="No") evaluates to True.

So entire function evaluates to True.

8. Click **OK** to close the dialog box and return to the workbook.

9. SAVE the workbook.

Take Note   As you add arguments, the Logical fields in the Function Arguments dialog box expand to allow you to enter multiple arguments.

PAUSE. LEAVE the workbook open for the next exercise.

Using NOT

The NOT function reverses the value of its arguments. Use NOT when you want to make sure a value is not equal to one particular value. If the logical value is FALSE, NOT returns TRUE. In the following exercise, you use the NOT function to answer the following question: Do we exclude this agent from the back office bonus?

STEP BY STEP **Use the NOT Function**

GET READY. USE the workbook from the previous exercise. The Performance worksheet should still be active.

1. Copy cell J4 to cell K4 and edit the label to say Not In Back Office.
2. Click cell K5. In the Function Library group, click the Logical button.
3. Select NOT from the list of logical formulas.
4. In the Function Arguments dialog box, type J5 and press Enter.
5. Copy cell K5 to cells K6 through K11. Notice that the values in K5 through K11 are the opposite of the values in column J.
6. SAVE the workbook.

PAUSE. LEAVE the workbook open for the next exercise.

Using IFERROR

An error message is returned when a formula does not contain sufficient or valid arguments to return a value. Use the IFERROR function to trap and handle errors in a formula. This function returns a value you specify if a formula evaluates to an error; otherwise, it returns the result of the formula. The syntax is IFERROR(Value, Value_if_error). In the IFERROR syntax, Value is the argument that is checked for an error. In the next exercise, you use this formula to determine eligible bonuses.

For this example, you change the functions in the Performance worksheet to no longer show #N/A because of the VLOOKUP function.

STEP BY STEP **Use the IFERROR Function**

GET READY. USE the workbook from the previous exercise and make sure the Performance worksheet is active.

1. Select cell E11 and click to place the insertion point after the = in the formula bar to edit the formula. You add the IFERROR formula to correct the formula error that gave the #N/A result in a previous exercise.
2. Type IFERROR(before VLOOKUP. Leave the existing formula intact. Press End to take you to the end of the formula.

Take Note Notice that we write function names such as IFERROR and VLOOKUP in all uppercase. These names are not case sensitive, but Microsoft always writes them in uppercase in the function lists and Help system because doing so makes reading functions much easier. Thus, it is best to get in the habit of using function names in uppercase.

3. At the end of the original formula, type ,0). As shown in Figure 10-18, the complete formula is =IFERROR(VLOOKUP(B11,Bonus,2,True),0). Be sure to include the closing parenthesis and the preceding comma or Excel returns an error that the formula is incorrect.

Troubleshooting When you start creating more complex formulas including functions within other functions, ensure that you use the same number of open parentheses as close parentheses.

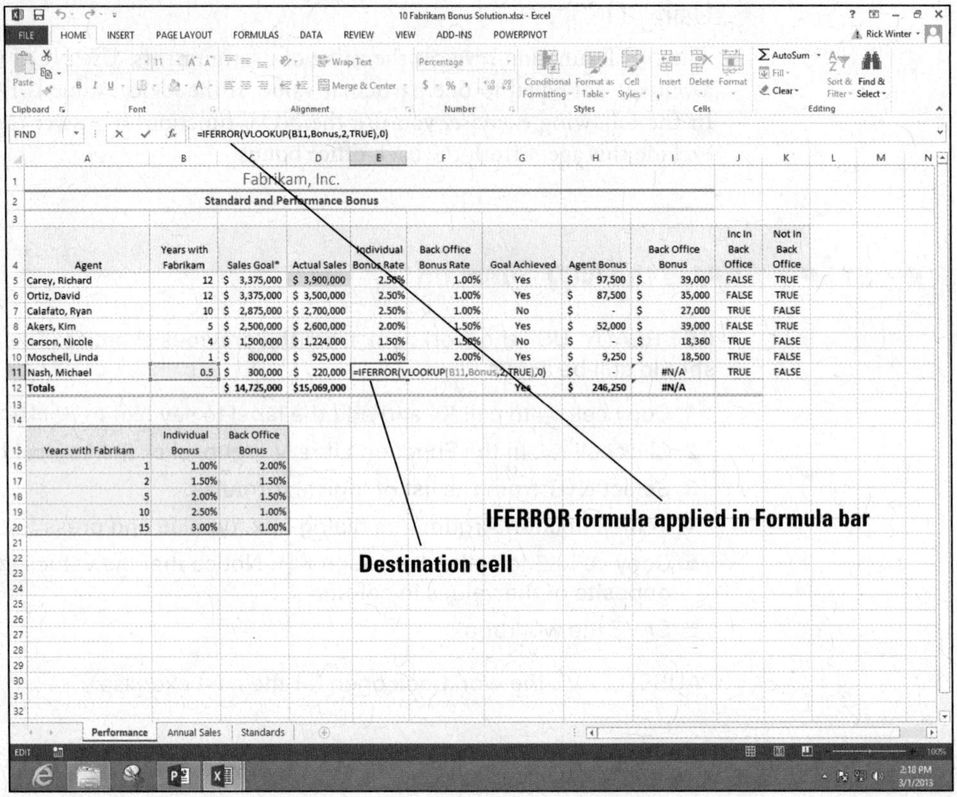

Figure 10-18

Editing a formula to enter 0
when an error occurs

4. Press **Enter**. The #N/A error message is replaced by 0. If you select cell **E11** and click
the **Insert Function** button next to the formula bar, the original VLOOKUP formula
appears in the Value box (first argument) in the IFERROR formula. As illustrated in
Figure 10-19, that argument returned a #N/A error. The Value_if_error box contains the
0 that replaces the error message.

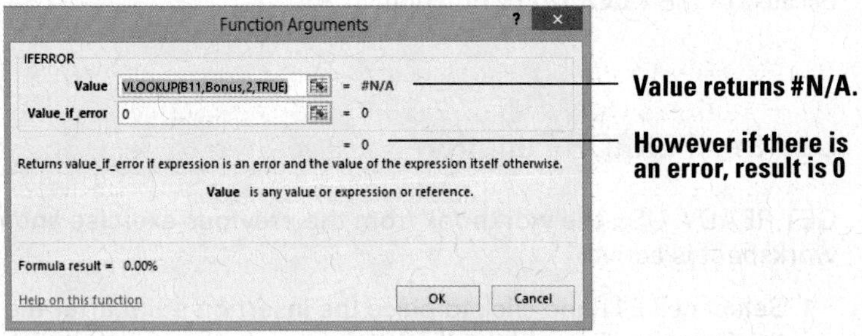

Figure 10-19

IFERROR function arguments

5. Click cell **F11** and edit the formula to include the IFERROR function
=IFERROR(VLOOKUP(B11,Bonus,3),0).

6. Copy the formulas in **E11:F11** to **E5** through **F10**. The workbook doesn't look like it
changes, but you should verify that this worked by changing B6 to 0 (as shown in
Figure 10-20).

Figure 10-20

Test of worksheet

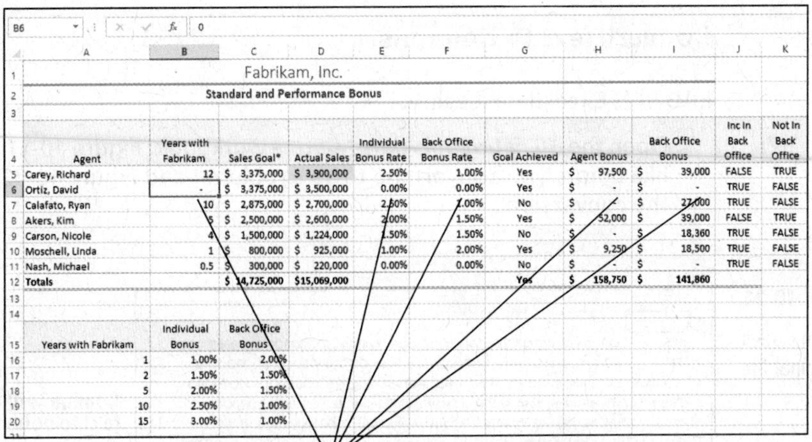

0 typed in B6 changed E6, F6, H6, and I6 to 0

7. Click **Undo** to reverse the change to cell B6 and return the worksheet to the proper values.

8. SAVE the workbook.

PAUSE. CLOSE the workbook and **LEAVE** Excel open for the next exercise.

IFERROR recognizes and evaluates the following errors: #N/A, #VALUE!, #REF!, #DIV/0!, #NUM!, #NAME?, or #NULL!. In this exercise, you replace the #N/A error message with 0".

USING FORMULAS TO MODIFY TEXT

Bottom Line

When you get files from other people or programs, you often have to do a significant amount of manipulation of the file. For example, sometimes you receive files in a text format with commas separating what should go in columns. The text is often not in the format that you need to use in Excel. Some text can be combined into one long string or other text can be all in lowercase or uppercase.

You might be familiar with Microsoft Word's Convert Text command that enables you to change the capitalization of text. Similarly, in Excel, you can use PROPER, UPPER, and LOWER formulas to capitalize the first letter in each word of a text string or to convert all characters to uppercase or lowercase. This section presents you with a text file from the alarm company. There is a lot of useful information in the file, but it is coded for the alarm system rather than for use in a spreadsheet. The company's president has asked you to keep the file confidential because it contains the codes for each employee, but he has also asked you to use your Excel knowledge to convert the information into a usable format.

Converting Text to Columns

You can use the Convert Text to Columns Wizard to separate simple cell content, such as first names and last names, into different columns. Depending on how your data is organized, you can split the cell contents based on a delimiter (divider or separator), such as a space or a comma, or based on a specific column break location within your data. In the following exercise, you convert the data in column A to two columns.

STEP BY STEP   **Convert Text to Columns**

LAUNCH Excel if necessary.

1. Open the *10 Fabrikam Alarm Codes* workbook. Figure 10-21 shows what the file looks like before you convert the rows to column and Figure 10-22 shows the same data after the conversion.

Figure 10-21

10 Fabrikam Alarm Codes original file

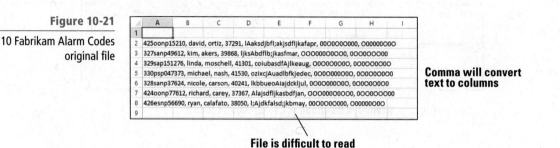

	A	B	C	D	E	F	G	H	I
1									
2	425oonp15210, david, ortiz, 37291, lAaksdjbfl;akjsdfljkafapr, 0000000000, O00000000								
3	327sanp49612, kim, akers, 39868, ljksAbdflb;jkasfmar, OO000000000, o00000000								
4	329sap151276, linda, moschell, 41301, coiubasdfAjlkeaug, 000000000, 000000000								
5	330psp047373, michael, nash, 41530, ozixcjAuadlbfkjedec, 0000000000, 000000000								
6	328sanp37624, nicole, carson, 40241, lkbbueoAiajdckljul, 0000000000, 000000000								
7	424oonp77612, richard, carey, 37367, Alajsdfljkasbdfjan, OO000000000, o00000000								
8	426esnp56690, ryan, calafato, 38050, l;Ajdkfalsd;jkbmay, 0000000000, O00000000								
9									

Comma will convert text to columns

File is difficult to read

2. Select cells **A2:A8**. Click the **DATA** tab and in the Data Tools group, click **Text to Columns**.

3. The Convert Text to Columns Wizard opens with Delimited selected as the default, because Excel recognizes that the data in the selected range is separated with commas. Click **Next** to move to the next step in the wizard.

4. Select **Comma** as the delimiter. If other delimiters are checked, deselect them

5. Click **Next**, and then click **Finish**.

6. Data is separated into seven columns. To help identify the columns, type the text in row 1 and increase the column widths so you can see the cell contents (see Figure 10-22).

Figure 10-22

Converted text

	A	B	C	D	E	F	G
1	ExtCodeEmpID	SpFirst	SpLast	Hire Date	Alarm	OCode1	Ocode2
2	425oonp15210	david	ortiz	37291	lAaksdjbfl;akjsdfljkafapr	0000000000	O00000000
3	327sanp49612	kim	akers	39868	ljksAbdflb;jkasfmar	OO000000000	o00000000
4	329sap151276	linda	moschell	41301	coiubasdfAjlkeaug	000000000	000000000
5	330psp047373	michael	nash	41530	ozixcjAuadlbfkjedec	0000000000	000000000
6	328sanp37624	nicole	carson	40241	lkbbueoAiajdckljul	0000000000	000000000
7	424oonp77612	richard	carey	37367	Alajsdfljkasbdfjan	OO000000000	o00000000
8	426esnp56690	ryan	calafato	38050	l;Ajdkfalsd;jkbmay	0000000000	O00000000
9							

Type column headers.

Double-click column borders to change column widths to match the widest column entries.

Another Way

You can also use text functions such as LEFT, MID, and RIGHT to convert text data from one column to multiple columns.

7. SAVE the workbook as *10 Fabrikam Alarm Codes Solution*.

PAUSE. LEAVE the workbook open for the next exercise.

USING LEFT

The LEFT function evaluates a string and takes any number of characters on the left side of the string. The format of the function is LEFT(Text, Num_chars). The first string in the Alarm Data workbook contains the employee's phone extension and floor number, which you grab by using the LEFT function.

STEP BY STEP   **Use the LEFT Function**

GET READY. USE the workbook from the previous exercise.

1. Click cell **H1**, type **Ext**, and in **I1**, type **Floor** to label the columns.

2. Select cell H2.

3. Click the FORMULAS tab. In the Function Library group, click Text and choose LEFT. The Function Arguments dialog box opens.

4. In the Text box, click A2 and press Tab.

5. In the Num_chars box, type 3 and press Tab. The preview of the result shows *425* (see Figure 10-23).

Figure 10-23

LEFT function arguments

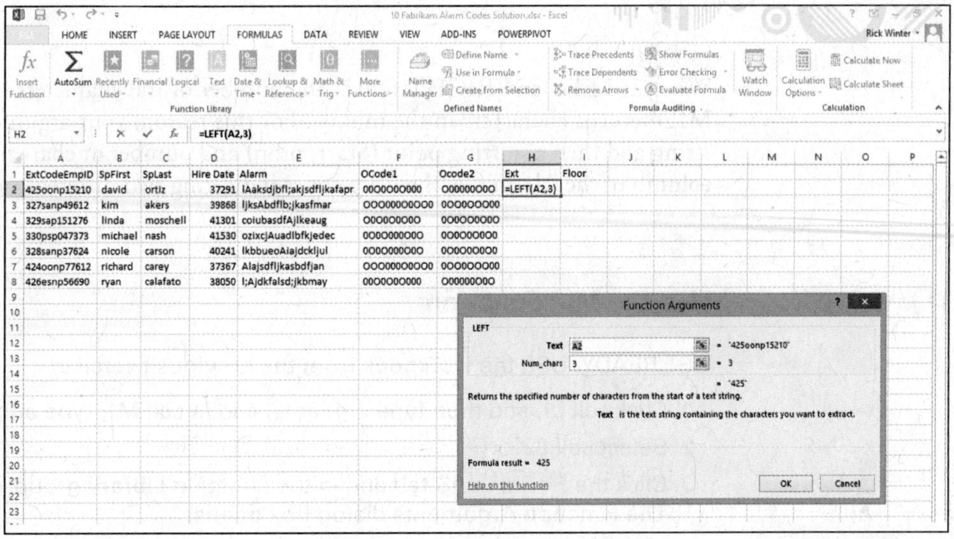

CERTIFICATION
READY? 4.4.1

How do you create a formula that extracts a certain number of characters on the left of a string?

6. Click OK and double-click on the fill handle in the bottom right of cell H2 to copy the formula in H2 from H3 to H8.

Take Note The result of this exercise on the LEFT function and the following exercises on the RIGHT and MID functions are shown in Figure 10-24.

7. Select cell I2, click the Recently Used button, and select LEFT.

8. In the Text box, type A2, press Tab, and in the Num_chars box, type 1. Click OK.

9. Copy the formula in I2 from I3 to I8.

10. SAVE the workbook.

PAUSE. LEAVE the workbook open for the next exercise.

USING RIGHT

The RIGHT function is almost identical to the LEFT function except that the function returns the number of characters on the right side of the text string. In the Alarm codes file, the first converted column contains the five-digit employee ID at the end, and the Alarm code in column E contains the employee's birth month.

STEP BY STEP **Use the RIGHT Function**

GET READY. USE the workbook from the previous exercise.

1. Click cell J1, and then type Birthday. In cell K1, type EmpID to label the columns.

2. Select cell J2.

3. Click the FORMULAS tab and in the Function Library group, click Text and choose RIGHT. The Function Arguments dialog box opens.

4. In the Text box, click E2 and press Tab.

5. In the Num_chars box, type 3 and press Tab. The preview of the result shows *apr*.
6. Click OK and copy the formula in J2 from J3 to J8.
7. Select cell K2, type =RIGHT(A2,5), and press Enter.
8. Copy the formula in K2 from K3 to K8.
9. SAVE the workbook.

PAUSE. LEAVE the workbook open for the next exercise.

Using MID

Whereas LEFT and RIGHT return the number of the characters on either side of a text string, MID returns characters in the middle. For this reason, your arguments need to include the Text string and then a starting point (Start_num) and number of characters (Num_chars). In the first column of the Alarm file, there are codes indicating two different categories of employees.

STEP BY STEP   **Use the Mid Function**

GET READY. USE the workbook from the previous exercise.

1. Click cell L1, and then type empcat1, and in cell M1, type empcat2 to label the columns.
2. Select cell L2.
3. Click the FORMULAS tab and in the Function Library group, click Text and choose MID. The Function Arguments dialog box opens.
4. In the Text box, click A2 and press Tab.

5. The starting point of the empcat1 value is the fourth character of (425oonp15210), so type a 4 in the Start_num text box.
6. In the Num_chars box, type 2. The preview of the result shows *oo*.
7. Click OK and copy the formula in L2 from L3 to L8.
8. Select cell M2, and type =MID(A2,6,2), and press Enter.
9. Copy the formula in M2 from M3 to M8.
10. SAVE the workbook. The worksheet should look like Figure 10-24.

Figure 10-24

Alarm Data workbook after
the MID functions are entered
and copied

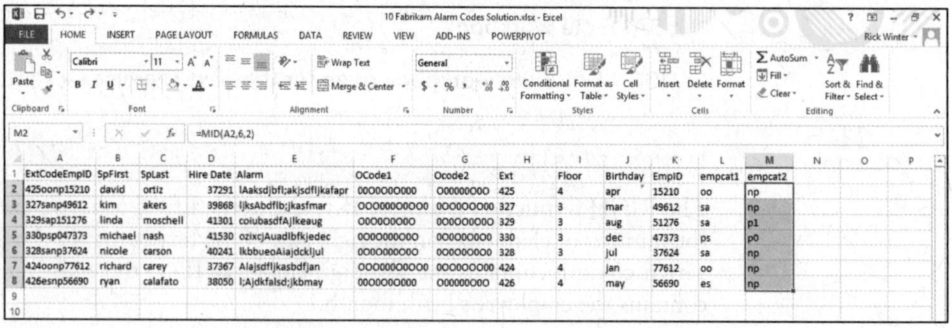

PAUSE. LEAVE the workbook open for the next exercise.

Using TRIM

Sometimes there are extra spaces in a cell—either at the end or the beginning of the string, especially after converting a text file like the alarm file—see the SPFirst and SPLast columns. The TRIM function removes characters at both ends of the string. There is only one argument: Text. Thus the syntax of the function is TRIM(Text).

| STEP BY STEP | **Use the TRIM Function** |

GET READY. USE the workbook from the previous exercise.

1. Click cell **N1**, type *first*, and in cell O1, type *last* to label the columns.
2. Click cell **N2**.
3. Click the **FORMULAS** tab and in the Function Library group, click Text and choose **TRIM**. The Function Arguments dialog box opens.
4. In the Text box, click **B2**. If you look closely, you see that the original value of cell B2 is "david" with a space before the first name.
5. Click **OK** and copy the formula in N2 from **N3** to **N8**.
6. Select cell **O2**, type =TRIM(C2), and press **Enter**.
7. Copy the formula in O2 from **O3** to **O8**.
8. SAVE the workbook. The results of the next few exercises appear in Figure 10-25.

PAUSE. LEAVE the workbook open for the next exercise.

CERTIFICATION READY?   **4.4.2**

How do you create a formula that removes blank characters at the beginning and/or end a string?

Using PROPER

The PROPER function capitalizes the first letter in a text string and any other letters in text that follow any character other than a letter. All other letters are converted to lowercase. In the PROPER(Text) syntax, Text can be text enclosed in quotation marks, a formula that returns text, or a reference to a cell containing the text you want to capitalize. In this exercise, you use PROPER to change lowercase text to initial capitals.

| STEP BY STEP | **Use the PROPER Function** |

GET READY. USE the workbook from the previous exercise.

1. Click cell **A11**, and then type First. In cell B11, type Last, and in cell C11, type Birthday to label the columns.
2. Select cell **A12**.
3. Click the **FORMULAS** tab and in the Function Library group, click Text and choose **PROPER**. The Function Arguments dialog box opens.
4. In the Text box, click **N2**. You see that *david* is converted to *David*.
5. Click **OK** and copy the formula in A12 from **A12** through **B18** (both First and Last name columns).
6. Select cell **C12**, type =PROPER(J2), and press **Enter**.
7. Copy the formula in C12 from **C13** to **C18**.
8. SAVE the workbook.

Take Note   You can see the results of this and the next few exercises in Figure 10-25 later in the lesson.

PAUSE. LEAVE the workbook open for the next exercise.

The PROPER function capitalizes the first letter in each word in a text string. All other letters are converted to lowercase. If you have an apostrophe such as David's, Excel recognizes the apostrophe as a break and capitalizes the result as David'S.

Using UPPER

The UPPER function allows you to convert text to uppercase (all capital letters) text. The syntax is UPPER(Text), with Text referring to the text you want converted to uppercase. Text can be a reference or a text string. In this exercise, you convert the employee category (empcat1 and empcat2) to uppercase.

| STEP BY STEP | Use the UPPER Function |

GET READY. USE the workbook from the previous exercise.

1. Click cell **D11**, type **EmpCat1**, and in cell **E11**, type **EmpCat2** to label the columns.
2. Click cell **D12**.
3. Click the **FORMULAS** tab and in the Function Library group, click **Text** and choose **UPPER**. The Function Arguments dialog box opens.
4. In the Text box, click **L2**. You see that *oo* is converted to *OO*.
5. Click **OK** and copy the formula in D12 from **D12** through **E18** (both EmpCat1 and EmpCat2 columns).
6. SAVE the workbook.

PAUSE. LEAVE the workbook open for the next exercise.

CERTIFICATION READY?   **4.4.3**

How do you create a formula that capitalizes all characters in a string?

Using LOWER

The LOWER function converts all uppercase letters in a text string to lowercase. LOWER does not change characters in text that are not letters. You use the LOWER formula in the following exercise to apply lowercase text in order to more easily tell an O (letter O) from a 0 (zero).

| STEP BY STEP | Use the LOWER Function |

GET READY. USE the workbook from the previous exercise.

1. Click cell **F11** and type **oCode1**. In cell **G11**, type **oCode2** to label the columns.
2. Click cell **F12**.
3. Click the **FORMULAS** tab and in the Function Library group, click **Text** and choose **LOWER**. The Function Arguments dialog box opens.
4. In the Text box, click **F2**. You see that *OOOOOOOOOO* is converted to *OOoOoOoOOO*.
5. Click **OK** and copy the formula in F12 from cell **F12** through **G18** (both oCode1 and oCode2 columns).
6. SAVE the workbook.

PAUSE. LEAVE the workbook open for the next exercise.

CERTIFICATION READY?   **4.4.3**

How do you create a formula that changes all the characters of a string to lowercase?

Using CONCATENATE

In some cases, you need to combine text strings together. Use CONCATENATE for this purpose. The syntax of the function is CONCATENATE(Text1, Text2, Text3 … up to Text30). In this case, you combine the first and last names into two different formats for future mail merges. In the first format, you use a comma to separate the last and first name but because the character can change to a semi-colon or other character, you type the comma in a cell and use the cell reference in the CONCATENATE formula.

| STEP BY STEP | Use the CONCATENATE Function |

GET READY. USE the workbook from the previous exercise.

1. Click cell **H11** and type **,** (a comma followed by a space), and in cell **I11**, type **First Last** to label the columns.
2. Click cell **H12**.
3. Click the **FORMULAS** tab and in the Function Library group, click **Text** and choose

CONCATENATE. The Function Arguments dialog box opens.

4. In the Text box, click cell B12 and press Tab. Click cell H11, press Tab, and click A12. In the preview area, you see "Ortiz, David."
5. Click OK and copy the formula in cell H12 from cell H13 through cell H18. The result is an error (see Figure 10-25). Notice that the string gets longer and longer and Ortiz is in every string.
6. In the Formula Bar, click the cell H11 reference and press F4 (Absolute). Cell H11 should become $H$11.

Figure 10-25

Copy formula for Last and First did not work.

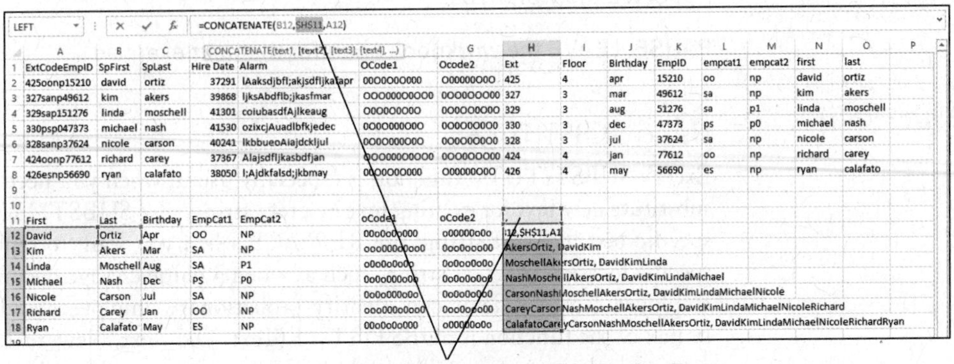

Comma string (H11) needs to become absolute.

7. Press Enter and copy the formula in cell H12 from cell H13 through cell H18 again. This time the formula is copied correctly.
8. Type a ; (a semi-colon followed by a space) in H11, and notice that all values in the column now have semi-colons instead of commas.
9. Select cell I12 and type =CONCATENATE(A12," ",B12). Notice that the second argument is a quote, space, and a quote. This separates the first and last names.
10. Press Enter and copy the formula in cell I12 from cell I13 through cell I18.
11. SAVE the workbook.

CERTIFICATION READY? 4.4.4

How do you create a formula that combines two strings together to form one string?

PAUSE. LEAVE the workbook open for the next exercise.

Using FIND

Use the FIND function to locate a specific string in a text string. The syntax of the function is FIND(Find_text, Within_text, *Start_num*). The Find_text argument can be one character as in this example or a longer string. The Within_text is usually a longer string and most often is a cell reference with a string. The Start_num argument tells you which position in the Within_text string to begin the counting. This argument is optional and if left off assumes you will begin searching at the beginning of the string. In the Alarm Data file, there are two hidden letters in one of the strings (A and B) whose position actually tells you the digits of the first entry code. The second entry is the month number of the employee's birthday.

STEP BY STEP **Use the FIND Function**

GET READY. USE the workbook from the previous exercise.

1. Click cell J11 and type APos, and in cell K11, type bPos to label the columns.
2. Click cell J12.
3. Click the FORMULAS tab and in the Function Library group, click Text and choose FIND. The Function Arguments dialog box opens.

4. In the Find_text box, type **A** and press **Tab**. Notice that the preview shows *"A"* (with quotes) in the row.

5. In the Within_text box, click **E2**. Notice that the result returns a 3 for the function. The first character in the string is a space, the second is an l (lowercase "L"), and the third is a capital A.

6. Click **OK** and copy the formula in cell J11 from cell **J12** through cell **J18**.

7. Select cell **K12**, type **=FIND("b",E2)**, and press **Enter**. In this case, you are looking for a lowercase b—the argument is case sensitive.

8. Copy the formula in cell K12 from cell **K13** to cell **K18**.

9. SAVE the workbook.

PAUSE. LEAVE the workbook open for the next exercise.

Using SUBSTITUTE

Excel's SUBSTITUTE function is especially useful when you need to edit data and you want to substitute new text for existing text in a text string. Use SUBSTITUTE when you want to replace specific text in a text string; use REPLACE when you want to replace any text that occurs in a specific location in a text string, such as when a name change occurs. In the Alarm Data file, the employee category fields can identify probationary employees and the level of probation. The syntax of the function is SUBSTITUTE(Text, Old_text, New_text, *Instance_num*). The Text argument is the string you will search. In this exercise you will replace the Old_text with New_text.

STEP BY STEP   **Use the SUBSTITUTE Function**

GET READY. USE the workbook from the previous exercise.

1. Click cell **L11** and type **S1**, and in M11, type **Probationary Level** to label the columns.

2. Select cell **L12**.

3. Click the **FORMULAS** tab and in the Function Library group, click **Text** and choose **SUBSTITUTE**. The Function Arguments dialog box opens.

4. In the Text box, click **E12** and press **Tab**.

5. In the Old_text box, type **NP**. This is a code for employees who are not probationary.

6. In the New_text box, type **Non** and press **Tab**. Because the first value is NP, the result of the formula will be Non.

7. Click **OK** and copy the formula in L11 from **L12** through **L18**.

8. Select cell **M12** and type **=SUBSTITUTE(L12,"P","Probationary Level ")** and press **Enter**. In this case, you are looking for the letter P and changing the string to Probationary Level with a space at the end because a number will follow.

9. Copy the formula in cell M12 from cell **M13** to cell **M18**. See Figure 10-26 to see the worksheet values.

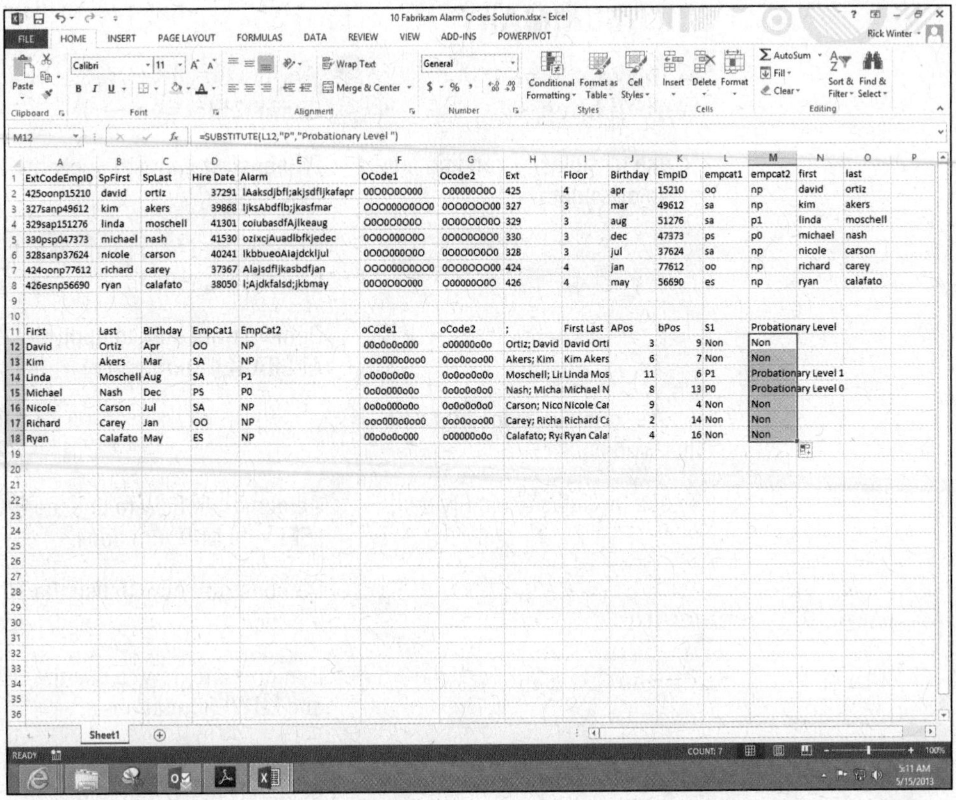

Figure 10-26

Text exercises

10. Press **Ctrl** + ` to display the formulas, as shown in Figure 10-27. Press **Ctrl** + ` again to switch back to the formula results.

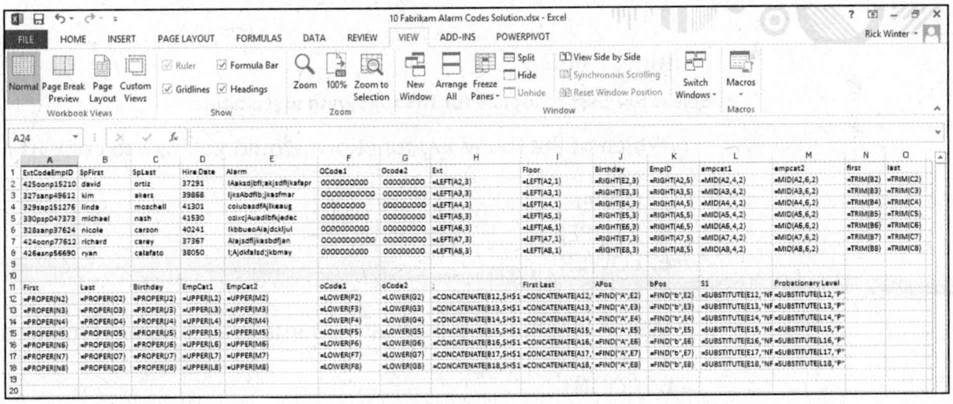

Figure 10-27

Text exercise worksheet formulas

11. SAVE the workbook.

CLOSE Excel.

To use existing text with small changes, you can use the SUBSTITUTE function. In the Function Arguments dialog box, Text can be the actual text you want to substitute, or it can be a cell reference.

SKILL SUMMARY

In this lesson you learned how:	Exam Objective	Objective Number
To use formulas to conditionally summarize data.	Demonstrate how to apply the SUMIF function.	4.3.1
	Demonstrate how to apply the COUNTIF function.	4.3.3
	Demonstrate how to apply the AVERAGEIF function.	4.3.2
To use formulas to look up data in a workbook.		
To use formulas to modify text.	Demonstrate how to use the RIGHT, LEFT, and MID functions.	4.4.1
	Demonstrate how to use the TRIM function.	4.4.2
	Demonstrate how to use the UPPER and LOWER functions.	4.4.3
	Demonstrate how to use the CONCATENATE function.	4.4.4

Knowledge Assessment

Multiple Choice

Select the best response for the following statements.

1. Which of the following functions would you use to convert text from uppercase to title case?
   a. UPPER
   b. PROPER
   c. LOWER
   d. SUBSTITUTE

2. Which function automatically counts cells that meet multiple conditions?
   a. COUNTIF
   b. COUNT
   c. COUNTIFS
   d. SUMIFS

3. Which function automatically counts cells that meet a specific condition?
   a. COUNTIF
   b. COUNT
   c. COUNTIFS
   d. SUMIFS

4. In the formula =SUMIFS(C5:C16, F5:F16, "<=60", B5:B16, ">200000"), what is the range of cells to be added?
   a. a.= C5:C16
   b. = F5:F16
   c. = B5:B16
   d. = C5:F16

5. In the formula =SUMIFS(C5:C16, F5:F16,"<=60", B5:B16, ">200000"), what does <=60 mean?
   a. If the value in C5:C16 is greater than or equal to 60, the value in C5:C16 will be included in the total.
   b. If the value in F5:F16 is greater than or equal to 60, the value in C5:C16 will be included in the total.
   c. If the value in B5:BF16 is less than or equal to 60, the value in C5:C16 will be included in the total.
   d. If the value in F5:F16 is less than or equal to 60, the value in C5:C16 will be included in the total.

6. What does criteria range in a formula refer to?
   a. The worksheet data to be included in the formula's results
   b. The range containing a condition that must be met in order for data to be included in the result
   c. The type of formula being used for the calculation
   d. The type of data contained in the cells to be included in the formula

7. Which function returns one value if a condition is true and a different value when the condition is not true?
   a. a.AND
   b. OR
   c. IF
   d. IFERROR

8. Which function returns a value if all conditions are met?
   a. AND
   b. OR
   c. IF
   d. IFERROR

9. Which function checks to see whether the result is something like #N/A (not available) and can return something else instead?
   a. AND
   b. OR
   c. NOT
   d. IFERROR

10. Which function reverses the value of the function arguments?
   a. AND
   b. NOT
   c. IF
   d. IFERROR

Matching

Match each term with its definition.

a. AND function

b. arguments

c. CONCATENATE function

d. COUNTIF

e. HLOOKUP

f. OR function

g. SUMIF

h. SUMIFS

i. table

j. VLOOKUP

_____ 1. A function used to look up information stored in the first column of an Excel table in the worksheet.
_____ 2. A function in which a True result is returned if data meets any condition specified in the formula.
_____ 3. The values that a function uses to perform operations or calculations.
_____ 4. A function in which a True result is returned if data meets all conditions specified in the formula.
_____ 5. A function that combines two or more strings together.
_____ 6. A formula component used to build single formulas that produce multiple results.
_____ 7. A function in which the result is determined by the state of multiple criteria.
_____ 8. A function that references the first row of an Excel table in the worksheet in order to look up information stored in the same column.
_____ 9. A function that returns the total number of cells that meet one condition.
_____10. A function in which the result is determined by the state of a particular condition.

Project 10-1: Separating Text into Columns

In this project, you take a text file of student grades and separate the information into seven columns rather than one.

GET READY. LAUNCH Excel if it is not already running.

1. OPEN the *10 SFA Grades Import* file.
2. Select cells A4:A41. Click the DATA tab and in the Data Tools group, click Text to Columns.
3. The Convert Text to Columns Wizard opens with Delimited selected as the default, because Excel recognized that the data in the selected range is separated with delimiters. Click Next.
4. Select Comma and Space as the delimiters. If other delimiters are checked (such as Tab), deselect them and click Next. Click Finish.
5. Label each of the columns in row 3 (A3 through G3): Last, First, Initial, ID, Final, Quarter, Semester.
6. SAVE the workbook in the Lesson 10 folder as *10 SFA Grades Import Solution*. CLOSE the workbook.

LEAVE Excel open for the next project.

Project 10-2: Creating SUMIF and SUMIFS Formulas to Conditionally Summarize Data

Salary information for Contoso, Ltd. has been entered in a workbook so the office manager can analyze and summarize the data. In the following exercise, you calculate sums with conditions.

GET READY. LAUNCH Excel if it is not already running.

1. OPEN the *10 Contoso Salaries* data file for this lesson.
2. Select cell C35. Click the FORMULAS tab and in the Function Library group, click Insert Function.
3. If the SUMIF function is not visible, type SUMIF in the Search for a function box and click Go. From the Select a function list, click SUMIF. Click OK.
4. In the Function Arguments dialog box, in the Range field select C4:C33.
5. In the Criteria box, type >100000.
6. Click OK. Because the range and sum range are the same, it is not necessary to enter a Sum_range argument.
7. Select C36 and click Insert Function. Select SUMIFS and click OK.
8. In the Function Arguments dialog box, select C4:C33 as the sum range.
9. Select D4:D33 as the first criteria range.
10. Type >=10 as the first criterion.
11. Select C4:C33 as the second criteria range.
12. Type <60000 as the second criterion. Click OK to finish the formula.
13. SAVE the workbook as *10 Contoso Salaries Solution*. CLOSE the file.

LEAVE Excel open for the next project.

Proficiency Assessment

Project 10-3: Using a Formula to Format Text

Use a formula to format text for employees to decide on 401K investments for Fabrikam, Inc.

GET READY. LAUNCH Excel if it is not already running.

1. OPEN the *10 Fabrikam Investments* data file for this lesson.
2. Enter formulas in column F to convert the text in column A to title case.
3. Copy the values from column F to column A and delete column F.
4. SAVE the workbook in the Lesson 10 folder as *10 Fabrikam Investments Solution* and then CLOSE the file.

LEAVE Excel open for the next project.

Project 10-4: Create COUNTIF and AVERAGEIF Formulas

In this exercise, you enter COUNTIF and AVERAGEIF formulas to analyze and summarize grades for a course at the School of Fine Arts.

GET READY. LAUNCH Excel if it is not already running.

1. OPEN the *10 SFA Grades* data file for this lesson.
2. In cell J2 enter a formula that counts the total number of students.
3. In the grades table on the right side of the worksheet, create formulas using COUNTIF that will count how many students got an A for the Final, Quarter, and Semester. In the Range field, use an absolute reference.
4. Create formulas for each of the other grades in the grades table.
5. SAVE the workbook as *10 SFA Grades Solution* and then CLOSE the file.

LEAVE Excel open for the next project.

Mastery Assessment

Project 10-5: Creating Conditional Logic Formulas

Professor Garrett Young has asked you to create formulas to identify the highest and lowest achieving students on his first test.

GET READY. LAUNCH Excel if it is not already running.

1. OPEN the *10 SFA Test Grades* file for this lesson.
2. In column F, use a function that will place the word "High" in each cell when the Test1 result is greater than 90. There will be a blank for all other values in this column.
3. In column G, use a function that will place the word "Low" in each cell when the test result is less than 70. There will be a blank for all other values in this column.
4. In cell A43, type Count, and then create two formulas that will count the High and Low labels in columns F and G. Best Practice Hint: Use the labels in F3 and G3 in your formulas instead of the word High or Low.
5. SAVE the workbook in the Lesson 10 folder as *10 SFA Test Grades Solution* and then CLOSE the file.

LEAVE Excel open for the next project.

Project 10-6: Creating COUNTIF, AVERAGEIF, and LOOKUP Formulas

In this project, you use a lookup table to determine an employee's end-of-year bonus.

GET READY. LAUNCH Excel if it is not already running.

1. OPEN the *10 Contoso Bonus* data file for this lesson.
2. In the table starting in row 35, create formulas to count the number of employees in each position in column B and the average salary of each position in column C.
3. Calculate the bonus by multiplying the Average salary by the rate/100.
4. Starting in F4, create a formula and copy it down that will look up the bonus for each position and put it in column F.
5. SAVE the workbook in the Lesson 10 folder as *10 Contoso Bonus Solution*, and then CLOSE the file.

CLOSE Excel.

LESSON SKILL MATRIX

Skills	Matrix Skill	Skill Number
Securing Your Work Before Sharing It with Others		
Distributing a Workbook by Email and the Cloud		
Tracking Changes to a Workbook		
Adding Comments to a Workbook		

KEY TERMS

- **change history**
- **password**
- **shared workbook**
- **strong password**
- **tracking changes**

©spxChrome / iStockphoto

327

©spxChrome / iStockphoto

Contoso, Ltd sees many patients every day. The clinic keeps confidential records about patient visits, medications, and medical issues. In addition, for employees, information about salaries, national identification numbers (social security numbers in the US, social insurance numbers in Canada, or national insurance numbers in the UK), and performance appraisals is stored. The back office staff must be able to share information, but it is critical that much of the information be kept confidential. In this lesson, you learn about Excel's tools for protecting and distributing documents, sharing them, tracking changes, and adding comments.

SOFTWARE ORIENTATION

The REVIEW Tab

Microsoft Excel provides several layers of security and protection that enable you to control who can access and change your Excel data. Commands on the REVIEW tab (Figure 11-1) enable you to protect an entire workbook file so that only authorized users can view or modify your data (the highest level of protection). You can also protect certain worksheet or workbook elements to prevent users from accidentally or deliberately changing, moving, or deleting important data. Data protection is especially important when files are shared and edited by multiple users.

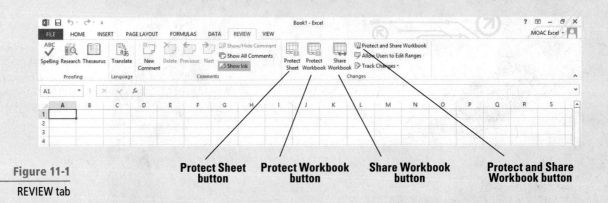

Figure 11-1

REVIEW tab

Protect Sheet button   Protect Workbook button   Share Workbook button   Protect and Share Workbook button

Use this illustration as a reference throughout this lesson as you learn to share and edit files using Excel's security and protection options.

SECURING YOUR WORK BEFORE SHARING IT WITH OTHERS

Bottom Line

A **password** is text that must be entered before a user can access a workbook, worksheet, or worksheet elements. You can secure an entire workbook by restricting who can open and/or use the workbook data and by requiring a password to view and/or save changes to the workbook. You can also provide additional protection for certain worksheets or workbook elements with or without applying a password.

Protecting a Worksheet

In a work environment, workbooks are frequently used by more than one employee. When you create a worksheet that is accessed by multiple users, you often need to protect it so that a user does not accidentally or intentionally change, move, or delete important data. In the next exercise, you use the RAND and RANDBETWEEN formulas to create unique ID numbers.

Excel has two random number functions: RAND and RANDBETWEEN. RAND does not require function arguments, so you cannot specify the number of digits you want in the number returned by a RAND formula. In contrast, RANDBETWEEN allows you to determine the beginning and ending numbers.

STEP BY STEP   **Protect a Worksheet**

GET READY. LAUNCH Excel.

1. OPEN *11 Contoso Employees* from the data files for this lesson.
2. On the SSN worksheet, select cell G4.
3. Click the FORMULAS tab, choose Math & Trig and select RANDBETWEEN. This formula creates a random number for each employee that can be used for identification purposes.
4. In the Function Arguments dialog box, in the Bottom box, type 10000 and in the Top box, type 99999, as shown in Figure 11-2. Click OK. As one of the first steps in information security, employees are usually assigned an Employee ID number that can replace replace Social Security numbers for US employees, Social Insurance numbers for Canadian employees, and National Insurance numbers for UK employees on all documents.

Figure 11-2

Generating a five-digit random number

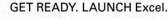

Function Arguments	?	✕
RANDBETWEEN		

Bottom 10000   = 10000
Top   99999   = 99999

= Volatile
Returns a random number between the numbers you specify.

           Top is the largest integer RANDBETWEEN will return.

Formula result = Volatile

Help on this function   OK   Cancel

5. Double-click the fill handle in cell G4 to copy the range to G5:G33. Each employee is now assigned a random five-digit ID number.
6. With the range G4:G33 already selected, on the HOME tab, click Copy. Click the Paste arrow, and then click Paste Values.

⚠ **Troubleshooting**   The RANDBETWEEN formula generates a new random number each time a workbook is opened or modified. To retain the Employee ID numbers created by the formula, you must replace the formula with the values.

7. With G4:G33 selected, on the HOME tab, click Format and then select Format Cells. Click the Protection tab and verify that Locked is checked. This prevents employee ID numbers from being changed when the worksheet has been protected. Click OK.

8. On the HOME tab, click the Sort & Filter button and select Sort Smallest to Largest. On the Sort Warning dialog box, select Continue with the current selection, and then click Sort.

9. Select cells C4:D33. On the HOME tab, click Format. Notice that the Lock Cell command appears selected, meaning the cells are locked by default. Click Lock Cell to turn off the protection on these cells to allow these cells to change.

10. Click on the REVIEW tab, and in the Changes group, click Protect Sheet.

11. In the Password to unprotect sheet box, type L11!e01. The password is not displayed in the Password to unprotect sheet box. Instead, asterisks (*) are displayed as shown in Figure 11-3. Click OK.

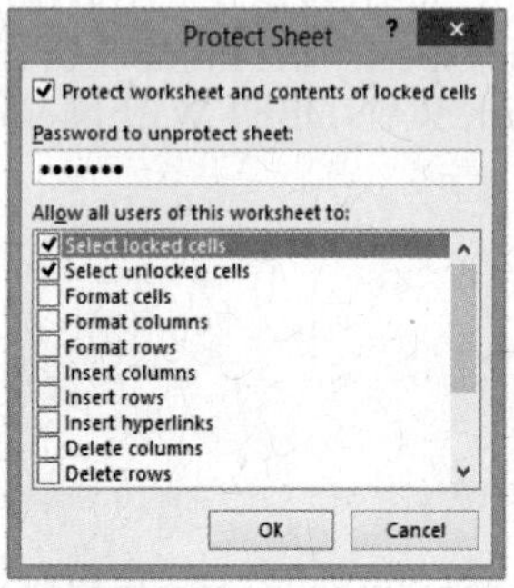

Figure 11-3

The Protect Sheet dialog box displays asterisks (*) as you type, to protect the password.

12. You are asked to confirm the password. Type L11!e01 again and click OK. You have just created and confirmed the password that will lock the worksheet. Passwords are meant to be secure. This means that all passwords are case sensitive. Thus, you must type exactly what has been assigned as the password—uppercase and lowercase letters, numbers, and symbols.

13. SAVE the workbook as *11 Payroll Data Solution*. CLOSE the workbook.

PAUSE. LEAVE Excel open for the next exercise.

Take Note   Workbook and worksheet element protection should not be confused with workbook-level password security. Element protection cannot protect a workbook from users who have malicious intent.

Protecting a Workbook

Assigning a password is an effective way to prevent any user who does not know the password from opening a workbook. To protect an entire workbook, you can require a password to open and view the workbook. You can also require one password to open and view the workbook and a second password to modify workbook data. Passwords that apply to an entire workbook provide optimal security for your data.

Currently, the 11 Payroll Data Solution workbook you saved in the previous exercise can be viewed by anyone who has access to the computer system. You restricted the modification of the file, but you did not restrict access to the data. In this exercise, you will limit access to the workbook by requiring a password to open the document.

Excel passwords can contain up to 255 letters, numbers, spaces, and symbols. Passwords are case sensitive, so you must type uppercase and lowercase letters correctly. If possible, select a strong password that you can remember so that you do not have to write it down. A **strong password** is one that combines uppercase and lowercase letters, numbers, and symbols—consider the example password of L11!e01 that you used in the previous exercise. A password that uses 14 or more characters, however, is considered to be more secure. Passwords that use birthdates, house numbers, pet names, and so on. provide little protection for anyone who can look up this information on social networks or the Internet.

Take Note It is vitally important that you remember passwords assigned to workbooks or worksheets. If you forget your password, Microsoft cannot retrieve it. If necessary, write down passwords and store them in a secure place away from the information you want to protect.

When you protect a worksheet, you can hide any formulas that you do not want to be visible in the formula bar. Select the cells that contain the formulas you want to hide. Then, on the Protection tab of the Format Cells dialog box, select the Hidden check box.

STEP BY STEP **Protect a Workbook**

GET READY. OPEN the *11 Payroll Data Solution* workbook that you saved and closed in the previous exercise.

1. Click cell G11 and try to type a new value in the cell. A dialog box informs you that you are unable to modify the cell because the worksheet is protected. Click OK to continue.

2. Click cell D4 and change the number to 1. You can make changes to cells in columns C and D because you unlocked the cells before you protected the worksheet. Click Undo to reverse the change.

3. Click the Performance worksheet tab and select cell D4.

4. On the HOME tab, in the Cells group, click the Delete arrow, and click Delete Sheet Rows. Dr. Bourne's data is removed from the worksheet because this worksheet was left unprotected.

5. Click Undo to return Dr. Bourne's data.

6. Click the SSN worksheet tab. Click the REVIEW tab, and in the Changes group, click Unprotect Sheet.

7. Type L11!e01 (the password you created in the previous exercise) and click OK.

8. Click cell D11. Type 8, press Tab three times, and then type 17000 (see Figure). Press Tab.

Figure 11-4

G11 is changed to 17000.

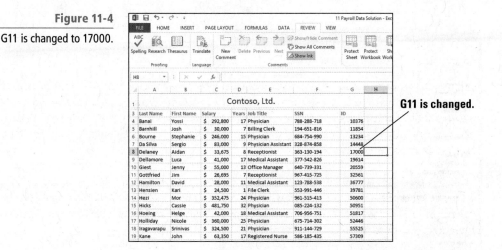

G11 is changed.

9. On the REVIEW tab, in the Changes group, click Protect Sheet. In the two dialog boxes, type the original password for the sheet L11!e01 to again protect the SSN worksheet.

10. On the REVIEW tab, in the Changes group, click **Protect Workbook**. The Protect Structure and Windows dialog box shown in Figure 11-5 opens. Select the **Protect workbook for Structure** check box in the dialog box , if it isn't already selected.

Figure 11-5

Protecting the structure of a workbook

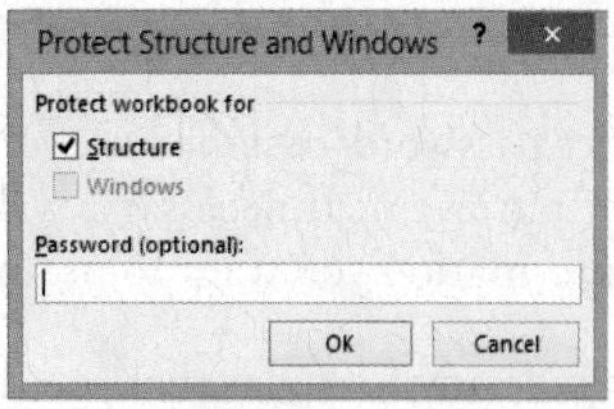

11. In the Password box, type **L11&E02**, and then click **OK**. Confirm the password by typing it again and click **OK**.

Take Note The workbook password is optional, but if you do not supply a password, any user can unprotect the workbook and change the protected elements.

12. To verify that you cannot change worksheet options, right-click the **Performance** worksheet tab and notice the dimmed commands shown in Figure 11-6.

Figure 11-6

Right-click on Performance worksheet and notice dimmed commands.

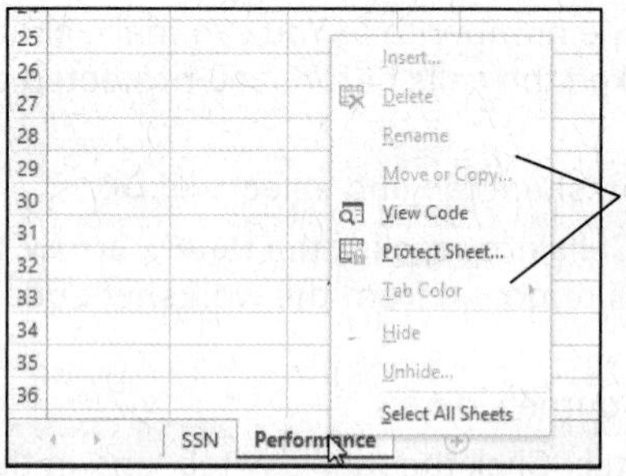

13. Press **Esc** and click the **FILE** tab. Select **Save As**, and then click the **Browse** button.
14. In the Save As dialog box, click the **Tools** button. The shortcut menu opens (see Figure 11-7).

Figure 11-7

Use the Tools options in the Save As dialog box to restrict access to the workbook.

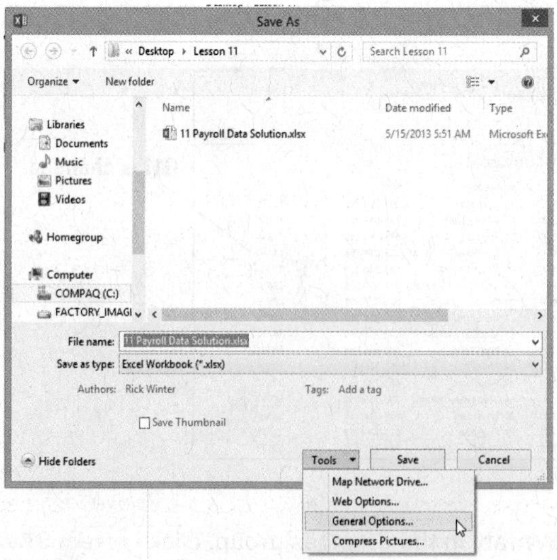

15. Select General Options. The General Options dialog box opens. In the General Options dialog box, in the Password to open box, type L11&E02. Asterisks appear in the text box as you type. Click OK.

16. In the Confirm Password dialog box, reenter the password, and then click OK. You must type the password exactly the same each time.

17. Click Save and click Yes to replace the document. As the document is now saved, anyone who has the password can open the workbook and modify data contained in the Performance worksheet because that worksheet is not protected. However, to modify the SSN worksheet, the user must also know the password you used to protect that worksheet in the first exercise.

Troubleshooting   When you confirm the password to prevent unauthorized viewing of a document, you are reminded that passwords are case-sensitive. If the password you enter in the Confirm Password dialog box is not identical to the one you entered in the previous dialog box, you will receive an error message. Click OK to close the error message and reenter the password in the Confirm Password dialog box.

18. CLOSE the workbook and OPEN it again.

19. In the Password box, type 111 and click OK. This is an incorrect password to test the security. You receive a dialog box warning that the password is not correct. Click OK.

PAUSE. LEAVE Excel open for the next exercise.

When you saved the Payroll Data Solution workbook in the first exercise in this section, it could be viewed by anyone with access to your computer system or network. As you saw when you opened the file in this exercise, the workbook could be viewed, but the SSN worksheet could not be modified except for the cells that were unlocked. If you saved the file with a different name, that file also would be protected, and you could not alter the data without the password that protects that worksheet.

Protecting the structure of a workbook prevents users from viewing worksheets that you have hidden; inserting new worksheets; or moving, deleting, hiding, or changing the names of worksheets. Selecting the Windows box on the Protect Structure and Windows dialog box (refer to Figure 11-5) prevents the user from changing the size and position of the windows when the workbook is opened.

Workplace Ready

PASSWORDS AND SECURITY

As you learned in this lesson, assigning a strong password is an important security precaution.

Visit http://www.microsoft.com/security/default.aspx and click Create better passwords, and then click Create stronger passwords to learn more about creating a strong password. The link also has valuable information about protecting yourself from hoaxes and spyware, and about protecting your privacy.

Based on your review of the suggestions for creating strong password, in a new workbook create a list of passwords that you need to change to secure your personal information and protect the integrity of data you create. Do not list your actual passwords; instead, identify the password usage. For example, you might indicate that you need to change the password that you use to access your college email account or your personal email account. Determine a safe storage vehicle for the new passwords you create (in case you forget them).

On the workbook, add a sheet similar to the one that follows that allows you to have your own strong password checklist. The passwords should have eight characters or more and include letters, punctuation, numbers, and symbols. In addition, you should change your passwords often, not share them with anyone unless absolutely required, and do not save individuals passwords or lists in a location that is easily accessed.

	A	B	C	D
1	Strong Password Checker		Goodol&1984^boys!	
2				
3	Objective	Criteria	My password	Meet?
4	Characters	8	17	yes
5	Letters	<Characters	10	yes
6	Punctuation	1	1	yes
7	Numbers	1	4	yes
8	Symbols	1	2	yes++
9	Change frequency (days)	90	No	No
10				
11				

Allowing Multiple Users to Edit a Workbook Simultaneously

Creating and updating workbooks is frequently a collaborative process. A worksheet or workbook is often routed to other employees so that they can verify data or make changes. In Excel, you can create a **shared workbook**, which is set up to allow multiple users on a network to view and make changes at the same time. When a user opens a shared workbook, he or she can see the changes made and saved by other users. The Protect and Share Workbook command prevents a user from disabling the Track Changes option.

For example, the workbook you create in this exercise is used by the medical assistants, who record all sample medications the physicians prescribe for patients. Sharing this workbook means that more than one medical assistant can access the workbook and enter data at the same time. In this exercise, you learn how to allow users to simultaneously edit workbooks.

STEP BY STEP   **Allow Multiple Users to Edit a Workbook Simultaneously**

GET READY. LAUNCH Excel if it is not already running.

1. CREATE a new blank workbook.
2. In cell A1, type Sample Drugs Dispensed and press Tab.
3. Select cells A1:D1. On the HOME tab, in the Alignment group, click Merge & Center.
4. Select cell A1, click Cell Styles, and in the Cell Styles gallery that appears, click Heading 1.
5. Beginning in cell A3, enter the following data:

Medical Assistant	Drug	Patient	Date
Dellamore, Luca	Cipro	Chor, Anthony	
Hamilton, David	Ketek	Brundage, Michael	
Hoeing, Helge	Lipitor	Charles, Matthew	
Murray, Billie Jo	Altace	Bishop, Scott	
Dellamore, Luca	Zetia	Anderson, Nancy	
Hamilton, David	Cipro	Coleman, Pat	
Hoeing, Helge	Avelox	Nayberg, Alex	
Murray, Billie Jo	Norvasc	Kleinerman, Christian	

6. In the Date column, apply today's date to the previous records.
7. Select cells A3:D3 and apply the Heading 3 style.

8. Increase the column widths to see all the data.

9. SAVE the workbook as *11 Sample Medications Solution*.

10. Click the REVIEW tab, and then, in the Changes group, click Share Workbook.

11. In the Share Workbook dialog box, click Allow changes by more than one user at the same time. Your identification will appear in the Who has this workbook open now box, as shown in Figure w. Click OK.

Figure 11-8

Sharing a workbook

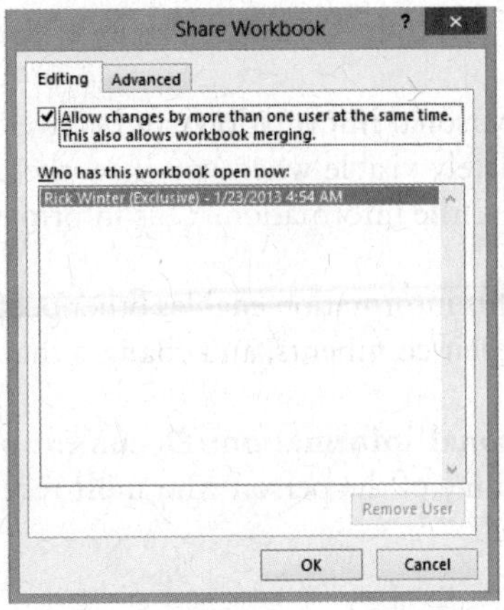

12. Click OK when prompted and the action will save the workbook.

13. In the Changes group, click Protect Shared Workbook. Select the Sharing with track changes check box in the Protect Shared Workbook dialog box. Click OK.

14. Notice that *[Shared]* appears in the title bar.

15. SAVE and CLOSE the workbook.

PAUSE. LEAVE Excel open for the next exercise.

In a shared workbook, information is maintained about changes each user makes when they edit the workbook. The **change history** includes the name of the person who made each change, when the change was made, and what data was changed.

🔍 **Cross Ref** Changes can also be turned on and off through the Track Changes button on the REVIEW tab. For more information and to see the result of track changes, see the "Tracking Changes to a Workbook" section later in this lesson.

A shared workbook does not support all Excel features. For example, you can include merged cells, conditional formats, data validation, charts, and so on before a workbook is shared, but these features cannot be added by those who edit a shared workbook.

When you protected your shared workbook, you prevented those who use the workbook from removing the change history. By default, changes made in the workbook will be retained for 30 days. You can increase that time frame on the Advanced tab of the Share Workbook dialog box (refer back to Figure 11-8).

 Troubleshooting If you want to assign a password to a shared workbook, you must assign it before the workbook is shared. You can also unshare a workbook and add the password. However, when you unshare a shared workbook, the change history is lost.

Using the Document Inspector

Before you share an important document with colleagues or individuals outside your organization, you should always spell check, proofread, and review the contents to ensure that everything is correct and the document does not contain anything you do not want to share with others. You should also review the document for hidden data or personal information that might be stored in the workbook or in the document properties. In Excel, the Document Inspector displays several different options that enable you to find and remove hidden data and personal information that is specific to Excel workbooks. The Document Inspector also locates custom XML data, hidden worksheets, and invisible content.

Several types of hidden data and personal information can be saved in an Excel workbook. This information might not be immediately visible when you view the document, but it still may be possible for others to view or retrieve the information. This information includes the following:

- **Comments and annotations:** This information enables other people to see the names of people who worked on your workbook, their comments, and changes that were made to the workbook.

- **Document properties and personal information:** Document properties include the author, subject, and title, as well as the name of the person who most recently saved the workbook and the date the workbook was created.

- **Headers and footers:** Headers and footers can include the author's name, the date the file was created, and so on.

- **Hidden rows, columns, and worksheets:** Columns can be hidden to protect salary and and social security (US), social insurance (Canada), or national insurance (UK) data. Before removing hidden rows or columns, be sure that their removal will not change calculations in your worksheet.

STEP BY STEP   **Use the Document Inspector**

GET READY. OPEN *11 Contoso Employee IDS* from the files for this lesson.

1. Click the FILE tab, click Save As, click Browse, and navigate to the Lesson 11 folder. In the File name box, type *11 Employee ID Doc Inspect Solution* to save a copy of the workbook. Click the SAVE button.

Troubleshooting   It is a good idea to perform an inspection on a copy of your workbook because you might not be able to restore hidden content that you remove in the inspection process. If you attempt to inspect a document that has unsaved changes, you will be prompted to save the document before completing the inspection.

2. Click the FILE tab. Then, with Info selected, click the Check for Issues button in the middle pane of the Backstage view. Next, click Inspect Document. The Document Inspector dialog box opens, as shown in Figure 11-9.

Figure 11-9

Document Inspector dialog box

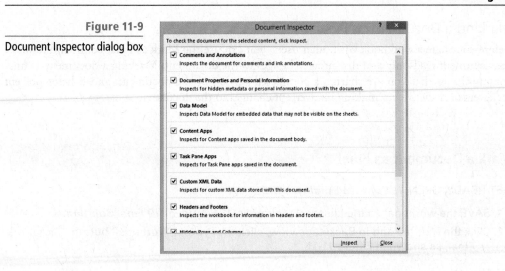

3. Click Inspect. The Document Inspector changes to include some Remove All buttons.

4. Click Remove All for Comments and Annotations.

Take Note You must remove each type of hidden data individually. You can inspect the document again after you remove items.

5. Click Remove All three times for Document Properties and Personal Information, Hidden Rows and Columns, and Hidden Worksheets. Headers and Footers should be the only hidden item remaining (see Figure 11-10).

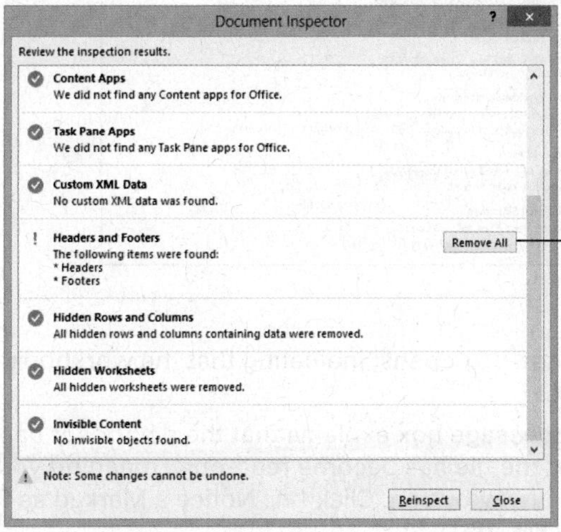

Figure 11-10

Remove All button for Headers and Footers

6. Click the Close button to close the Document Inspector dialog box.

7. SAVE the workbook.

PAUSE. CLOSE the workbook.

When you opened the file in this exercise, it contained hidden columns as well as other information that you didn't want to share with others. You first created a copy of your original workbook because it is not always possible to restore data that the Document Inspector removes. For that reason, you removed sensitive information from the copy; the complete data is retained in the original workbook. If the original workbook was protected, the copy would also be protected, and some of the items in the workbook would not be able to be changed through the Document Inspector. You would have to unprotect the workbook first to run the Document Inspector.

Marking a Document as Final

Before you share a workbook with other users, you can use the Mark as Final command to make the document read-only and discourage changes to the document. Marking a document as final communicates that you are sharing a completed version of the document, and it helps prevent reviewers or readers from making inadvertent changes to the document.

STEP BY STEP   **Mark a Document as Final**

GET READY. OPEN *11 Contoso Employee IDS*.

1. SAVE the workbook in the Lesson 11 folder as *11 Employee ID Final Solution*.

2. Click the FILE tab and in Backstage view, click the Protect Workbook button. Click Mark as Final, as shown in Figure 11-11.

Figure 11-11

Mark as Final

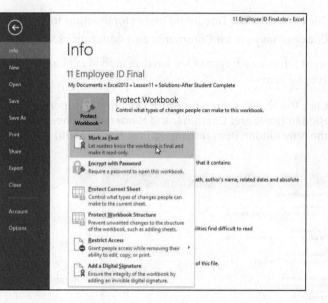

3. An Excel message box opens, indicating that the workbook will be marked as final and saved. Click OK.

4. Another Excel message box explains that the document has been marked as final. This also means that the file has become read-only, meaning you can't edit it unless you click the Edit Anyway button. Click OK. Notice a Marked as Final icon appears in the status bar (See Figure 11-12).

Figure 11-12

Marked as Final icon on the
status bar

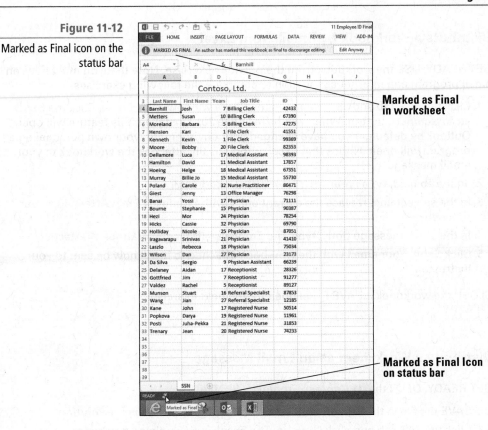

**Marked as Final
in worksheet**

**Marked as Final Icon
on status bar**

PAUSE. LEAVE the workbook open for the next exercise.

The Mark as Final command is not a security feature. Anyone who opens a workbook that has been marked as final can edit the document by removing the Mark as Final status from the document by clicking the Edit Anyway button.

DISTRIBUTING A WORKBOOK BY EMAIL AND THE CLOUD

Bottom Line

The most common ways to share Excel data are by sending workbooks through email, by faxing workbooks, and by printing and distributing hard copies. Email allows you to share a workbook by routing it to one user who can make changes or add comments and then route the workbook to the next user. Changes can then be incorporated into a final document. You can email a workbook as an attachment from Excel or from your email program. You can also send a worksheet as an email message rather than as an attachment.

Distributing a Workbook by Email

The option to send a worksheet as an email message is available only from the Send to Mail Recipient command on the Quick Access Toolbar. When you add this command to the toolbar, you also can use this option as a shortcut to send a workbook as an attachment. In the next set of exercises, you will learn how to send a workbook as part of the message body and send a workbook as an attached file.

| STEP BY STEP | Distribute a Workbook by Email From Excel |

GET READY. USE the workbook from the previous exercise. Note that you must have an email program and Internet connection to complete the following exercises.

1. Click the FILE tab and click Share. In the Share window, click Email. Click the Send as Attachment button. When you have Office 2013 installed, this feature will open Outlook by default. If you have changed your environment, your own personal email program will open. Notice that Excel automatically attaches the workbook to your email message.

2. In the To field, type [your instructor's email address].

3. In the subject line, replace the current entry with Employee Final Attached as per request.

4. In the email message body, type The Employee ID Final workbook is attached.

5. Click Send. Your email with the workbook attached to it will now be sent to your instructor.

CLOSE the workbook. LEAVE Excel open for the next exercise.

| STEP BY STEP | Distribute a Worksheet as an Email Message |

GET READY. OPEN the *11 Contoso Employee IDS* file.

1. SAVE the file in the Lesson 11 folder as *11 Employee ID Recipient Solution*.

2. Click the FILE tab and click Options. The Excel Options dialog box opens.

3. Click Quick Access Toolbar. In the Choose commands from field, click Email. In the center bar between the left and right fields, click Add. This step adds the Email button to the Quick Access Toolbar.

4. In the Choose commands from drop-down box, click All Commands. Click in the list and type the letter s, and then scroll and find Send to Mail Recipient and click to highlight it. In the center bar between the left and right fields, click Add. This step adds this command to the Quick Access Toolbar.

5. Click OK to save both commands to the Quick Access Toolbar.

6. On the Quick Access Toolbar, click Send to Mail Recipient. The E-mail dialog box opens as shown in Figure 11-13.

Figure 11-13

E-mail dialog box

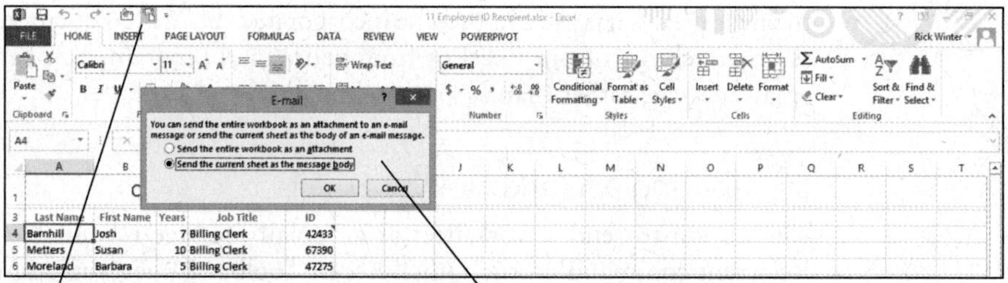

Send to Recipient button on Quick Access Toolbar   E-mail dialog box

7. Click the Send the current sheet as the message body option, and then click OK. The email window is now embedded in your Excel screen with the current worksheet visible as the body of the email.

8. In the To field, type [your instructor's email address] and keep the name of the file in the Subject line. This is automatically added for you.

9. In the Introduction, type Please Review (see Figure 11-14).

Figure 11-14

Send to recipient

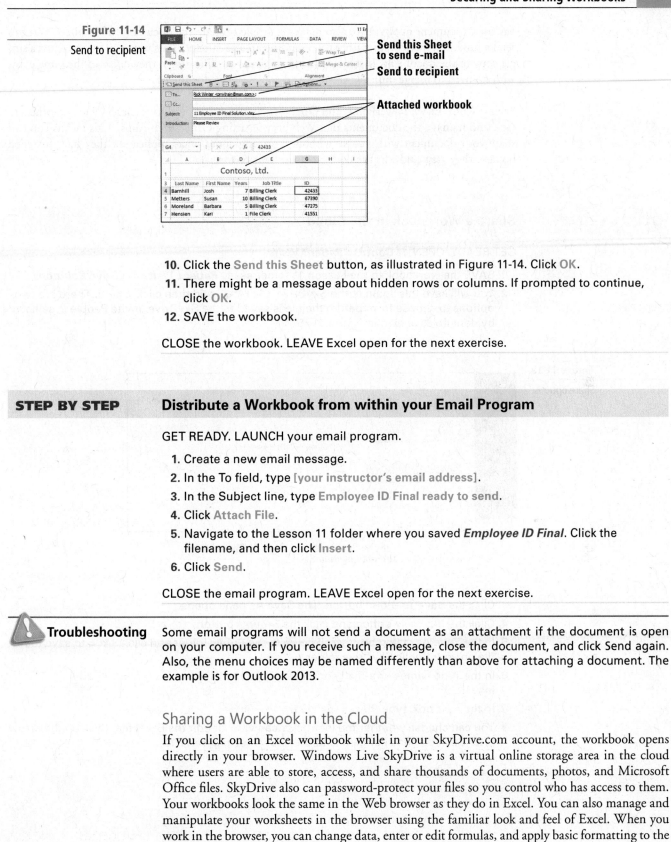

Send this Sheet to send e-mail

Send to recipient

Attached workbook

10. Click the Send this Sheet button, as illustrated in Figure 11-14. Click OK.

11. There might be a message about hidden rows or columns. If prompted to continue, click OK.

12. SAVE the workbook.

CLOSE the workbook. LEAVE Excel open for the next exercise.

STEP BY STEP   **Distribute a Workbook from within your Email Program**

GET READY. LAUNCH your email program.

1. Create a new email message.

2. In the To field, type [your instructor's email address].

3. In the Subject line, type Employee ID Final ready to send.

4. Click Attach File.

5. Navigate to the Lesson 11 folder where you saved *Employee ID Final*. Click the filename, and then click Insert.

6. Click Send.

CLOSE the email program. LEAVE Excel open for the next exercise.

Troubleshooting Some email programs will not send a document as an attachment if the document is open on your computer. If you receive such a message, close the document, and click Send again. Also, the menu choices may be named differently than above for attaching a document. The example is for Outlook 2013.

Sharing a Workbook in the Cloud

If you click on an Excel workbook while in your SkyDrive.com account, the workbook opens directly in your browser. Windows Live SkyDrive is a virtual online storage area in the cloud where users are able to store, access, and share thousands of documents, photos, and Microsoft Office files. SkyDrive also can password-protect your files so you control who has access to them. Your workbooks look the same in the Web browser as they do in Excel. You can also manage and manipulate your worksheets in the browser using the familiar look and feel of Excel. When you work in the browser, you can change data, enter or edit formulas, and apply basic formatting to the spreadsheet. You can also work with others on the same workbook at the same time.

When you save a document in Windows Live SkyDrive, your document is stored in a central location that you can access from almost anywhere. Even if you're away from your primary computer, you can work on your document whenever you have a connection to the Web even if you don't have Excel on that computer.

Saving a document in SkyDrive also makes it simple to share the document with others. You can send a link directly to them, rather than sending an attachment. This way, you preserve just a single copy of the document. If someone needs to make modifications, they do so in the same copy, with no need to merge multiple versions and copies of the document.

Saving Word, Excel, PowerPoint, and OneNote documents in SkyDrive enables you and others to view and manage the documents in a Web browser using Office Web Apps. This means you can share your document with people without worrying about what application they have installed because they view and edit the documents in their browsers.

STEP BY STEP   **Share a Workbook in the Cloud**

GET READY. OPEN *11 Contoso Patient Visits*.

1. SAVE the workbook to the Lesson 11 folder as *11 Patient Visits SkyDrive Solution*.
2. You will save this again to the SkyDrive. Click FILE and then click Share. There are two options to choose from before the file is saved to the SkyDrive. Invite People is selected by default, as shown in Figure 11-15.

Figure 11-15

Share options.

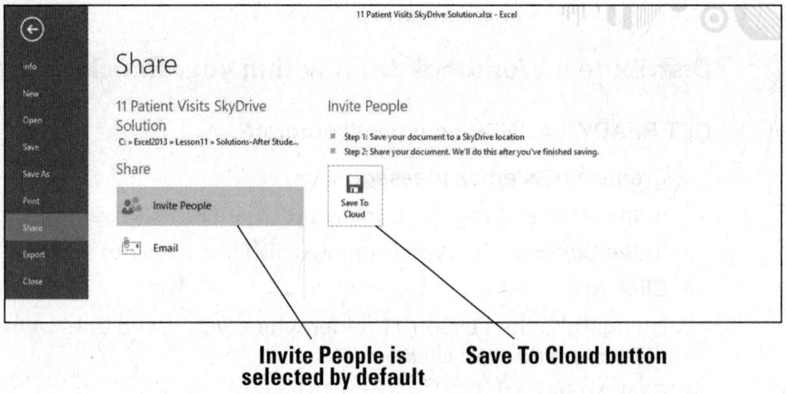

Invite People is selected by default

Save To Cloud button

3. Click the Save To Cloud button. The Save As pane opens.
4. Click the SkyDrive option and click the Browse button.
5. In the Save As dialog box, scroll down to the Public folder and click SAVE to save the file on your Public SkyDrive folder.
6. In the Type names or e-mail addresses box, type [the email address of your instructor].
7. In the next box, type Please review my assignment.
8. You can choose whether the instructor can view or edit the Excel file. Click on the arrow after Can edit and change this to Can view (see Figure 11-16).

Figure 11-16

Invite People option

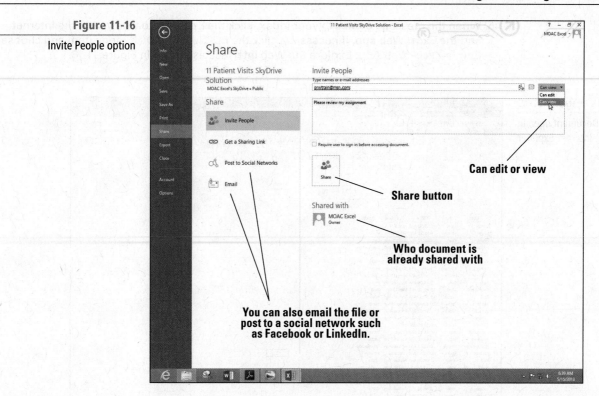

- **Can edit or view**
- **Share button**
- **Who document is already shared with**
- **You can also email the file or post to a social network such as Facebook or LinkedIn.**

9. Click the Share button.

10. Open a new email message in your email program and address the email to yourself with a CC to your instructor. Type Patient Visits for the Subject. In the Body of the message, type View, press Enter, and type Edit.

11. Return to Excel and click the Get a Sharing Link button.

12. Under View Link, click the Create Link button, and then after the word View, COPY and PASTE the link shown to your email message, and then press Enter after the link in the email. The link should change to a hyperlink depending on your email program.

13. Return to Excel. Under Edit Link, click the Create Link button. Both links show on the screen (see Figure 11-17).

Figure 11-17

Get a Sharing Link options

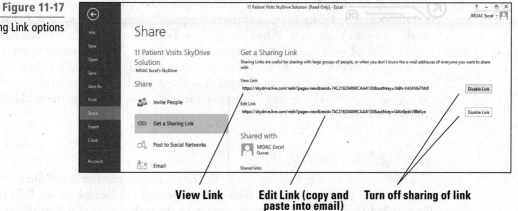

- **View Link**
- **Edit Link (copy and paste into email)**
- **Turn off sharing of link**

14. COPY and PASTE the Edit Link after the word Edit in your email message and press Enter after the link. SEND the email message.

15. When the message comes to your Inbox, click the Edit Link to take you to the Internet and the Excel Web app. If necessary, click the EDIT WORKBOOK menu item and choose Edit in Excel Web App. Explore the Web interface as shown in Figure 11-18.

Figure 11-18

Document open in Internet Explorer

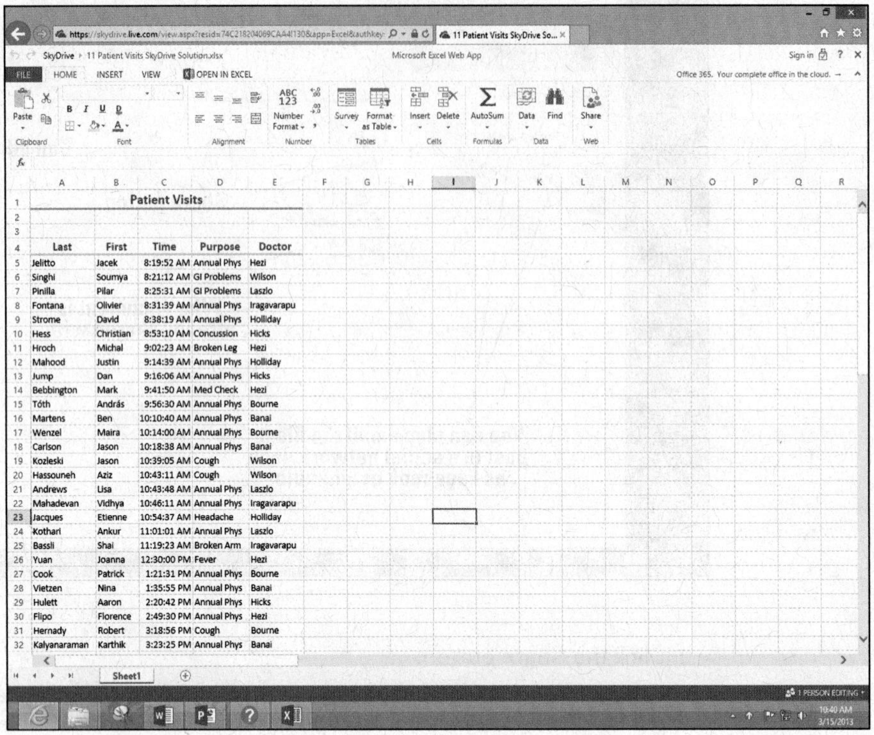

16. CLOSE the Web browser without saving the document, close your email program, and click the Return to Document button in Excel.

SAVE and CLOSE the workbook. LEAVE Excel open for the next exercise.

TRACKING CHANGES TO A WORKBOOK

Tracking changes is the ability to mark who makes what changes that have been made to a workbook. The ability to track changes is especially helpful in a workbook that is shared and modified by multiple users. When you turn on Track Changes, the workbook automatically becomes a shared workbook. You can customize the Track Changes feature to track specific types of changes, you can allow the feature to be turned on and off at will by various users, or you can specify a password to protect the changes. You also can decide whether to accept or reject changes to your original workbook data. When you turn off change tracking, the workbook is no longer a shared workbook.

Turning Track Changes On and Off

You can turn on change tracking using the Track Changes command, the Share Workbook command, or the Protect and Share Workbook command (all located on the REVIEW tab). The Protect and Share Workbook command provides the highest level of security because you can add a password. When workbooks are shared, it is often important to know what changes were made by each user. The owner (creator) of the workbook can use change-tracking functions to manage the data in a shared workbook. The owner can use the change history record to manage the shared workbook by adding or removing users and resolving conflicting changes. In the next exercise, you will learn to track changes.

STEP BY STEP	**Turn Track Changes On and Off**

GET READY. OPEN the *11 Contoso Assignments* workbook for this lesson.

1. SAVE the workbook as *11 Assignments Solution* in the Lesson 11 folder.
2. On the REVIEW tab, in the Changes group, click the Protect and Share Workbook button. The Protect Shared Workbook dialog box opens.
3. In the dialog box, click Sharing with track changes. When you choose this option, the Password text box becomes active. You can assign a password at this time, but it is not necessary. Click OK.
4. Click OK when asked if you want to continue and save the workbook. You have now marked the workbook to save tracked changes.

PAUSE. LEAVE the workbook open for the next exercise.

You can turn change tracking off by clicking the Unprotect Shared Workbook button, which was named Protect Shared Workbook before you completed the preceding exercise.

Cross Ref The Track Changes command enables you to manage how changes are displayed on your screen. You use this option in an upcoming exercise.

Take Note Turning off Track Changes removes the change history and removes the shared status of the workbook, but changes already shown in the document will remain until you accept or reject them.

Setting Track Change Options

The Advanced tab of the Share Workbook dialog box allows you to customize the shared use of the workbook. These options are normally set by the workbook author before the workbook is shared. In this exercise, you modify these options.

STEP BY STEP	**Set Track Change Options**

GET READY. USE the workbook from the previous exercise.

1. On the REVIEW tab, in the Changes group, click Share Workbook. The Share Workbook dialog box opens.
2. Click the Advanced tab (see Figure 11-19).

Figure 11-19

Share Workbook Advanced tab

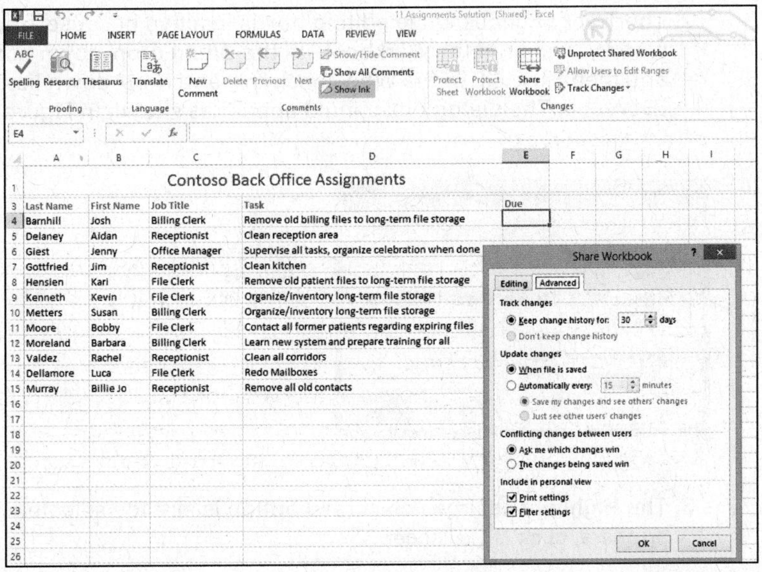

3. In the Keep change history for box, click the scroll arrow to display 35.

4. Click the Automatically every option button so the file automatically saves every 15 minutes (the default).

5. Click OK to accept the default settings for the remainder of the options.

PAUSE. SAVE the workbook and LEAVE it open for the next exercise.

The Advanced tab contains four options:

- **Track changes** determines whether a change history is kept and the length of time it is kept. In a shared workbook, the change history documents changes made in past editing sessions. The information includes the name of the person who made each change, when the changes were made, and what data was changed. The default setting is 30 days. Contoso maintains a monthly record of the distribution of samples. Setting the change history to 35 days ensures that the office manager has sufficient time to review the workbook and resolve any conflicting changes before the change history is deleted.

- **Update changes** controls when changes made to the shared workbook are incorporated into the workbook.

- **Conflicting changes between users** determines whose edits become part of the file if two or more people attempt to edit at the same time. The workbook owner's changes usually take precedence.

- **Include in personal view** enables each user who edits the workbook to see a personal view of the workbook.

Inserting Tracked Changes

When you open a shared workbook, Track Changes is automatically turned on. In most cases, the workbook owner has entered a password to prevent a user from turning off Track Changes. Thus, any text you type in the workbook is tracked.

STEP BY STEP   **Insert Tracked Changes**

GET READY. USE the workbook from the previous exercise.

1. On the REVIEW tab, in the Changes group, click Track Changes. In the drop-down list that appears, click Highlight Changes. The Highlight Changes dialog box appears.

2. The Track changes while editing box is inactive because Track Changes was activated when you shared the workbook. In the When drop-down box, click the down arrow, and then click All. In the Who check box and drop-down list, check the box and select Everyone. The dialog box should appear as shown in Figure 11-20.

Figure 11-20

Inserting tracked changes

Highlight Changes

☑ Track changes while editing. This also shares your workbook.

Highlight which changes

☑ When: All

☑ Who: Everyone

☐ Where:

☑ Highlight changes on screen

☐ List changes on a new sheet

OK   Cancel

Track Changes options

Highlight Changes dialog box

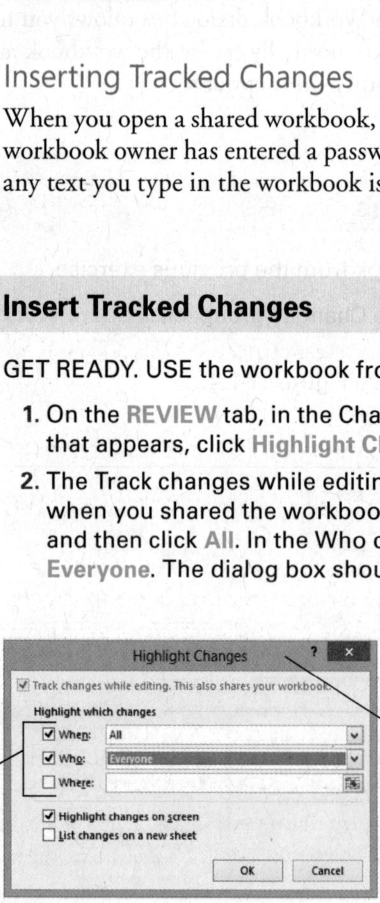

3. The Highlight changes on screen option is already selected. Click OK. If a warning box appears, click OK to accept.

4. Click the FILE tab and click Options. The Excel Options dialog box opens.

5. In the General category, under Personalize your copy of Microsoft Office, in the User name box, type Luca Dellamore. Click OK. You have changed the document user name that will be listed in the Track Changes.

Take Note Make a note of the name that you remove. You will restore the original user name at the end of this lesson.

6. Click cell A14 and type the following information in each of the columns:

   Dellamore   Luca   File Clerk   Redo Mailboxes

7. As you enter these changes, a colored triangle and comment box appear for each entry made. This makes it easy to view the changes later.

8. On the Quick Access Toolbar, click Save to save the changes you made under the user name Luca Dellamore.

9. Click the FILE tab and select Options.

10. In the User name box, type Billie Jo Murray. Click OK. You are once again changing the user name and applying it to the document.

11. Click cell A15 and type the following information in each of the columns:

    Murray   Billie Jo   Receptionist   Remove all old contacts

12. Move the mouse pointer to cell D15. The person's name who made the change, the date of the change, and the change itself appear in a ScreenTip as shown in Figure 11-21.

Figure 11-21

Tracked changes in a worksheet

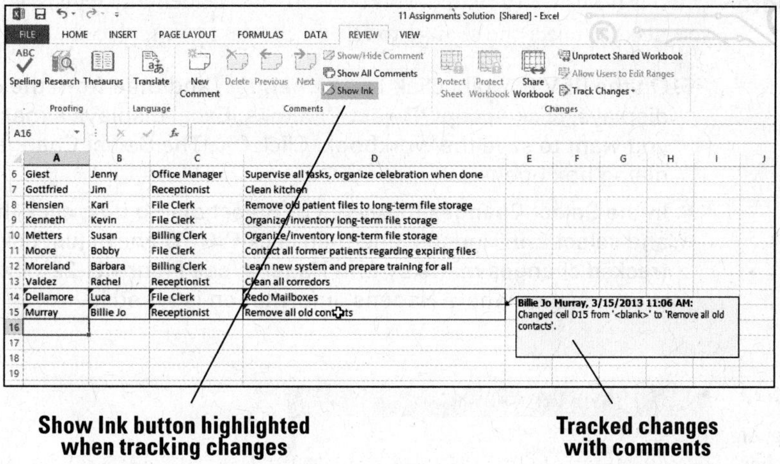

Show Ink button highlighted when tracking changes

Tracked changes with comments

13. Look at the ScreenTips for the other cells in rows 14 and 15.

PAUSE. SAVE the workbook and LEAVE it open for the next exercise.

On a network, you do not see changes made by other users until both they and you save your changes. To save your changes to a shared workbook and to see the changes that other users have saved since your last save, click Save on the Quick Access Toolbar or choose other save options such as Ctrl + S. Note that when you work in a network environment, you can click Share Workbook in the Changes group and see a list of other users who have the workbook open.

Sometimes conflicts occur when two users edit a shared workbook and try to save changes that affect the same cell. When the second user tries to save the workbook, Excel displays the Resolve Conflicts dialog box. Depending on the options established when the workbook was created and shared, you can either keep your change or accept the change made by the other user.

You can also display a list that shows how past conflicts have been resolved. These can be viewed on a separate worksheet that displays the name of the person who made the change, when and where it was made, what data was deleted or replaced, and how conflicts were resolved.

Deleting Your Changes

As noted previously, the changes you make in a shared workbook are not visible to other users until you save your work. Changes become a part of the change history only when you save. If you change your mind before saving, you can edit or delete changes. Changes must be saved before you can accept or reject them. If you do not save, Excel displays a message that the workbook must be saved before you can accept or reject changes. When you have saved your workbook and you want to delete a change, you can either enter new data or reject the change you made before saving.

STEP BY STEP   **Delete Your Changes**

GET READY. USE the workbook from the previous exercise.

1. Click the FILE tab and click Options.
2. In the General category, under Personalize your copy of Microsoft Office, in the User name box, type Erin Hagens. Click OK. You have again changed the user of the workbook for change tracking purposes.
3. Select cell A16 and type the following information in each of the columns:

   Hagens   Erin   Receptionist   Clean all corridors

4. Click cell D13, and then edit the cell so corridors is spelled correctly. Change corredors to corridors.

Take Note   Undo is inactive in a shared workbook. If you accidentally replace your data or another user's data, you need to reject the change to restore the data you replaced.

5. On the REVIEW tab, click Track Changes, and then from the drop-down menu that displays, click Accept/Reject Changes. Excel displays a message box confirming that you want to save the workbook. Click OK. The Select Changes to Accept or Reject dialog box opens.
6. In the Select Changes to Accept or Reject dialog box, click the Who drop-down arrow and select Erin Hagens, and then click OK. You have just asked Excel to return only the tracked changes made by Erin Hagens (see Figure 11-22). Excel highlights row 16 with green dashes where Hagens' information is typed in.

Figure 11-22

Select Changes to Accept or Reject dialog box

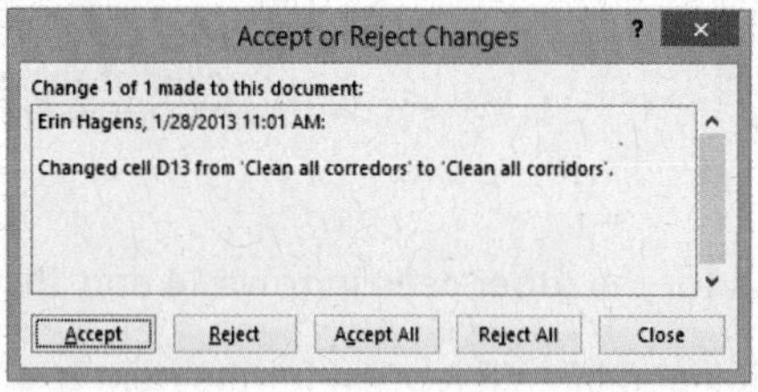

Take Note   The order of the accept or reject changes may appear differently. Accept the change in D13 but reject all other changes.

7. Click Reject. All four entries are removed.
8. When cell D13 is selected for the correction of the spelling of corridors, click Accept.

PAUSE. SAVE the workbook and LEAVE it open for the next exercise.

If you replace another user's data and you want to restore the original data, you should reject your change. If you instead delete text you entered as a replacement for other text, you will leave the cell or range blank. Rejecting your change restores the entry that you replaced.

Accepting Changes from Another User

After a shared workbook has been edited, you can easily identify which cells have been changed and determine whether you want to keep or reject the changes. You can choose to accept or reject all changes at one time without reviewing each change, or you can accept or reject them individually. In the following exercise you will learn how to accept changes from other users.

STEP BY STEP   **Accept Changes from Another User**

GET READY. USE the workbook from the previous exercise.

1. Click the FILE tab and click Options.
2. In the General category, under Personalize your copy of Microsoft Office, in the User name box, type Jim Giest. Click OK.
3. Click Track Changes and select Accept/Reject Changes from the drop-down list.
4. Not yet reviewed will be selected by default. In the Who box, select Luca Dellamore. Click OK. The Accept or Reject Changes dialog box is displayed.
5. Click Accept to accept each of the changes Luca made. The Accept or Reject Changes dialog box closes when you have accepted all changes made by Luca Dellamore.

PAUSE. SAVE the workbook and LEAVE it open for the next exercise.

You can also click the Collapse Dialog button in the Where box on the Select Changes to Accept or Reject dialog box and select the cells that contain changes. You can then accept or reject the changes in their entirety. In this exercise, some changes were highlighted by cell and others were highlighted by row, and you could accept or reject changes to the selected cell or range.

Rejecting Changes from Another User

As the owner of the Assignments workbook, the office manager in the following exercise has the authority to accept or reject changes by all users. Rejecting changes, however, does not prohibit a user from changing the data again. When all users have made the necessary changes, the owner can remove users and unshare the workbook.

STEP BY STEP   **Reject Changes from Another User**

GET READY. USE the workbook from the previous exercise.

1. Click Track Changes and click Accept/Reject Changes.
2. On the right side of the Where box, click the Collapse Dialog button.
3. Select the data in row 15 and click the Expand Dialog button. Click OK to close the Select Changes to Accept or Reject dialog box. The Accept or Reject Changes dialog box is displayed.
4. Click Reject All. A dialog box will open to ask you if you want to remove all changes and not review them. Click OK. The data is removed and row 15 is now blank.
5. SAVE the workbook in the Lesson 11 folder as *11 Assignments Edited Solution*.

PAUSE. LEAVE the workbook open for the next exercise.

When you have the opportunity to work with a shared workbook that is saved on a network, you will likely encounter conflicts when you attempt to save a change that affects the same cell as another user's changes. In the Resolve Conflicts dialog box, you can read the information about each change and the conflicting changes made by another user. The options set on the Advanced tab of the Share Workbook dialog box determine how conflicts are resolved.

Removing Shared Status from a Workbook

Before you stop sharing a workbook, make sure that all other users have completed their work and that you have accepted or rejected all changes. Any unsaved changes will be lost when you stop sharing and the history worksheet is deleted. Thus, before you remove the shared status from a workbook, you should print the history worksheet and/or copy it to another workbook. In this exercise, you remove shared status from a workbook.

STEP BY STEP   **Remove Shared Status from a Workbook**

GET READY. USE the workbook from the previous exercise.

1. On the REVIEW tab, in the Changes group, click Track Changes, and then click Highlight Changes.

2. In the When box, All is selected by default. This tells Excel to search through all tracked changes made to the worksheet.

3. Clear the Who and Where check boxes if they are selected.

4. Click the List changes on a new sheet check box. Click OK. A History sheet is added to the workbook.

5. On the History worksheet, in the corner of the worksheet adjacent to the first column and first row, click the Select All button. Click the HOME tab, and then in the Clipboard group, click the Copy button.

6. Press Ctrl + N to open a new workbook.

7. In the new workbook, on the HOME tab, in the Clipboard group, click Paste.

8. SAVE the new workbook as *11 Assignments History Solution*. CLOSE the workbook.

Take Note   It is a good idea to print the current version of a shared workbook and the change history, because cell locations in the copied history may no longer be valid if additional changes are made.

9. In the shared workbook, click on the REVIEW tab, click Unprotect Shared Workbook and then click Share Workbook. The Share Workbook dialog box is displayed. On the Editing tab, make sure that Jim Giest (the last user name changed in File Options) is the only user listed in the Who has this workbook open now list.

10. Clear the Allow changes by more than one user at the same time. Click OK to close the dialog box.

11. A dialog box opens to prompt you about removing the workbook from shared use. Click Yes to turn off the workbook's shared status. The word Shared is removed from the title bar.

12. SAVE and CLOSE the workbook.

PAUSE. LEAVE Excel open for the next exercise.

When shared status has been removed from a workbook, changes can be made like they are made in any workbook. You can, of course, turn change tracking on again, which will automatically share the workbook.

ADDING COMMENTS TO A WORKBOOK

In Excel, you can add a note to a cell by inserting a comment. You can also edit the text in comments and delete any comments that you no longer need. Comments are marked by a red triangle in the upper-right corner of the cell. When you point to this triangle, the comment appears in a box next to the cell, along with the name of the user logged on to the computer at the time the comment was created.

Inserting a Comment

Comments are a useful technique for calling attention to important or significant data and providing insights from the user that explain more about the data. For example, say that Contoso's employees are evaluated on three performance measures. The manager uses comments to note incidents related to these measures. In this exercise, you learn how to insert comments.

STEP BY STEP	Insert a Comment

GET READY. OPEN the *11 Contoso Personnel Evaluations* file for this lesson.

1. Select cell **E11**. On the **REVIEW** tab, in the Comments group, click **New Comment**. The comment text box opens for editing.

2. Type **Frequently late to work** as shown in Figure 11-23.

Figure 11-23

New comment text box

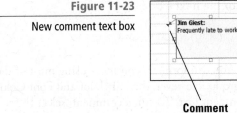

Comment text box

Comment marker

3. Click cell **D8**. Press **Shift + F2** and type **Currently completing Masters degree program for additional certification**. Click outside the comment box. The box disappears and a red triangle remains in the upper-right corner of the cell the comment was placed in.

4. Click cell **E4**. Click **New Comment** and type **Adjusted hours for family emergency**.

5. Click cell **F10**. Click **New Comment** and type **Consider salary increase**.

6. SAVE the file as *11 Evaluations Solution*.

PAUSE. SAVE the workbook and LEAVE it open for the next exercise.

As previously mentioned, Contoso, Ltd. conducts an annual employee performance review. In this workbook, the manager uses comments to note events or actions that he wants to recall when he conducts employees' annual reviews. When you add comments, Excel automatically displays the name that appears in the Name box under General Office settings in the Excel Options dialog box. If you don't want to use a name, you can select it in the comment and press Delete.

Viewing a Comment

When you rest your pointer over the red triangle that indicates that a cell has a comment attached to it, the comment is displayed. You can keep selected comments visible as you work, or you can display all comments using commands in the Comments group on the REVIEW tab. The Show/Hide Comment and Show All Comments commands allow you to display or hide comments as needed. The Previous and Next commands allow you to move from one comment to another without selecting the cells.

STEP BY STEP **View a Comment**

GET READY. USE the workbook from the previous exercise.

1. Click cell F10 and on the REVIEW tab, in the Comments, group, click Show/Hide Comment. Note that the comment remains visible when you click outside the cell.

2. Click cell E4 and click Show/Hide Comment. Again, the comment remains visible when you click outside the cell.

3. Click cell F10 and click Show/Hide Comment. The comment is hidden.

4. In the Comments group, click Next twice to navigate to the next available comment. The comment in cell E11 is displayed.

5. In the Comments group, click Show All Comments. All comments are displayed.

6. In the Comments group, click Show All Comments again to hide all comments and make sure they are no longer displayed.

PAUSE. SAVE the workbook and LEAVE it open for the next exercise.

Editing a Comment

Comments can be edited and formatted as needed. You can format a comment using most of the formatting options on the HOME tab in the Font group. However, the Fill Color and Font Color buttons on the HOME tab are not available for comment text. To edit a comment, select the cell containing the comment and click Edit Comment.

STEP BY STEP **Edit a Comment**

GET READY. USE the workbook from the previous exercise.

1. Click cell E11 and move the mouse pointer to the Edit Comment button on the REVIEW tab. The ScreenTip also shows Shift + F2 as an option, as shown in Figure 11-24.

Figure 11-24

Edit Comment button and ScreenTip

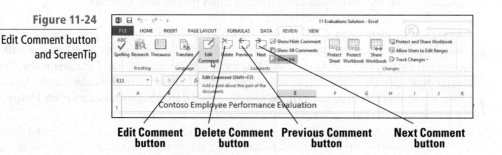

2. Click the Edit Comment button.

3. Following the existing comment text, type a . (period) followed by a space and then Placed on probation. Then click any cell between F4 and D8.

4. Click Next. The comment in D8 is displayed.

5. Select the existing comment text in D8 and type MA completed; can now prescribe medications.

6. Click cell E4 and click Edit Comment.

7. Select the text in the comment attached to E4. On the HOME tab, click Bold.

8. Click cell E11, click the REVIEW tab, and click Edit Comment.

9. Select the name and the comment text. Click the HOME tab and notice that the Fill Color and Font Color options are dimmed. Right-click on the selected text and select Format Comment.

10. In the Format Comment dialog box, click the arrow in the Color box and click Red. Click OK to apply the format and close the dialog box. There is no fill option for the comment box.

PAUSE. SAVE the workbook and LEAVE it open for the next exercise.

Deleting a Comment

Of course, you can delete comments from a workbook when they are no longer needed. Unless the workbook is protected, any user can delete comments, so you should consider protecting a workbook that contains sensitive or confidential information. In this exercise, you learn to delete a comment.

STEP BY STEP **Delete a Comment**

Another Way To delete a comment, you can click Show/Hide Comment on the REVIEW tab to display the comment and then select the edge of the comment text box and press Delete.

GET READY. USE the workbook from the previous exercise.

1. Click cell E4. The comment for this cell is displayed.

2. On the REVIEW tab, in the Comments group, click Delete.

PAUSE. SAVE the workbook and LEAVE it open for the next exercise.

Printing Comments in a Workbook

Anyone with access to a workbook can view the comments made by all users. As you learned in a previous exercise, comments can be removed from a workbook before the workbook is shared or copies are distributed. Comments can also be printed as they appear in the worksheet or on a separate page following the workbook. You will learn how to print comments in this exercise.

STEP BY STEP **Print Comments in a Workbook**

GET READY. USE the workbook from the previous exercise.

1. On the REVIEW tab, click Show All Comments. Notice that the comments slightly overlap each other.

2. In cell D8, click the border of the comment box. Select the center sizing handle at the bottom of the box and drag upward until the comment in cell E11 is completely visible.

3. Move the mouse pointer until it is a four-headed arrow on the border of the comment in cell F10. Drag the comment so it no longer overlaps the comment in cell E11 (see Figure 11-25).

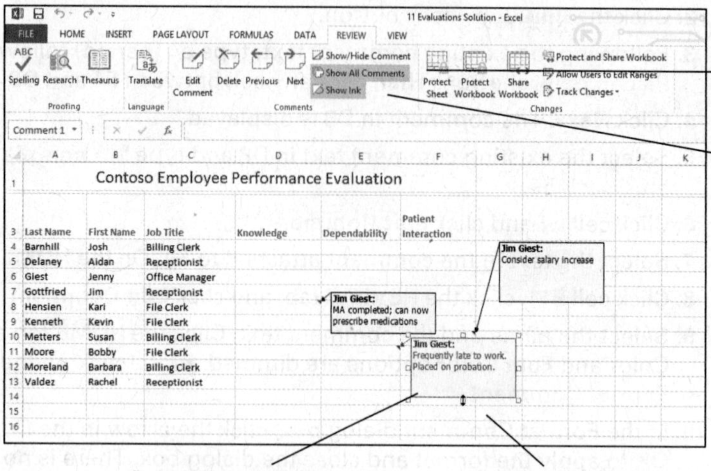

Figure 11-25

Setting up a workbook to print with comments

4. Click the PAGE LAYOUT tab, and in the Page Setup group, click Orientation. Click Landscape.

5. In the Page Setup group, click the Page Setup dialog box launcher.

6. On the Sheet tab, in the Comments box, click As displayed on sheet.

7. Click Print Preview. The Print Options window in Backstage opens.

8. Click Print.

9. SAVE and CLOSE the workbook.

CLOSE Excel.

When you print comments as they appear on the worksheet, the data in some cells may be covered. To print comments on a separate page, select At end of sheet in the Comments box on the Sheet tab of the Page Setup dialog box.

SKILL SUMMARY

In this lesson, you learned how:	Exam Objective	Objective Number
To secure your work before sharing it with others.		
To distribute a workbook by email and the cloud.		
To track changes to a workbook.		
To add comments to a workbook.		

Knowledge Assessment

Multiple Choice

Select the best response for the following statements.

1. Adding, deleting, moving, and viewing comments are performed from the commands on which ribbon tab?
   a. COMMENTS
   b. REVIEW
   c. FILE
   d. VIEW

2. The Protect and Share Workbook button is on which ribbon tab?
   a. COMMENTS
   b. REVIEW
   c. FILE
   d. VIEW

3. Which is NOT an option in the Comments group?
   a. New Comment
   b. Delete
   c. Show Ink
   d. Edit Comment

4. You can turn on track changes with all of the following EXCEPT:
   a. Track Changes button
   b. Share Workbook button
   c. Protect Sheet button
   d. Protect and Share Workbook button

5. All of the following are on the REVIEW tab except which of the following?
   a. Track Changes button
   b. Share Workbook button
   c. Protect Cells button
   d. Protect and Share Workbook button

6. Which of the following would be the strongest password?
   a. 02Feb2011 (your dog's birthdate)
   b. DenVer (the city in which you were born, with odd capitalization)
   c. 679KrDj! (the last three digits of your social security or social insurance number and first names of each of your siblings with an exclamation point)
   d. BruinsO6 (your high school mascot and year you graduated using the letter O for a zero)

7. In Excel, you can require a password for all of the following except which of the following?
   a. Opening a file
   b. Formatting cells, columns, and rows on a worksheet
   c. Adding a new worksheet, deleting a worksheet
   d. Deleting a file

8. You can send a workbook to someone by all of the following methods except which of the following?
   a. Use the FILE, Insert, Email command from Backstage view.
   b. Open a third-party email program and attach the Excel file.
   c. Save the workbook on SkyDrive and send a link to the file for viewing only.
   d. Through a Send to Mail Recipient button you've added to the Quick Access Toolbar.

9. Which of the following functions allows you to have Excel put any number in by chance from 10000 to 99999?
   a. RAND()
   b. RANDBETWEEN(10000,99999)
   c. BYCHANCE(10000,99999)
   d. RANDOM(10000,99999)

10. You can do all of the following with comments except which of the following?
   a. Format the text using a different color
   b. Change the background comment box color
   c. Not include the user name who made the comment
   d. Hide the comment

Fill in the Blank

Complete the following sentences by writing the correct word or words in the blanks provided.

1. A strong _____ protects the document because it contains upper and lower case letters, numbers, and symbols.

2. The _____ feature allows you to see what each user adds, deletes, or edits in a workbook.

3. The _____ includes the name of the person who made each change, when the change was made, and what data was changed.

4. The _____ tab contains commands for comments, protecting the worksheet and workbook, sharing the workbook, and track changes.

5. If you want Excel to assign number by chance from 100 to 999, use the _____ function.

6. When you want to add a note to a cell without entering cell contents, use cell _____ .

7. If you want to check the document for hidden properties or personal information, use the _____.

8. Use the _____ option on the Backstage view to send an email message.

9. You can use the Shift+F2 or _____ button to add a note to a cell.

10. The _____ tab of the Page Setup dialog box allows you to print comments.

Competency Assessment

Project 11-1: Protect a File with a Password

In this project, the office manager has asked you to create an inventory of company credit cards and save the file with a password.

GET READY. LAUNCH Excel if it is not already open.

1. Open a Blank workbook and type Contoso Credit Card Inventory in cell A1.

2. Type and format the information in Figure 11-26. The title in cell A1 is merged and centered, with Cell Style Heading 1 applied. The labels in row 3 are centered, with Cell Style Heading 3 applied.

Figure 11-26

Creating the Credit Cards
workbook.

	A	B	C	D	E
1		Contoso Credit Card Inventory			
2					
3	Issuer	Name on Card	Exp Date	Card	CVC
4	MasterCard	Jenny E. Giest	1/1/2015	9806-7415-9741-7237	274
5	MasterCard	Cassie A. Hicks	12/31/2020	7491-8877-4743-3608	798
6	MasterCard	Dan A. Wilson	1/1/2017	9512-1164-4689-8911	703
7	MasterCard	Mor O. Hezi	1/2/2017	1925-4341-8239-4914	787
8	MasterCard	Nicole I. Holliday	5/9/2019	9357-8825-4945-3995	614
9	Visa	Rebecca E. Laszlo	2/6/2016	8283-1378-3595-8119	569
10	Visa	Srinivas R. Iragavarapu	4/25/2018	1259-3980-3012-4877	661
11	Visa	Stephanie T. Bourne	7/21/2017	2716-2332-2847-3247	142
12	Visa	Yossi O. Banai	12/26/2017	1621-4398-6763-2687	918
13					
14					
15	MasterCard Customer Service 1-800-732-9194				
16	Visa Customer Service 1-800-537-7783				
17					

3. SAVE the file as *11 Credit Cards Solution* for use in each of the other exercises.

4. Click the FILE tab and Info is automatically selected; click Protect Workbook and choose Encrypt with Password.

5. In the Encrypt Document dialog box, type 11P1!s5 and reenter the same password in the Confirm Password dialog box.

6. SAVE and CLOSE the workbook.

LEAVE Excel open for the next project.

Project 11-2: Email and Save a File to SkyDrive

In this project, you will email your workbook to your instructor and save the file to the SkyDrive.

GET READY. LAUNCH Excel if it is not already open.

1. OPEN the *11 Credit Cards Solution* file you created in the first project. Use the password you created in Project 11-1.

2. SAVE the file as *11 Credit Cards Email Solution*.

3. Select the FILE tab, and then Share.

4. Invite People is already selected. Click Save to Cloud.

5. Click on your SkyDrive icon and then Browse, and select the SkyDrive folder for this lesson.

6. Click Save. You return to the Share screen.

7. Type the [email address of your instructor], in the personal message box, type Project 2 Assignment and click the Share button SEND the email message.

CLOSE the workbook and LEAVE Excel open for the next project.

Proficiency Assessment

Project 11-3: Send Links for Editing and Viewing a File on the Web

In this project, you will send the links for viewing and editing the file on the Web to your instructor and yourself.

GET READY. LAUNCH Excel if it is not already open.

1. OPEN the *11 Credit Cards Solution* file you created in the first project. Use the password you created in Project 11-1.

2. SAVE the file as *11 Credit Cards Links Solution*.

3. Use the Share option on the Backstage view to save the file to the cloud.

4. Open your email program and add your instructor's email address. In the body of the message, type View and press Enter and then type Edit.

5. Return to Excel's Backstage view Share page and click Get a Sharing Link for viewing, copy this in the email message after the word View, and then copy the link for editing and copy this in the email message after the word Edit. SEND the email message.

6. SAVE and CLOSE all open workbooks.

LEAVE Excel open for the next project.

Project 11-4: Add Comments to a File

In this project, you will add comments to a file.

GET READY. LAUNCH Excel if it is not already open.

1. OPEN the *11 Credit Cards Solution* file you created in the first project. Use the password you created in Project 11-1.

2. SAVE the file as *11 Credit Cards Comments Solution*.

3. In cell B4, type a new comment Initial E will be removed on next card.

4. In cell D9, type a new comment Card lost – need to cancel if not found by tomorrow.

5. In cell B12, type a new comment Yossi will be leaving at the end of the quarter – make sure to cancel card.

6. Edit the comment in D9 to just say Card lost and found [today's date].

7. Make sure all comments are hidden.

8. PRINT the worksheet with the comments displayed at the end of the sheet.

9. SAVE and CLOSE the workbook.

LEAVE Excel open for the next project.

Mastery Assessment

Project 11-5: Track Changes

In this project, you will open the credit card file and track changes with different users.

GET READY. LAUNCH Excel if it is not already open.

1. OPEN the *11 Credit Cards Solution* file you created in the first project. Use the password you created in Project 11-1.

2. SAVE the file as *11 Credit Cards Changes Solution*.

3. In cell F3, type Balance and continue the formatting for row 3.

4. Format column F to be Accounting Number Format.

5. Change the label in row 1 to be merged and centered across A1:F1.

6. Track changes for all users.

7. Change the username prior to each change to be the user whose name is on the card in row 4 and enter the balances below for each user in column F. SAVE the workbook after each balance is entered.

Jenny E. Geist	$3,533.15
Cassie A. Hicks	$9,929.25
Dan A. Wilson	$952.92
Mor O. Hezi	$9,768.55
Nicole I. Holliday	$1,669.72
Rebecca E. Laszlo	$166.00
Srinivas R. Iragavarapu	$6,186.08
Stephanie T. Bourne	$8,662.97
Yossi O. Banai	$1,621.48

8. List the changes on a new sheet.

9. Create a copy of the History sheet to a new workbook and save the workbook as *11 Credit User Changes Solution*.

10. Accept everyone's changes except Dan's in F6 and Rebecca's in F9.

11. SAVE and CLOSE both workbooks.

LEAVE Excel open for the next project.

Project 11-6: Lock Cells and Protect Worksheet Elements

This project will put together various features of worksheet security and annotation, and then have you share the workbook with other users.

GET READY. LAUNCH Excel if it is not already open.

1. OPEN the *11 Credit Cards Solution* file you created in the first project. Use the password you created in Project 11-1.

2. SAVE the file as *11 Credit Cards Passwords Solution*.

3. Turn off the password for the file (delete all characters).

4. Add a label in F3: Birthday and one in G3: Mom Name. Format these two labels the same as other labels in the row and increase column width to fit.

5. Change the title of the workbook in A1 to read Contoso Credit Card Passwords and center across A1:G1.

6. Add a label in A17: Password is Birthday in yyyymmdd format + first 4 characters of Mom's Maiden name.

7. Unlock the input for Birthday and Mom Name columns (F4:G12).

8. Protect Sheet with the password of the company name: Contoso.

9. Send this workbook in an email to your instructor. The subject should read: CC Passwords. The body text should read Go to your row. In column F type your birth date. In column G type your mother's maiden name. After you complete these changes, make sure to email the workbook back to me on Friday.

10. The following will simulate getting each workbook back. Enter the following data:

Name on Card	Birthday	Mom Name
Jenny E. Giest	4/7/1955	Soon
Cassie A. Hicks	11/6/1953	Banti
Dan A. Wilson	11/27/1949	Meadows
Mor O. Hezi	5/27/1950	Mayo
Nicole I. Holliday	7/20/1952	Kim
Rebecca E. Laszlo	2/23/1970	Untch
Srinivas R. Iragavarapu	2/1/1959	Chia
Stephanie T. Bourne	6/10/1945	Brauninger
Yossi O. Banai	7/5/1948	Posti

11. In the Excel Options dialog box, change the User name to the original name for this computer.

12. Put a comment in cell G4: **Password would look like 19550407Soon**.

13. Click the **FILE** tab, choose **Options**, select **Quick Access Toolbar**, click the **Reset** button, and select the **Reset all customizations** option to return your Excel settings to normal.

14. Send an email to your instructor with a critique of this worksheet. In the email text, tell your instructor how you would improve the worksheet or the process of creating it.

CLOSE Excel.

Creating Charts 12

LESSON SKILL MATRIX

Skills	Exam Objective	Objective Number
Building Charts	Create charts and graphs.	5.1.1
Formatting a Chart with a Quick Style or Layout		
Formatting the Parts of a Chart Manually	Add legends.	5.2.1
	Modify chart and graph parameters.	5.2.3
Modifying a Chart	Add additional data series.	5.1.2
	Switch between rows and columns in source data.	5.1.3
	Position charts and graphs.	5.2.5
	Resize charts and graphs.	5.2.2
	Apply chart layout and styles.	5.2.4
Using New Quick Analysis Tools	Insert sparklines.	2.3.2
	Demonstrate how to use Quick Analysis.	5.1.4
Creating PivotTables and PivotCharts		

© kgelati1 / iStockphoto

KEY TERMS

- axis
- chart
- chart area
- chart sheet
- data labels
- data marker
- data series
- embedded chart
- legend
- PivotChart
- PivotTable
- plot area
- sparklines
- title

361

© kgelati1 / iStockphoto

Fourth Coffee owns espresso cafes in 15 major markets. Its primary income is generated from the sale of trademarked, freshly brewed coffee, and espresso drinks. The cafes also sell a variety of pastries, packaged coffees and teas, deli-style sandwiches, and coffee-related accessories and gift items. In preparation for an upcoming budget meeting, the corporate manager wants to create charts to show trends in each of the five revenue categories for a five-year period and to project those trends to future sales. Because Excel enables you to track and work with substantial amounts of data, it is sometimes difficult to see the big picture by looking at the details in a worksheet. With Excel's charting capabilities, you can summarize and highlight data, reveal trends, and make comparisons that might not be obvious when looking at the raw data. You will use charts, Quick Analysis tools, PivotTables, and PivotCharts to present the data for Fourth Coffee.

SOFTWARE ORIENTATION

The INSERT Tab

The INSERT tab contains the command groups you'll use to create charts in Excel (see Figure 12-1). To create a basic chart in Excel that you can modify and format later, start by entering the data for the chart on a worksheet. Then, you select that data and choose a chart type to graphically display the data. Simply by choosing a chart type, a chart layout, and a chart style—all of which are within easy reach on the ribbon's INSERT and CHART TOOLS tabs—you will have instant professional results every time you create a chart.

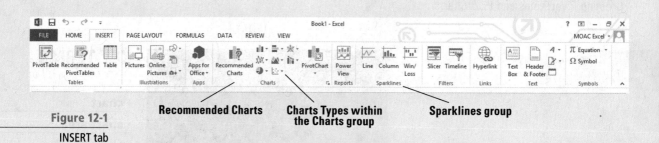

Recommended Charts   **Charts Types within**   **Sparklines group**
                              the Charts group

Figure 12-1

INSERT tab

Use this illustration as a reference throughout this lesson as you become familiar with and use Excel's charting capabilities to create attention-getting illustrations that communicate an analysis of your data.

BUILDING CHARTS

Bottom Line

A **chart** is a graphical representation of numeric data in a worksheet. Data values are represented by graphs with combinations of lines, vertical or horizontal rectangles (columns and bars), points, and other shapes. When you want to create a chart or change an existing chart, you can choose from 11 chart types with numerous subtypes and combo charts. Table 12-1 gives a brief description of each Excel chart type.

Table 12-1

Ribbon Buttons and Options

Ribbon Button and Options	Chart Name	Function	Usual Data Arrangement
	Column	Useful for comparing values across categories or a time period. Data points are vertical rectangles.	Categories (in any order) or time are usually on horizontal axis and values are on vertical axis.
	Line	Useful for showing trends in data at equal intervals. Displays continuous data over time set against a common scale. Values are represented as points along a line.	Time in equal units on horizontal axis and values on vertical axis.
	Pie	Useful for comparing the size of items in one data series and how each slice compares with the whole. Data points are displayed as a percentage of a circular pie.	Only one data series and none of the values are negative or are zero.w
	Doughnut	Useful for displaying the relationship of parts to a whole. Can contain more than one data series. Values are represented as sections of a circular band.	Categories are colors of circular bands and the size of the bands are the values of each band.
	Bar	Useful for illustrating comparisons among individual items when axis labels are long. Values are represented as horizontal rectangles.	Categories or time are along the vertical axis and values are along the horizontal axis.
	Area	Useful for emphasizing magnitude of change over time. It can be used to draw attention to the total value across a trend. Shows relationships of parts to the whole. Values represented as shaded areas.	Categories or time are on the horizontal axis and values are on the vertical axis.

Table 12-1

Ribbon Buttons and Options

Ribbon Button and Options	Chart Name	Function	Usual Data Arrangement
	Scatter	Useful for showing relationships of one numeric set of data against another numeric set of data to see whether there is a correlation between two variables. Values are represented as single data points that are the intersection of a value on one axis against the other value on the other axis.	The independent variable is usually on the horizontal axis and the dependent variable is on the vertical axis.
	Bubble	Useful for comparing three sets of values.	First value is horizontal distance, second value is vertical distance, and third value is the size of bubble.
	Stock	Useful for illustrating the fluctuation of stock prices or scientific data when there is a start, end, high, and low value during each period. There can also be a separate value attached to each time period (such as volume).	For each time period, there are three to five numbers.
	Surface	Useful for finding optimum combinations between two sets of data. The resulting plot looks similar to a topographic map or piece of cloth draped over points.	Both categories and values are numeric values.
	Radar	Useful for showing multiple variables for each subject. Variables are often unrelated but standardized to the same scale. The value of each variable is the distance from a center point. Represents values as points that radiate on spikes from the center.	First column is label of spike. First row is label of units. Values for each unit go down each column starting in the second column after the row labels. The maximum value is the outer edge of chart. The minimum value is in the center of the chart.
	Combo	Two or more chart types such as line and column.	

Take Note When building a worksheet for a chart, the time period is normally displayed in the first row and the categories are in the first column. There is a Switch Row/Column button on the DESIGN tab that allows you to change the orientation of the data as it appears in the chart. The fourth column in Table 12-1 assumes the default setup for data in a chart. You should know what your organization's standards are because charts are meant for quickly telling a story and if they are laid out differently than the standards, the charts may defeat their purpose and confuse rather than enlighten your audience.

Workplace *Ready*

PERSONAL CHARTS

As you see throughout this lesson, in addition to looking good, charts can be tools for communicating a lot of information in an easy-to-read format and they help make decisions. As you go through this chapter, consider the financial decisions you make throughout your life. It might feel impossible to save $1,000 now to put toward the future; however, it might also feel impossible when you have children in college. It's hard to say. To get about $100,000 by the age of 80, you could put $1,000 in a stock market fund (assuming historic rates of return) one time at age 20 or you can put $1,000 a year for 18 years from age 50 to 67).

Try to put your major life financial decisions in workbooks to see the impact of your decisions on your pocketbook. Obviously, you have to make decisions based on many more factors, but at least you will have one objective viewpoint covered.

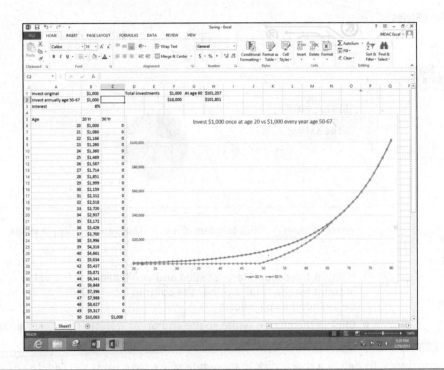

Selecting Data to Include in a Chart

Excel's ribbon interface makes it simple to create a chart. As you will see in the following exercise, you can create one of the common chart types by clicking its image on the INSERT tab. More important than the chart type, however, is the selection of the data you want to display graphically. What aspects of the data do you want viewers to notice? The answer to that question is a major factor in selecting an appropriate chart type. In this exercise, you will learn to select data for use in an Excel chart that returns your calculations and data in a color-coded pie chart with sections identified by numbers or labels.

There are two approaches to identifying the data for your chart. If you lay out your worksheet efficiently, you can select multiple ranges at one time that will become the different chart elements. The second way is to identify the chart type and then select the data for each chart element. If you create many charts and eventually identify your own chart types, you might benefit by using the former method. If your charts are more complex, you will benefit by using the latter method. The first part of this lesson walks you through choosing the ranges first and the second part of the lesson walks you through adding and removing certain chart elements.

STEP BY STEP   Select Data to Include in a Chart

GET READY. LAUNCH Excel.

1. OPEN the *12 4thCoffee Financial History* file for this lesson.
2. Select **B2:B8** (the 2010 data).
3. Click the **INSERT** tab, and in the Charts group, click the **Pie** button. Click the **first** 2-D Pie chart. A color-coded pie chart with sections identified by number is displayed.
4. Move the mouse pointer to the largest slice. The ScreenTip shows *Series 1 Point 1 Value: 2010 (39%)*, as shown in Figure 12-2. This corresponds to the label 2010 rather than actual data.

Figure 12-2

Pie chart created with incorrect data

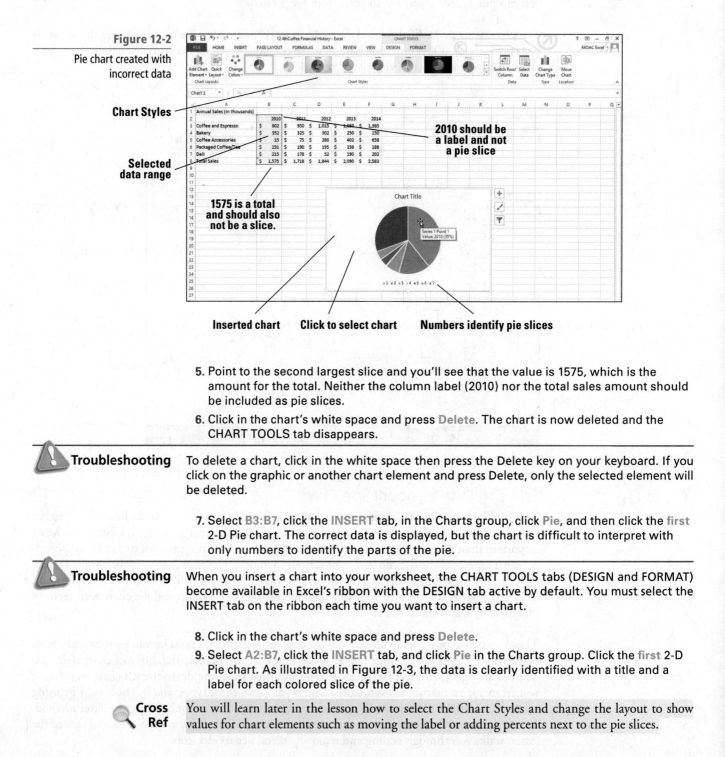

Chart Styles

Selected data range

2010 should be a label and not a pie slice

1575 is a total and should also not be a slice.

Inserted chart   Click to select chart   Numbers identify pie slices

5. Point to the second largest slice and you'll see that the value is 1575, which is the amount for the total. Neither the column label (2010) nor the total sales amount should be included as pie slices.
6. Click in the chart's white space and press **Delete**. The chart is now deleted and the CHART TOOLS tab disappears.

Troubleshooting   To delete a chart, click in the white space then press the Delete key on your keyboard. If you click on the graphic or another chart element and press Delete, only the selected element will be deleted.

7. Select **B3:B7**, click the **INSERT** tab, in the Charts group, click **Pie**, and then click the **first** 2-D Pie chart. The correct data is displayed, but the chart is difficult to interpret with only numbers to identify the parts of the pie.

Troubleshooting   When you insert a chart into your worksheet, the CHART TOOLS tabs (DESIGN and FORMAT) become available in Excel's ribbon with the DESIGN tab active by default. You must select the INSERT tab on the ribbon each time you want to insert a chart.

8. Click in the chart's white space and press **Delete**.
9. Select **A2:B7**, click the **INSERT** tab, and click **Pie** in the Charts group. Click the **first** 2-D Pie chart. As illustrated in Figure 12-3, the data is clearly identified with a title and a label for each colored slice of the pie.

Cross Ref   You will learn later in the lesson how to select the Chart Styles and change the layout to show values for chart elements such as moving the label or adding percents next to the pie slices.

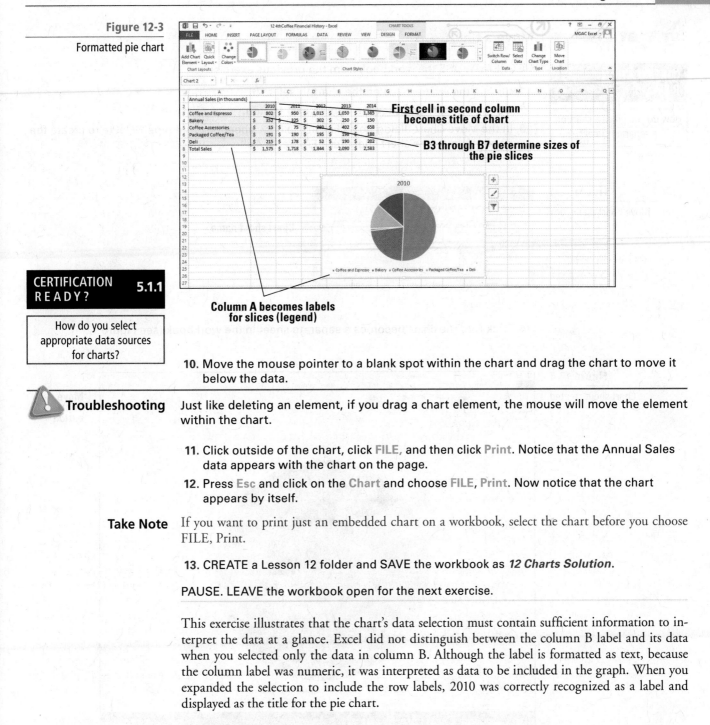

Figure 12-3

Formatted pie chart

First cell in second column becomes title of chart

B3 through B7 determine sizes of the pie slices

Column A becomes labels for slices (legend)

10. Move the mouse pointer to a blank spot within the chart and drag the chart to move it below the data.

Troubleshooting   Just like deleting an element, if you drag a chart element, the mouse will move the element within the chart.

11. Click outside of the chart, click FILE, and then click Print. Notice that the Annual Sales data appears with the chart on the page.

12. Press Esc and click on the Chart and choose FILE, Print. Now notice that the chart appears by itself.

Take Note   If you want to print just an embedded chart on a workbook, select the chart before you choose FILE, Print.

13. CREATE a Lesson 12 folder and SAVE the workbook as *12 Charts Solution*.

PAUSE. LEAVE the workbook open for the next exercise.

This exercise illustrates that the chart's data selection must contain sufficient information to interpret the data at a glance. Excel did not distinguish between the column B label and its data when you selected only the data in column B. Although the label is formatted as text, because the column label was numeric, it was interpreted as data to be included in the graph. When you expanded the selection to include the row labels, 2010 was correctly recognized as a label and displayed as the title for the pie chart.

When you select data and create a pie chart, the chart is placed on the worksheet. This is referred to as an **embedded chart**, meaning it is placed on the worksheet rather than on a separate **chart sheet**, a sheet that contains only a chart.

Moving a Chart

When you insert a chart, by default it is embedded in the worksheet. You can click a corner of a chart or the midpoint of any side to display sizing handles (two-sided vertical, horizontal, or diagonal white arrows). You can use the sizing handles to change the size of a chart. To move the chart, you need to click and drag the four-headed black mouse pointer in the white space. You might want a chart to be reviewed with the worksheet data or you might want the chart to stand on its own. In this exercise, you move a chart to a new sheet in the workbook.

STEP BY STEP   **Move a Chart**

CERTIFICATION READY?   5.2.5

How do you place a chart on a separate sheet?

GET READY. USE the workbook from the previous exercise.

1. Click in the white space on the chart to select it.
2. On the DESIGN tab, click the Move Chart button.
3. In the Move Chart dialog box, click in the New sheet box and type 2010Pie to create the name of your new chart sheet (see Figure 12-4).

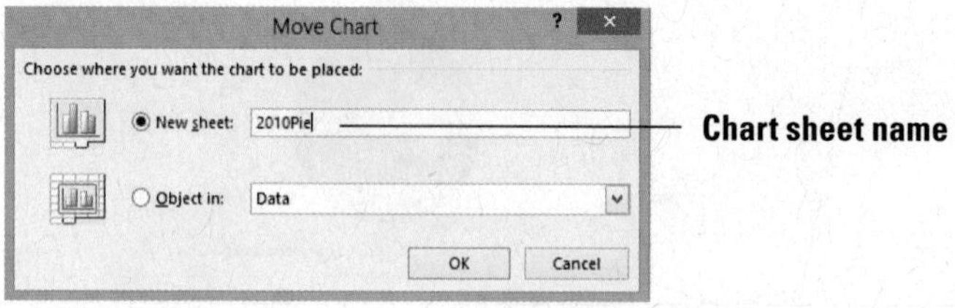

Figure 12-4

Move Chart dialog box

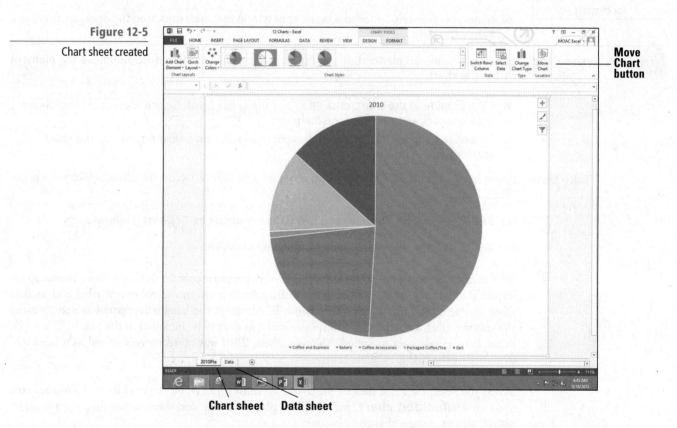

4. Click OK. The chart becomes a separate sheet in the workbook (see Figure 12-5).

Figure 12-5

Chart sheet created

5. Click on the Data worksheet tab to return to the data portion of the workbook.
6. SAVE the workbook.

PAUSE. LEAVE the workbook open for the next exercise.

If you want to return the chart to the Data sheet, you could go to the 2010Pie tab, click the Move Chart button again, and in the Object in box, select Data (the name of the sheet). Refer back to Figure 12-4.

Choosing the Right Chart for Your Data

You can create most charts, such as column and bar charts, from data that you have arranged in rows or columns in a worksheet. Some charts, such as pie and bubble charts, require a specific data arrangement. A single pie chart cannot be used for comparisons across periods of time or for analyzing trends. The column chart works well for comparisons. In a 2-D or 3-D column chart, each data marker is represented by a column. In a stacked column, data markers are stacked so that the top of the column is the total of the same category (or time) from each data series. A line chart shows points connected by a line for each value. The line chart emphasizes the trend or change over time and the column chart highlights differences between categories. In this exercise, you learn how to create a column chart and a line chart to illustrate the increase in coffee and espresso sales at Fourth Coffee during a five-year period.

STEP BY STEP   **Choose the Right Chart for Your Data**

GET READY. USE the workbook from the previous exercise.

1. Select cells **A2:F7**.

⚠ Troubleshooting   Make sure you do not include row 8, the Total Sales row. Otherwise, the last column in each year will be huge and dwarf the other columns. It is standard practice not to include totals in column and bar charts. In some instances it may be helpful to add a line with the totals as a separate axis on the right.

CERTIFICATION READY?   5.1.1

How do you pick the chart type for your chart?

2. Click the **INSERT** tab, and in the Charts group, click **Column**. In the Column drop-down list, move to each of the options. When you pause on an option, Excel shows a preview of the chart on the worksheet and a description and tips for the selected chart type. Under 3-D Column, move to the first option. As shown in Figure 12-6, the ScreenTip shows that the type of chart is a 3-D Clustered Column and it is suggested to compare values when the order of categories is not important.

Figure 12-6

ScreenTip and chart preview

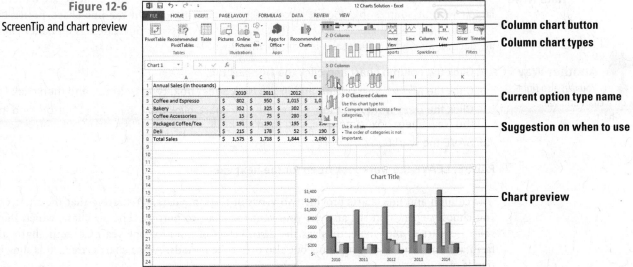

— Column chart button
— Column chart types
— Current option type name
— Suggestion on when to use
— Chart preview

---

3. In the drop-down list, click **3-D Clustered Column**. The column chart illustrates the sales for each of the revenue categories for the five-year period. The CHART TOOLS tab appears with the DESIGN tab active.

4. Anywhere in a blank area on the chart, click and drag the chart below the worksheet data and position it at the far left.

5. Click outside the column chart to deselect it. Notice that the CHART TOOLS tab disappears.

CERTIFICATION READY?   5.1.1

How do you select appropriate chart types to represent data sources?

6. Select **A2:F7**, click the **INSERT** tab, and in the Charts group, click **Line**. In the 2-D Line group, click the **Line with Markers** option (first chart in the second row). Position the line chart next to the column chart. Note that the CHART TOOLS tab is on the ribbon with the DESIGN tab active. Refer to Figure 12-7.

Figure 12-7

Column chart and line chart

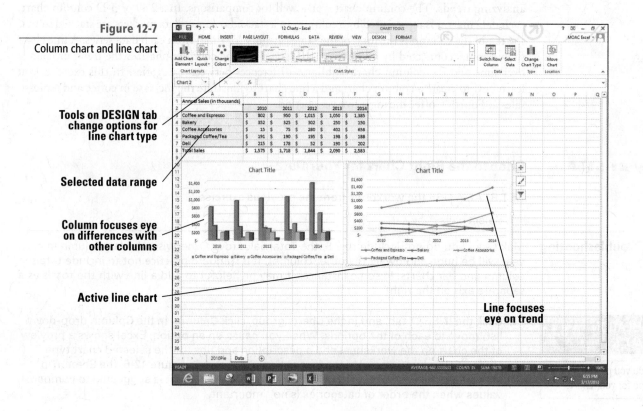

Tools on DESIGN tab change options for line chart type

Selected data range

Column focuses eye on differences with other columns

Active line chart

Line focuses eye on trend

Take Note   Take a minute to study the two charts. In the column chart, Coffee and Espresso are by far the largest revenue sources, but Coffee Accessories are catching up. On the line chart, notice that Coffee and Espresso increase over time, but that Coffee Accessories increases faster. Bakery items are decreasing, and the Deli sales is a bit up and down.

Another Way
You can also right-click on a chart and select Move Chart.

7. Click the column chart and click the **DESIGN** tab.

8. Click the **Move Chart** button and in the New sheet box, type **Column**, and then click **OK**.

9. Click the **Data** worksheet tab, select the **line** chart, click the **Move Chart** button, and in the New sheet box, type **Line**, and then click **OK**.

10. SAVE the workbook.

PAUSE. LEAVE the workbook open for the next exercise.

The column and line charts provide two views of the same data, illustrating that the chart type you choose depends on the analysis you want the chart to portray. The pie chart, which shows values as part of the whole, displays the distribution of sales for one year. Column charts also facilitate comparisons among items but also over time periods. A line chart's strength is showing trends over time.

The line chart you created in this exercise is shown in Figure 12-8. The chart includes data markers to indicate each year's sales. A **data marker** is a bar, area, dot, slice, or other symbol in a chart that represents a single data point or value that originates from a worksheet cell. Related data markers in a chart constitute a **data series**.

Figure 12-8

Line chart with data markers

Data marker

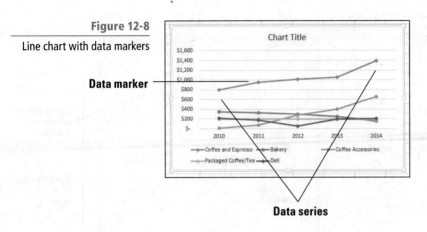

Data series

Using Recommended Charts

If you are new to charting, it can be overwhelming with up to 11 options on each of the 8 chart buttons, not to mention the more chart type choices on each button. Excel 2013 has a new feature to help narrow the choices depending on the data that you select. It is the Recommended Charts button. In this exercise, you will select different sets of data and observe what choices Recommended Charts displays.

STEP BY STEP   **Use Recommended Charts**

GET READY. USE the workbook from the previous exercise.

1. Click the Data worksheet tab.
2. Select the Year labels and Coffee and Espresso cells A2:F3, click the INSERT tab, and then click the Recommended Charts button. Notice that Excel recommends four chart types (see Figure 12-9). Excel explains when you use each of the charts underneath the example.

Figure 12-9

Recommended charts for
two rows of data (labels and
values)

Coffee and Espresso becomes title of chart.

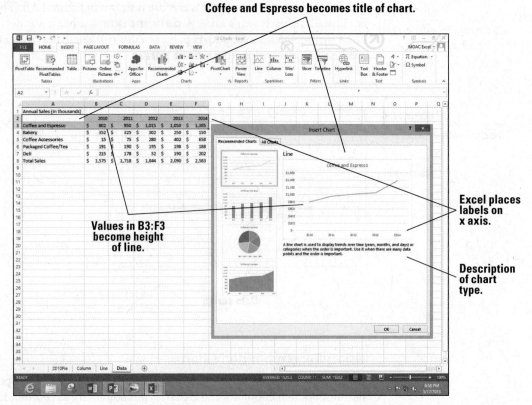

**Values in B3:F3
become height
of line.**

**Excel places
labels on
x axis.**

**Description
of chart
type.**

3. Click the other three chart types and read each description. Click the Line chart, and then click OK.

4. Click the Move Chart button, and in the New sheet box, type CoffeeLine, and then click OK.

5. Click the Data worksheet tab, select cells A2:B7 to include the labels and data for 2010, and then on the INSERT tab, click the Recommended Charts button. Notice the three chart types recommended this time (see Figure 12-10).

Figure 12-10

Recommended charts for text in one column and values in next column

2010 becomes
title of chart.

Values in B3:B7
become length
of bars.

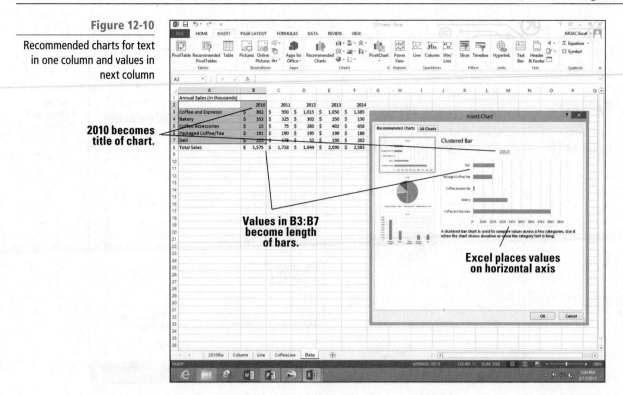

Excel places values
on horizontal axis

Take Note   Notice that three charts are recommended this time compared to the four different charts in   .
Because 2010-2014 is in the first row in the previous example, charts that show trends are included
(line and column). Because the first column is selected this time, charts that compare items are
selected (bar, pie, and column charts). There is some overlap in the recommended chart types;
column charts are suggested in both cases.

6. Click Cancel. Select A2:F7 and click the Recommended Charts button. Look at each of
the suggested choices and scan the description. Click Cancel.

7. Select A8:F8 and click the Recommended Charts button. Notice that the choices are
even different from the options in Figure 12-9. Click Cancel.

8. Select A2:F2, hold down Ctrl, and select A8:F8. You do not have to choose adjacent
ranges for your data.

9. Click the Recommended Charts button. Notice that the recommended choices in Figure
12-11 are the same as Figure 12-9 because the first row includes years and the second
row includes values. Click OK.

Figure 12-11

Nonadjacent ranges used prior to choosing Recommended Charts

Range A2:F2 —

Range A8:F8 —

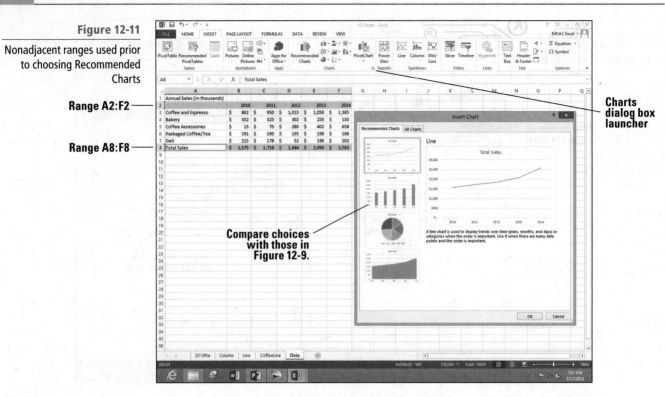

Compare choices with those in Figure 12-9.

Charts dialog box launcher

Another Way
You can also select the data and press F11. Excel tries to determine the best chart for the selected data and places this chart on a separate sheet in one step.

10. Click the **Move Chart** button, and in the New sheet box, type **TotalLine**, and then click **OK**.

11. SAVE the workbook.

PAUSE. LEAVE the workbook open for the next exercise.

Creating a Bar Chart

Bar charts are similar to column charts and can be used to illustrate comparisons among individual items. Data that is arranged in columns or rows on a worksheet can be plotted in a bar chart. Clustered bar charts compare values across categories. Stacked bar charts show the relationship of individual items to the whole of that item. The side-by-side bar charts you create in this exercise illustrate two views of the same data. You can experiment with chart types and select the one that best portrays the message you want to convey to your target audience.

STEP BY STEP | **Create a Bar Chart**

GET READY. USE the workbook from the previous exercise.

1. Click the **Data** worksheet tab.

2. Select cells **A2:F7** and on the INSERT tab, in the Charts group, click the **Bar** button.

Take Note A ScreenTip displays the chart type name when you hover the mouse pointer on its button or subtype option.

3. Click the **3-D Clustered Bar** subtype. The data is displayed in a clustered bar chart and the DESIGN tab is active on the CHART TOOLS tab.

4. Drag the clustered bar chart to the left, below the worksheet data.

5. Select **A2:F7**. On the INSERT tab, in the Charts group, click the **Bar** button.

6. Click the **3-D Stacked Bar** subtype.

7. Position the stacked bar graph next to the 3-D bar graph. Your worksheet should look like Figure 12-12.

Figure 12-12

A clustered bar and stacked bar using the same data as the line and column charts earlier in the lesson (see Figure 12-7).

Each part of bar adds together to show total in the stacked bar.

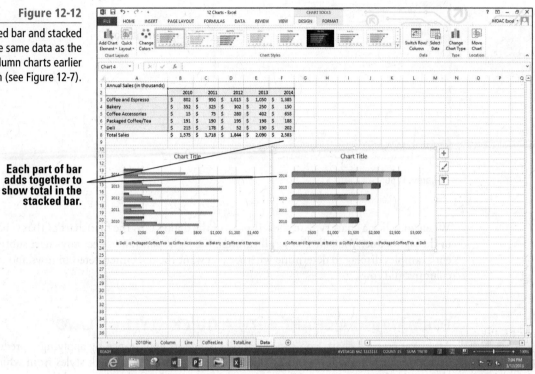

Another Way
You can open the Insert Chart dialog box by clicking Recommended Charts, and then clicking the All Charts tab. You can also choose any chart button and click the More Charts button on the bottom of any menu.

8. Click the **Move Chart** button, and in the New sheet box, type **StackedBar** and click **OK**.

9. Click the **Data** worksheet tab, click the clustered bar chart, click the **Move Chart** button, and in the New sheet box, type **ClusteredBar**, and then click **OK**.

10. SAVE the workbook.

PAUSE. LEAVE the workbook open for the next exercise.

The Charts group on the INSERT tab contains eight buttons leading to multiple chart types (including a combined chart type). To create one of these charts, select the worksheet data and click the button and choose one of the chart type options. You can select from any chart type by clicking the Charts dialog box launcher (see Figure 12-11) to open the Insert Chart dialog box. The Recommended Charts shows in the first tab. Click on the All Charts tab in the dialog box as shown in Figure 12-13 to see samples of all types and subtypes of charts.

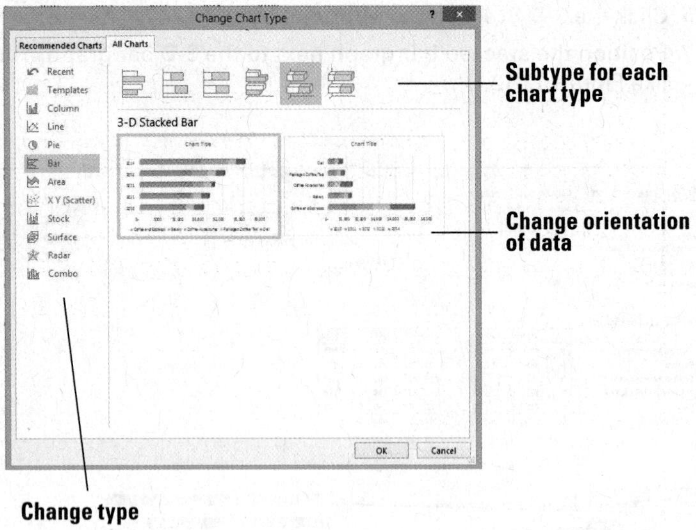

Figure 12-13

All Charts tab of the Insert Chart dialog box

When you click a chart type in the left pane of the dialog box, the first chart of that type is selected in the right pane. You can also scroll through the right pane and select any chart subtype. Different examples display to determine whether you want the data interpreted in rows and columns vs. columns and rows.

FORMATTING A CHART WITH A QUICK STYLE OR LAYOUT

Bottom Line

After you create a chart, you can instantly change its appearance by applying a predefined style or layout. Excel provides a variety of useful quick layouts and quick styles from which you can choose. As shown in Figure 12-14, when you create a chart, the chart tools become available and the DESIGN and FORMAT tabs and Quick Layout button appears on the ribbon.

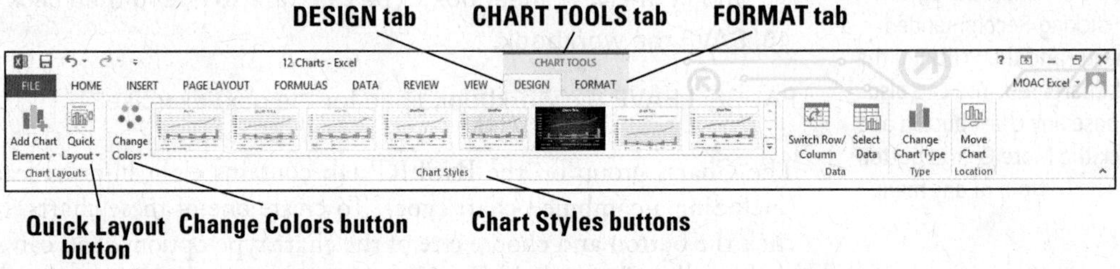

Figure 12-14

The CHART TOOLS tab activates when a chart is inserted.

Formatting a Chart with a Quick Style

Predefined layouts and styles are timesaving features that you can use to enhance the appearance of your charts. Quick Styles, as defined by Microsoft, are the chart styles available in the Chart Styles group of the DESIGN tab in the CHART TOOLS tab. They are Quick Styles because you can click them in an instant instead of searching through the Chart Styles gallery. In this exercise, you apply a Quick Style to your chart.

STEP BY STEP   **Format a Chart with a Quick Style**

GET READY. USE the workbook from the previous exercise.

1. Click on the 2010Pie chart tab. If the DESIGN tab is not visible and the buttons active, click the white space inside the chart boundary and click the DESIGN tab if necessary.

2. One of the Chart Styles is already selected. Click each of the styles until you come to the style shown in Figure 12-15 with the labels and percentages shown next to each pie slice. If necessary, click the down arrow to select more styles.

Figure 12-15

Pie chart with labels next
to each slice

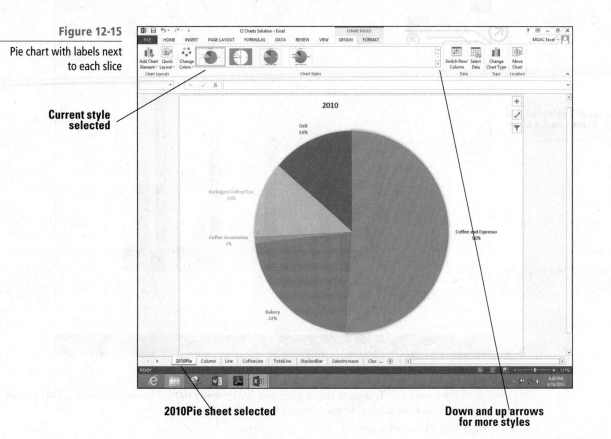

Current style
selected

2010Pie sheet selected   Down and up arrows
                                                                for more styles

3. The chart colors are determined by the theme of your worksheet. Click the Change Colors button and move the mouse pointer over each of the different rows to see the preview of the pie change.

4. Click Color 3 to make the change.

5. SAVE the workbook.

PAUSE. LEAVE the workbook open for the next exercise.

Take Note   You can use the Chart Styles buttons as you are first creating an embedded chart on a worksheet or use them while editing a chart whether it is embedded or a separate chart sheet as shown here.

Formatting a Chart with Quick Layout

In addition to the colors and patterns, you can change which elements appear on your chart and where they appear. This includes items such as axis titles, data tables, and where the legend goes. In this exercise, you will apply a Quick Layout to your chart to display a data table under the chart.

STEP BY STEP Format a Chart with Quick Layout

CERTIFICATION READY? 5.2.4

How do you quickly change the layout of a chart?

GET READY. USE the workbook from the previous exercise.

1. Click on the **Column** chart tab.
2. On the **DESIGN** tab, click the **Quick Layout** button. As you move to each of the options, the chart changes to preview what the option will look like (see Figure 12-16).

Figure 12-16

Quick Layout choices

Layout 5 selected and shown on the chart

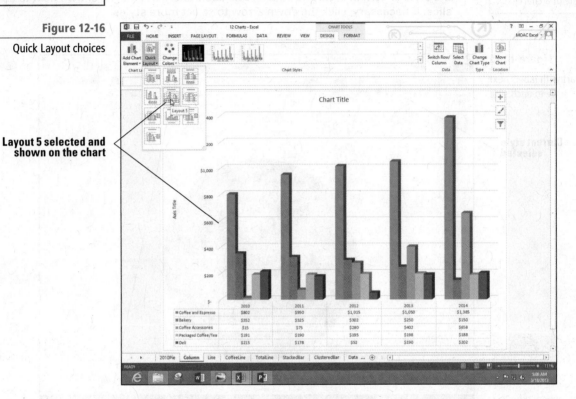

3. Click **Layout 5**. The data table appears under the chart. The years (2010-2014) act as both the x-axis labels and column headers of the data table.
4. SAVE the workbook.

PAUSE. LEAVE the workbook open for the next exercise.

You can also use the design buttons on the right of a selected chart to change the style and color and which elements appear on the chart. Click on the chart and click the first button to select which items appear on the chart as shown in Figure 12-17.

Figure 12-17

Chart Elements button

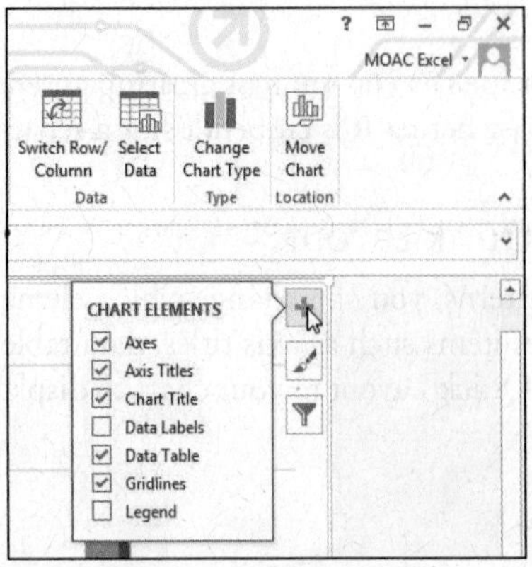

Click the second button and choose which style and color you want (see Figure 12-18).

Figure 12-18

The Chart Style button: Style and color options

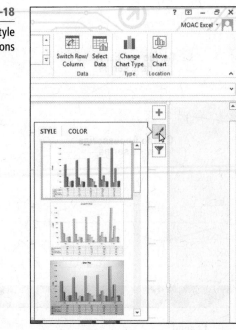

FORMATTING THE PARTS OF A CHART MANUALLY

The FORMAT tab provides a variety of ways to format chart elements. To format a chart element, click the chart element that you want to change, and then use the appropriate commands from the FORMAT tab.

The following list defines some of the chart elements you can manually format in Excel. These elements are illustrated in Figure 12-19:

• **Chart area:** The entire chart and all its elements.

• **Plot area:** The area bounded by the axes.

• **Axis:** A line bordering the chart plot area used as a frame of reference for measurement.

• **Data Series:** Row or column of data represented by a line, set of columns, bars or other chart type

• **Title:** Descriptive text that is aligned to an axis or at the top of a chart.

• **Data labels:** Text that provides additional information about a data marker, which represents a single data point or value that originates from a worksheet cell.

• **Legend:** A box that identifies the patterns or colors that are assigned to the data series or categories in a chart.

Figure 12-19

Chart elements

Select Chart
Element

Chart Title

Chart area

Plot area

Vertical
(Value) Axis

Horizontal
(Category) Axis

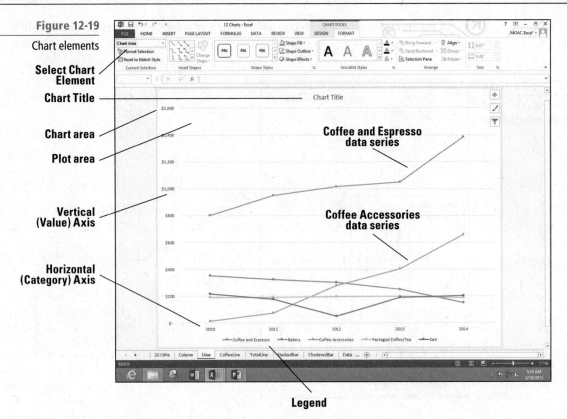

Legend

Take Note   To learn the elements of the chart, click the Chart Elements drop-down list and select each of the elements on the sample charts in your workbook.

Editing and Adding Text on Charts

wUp until now we have accepted the default labels on the charts created. You can edit existing labels in a similar way that you do in a worksheet. Click the label, select the text, and type the new text. If the element isn't visible, you can add it by checking the CHART ELEMENTS option or inserting a text box.

STEP BY STEP   **Edit and Add Text on Charts**

GET READY. USE the workbook from the previous exercise.

1. Click the 2010Pie chart tab.

2. Click the 2010 title, move the insertion point to the end of the label and click. Type a space and then type Annual Sales. The text appears in all caps based on the current layout.

3. Select the label text. Click the HOME tab and click the Font dialog box launcher. The Font dialog box appears (see Figure 12-20).

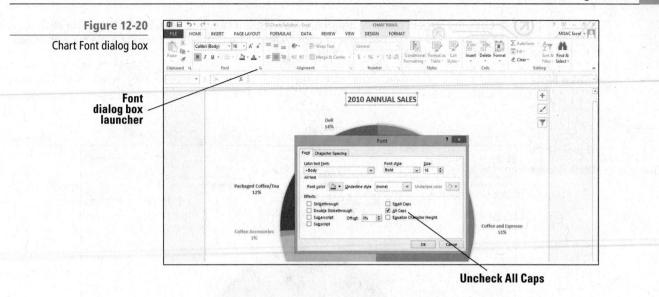

Figure 12-20

Chart Font dialog box

Font dialog box launcher

Uncheck All Caps

4. Click the All Caps check box to uncheck this option. Click OK.

5. Click on the FORMAT tab and click the Text Box button. Click the bottom left corner of the chart area and type your initials and today's date in the text box.

6. Edit the chart titles on each of the charts as follows:

Chart	Title	Text
Column	Chart Title	Annual Sales
Column	Axis Title	Thousands
Line	Chart Title	Annual Sales (Thousands)
StackedBar	Chart Title	Annual Sales
ClusteredBar	Chart Title	Annual Sales

7. SAVE the workbook.

PAUSE. LEAVE the workbook open for the next exercise.

Formatting a Data Series

Use commands on the FORMAT tab to add or change fill colors or patterns applied to chart elements. Select the element to format and click on one of the buttons on the ribbon or display the Format pane to add fill color or a pattern to the selected chart element.

STEP BY STEP **Format a Data Series**

GET READY. USE the workbook from the previous exercise.

1. Click the 2010Pie chart tab.

2. Click in the largest slice of the pie. You can see data selectors around each of the pie slices.

3. Click the FORMAT tab, click the Shape Fill button, and then choose Red in the Standard Colors section. All the slices of the pie change to red. Click Undo. You want to select the largest pie slice instead of all of the pie slices.

4. Click the largest pie slice again and you should see data selectors only on the slice. Click the Shape Fill button and choose Red. The Coffee and Espresso pie slice changes to Red, as shown in Figure 12-21.

Take Note The first click on a data series selects the whole series. The second click selects the individual marker for the series.

Figure 12-21

Change color of data element

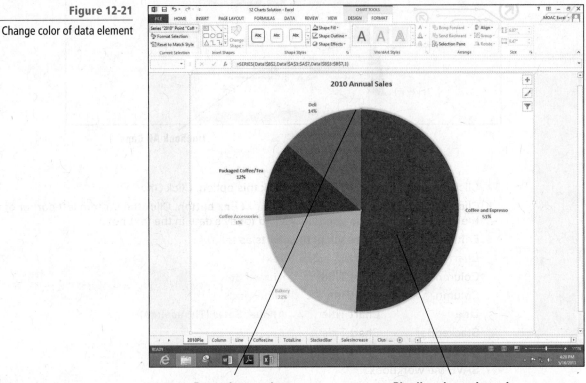

Data selectors show only one pie slice selected

Pie slice changed to red

5. Click the Column chart tab.
6. Click the tallest bar (Coffee and Espresso). Notice that the five bars have data selectors. Click the Shape Fill button and select Red. All five bars and the legend color for Coffee and Espresso changes to red.
7. Click the Shape Effects button, click Bevel and notice the options available (see Figure 12-22).

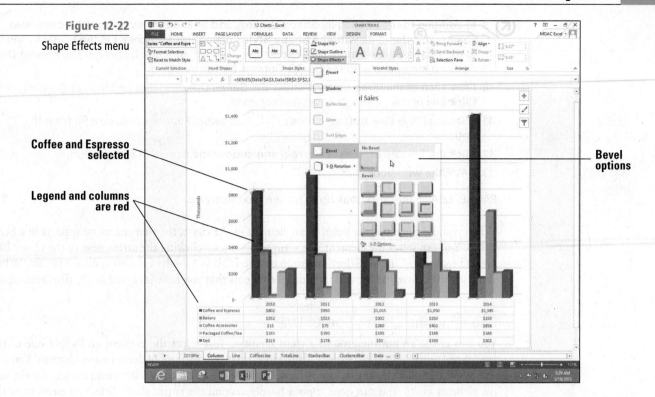

Figure 12-22

Shape Effects menu

Coffee and Espresso selected

Legend and columns are red

Bevel options

8. Click the **first** Bevel option (Circle). Repeat this option for each of the data series. The chart now looks like Figure 12-23.

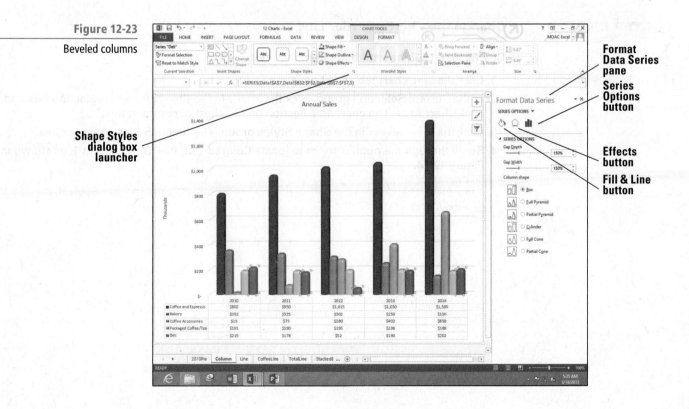

Figure 12-23

Beveled columns

Shape Styles dialog box launcher

Format Data Series pane

Series Options button

Effects button

Fill & Line button

9. In addition to the Shape Fill, Shape Outline, and Shape Effects buttons, you can also change the elements with the Shape Styles dialog box launcher. On the FORMAT tab, in the Shape Styles group, click the Shape Styles dialog box launcher. The Format Data Series pane opens with the Series Options button selected.

10. Click each of the three buttons under the Series Options label and look at the choices. Click one of the Coffee Accessories columns.

11. Click the Fill & Line button, choose FILL, and select Picture or texture fill from the options.

12. Click the Texture drop-down arrow and choose the Brown Marble option.

13. SAVE the workbook.

PAUSE. LEAVE the workbook open for the next exercise.

When you use the mouse to point to an element in the chart, the element name appears in a ScreenTip. You can select the element you want to format by clicking the arrow next to the Chart Elements box in the Current Selection group on the FORMAT tab. This list is chart specific. When you click the arrow, the list will include all elements that you have included in the displayed chart.

Changing the Chart's Border Line

You can create an outline around a chart element. Just select the element and apply one of the predefined outlines or click Shape Outline to format the shape of a selected chart element. You can also click the Shape Styles dialog box launcher to bring up the pane with menu choices for the way the element looks. You can even apply a border around the entire chart. Select an element or the chart and use the colored outlines in the Shape Styles group on the FORMAT tab, or click Shape Outline and choose a Theme or Standard color for the border.

STEP BY STEP   **Change the Chart's Border Line**

GET READY. USE the workbook from the previous exercise.

1. Click the Line chart tab and choose the FORMAT tab.

2. In the Current Selection group, click the arrow in the Chart Elements selection box and click Chart Area. The chart area section on the chart becomes active.

3. Click the More arrow in the Shape Styles group. The Shape Styles gallery opens.

4. Scroll through the outline styles to locate Colored Outline – Blue, Accent 1, as shown in Figure 12-24.

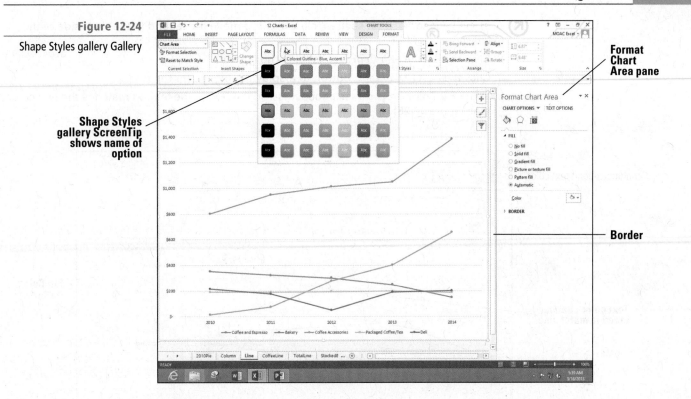

Figure 12-24

Shape Styles gallery Gallery

Shape Styles gallery ScreenTip shows name of option

Format Chart Area pane

Border

5. Click **Colored Outline – Blue, Accent 1**. You might not notice a change. This is because the Width of the line may be set so thin you can't see it.

6. In the Format Chart Area pane, click the **BORDER arrow** to expand that section.

7. Click the **Width up arrow**, until you get to 2.5 pt. Now you can see that the chart is outlined with a light blue border.

8. Click the **Coffee and Espresso** line.

9. In the **Color** drop-down, under the LINE section, choose **Red**.

10. SAVE your workbook.

PAUSE. LEAVE the workbook open for the next exercise.

Modifying a Chart's Legend

You can modify the content of the legend, expand or collapse the legend box, edit the text that is displayed, and change character attributes. A finished chart should stand alone—that is, the chart should contain sufficient data to convey the intended message. In the chart you modify in this exercise, changing the font colors in the legend to match the blocks in the columns provides an additional visual aid that enables the viewer to quickly see the income contribution for each category.

STEP BY STEP   **Modify a Chart's Legend**

GET READY. USE the workbook from the previous exercise.

1. Click the **Line** chart tab.

2. On the **FORMAT** tab, click the **Chart Elements drop-down arrow**, and choose **Legend**.

3. If the Format Legend pane does not appear, click the **Shape Styles dialog box launcher**.

4. Click the **Legend Options** button.

CERTIFICATION READY?   5.2.1

How do you add a chart legend?

5. In the Legend Position section, click **Right** to move the legend to the right side of the chart.

6. Click the **Coffee and Espresso** label in the legend.

7. Click the **TEXT OPTIONS** button to display the menus for the text.

8. In the Fill Color drop-down, choose **Red** so the text in the legend matches the line color (see Figure 12-25).

Figure 12-25

Changing Legend text color

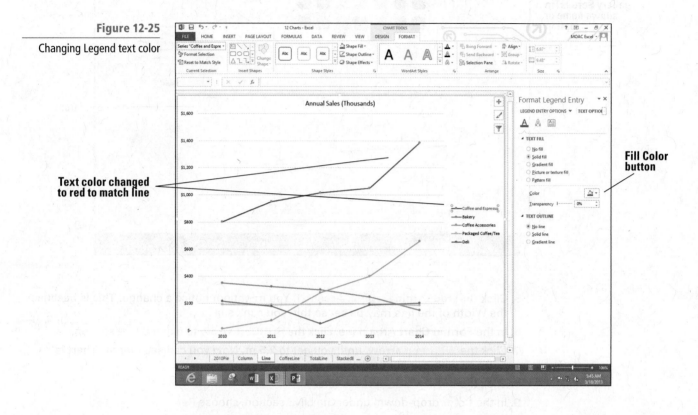

9. Click the **2010Pie** chart tab.

10. Click the **Coffee and Espresso** label twice. If necessary, click the **TEXT OPTIONS** button and underneath TEXT FILL, click the **Color** button, and choose **Red** to change the text color.

11. CLOSE the Format Data Label pane and SAVE the workbook.

PAUSE. LEAVE the workbook open for the next exercise.

MODIFYING A CHART

Bottom Line

Sometimes the chart that you add from the INSERT tab and modify through the Quick Layout and Chart Styles still isn't exactly what you want. In addition to using the creation and design features mentioned previously, you can modify a chart by adding or deleting individual elements or by moving or resizing the chart. You can also change the chart type without having to delete the existing chart and create a new one or change how Excel selects data as its data elements by changing rows to columns.

Adding Elements to a Chart

Adding elements to a chart can provide additional information that was not available in the data you selected to create the chart. In some cases adding data labels helps make the charts more understandable. In this exercise, you learn to use the CHART ELEMENTS button to add items to a chart.

STEP BY STEP   **Add Elements to a Chart**

GET READY. USE the workbook from the previous exercise.

1. Click the StackedBar chart tab.

2. If necessary, click in a white space of the chart to select the chart and make the buttons in the upper right hand corner appear.

3. Click the CHART ELEMENTS button. A menu appears showing which elements are currently on the chart (checked boxes) and which are not (unchecked boxes). See Figure 12-26.

Figure 12-26

Current Chart Elements

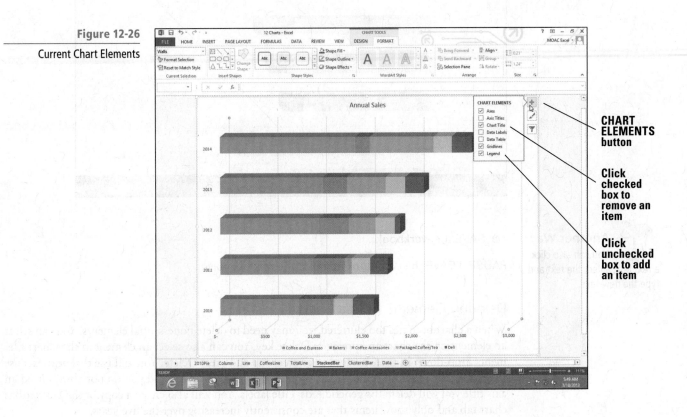

4. Click the Axis Titles box to check the box and add both a vertical and horizontal axis placeholder.

5. The Axis Title on the bottom of the screen has selection indicators to indicate it is selected. Type Thousands and press Enter.

6. Click the TotalLine chart tab, click the CHART ELEMENTS button, and select the Axis Titles option. This time the vertical Axis Title is selected. You can click any label placeholder to select it if it is already on a chart. Type Thousands for the vertical title.

7. Repeat the previous step to add a vertical axis title of Thousands for the CoffeeLine chart and the horizontal axis title for the ClusteredBar chart.

8. Click the StackedBar chart tab, click the CHART ELEMENTS button, and select the Data Labels option. Labels appear for each of the bars on the chart as shown in Figure 12-27.

Figure 12-27

Data Labels added to the
chartw

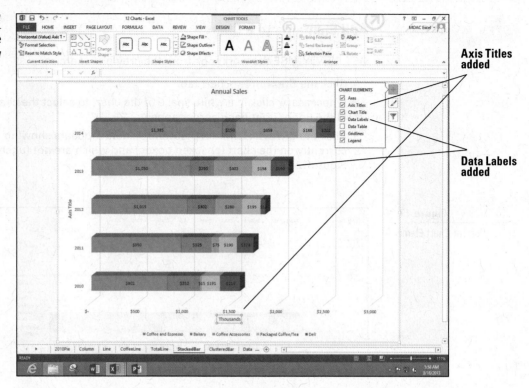

Another Way
You can also click
a text box, select the text and
type the new text.

9. SAVE the workbook.

PAUSE. LEAVE the workbook open for the next exercise.

Deleting Elements from a Chart

When a chart becomes too cluttered, you may need to delete nonessential elements. You can select
an element on the chart and press the Delete key. You can also select an element in the Chart Elements drop-down in the Current Selection group and press Delete. You will use this next exercise
to delete elements from some charts. Since the years are obvious and you do not always need an
axis title you will delete the generic Axis Title labels. You will also create a copy of the StackedBar
chart tab and only show items that are consistently increasing over the five years.

STEP BY STEP   **Delete Elements from a Chart**

GET READY. USE the workbook from the previous exercise.

1. On the StackedBar chart sheet tab, click the vertical Axis Title and press Delete.

2. Repeat Step 1 to delete the following generic Axis Title labels:

Chart tab	Vertical or Horizontal Axis Title
CoffeeLine	Horizontal
TotalLine	Horizontal
ClusteredBar	Vertical

3. Right-click the StackedBar chart tab and select Move or Copy. In the Before sheet list
   box, Select ClusteredBar, click the Create a copy check box, and then click OK to create
   another copy of the StackedBar chart.

4. Double-click the StackedBar (2) label for the tab and type SalesIncrease for the new
   name.

5. Click the $150 data label for the Bakery in 2014. All data labels for bakery have selection
   indicators. Press Delete.

6. Repeat Step 5 for Coffee Accessories, Packaged Coffee/Tea, and Deli data labels.

7. Click the Annual Sales title and type Coffee, Espresso, and Accessories only Consistent Sales Increase. Press Enter.

8. You can also hide data series. Click the Chart Filters button on the right side of the chart and in the SERIES group, click Bakery to uncheck it (see Figure 12-28).

Figure 12-28

Uncheck series you do not want to appear on the chart.

When mouse is on series, chart highlights just that series

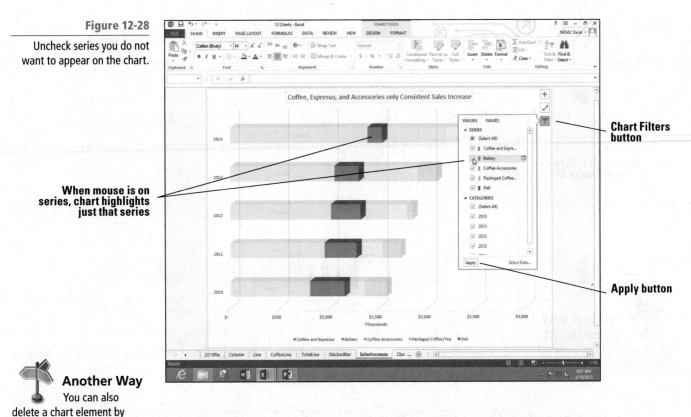

Chart Filters button

Apply button

Another Way
You can also delete a chart element by right-clicking on the element and selecting Delete.

9. Repeat step 8 for Packaged Coffee/Tea and Deli and click the Apply button.

10. After looking at the chart, you might decide it is better to keep all of the data series. Repeat Steps 8 and 9 to recheck the Bakery, Packaged Coffee /Tea, and Deli series.

Take Note Compare this to previous versions of Excel when you removed series from a chart. The Chart Filters button is much easier to put the series back on.

11. SAVE the workbook.

PAUSE. LEAVE the workbook open for the next exercise.

Take Note It is important to remember that whether the chart is embedded in the worksheet or located on a chart sheet, the chart is linked to the worksheet data. Any changes in the worksheet data are reflected in the chart. Likewise, if the worksheet data is deleted, the chart is also deleted.

Adding Additional Data Series

You might need to add additional data to a chart. In this case the CEO of the company has asked you to create a new data sheet that breaks out coffee and espresso and packaged coffee and tea to see if you can see any new trends.

STEP BY STEP   Add Additional Data Series

GET READY. USE the workbook from the previous exercise.

1. Right-click the Data worksheet tab, select Move or Copy, scroll to the bottom of the Before sheet list, and select (move to end). Click the Create a copy checkbox and click

OK. Double-click the Data (2) tab, type DataExp, and then press Enter.

2. Select A2:F7, click the INSERT tab, click the Insert Column Chart button, and then under 2-D Column, click the Clustered Column option.

3. Insert rows below Coffee and Espresso and Packaged Coffee/Tea. Edit the labels and values as shown in Figure 12-29.

Figure 12-29

Edited Annual Sales with new categories

New rows of data do not appear in chart

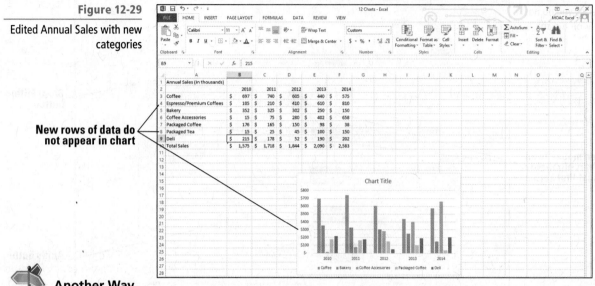

Another Way
You can also click the DESIGN tab and the Select Data button.

4. Right-click in a blank area of the chart, and choose Select Data. The Select Data Source dialog box opens (see Figure 12-30).

Figure 12-30

Select Data Source dialog box

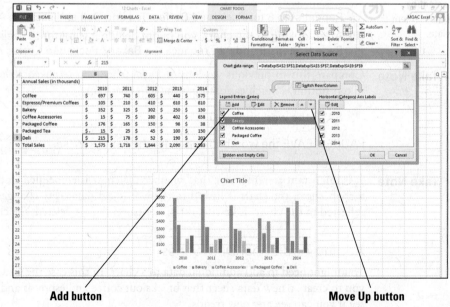

Add button   Move Up button

Take Note   In the previous section, you used the Chart Filter button to remove data series. You can also use this Select Data Source dialog box to remove data series.

5. Click the Add button and in the Series name box, click cell A4. In the Series values box, delete the entry and drag on the worksheet to select cells B4:F4. The Edit Series dialog box looks like Figure 12-31.

Figure 12-31

Edit Series dialog box

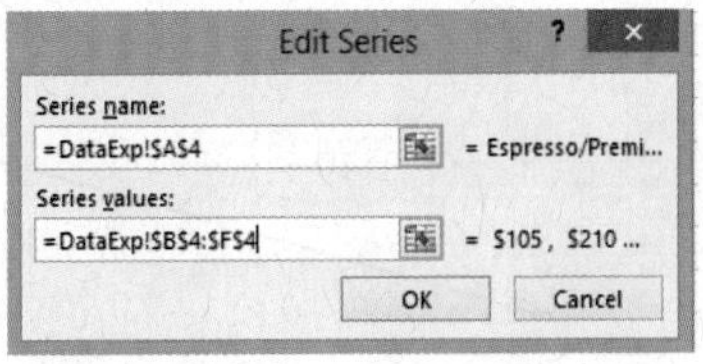

Edit Series	? ×
Series name:	
=DataExp!$A$4	= Espresso/Premi...
Series values:	
=DataExp!$B$4:$F$4	= $105 , $210 ...
	OK Cancel

CERTIFICATION READY?   5.1.2

How do you add additional data series?

6. Click OK, then click the Move Up button multiple times to move the Espresso/Premium Coffees label below Coffee.

7. Repeat Steps 5 and 6 with Packaged Tea in A8 and the data in B8:F8 so the label is below Packaged Coffee. Click OK to accept the changes and return to the sheet.

8. SAVE the workbook.

Another Way
You can also highlight the data in the worksheet, click Copy, click on the chart, and click Paste to add a data series to a chart.

PAUSE. LEAVE the workbook open for the next exercise.

Resizing a Chart

You can point to a corner of a chart or the midpoint of any side to display sizing handles (two-sided arrows). Use the side handles to change the chart height or width. Use the corner sizing handles to change both height and width. Increasing the size of a chart makes it easier to read, especially if it is an embedded chart. Be cautious when you reduce the size of a chart, however. Titles and legends must be readable. In this exercise, you learn to resize the chart.

STEP BY STEP   **Resize a Chart**

GET READY. USE the workbook from the previous exercise. The DataExp sheet should be selected.

CERTIFICATION READY?   5.2.2

How do you change the size of a chart?

1. Move the mouse to the white space to the left of the chart title. The mouse is a black four-headed arrow. Drag to move the chart to the left edge of the sheet and below row 11.

2. Move the mouse to the bottom right corner of the chart. The mouse pointer is a two-headed diagonal arrow on the resize handle. Drag the mouse so it is in the bottom right corner of the screen. The chart expands to take up more of the screen and you can see the columns and legend easier.

3. Click the Chart Title and type Detailed Annual Sales. Click back in the chart to select the chart and move to the right center resize handle. Your screen should look similar to Figure 12-32.

Figure 12-32

Resized chart

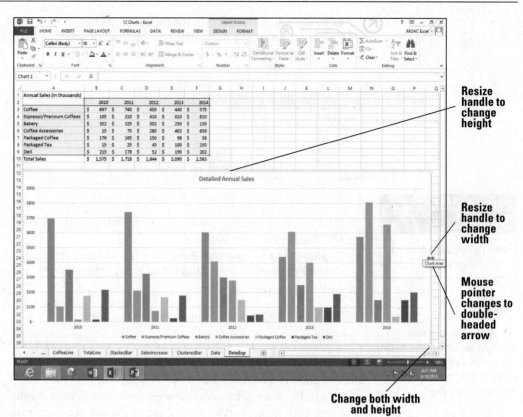

Take Note   You can click any selection handle on the chart border and drag to increase the height, width, or both.

   4. SAVE the workbook.

PAUSE. LEAVE the workbook open for the next exercise.

Choosing a Different Chart Type

For most 2-D and 3-D charts, you can change the chart type and give it a completely different look. If a chart contains multiple data series, you can also select a different chart type for any single data series, creating a combined chart. You cannot combine a 2-D and a 3-D chart, however.

STEP BY STEP   **Choose a Different Chart Type**

GET READY. USE the workbook from the previous exercise. The DataExp sheet should be visible and the chart selected.

   1. Click the DESIGN tab and select the Change Chart Type button. The Change Chart Type dialog box opens.
   2. Click each of the chart types on the left and you will see a set of different icons representing subtypes for each of the chart types. Click the Column button. Click the Stacked Column subtype (second icon in the right pane, at the top of the dialog box). The screen should look like Figure 12-33.

Figure 12-33

Change Chart Type dialog box

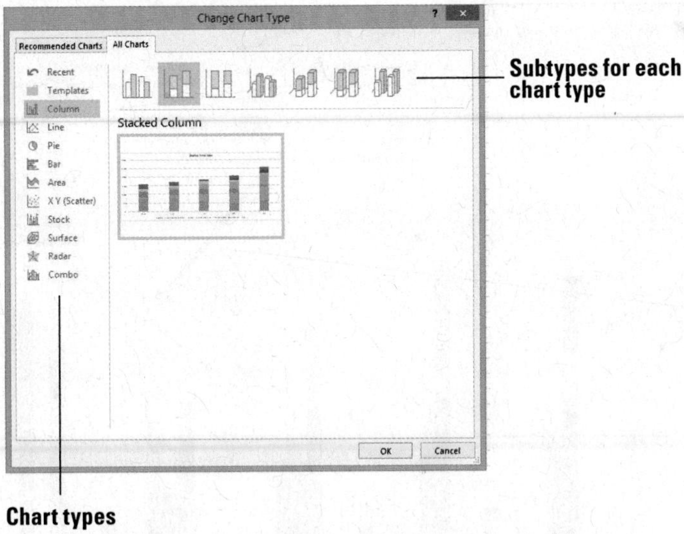

Subtypes for each chart type

Chart types

3. Click OK.

4. Click the Move Chart button and in the New sheet box, type DetSales, and then click OK.

5. COPY the DetSales chart sheet before the DataExp sheet and name the tab DetSalesEs.

6. On the DESIGN tab, using the Change Chart Type button, change the chart back to a Clustered Column.

7. Click just one of the Espresso/Premium Coffees columns.

8. On the DESIGN tab, click the Change Chart Type button.

9. The Change Chart Type box opens to the Combo chart type. In the Espresso/Premium Coffees Chart Type box, select Line (see Figure 12-34).

Figure 12-34

Change Chart Type with Combo chart type

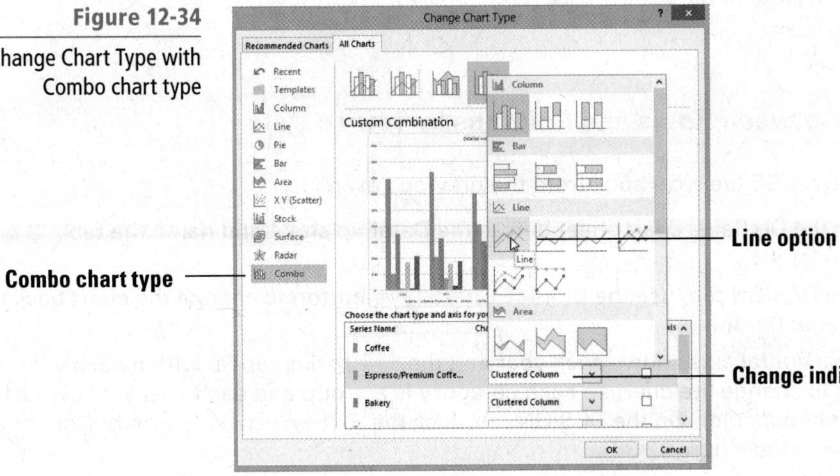

Combo chart type

Line option

Change individual data series

10. Click OK and edit the chart title to read WOW! Look at Espresso/Premium Coffee Sales!

11. Click the FORMAT tab and in the Insert Shapes group, click the Arrow button and drag the arrow from the chart title to the Espresso line. Use the Shape Outline button to change the arrow to Red and the Weight to 6 pt. Your chart should look similar to Figure 12-35.

Figure 12-35

Espresso/Premium Coffee
Sales chart

Arrow button

Shape
Outline
button

Arrow

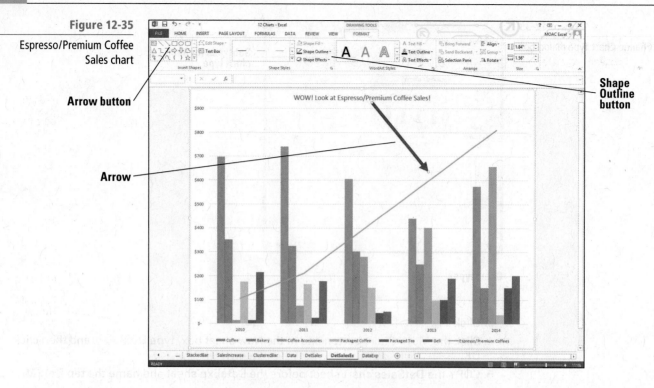

12. SAVE the workbook.

PAUSE. LEAVE the workbook open for the next exercise.

Switching Between Rows and Columns in Source Data

You might want to change the orientation of your chart so that the categories are along the horizontal axis instead of the years or vice versa.

| STEP BY STEP | **Switch Between Rows and Columns in Source Data** |

GET READY. USE the workbook from the previous exercise.

**CERTIFICATION
READY?**   5.1.3

How do you switch between
rows and columns in source
data?

1. COPY the DetSales chart sheet before the DataExp sheet and name the tab **DetSalesCat**.

2. On the DESIGN tab, use the Change Chart Type button to change the chart back to a **Clustered Column**.

3. The horizontal axis shows each year and the categories repeat within each year. We're going to change the chart so each category is a group and each year is shown as a different bar color. On the DESIGN tab, click the Switch Row/Column button. The chart changes (see Figure 12-36).

Figure 12-36

Rows and columns switched (legend and categories changed)

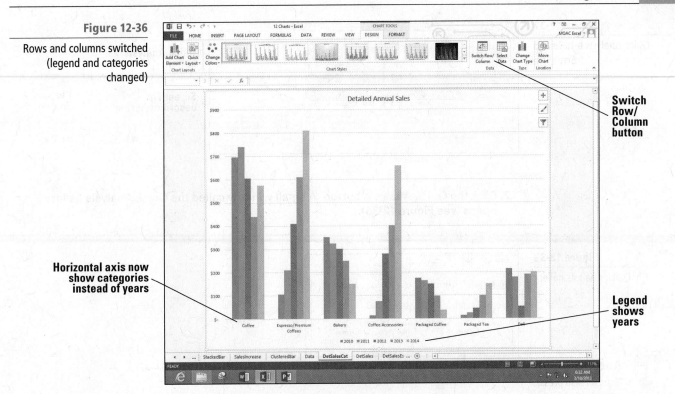

Switch Row/Column button

Horizontal axis now show categories instead of years

Legend shows years

4. SAVE the workbook.

PAUSE. LEAVE the workbook open for the next exercise.

USING NEW QUICK ANALYSIS TOOLS

Bottom Line

Excel 2013 includes a new feature that allows analysis of data with a few clicks of the mouse. You select a data range, and the new Quick Analysis button appears, allowing you to quickly create charts, add tiny miniature graphs called **sparklines**, work with totals, format the data with conditional formatting, and create PivotTables.

Adding a Chart or Sparklines

In addition to the INSERT tab and F11 key, the new Quick Analysis button allows you to quickly add charts to your workbook. After you add the chart, you can modify it using the exercises above.

STEP BY STEP   **Add a Chart or Sparklines**

GET READY. USE the workbook from the previous exercise.

1. Click the **DataExp** worksheet tab. Select cells **A2:F9**. The new Quick Analysis icon appears at the bottom right of the selected range. Move the mouse pointer to the button and the ScreenTip displays (see Figure 12-37).

Figure 12-37

Quick Analysis button and ScreenTip

	A	B	C	D	E	F	G	H	I	J
1	Annual Sales (in thousands)									
2		2010	2011	2012	2013	2014				
3	Coffee	$ 697	$ 740	$ 605	$ 440	$ 575				
4	Espresso/Premium Coffees	$ 105	$ 210	$ 410	$ 610	$ 810				
5	Bakery	$ 352	$ 325	$ 302	$ 250	$ 150				
6	Coffee Accessories	$ 15	$ 75	$ 280	$ 402	$ 658				
7	Packaged Coffee	$ 176	$ 165	$ 150	$ 98	$ 38				
8	Packaged Tea	$ 15	$ 25	$ 45	$ 100	$ 150				
9	Deli	$ 215	$ 178	$ 52	$ 190	$ 202				
10	Total Sales	$ 1,575	$ 1,718	$ 1,844	$ 2,090	$ 2,583				
11										
12										
13										
14										
15										
16										

Quick Analysis button

ScreenTip describes button

Quick Analysis (Ctrl+Q)
Use the Quick Analysis tool to quickly and easily analyze your data with some of Excel's most useful tools, such as charts, color-coding, and formulas.

2. Click the Quick Analysis button. A small window called the Quick Analysis gallery opens (see Figure 12-38).

Figure 12-38

Quick Analysis gallery

1,844	$ 2,090	$ 2,583	

FORMATTING   CHARTS   TOTALS   TABLES   SPARKLINES

Data Bars   Color Scale   Icon Set   Greater Than   Top 10%   Clear Format

Conditional Formatting uses rules to highlight interesting data.

Another Way
You can also press Ctrl + Q to open the Quick Analysis gallery.

3. Click the CHARTS tab in the gallery. The options change in the lower part of the gallery. Move the mouse pointer to each of the charts and a preview appears on the screen above the Quick Analysis gallery. For example, move the mouse pointer to the Stacked Area option and you'll see a preview showing this type of chart (see Figure 12-39).

Figure 12-39

Stacked Area chart previewed

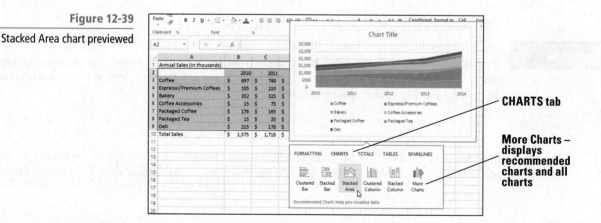

CHARTS tab

More Charts – displays recommended charts and all charts

Take Note If you click the More Charts option, Excel displays the Insert Chart dialog box, with the Recommended Charts and All Charts tabs discussed earlier in this lesson.

CERTIFICATION READY? 2.3.2

How do you add sparklines to a data range?

4. We will not add any charts from the CHARTS menu at this time. Click the SPARKLINES tab. Move the mouse pointer to preview the Column option. A set of tiny column charts shows in column G.

5. Click the Line option. A series of lines appear in your worksheet in column G.

6. Row 2 (years) should not have a sparkline. Click cell G2 and on the DESIGN tab, click the Clear button. The sparkline is removed in that cell. In cell G2, type Sparkline.

7. Click cell G9. Use the fill handle to drag to cell G10. A sparkline appears for the total.

8. Select G3:G10 and click the DESIGN tab. There are a number of options you can do with the sparklines.

9. In the Show group, click High Point and Low Point and in the Style gallery, choose

Sparkline Style Dark #3 (see Figure 12-40).

Figure 12-40

Sparklines in column G

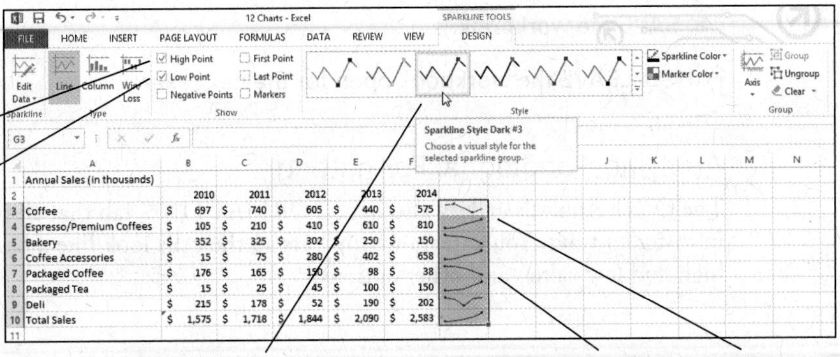
High Point
Low Point
Sparkline Style Dark #3
Decreasing sales
Increasing sales

Take Note The DESIGN tab changes to SPARKLINE TOOLS when you have sparklines selected. Take the time to explore the options on the ribbon shown in Figure 12-40.

10. SAVE the workbook.

PAUSE. LEAVE the workbook open for the next exercise.

Working with Totals

The Quick Analysis button can also quickly add SUM, AVERAGE, and COUNT functions as well as %of Total and Running Totals to either the bottom row or to the right of the data.

STEP BY STEP

Work with Totals

GET READY. USE the workbook from the previous exercise and click on the Data worksheet tab.

CERTIFICATION READY? 5.1.4

How do you use Quick Analysis to add totals?

1. Select **A3:F7**. Click the **Quick Analysis** button and select the **TOTALS** tab.
2. Move to the first icon, Sum (with the blue row highlighted in the icon). You'll see a preview on the worksheet of Sum overwriting the Total Sales row that was already there.
3. Move to the next icon and you'll see row 8 previewed with Averages for each column. Move to each of the Count, % Total, and Running total icons and watch the preview of the worksheet change.
4. Move to the second Sum icon (with the orange column highlighted). Notice that the worksheet preview changes to show totals in column G.
5. Click the **arrow** on the right to show more options. Preview each of the options and return to % Total (see Figure 12-41).

Figure 12-41

% Total appears in column G

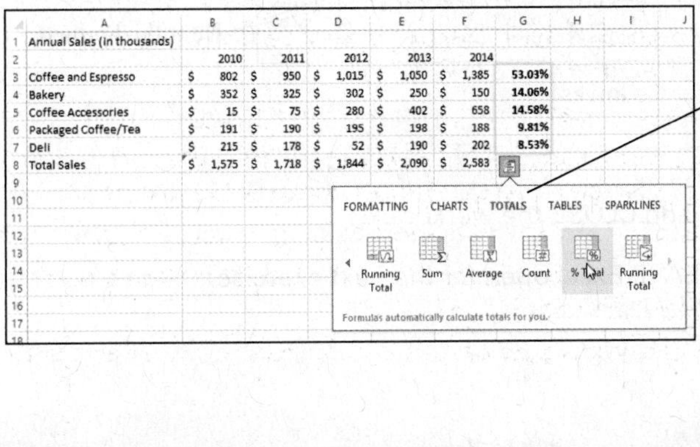
TOTALS tab

6. Click the % Total option. Click cell G3 and notice that the formula =SUM(B3:F3)/SUM($B$3:$F$7) appears in the formula bar.

7. In cell G2, type Average.

8. SAVE the workbook.

PAUSE. LEAVE the workbook open for the next exercise.

Applying Conditional Formatting

The Quick Analysis gallery also has a FORMATTING tab that allows you to format the cell data in different ways. You can show tiny bars so the cells look like a bar chart, change the colors for high and low values and other options.

STEP BY STEP   **Apply Conditional Formatting**

GET READY. USE the workbook from the previous exercise. You should still be on the Data worksheet tab.

1. Select A3:F7. Click the Quick Analysis icon. The FORMATTING tab is selected.

2. Move to the first icon, Data Bars. You can see a preview on the worksheet of small bars in each cell indicating the relative value in the cell. The largest value is in F3 and the bar shows the largest width (see Figure 12-42).

Figure 12-42

Data Bars preview

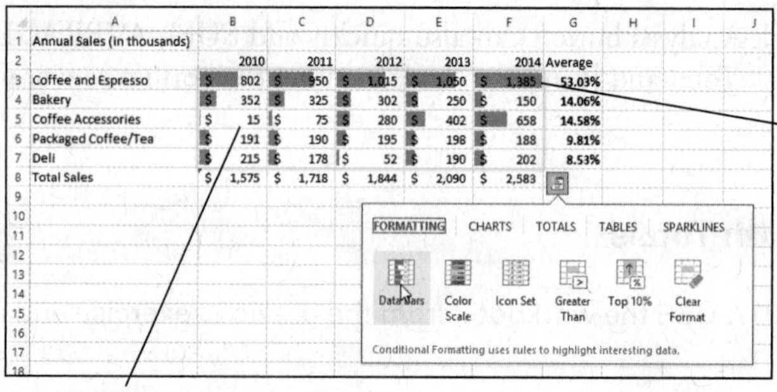

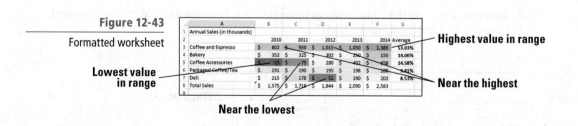

CERTIFICATION READY?   5.1.4

How do you use Quick Analysis to apply conditional formatting?

3. Click the Color Scale option to make this choice. Click in a cell outside the range so the formatting is clearer. The worksheet is formatted (see Figure 12-43) with the highest values in green with the highest value in dark green. The lowest values are in red.

4. If the value is close to the highest or lowest value, the color or the cell is less dark. As the values move away from the value, the color becomes lighter.

Figure 12-43

Formatted worksheet

5. SAVE and CLOSE the workbook.

PAUSE. LEAVE Excel open for the next exercise.

CREATING PIVOTTABLES AND PIVOTCHARTS

Bottom Line

A **PivotTable** report and **PivotCharts** are collaborative ways to quickly condense and rearrange large amounts of data. Use a PivotTable report to analyze and display the numerical data in detail and to answer unforeseen questions about your data. In this exercise, you will learn to create basic PivotTables.

A PivotTable report and Pivot Charts are especially designed for:

• Querying large amounts of data in many different ways.

• Subtotaling and gathering numeric data, summarizing data by categories and subcategories, and creating custom calculations and formulas.

• Expanding and collapsing levels of data to filter your results, and drilling down finer points from the summary data for areas of importance.

• Moving rows to columns or columns to pivot rows to examine different summaries of the data.

• Filtering, sorting, grouping, and conditionally formatting the most useful and interesting subset of data to enable you to focus on the information that you want.

• Providing concise, eye-catching, and interpreted online or printed information.

Creating a Basic PivotTable

PivotTable reports are used to examine and analyze related totals. Examples are calculating a long list of figures or comparing several facts about each piece of numerical data. In this exercise, you create a basic PivotTable report.

STEP BY STEP   **Create a Basic PivotTable**

GET READY. OPEN *12 School Test Data* from the student data files.

1. Click cell **A1**. Press **End** and then press the **down arrow**. Notice that there are 139,129 rows of data.
2. Press **Ctrl + Home** to return to the top of the worksheet.
3. On the **INSERT** tab, click the **Recommended PivotTables** button.
4. Scroll to the bottom and click **Count of ScaleScore by Proficiency Level** (see Figure 12-44).

Figure 12-44

Recommended PivotTables
dialog box

PivotTable
button

Recommended
PivotTables
button

PivotChart
button

Recommended
PivotTables
dialog box

Select last
choice

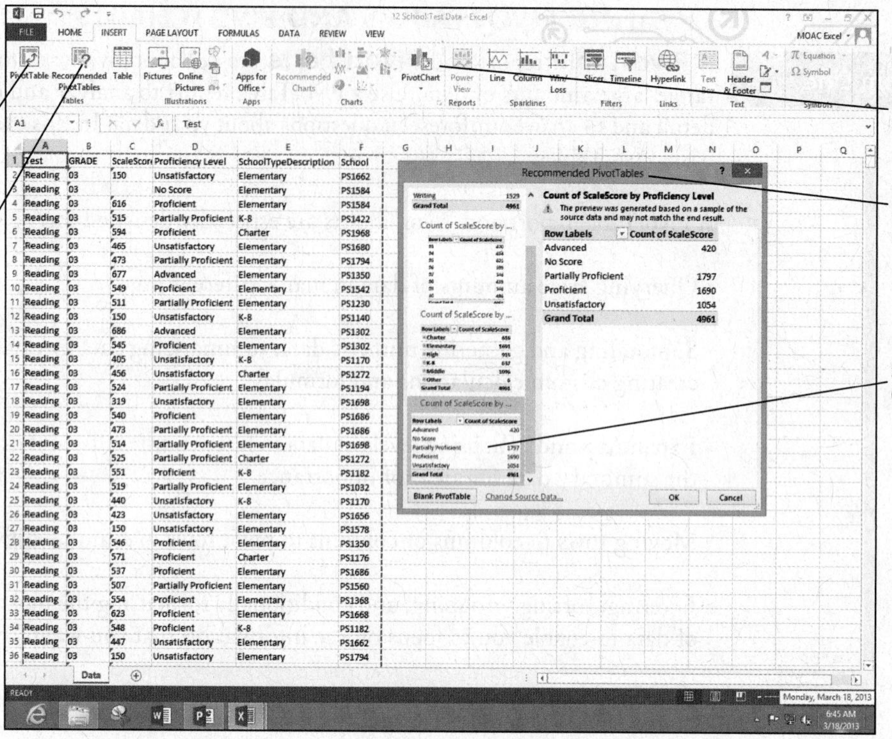

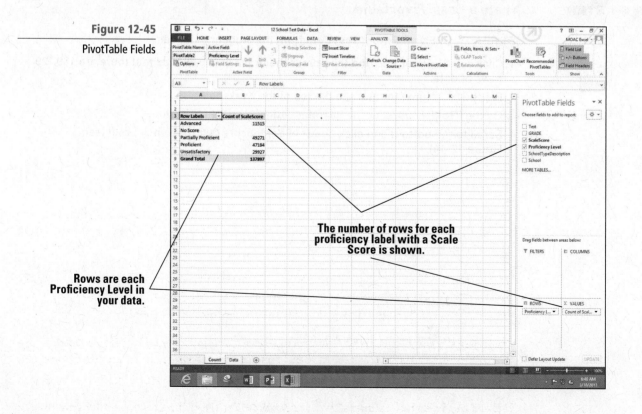

5. Click **OK** and **NAME** the new sheet **Count**. The PivotTable Fields pane opens on the right side of your screen and the data appears on the worksheet (see Figure 12-45). Notice that the data for No Score is blank. That is because the count of the rows is based on the Scale Score, which is empty for unavailable scores. You will want to change the field to count to a field that has data. If you look back on the Data tab, every row is filled by a grade so you can use this column so every row is counted.

Figure 12-45

PivotTable Fields

The number of rows for each proficiency label with a Scale Score is shown.

Rows are each
Proficiency Level in
your data.

6. Return to the Counts sheet and drag the Grade field in the PivotTable Fields pane down to the VALUES section.

7. Drag the Count of ScaleScore from the VALUES section into the worksheet to remove it. Notice that the No Score row now counts each missing score.

8. Drag the Grade field to the COLUMNS area. You'll see each grade summarized.

9. Drag the Test field to the FILTERS area.

10. Cell B1 currently shows *(All)*. Click the Filter drop-down arrow, choose Math, and click OK.

11. On the Filter button, click cell B1 and choose Reading. Click OK. Your data should look similar to Figure 12-46.

Figure 12-46

Results of PivotTable

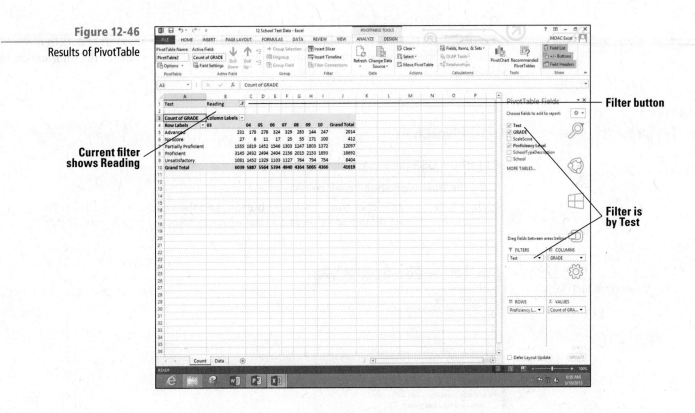

12. SAVE the workbook to the Lesson 12 folder as *12 Test PivotTable Solutions*.

PAUSE. LEAVE the workbook open for the next exercise.

Take Note When you click any empty cell on the PivotTable, the Field list disappears. To make it reappear, you simply need to click on any active cell that is showing data.

After you create the initial PivotTable report by defining the data source, arranging fields in the PivotTable Field List, and choosing an initial layout, you can perform additional tasks as you work with and improve a PivotTable report, including:

• **Exploring the data:** Once initially created, you can expand and collapse data, and show the essential facts that pertain to the data. You can sort, filter, and group fields and data items. You can edit summary functions, and create custom calculations and formulas.

• **Changing the form layout and field arrangements:** You can edit the PivotTable report to display it in compact, outline, or tabular form. You can add, rearrange, and remove fields and also edit the order of the fields or items.

• **Change the layout of columns, rows, and subtotals:** Excel enables you to turn column and row field headers on or off, display or hide blank rows, display subtotals above or below their rows, and adjust column widths on refresh. You also can move a column field to the row area or a row field to the column area, and merge or unmerge cells for outer row and column items.

• **Change the display of blanks and errors:** You can change how errors and empty cells are displayed, change how items and labels without data are shown, and display or hide blank lines.

• **Changing the format of the PivotTable:** You can apply manual and conditional formatting to cells and ranges, and you can edit the overall look by applying a PivotTable format style.

Take time to explore these options for PivotTables on your own.

Adding a PivotChart

A **PivotChart** is an essential tool to help organize and arrange large amounts of data from worksheets. In addition to summarizing a huge amount of data, you can visualize the information in a simple graph.

STEP BY STEP   **Add a PivotChart**

GET READY. USE the workbook from the previous exercise.

1. On the Data worksheet, click cell A1.
2. On the INSERT tab, click the PivotChart button, and then choose PivotChart. The Create PivotChart dialog box opens and the range is selected (see Figure 12-47).

Figure 12-47

Create PivotChart dialog box

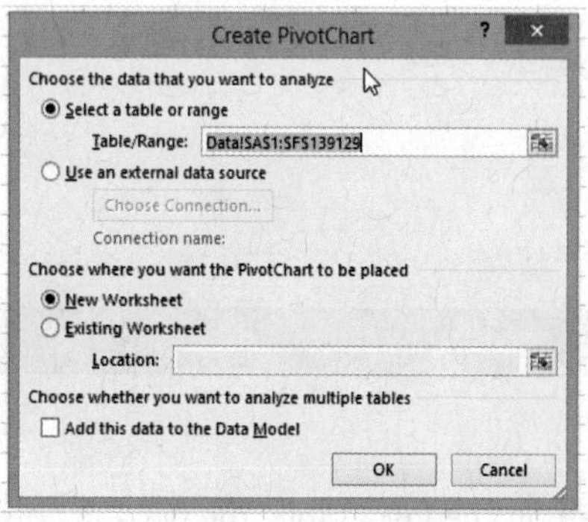

3. The default location is for a New Worksheet so click OK. Name the new sheet tab PivotChart.
4. Drag the Test field to the FILTERS area.
5. Drag Grade to the VALUES area (count number of items).
6. Drag Grade again to the AXIS area.
7. Drag Proficiency Level to the LEGEND area.
8. MOVE the chart to the left edge of the worksheet, below the data, and then resize the chart (see Figure 12-48).

Figure 12-48

PivotChart of student test scores created

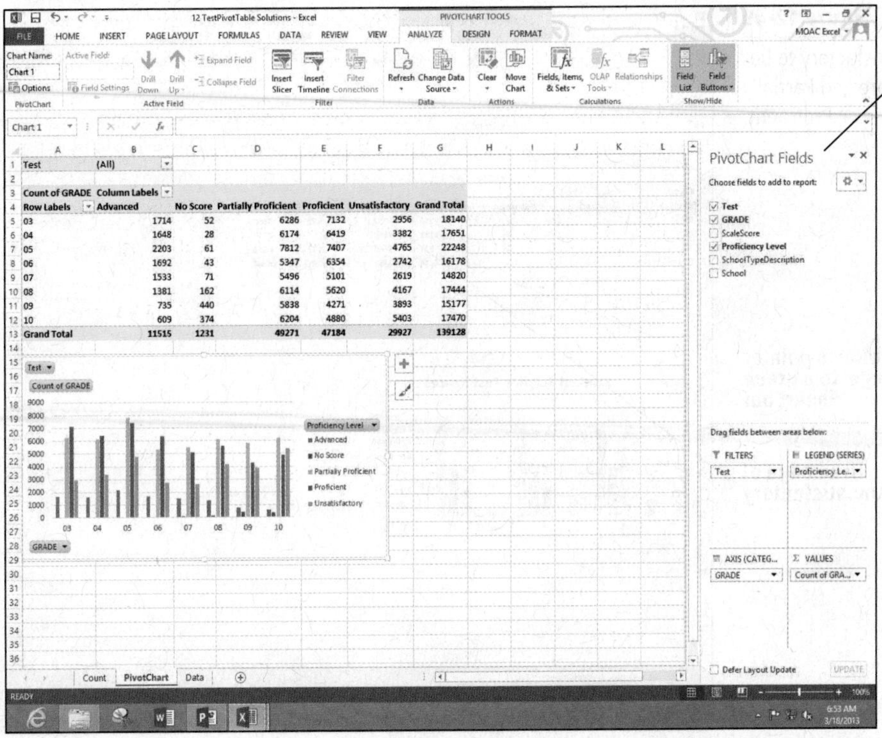

PivotChart Fields pane

9. On the Test drop-down arrow on the chart, choose Science and click OK. Notice that only 5th, 8th, and 10th grades are available because only those grades take the Science test.

10. Click the FORMAT tab, click the Text Box button, and click the top of the chart. Add a label that says Student Science Test Scores and make this label Bold and 18 points.

11. Click cell A3 and change the label to just say Count.

12. In F4, click on the label for Unsatisfactory.

13. Move the mouse pointer to the left edge of the cell until the mouse pointer changes to a four-headed black arrow and drag the mouse between columns C and D (see Figure 12-49).

Figure 12-49

Drag Unsatisfactory to between No Score and Partially Proficient.

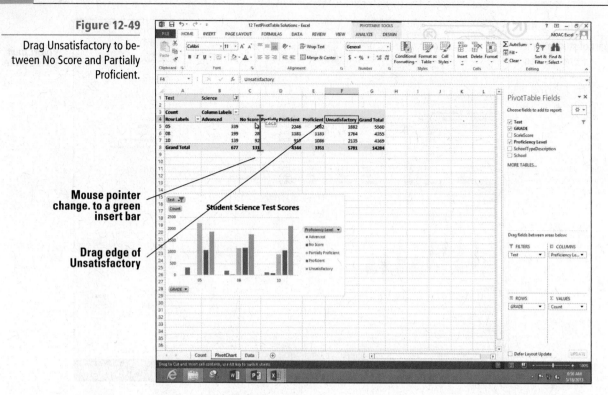

14. Repeat Step 13 and move the Advanced column to between Proficient and Grand Total.

15. Resize the PivotChart so it goes to column L.

16. SAVE the workbook as *12 Test PivotChart Solution*. Your final sheet should look like that shown in Figure 12-50.

Figure 12-50

PivotChart completed

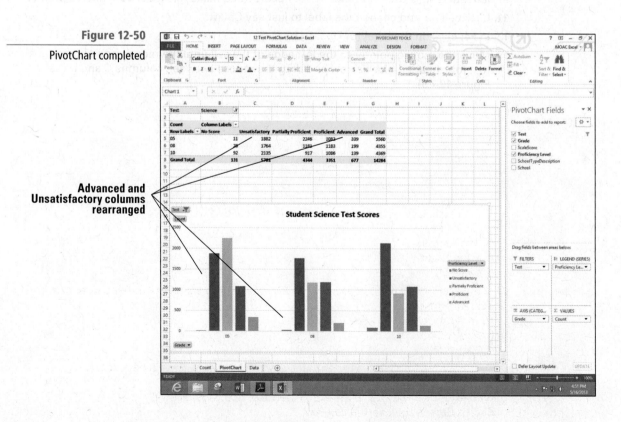

PAUSE. CLOSE the workbook and LEAVE Excel open for the next exercise.

SKILL SUMMARY

In this lesson you learned how to:	Exam Objective	Exam Number
Build charts	Create charts and graphs	5.1.1
Format a Chart with a Quick Style or Layout		
Format the parts of a chart manually	Add legends	5.2.1
	Modify chart and graph parameters	5.2.3
Modify a chart	Add additional data series	5.1.2
	Switch between rows and columns in source data	5.1.3
	Position charts and graphs	5.2.5
	Resize charts and graphs	5.2.2
	Apply chart layout and styles	5.2.4
Use new Quick Analysis Tools	Insert sparklines	2.3.2
	Demonstrate how to use Quick Analysis	5.1.4
Create PivotTables and PivotCharts		

Knowledge Assessment

Multiple Choice

Select the best response for the following statements.

1. Which chart type shows values as parts of a whole?
   a. Column
   b. Bar
   c. Area
   d. Pie

2. Which type of chart appears on a worksheet with other data?
   a. Chart sheet
   b. Embedded
   c. PivotChart
   d. Mixed

3. Which part of a chart do you click when you want to select the entire chart?
   a. Chart area
   b. Plot area
   c. Chart title
   d. Legend

4. Which of the following happens to a chart if the source data is deleted?
   a. Nothing.
   b. The chart will move to the area where the data was located.
   c. The data in the chart is deleted.
   d. You will be asked if you want the chart deleted.

5. Which is the first step that should be taken when creating a chart?
   a. Providing a name for the chart
   b. Selecting the chart type
   c. Selecting the range of cells that contain the data the chart will use
   d. Choosing the data labels that will be used in the chart

6. If you want to print only the chart in a worksheet, which of the following should you do before printing?
   a. Click the chart to select it and then print.
   b. Select the Print chart only option in the Page Setup dialog box.
   c. Move the chart to a new sheet by itself and then print that sheet.
   d. You cannot print only the chart if it is part of a larger worksheet.

7. A bar chart represents values as which of the following?
   a. Horizontal bars
   b. Vertical bars
   c. Horizontal lines
   d. Vertical lines

8. A column chart represents values as which of the following?
   a. Horizontal bars
   b. Vertical bars
   c. Horizontal lines
   d. Vertical lines

9. To move a chart from a worksheet to a chart sheet, perform which of the following?
   a. Use the move handles and drag it to the new location.
   b. Use the Move Chart button on the DESIGN tab.
   c. Cut the chart from the worksheet and paste it to a new workbook sheet.
   d. You cannot move the chart after it has been created.

10. Which of the following statements is not true?
   a. You can change both the height and width of a chart with commands on the FORMAT tab.
   b. You can use the sizing handles to change the height and width of a chart.
   c. You must delete an existing chart in order to have the data displayed in a different chart type.
   d. When a chart sheet is created, it no longer appears on the worksheet containing the data series.

Matching

Match each vocabulary term with its definition.

a. axis _____ 1. A box that identifies the patterns or colors that are assigned to a data series or categories in a chart.

b. chart _____ 2. A graphical representation of numeric data in a worksheet.

c. chart area _____ 3. A bar, area, dot, slice, or other symbol in a chart that represents a single data point or value that originates from a worksheet cell.

d. chart sheet _____ 4. A chart that is placed on a worksheet rather than on a separate sheet.

e. data label _____ 5. A sheet in a workbook that contains only a chart.

f. data marker _____ 6. The entire chart and all its elements.

g. data series _____ 7. Related data points that are plotted in a chart.

h. embedded chart _____ 8. A line bordering the chart plot area used as a frame of reference for measurement.

i. legend _____ 9. Descriptive text that is automatically aligned to an axis or centered at the top of a chart.

j. title _____ 10. A label that provides additional information about a data marker, which represents a single data point or value that originates from a worksheet cell.

Project 12-1: **Create a Pie Chart**

The Blue Yonder Airlines boss has asked you to do an analysis of your time for the past month.

GET READY. LAUNCH Excel if it is not already running.

 1. CREATE the following workbook as shown in Figure 12-51. Use a SUM function in B9.

Figure 12-51

Data for pie chart

	A	B
1	Blue Yonder Airlines	
2	Monthly Time Analysis	
3	Labor Council Presentation	23.75
4	VP Staff Meetings	19.25
5	BOD Meetings	25.00
6	Terrorism Impact Analysis	75.00
7	Pilot Wages	25.00
8	Misc	12.75
9	Total	180.75
10		

 2. Select A3:B8.
 3. Click the INSERT tab. Click Pie and click 3-D Pie.
 4. On the DESIGN tab, click Quick Layout and choose Layout 4.
 5. Click the Move Chart button.
 6. In the New Sheet box, type TimePie and click OK.
 7. Click the CHART ELEMENTS button and check Chart Title.
 8. For the selected Chart Title type Monthly Time Analysis.
 9. SAVE the workbook to the Lesson 12 folder as *12 My Time Solution*.
 10. CLOSE the workbook.

PAUSE. LEAVE Excel open for the next project.

Project 12-2: **Create a Column Chart**

Your friends have asked you to do a summary of salaries for selected occupations. You are going to meet as a group and discuss the pros and cons of each position. Salary is only one of the issues you will talk about, but it is significant.

GET READY. LAUNCH Excel if it is not already running.

 1. CREATE the following workbook as shown in Figure 12-52.

Figure 12-52

Data for column chart

	A	B
1	Salaries for Entry Level Positions	
2		US
3	Accountant	44,911
4	Attorney	85,669
5	Biologist	44,116
6	Budget Analyst	49,420
7	Teller	23,112
8	Trader	44,472
9	Community Organizer	32,266
10	Database Analyst	56,284
11		

2. Select A3:B10.

3. Click the INSERT tab. Click Column and click Clustered Column.

4. Edit the chart title to read Entry Level Salaries.

5. Right-click in a blank area of the chart, choose Move Chart, and in the New sheet box, type Salaries. Click OK.

6. Right-click on the Vertical (Value) axis and select Format Axis.

7. In the Format Axis pane, choose NUMBER and in the Category drop-down, choose Currency.

8. SAVE the workbook to the Lesson 12 folder as *12 Salaries Solution*.

PAUSE. LEAVE the workbook open for the next project.

Proficiency Assessment

Project 12-3: Convert and Modify a Chart

In the previous project, you created a column chart to display entry level salaries. In this project you will change the chart type, add data, and format the chart.

GET READY. USE the workbook from the previous exercise.

1. Click on Sheet1. In cell A11, type Engineer and in cell B11, type 57,894.

2. Modify the chart to include row 11 .

3. Change the chart type to Clustered Bar.

4. Add a text box in the lower left corner to read US Average (salary.com).

5. Change the bars using the Green marble Texture fill.

6. Change the Chart title to Green Accent 6, Darker 50%, and then apply Bold, 24 point.

7. Drag the plot area up slightly so the text box you added in step 4 does not overlap the horizontal axis.

8. SAVE the workbook to the Lesson 12 folder as *12 Salaries2 Solution*.

9. CLOSE the file.

PAUSE. LEAVE Excel open for the next project.

Project 12-4: Create a Radar Chart

In this exercise, you will plot the evaluations from three teachers to discuss your next semester schedule with your study group.

GET READY. LAUNCH Excel if it is not already running.

1. CREATE the workbook shown in Figure 12-53.

Figure 12-53

Data for radar chart

	A	B	C	D
1	Teacher Evaluations			
2		T1	T2	T3
3	Clear Presentation	83	76	46
4	Knowledgable	75	45	95
5	Available	100	48	45
6	Answered Questions	82	67	46
7	Stimulating	50	89	43
8	Encourage Participation	93	64	50

2. Create a Radar chart for the three teachers.

3. Move the chart to a sheet called Evaluations.

4. Change the Chart Title to read Teacher Evaluations.

5. Using the CHART STYLES button, change the chart to Style 7.

6. Move the legend to the bottom right of the chart.

7. Add a text box on the bottom left: Fall Semester Evals.

8. Change the text box font color to gray to match the other labels and make the font italic.

9. Decide which teacher you want and change the Legend so the teacher has an asterisk (*) after the number (on T1, T2, or T3).

10. SAVE the workbook to the Lesson 12 folder as *12 Teachers Solution*.

11. CLOSE the file.

PAUSE. LEAVE Excel open for the next project.

Mastery Assessment

Project 12-5: Create Sparklines on a Worksheet

Your International Studies professor asked you to compare data from Gapminder about the changing number of years of education of women throughout the world.

GET READY. LAUNCH Excel if it is not already running.

1. OPEN the *12 School International Women* file for this lesson.

2. Create Line sparklines in column AP.

3. Change the sparklines to Column.

4. Identify the High Point on each sparkline.

5. Change both axes on each sparkline to Same for All Sparklines.

6. Type Sparkline in AP1.

7. Select A2:AO176 and using the Quick Analysis button add an Average to the bottom of the chart.

8. Change the number of decimals in row 177 to 1 decimal.

9. SAVE the workbook to the Lesson 12 folder as *12 International Schooling Women Solution*.

PAUSE. LEAVE the workbook open for the next project.

Project 12-6: Create Line Charts

You've decided to continue the analysis of international women's education for your final paper. To prepare for your report you create several line charts of example countries from each part of the world.

GET READY. USE the workbook from the previous exercise.

1. CREATE a line chart of the average years of women's education for the world from 1970-2009.

2. Move the chart to a separate sheet and name the chart sheet International Average and title the chart International Women's Education. You do not need a legend since there is only one line.

3. Label only the vertical axis Average Years of Education.

4. Copy the chart 5 times and add data to compare the international average with a selected country. Use the following for the chart sheet name and data for each of the following countries:

US

Afghanistan

Zimbabwe

Taiwan

Mexico

5. Change the chart title of each of the charts to read [Country name] Women's Education.

6. Add a legend to each of the charts in Step 4 to compare the country with the international average.

7. SAVE the workbook to the Lesson 12 folder as *12 Women Final Solution* and then CLOSE the file.

CLOSE Excel.

LESSON SKILL MATRIX

Skills	Exam Objective	Objective Number
Inserting Pictures	Insert images.	5.3.3
Adding Shapes, Lines, Text Boxes, and WordArt	Insert text boxes.	5.3.1
	Change text to WordArt.	2.2.9
Deleting, Copying, and Moving Graphics		
Formatting Graphics	Change object colors.	5.3.6
	Position objects.	5.3.8
Adding Graphic Enhancements Using Picture Tools	Add styles and effects to objects.	5.3.5
	Add borders to objects.	5.3.4
	Modify object properties.	5.3.7
Using SmartArt Graphics	Insert SmartArt.	5.3.2

KEY TERMS

- **artistic effect**
- **clip art**
- **duotone**
- **graphic**
- **handle**
- **metadata**
- **saturation**
- **shape**
- **SmartArt graphic**
- **text box**
- **WordArt**

© kate_sept2004 / iStockphoto

Tailspin Toys creates unique toys and games aimed at childhood education. The company is also highly involved in charitable giving and fundraising for community organizations, especially to support the local food pantry. Tailspin Toys works with the pantry to run various fundraising activities throughout the year, as well as to provide educational opportunities to train volunteers and the public to assist with feeding the hungry and ending hunger in the community. They also collect donated food for distribution to the needy. Throughout this lesson, you will add graphics to a worksheet that reports on fundraising activities. You'll learn to manipulate those graphics using Excel's many tools to place, resize, reposition, and reformat photos, clip art, shapes, SmartArt, and WordArt.

SOFTWARE ORIENTATION

The INSERT Tab's Illustration and Text Tools

Excel isn't just for crunching numbers or storing rows and rows of records. It contains a robust set of tools for turning data into charts; concepts and processes into diagrams; and adding photos, clip art, shapes, and other drawn content to make worksheets more interesting and more quickly understood. In this lesson, you focus on diagrams, images, shapes, and text-based graphics such as WordArt and text boxes, which are used to enhance a worksheet and help those viewing it to understand its content.

Most of the graphical elements you can add to an Excel worksheet are generated from the INSERT tab, shown in Figure 13-1, in the Illustrations and Text groups. Everything from pictures, clip art, SmartArt, shapes, text boxes, and WordArt are found in these two clusters of buttons. Once you've inserted the graphical element you need, tools are presented to allow you to format, size, and position them to meet your needs.

Illustrations group   **Text group**

Figure 13-1

The INSERT tab's Illustrations and Text groups

INSERTING PICTURES

Bottom Line

As the saying goes, "A picture's worth a thousand words," and in the case of Excel, pictures can be worth a thousand cells filled with text and numbers. Adding everything from photos to clip art is easy in Excel, helping you take a mind-numbing worksheet packed with numbers and text and turn it into something interesting to look at, compelling to read, and easy to navigate.

Inserting a Picture from a File

A **graphic** is an art-related object, such as a drawing (including clip art), image, or shape. Perhaps the most common graphical item added to a worksheet, aside from pie charts and bar graphs, is the picture. Using the Pictures button on the INSERT tab, it's quick and easy to add any picture you have stored on your computer (or on a network drive to which you have access), simply by navigating to the folder where that picture is stored and selecting it via the Insert Picture dialog box.

STEP BY STEP   **Insert a Picture from a File**

GET READY. LAUNCH Excel and open a new, blank workbook. Download the image files for this lesson and SAVE them in the My Pictures folder. Alternatively, you can create a subfolder in your student data folder named Lesson 13 Images and save the images in that subfolder.

1. On the INSERT tab, in the Illustrations group, click the Pictures button. The Insert Picture dialog box opens (see Figure 13-2).

Figure 13-2

The Insert Picture dialog box

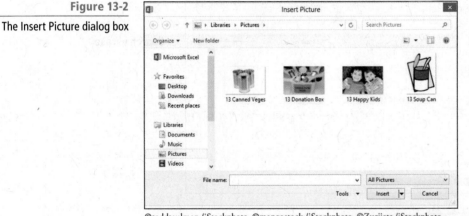

©toddtaulman /iStockphoto, ©mangostock /iStockphoto, ©Zurijeta /iStockphoto, ©mikessss /iStockphoto

2. Navigate to the folder that holds the image files for this lesson. Double-click the *13 Happy Kids* image, or click it once and then click the Insert button. The picture is inserted into your worksheet.

Troubleshooting

If you don't see your picture file listed in the Insert Picture dialog box after navigating to the folder where the picture is stored, click the All Pictures drop-down list to the right of the File Name box. Excel displays all pictures that it supports, such as BMP, JPG, PNG, TIFF, and more.

3. SAVE the workbook in the Lesson 13 folder as *13 Insert Pictures Solution*.

PAUSE. LEAVE the workbook open to use in the next exercise.

CERTIFICATION READY?   5.3.3

How do you insert an image into a worksheet?

When you insert a graphic into Excel, the upper-left corner of the graphic aligns with the active cell. However, the graphic appears on top of the worksheet grid. Although the graphic might cover up content in the grid, it doesn't affect that content and is not actually inserted into any cell in the worksheet. You can move the graphic in the worksheet without affecting any existing data or other inserted graphics.

If you decide you want to use a different photo, select the current picture and on the FORMAT tab, in the Adjust group, click the Change Picture button. In the Insert Pictures dialog box, choose an alternate image to replace the selected picture on your worksheet.

Inserting an Online Picture

Pictures and **clip art** (drawings and illustration files) can increase the appeal of many worksheets. You can easily obtain royalty-free images from Office.com or search Bing's image library, both through a simple keyword search. In lieu of that, you can browse your own SkyDrive (which is part of Office 365) to insert an image you've stored there. It's all done through the Online Pictures button in the INSERT tab's Illustrations group.

STEP BY STEP	Insert Office.com Clip Art

GET READY. USE the workbook from the previous exercise.

1. Click in cell **J1**.
2. On the INSERT tab, in the Illustrations group, click the Online Pictures button. The Insert Pictures dialog box appears.
3. To the right of Office.com Clip Art, click in the Search box. Type a keyword or phrase, such as canned food (see Figure 13-3).

Figure 13-3

Entering a search phrase in the online version of the Insert Pictures dialog box

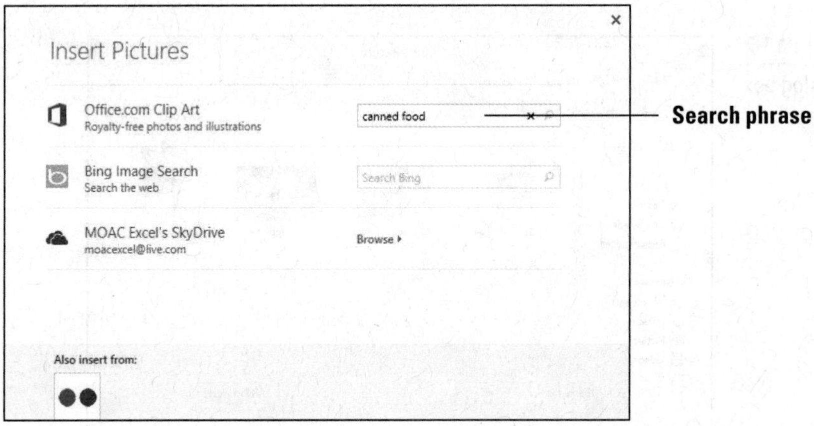

4. Click the magnifying glass icon at the right end of the search box or press Enter to begin the search. Excel searches the online Office clip art database for images containing the keywords "canned food" in their metadata.
5. The dialog box displays the images that meet the search criteria. To insert one of the images, click on it and then click the Insert button in the dialog box. You can also double-click the desired image to insert it into your worksheet. When an image is inserted, the dialog box closes automatically. Figure 13-4 shows a clip art image inserted into the worksheet.

Figure 13-4

A clip art image inserted into a worksheet

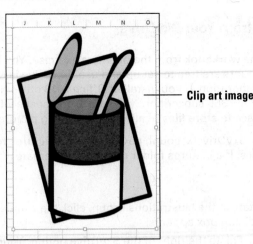

— **Clip art image**

©mikessss /iStockphoto

6. SAVE the workbook.

PAUSE. LEAVE the workbook open to use in the next exercise.

After searching for an image, if none of the images returned by Office.com meet your needs, type new search criteria into the search box and press the Enter key to initiate a new search.

Metadata is information stored about images—keywords that describe the content of the image, the name of the photographer, the type of image, the date the image was taken or last edited, and so on. Any image search, through Office.com or a web browser's image search feature, relies on the metadata stored about each image to return results when a user searches for an image to meet his needs.

STEP BY STEP   **Insert an Image via a Bing Image Search**

GET READY. USE the workbook from the previous exercise.

1. On the INSERT tab, in the Illustrations group, click the Online Pictures button. The Insert Pictures dialog box appears.

2. Click in the Search Bing box to the right of Bing Image Search.

3. Type a keyword or phrase, such as children eating lunch to search the Internet via the Bing web browser for images containing those keywords in their metadata.

4. Click the magnifying glass icon at the right end of the search box or press Enter to begin the search.

5. The dialog box displays the images that meet the search criteria. To insert one of the images, click on it and click the Insert button in the dialog box. You can also double-click the desired image. Once an image is inserted, the dialog box closes automatically. Notice that the image was inserted over the top of the clip art image.

6. Click the newly inserted image to select it, and then press the Delete key on your keyboard.

Take Note   Most images you find on the Internet are copyrighted, even if you don't see a copyright symbol or copyright text associated with the image. If you intend to use an image you find on the Internet, you need to contact the image owner and seek permission. As an alternative, you can search for "public domain images" to find images that are not restricted by copyright, or purchase images from any number of stock image websites.

PAUSE. LEAVE the workbook open to use in the next exercise.

Insert an Image from Your SkyDrive

GET READY. USE the workbook from the previous exercise. You must have an account at SkyDrive.com. Accounts are free to set up and use. SkyDrive is Microsoft's cloud solution for sharing and collaboration. If you installed Office 2013 on your own computer, you most likely became an Office 365 subscriber, which gave you space within the SkyDrive cloud. You can use this space to store files of all kinds, including pictures.

1. Connect to your SkyDrive account, navigate to the Pictures folder, and upload the Lesson 13 images. If a Pictures folder doesn't exist, create it and then upload the images.

2. Click in cell Q1.

3. On the INSERT tab, in the Illustrations group, click the Online Pictures button. The Insert Pictures dialog box appears.

4. Click the Browse link to the right of the SkyDrive option. Your SkyDrive folders, including a Public folder, appear.

5. Double-click the Pictures folder or whichever folder contains the picture you want to insert. The folder opens, displaying the images it contains (see Figure 13-5).

Figure 13-5

Any image stored in your SkyDrive folders is available for insertion in an Office document.

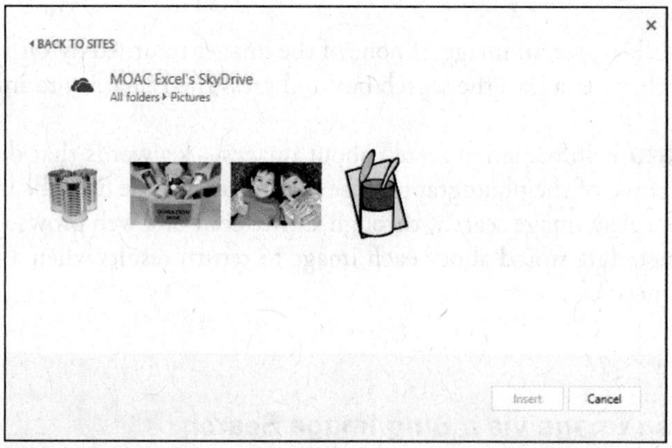

‹ BACK TO SITES

MOAC Excel's SkyDrive
All folders ▸ Pictures

Insert   Cancel

©toddtaulman /iStockphoto, ©mangostock /iStockphoto, ©Zurijeta /iStockphoto, ©mikessss /iStockphoto

6. Scroll through the images, select the 13 Canned Veges image, and then click the Insert button. You can also double-click the desired image.

7. Once an image is inserted, the dialog box closes automatically.

8. SAVE the workbook and CLOSE the file.

PAUSE. LEAVE Excel open to use in the next exercise.

ADDING SHAPES, LINES, TEXT BOXES, AND WORDART

Nothing directs a worksheet user's attention to key information faster than an arrow or line that literally points to important data. Microsoft offers **shapes** in several Office products, which are editable lines, circles, arrows, stars, and more used to draw the user's focus to a particular part of the worksheet. You can add text to shapes to provide additional information to someone trying to understand complex data, making the worksheet data more friendly and accessible. You can also insert a standard **text box**, a box that may contain text or graphics and that you can insert anywhere in a worksheet. A text box may be used to explain complex content or provide the history or source of data, or create an eye-catching title through the use of WordArt.

Adding Shapes

Excel, like Word and PowerPoint, offers the capability to insert and modify shapes in worksheets. The Shapes feature offers eight different categories of shapes, along with a group entitled Recently Used Shapes so you can quickly draw the same shapes over and over. The categories—Lines, Rectangles, Basic Shapes, Block Arrows, Equation Shapes, Flowchart, Stars and Banners, and Callouts—provide the capability to draw nearly any shape.

STEP BY STEP

Add a Shape

GET READY. LAUNCH Excel if it's not already running.

1. OPEN ***13 Add Shapes*** from the data files for this lesson.
2. On the INSERT tab, in the Illustrations group, click the **Shapes** button. A menu of shape categories appears, as shown in Figure 13-6.

Figure 13-6

The Shapes list

Up Arrow icon

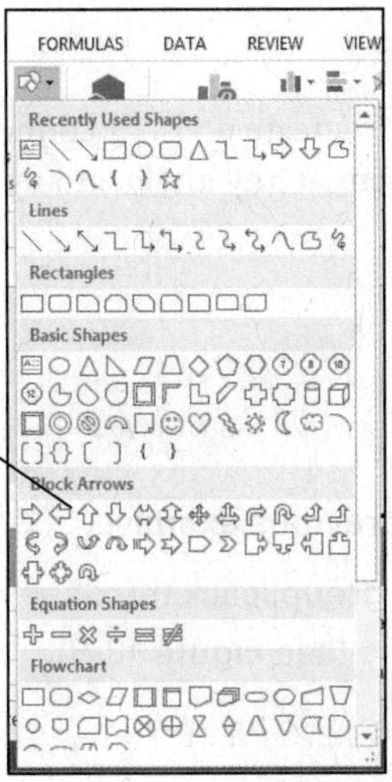
FORMULAS
DATA
REVIEW
VIEW
Recently Used Shapes
Lines
Rectangles
Basic Shapes
Block Arrows
Equation Shapes
Flowchart

3. In the Block Arrows section, click the **Up Arrow** shape. The Up Arrow shape is probably located on the first line in the Block Arrows section, third from the left.
4. Move the mouse pointer onto the worksheet, just below the FUNDS RAISED column. The mouse pointer appears as a crosshair. Draw the shape by clicking and dragging down and a little to the right. The shape appears as you drag.
5. When the shape is the desired size (both size and proportions can be changed later, so don't worry about being perfect), release the mouse button. Your block arrow should look similar to Figure 13-7.

Figure 13-7

A block arrow drawn in a worksheet

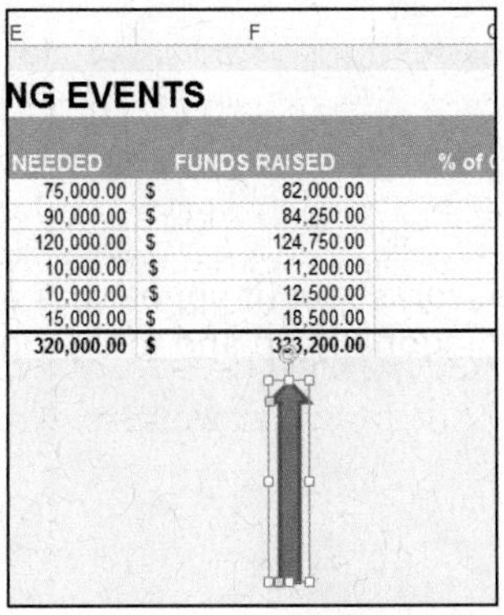
E
F
NG EVENTS
NEEDED
FUNDS RAISED
% of
75,000.00 $ 82,000.00
90,000.00 $ 84,250.00
120,000.00 $ 124,750.00
10,000.00 $ 11,200.00
10,000.00 $ 12,500.00
15,000.00 $ 18,500.00
320,000.00 $ 323,200.00

6. Click any blank cell.

7. SAVE the workbook in the Lesson 13 folder as *13 Add Shapes Solution*.

PAUSE. LEAVE the workbook open to use in the next exercise.

When inserting a shape, the direction you drag from the starting point controls the size of the shape and its proportions. You can, by controlling the angle, create a nearly perfect square or a very round, almost circular ellipse. But why do it by eye? Instead, hold down the Shift key as you drag, and you draw a shape that's equal in width and height. This applies to any shape, but is essential for squares and circles. The trick to successful use of this technique is to release the mouse button and then the Shift key.

When a shape is drawn, it has white handles on its perimeter. For graphics, a **handle** is a white box on the side and/or corner of the graphic that you click and drag to increase or decrease the size of the graphic. You can also click inside a graphic and drag to move it, and change the color of its fill and/or outline, assuming the default blue isn't what you need. You'll learn the specifics of these formatting changes later in this lesson.

Drawing Lines

Lines can be used to point to something or to create a visual connection between two shapes or two areas of the worksheet. You can draw them at any angle, at any length, and once drawn, format their appearance.

STEP BY STEP   **Draw Lines**

GET READY. USE the workbook from the previous exercise.

1. On the INSERT tab, in the Illustrations group, click the Shapes button.

2. In the Lines section, click the Arrow line (see Figure 13-8).

Figure 13-8

The arrow line in the Shapes list

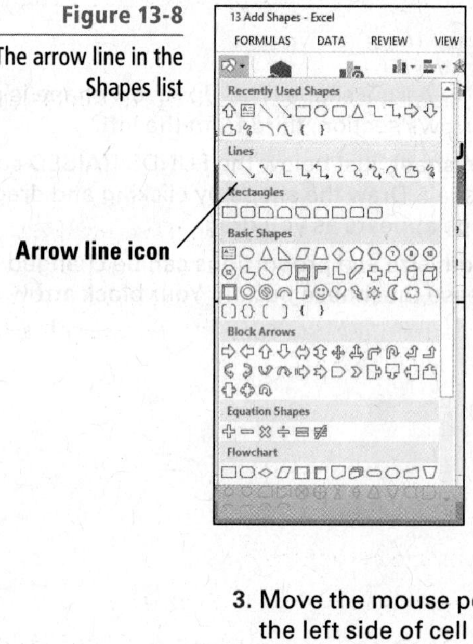

Arrow line icon

3. Move the mouse pointer onto the worksheet (it appears as a crosshair), and click over the left side of cell D22 and drag diagonally up and to the right, toward cell D19.

Take Note   When drawing straight lines, with or without arrowheads, to constrain the line to a 45° or 90° angle, hold the Shift key as you drag to draw the line. Release the mouse button before releasing the Shift key to maintain the angle after the line is completed.

4. When your line is complete, release the mouse button and click a blank cell. A finished line is shown in Figure 13-9.

Figure 13-9

An arrow line in the worksheet

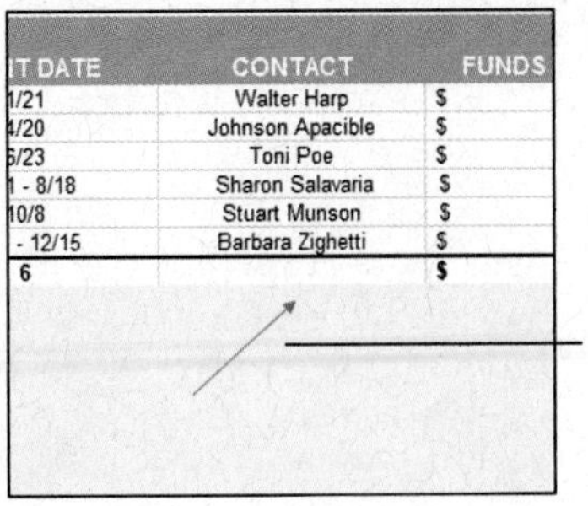

Arrow line

5. SAVE the workbook.

PAUSE. LEAVE the workbook open to use in the next exercise.

Use the following methods, depending on the type of line you choose to draw:

- To draw a straight, elbow, or curve line, click and drag the mouse in the direction you want the line to follow.

- To draw a freeform line, hold the mouse button down, so that you're drawing the line in the path of the mouse.

- To draw a freeform shape, continue dragging and drawing the line as you would for a freeform line, but come back to your line's starting point to close the shape (the shape then fills with the default blue).

- To draw a line with an arrowhead at one end, drag toward the spot that the line should point to.

Adding Text to a Shape

Shapes of all kinds can be turned into geometric text boxes by typing text directly into the shape. Once in place, the text can be formatted to any font, size, or color, and positioned within the shape using the same alignment tools that align text in your worksheet cells. All of this makes it possible to place eye-catching annotations right on the worksheet, offering short phrases or longer descriptions or instructions for use, right along with the data.

STEP BY STEP   **Add Text to a Shape**

GET READY. USE the workbook from the previous exercise.

1. On the INSERT tab, in the Illustrations group, click the Shapes button.

2. In the Stars and Banners section, click the Explosion 1 shape (see Figure 13-10).

Figure 13-10

The Explosion 1 shape in the
Shapes list

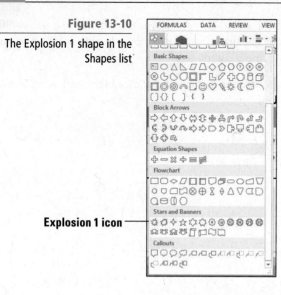

Explosion 1 icon

3. Click and drag the mouse pointer under the FUNDS NEEDED column, so the shape looks similar to Figure 13-11.

Figure 13-11

Drawing the Explosion 1 shape

	FUNDS NEEDED	FUNDS
	$	75,000.00	$
ible	$	90,000.00	$
	$	120,000.00	$
aria	$	10,000.00	$
on	$	10,000.00	$
etti	$	15,000.00	$
	$	320,000.00	$

4. With the shape still selected, type Goal Exceeded!. The text begins in the upper left of the shape and wraps within the shape if the width is too small to display all text on one line. Don't press Enter unless you want to force the text onto a new line to create a new paragraph or to place words or phrases on separate lines.

5. To format the text in the shape, select the text by clicking just to the left of the "G" in Goal and dragging through all text. Note that when you're within the shape that contains text, the mouse pointer turns to an I-beam cursor.

6. With the text selected, use the formatting tools on the Mini Toolbar or on the HOME tab to bold and center the text, and change the font size to 14. Grab a sizing handle on either side of the shape and pull to the left, right, or down a bit until all text appears, as shown in Figure 13-12.

 Cross Ref   You learned how to format text in Lesson 6 , "Formatting Cells and Ranges.".

Figure 13-12

A shape with text added

Figure 13-12

A shape with text added

7. SAVE the workbook.

PAUSE. LEAVE the workbook open to use in the next exercise.

When you select text within a shape, you can use the formatting tools on the Mini Toolbar or on the HOME tab to change the font, font size, text color, and alignment of the text.

You can apply special effects to a shape by right-clicking the shape and choosing Format Shape from the shortcut menu. The Format Shape pane appears on the right side of the workspace. Click the Text Options tab, and use the Text Fill & Outline, Text Effects, and Textbox icons shown in Figure 13-13 to apply various special effects, using the commands that appear below the icons as you select each one.

Figure 13-13

Special effect icons for formatting shapes

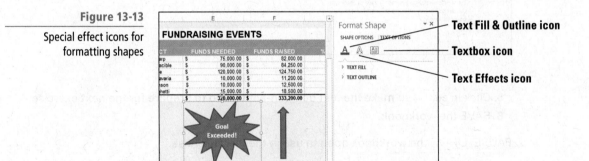

Adding a Text Box

Shapes with text in them can function as a text box, but give you the freedom to make that box appear as a circle, a star, an arrow, a banner, or any polygon. If all you need is a basic white box that contains text, however, there's no need to draw a shape and then have to format it and add text to it. Instead, insert a Text Box and type the text into it.

STEP BY STEP Add a Text Box

GET READY. USE the workbook from the previous exercise.

1. On the INSERT tab, in the Text group, click the **Text Box** button, as shown in Figure 13-14.

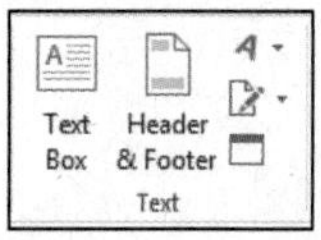

Figure 13-14

The Text group of tools on the INSERT tab

CERTIFICATION READY? 5.3.1

How do you insert a text box into a worksheet?

2. Move the mouse pointer onto the worksheet over cell **B20**. The mouse pointer turns into a vertical cursor.
3. Click and drag to cell **C24** to draw a small box. If you draw a box that's too big or too small for the text you will type into the box, you can resize the box after typing the text.
4. The text box contains a blinking cursor. Type **These numbers are preliminary. I need to check with the director before releasing the worksheet to the board for review.** See Figure 13-15.

Figure 13-15

Entering text into a text box

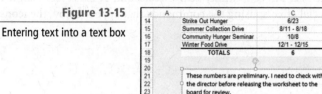

5. Click in cell **A1** to make the text box non-active and to prepare for the next exercise.
6. SAVE the workbook.

PAUSE. LEAVE the workbook open to use in the next exercise.

You can use the formatting tools on the HOME tab or on the Mini Toolbar to format text in a text box.

Using WordArt

Looking for a way to add text to your worksheet and catch everyone's eye? **WordArt**, a Microsoft Office feature that combines words and artistic effects, may be just what you need. Utilizing an extensive series of preset colored fills, drop shadows, outlines, and 3D looks, WordArt makes it easy to create a specialized text object quickly. You can use them to add phrases like "Great job!" next to high sales numbers or to include staff or product names and short titles on your worksheet, unbound by the limited formatting tools available through the Font group on the HOME tab.

STEP BY STEP Use WordArt

GET READY. USE the workbook from the previous exercise.

1. On the INSERT tab, in the Text group, click the **Insert WordArt** button. The WordArt styles gallery appears, as shown in Figure 3-16.

Figure 13-16

The WordArt styles gallery

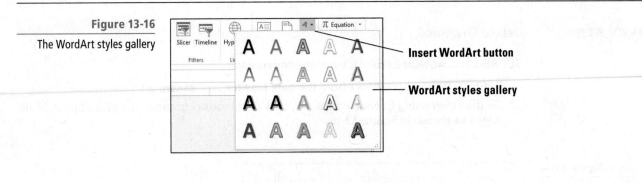

Insert WordArt button

WordArt styles gallery

1. Select the Fill - Blue, Accent 1, Shadow style.

2. A box of sample text appears on the worksheet. Triple-click in the box to select all sample text and type Great Fundraisers!. Notice in Figure 13-17 that the style you chose in Step 2 is applied to the sample text.

Figure 13-17

WordArt in a worksheet

EVENT NAME	EVENT DATE	CONTACT	FUNDS NEEDED	FUNDS RAISED	% of GOAL	EVENT TYPE
Winter Carnival	1/21	Walter Harp	$ 75,000.00	$ 82,000.00	109%	Fundraising
Spring Banquet	4/20	Johnson Apacible	$ 90,000.00	$ 84,250.00	94%	Fundraising
Strike Out Hunger	6/23	Toni Poe	$ 120,000.00	$ 124,750.00	104%	Fundraising
Summer Collection Drive	8/11 - 8/18	Sharon Salavaria	$ 10,000.00	$ 11,200.00	112%	Collection
Community Hunger Seminar	10/8	Stuart Munson	$ 10,000.00	$ 12,500.00	125%	Education
Winter Food Drive	12/1 - 12/15	Barbara Zighetti	$ 15,000.00	$ 18,500.00	123%	Collection
TOTALS	6		$ 320,000.00	$ 333,200.00	111%	

WordArt

3. SAVE the workbook as *13 Add Shapes Solution* and CLOSE the file.

PAUSE. LEAVE Excel open to use in the next exercise.

You can change your WordArt style, simply by selecting the WordArt object on your worksheet and then displaying the WordArt Styles gallery on the FORMAT tab. Choose a different style, and the text you typed appears in that new style. If you want to get rid of the style entirely and just use plain text, choose Clear WordArt from the WordArt Styles gallery on the FORMAT tab.

If you need to correct a typo, or add or remove text, you can edit your text at any by selecting some or all of the WordArt text and typing the correction. You can also move and resize the graphic at any time, so placement and size are entirely up to you. You learn more about how to move and resize graphics of any kind later in this lesson.

DELETING, COPYING, AND MOVING GRAPHICS

Bottom Line

Once you add a graphic to a worksheet, you'll probably want to move it to the perfect spot. You may also want to reuse it in another location, to improve yet another worksheet through the use of interesting and helpful visuals. Conversely, you may want to get rid of it all together. No matter what you want to do, fortunately, moving, copying, and deleting graphics are incredibly simple.

Deleting Graphics

To delete a graphic, just select the graphic and then press the Delete key on your keyboard. The same concept applies to nearly any object, such as a shape, line, text box, or WordArt.

STEP BY STEP **Delete Graphics**

GET READY. LAUNCH Excel if it's not already running.

1. OPEN *13 Delete Copy Move* from the data files for this lesson.
2. On the Fundraising Events worksheet, click the WordArt graphic. Handles appear on its edges as shown in Figure 13-18.

Figure 13-18

Handles on the selected graphic

Great Fundraisers!   → **WordArt handles**

DATE	CONTACT	FUNDS NEEDED	FUNDS RAISED
1	Walter Harp	$ 75,000.00	$ 82,000.00
0	Johnson Apacible	$ 90,000.00	$ 84,250.00
3	Toni Poe	$ 120,000.00	$ 124,750.00

3. Press the Delete key on your keyboard. Excel deletes the graphic.
4. Click the block arrow graphic and press the Delete key.
5. SAVE the workbook in the Lesson 13 folder as *13 Delete Copy Move Solution*.

PAUSE. LEAVE the workbook open to use in the next exercise.

When deleting text boxes, WordArt, and shapes to which you've added text, it's important to select the object and not the text. If your cursor is active in the text, that's what you'll delete when you press the Delete key. You'll remove text rather than the whole object. To be sure your entire object is selected, click once on the object and then click the edge of it, so that the line around the object is solid. If the contents of the object are selected or active for editing, the bounding box will appear as a dashed line.

Moving Graphics

Rarely do we insert a graphic in the exact spot where we need it. This isn't a big deal, however, considering how simple it is to move the graphic to where it belongs, whether you're nudging it just a bit or dragging it to an entirely new spot in the worksheet. You can also move objects to another worksheet or workbook using the Clipboard.

STEP BY STEP **Move Graphics**

GET READY. USE the workbook from the previous exercise.

1. Click the starburst shape. Handles appear on its edges.
2. Point the mouse pointer inside the graphic. The mouse pointer should change to a four-headed arrow, as shown in Figure 13-19.

Figure 13-19

The mouse pointer is a four-headed arrow, which indicates you can move the graphic.

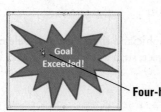

Goal Exceeded!

Four-headed arrow

3. Click and drag the graphic so it appears under the % of GOAL column. Release the mouse button.

Take Note While the object is selected, you can move it without using the mouse. Just tap the arrow keys on your keyboard to nudge the object in small increments—up, down, left, or right.

4. Click and drag the arrow shape so it points to the FUNDS RAISED column, as shown in Figure 13-20.

Figure 13-20

The result of moving graphics

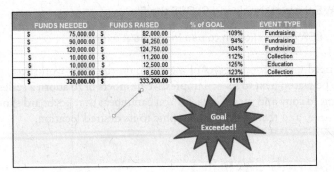

FUNDS NEEDED	FUNDS RAISED	% of GOAL	EVENT TYPE
$ 75,000.00	$ 82,000.00	109%	Fundraising
$ 90,000.00	$ 84,250.00	94%	Fundraising
$ 120,000.00	$ 124,750.00	104%	Fundraising
$ 10,000.00	$ 11,200.00	112%	Collection
$ 10,000.00	$ 12,500.00	125%	Education
$ 15,000.00	$ 18,500.00	123%	Collection
$ 320,000.00	$ 333,200.00	111%	

Goal Exceeded!

5. SAVE the workbook.

PAUSE. LEAVE the workbook open to use in the next exercise.

When selecting the graphic, be careful not to point to a handle by accident, which will resize the graphic instead of moving it.

Another way to move a graphic of any kind, especially if you want to use it on another worksheet instead of the one where it currently resides, is to cut it. Once the object is cut, you can paste it where you want it, moving it from point A to point B.

To cut, click the object and then right-click. Select Cut from the shortcut menu, and the object disappears. You can also select the object and press Ctrl + X, which also cuts the selection.

Then, go to the other worksheet where you want to use the graphic, and either right-click anywhere on the worksheet and select one of the paste options from the shortcut menu or press Ctrl + V. The Paste Options section of the shortcut menu includes icons for Use Destination Theme, Keep Source Formatting, and Picture.

Copying Graphics

You designed a WordArt banner, or formatted a shape with text in it, and it's so great you want to use it in another worksheet, or in a Word document or a PowerPoint presentation. Making a copy of the graphic is easy, as is placing it in a different location where you want it to appear.

STEP BY STEP **Copy a Graphic**

GET READY. USE the workbook from the previous exercise.

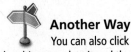

Another Way
You can also click the object to select it and then press Ctrl + C to copy it to the Clipboard.

1. On the Fundraising Events worksheet, click the text box to select it.
2. Right-click a border of the text box and select Copy from the shortcut menu.
3. Click the Volunteers tab.
4. Right-click in cell A1 and under Paste Options in the shortcut menu, select the Use Destination Theme icon.
5. Triple-click inside the text box to select all text, and then type Confidential. Do not share this information without permission from a committee chair. The text box is shown in Figure 13-21.

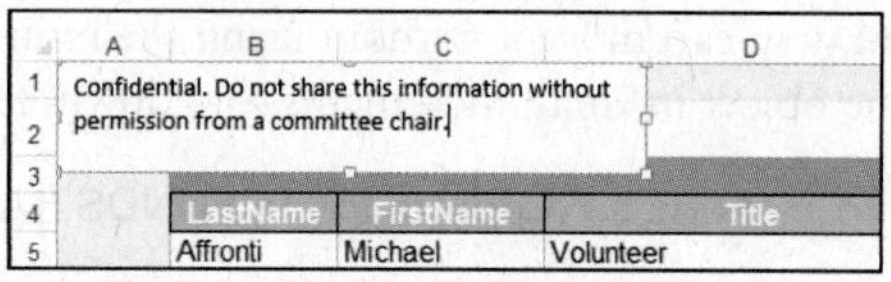

Adding Pictures and Shapes to a

Figure 13-21

The copied text box with new text

	A	B	C	D
1	Confidential. Do not share this information without			
2	permission from a committee chair.			
3				
4	**LastName**	**FirstName**	**Title**	
5	Affronti	Michael	Volunteer	

6. SAVE the workbook and CLOSE the file.

PAUSE. LEAVE Excel open to use in the next exercise.

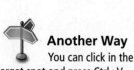

Another Way You can click in the target spot and press Ctrl+V to paste the object from the Clipboard.

If you need one or more copies of a graphic on the same worksheet, perhaps to create a series of stars to be placed next to several impressive numbers or to adorn a series of charts, click the graphic you want to copy and press Ctrl + D. You can repeat that keyboard shortcut for as many duplicates as you need, and then move each graphic to its desired location.

FORMATTING GRAPHICS

Bottom Line

In addition to moving or copying graphics, you will most likely need to change their appearance at some point. From styles to the use of the mouse and keyboard to change the appearance, placement, and stacking order of overlapping graphics, Excel offers great tools to make your graphics look exactly as you'd imagined them.

Applying Styles to Shapes and Changing Styles

Once you've drawn a shape, the Excel ribbon changes to display DRAWING TOOLS with the FORMAT tab selected. In the steps below, you learn to apply Shape Styles and to customize shapes by choosing your own fill color, outline, and effects.

STEP BY STEP **Apply a Style to a Shape**

GET READY. LAUNCH Excel if it's not already running.

1. OPEN *13 Format Graphics* from the data files for this lesson.
2. In the Fundraising Events worksheet, click the starburst shape to select it.
3. On the DRAWING TOOLS FORMAT tab, in the Shape Styles group, hold your mouse over each of the styles in the Shape Styles mini gallery. Excel previews each style using the selected shape.
4. To see the full list of styles, click the More arrow in the lower right corner of the Shape Styles mini gallery. The Shape Styles gallery appears (see Figure 13-22).

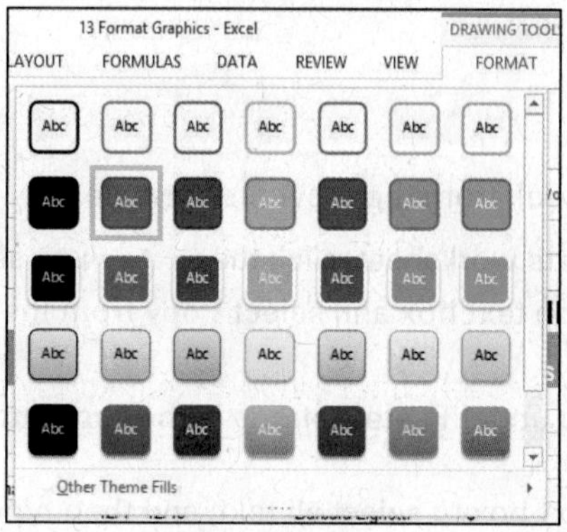

Figure 13-22

The Shape Styles gallery

CERTIFICATION READY?   **5.3.6**

How do you use Shape Fill to change the color of an object?

5. From the gallery, select Light 1 Outline, Colored Fill - Olive Green, Accent 3.

6. To change the shape's fill color, in the Shape Styles group, click the Shape Fill button. The color palette appears.

7. From the palette under Theme Colors, select Dark Blue, Text 2. The object's background color changes to dark blue (see Figure 13-23).

Figure 13-23

Changing the fill color of your shape

8. SAVE the workbook in the Lesson 13 folder as *13 Format Graphics Solution*.

PAUSE. LEAVE the workbook open to use in the next exercise.

In addition to a shape's fill color, you can also change a shape's outline and effects. To change a shape's outline, click the Shape Outline button in the Shape Styles group, and then select an outline color from the palette that appears. To make the outline thicker or apply a dashed or other non-solid outline, use the Weight and Dashes commands in the Shape Outline menu and make a selection from their respective submenus.

To apply a shape effect, in the Shape Styles group, click the Shape Effects button and select an effect from the gallery that appears. Examples of effects are Shadow, Reflection, and Glow.

Resizing a Graphic

You can control the size of the graphics you draw, such as the width and height of polygons, the length of lines, and the size of text boxes and WordArt objects, through your original creation of the graphic and how far you click and drag the mouse. Once created, however, it's easy to resize graphics to meet your needs, making them fit where you intend to place them, to make them large enough to house the text you type, and so that they attract the amount of attention you need them to. The same techniques work to resize pictures, too.

STEP BY STEP   **Resize a Graphic**

GET READY. USE the workbook from the previous exercise.

1. Select the starburst shape.

2. Point to the lower-left corner handle. When the mouse pointer turns to a two-headed arrow, drag inward to make the graphic smaller. With the handle still selected, drag outward to make the graphic larger. By pressing the Shift key while using a corner handle, you maintain the current width-to-height ratio when resizing a graphic.

3. To change the height of the shape, drag a top or bottom handle. This allows you to stretch the shape vertically.

4. To change the width of the shape, drag a side handle—drag outward to widen it and inward to make it narrower. Adjust your starburst shape so it resembles Figure 13-24.

Figure 13-24

The starburst shape after resizing it

5. SAVE the workbook.

PAUSE. LEAVE the workbook open to use in the next exercise.

To change the length of a line you've drawn, select the line and then point to either of its two handles. When the mouse pointer turns to a two-headed arrow, drag outward to lengthen the line, or drag toward the center of the line to shorten it. To keep the line at a 45° or 90° angle, hold the Shift key as you drag, and release the mouse button before releasing the Shift key.

Certain polygons, such as stars, block arrows, and triangles have more than just the standard white handles on their corners and sides when selected. These shapes also have control handles, which are yellow boxes used to change the depth of sides. Use these yellow handlesto make your block arrow pointier or to deepen the sides of your stars, dragging inward to make the angles more acute, or outward to make the angles more obtuse or shallow.

Rotating a Graphic

You can change the rotation of any shape with the mouse using the rotation handle that appears just outside the shape, above the top side handle.

STEP BY STEP	Rotate a Graphic

GET READY. USE the workbook from the previous exercise.

1. Select the **starburst** shape.
2. Point to the rotation handle (see Figure 13-25). The mouse pointer turns to a circular arrow.

Figure 13-25

The rotation handle

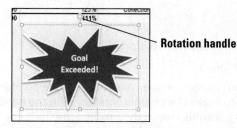

Rotation handle

3. Drag the mouse counterclockwise. As you drag, the mouse pointer changes to a series of arrows in a circle.
4. When the shape is rotated to the desired angle, similar to Figure 13-26, release the mouse button.

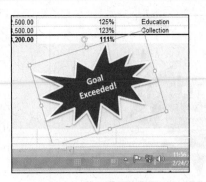

5. SAVE the workbook.

PAUSE. LEAVE the workbook open to use in the next exercise.

Stacking Overlapping Graphics

When graphics overlap, their stacking order is determined, by default, by the order in which they were drawn or inserted. So if you insert a photo and then draw a block arrow that points from it to a portion of the worksheet, if the objects overlap, the arrow will be on top of the photo. If you want to change this stacking order, use the Arrange group of tools on the DRAWING TOOLS FORMAT tab.

STEP BY STEP | **Control Stacking Order when Graphics Overlap**

GET READY. USE the workbook from the previous exercise.

1. In the Format Graphics workbook, click the Overlap sheet tab. The worksheet contains several overlapping graphics.

2. Select the border of the WordArt graphic (Great Fundraisers), which has other graphics stacked on top of it. Figure 13-27 shows the stack of graphics. The WordArt object, which is further down in the stack, is selected.

Figure 13-27

A stack of objects

©toddtaulman /iStockphoto

3. On the DRAWING TOOLS FORMAT tab, in the Arrange group, click the Bring Forward button. The WordArt graphic moves up one level in the stack.

4. Click the Bring Forward arrow button and select Bring to Front. The WordArt graphic appears at the top of the stack (see Figure 13-28).

Figure 13-28

The WordArt graphic is now on the top of the st0ack.

©toddtaulman /iStockphoto

5. With the WordArt graphic still selected, click the Send Backward button to move it back one level. The Food Drive shape is now on top.

Take Note   You can use the Bring Forward and Send Backward commands repeatedly, so that, for example, a shape can go from sixth place in a stack of six items to third. To use these buttons without having to display the drop-down menu and make a choice there, just click the Send Backward or Bring Forward buttons rather than clicking their button arrows.

6. SAVE the workbook and CLOSE the file.

PAUSE. LEAVE Excel open to use in the next exercise.

What if you can't see the shape that's beneath another graphic on the worksheet? That's where the Selection pane comes in. To display it, select any graphic, and on the FORMAT tab, in the Arrange group, click the Selection Pane button. The pane appears on the right side of the workspace and contains a list of the graphics on the active worksheet. To restack the shapes using this pane, drag them, by name (such as "Rectangle 1") up or down in the list, with the mouse (see Figure 13-29).

Rectangle 1   Picture 3   Sun 4   Explosion 1 2   Selection pane

Figure 13-29

The Selection pane gives you a list of graphics and lets you drag them up and down in the list to change their stacking order.

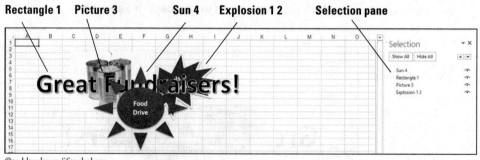

©toddtaulman /iStockphoto

CERTIFICATION READY?   5.3.8

How do you align objects so they're distributed evenly in a group?

If your graphics don't overlap, or overlap only slightly, you might want to arrange them in a tidy row or column, or make sure they're distributed evenly in a group. To do this, use the Align button in the Arrange group after having selected all of the graphics you want to align. Select them first (Shift + Click on the graphics you want to include in the alignment) and then click the Align button to choose from aligning them by their sides, tops, bottoms, or centers. The Distribute options are found in the Align drop-down menu, too. If you want to keep them together when copying or moving them, select Group from the Arrange tools right below the Align button.

ADDING GRAPHIC ENHANCEMENTS USING PICTURE TOOLS

Bottom Line

You don't need a separate image-editing application to change the colors, sharpness, and contrast of images you add to a worksheet. Excel provides simple tools for making quick changes to any photo, drawing, or clip art you might add. In addition, it makes it easy to take a screenshot of any part of the interface and include that as a graphic element.

Making Corrections to a Graphic

One of your photos doesn't look good. Maybe it was taken with a low-quality camera, it's a little blurry, or it's too dark or too light. You don't need to make it perfect, but it needs to be better, sharper, clearer, and more professional looking. Use the Corrections options on the PICTURE TOOLS FORMAT tab to correct lighting and sharpness. You can also use options in the Format Picture pane to make further corrections.

STEP BY STEP | **Make Corrections to a Graphic**

GET READY. LAUNCH Excel if it's not already running.

1. OPEN *13 Enhancements* from the data files for this lesson.
2. In the Correction worksheet, select the photo of two boys.
3. On the PICTURE TOOLS FORMAT tab, in the Adjust group, click the Corrections button. The menu shown in Figure 13-30 appears.

Figure 13-30

The Corrections menu provides commands for making quick changes to improve your photo.

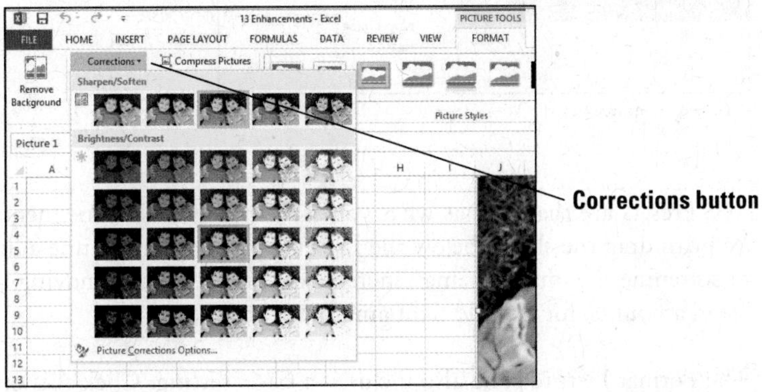

Corrections button

©Zurijeta /iStockphoto

4. Using the thumbnails of your selected photo from the Sharpen/Soften corrections section, make a choice that represents the adjustment you're looking for—more sharpness for a blurry picture or perhaps softening for an image that's too sharp or where the exposure was too harsh. At the far right end of the Sharpen/Soften section, select Sharpen: 50%. Figure 13-31 shows two side-by-side images—the image on the left before applying 50% sharpening and the image on the right after.

Figure 13-31

Sharpen a blurry photo with one click.

©Zurijeta /iStockphoto

Take Note   Excel allows you to hover your mouse over the thumbnails that represent various corrections and see the effect in your selected photo before committing to the change. Point to any thumbnail in the Corrections menu, wait a second, and observe the change in your photo. If you like the effect, click the thumbnail. If not, move on and preview another.

5. To adjust a photo that's too dark or too light, use the Brightness/Contrast settings, also represented by thumbnails showing your selected photo in varying stages of correction. Hold your mouse over each of the settings to see their effect on your photo, but don't select any of the settings.

6. SAVE the workbook in the Lesson 13 folder as *13 Enhancements Solution*.

PAUSE. LEAVE the workbook open to use in the next exercise.

The Format Picture pane, shown in Figure 13-32, lets you make more fine-tuned adjustments to an image. To access the Format Picture pane, at the bottom of the Corrections menu, click the Picture Corrections Options command. The right-most icon across the top of the pane is selected, showing more detailed controls for adjusting brightness and contrast.

Figure 13-32

The Picture Corrections pane

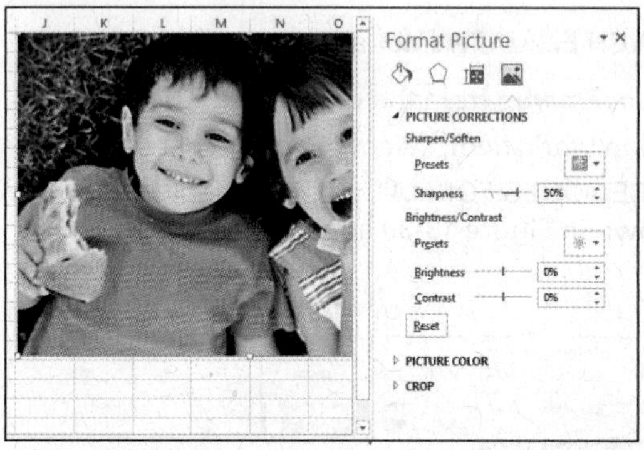

©Zurijeta /iStockphoto

The Presets are the same as what you saw in the Corrections menu for each type of correction. You can drag the sliders below the Presets options to make fine adjustments, such as sharpening or softening the image in small increments, or adding or removing brightness/contrast in equally small amounts, for just the right amount of correction.

The Format Picture pane also includes a Crop setting. Click this option and enter values for desired width and height and the offset (amount and location of cropping), or use the Crop tool, found in the Size group on the FORMAT tab. With the Crop tool, you use crop handles, shown in Figure 13-33, to crop away unwanted portions of the photo.

Figure 13-33

Cropping handles

Cropping handles like this one appear on the sides and all four corners.

©Zurijeta /iStockphoto

You can apply picture corrections to clip art as well, but corrections are intended for use in photos where brightness, contrast, and sharpness may need adjustments.

Using the Color Feature to Enhance Images

To make improvements to a photo's color or to apply special color effects, such as turning a four-color image into a **duotone** (an image with two colors), you need to start with a photo. You can also apply these color adjustments to clip art, but they're intended for use in photos where changing from color to black and white or to greater or reduced levels of color (also known as **saturation**) are more useful.

STEP BY STEP	Change the Color of an Image

GET READY. USE the workbook from the previous exercise.

1. Click the Color sheet tab and select the top photo, which shows a baby holding a spoon.
2. On the PICTURE TOOLS FORMAT tab, in the Adjust group, click the Color button. The menu shown in Figure 13-34 appears.

Figure 13-34

The Color menu offers a series of color adjustments.

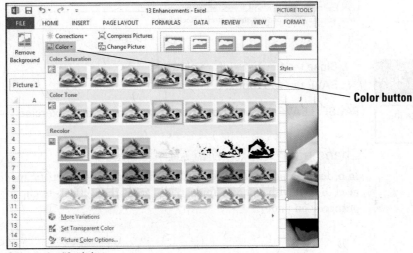

©zest_marina /iStockphoto

3. Hold your mouse over each thumbnail of your photo to see its effect. The options include:
   - **Color Saturation:** This set of options adds or removes color depth. You can use it to fade the colors in an image or to create a more intensely colored image. The lowest level of saturation makes a color photo appear to be black and white or grayscale.
   - **Color Tone:** This adjusts *temperature*, which essentially adds more blue for a cooler, lower-temperature image or more red for a more vibrant, higher-temperature image.
   - **Recolor:** This set of options provides several preset color changes, ranging from grayscale to true black and white (which looks like a bad photocopy) to a variety of *duotones*, which means the image is comprised of two colors—black and one other color.
   - **More Variations:** This is an expansion of the duotone options presented by some of the Recolor presets.
   - **Set Transparent Color:** Use this if you want to remove a particular color from the image. This is handy for photos on a white background, such as product images, allowing you to remove that background and have everything but the product be see-through (making the underlying worksheet visible).
   - **Picture Color Options:** This displays the Format Picture pane and opens a set of sliders for Saturation, Tone, and Recolor, allowing fine adjustments to those settings, rather than relying on thumbnails with set amounts of color added or removed.

4. In the Recolor section of the Color menu, on the first line of the gallery, select Sepia. The image takes on brown tones.

5. On the PICTURE TOOLS FORMAT tab, in the Adjust group, click the Color button, and then select Picture Color Options at the bottom of the menu.

6. In the Format Picture pane on the right, move the Sharpness slider to the right until you reach the 33% value. Your photo should look similar to Figure 13-35.

Figure 13-35

The enhanced photo

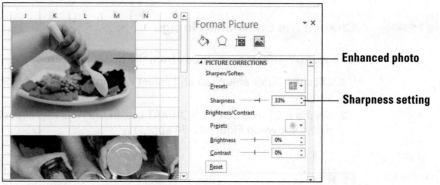

©zest_marina /iStockphoto, ©mangostock /iStockphoto

7. Close the Format Picture pane.

8. SAVE the workbook.

PAUSE. LEAVE the workbook open to use in the next exercise.

Changing a Graphic with Artistic Effects

In order to apply **artistic effects**, which are various artistic mediums and special effects, you need to start with a photo. You can also apply these effects to clip art, but they're designed for use primarily on photos.

STEP BY STEP   **Apply Artistic Effects**

GET READY. USE the workbook from the previous exercise.

1. In the Color worksheet, select the donation box photo.

2. On the PICTURE TOOLS FORMAT tab, in the Adjust group, click the Artistic Effects button. The gallery of effects thumbnails is shown in Figure 13-36.

Figure 13-36

Choose from over 20 different artistic effects.

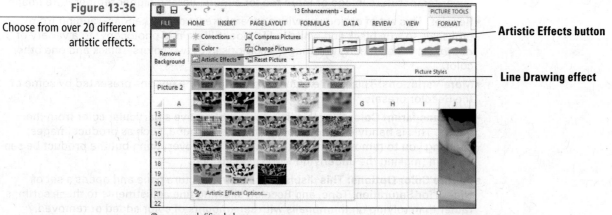

©mangostock /iStockphoto

3. Hold your mouse pointer over each effect to see its preview on the photo. Select the Line Drawing effect. Figure 13-37 shows the Line Drawing effect applied.

©mangostock /iStockphoto

4. You can customize the applied effect using the Format Picture pane. To display the pane, open the Artistic Effects menu and select Artistic Effects Options. In the Format Picture pane that appears on the right, move the Pencil Size slider to the right to observe its effect on the photo, stopping at the value 28. Then move the Transparency slider to the right, stopping at the value 51%.

5. CLOSE the Format Picture pane.

6. SAVE the workbook.

PAUSE. LEAVE the workbook open to use in the next exercise.

Applying a Picture Style

Picture styles add borders, frames, shadows, and similar effects with one click of any of the Picture Style icons on the PICTURE TOOLS FORMAT tab. Use one or more to make your photos "pop" with the appearance of a picture frame or 3D effect.

STEP BY STEP   **Apply Picture Styles**

GET READY. USE the workbook from the previous exercise.

1. In the Color worksheet, select the donation box photo.

2. On the PICTURE TOOLS FORMAT tab, in the Picture Styles group, hold your mouse over each of the styles in the mini gallery to see their effect on your photo.

3. In the lower-right corner of the mini gallery, click the More button to display the Picture Styles gallery (see Figure 13-38).

©mangostock /iStockphoto

4. Select **Drop Shadow Rectangle**, which is probably located on the first row, fourth from the left. The style is applied to your picture.

5. To change the picture border, click the **Picture Border button**, point to **Weight**, and select **3 pt** (see Figure 13-39).

Figure 13-39

Modifying a picture border

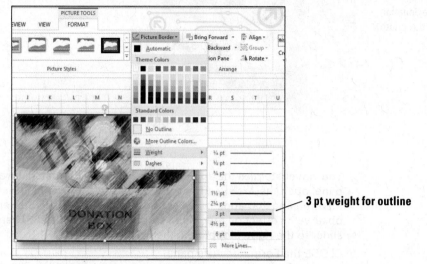

3 pt weight for outline

©mangostock /iStockphoto

6. SAVE the workbook.

PAUSE. LEAVE the workbook open to use in the next exercise.

You can change the color of a picture border, make the border thicker or thinner, and change the border from a solid line to a dashed or dotted line.

To change a picture's effects, click the Picture Effects button arrow and choose an effect from the palette that appears.

To apply a picture layout, click the Picture Layout button and make a selection from the palette of 30 layouts of pictures, captions, connectors, and so on.

Resetting a Picture to Its Original State

You've applied corrections, you've changed colors, and you've chosen an artistic effect for a photo in your worksheet, and you've resized an image, too. Now you regret one or more of those changes and want to go back to its original state. What to do? Well, you could delete and re-insert the image, but it's much easier to use the Reset Picture button, found on the PICTURE TOOLS FORMAT tab in the Adjust group.

STEP BY STEP   **Reset a Picture**

GET READY. USE the workbook from the previous exercise.

1. On the Color worksheet, scroll down and select the third photo (Give, Gain, Grow).

2. On the PICTURE TOOLS FORMAT tab, in the Adjust group, click the **Reset Picture arrow** button. Two options appear (see Figure 13-40).

Figure 13-40

The Reset Picture options

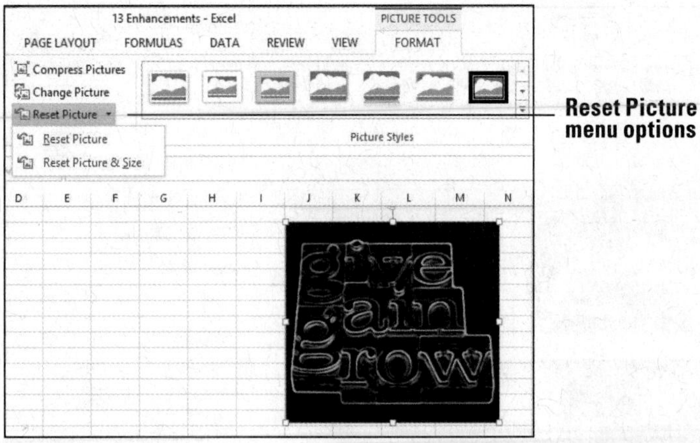

©marekuliasz /iStockphoto

3. Select Reset Picture & Size to remove all changes made since insertion.

4. SAVE the workbook.

PAUSE. LEAVE the workbook open to use in the next exercise.

The Reset Picture option removes corrections, color, styles, and effects.

If instead of reverting or resetting the picture to its pre-correction and pre-color adjustment status you want to permanently apply the changes you've made to the image size and quality, click Compress Pictures in the Adjust group. A dialog box appears through which you can choose which of the changes you want to keep. This compression reduces the size of your worksheet file, which is especially useful if you inserted a very high-resolution photo and then reduced its size and removed color from it.

Using Picture Properties

Picture Properties tell Excel how you want it to deal with the graphics you add to your worksheets, how they should relate to the worksheet itself, whether or not they'll print with the worksheet content, and whether or not the text in shapes or text boxes can be edited after insertion. This section walks you through Picture Properties options.

STEP BY STEP | **Modify a Picture's Properties**

GET READY. USE the workbook you modified in the previous exercise.

1. Click the Color sheet tab.

2. Right-click the baby feeding photo and select Size and Properties from the shortcut menu. The Format Picture pane appears on the right side of the workspace, as shown in Figure 13-41.

Figure 13-41

Control the relationship between the worksheet and your graphic using the Format Picture pane.

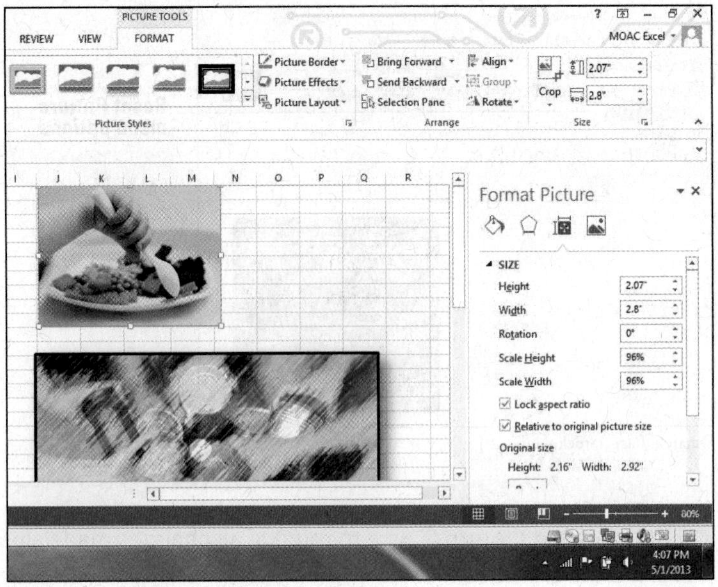

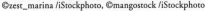

©zest_marina /iStockphoto, ©mangostock /iStockphoto

CERTIFICATION READY? **5.3.7**

How do you modify an object's properties?

3. Scroll down if necessary and click the PROPERTIES category.

4. Select the Move and size with cells option. This option associates the object with the cells it overlays.

5. Close the Format Picture pane.

6. Grab the column border between column headings J and K, and then drag to the right to widen column J. Notice that the picture becomes wider as well.

7. On the Quick Access Toolbar, click the Undo icon to undo the column width setting.

8. SAVE the workbook and CLOSE the file.

PAUSE. LEAVE Excel open to use in the next exercise.

The picture properties are described as follows:

• **Move and size with cells:** This option is off by default, but if selected (by clicking the option button), if you change the width of columns or the height of rows, the adjacent graphic changes as well. Moving cells from one section of the worksheet to another or to another worksheet or workbook takes the graphic along for the ride.

• **Move but don't size with cells:** This option, which is on by default, only connects the graphic with adjacent data. Changes to cell sizes won't impact the size of the graphic.

• **Don't move or size with cells:** This option, also off by default, makes the graphics entirely independent of the worksheet content and leaves them behind if content is moved, and doesn't cause any automatic resizing in response to the resizing of worksheet cells.

• **Print object:** This checkbox is selected by default, and simply means that if you choose to print the worksheet or set a print area that contains the graphic, the graphic is printed.

• **Locked:** Selected by default, this option pins the graphic to its current location until and unless the Locked option is unchecked. Note, however, that this option doesn't take effect unless you also have the worksheet protected. To protect the worksheet, go to the HOME tab and use the Format button menu and choose Protect Sheet. The resulting dialog box gives you your protection options.

• **Lock text:** This option pertains only to shapes that contain text or to Text Box objects and it prevents changes to the text.

Using a Screenshot to Capture and Crop Images

There are many reasons you might take a screenshot and place it in an Excel worksheet. For example, you might want to show a portion of a Word document that contains relevant information, or provide a picture of a PowerPoint slide. Whatever your reason, it's easy to take and insert a screenshot of any aspect of your workspace, even the workspace of another open application or your Windows desktop and make it a graphical element in your worksheet.

STEP BY STEP **Capture a Screenshot**

GET READY. LAUNCH Excel if it's not already running.

1. OPEN *13 Screenshot* from the data files for this lesson.

2. OPEN *13 Fundraising Flash* from the data files for this lesson. This is a Microsoft Word document. You will capture a screenshot of some content in this document and insert it into an Excel worksheet. Click Enable Editing if the message appears.

3. On the taskbar, click the Excel icon to switch to the Excel workbook. Click in cell A1.

4. On the INSERT tab, in the Illustrations group, click the Take a Screenshot button arrow. The screenshot menu appears, as shown in Figure 13-42.

Figure 13-42

The Take a Screenshot menu

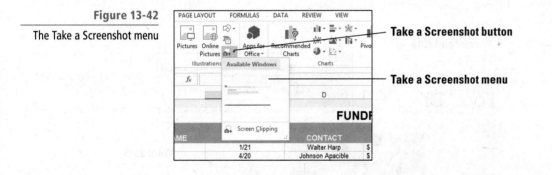

5. Your options include the windows of other applications currently open (in this case, Word), or to implement Screen Clipping, which allows you to draw a box around any space within any open application and make that the inserted graphic. Select Screen Clipping.

6. The Word document appears. Drag the mouse pointer, which looks like a crosshair, over the text and release the mouse button. The screenshot appears automatically in the Excel document.

7. Figure 13-43 shows the inserted screenshot, which is a section of a Word document pertaining to the year's fundraising events.

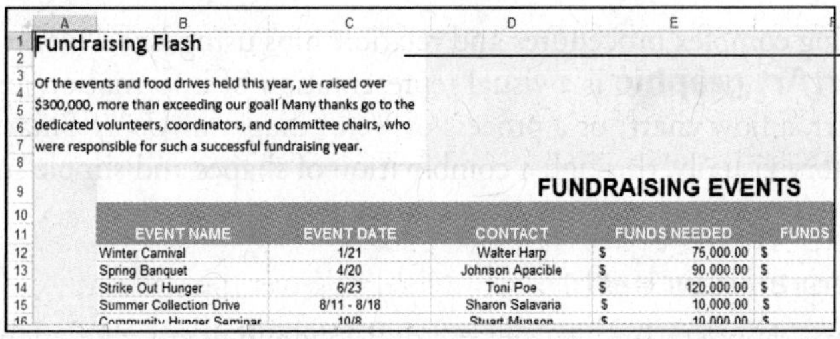

Figure 13-43

Bring in useful information by adding a screenshot of a relevant document.

8. SAVE the workbook in the Lesson 13 folder as *13 Screenshot Solution* and CLOSE the file. CLOSE the Word program.

PAUSE. LEAVE Excel open to use in the next exercise.

Workplace *Ready*

USING GRAPHICS IN EXCEL AND OTHER OFFICE APPLICATIONS

The Excel Picture tools enable you to insert, modify, and use more creative and profession-al-looking graphics in your workbooks.

Microsoft incorporated Picture tools across the Microsoft Office suite, so images you format in one application are portable and editable in another. For example, screenshots you use in an Excel document can be copied and pasted to PowerPoint and Word.

The Picture tools also promote more consistent and professional image branding. In a business set-ting, you can use the tools to refine images for company logos, brochure photos, employee photo ID pictures, and so on. You can edit photos in Excel and insert them into Word and PowerPoint. You can also add them to emails in Outlook. An individual can edit family photos to create al-bums, calendars, cards, and many other items that once needed a separate graphics application to create them.

Consider all the possibilities that picture-editing features have to offer. Be creative and enjoy mas-tering the possibilities.

©mangostock /iStockphoto

USING SMARTART GRAPHICS

Bottom Line

Explaining complex procedures and relationships using Excel worksheet data can be challenging. A **SmartArt graphic** is a visual representation of information and ideas, such as an organiza-tion chart, a flow chart, or a process or Venn diagram. Using SmartArt, you can tell your work-sheet's story visually, through a combination of shapes and simple strings of text.

Creating a Flowchart

Flowcharts show a series of events and decisions and how activity flows through that process. From designing software to making profitable sales to developing a budget, any activity can be depicted through a flowchart. Excel's SmartArt feature makes it easy to build one through an interactive set of shapes and text tools.

STEP BY STEP	Create a Flowchart

GET READY. LAUNCH Excel if it's not already running.

1. OPEN *13 SmartArt* from the data files for this lesson.

2. At the bottom of the workbook, click the New sheet icon to create a new sheet. Rename it Process and move it to the end of the row of worksheets.

3. On the INSERT tab, in the Illustrations group, click the Insert a SmartArt Graphic button. The Choose a SmartArt Graphic dialog box opens.

4. The list of SmartArt categories appears on the left side of the dialog box. Click the Process category.

5. From the options, select the flowchart that best suits your needs for the process you want to depict. Chosen in Figure 13-44 is the Alternating Flow, which pairs a colored box with the name of a step in the process with a bulleted list of the tasks related to the process.

Figure 13-44

Each diagram is previewed and explained to help you make a choice.

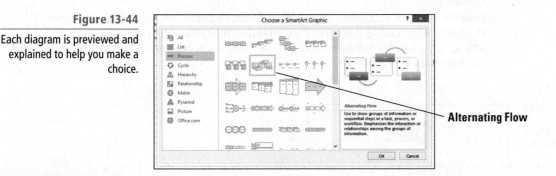

Alternating Flow

CERTIFICATION READY?	5.3.2

How do you insert a SmartArt graphic into a worksheet?

6. Click OK to begin building the flowchart.

7. On the left edge of the SmartArt graphic, click the arrow control to open the Text pane. In the Text pane, enter the names of each step in the process (the top-most bullet) and the tasks related to each one (the sub-bullets under each main bullet). Excel builds the flowchart as you type text. See Figure 13-45 for the text to be entered.

Figure 13-45

The Alternating Flow chart combines shapes, bulleted lists, and arcs that show relationships between steps in the process.

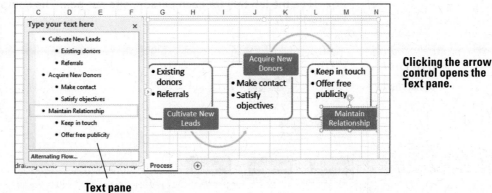

Clicking the arrow control opens the Text pane.

Text pane

8. SAVE the workbook in the Lesson 13 folder as *13 SmartArt Solution*.

PAUSE. LEAVE the workbook open to use in the next exercise.

Each SmartArt diagram starts with a default number of objects. You can add more objects quickly by clicking the Add Shape button in the Create Graphic group on the DESIGN tab (under SMARTART TOOLS). If your diagram also requires text beyond the label that will appear in the shape you're adding, an Add Bullet button is available as well.

Creating an Organization Chart

In organizations, someone's in charge, someone reports to someone else, departments or groups have leaders and staff, and so on. Creating an organization chart to show the relationship between departments or groups within a company is easily accomplished through an organization chart, built through the SmartArt feature's Hierarchy category.

STEP BY STEP   **Create an Organization Chart**

GET READY. USE the workbook from the previous exercise.

1. Insert a new worksheet, naming the tab Organizational Chart.
2. On the INSERT tab, in the Illustrations group, click the SmartArt button. The Choose a SmartArt Graphic dialog box opens.
3. In the list of SmartArt categories on the left side of the dialog box, click the Hierarchy category.
4. Select the Name and Title Organization Chart and click OK. Figure 13-46 shows the chart, which pairs a colored box intended to contain the person's name and a smaller text box for the person's job title. The boxes are connected by lines to show relationships and structure.

Figure 13-46

The Name and Title Organization Chart in SmartArt

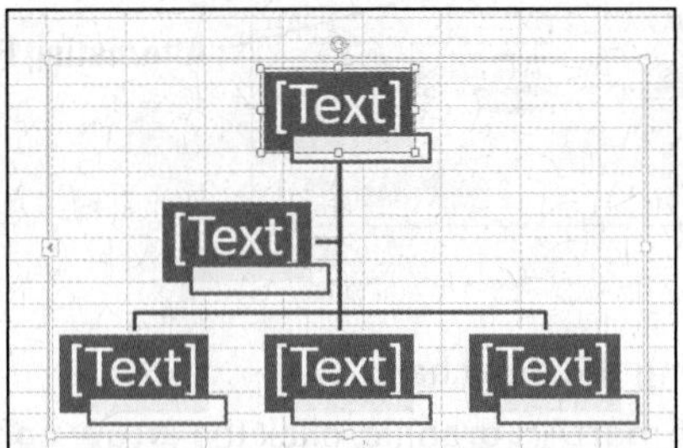

5. Using the Text pane, type the names of the people to be included in the chart. Enter job titles for each person by clicking the white box underneath the larger color-filled name box. Type the job title for each person, one per box. The completed chart is shown in Figure 13-47.

Figure 13-47

The final chart

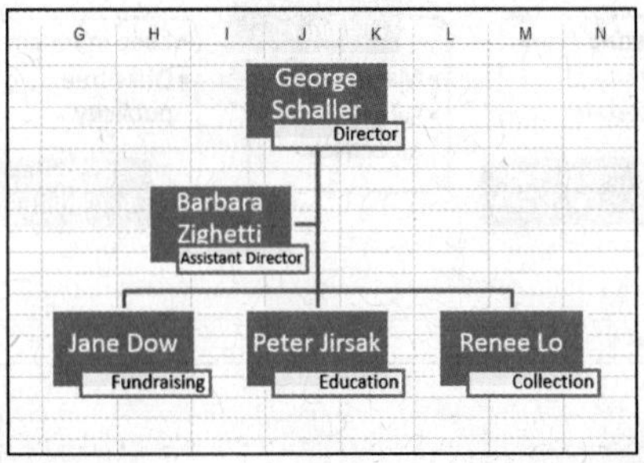

6. SAVE the workbook and CLOSE the file.

CLOSE Excel.

Organization charts allow for moving people up or down on the company ladder. Using the Promote and Demote buttons on the DESIGN tab in the Create Graphic group, click on one of the people in the chart and click Promote to move them up in the structure or Demote to move them down.

You certainly aren't stuck with the default colors of any SmartArt diagram. You can recolor the entire diagram using the Change Colors button (on the DESIGN tab in the SmartArt Styles group), or recolor individual parts by selecting them and then using the Shape Fill button on the FORMAT tab.

SKILL SUMMARY

In this lesson you learned how:	Exam Objective	Objective Number
To insert pictures and other objects.	Insert images.	5.3.3
To add shapes, lines, text boxes, and WordArt.	Insert text boxes.	5.3.1
	Change text to WordArt.	2.2.9
To delete, copy, and move graphics.		
To change the color of shapes and other graphics.	Change object colors.	5.3.6
To reposition shapes and other graphics.	Position objects.	5.3.8
To use picture tools to enhance graphics and other objects.	Add styles and effects to objects.	5.3.5
	Add borders to objects.	5.3.4
	Modify object properties.	5.3.7
To insert and modify SmartArt graphics.	Insert SmartArt.	5.3.2

Knowledge Assessment

Multiple Choice

Select the best response for the following statements.

1. The Shape Styles group is found on which tab?
   a. INSERT
   b. DRAWING TOOLS FORMAT
   c. HOME
   d. STYLES

2. Which object resizing handle do you use to resize a shape or picture proportionally?
   a. Top center
   b. Left or right side
   c. Corner
   d. Rotate

3. Which button do you click to apply a shadow to a shape or line?
   a. Shape Effects
   b. Picture Effects
   c. Artistic Effects
   d. 3D Effects

4. When you type text into a shape, which paragraph alignment is applied by default?
   a. Center
   b. Full Justify
   c. Right
   d. Left

5. Which button gives you access to the Office.com Clip Art collection?
   a. Online Pictures
   b. Pictures
   c. Online Clip Art
   d. Clip Art

6. If you want to move a shape up one level within a stack of overlapping graphics, which button do you click?
   a. Restack
   b. Bring to Front
   c. Rearrange
   d. Bring Forward

7. Which of the following is not found in the Illustrations group on the INSERT tab?
   a. WordArt
   b. Shapes
   c. Online Pictures
   d. Screenshot

8. Where does the Format Picture pane appear by default?
   a. As a free-floating pane
   b. On the right side of the workspace
   c. On the left side of the workspace
   d. Centered across the bottom of the workspace

9. The Crop tool is found on which ribbon tab?
   a. DRAWING TOOLS FORMAT
   b. INSERT
   c. PICTURE TOOLS FORMAT
   d. HOME

10. When drawing lines, how do you change their thickness?
    a. Right-click the line and choose Thickness.
    b. In the Shape Outline menu, select Weight.
    c. You must set the thickness before drawing the line.
    d. In the Shapes menu, select the Thicker Line option.

Fill in the Blank

Complete the following sentences by writing the correct word or words in the blanks provided.

1. The Illustrations group is found on the _____ tab.

2. When you select a graphic, _____ are found on the corners and sides.

3. In Excel, a(n)_____ is a picture of any part of the screen in an open application.

4. Locking a graphic works only if your worksheet is _____.

5. Press and hold the _____ key as you draw an object to make the width and height equal.

6. Online pictures can be found in the Office 365 _____.

7. Combine graphics with captions and connectors with the _____ button's options.

8. _____ apply various borders, shadows, and other effects with a single click.

9. Text can be added to a text box or a(n) _____.

10. A(n) _____ is a visual representation of information and ideas, such as an organization chart, a flow chart, or a process or Venn diagram.

Project 13-1: Adding Text to a Shape

Practice adding graphics to a worksheet to enhance the document.

GET READY. LAUNCH Excel.

1. OPEN the *13 Cruises* data file for this lesson.
2. On the INSERT tab, in the Illustrations group, click the Shapes button.
3. In the Basic Shapes section, click the Sun shape.
4. Draw the shape to the right of the Mexico section. The star should be roughly the same height as all of the rows in the Mexico section.
5. With the shape selected, click the DRAWING TOOLS FORMAT tab, open the Shape Outline menu, and select No Outline.
6. Right-click the shape and select Edit Text. Type ON SALE inside the shape.
7. Bold and center the text.
8. Click and grab a corner handle and adjust the size of the graphic so you can see all of the words.
9. SAVE the workbook as *13 Cruises Solution* and CLOSE the file.

LEAVE Excel open for the next project.

Project 13-2: Enhancing a Photo

Practice using your photo-enhancement skills.

GET READY. LAUNCH Excel if it is not already running.

1. OPEN the *13 Enhance Photo* data file for this lesson.
2. Select the photo.
3. On the PICTURE TOOLS FORMAT tab, in the Adjust group, open the Color menu and select Set Transparent Color.
4. Click the white background of the photo. The background becomes transparent, blending into the blue background behind it.
5. With the photo still selected, open the Artistic Effects menu in the Adjust group.
6. Select the Crisscross Etching effect.
7. With the photo still selected, on the PICTURE TOOLS FORMAT tab, in the Picture Styles group, select the Drop Shadow Rectangle style.
8. SAVE the workbook as *13 Enhance Photo Solution* and CLOSE the file.

LEAVE Excel open for the next project.

Proficiency Assessment

Project 13-3: Creating a SmartArt Organization Chart

Create a SmartArt graphic that lists goals for a non-profit organization.

GET READY. LAUNCH Excel if it is not already running, and open a new, blank workbook.

1. On the INSERT tab, in the Illustrations group, click the Insert a SmartArt Graphic button.
2. In the Choose a SmartArt Graphic dialog box, in the List category, select Vertical Arrow List and click OK.
3. In the Text pane, click in the top-most Text bullet position.
4. Type Short-term Goals.
5. Click in the next bullet position, and type Acquire four new donors.
6. In the next bullet position, type Publicize spring fundraiser.
7. In the next major bullet position, type Long-term Goals.
8. Click in the next bullet position, and type Raise $1 million.
9. In the last bullet position, type Build new warehouse.
10. Close the text box on the left.
11. On the SMARTART TOOLS DESIGN tab, in the SmartArt Styles group, click the Intense Effect style in the mini gallery.
12. SAVE the workbook as *13 Goals Solution* and CLOSE the file.

LEAVE Excel open for the next project.

Project 13-4: Stacking, Moving, and Deleting Graphics

Use the skills you learned in this lesson to work with a stack of graphics.

GET READY. LAUNCH Excel if it is not already running.

1. OPEN the *13 Stack and Move* data file for this lesson.
2. Click the photo of canned vegetables.
3. On the PICTURE TOOLS FORMAT tab, in the Arrange group, click the Bring Forward button arrow and select Bring to Front.
4. Point inside the graphic, and then click and drag it horizontally to column L.
5. Click the blue starburst graphic.
6. On the DRAWING TOOLS FORMAT tab, in the Arrange group, click the Bring Forward button twice to bring the graphic to the top of the stack.
7. Select the graphic, right-click an edge of the graphic, and select Cut from the shortcut menu.
8. Click in cell A23 and then press Ctrl + V.
9. Click the border of the Great Fundraisers! WordArt graphic and press the Delete key on your keyboard.
10. SAVE the workbook as *13 Stack and Move Solution* and CLOSE the file.

LEAVE Excel open for the next project.

Project 13-5: Combining WordArt and Photos in a Fundraising Report

Add a WordArt title, a photo, and a shape to a worksheet to create a more interesting fundraising report.

GET READY. LAUNCH Excel if it is not already running.

1. OPEN the *13 Fundraising Report* data file for this lesson.
2. Insert a WordArt graphic with the Fill - White, Outline - Accent 1, Shadow style.
3. Replace the placeholder text with Fundraising Report.
4. Position the resulting WordArt above the worksheet, centering it horizontally, by eye.
5. Insert the 13 Donation Box photo below the table.
6. Resize the photo proportionally smaller, so that it fits within the gray-shaded area below the table.
7. Insert a 24-point star to the right of the photo. Insert the text GREAT WORK! in the star. BOLD and CENTER the text, and change the font size to 36 points. You might need to enlarge the star and reposition it after adding and formatting the text.
8. Remove the outline from the star shape.
9. Rotate the star shape clockwise, slightly.
10. SAVE the workbook as *13 Fundraising Report Solution*.

LEAVE the workbook open for the next project.

Project 13-6: Enhancing the Graphics in a Fundraising Report

Modify the graphics in the fundraising report.

GET READY. USE the workbook from the previous project.

1. Modify the WordArt graphic to change the text fill color to Red, Accent 2, Darker 25%.
2. Remove the outline from the WordArt graphic text.
3. Apply a Shadow, Outer, Offset Diagonal Bottom Right text effect to the WordArt graphic.
4. Apply a Drop Shadow Rectangle picture style to the donation box photo.
5. SAVE the workbook as *13 Fundraising Report Solution 2* and CLOSE the file.

CLOSE Excel.

Circling Back 3

The CFO and the president of the Graphic Design Institute need you to modify the Contributions and Student Roster workbooks. You will add a few advanced formulas to the Contributions workbook in addition to creating charts that show contributions from organizations and individuals. You will also add graphics to the Student Roster workbook, protect the worksheet, and share it via email.

Project 1: Using Advanced Formulas

In this project, you will add some formulas that use advanced functions to the Contributions workbook. The formulas you will work with are COUNTIF and AVERAGEIF.

GET READY. LAUNCH Excel if it is not already running.

1. OPEN *Contributions Adv Functions* from the student data files.
2. Click in cell B40.
3. On the FORMULAS tab, in the Function Library group, click the Insert Function button.
4. In the Search for a function box, type COUNTIF and click Go.
5. In the Select a function box, select COUNTIF and click OK.
6. In the Function Arguments dialog box, for Range, click the Collapse Dialog button, and then select C4:C32. The word *Amount* appears in the dialog box because this range was named in a previous exercise. Click the Expand Dialog button.
7. In the Criteria box, type <1000 and click OK. The steps use the COUNTIF function to create a formula that counts the number of contributions that are less than $1,000.
8. In B41, type =COUNTIF(C4:C32,">=10000") and press Enter. This formula counts the number of contributions that are equal to or greater than $10,000.
9. In B42, type =AVERAGEIF(C4:C32,"<1000") and press Enter. This formula averages the dollar amount of contributions that are less than $1,000.
10. In B43, type =AVERAGEIF(C4:C32,">=10000") and press Enter. This formula averages the dollar amount of contributions that are equal to or greater than $10,000.
11. SAVE the workbook as *Contributions Adv Functions Solution* in the Circling Back folder, and then CLOSE the file.

LEAVE Excel open for the next project.

Project 2: Creating Charts

The CFO has requested that you add some charts to the Contributions workbook to help readers see at a glance the relative amount of contributions to each of the Graphic Design Institute funds. You should create a chart for dollar amounts from organizations and from individuals.

GET READY. LAUNCH Excel if it is not already running.

1. OPEN *Contributions Chart* from the student data files.
2. In the left margin, above the groups, collapse the groups by clicking the 2.
3. Select B10:C26.
4. On the INSERT tab, in the Charts group, click the Pie Chart button arrow and select 3-D Pie. A 3-D pie chart appears.
5. Right-click an edge of the chart frame and select Move Chart. In the Move Chart dialog box, select New Sheet and click OK. The chart appears on a new sheet named *Chart1*.
6. Move the Chart1 sheet to appear after Sheet1.
7. On the Chart1 sheet, triple-click in the Chart Title placeholder and type Contributions by Organizations.

8. Select the title text, and using the tools on the HOME tab, in the Font group, change the font size to 24 and BOLD the text.

9. Click the chart, on the right, click the Chart Elements button (the plus sign), and then select Data Labels.

10. Click the Chart Styles button (the paint brush), and then select Style 3.

11. Click a data label in the pie chart to select all data labels. On the HOME tab, in the Font group, in the Font Size list, increase the font size of the data labels to 16.

12. Reapply the 24-point font size to the chart title.

13. Create the same type of chart for the data in B31:C43. Use Contributions by Individuals as the chart title.

14. Double-click one of the data labels. In the Format Data Labels pane that appears on the right, click the Label Options icon to display those settings, if necessary, and select Outside End under Label Position. Click and move each of the three data labels near the top of the pie chart to prevent overlapping. The labels should have leader lines that connect to their wedge of the pie chart.

15. Move Chart2 to the end of the series of worksheets.

16. SAVE the workbook as *Contributions Chart Solution* in the Circling Back folder, and then CLOSE the file.

LEAVE Excel open for the next project.

Project 3: Adding Graphics to a Worksheet

In this project, you add a text box to the Student Roster workbook to warn people that they're reading confidential information. You also create a SmartArt graphic that reminds readers of the various disciplines taught at the Graphic Design Institute.

GET READY. LAUNCH Excel if it is not already running.

1. OPEN *Student Roster Graphics* from the student data files.

2. On the INSERT tab, in the Text group, click the Text Box button.

3. Beginning in F2, draw a text box approximately three columns wide and four rows in height. In the text box, type Confidential Information.

4. Highlight the text. Using the tools on the HOME tab in the Font group, change the font color to Red and the font size to 24. In the Alignment group, click the Center button to center the text.

5. On the right of Sheet1, click the New sheet button (the plus sign).

6. Ensure you're on Sheet2. On the INSERT tab, in the Illustrations group, click the Insert a SmartArt Graphic button. Select the Basic Block List graphic, and then click OK.

7. In the five graphic boxes, starting in the upper-left corner, type the following text:
   Visual Arts
   Graphic Design
   Typography
   Digital Media
   Photography

8. Click an edge of the SmartArt graphic to display the frame. Right-click the frame and select Format Object. In the Format Shape pane that appears on the right, click the Size & Properties icon, and then click Size. Change the Height setting to 3.75, press Tab, and then change the Length setting to 6.75. Press Enter. Close the Format Shape pane.

9. To move the graphic, click and hold the bottom edge of the frame, and drag up to the top of the spreadsheet. Click and hold the left edge of the frame and drag to the left, so the frame aligns with the border between columns B and C.

10. With the SmartArt still selected, click the SMARTTOOLS DESIGN tab. In the SmartArt Styles group, click the Change Colors button and in the Colorful section, select Colorful - Accent Colors.

11. SAVE the workbook as *Student Roster Graphics Solution* in the Circling Back folder.

LEAVE the workbook open for the next project.

Project 4: Securing and Sharing Workbooks

You need to share the student roster with others, and the file should be as secure as possible to avoid unauthorized viewing. In this project, you protect the worksheet that includes students' names, and then you send the worksheet to an associate.

GET READY. USE the workbook you saved in the previous project.

1. Click Sheet1.

2. On the REVIEW tab, in the Changes group, click Protect Sheet.

3. In the Password to unprotect sheet box, type CB!sr01. Click OK.

4. You are prompted to confirm the password. Type CB!sr01 again and click OK.

5. SAVE the workbook as *Student Roster Protected Solution* in the Circling Back folder.

6. Check the Quick Access Toolbar for the Email tool. If it is not visible, on the right side of the Quick Access Toolbar, click the Customize Quick Access Toolbar button. Select Email.

7. On the Quick Access Toolbar, click Email. An email window appears.

8. In the To field, type [your instructor's email address]. Leave the name of the file in the Subject line.

9. In the email message window, type The latest student roster is attached for your records. I will send you the password to access the student list in the workbook via an instant message. Press Enter twice, and then type your name and title.

10. In the email message window, click the Send button.

11. SAVE the workbook and CLOSE the file.

12. (Optional) If you to want to reset the Quick Access Toolbar to the default settings, which will remove any buttons you added to the toolbar, click the Customize Quick Access Toolbar button, and then select More Commands. In the Excel Options dialog box, click the Reset button, select Reset only Quick Access Toolbar, click Yes, and click OK.

CLOSE Excel.

Matrix Skill	Objective Number	Lesson Number
Create and manage worksheets and workbooks.	**1**	
Create worksheets and workbooks.	1.1	
Create new blank workbooks.	1.1.1	1, 2
Create new workbooks using templates.	1.1.2	3
Import files.	1.1.3	9
Open non-native files directly in Excel.	1.1.4	9
Add worksheets to existing workbooks.	1.1.5	8
Copy and move worksheets.	1.1.6	8
Navigate through worksheets and workbooks.	1.2	
Search for data within a workbook.	1.2.1	8
Insert hyperlinks.	1.2.2	6
Change worksheet order.	1.2.3	8
Demonstrate how to use Go To.	1.2.4	1
Demonstrate how to use Name Box.	1.2.5	1
Format worksheets and workbooks.	1.3	
Change worksheet tab color.	1.3.1	8
Modify page setup.	1.3.2	7
Insert and delete columns and rows.	1.3.3	7
Change workbook themes.	1.3.4	7
Adjust row height and column width.	1.3.5	2, 7
Insert watermarks.	1.3.6	7
Insert headers and footers.	1.3.7	7
Set data validation.	1.3.8	9
Customize options and views for worksheets and workbooks.	1.4	
Hide worksheets.	1.4.1	8
Hide columns and rows.	1.4.2	7
Customize the Quick Access Toolbar.	1.4.3	1, 3
Customize the ribbon.	1.4.4	3

Matrix Skill	Objective Number	Lesson Number
Manage macro security.	1.4.5	9
Change workbook views.	1.4.6	1
Record simple macros.	1.4.7	9
Add values to workbook properties.	1.4.8	2
Demonstrate how to use zoom.	1.4.9	8
Display formulas.	1.4.10	4
Freeze panes.	1.4.11	8
Assign shortcut keys.	1.4.12	9
Split the window.	1.4.13	1
Configure worksheets and workbooks to print or save.	1.5	
Set a print area.	1.5.1	3
Save workbooks in alternate file formats.	1.5.2	2
Print individual worksheets.	1.5.3	3
Set print scaling.	1.5.4	3, 7
Repeat headers and footers.	1.5.5	7
Maintain backward compatibility.	1.5.6	2
Configure workbooks to print.	1.5.7	3, 7
Save files to remote locations.	1.5.8	2
Create cells and ranges.	**2**	
Insert data in cells and ranges.	2.1	
Append data to worksheets.	2.1.1	2, 9
Find and replace data.	2.1.2	2, 8
Copy and paste data.	2.1.3	2
Demonstrate how to use AutoFill tool.	2.1.4	2
Expand data across columns.	2.1.5	2
Insert and delete cells.	2.1.6	2, 6
Format cells and ranges.	2.2	
Merge cells.	2.2.1	6
Modify cell alignment and indentation.	2.2.2	6
Change font and font styles.	2.2.3	6
Use Format Painter.	2.2.4	6
Wrap text within cells.	2.2.5	6
Apply number formats.	2.2.6	6

Matrix Skill	Objective Number	Lesson Number
Apply highlighting.	2.2.7	6
Apply cell styles.	2.2.8	6
Change text to WordArt.	2.2.9	13
Order and group cells and ranges.	2.3	
Apply conditional formatting.	2.3.1	6
Insert sparklines.	2.3.2	12
Transpose columns and rows.	2.3.3	7
Create named ranges.	2.3.4	4
Create outlines.	2.3.5	9
Collapse groups of data in outlines.	2.3.6	9
Insert subtotals.	2.3.7	9
Create tables.	**3**	
Create a table.	3.1	
Move between tables and ranges.	3.1.1	9
Add and remove cells within tables.	3.1.2	9
Define titles.	3.1.3	9
Modify a table.	3.2	
Apply styles to tables.	3.2.1	9
Band rows and columns.	3.2.2	9
Insert total rows.	3.2.3	9
Remove styles from tables.	3.2.4	9
Filter and sort a table.	3.3	
Filter records.	3.3.1	9
Sort data on multiple columns.	3.3.2	9
Change sort order.	3.3.3	9
Remove duplicates.	3.3.4	9
Apply formulas and functions.	**4**	
Apply cell ranges and references in formulas and functions.	4.1	
Demonstrate how to use references (relative, mixed, absolute).	4.1.1	4
Define order of operations.	4.1.2	4
Reference cell ranges in formulas.	4.1.3	4
Summarize data with functions.	4.2	
Demonstrate how to apply the SUM function.	4.2.1	5

Matrix Skill	Objective Number	Lesson Number
Demonstrate how to apply the MIN and MAX functions.	4.2.2	5
Demonstrate how to apply the COUNT function.	4.2.3	5
Demonstrate how to apply the AVERAGE function.	4.2.4	5
Apply conditional logic in functions.	4.3	
Demonstrate how to apply the SUMIF function.	4.3.1	10
Demonstrate how to apply the AVERAGEIF function.	4.3.2	10
Demonstrate how to apply the COUNTIF function.	4.3.3	10
Format and modify text with functions.	4.4	
Demonstrate how to use the RIGHT, LEFT and MID functions.	4.4.1	10
Demonstrate how to use the TRIM function.	4.4.2	10
Demonstrate how to use the UPPER and LOWER functions.	4.4.3	10
Demonstrate how to use the CONCATENATE function.	4.4.4	10
Create charts and objects.	5	
Create a chart.	5.1	
Create charts and graphs.	5.1.1	12
Add additional data series.	5.1.2	12
Switch between rows and columns in source data.	5.1.3	12
Demonstrate how to use Quick Analysis.	5.1.4	12
Format a chart.	5.2	
Add legends.	5.2.1	12
Resize charts and graphs.	5.2.2	12
Modify chart and graph parameters.	5.2.3	12
Apply chart layouts and styles.	5.2.4	12
Position charts and graphs.	5.2.5	12
Insert and format an object.	5.3	
Insert text boxes.	5.3.1	13
Insert SmartArt.	5.3.2	13
Insert images.	5.3.3	13
Add borders to objects.	5.3.4	13
Add styles and effects to objects.	5.3.5	13
Change object colors.	5.3.6	13
Modify object properties.	5.3.7	13
Position objects.	5.3.8	13

A

absolute cell reference   A reference to a specific cell or range of cells regardless of where the formula is located in the worksheet. An absolute cell reference uses a dollar sign in front of the column and row markers in a cell address.

active cell   A cell that is highlighted or outlined by a bold black rectangle. This is also called the current or highlighted cell.

align   Arrange in a line or bring into alignment.

argument   The parameters of a function.

arguments   The values a function uses to perform operations or calculations in a formula.

artistic effect   Various artistic mediums and special effects designed for use on photos in Excel.

attribute   A formatting characteristic, such as bold, italic, or underlined text.

Auto Fill   An Excel feature that automatically fill cells with data, formatting, or both.

Auto Outline   A feature that automatically groups selected rows in Excel.

AutoComplete   An Excel feature that automatically enters the remaining characters of an entry when the first few typed characters match an entry made previously.

AutoFilter   A built-in set of filtering capabilities.

AutoSum   A formula that calculates (by default) the total from the adjacent cell through the first nonnumeric cell using the SUM function.

AVERAGE function   A function that calculates (by default) the total from the adjacent cell through the first nonnumeric cell using the SUM function in its formula.

axis   A line bordering the chart plot area used as a frame of reference for measurement.

B

Backstage view   A view that shows you behind-the-scenes options for managing files such as opening, saving, printing, and documenting files.

boundary   The line between rows or columns.

C

calculation operator   Operators that specify the calculations to be performed.

cell reference   A reference that identifies a cell's location in the worksheet based on its row number and column letter.

cell   A box on the grid identified by the intersection of a column and a row.

change history   In a shared workbook, a feature that includes the name of the person who made each change, when the change was made, and what data was changed.

chart area   The entire chart and all its elements.

chart sheet   A sheet that contains only a chart.

chart   A graphical representation of numeric data in a worksheet.

clip art   Drawings and illustration files available in Excel.

collapse   To condense groups into single-row headings called outlines.

column heading   The identifying letter of a column.

column width   The left-to-right measurement of a column.

column   Cells that run from top to bottom in a worksheet and are identified by letters.

command group   Task-specific groups divided among the command tabs appropriate to the work a user currently performs.

command tabs   Task-oriented tabs that are organized on the ribbon.

conditional formatting   An Excel feature that enables you to specify how cells that meet one or more given conditions should be displayed.

conditional formula   A formula in which the result is determined by the presence or absence of a particular condition.

constant   A number or text value entered directly into a formula.

copy pointer   A mouse pointer, resembling an arrow with a plus sign, that allows users to drag a cell or range of cells to a new location.

copy   To duplicate data from a worksheet to the Clipboard.

COUNT function   A function that determines how many cells in a range contain a number.

COUNTA function   A function that returns the number of cells in the selected range that contain text or values, but not blank cells.

criteria   See criterion.

criterion   A condition you specify to limit which records are returned when filtering data. The plural of criterion is criteria.

cut   To remove data from a worksheet. Cut data may be pasted into a new location or locations in a worksheet.

D

data file   An electronic file that stores a series of records in a relatively simple format.

data label   Text that provides additional information about a data marker, which represents a single data point or value that originates from a worksheet cell.

data marker   A bar, area, dot, slice, or other symbol in a chart that represents a single data point or value that originates from a worksheet cell.

data series   A row or column of data represented by a line, set of columns, bars, or other chart types.

database   A comparatively complex system that can store a large amount of related data, which requires a program to be able to assess and render that data.

default settings   Pre-set settings that determine how Excel behaves when performing an action.

delimiter   A character that separates data entries from one another.

Dialog Box Launcher   An arrow in the lower, right corner of some command groups on the ribbon that opens a dialog box related to the command group.

document theme   A predefined set of colors, fonts, and effects that can be applied to an entire workbook or to specific items in a workbook.

duotone   An image with two colors.

E

effects   Something that modifies the appearance of an object.

embedded chart   A chart placed on a worksheet rather than on a separate chart sheet.

external reference   A cell or range in a worksheet in another Excel workbook, or a defined name in another workbook.

F

FILE tab   In Office 2013, the tab that takes you to Backstage view to access Save, Print, Options, and other commands.

fill handle   A small square in the lower, right corner of a selected cell or range of cells. Used mainly to copy data to adjacent cells.

filter   A restriction that Excel uses to determine which worksheet rows to display.

Find   A command to help you search for certain content.

Flash Fill   A new feature in Excel that is similar to AutoFill. When Excel recognizes a pattern based on other information in your workbook, it uses the pattern to enter data into several cells at once.

font   A set of text properties that affects the typeface, size, and similar aspects of text.

footer   Lines of text that appear at the bottom of each page.

Format Painter   A feature found in most Office applications that allows you to quickly copy formatting attributes that you have already applied and "paint" those attributes onto other text, shapes, pictures, and worksheet cells.

formula bar   A bar located between the ribbon and the worksheet in which users can edit the contents of a cell.

formula   An equation that performs calculations, such as addition, subtraction, multiplication, and division, on values in a worksheet.

freeze   To prevent portions of a worksheet from moving on the screen. When you freeze panes, such as a row of column headings, the column headings remain visible as you scroll down the worksheet or change magnification.

function   A predefined formula that performs a calculation.

G

graphic   An art-related object, such as a drawing, image, or shape.

gridlines   The lines that display around worksheet cells.

group   Commands on the default ribbon tabs that are related in functionality.

grouping   Organizing data so it can be viewed as a collapsible and expandable outline.

H

handle   A small box on the side and/or corner of the graphic that you click and pull to increase or decrease the size of a graphic.

header   A line of text that appears at the top of each page of a printed worksheet.

Help system   A system in Excel that is rich in information, illustrations, and tips that can help you complete any task as you create worksheets and workbooks.

hide   To make a worksheet invisible.

hotkey   Another name for KeyTip.

hyperlink   A shortcut that enables you to navigate to a web page or a location in another file in just one click of the mouse.

K

KeyTip   Small "badges" displaying keyboard shortcuts for specific tabs and commands on the ribbon and Quick Access Toolbar. Also referred to as hotkeys.

keyword   A word assigned to a document's properties that makes it easier to organize and find documents.

L

label   Text entered in a worksheet that identifies numeric data and is the most common type of text entered in a worksheet. Labels are also used to sort and group data.

legend   An explanatory list that identifies the patterns or colors assigned to the data series or categories in a chart.

lookup function   An efficient way to search for and insert a value in a cell when the desired value is stored elsewhere in the worksheet or even in a different workbook.

M

macro   A series of steps you record that you might want to repeat frequently to save time.

MAX function   A function that returns the largest value in a set of values.

merged cells   Two or more cells combined into a single cell.

MIN function   A function that determines the minimum value in a range of cells.

Mini toolbar   A formatting tool that appears above or below the shortcut menu when you right-click a cell and that displays the most commonly used formatting commands.

mixed cell reference   A cell reference that uses an absolute column or row reference, but not both.

move pointer   A mouse pointer that enables users to drag a cell or range of cells to a new location, replacing any existing data in the destination cells.

N

Name Box   Located below the ribbon at the left end of the formula bar. When a user types a cell location into this box and presses Enter, the insertion point moves to that cell.

named range   A group of cells, and occasionally a single cell, with a designated name.

natural series   A formatted series of text or numbers that are in a normal sequence such as months, weekdays, numbers, or times.

navigation pane   A pane found on the left side of Backstage view. It provides you access to workbook and file-related commands through a series of tabs.

nested parentheses   Parentheses inside of parentheses within a formula.

NOW function   A function that returns today's date and the current time, in the default format of mm/dd/yyyy hh:mm.

O

Office Clipboard   A location that collects and stores up to 24 copied or cut items that are then available to be used in the active workbook, in other workbooks, and in other Office programs.

operand   An element that identifies the values to be used in a calculation.

order of operations   The rules Excel follows to calculate any formula that contains two or more operators.

orientation   The position of the content in a worksheet, so that it prints either vertically or horizontally on a page.

outline symbols   Symbols that add controls next to the row and column headings to change the view of an outlined worksheet.

outline   Single-row headings.

P

page break   A divider that breaks a worksheet into separate pages for printing.

Page Break Preview   An Excel view in which you can quickly adjust automatic page breaks to achieve a more desirable printed document.

parse   To separate into components. Also, to interpret character by character.

password   Text that must be entered before a user can access a secured workbook, worksheet, or worksheet elements.

Paste Special   A tool that enables you to control specifically what you want to paste after using the Copy or Cut commands, such as cell content, formulas, values, formatting, and much more.

paste   To insert data from the Clipboard to a new location in a worksheet.

PivotChart   A graphical representation of the data in a PivotTable.

PivotTable   A highly configurable table that condenses large amounts of data. A PivotTable is used to analyze and display numerical data in detail and to answer unforeseen questions about data.

plot area   The area bounded by axes in a chart.

PMT function   A function that requires a series of inputs regarding interest rate, loan amount (principal), and loan duration, and then calculates the resulting loan payment.

print options   Several settings that enable you to change how a document prints.

Print Preview   An Excel view that enables you to see what your document will look like before sending it to the printer.

Q

Quick Access Toolbar   A toolbar that gives you fast and easy access to the tools you use most often in Excel.

quick format   Predefined formatting in Excel that enables you to apply an elaborate format that makes a table look sleek and professional.

R

range   A group of adjacent cells you select to perform operations on all of the selected cells.

relative cell reference   A cell reference that adjusts the cell identifier automatically if you insert or delete columns or rows, or if you copy the formula to another cell.

Replace   An Excel feature that allows you to add content to a text box and replace any matches Excel finds.

ribbon   A broad band that runs across the top of the Excel window that organizes commands and tools into an easy-to-use interface. The ribbon was introduced in Office 2007.

row heading   The identifying letter of a row.

row height   The top-to-bottom measurement of a row.

row   A line of cells that start at the left edge of a worksheet, continue to the right, and are identified by numbers.

Rules Manager   A tool that enables you to set the order of multiple rules, fine-tune rule settings, and more.

S

saturation   Changing from color to black and white or to greater or reduced levels of color.

scaling   Shrinking or stretching printed output to a percentage of its actual size.

scope   The location within which Excel recognizes a named range, which is either a specific worksheet or the entire workbook. If you set the scope of a named range to Workbook, you can reference the named range on any sheet in the workbook.

ScreenTip   A small, onscreen rectangle that displays descriptive text when you rest the pointer on a command or control.

selecting text   Highlighting text that is to be changed.

shape   An editable line, circle, arrow, star, or other form.

shared workbook   A workbook set up to allow multiple networked users to view and make changes simultaneously.

slicer   One of the ways to filter a table so that it shows only records containing a certain object. A slicer is a selection panel that floats above a worksheet (the way a chart does).

SmartArt graphic   A visual representation of information and ideas, such as an organization chart, a flow chart, a process, or a Venn diagram.

sparklines   Miniature graphs that summarize data; typically used to graphically describe trends in data.

strong password   A password that combines uppercase and lowercase letters, numbers, and symbols, making the password difficult to guess.

style   A set of formatting attributes that you can apply to a cell or range of cells more easily than by setting each attribute individually.

SUBTOTAL function   A function that returns a subtotal for a list.

subtotals   The sum of values that are grouped together.

SUM function   A function that totals all of the cells in a range.

T

tab   An area on the ribbon that contains groups of related commands. See command tab. Or an area of the Backstage navigation pane that contains groups of related commands.

table array   Data in a table arranged in rows and columns.

table   A range of cells in a worksheet that contains related data and can be used by a lookup function.

template   A file that includes formatting and formulas complete with designs, tools, and specific data types.

text box   A floating box in a worksheet that can contain text or graphics.

title   Descriptive text that is aligned to an axis or at the top of a chart.

TODAY function   A function that returns the current date in a worksheet.

trace arrow   An arrow that shows the relationship between formulas and the cells they refer to in order to resolve a formula error.

Track Changes   A feature that marks and records changes made to a workbook.

transposing   Changes your cell data to change orientation.

U

unhide   To make a worksheet visible again.

V

Validation A feature in Excel that ensures data is entered correctly, before it is processed incorrectly.

value A number, a cell address, a date, text, or Boolean data in Excel. Regarding formulas, it is usually a number or cell address.

variable A symbol or name that represents something else; it can be a cell address, a range of cells, and so on.

W

watermark Text or a picture that appears in the background of a document; it is similar to a sheet background in Excel.

white space The empty area of a document in which no content appears.

WordArt An Office feature that combines text and artistic effects.

workbook properties Items you directly change, such as keywords.

workbook A collection of worksheets in a single file.

worksheet A page in a workbook that consists of a grid of rows and columns in which you can enter text, values, and formulas, and perform calculations.

wrap To automatically display data on the next line when it is too long to display within the cell's width. Wrapping automatically increases a cell's height.

Z

zoom An Excel feature that enables you to make a worksheet appear bigger (zoom in) or smaller (zoom out).